Numerical Analysis and Graphic Visualization with MATLAB

Second Edition

Shoichiro Nakamura

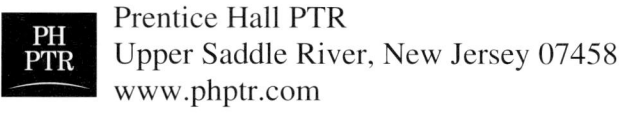

Prentice Hall PTR
Upper Saddle River, New Jersey 07458
www.phptr.com

ISBN 0-13-065489-2

Library of Congress Cataloging-in-Publication Data
Nakamura, Shoichiro
    Numerical analysis and graphic visualization with matlab / Shoichiro Nakamura.—2nd ed.
        p. cm.
    Includes index.
    ISBN 0-13-065489-2
        1. Computer graphics. 2. MATLAB. I. Title.

T385 .N34 2001
519.4'0285'53—dc21   2001033848

Editorial/Production Supervision: Carol Wheelan
Acquisitions Editor: Mary Franz
Marketing Manager: Dan DePasquale
Manufacturing Buyer: Maura Zaldivar
Cover Design: Anthony Gemmellaro
Cover Design Direction: Jerry Votta
Interior Series Design: Gail Cocker-Bogusz

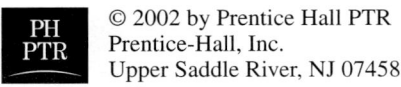
© 2002 by Prentice Hall PTR
Prentice-Hall, Inc.
Upper Saddle River, NJ 07458

Prentice Hall books are widely used by corporations and government agencies for training, marketing, and resale.

The publisher offers discounts on this book when ordered in bulk quantities. For more information, contact Corporate Sales Department, phone: 800-382-3419; fax: 201-236-7141; email: corpsales@prenhall.com Or write Corporate Sales Department, Prentice Hall PTR, One Lake Street, Upper Saddle River, NJ 07458.

Product and company names mentioned herein are the trademarks or registered trademarks of their respective owners.

All rights reserved. No part of this book may be reproduced, in any form or by any means, without permission in writing from the publisher.

Printed in the United States of America

10 9 8 7 6 5 4 3 2 1

ISBN 0-13-065489-2

Pearson Education LTD.
Pearson Education Australia PTY, Limited
Pearson Education Singapore, Pte. Ltd
Pearson Education North Asia Ltd
Pearson Education Canada, Ltd.
Pearson Educación de Mexico, S.A. de C.V.
Pearson Education—Japan
Pearson Education Malaysia, Pte. Ltd
Pearson Education, Upper Saddle River, New Jersey

CONTENTS

PREFACE		**viii**
1	**MATLAB PRIMER**	**1**
	1.1 Before Starting Calculations	2
	1.2 How to Do Calculations	7
	1.3 Branch Statements	10
	1.4 Loops with for/end or while/end	12
	1.5 Reading and Writing	16
	1.6 Array Variables	18
	1.7 Unique Aspect of Numbers in MATLAB	30
	1.8 Mathematical Functions of MATLAB	32
	1.9 Functions That Do Chores	35
	1.10 Developing a Program as an M-File	37
	1.11 How to Write Your Own Functions	39
	1.12 Saving and Loading Data	41
	1.13 How to Make Hard Copies	44
2	**GRAPHICS WITH MATLAB**	**50**
	2.1 Simple Plotting	51
	2.2 Interactive Editing of Figures	65
	2.3 How to Print or Record Graphs	67
	2.4 Plotting of Two-Dimensional Functions	68
	2.5 Triangular Grid and Contours	73
	2.6 Curvilinear Grid and Contours	75
	2.7 Plotting Curved Surfaces	76
	2.8 MATLAB as a Drawing Board	85

	2.9	Interactive Graphics	91
	2.10	M-Files	92
3	**LINEAR ALGEBRA**		**110**
	3.1	Matrices and Vectors	110
	3.2	Matrix and Vector Operations in MATLAB	117
	3.3	Inverse Matrix	118
	3.4	Linear Equations	120
	3.5	Unsolvable Problems	124
	3.6	The Determinant	127
	3.7	Ill-conditioned Problems	130
	3.8	Gauss Elimination	135
	3.9	Gauss-Jordan Elimination and Matrix Inversion	141
	3.10	LU Decomposition	145
	3.11	Iterative Solution	149
	3.12	Matrix Eigenvalues	152
4	**POLYNOMIALS AND INTERPOLATION**		**161**
	4.1	MATLAB Commands for Polynomials	161
	4.2	Linear Interpolation	166
	4.3	Polynomial Interpolation with Power Series	170
	4.4	Lagrange Interpolation Polynomial	173
	4.5	Error of Interpolation Polynomials	177
	4.6	Differentiation and Integration of Lagrange Interpolation Formula	181
	4.7	Interpolation with Chebyshev Points	183
	4.8	Cubic Hermite Interpolation	188
	4.9	Two-Dimensional Interpolation	193
	4.10	Transfinite Interpolation	194
	4.11	M-Files	199
5	**NUMERICAL INTEGRATION**		**205**
	5.1	Trapezoidal Rule	205
	5.2	Simpson's Rules	211
	5.3	Other Quadratures	215
	5.4	Numerical Integration with Infinite Limits or Singularities	221
		5.4.1 Use of the Extended Trapezoidal Rule	222

	5.4.2	Exponential Transformation	224
	5.4.3	Double-Exponential Transformation	228
5.5	MATLAB Commands for Integrations		230
5.6	Numerical Integration on a Two-Dimensional Domain		231
5.7	M-Files		237

6 NUMERICAL DIFFERENTIATION 250
- 6.1 Derivatives of Interpolation Polynomials — 250
- 6.2 Difference Approximations — 252
- 6.3 Taylor Expansion Method — 257
- 6.4 Algorithms to Automate Derivations — 263
  - 6.4.1 Algorithm 1 — 264
  - 6.4.2 Algorithm 2 — 265
- 6.5 Difference Approximation for Partial Derivatives — 267
- 6.6 Numerical Evaluation of High-Order Derivatives — 268
- 6.7 M-Files — 271

7 ROOTS OF NONLINEAR EQUATIONS 279
- 7.1 Graphical Method — 279
- 7.2 Bisection Method — 282
- 7.3 Newton Iteration — 285
- 7.4 Secant Method — 290
- 7.5 Successive Substitution Method — 291
- 7.6 Simultaneous Nonlinear Equations — 295
- 7.7 M-Files — 300

8 CURVE FITTING TO MEASURED DATA 309
- 8.1 Line Fitting — 309
- 8.2 Nonlinear Curve Fitting with a Power Function — 314
- 8.3 Curve Fitting with a Higher-Order Polynomial — 316
- 8.4 Curve Fitting by a Linear Combination of Known Functions — 319

9 SPLINE FUNCTIONS AND NONLINEAR INTERPOLATION 324
- 9.1 C-Spline Interpolation — 324
- 9.2 Cubic B-Spline — 331
- 9.3 Interpolation with a Nonlinear Function — 338
- 9.4 M-Files — 346

10 INITIAL-VALUE PROBLEMS OF ORDINARY DIFFERENTIAL EQUATIONS   351
   10.1 First-Order ODEs   352
   10.2 Euler Methods   355
      10.2.1 Forward Euler Method   355
      10.2.2 Modified Euler Method   358
      10.2.3 Backward Euler Method   361
      10.2.4 Accuracy of Euler Methods   362
      10.2.5 Second-Order ODEs   363
      10.2.6 Higher-Order ODEs   367
   10.3 Runge-Kutta Methods   371
      10.3.1 Second-Order Runge-Kutta Method   372
      10.3.2 Accuracy of the Second-Order Runge-Kutta Method   376
      10.3.3 Higher-Order ODEs   377
      10.3.4 Third-Order Runge-Kutta Method   383
      10.3.5 Fourth-Order Runge-Kutta Method   385
      10.3.6 Error, Stability, and Time-Interval Optimization   395
   10.4 Shooting Method   399
   10.5 Method of Lines   402

11 BOUNDARY-VALUE PROBLEMS OF ORDINARY DIFFERENTIAL EQUATIONS   414
   11.1 Introduction   414
   11.2 Boundary-Value Problems for Rods and Slabs   417
   11.3 Solution of Tridiagonal Equations   422
   11.4 Variable Coefficients and Nonuniform Grids   424
   11.5 Cylinders and Spheres   427
   11.6 Nonlinear Ordinary Differential Equations   429
      11.6.1 Successive Substitution   430
      11.6.2 Newton Iteration   430

A COLORS   439

B DRAWING THREE-DIMENSIONAL OBJECTS   443

C MOVIES   453

D IMAGE PROCESSING   456

E	**GRAPHICAL USER INTERFACE**	**467**
F	**ANSWER KEY**	**497**
SUBJECT INDEX		**515**

PREFACE

WHAT THIS BOOK DESCRIBES

This book is intended to introduce numerical analysis and graphic visualization using MATLAB to college students majoring in engineering and science. It can also be a handbook of MATLAB applications for professional engineers and scientists. The goal is not to teach the mathematics of numerical analysis, but rather to teach the knowledge and skills of solving equations and presenting them graphically so that readers can easily handle equations and results of the computations.

With its unique and fascinating capabilities, MATLAB has changed the concept of programming for numerical and mathematical analyses. Therefore, MATLAB is a superb vehicle to achieve our goal. This book fully implements the mathematical and graphic tools in the most recent version of MATLAB.

The following four fundamental elements are integrated in this book: (1) programming in MATLAB, (2) mathematical basics of numerical analysis, (3) application of numerical methods to engineering, scientific, and mathematical problems, and (4) scientific graphics with MATLAB.

The first two chapters are comprehensive tutorials of MATLAB commands and graphic tools, particularly for the beginner or entry-level college student. Indeed, these two chapters have been most significantly enhanced in this edition compared to the first edition. In Chapter 1, understanding and developing programming skills on MATLAB are emphasized particularly because, unless the reader has knowledge and experience with another programming language, these are tough hurdles for the beginner to overcome. To aquire the knowledge and skills necessary to read the rest of the book, solving the problems at the end of each chapter is very important.

Chapter 2 starts out with the elements of graphics on MATLAB, which is easy to follow. Yet, toward the end of the chapter, three-dimensional graphics on the professional level are achieved. Not only is the programming technique of plotting functions mentioned, but also skills of presenting mathematical and scientific material using graphics are developed throughout the chapter. The graphics knowledge acquired in this chapter are foundations in learning and applying the numerical methods described in the remainder of the book. Again, practice on the computer is important. Some students try to memorize scripts without understanding why and how they work, but such an effort is utterly meaningless. More important is to play with a few new commands, understand how they work and how they may fail, and finally become a master of the commands.

Chapters 3 through 11 cover numerical methods and their implementations with MATLAB. All the numerical methods described are illustrated with applications on MATLAB. Appendices describe special topics, including advanced three-dimensional graphics with colors, motion pictures, image processing, and graphical user interface. Readers should feel free to use the scripts in this book in any way desired. However, the beginning students are advised not to use these scripts blindly. The students should write their own scripts.

Using the lists of the scripts and functions, readers can run most examples and figures on their own computers. The m-files of the scripts can be downloaded as mentioned later.

WHAT IS UNIQUE ABOUT MATLAB?

MATLAB may be regarded as a programming language like Fortran or C, although describing it in a few words is difficult. Some of its outstanding features for numerical analyses, however, are:

> Significantly simpler programming
> Continuity among integer, real, and complex values
> Extended range of numbers and their accuracy
> A comprehensive mathematical library
> Extensive graphic tools including graphic user interface functions
> Capability of linking with traditional programming languages
> Transportability of MATLAB programs

An extraordinary feature of MATLAB is that there is no distinction among real, complex, and integer numbers. All numbers are in double precision. In MATLAB, all kinds of numbers are continuously connected, as they should be. It means that in MATLAB, any variable can take any type of number without special declaration in programming. This makes programming faster and more productive. In Fortran, a different subroutine is necessary for each single, double, real or complex, or integer variable, while in MATLAB there is no need to separate them.

The mathematical library in MATLAB makes mathematical analyses easy. Yet the user can develop additional mathematical routines significantly more easily than in other programming languages because of the continuity between real and complex variables. Among numerous mathematical functions, linear algebra solvers play central roles. Indeed, the whole MATLAB system is founded upon linear algebra solvers.

IMPORTANCE OF GRAPHICS

Graphic presentation of mathematical analysis helps the reader to understand mathematics and makes it enjoyable. Although this advantage has been well known, presenting computed results with computer graphics was not without substantial extra effort in the past. With MATLAB, however, graphic presentations of mathematical material is possible with just a few commands. Scientific and even artistic graphic objects can be created on the screen using mathematical expressions. It has been found that MATLAB graphics motivate and excite students to learn mathematical and numerical methods that could otherwise be dull.

MATLAB graphics are easy and great fun for readers. This book also illustrates image processing and production of motion pictures for scientific computing as well as for artistic or hobby material.

COMMAND AND FUNCTION NAMES IN THIS BOOK

The command and function names peculiar to this book all include an underscore, for example, rotx_.m. The functions and commands that do not include an underscore are original from MATLAB.

WILL MATLAB ELIMINATE THE NEED FOR FORTRAN OR C?

The answer is no. Fortran and C are still important for high-performance computing that requires a large memory or long computing time. The speed of MATLAB computation is significantly slower than that with Fortran or C because MATLAB is paying the high price for the nice features. Learning Fortran or C, however, is not a prerequisite for understanding MATLAB.

REFERENCE BOOKS THAT ARE HELPFUL TO LEARN MATLAB

This book explains many MATLAB commands but is not intended to be a complete guide to MATLAB. Readers interested in further information on MATLAB are advised to read *User's Guide* and *Reference Guide*. Also, you should know that over 400 books for use with MATLAB, Simulink, Toolboxes, and Blocksets have been written. See

http://www.mathworks.com/support/books

WEB SITE FOR READERS OF THIS BOOK

A Web site for readers of this book has been opened at

http://olen.eng.ohio-state.edu/matlab

This Web site includes additional examples, hints, and color graphics that cannot be printed in the book. If there are corrections to the text material, they will appear on this Web site. Links to other relevant sites are also provided.

HOW TO OBTAIN M-FILES PACKAGE

The m-files package that includes all the scripts and functions developed in the present book are available from the download site of the publisher, which can be accessed via the Web site in the foregoing paragraph. The package includes the following files:

(1) All m-files listed at the end of chapters.
(2) All scripts illustrated in the book (except short ones).
(3) Scripts to plot typical figures in the book.

SOLUTION KEYS

Solution keys for the problems for each chapter are available at the end of this book. Further help may also be available at the Web site for the readers.

HOW TO OBTAIN MORE INFORMATION ABOUT MATLAB

The best way to start collecting more information about MATLAB is to visit the Web site of MATHWORKS at http://www.mathworks.com.

For other communication with MathWorks, their address is: The MathWorks, Inc., 3 Apple Hill Drive, Natick, MA 01760-2098, United States

Phone: 508-647-7000, Fax: 508-647-7001.

LIST OF REVIEWERS
The first edition of this book was reviewed by:

Professor T. Aldemir, Nuclear Engineering,
The Ohio State University, Columbus, Ohio

Professor M. Darwish, Mechanical Engineering Department,
American University of Beirut, Beirut, Lebanon

The MathWorks Inc., Natick, Massachusetts

Professor J. K. Shultis, Nuclear Engineering,
Kansas State University, Manhattan, Kansas

Professor S. V. Sreenivasan, Department of Mechanical Engineering,
University of Texas, Austin, Texas

TRADE NAMES
Image Alchemy is a registered trademark of Handmade Software, Inc.
Digital Mavica is a trademark of Sony Corporation.
MATLAB is a registered trademark of MathWorks, Inc.
Qtake is a registered trademark of Apple, Inc.
Unix is a registered trademark of AT&T Bell Laboratories.
Windows is a registered trademark of Microsoft, Inc.

ACKNOWLEDGEMENTS
Editor Mary Franz originally suggested the idea of developing this book. Her initial suggestion was coincident with the time the author started teaching numerical methods with MATLAB. Without her continuous encouragement and administrative assistance, this book would have been impossible. The author is grateful for the full support of this book by MathWorks. Paul Costa, Allison Babb, and John Galenski of MathWorks have given the author substantial technical support. Support to the authors provided by Cristina Palumbo and Naomi Fernandes of MathWorks have also been indispensable.

Several university professors have provided useful example problems, which are acknowledged in the footnotes below the material. Former graduate students at The Ohio State University, including David Smith, Keiji Yano, Y.C. Su, and R. Chong, assisted the author to finish the manuscript. Comments from the instructors and students of the first edition were invaluable.

The manuscript for this second edition was written in PCTeX32. All figures except a few were created by MATLAB, saved in PostScript form, and then taken into LaTex manuscript files.

Robert Chong of The Ohio State University typed a major part of the first draft in LaTex. The author owes much to Professor Shultis, who not only reviewed the manuscript, but was also helpful in conjunction with his book, *LaTex Notes* (Prentice-Hall 1994), in typesetting using LaTex.

Finally, the author sincerely hopes that the reader will enjoy the study of *Numerical Analysis and Graphic Visualization with MATLAB*.

S. Nakamura
Columbus, Ohio

Chapter 1

MATLAB PRIMER

This chapter will serve as a hands-on tutorial for beginners who are unfamiliar with MATLAB. We assume that readers have either the student edition or a full version of MATLAB.[1] Before reading this chapter, the reader should set up MATLAB on the computer, open the command window, and try to type and execute the commands as they are explained. Although this book tries to explain the MATLAB commands as clearly as possible, keep in mind that learning a new language is confusing and tedious in the beginning. Trying the commands and practicing them on the computer will help you to understand them.

Readers are encouraged to solve most of the problems at the end of this chapter. Each one is simple, but your knowledge and skill will increase by a continuous effort to solve them. Readers may also seek help by looking at answer keys at the end of the book, as well as similar problems and answers posted at the author's web site.[2]

Throughout this book you will see `log` represented as $\log_e$. The log function to the base 10, namely $\log_{10}$, will be specifically denoted as `log10`. Trigonometric functions use *radians* but not degrees; however, the angles in graphic views are in degrees.

The results of some computations may vary slightly on different computers, but the differences are typically negligible. Some calculations, however, are sensitive to rounding errors and can produce significantly disparate results on different computers. Such problems are often called ill-conditioned problems and are usually difficult to solve on any computer.

---

[1] MATLAB-6. However, most explanations are applicable to MATLAB 4 and 5 except for a small number of commands. The features available only with MATLAB-6 are indicated in the text.

[2] http://olen.eng.ohio-state.edu/matlab

1.1 BEFORE STARTING CALCULATIONS

how to open MATLAB: On a Unix workstation, MATLAB can be opened by typing

> matlab

On a PC, MATLAB can be started by clicking on the start-up menu or a shortcut icon for MATLAB. When MATLAB-6 is started, the window, as illustrated in Figure 1.1, will open. The left side is divided into two subwindows. The right side is the command window, where the most important work for MATLAB is done. Earlier versions did not have such divided subwindows on the left side.

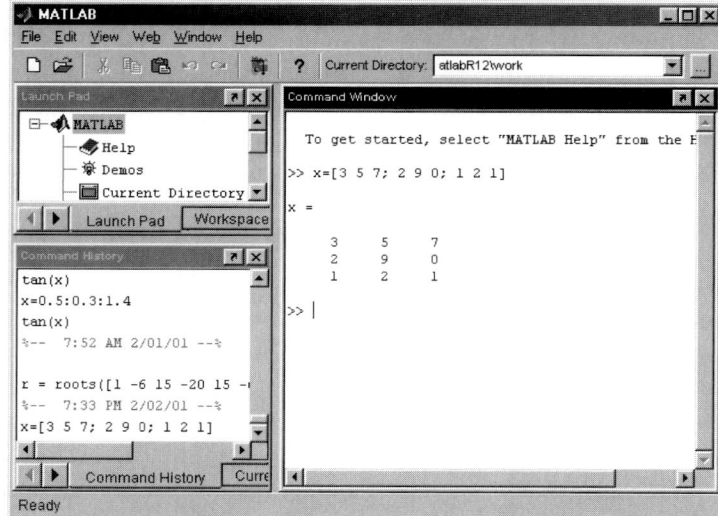

Figure 1.1 MATLAB-6 Desktop.

Once the prompt sign ">>" appears in the command window, type the commands that are explained throughout this section. On Windows, the initial (default) working directory is C:/MATLAB/bin. If you wish to use a floppy disk as a working directory, type the command to change directory, namely "cd a:", in after the >> sign, for example

>> cd a:

If the working directory is C:/my_directory, type

>> cd ../..
>> cd my_directory

Section 1.1 Before Starting Calculations

On Unix, MATLAB can be opened from any directory. To quit MATLAB, type

```
>> quit
```

help: When the meaning of a command is not clear, type help followed by any command in question. The help command will give you a concise but precise explanation and will be one of the most frequently used commands as you proceed. If you type help date or help format as examples, responses are, respectively, as follows:

```
>> help date
   DATE   Current date as date string.
   S = DATE returns a string containing the date in dd-mmm-yyyy format.
   See also NOW, CLOCK, DATENUM.

>> help format
   FORMAT Set output format.
   All computations in MATLAB are done in double precision.
   FORMAT may be used to switch between different output
   display formats as follows:
      FORMAT          Default. Same as SHORT.
      FORMAT SHORT    Scaled fixed point format with 5 digits.
      FORMAT LONG     Scaled fixed point format with 15 digits.
      FORMAT SHORT E  Floating point format with 5 digits.
      FORMAT LONG E   Floating point format with 15 digits.
      FORMAT SHORT G  Best of fixed or floating point format
                      with 5 digits.
      FORMAT LONG G   Best of fixed or floating point format
                      with 15 digits.
      FORMAT HEX      Hexadecimal format.
      FORMAT +        The symbols +, - and blank are printed
                      for positive, negative, and zero elements.
                      Imaginary parts are ignored.
      FORMAT BANK     Fixed format for dollars and cents.
      FORMAT RAT      Approximation by ratio of small integers.

   Spacing:
      FORMAT COMPACT Suppress extra line-feeds.
      FORMAT LOOSE   Puts the extra line-feeds back in.
```

In the online help, keywords are capitalized to make them stand out. Always type commands in lowercase as all command and function names are actually in lowercase.

Be aware that the `help` command is limited to the questions regarding the commands. If you have a question that is more general in nature, click the *Help* menu on the top menu bar and then click on *MATLAB Help*. A window as shown in Figure 1.2 will open with the index page already in front. Type the keyword for your question in the small white box under *Search index for*. The remainder of the process is similar to that of `help` in MS Windows.

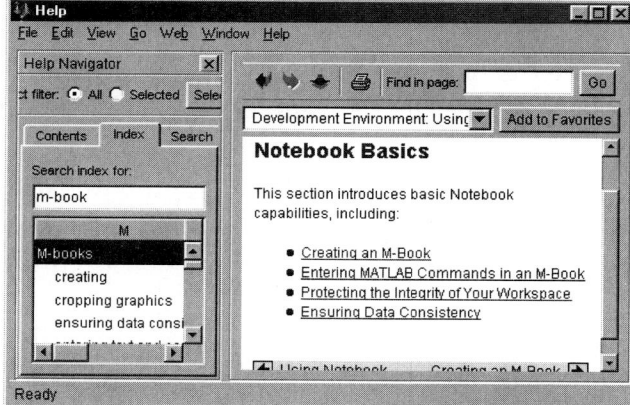

Figure 1.2 Help window.

version: The first thing you should know about MATLAB is what version you are using. To get this information, type `version`.

pwd: `pwd` prints out the current working directory name.

dir: `ls` or `dir` lists all the filenames in the current directory.

cd: `cd` changes the directory.

what: `what` will list M-, MAT-, and MEX-files in the current working directory.[3] The command `what dirname` lists the files in directory `dirname` on the `matlabpath`. It is not necessary to give the full pathname in the position of `dirname`; the last component or last several components are sufficient. For example, `what general` and `what matlab/general` both list the m-files in

---

[3] m-file: a script or function file (its format is `filename.m`); MAT-file: a file containing binary data (its format is `filename.mat`); MEX-file: MATLAB executable file compiled from Fortran or C (`filename.mex`).

directory `toolbox/matlab/general`.

who: `who` lists the variables in the current workspace. `whos` lists more information about each variable. `who global` and `whos global` list the variables in the global workspace.

clock: The `clock` command prints out numbers such as

```
ans =
    1.0e+03 *
    2.001  0.0030  0.0050  0.0150  0.0140  0.0091
```

The first number, 1.0e+03, is a multiplier. The numbers in the second line have the following meaning:

```
[year, month, day, hour, minute, second]
```

The clock values can also be printed out in the integer form by `fix(clock)`. The answer is

```
ans =
    2001    3    5    15    19    56
```

where time was year 2001, 3rd month, 5th day, 15 hr, 19 min and 56 sec, approximately six minutes after the first example of `clock` was printed out. The elapsed time of an execution may be measured by `clock`. For example, set t_0=`clock` before a computation starts and t_1=`clock` when completed. Then, $t\_1 - t\_0$ gives the time elapsed for the computation. You can also use `tic` and `toc` to measure the elapsed time.

The `date` command gives similar information, but in a more concise format:

```
ans =
    5-Mar-01
```

path: `path` or `matlabpath` prints MATLAB's current search path. Command `p = path` returns a string p containing the path. Command `path(p0)` changes the path to p0, which is a string containing the new path. Command `path(p1,p2)` changes the path to the concatenation of the two path strings, p1 and p2. Therefore, `path(path, p3)` appends a new directory, p3, to the current path and `path(p3, path)` prepends the new path.

getenv: `getenv('matlabpath')` will show current MATLAB paths. If you have not set any path, the response of the computer is simply two dots.

diary on, diary off: with `diary` you can record all activities on the MATLAB window. The `diary on` command starts writing all keyboard input as well as most screen output to a file named `diary`. `diary off` terminates writing. If file `diary` already exists, the screen output is appended to the existing diary file. A filename other than `diary` may be specified by writing the intended filename after `diary`. Without `on` or `off`, `diary` itself toggles `diary on` and `diary off`. The file may be printed as a hard copy or may be edited later.

!(escape): The ! mark is the operator to escape from MATLAB. With this mark, you have access to the DOS or Unix commands. A text editing software like the *vi* editor may be opened from within MATLAB by using `!vi filename` if you are on an Unix computer. Escape may be used similarly on a PC for some DOS commands. `!erase filename` deletes the file named `filename` on a PC. A subdirectory named `d.subdir` on PC can be created by using `!mkdir d.subdir`. Formatting a diskette from MATLAB on a PC is possible by using `!format a:`. Executing PC or Unix software in this way is not recommended, however, because some programs, particularly graphic or communication software, may harm the computing environment.

demo: The `demo` command guides the user to numerous demonstrations that are selectable from a menu. The MATLAB demonstrations are fun. Visit them often until you understand them in detail.

pathological symptom: MATLAB can get sick for various reasons. Possible causes may include: (1) wrong combination of commands given by the user, (2) its own bug, or (3) software instability due to insufficient memory. Pathological symptoms tend to occur more frequently with an early edition of an updated version that is loaded with many new features. If strange behavior is suspected, shut down MATLAB and restart. If a software error is found, it should be reported to the company. Often, the company's web site will explain and provide a patch to update the software.

1.2 HOW TO DO CALCULATIONS

arithmetic operators: Arithmetic operators +, -, *, and / are, respectively, *plus*, *minus*, *multiply*, and *divide*, the same as in traditional programming languages. To express power, the operator ^ is used. MATLAB uses one untraditional operator, \, which may be named *inverse division*. This operator yields the reciprocal of division, that is, a\b equals b/a. For example,

```
c = 3\1
c =
    0.3333
```

It is not recommended that readers use this operator in typical computations, but it will become important in Chapter 3, "Linear Algebra."

calculation with single variables: When a command window is opened, a prompt sign >> is seen at the upper left corner of the window. Any command can be written after the prompt sign. In the explanation of the commands, however, the prompt sign will be omitted for simplicity.

As a simple example, let us evaluate:

$$\text{Volume} = \frac{4}{3}\pi r^3, \quad \text{with } r = 2$$

The commands to type on the screen are:

List 1.1a
```
r = 2;
vol = (4/3)*pi*r^3;
```

where $\text{pi} = \pi$, that is, 3.14159265358979, in MATLAB. Each line is typed after the prompt sign >> and the return key is hit when finished typing. Notice in the preceding script that each line is a command and completed by a semicolon. The caret symbol ^ after r is the power operator.

When we work in the command window, the computer calculates the answer for each command immediately after the return key is hit. Therefore, the value of vol is already in the computer. How can we get the result printed out on the screen?

The quickest way of printing out the result is to type vol and hit return. Then the computer prints out

```
vol =
     33.510
```

Another way of printing out the value of `vol` is to omit the semicolon at the end of the second command

List 1.1b
```
r = 2;
vol = (4/3)*pi*r^3
```

Without a semicolon, the result is printed out immediately after the computation. Because displaying every result is cumbersome, however, we generally place a semicolon after each command.

Multiple commands may be written in a single line separated by semicolons. If the results are to be printed out for each command executed, separate commands by commas. The line may be terminated with or without a comma. For example, if you write

```
r = 2,   vol = (4/3)*pi*r^3
```

the values of `r` and `vol` are printed out, but if you write

```
r = 2;   vol = (4/3)*pi*r^3;
```

no results are displayed.

A long command may be split into multiple lines. In Fortran, it is done by a continuation mark on column 6. In MATLAB, the continuation mark is ... and it is placed at the end of the line to be continued; for example,

List 1.2
```
r = 2;
vol = (4/3)*3.14159 ...
      *r^3;
```

The prompt sign will not appear in the line following the continuation mark.

variables and variable names: Variable names and their types do not have to be declared. This is because variable names in MATLAB make no distinction among integer, real, and complex variables. Any variable can take real, complex, and integer values.

In principle, any name can be used as long as it is compatible in MATLAB. We should, however, be aware of two incompatible situations. The first is that the name is not accepted by MATLAB. The second is that the

Section 1.2 How to Do Calculations 9

name is accepted, but it destroys the original meaning of a reserved name. These conflicts can occur with the following types of names:

(a) Names for certain values
(b) Function (subroutine) names
(c) Command names

One method to examine compatibility of the variable name is to test it on the command screen. A valid statement such as x=9 is responded to as

```
x =
    9
```

which means that the variable is accepted. If end=4 (a bad example) is attempted, however, it is ignored.

An example of the second conflict is as follows: If sin and cos are used (as poor examples of variables) with no relation to the trigonometric functions, for example,

```
sin = 3;
cos = sin^2;
```

the calculations proceed; however, sin and cos can never be used as trigonometric functions thereafter until variables are cleared by issuing the clear command or MATLAB is shut down. If any error message concerning a conflict appears, the reader should investigate the cause.

Traditionally, symbols i, j, k, l, m, and n have been used as integer variables or indices. At the same time, i and j are used to denote a unit imaginary value, or $\sqrt{-1}$. In MATLAB, i and j are reserved as unit imaginary value. Therefore, if the computation involves complex variables, it is advisable to avoid i and j as user-defined variables.

Table 1.1 lists samples of reserved variable names that have special meanings. Whether a variable or filename exists may also be checked by using the exist command. For more details, type help exist.

format: Numbers displayed are five-digit numbers by default:

```
pi
ans =
    3.1416
```

The same numbers, however, may be displayed with 16 digits after the command format long; for example,

Table 1.1 Special Numbers and Variable Names

Variable name	Meaning	Value
eps	Machine epsilon	2.2204e-16
pi	π	3.14159...
i and j	Unit imaginary	$\sqrt{-1}$
inf	Infinity	∞
NaN	Not a number	
date	Date	
flops	Floating point operation count	
nargin	Number of function input arguments	
nargout	Same for output	

```
format long
pi
ans =
     3.141592653589793
```

In order to return to the short format, use `format short`. Also, with `format short e` and `format long e`, respectively, short and long numbers are printed in floating-point format.

clear: As you execute commands, MATLAB memorizes the variables used. Their values stay in memory until you quit MATLAB or clear the variables. To clear all the variables, use the `clear` command. If only certain variables are to be cleared, name the variables after `clear`; for example,

```
clear x y z
```

clc: If you wish to clear a window, use the command `clc`.

1.3 BRANCH STATEMENTS

if, else, elsif, end: An `if` statement is always closed with an `end` statement; for example,

List 1.3
```
n = 2;    %(Assume n is a user input so it may be changed)
if     n<=5,  price=15;
elseif n>5,   price=12;
end
```

Here the line starting `elseif` can be eliminated if not needed. Do not separate `elseif` into two words. Of course, `elseif` can be repeated when necessary. Notice also in writing the foregoing script that the prompt sign does not appear after `if` until `end` is typed. The foregoing script may be equivalently written as

```
n = 2;    %(Assume n is a user input so it may be changed)
if    n<=5,   price=15;
else  price=12;
end
```

When the `if` statement needs to examine the equality of two terms, use "==" as in the C language; for example,

List 1.4
```
n = 2;
if n==2, price=17;
end
```

The *not equal* operator is written as "~=," for example,

List 1.5
```
r = 2;
if r ~= 3, vol = (4/3)*pi*r^3;
end
```

The *greater than, less than, equal or greater than,* and *equal or less than* operators are, respectively,

```
>
<
>=
<=
```

The logical statements *and* and *or* are denoted by `&` and `|`, respectively. For example, the conditional equation,

$$\text{if } g > 3 \text{ or } g < 0, \text{ then } a = 6$$

is written as

```
if g>3 | g<0, a = 6; end
```

Also, the conditional equation

$$\text{if } a > 3 \text{ and } c < 0, b = 19$$

is stated as

```
if a>3 & c<0, b=19; end
```

The & and | operators can be used in a clustered form, for example,

```
if ((a==2 | b==3) & c<5)    g=1; end
```

Example 1.1

Assuming two arbitrary integers, R and D, are given in the beginning of the script, write a script that prints out only if R is divisible by $D = 3$.

Solution

Two equivalent ways to examine if R is divisible by another number are: (1) `fix(R/D)=R/D`, and (2) `mod(R,D)=0`. Here, `fix(x)` returns the integer part of the number x, while `mod(x,y)` returns the remainder on division of x by y. Therefore, a script based on (1) is:

List 1.6a
```
R=45; D=3;
if fix(R/D) == R/D, R, end
```

A script based on (2) is

List 1.6b
```
R=45; D=3;
if mod(R,D) == 0, R, end
```

1.4 LOOPS WITH for/end OR while/end

loops: MATLAB has `for/end` and `while/end` loops. To illustrate a `for/end` loop, let us look at the following script that calculates $y = x^2 - 5x - 3$ for each of $x = 1, 2..9$ in increasing order.

List 1.7a
```
for x=1:9
    y=x^2 - 5*x - 3
end
```

Section 1.4 Loops with for/end or while/end

Notice that `for` is terminated by `end`. In the first cycle, x is set to 1, and y is calculated. In the second cycle, x is set to 2 (with an increment of 1), and y is calculated. The same is repeated until the calculation of y is completed for the last value of x.

If x is to be changed with a different increment, the increment can be specified between the initial and last number as follows:

List 1.7a
```
for x=1:0.5:9
    y=x^2 - 5*x - 3
end
```

where the increment is now 0.5.

The order of calculation in the loop can be reversed as follows:

List 1.7b
```
for x=9:-1:1
    y=x^2 - 5*x - 3
end
```

Here, the middle number -1 in 9:-1:1 is the increment in changing x.

It is also possible to compute for any sequence of specified values of x, for example:

List 1.7c
```
for x=[-2 0 15 6]
    y=x^2 - 5*x - 3
end
```

Here, y is computed for $x = -2$ first, which is followed by $x = 0$, 15, and 6.

The `if/end` statement can be inserted in the loop. In the following example, $y = \sin(x)$ if $\sin(x) > 0$ but $y = 0$ if $\sin(x) < 0$.

List 1.7d
```
for x=0:0.1:10
    y=sin(x);
    if y<0, y=0;end
    y
end
```

In the following script, c=0 initializes the counter c to zero, x=[-8, ..] defines an array of the numbers, and `length(x)` is the length of the array x. In the `for/end` loop the counter c is incremented by one if x(i) is negative. Finally, c prints out the count of the negative elements.

List 1.7e
```
c=0; x=[-8, 0, 2, 5, 7, 2, 0, 0, 4, 6, 6, 9];
for i=1:length(x)
   if x(i)<0, c=c+1; end
end
c
```

The loop index can be decremented as

List 1.8
```
c=0; x=[-8, 0, 2, 5, 7, 2, 0, 0, 4, 6, 6, 9];
for i=length(x):-1:1
   if x(i)<0, c=c+1; end
end
c
```

In this example, -1 between two colon operators is the decrement of the parameter i after each cycle of the loop operation.

An alternative way of writing a loop is to use the while/end; for example,

List 1.9
```
i = 0;c=0; x=[-8, 0, 2, 5, 7, 2, 0, 0, 4, 6, 6, 9];
while i<length(x)+1
   i=i+1
   if x(i)<0, c=c+1; end
end
c
```

Example 1.2

Write a script that removes the numbers divisible by 4 from an array x. Assume the array x is given by

x=[-8, 0, 2, 5, 7, 2, 0, 0, 4, 6, 6, 9]

Solution

The script to the answer is

List 1.9
```
x=[-8, 0, 2, 5, 7, 2, 0, 0, 4, 6, 6, 9];
y=[];
for n=1:length(x)
   if x(n)/4 - fix(x(n)/4)~=0  y=[y,x(n)]; end
end
y
```

In the foregoing script, fix(x(n)/4) equals the integer part of x(n)/4, so fix(x(n)/4)-x(n)/4=0 is satisfied if x(n) is divisible by 4. Equivalently, mod(a,b) may be used that equals zero if a is divisible by b. The following script shows alternative programming to achieve the same end:

List 1.9
```
x=[-8, 0, 2, 5, 7, 2, 0, 0, 4, 6, 6, 9];
for n=1:length(x)
    if mod(x(n),4)=0  x(n)=[]; end
end
x
```

The result is

```
y =
     2    5    7    2    6    6    9
```

break: The break terminates the execution of a for or while loop. When used in nested loops, only the immediate loop where break is located is terminated. In the next example, break terminates the inner loop as soon as j>2*i is satisfied once, but the loop for i is continued until i=6:

List 1.10
```
for i=1:6
    for j=1:20
        if j>2*i, break, end
    end
end
```

Another example is

List 1.11
```
r=0
while r<10
    r = input('Type radius (or -1 to stop): ');
    if  r< 0, break, end
    vol = (4/3)*pi*r^3;
    fprintf('Volume = %7.3f\n', vol)
end
```

In the foregoing loop, the radius r is typed through the keyboard. The fprintf statement is to print out vol with a format, %7.3f, which is equivalent to F7.3 in Fortran. If $0 \leq r < 10$, vol is computed and printed out, but if $r < 0$ the loop is terminated. Also, if $r < 10$ is dissatisfied once, the while loop is terminated. More explanations for `input` and `fprintf` are given in later subsections.

In a programming language that has no break command, `goto` would be used to break a loop. MATLAB, on the other hand, has no `goto` statement.

infinite loop: Sometimes a loop that can continue infinitely is used, which may be terminated when a certain condition is met. The following example shows an infinite loop that is broken only if the condition $x > x \text{limit}$ is met:

```
while 1
   .
   .
   if x > xlimit, break; end
   .
   .
end
```

1.5 READING AND WRITING

Passing data to and from MATLAB is possible in several different ways. The methods may be classified into three classes:

(a) Interactive operation by keyboard or mouse
(b) Reading from or writing to a data file
(c) Using `save` or `load`

In the remainder of this subsection, only a minimal amount of information regarding reading and writing is introduced. More information can be found in Section 1.8.

input: MATLAB can take input data through the keyboard using the input command. To read a number, the synopsis would be

```
z = input('Type your input: ')
```

The string between quote signs, namely, `Type your input:`, is a prompting message to be printed out on the screen. As a value is typed and a return key is hit, the input is saved in `z`. A string input can be typed from the keyboard. The synopsis is

Section 1.5 Reading and Writing

```
z = input('Your name please: ', 's')
```

The second argument 's' indicates that the input from the keyboard is a string. The variable z becomes an array variable (row vector) unless the string has only one character. A string input can be taken by input without 's' if the typed string is enclosed by single quote signs. In this case, a prompt message may be written as

```
z = input('Type your name (in single quote signs):')
```

fprintf: Printing out formatted messages and numbers is possible using fprintf; for example,

```
fprintf('The volume of the sphere %12.5f.\n', vol)
```

Included between two single quote signs are a string to be printed out, the format for the volume, and a new-line operator. The style of the format is familiar to those who know the C language: The volume of the sphere is the string to be printed out, %12.5f is the format and similar to F12.5 in Fortran, and \n is the new-line operator that advances the screen position by one line. The new-line operator can be placed anywhere within the string. Finally, vol is the variable to be printed out in accordance with the format %12.5f. If \n is omitted, the next print starts without advancing a line.

The command

```
fprintf('e_format: %12.5e\n', 12345.2)
```

will print out

```
e_format:  1.23452e+04
```

If two print statements are consecutively written without \n in the first statement, for example,

```
fprintf('e_format: %12.5e', 12345.2);
fprintf('f_format: %12.3f\n', 7.23462)
```

then all the output will be printed out in a single line as

```
e_format: 1.23452e+04  f_format: 7.235
```

An integer value can be typed using the same format, except that 0 is placed after the decimal point; for example,

```
fprintf('f_format: %12.0f\n', 93)
```

yields

```
f_format: 93
```

When multiple numbers are to be printed on a single line, `fprintf` may be repeatedly used without `\n`, except in the last statement.

With the `fprintf` command, it is possible to write formatted output into a file. To do this, the named file has to be opened by the `fopen` command, for example,

```
vol=55.0
fileid = fopen('file_x','w');
fprintf(fileid,'Volume=  %12.5f\n', vol);
fclose(fileid);
```

will write the output in the file named `file_x`. If no such file exists, a new file is created. If the file exists, the output is appended. If necessary, the existing file `file_x` can be deleted by `!rm file_x` on Unix, or `!erase file_x` on Windows.

disp: Command `disp` displays a number, vector, matrix, or a string on the command window without variable name. Therefore, it may be used to display messages or data on the screen. For example, `disp(pi)` and `disp pi` both print 3.14159 on the command screen. Try also `disp 'This is a test for disp.'`.

sprintf: Writing `sprintf` is very similar to `fprintf` except that `sprintf` writes the output into a string. This statement is often used to create a command in a string that can be executed as `eval(s)`. It is useful when a command is to be created or edited automatically and executed within an m-file.

1.6 ARRAY VARIABLES

one-dimensional array variables: One-dimensional array variables are in a column or a row form, and are closely related to vectors and matrices. In MATLAB, *row array* is synonymous with *row vector*, and *column array* is synonymous with *column vector*. The variable x can be defined as a row vector by specifying its elements; for example:

```
x = [0, 0.1, 0.2, 0.3, 0.4, 0.5];
```

Section 1.6 Array Variables

To print a particular element, type x with its subscript. For example, typing x(3) as a command will show

```
ans =
      0.2
```

An equivalent way of defining the same x is

```
for i=1:6
   x(i) = (i-1)*0.1;
end
```

The size of the vector does not have to be predeclared as it is adjusted automatically. The number of elements of x can be increased by defining additional elements, for example,

```
x(7) = 0.6;
```

A row array variable with a fixed increment or decrement may be equivalently written as

```
x = 2:-0.4:2
```

It yields

```
x =  2.0000  1.6000  1.2000  0.8000  0.4000  -0.0000
```

The definition of a column array is similar to a row array except that the elements are separated by semicolons; for example,

```
z = [0; 0.1; 0.2; 0.3; 0.4; 0.5];
```

An alternative way of defining the same thing is to put a prime after a row array:

```
z = [0, 0.1, 0.2, 0.3, 0.4, 0.5]';
```

The prime operator is the same as the transpose operator in the matrix and vector calculus, so it converts a column vector to a row vector and vice versa. Typing z as a command yields

```
z =
    0
    0.1
    0.2
    0.3
    0.4
    0.5
```

If a single element of an array c is specified, for example,

```
c(8) = 11;
```

c(i) = 0 is assumed for i=1 through 7. Therefore, typing c yields

```
c =
    0   0   0   0   0   0   0   11
```

Likewise

```
clear c
c(1:5)=7
```

produces

```
c =
    7   7   7   7   7
```

Also

```
clear c
c(1:2:7)=5
```

yields

```
c =
    5   0   5   0   5   0   5
```

which can be further changed by

```
c(2:2:7)=1
```

to

```
c =
    5   1   5   1   5   1   5
```

When y and x have the same length and the same form (row or column), the vector y and x can be added, subtracted, multiplied, and divided using the array arithmetic operators as

```
z = x + y
z = x - y
z = x .* y
z = x ./ y
```

which are equivalent, respectively, to

List 1.12
```
for i=1:6;   z(i) = x(i) + y(i);   end
for i=1:6;   z(i) = x(i) - y(i);   end
for i=1:6;   z(i) = x(i)*y(i);     end
for i=1:6;   z(i) = x(i)/y(i);     end
```

The rules for addition and subtraction are the same as for vectors in linear algebra. However, .* and ./ are named array multiplication operators and array division operators, respectively, which are not the same as multiplication and division for matrices and vectors. If the period in .* or ./ is omitted, the meaning becomes entirely different (see Chapter 3, "Linear Algebra," for more details).

The array power operator is illustrated by

```
g = z.^1.2;
```

where z is a vector of length 6, a period is placed before the ^ operator, and g becomes a vector of the same length. The foregoing statement is equivalent to

```
for i=1:length(g);   g(i) = z(i)^1.2;   end
```

where no period is placed before the ^ operator.

The size of an array can be increased by appending an element or a vector (or vectors). As an example, assume

```
x =
     2   3
```

The following command appends 5 to x and makes its length 3:

```
x = [x, 5]
```

which returns

```
x =
     2   3   5
```

A column vector may be appended with a number or a vector or vectors. Suppose y is a column vector,

```
y =
     2
     3
```

then

```
    y = [y; 7]
```

yields

```
    y =
        2
        3
        7
```

Here, 7 is appended to the end of the column vector. Notice that a semicolon is used to append to a column vector. An element can be prepended to a vector also, for example, x = [9,x] yields

```
    x =
        9   2   3   5
```

where x on the right side was defined earlier. Similarly, [-1;y] yields

```
    y =
        -1
         2
         3
         7
```

A reverse procedure is to extract a part of a vector. For the foregoing y,

```
    w = y(3:4)
```

will define w that equals the 3rd and 4th elements of y, namely

```
    w =
        3
        7
```

length, size: If you don't remember the size of a vector, ask the computer. For a vector

```
    x = [9, 2, 3, 5]
```

the inquiry

```
    length(x)
```

is responded to by

Section 1.6 Array Variables

```
ans =
     4
```

The answer is the same for a column array. Let us define y = [9, 2, 3]'. Then, `length(y)` returns `ans = 3`; however, when you want to know if the vector is a column or row type in addition to the length, use `size`. For example, `size(y)` will return

```
ans =
     3    1
```

where the first number is the number of rows and the second number is the number of columns. From this answer, we learn that y is a 3×1 array, that is, a column vector of length 3. For `z=[9,2,3,5]`, `size(z)` will return

```
ans =
     1    4
```

that is, z is a row vector of length 4.

deletion of array elements: An element of an array may be deleted as follows. Assume `z=[3, 5, 7, 9]`, and the third element is to be deleted from the array. Then

```
z(3)=[]
```

yields

```
z =
    [3, 5, 9]
```

string variables: String variables are arrays. For example, a string variable v defined by

```
v = 'glacier'
```

is equivalent to

```
v = ['g', 'l', 'a', 'c', 'i', 'e', 'r']
```

The variable v can be converted to a column string by

```
v = v'
```

which is

glacier

two-dimensional array variables: A two-dimensional array, which is synonymous with a matrix in MATLAB, can be defined by specifying its elements. For example, a 3×3 array can be defined by

```
m = [0.1, 0.2, 0.3; 0.4, 0.5, 0.6; 0.7, 0.8, 0.9];
```

Notice that the elements for a row are terminated by a semicolon. Of course, the number of elements in each row must be identical. Otherwise the definition will not be accepted. The statement is equivalent to writing

List 1.13
```
m(1,1)=0.1;
m(1,2)=0.2;
m(1,3)=0.3;
m(2,1)=0.4;
m(2,2)=0.5;
m(2,3)=0.6;
m(3,1)=0.7;
m(3,2)=0.8;
m(3,3)=0.9;
```

Typing m as a command yields

```
m =
     0.1000    0.2000    0.3000
     0.4000    0.5000    0.6000
     0.7000    0.8000    0.9000
```

A whole column or a row of a two-dimensional array can be expressed using a colon. For example, m(1,:) and m(:,3) are the first row of m and the third column of m, respectively, and treated as vectors. For example,

```
c(1,:) = m(3,:);
c(2,:) = m(2,:);
c(3,:) = m(1,:);
```

yields

Section 1.6 Array Variables

```
c =
     0.7000    0.8000    0.9000
     0.4000    0.5000    0.6000
     0.1000    0.2000    0.3000
```

Two-dimensional arrays can be added, subtracted, multiplied, and divided using the array arithmetic operators:

List 1.14a
```
c = a + b
c = a - b
c = a .* b
c = a ./ b
```

Here, a and b are two-dimensional arrays of the same size. The foregoing statements are equivalent to, respectively,

List 1.14b
```
for i=1:3
   for j=1:3
      c(i,j) = a(i,j) + b(i,j);
   end
end

for i=1:3
   for j=1:3
      c(i,j) = a(i,j) - b(i,j);
   end
end

for i=1:3
   for j=1:3
      c(i,j) = a(i,j)*b(i,j);
   end
end

for i=1:3
   for j=1:3
      c(i,j) = a(i,j)/b(i,j);
   end
end
```

Note that the expressions in List 1.14a are significantly more compact and clearer than the expressions in List 1.14b.

The statement with the array power operator,

```
    g = a.^3
```
is equivalent to
```
    for i=1:3
        for j=1:3
            g(i,j) = a(i,j)^3;
        end
    end
```

Column vectors and row vectors are both special cases of a matrix. Therefore, array operators work equally on vectors and matrices. There are two advantages in using the array arithmetic operators. First, programming becomes short. Second, the computational efficiency of MATLAB is higher with the short form than writing the same using loops.

if and arrays: Array variables may be compared in an `if` statement, assuming that `a` and `b` are matrices of the same size:

(1) `if a==b` is satisfied only if `a(i,j)=b(i,j)` for all the elements.

(2) `if a>=b` is satisfied only if `a(i,j)>=b(i,j)` for all the elements.

(3) `if a~=b` is satisfied if `a(i,j)~=b(i,j)` for at least one element.

If two string variables of different lengths are compared by an `if` statement, an arithmetic error occurs because the two arrays must have the same length. In order to compare string variables in `if` statements, all the string variables must be adjusted to a predetermined length by appending blank spaces. For example, instead of

```
    a = 'echinopsis'
    b = 'thithle'
    c = 'cirsium'
    d = 'onopordon'
```
write as
```
    a = 'echinopsis'
    b = 'thithle   '
    c = 'cirsium   '
    d = 'onopordon '
```

Then, a, b, and c may be compared in `if` statements.

This task may be more easily achieved, however, by `str2mat`. For example, suppose string variables have been given by

Section 1.6 Array Variables

```
t1 = 'digitalis'
t2 = 'nicotiana'
t3 = 'basilicum'
t4 = 'lychnis'
t5 = 'chrysanthemum'
```

Then they may be organized in a single string matrix by

```
s = str2mat(t1,t2,t3,t4,t5)
```

The first row of s becomes t1, the second row t2, and so on, with an identical length because blank spaces are added to shorter strings.

Example 1.3

(a) An array of numbers is given by
```
x=[9, 2, -3, -6, 7, -2, 1, 7, 4, -6, 8, 4, 0, -2];
```
Write a script to count the number of negative entries.

(b) Write a script to find the minimum and maximum values in the array given in (a). (Do this in a primitive way without using min or max commands.)

Solution

(a) The key for the script writing is to use for/end and if/end. The counter c is initialized to 0 in the beginning. Then, x(i)<0 is examined for each of x(i). If the condition is satisfied, the counter is increased by one. The final answer is typed simply by c.
```
x=[9, 2, -3, -6, 7, -2, 1, 7, 4, -6, 8, 4, 0, -2];
c=0;
for i=1:length(x);
   if x(i)<0 c=c+1;end
end
c
```
The answer is
```
c =
    5
```

(b) In the following script, xmin and xmax are initialized to a large positive and large negative number, respectively. Then, xmin and xmax are compared to each x(i). If xmin is greater than x(i), xmin is set to x(i), and, similarly, if xmax is smaller than x(i), xmax is set to x(i).

```
x=[9, 2, -3, -6, 7, -2, 1, 7, 4, -6, 8, 4, 0, -2];
xmin=999;  xmax=-999;
for i=1:length(x);
   if xmin>x(i), xmin=x(i);end
   if xmax<x(i), xmax=x(i);end
end
[xmin,xmax]
```

The answer is

```
ans =
      -6     9
```

Comment: Be aware that `min` and `max` commands find the minimum and maximum, respectively, and make the task easier.

Example 1.4

(a) Write a script to examine if a given number is a prime number or not. Read the integer to be examined by the `input` command. Do not use `factor` or `isprime` commands. (Hint: Check to see if the number is divisible by all the lower numbers except unity).

(b) Write a script to print out the prime numbers less than 100 in increasing order. Print out the total number of the prime numbers found, a list of the prime numbers, and the sum of the prime numbers less than 100. (Do not use `factor` or `isprime` commands).

Solution

(a) In the following script, the number to be examined, `i`, is given through the `input`. The `ans` is initialized to 1. Then the number `i` is divided by 2 through i-1. If `fix(i/n)` equals `i/n` for any n, `ans` is set to 0 and the loop is terminated by `break`. If the loop is completed without resetting `ans=1`, the `i` is a prime number.

```
clear
i=input('Type an integer greater than 1: ');
ans=1;
for n=2:i-1
    if i/n==fix(i/n), ans=0; break;end
```

```
        end
        if ans==0, fprintf('No, %2.0f is not a prime number.\n',i)
        else       fprintf('Yes, %2.0f is a prime number.\n',i)
        end
```

A sample output is

```
Type an integer greater than 1: 5
Yes,  5 is a prime number.
```

(b) The script for this part is essentially the same as for (a), except the prime number tested is changed in another loop from 2 to 99. The array prime is initialed to 2 because it is the first prime number. If i examined is a prime number, then it is appended to prime.

```
clear
prime=[2];
for i=3:99
  ans=1;
  for n=2:i-1
    if i/n==fix(i/n), ans=0; break ;end
  end
  if ans==1, prime=[prime,i];end
end
k=length(prime);
fprintf('\n\nPart (b) answer\n')
fprintf('Number of prime numbers = %3.0f\n',k)
fprintf('Prime numbers less than 100\n',k)
for j=1:length(prime)
  fprintf('%4.0f',prime(j));
  if j==fix(j/10)*10, fprintf('\n');end
end
fprintf('\nThe sum of the prime numbers = %4.0f\n',sum(prime))
```

The results are

```
Part (b) Answer
Number of prime numbers =  25
Prime numbers less than 100
   2   3   5   7  11  13  17  19  23  29
  31  37  41  43  47  53  59  61  67  71
  73  79  83  89  97
The sum of the prime numbers = 1060
```

1.7 UNIQUE ASPECT OF NUMBERS IN MATLAB

In ordinary programming languages, numbers are classified into several categories such as single, double, real, integer, and complex. In MATLAB, all variables are treated equally in double precision. There is no distinction between integer and real variables, nor between real and complex variables. How to assign a value to a variable is entirely up to the user. If a variable is to be used as an integer, just set the value as an integer. Integers are recognized as far as they are recognizable from the mantissa and exponents in the memory. No distinction between real and complex variables is unique to MATLAB, but it provides great advantages. In Fortran, for example, real variables and complex variables cannot share the same subroutines.

As a simple example, consider roots of a quadratic polynomial

$$ax^2 + bx + c = 0$$

The solution may be written as

$$x = \frac{-b \pm \sqrt{b^2 - 4ac}}{2a}$$

In Fortran or C, one has to separate the solutions to two cases:

(a) $b^2 \geq 4ac$,

$$x = \frac{-b \pm \sqrt{b^2 - 4ac}}{2a}$$

(b) $b^2 < 4ac$,

$$x = \frac{-b \pm i\sqrt{4ac - b^2}}{2a}$$

where i equals $\sqrt{-1}$, and the solutions in the second case are complex values. In MATLAB, however, no separation is necessary. Regardless of the sign of the value inside the square root, the roots are computed by

```
x1 = (-b + sqrt(b^2 - 4*a*c))/(2*a)
x2 = (-b - sqrt(b^2 - 4*a*c))/(2*a)
```

If the roots are complex, MATLAB automatically treats the variables as complex.

Accuracy of computations is affected by a number of factors. The key parameters that affect computational accuracy in a programming language are

Section 1.7 Unique Aspect of Numbers in MATLAB

Smallest positive number: x_min
Largest positive number: x_max
Machine epsilon: eps[4]

In Table 1.2, these three numbers in MATLAB are compared to those in Fortran on a few typical computers.

Table 1.2 Comparison of the Range of Numbers and Machine Epsilon

Software Precision	MATLAB	Fortran(workstation) Single (Double)	Fortran(Cray)
x_min	4.5e-324	2.9e-39(same)	4.6e-2476
x_max	9.9e+307	1.7e+38(same)	5.4e+2465
eps	2.2e-16	1.2e-7(2.8e-17)	1.3e-29

The foregoing table shows that the machine epsilon (eps) of MATLAB is equivalent to that of double precision in Fortran on typical workstations.[5] MATLAB treats all numbers in double precision. The x_min of MATLAB is significantly smaller than in Fortran on workstations and PCs, and x_max is significantly larger. Indeed, x_min and x_max are next to those of Cray. The wide range of numbers on MATLAB is indeed a significant advantage when exponential functions or functions with singularities are computed.

If the reader would like to verify x_min, x_max, and eps, run the following scripts (the last number appearing on the screen is the answer):

List 1.15

```
% To find x_min
x=1; while x>0, x=x/2, end
```

List 1.16

```
% To find x_max
x=1; while x<inf, x=x*2, end
```

---

[4] Machine epsilon is the difference between 1 and the next floating value greater than 1. In other words, no floating value between 1 and 1+eps can be expressed. Any number that falls in between is, therefore, rounded to 1 or 1+eps. One half of the machine epsilon can be interpreted as a maximum relative rounding error associated with a floating value. Obviously, the smaller the eps, the more accurate the numbers in the computing environment.

[5] S. Nakamura, *Applied Numerical Methods in C*, Prentice-Hall, 1992.

List 1.17
```
% To find machine epsilon
x=1;   while x>0,    x=x/2; ex = x*0.98 + 1; ex=ex - 1;
       if ex > 0, ex, end
   end
```

If a value becomes greater than x_max, the number is treated (in MATLAB) as ∞, denoted by `inf`. If you type `inf` on the command window, the response is

```
ans =
    inf
```

Typing `x = 1/inf` will yield

```
ans =
    0
```

Sometimes, however, the answer becomes `NaN`, which means *not a number*. For example, if you try to compute `i*inf`, the answer of MATLAB is

```
ans =
    NaN
```

1.8 MATHEMATICAL FUNCTIONS OF MATLAB

Like any other programming language, MATLAB has numerous mathematical functions ranging from elementary to high levels. Elementary functions may be classified into the following three categories:

   (a) Trigonometric functions
   (b) Other elementary functions
   (c) Functions that do chores

Table 1.3 shows the functions in the first two categories. The functions in the third category are explained in Section 1.9.

Mathematical functions in MATLAB have two distinct differences from those in other programming languages such as Fortran and C: (1) mathematical functions work for complex variables without any discrimination, and (2) mathematical functions work for vector and matrix arguments.

complex arguments: To show how the functions of MATLAB work for imaginary or complex variables, let us try

```
cos(2 + 3*i)
```

where `i` equals the unit imaginary number, or equivalently square root of -1. Then the answer is

Table 1.3 Elementary Mathematical Functions

Trigonometric functions	Remarks
`sin(x)`	
`cos(x)`	
`tan(x)`	
`asin(x)`	
`acos(x)`	
`atan(x)`	$-\pi/2 \geq \text{atan}(x) \geq \pi/2$
`atan2(y,x)`	Same as `atan(y/x)` but $-\pi \geq \text{atan}(y,x) \geq \pi$
`sinh(x)`	
`cosh(x)`	
`tanh(x)`	
`asinh(x)`	
`acosh(x)`	
`atanh(x)`	
Other elementary functions	**Remarks**
`abs(x)`	Absolute value of x
`angle(x)`	Phase angle of complex value:
	If $x = $ real, angle $= 0$
	If $x = \sqrt{-1}$, angle $= \pi/2$
`sqrt(x)`	Square root of x
`real(x)`	Real part of complex value x
`imag(x)`	Imaginary part of complex value x
`conj(x)`	Complex conjugate x
`round(x)`	Round to the nearest integer
`fix(x)`	Round a real value toward zero
`floor(x)`	Round toward $-\infty$
`ceil(x)`	Round x toward $+\infty$
`sign(x)`	$+1$ if $x > 0$; -1 if $x < 0$
`mod(x,y)`	Remainder upon division: x - y*fix(x/y)
`rem(x,y)`	Remainder upon division: x - y*fix(x/y). Different from `mod` if $y \leq 0$
`exp(x)`	Exponential base e
`log(x)`	Log base e
`log10(x)`	Log base 10
`factor(x)`	Factorize x into prime numbers
`isprime(x)`	1 if x is a prime number, 0 if not
`factorial(x)`	$x!$

```
ans =
    -4.1896 - 9.1092i
```

For another example, consider the arccosine function, which is the inverse of the cosine function defined by

$$y = \mathrm{acos}(x) = \cos^{-1}(x)$$

The command

```
acos(0.5)
```

yields

```
ans =
    1.0472
```

The argument x in acos(x) is ordinarily limited to the range $-1 \leq x \leq 1$ (this is the way acos function works in Fortran). In MATLAB, however, acos accepts any value in $-\infty < x < \infty$ because the values of acos(x) are not restricted to real values. Indeed, if we try

```
acos(3)
```

then

```
ans =
    0 + 1.7627i
```

array arguments: Most functions in MATLAB can take vectors and matrices as argument. For example, if

```
x =
    1    2    3
    9    8    7
```

then sin(x) will yield

```
ans =
    0.8415    0.9093    0.1411
    0.4121    0.9894    0.6570
```

which is a matrix of the same size as x. The computation performed here is equivalent to

List 1.18

```
for i=1:2
  for j=1:3
    x(i,j) = sin(x(i,j))
  end
end
```

If x is a column or row array, sin(x) becomes a column or row array accordingly.

1.9 FUNCTIONS THAT DO CHORES

Besides functions that compute straightforward mathematical functions listed in Table 1.3, there are several functions that do chores.

sort: sort reorders elements of a vector to ascending order. This command is useful if data in a random order have to be reordered in ascending order. The argument x can be a row vector, column vector, or a matrix. If x is a matrix, reordering is performed for each column. A few examples are given here:

```
sort([2 1 5])
ans =
     1     2     5

sort([2 1 5]')
ans =
     1
     2
     5

sort([9 1 5; 2 8 4])
ans =
     2     1     4
     9     8     5
```

sum: sum(x) computes the summation of the elements of a vector or matrix x. For both a column vector or a row vector, sum computes the total of the elements. If x is a matrix, the sum of each column is computed and a row vector consisting of the summation of each column is returned. A few examples are given here:

```
sum([2 1 5])
ans =
    8

sum([2 1 5]')
ans =
    8

sum([2 1 5; 9 8 5])
ans =
    11    9   10
```

max, min: `max(x)` finds the maximum in vector x, and `min(x)` finds the minimum. Argument x can be a row or column vector, or a matrix. If x is a matrix, the answer is a row vector containing the maximum or minimum of each column of x. (The rule is the same as that for `sort` and `sum`.)

mod: `mod(x,y)` returns the remainder of division of x by y. Therefore, the returned values becomes zero if x is divisible by y. In other words, `mod(x,y)` becomes zero if x is an integer multiple of y.

rand: Random numbers can be generated by `rand`. Its synopsis is `rand(n)`, where n specifies the size of the matrix of random numbers to be returned. If n = 1, a single random number is returned. For n > 1, a $n \times n$ matrix of random numbers is returned. Unless otherwise specified, the random numbers generated in this way are in $0 \leq x \leq 1$. If `rand` is called repeatedly, a sequence of random numbers is generated. The random number generator may be initialized by giving a seed number. The synopsis of initialization is

```
rand('seed', k)
```

where k is the seed number. It must be greater than unity. When the seed number is the same, the sequence of the random numbers becomes the same. If, however, the sequence is desired to be randomly different whenever the random generator is started, a randomly chosen seed number must be given. It could be the pollen count of the day, or the time in seconds, or a number drawn at a state lottery during the week, although finding a truly random number from natural phenomena or our daily life is not easy (see Example 1.2).

Section 1.10 Developing a Program as an M-File   **37**

eval: Commands can be edited as a string and then executed by `eval`. The string can be read as input, or created within a script. For example

```
x=0:0.1:10
string=input('Type a function name, and hit return:   ','s');
s=['plot(', 'x,',string,'(x))'];
eval(s)
```

If the input is `cos`, for example, the script plots `y=cos(x)` for `x=0:0.1:10`.

1.10 DEVELOPING A PROGRAM AS AN M-FILE

Executing commands from a window is suitable only if the amount of typing is small, or if you want to explore ideas interactively. When commands are more than a few lines long, however, the user should write a script m-file, or a function m-file, because the m-files are saved to disk and can be corrected as many times as needed.[6] The m-file can include anything the user would write directly in the command window. Beginners should try to develop short m-files first and execute them.

In MATLAB-6, an m-file can be executed from the editor window. Click `Save and run` in the *Debug* menu.

echo on, echo off: When an m-file is executed, the statements in the m-file are not usually printed on the screen. After echo is turned on with the `echo on` command, however, the statements are printed out. By doing this, the user can see which part of the m-file is being executed. To turn off echo, type `echo off`.

comment statements: The percent sign in m-files indicates that any statements after this sign on the same line are comments and are to be ignored for computations. Comments added to m-files in this way can help explain the meaning of variables and statements.

Example 1.5

Random numbers may be used to play a game. The `x=rand(1)` command generates a random number between 0 and 1 and sets x to that

---

[6]m-files are classified into two categories: script m-file and function m-file. Script corresponds to a main program in traditional programming languages, while function corresponds to subprogram, subroutine, or function in traditional languages.

number. Consider 13 spade cards which have been well shuffled. The probability of picking up one particular card from the stack is 1/13. Write a program to emulate the action of picking up one spade card by a random number. The game is to be continued by returning the card to the stack and shuffling again after each game is over.

Solution

Suppose the interval between 0 and 1 is divided into 13 equally spaced subintervals. Each is defined by $(n-1)/13 < x < n/13$ where $n = 1, 2, ..13$. Then, if a random number falls in the nth interval, we can say that the nth card is drawn. Actually, n can be found by multiplying x by 13 and rounding up to the nearest higher integer.

Of course, before using `rand`, we have to initialize `rand` with a seed number. If the same seed is used, an identical sequence of random numbers is generated. One way to pick up a seed number is to use the `clock` command. For example, `c=clock` will set `c` to a row vector of length 6. The product of the second through the last numbers, namely `c(2)*c(3)*c(4)*c(5)*c(6)`, has approximately 3×10^7 combinations and changes every second throughout one year.

The following m-file determines a card every time it is executed. The game is repeated by answering the prompted question by `r`, but is terminated by typing any letter other than `r`. This m-file is saved by `List1_19.m`, so it can be executed from the command window by typing `List1_19`.

```
List 1.19
c=clock;
k=c(2)*c(3)*c(4)*c(5)*c(6);
rand('seed', k)
for k=1:20
  n=ceil(13*rand(1));
  fprintf('Card number drawn:    %3.0f\n', n)
  disp(' ')
  disp('Type r and hit Return to repeat')
  r = input('or any letter to terminate   ','s');
  if r ~= 'r', break, end
end
```

One interesting but useful feature of an m-file is that it can call other m-files. The calling m-file is a parent m-file, while the called m-files are children m-files. This implies that one script may be broken into one parent m-file and multiple children m-files. The children m-files are similar to function m-files, which are explained in the next section. The difference, however, is that the parent and children m-files can see all the variables among them while function m-files can see only those variables given through arguments.

1.11 HOW TO WRITE YOUR OWN FUNCTIONS

Functions in MATLAB, which are saved as separate m-files, are equivalent to subroutines and functions in other languages.

function that returns only one variable: Let us consider a function m-file for the following equation:

$$f(x) = \frac{2x^3 + 7x^2 + 3x - 1}{x^2 - 3x + 5e^{-x}} \qquad (1.11.1)$$

Assuming the m-file is saved as `demof_.m`, its script is illustrated by

List 1.20
```
function y = demof_(x)
y = (2*x.^3+7*x.^2+3*x-1)./(x.^2-3*x+5*exp(-x));
```

Notice that the name of the m-file is identical to the name of the function, which appears on the right side of the equality sign. In the m-file, array arithmetic operators are used, so the argument x can be a scalar as well as a vector or matrix. Once `demof_.m` is saved as an m-file, it can be used in the command window or in another m-file. The command

```
y = demof_(3)
```

yields

```
y =
    502.1384
```

If the argument is a matrix, for example,

```
demof_([3,1; 0, -1])
```

the result becomes a matrix also:

```
ans =
    502.1384   -68.4920
     -0.2000     0.0568
```

function that returns multiple variables: A function may return more than one variable. Suppose a function that evaluates mean and standard deviation of data. To return the two variables, a vector is used on the left side of the function statement, for example,

List 1.21
```
function [mean,stdv] = mean_st(x)
n=length(x);
mean = sum(x)/n;
stdv = sqrt(sum(x.^2)/n - mean.^2);
```

To use this function, the left side of the calling statement should also be a vector. The foregoing script is to be saved as mean_st.m. Then,

```
x = [ 1 5 3 4 6 5 8 9 2 4];
[m, s] = mean_st(x)
```

yields

```
m =
    4.7000
s =
    2.3685
```

function that uses another function: The argument of a function may be the name of another function. For example, suppose a function that evaluates a weighted average of a function at three points as

$$f_{av} = \frac{f(a) + 2f(b) + f(c)}{4} \qquad (1.11.2)$$

where $f(x)$ is the function to be named in the argument. The following script illustrates a MATLAB function f_av.m that computes Eq.(1.11.2):

List 1.22
```
function wa = f_av(f_name, a, b, c)
wa = (feval(f_name,a) + 2*feval(f_name,b) ...
                     + feval(f_name,c))/4;
```

In the foregoing script, f_name (a string variable) is the name of the function $f(x)$. If $f(x)$ is the sine function, f_name equals 'sin'. The feval(f_name,x) is a MATLAB command that evaluates the function named f_name for the argument x. For example, y = feval('sin',x) becomes equivalent to y=sin(x).

Example 1.6

Evaluate Eq.(1.11.2) for the function defined by Eq.(1.11.1) with $a = 1, b = 2,$ and $c = 3$. Equation (1.11.1) has been written as `demof_.m` in List 1.20.

Solution

We assume `f_av.m` (List 1.22) has been saved as an m-file. Then, the command

```
A = f_av('demof_', 1, 2, 3)
```

yields

```
89.8976
```

The number of input and output arguments of `feval` must be consistent with the input and output format of the function `f_name`. For example, if the function `f_name` needs four input variables and returns three output variables, the statement to call `feval` would be:

```
[p, q, s] = feval( f_name, u, v, w, z)
```

where p, q, and s are output, while `f_name`, u, v, w, and s are input.

debugging of function m-files: Debugging function m-files is more difficult than script m-files. One reason is that you cannot see the values of variables by typing the variable names unless debugging commands are used. The most basic but effective method of developing a function m-file is to comment-out the function statement on the first line by placing % before `function` and then test the m-file as a script m-file. Put the function statement back after a thorough examination of the m-file.

Using debugging commands is recommended only for advanced MATLAB users.

1.12 SAVING AND LOADING DATA

save, load: If save is used by itself, as in

```
save
```

all the variables are saved in the default file `matlab.mat`. The `load` command is the inverse of the `save` command and retrieves all the variables saved by `save`.

The filename may be specified by placing it after `save`; for example:

```
save file_name
```

saves all the variables in the file named `file_name.mat`. When you wish to retrieve the variables, write

```
load file_name
```

If only selected variables are to be saved, write the variable names after `file_name`; for example:

```
save file_name a b c
```

In this example, `a`, `b`, and `c` are saved in the file named `file_name`. Do not separate `file_name` and variables by a comma. All the variables are saved in double precision binary. When you wish to load the data in `file_name.mat`, type

```
load file_name
```

without variable names. Then, all of `a`, `b`, and `c` are retrieved.

save filename data -ascii: `save` can be used to save data in ASCII format. Both `save` and `load` with the ASCII option are important because they make possible export and import of data from MATLAB.

To use the ASCII format, `-ascii` or `/ascii` is appended after the variable names. For example,

```
save data.tmp   x   -ascii
```

saves variable `x` in 8-digit ASCII to the file named `data.tmp`. The `save` command can save more than one variable; for example,

```
x = [1, 2, 3, 4 ]
y = [-1, -2, -3]'
save data2.tmp   x   y   -ascii
```

If you open the `data2.tmp` file, it looks like

```
  1.0000000e+00   2.0000000e+00   3.0000000e+00   4.0000000e+00
 -1.0000000e+00
 -2.0000000e+00
 -3.0000000e+00
```

Section 1.12 Saving and Loading Data

The `load` command allows you to convert a data file into a variable, but loading a file in ASCII format is not quite the inverse of `save` in ASCII format. The reason is that while `save` in ASCII can write multiple variables, `load` reads the entire data file into only one variable. Furthermore, the filename becomes the variable's name. For example, if a file named y_dat.e is loaded by

```
load y_dat.e
```

the content is loaded to the variable named y_dat regardless of the extension name.

Therefore, the data file y_dat must be in one of the following data forms only:

(a) a single number

(b) a row vector

(c) a column vector

(d) a matrix

If multiple variables have to be loaded, each variable should be prepared in a separate ASCII data file.

Data files prepared by Fortran or C in ASCII (or text) format can be loaded by `load` as long as the data structure is one of the four forms. For more advanced methods of exporting and importing data files, consult the MATLAB User's Guide.

creating file name automatically: it often becomes desirable to create filenames automatically within an m-file. If a whole command, including the filename, is written as a string, it may be executed by `eval`. In the following script, xdata is assumed to be computed for each k and saved in separate files named fname001, fname002, ... in ASCII format.

```
for k=1:kmax
  %Here are some statements to produce xdata for each k.
  %kmax is the maximum number of k (less than 1000).
  if k<10, s=['save fname00',num2str(k), ' xdata -ascii']
    elseif k>=10 & k<100, s=['save fname0',num2str(k), ' xdata -ascii']
    elseif k>=100, s=['save fname',num2str(k), ' xdata -ascii']
  eval(s)
end
```

1.13 HOW TO MAKE HARD COPIES

One frequently asked question is how to make hard copies of the prints on the screen. To produce a copy of prints on the screen, use `diary` introduced in Section 1.1. If `diary` is used without a specific filename, the filename becomes `diary` in the directory. The file can be printed out as a text file. Graphic figures are not captured in `diary`.

PROBLEMS

In resolving the problems that follow, prepare your answers using MATLAB. Run the statements or scripts on MATLAB. Make sure you correct your script until you get the right answers. If you are required to submit your answers for the problems, do not submit the printout without attaching a short summary by hand in case your instructors have trouble understanding it. Highlight the key numbers (final answers) in the printout so the instructor can find them without a struggle. If the problems are difficult and you need assistance, look at similar problems and answers given in *Additional Exercises* at http://olen.eng.ohio-state.edu/matlab

(1.1) Guess the MATLAB response to the following statements. Examine your answers by executing them on MATLAB.

```
a = [1 2 3; 4 5 6]'
b = [9;7;5;3;1]
c = b(2:4)
d = b(4:-1:1)
e = sort(b)
f = [3,b']
```

(1.2) Arrays x and y are defined by

```
x=[7 4 3]
y=[-1 -2 -3]
```

(a) Define a new array u by prepending y to x.
(b) Define a new array v by appending y to x.

(1.3) On MATLAB, make a two-dimensional array such that the first row equals x and the second row equals y, where both x and y are defined in the previous problem.

(1.4) Eliminate the `for/end` loop in the following script by using the array arithmetic operators:

```
x=11:15
for k=1:length(x)
z(k)=x(k)^2 + 2.3*x(k)^0.5;
end
z
```

(1.5) Rewrite the following script without using the array arithmetic operators:

```
x=[4 1 2]
z=1./(1 + x.^2)
```

(1.6) A vector is given by

$$a = [4\ -1\ 2\ -8\ 4\ 5\ -3\ -1\ 6\ -7]$$

Write a script that doubles the negative numbers in **a**. Run the script and show your output.

(1.7) Write a script that removes positive numbers from **a** given in Problem (1.6). Run the script and show your printout of the answer.

(1.8) Write a script that generates an array such as

x=[1 4 2 4 2 4 .. 4 1]

where the length of the array is an odd number, the numbers in the even addresses are 4, and the numbers in the odd addresses are 2 (except the first and the last numbers are 1). Run your script and show how it works for any odd length of **x**, given by input, which is equal to 3 or greater.

(1.9) Write a script that generates an array such as

x=[1 3 3 2 3 3 2 3 3 .. 2 3 3 1]

where the length of the array is 3n+1 with an integer **n**, 3 always repeats two times following 2 except for the first number 1, and the last number is 1. Run your script and show how it works for any **n**.

(1.10) A vector is given by

$$a = [4\ -1\ 2\ -8\ 4\ 5\ -3\ -1\ 6\ -7]$$

Write a script that calculates the sum of positive numbers of **a**. Run the script and show your printout of the answer.

(1.11) The pricing scheme of computer printers sold by a company is as follows:

(a) the basic price of a printer is $150 if the customer buys only one printer

(b) the second printer is $120 if the customer buys more than 1 printer

(c) the third printer and beyond is $110.

Write a script that calculates the total price for up to 10 printers purchased by one customer.

The number of printers should be specified at the beginning of the script. The number of printers may be read by the input command. Calculate the total price for 10 printers by running your script.

(1.12) Develop a script that generates a price chart for up to 10 printers for the printer store described in the previous problem. (Use the `fprintf` command to print out the table. Utilizing a price table recalculated by hand calculations is not acceptable.)

(1.13) A company selling printer cartridges has the following price policy. The first cartridge is $50, the second is $35, but the third one is free. This pricing pattern repeats as the number of cartridges sold increases, namely, the fourth is $50, the fifth is $35 and the sixth is free, and so on. Most customers buy multiples of three to take advantage of every third. However, large organizations like universities and government agencies buy the exact number of cartridges they need regardless of the advantage of the free phurchase. Thus, the company must prepare a price chart for any number of cartridges sold. Write a script to prepare a price chart for up to 20 cartridges. Make sure the output of your chart is correct by hand calculations.

(1.14) Bubble sort is an iterative method for reordering a sequence of numbers in increasing order. For example, consider x=[7 1 2 4 8 5]. In the first iteration cycle, 7 in the first position and 1 in the second position are compared. Since 7 is greater than 1, they are exchanged in the array. Next, 7, which is now in the second position, is compared to 2 in the third position. Then an exchange takes place because 7 is greater than 2. The same procedure is repeated until the last position is involved. The second cycle is the same using the result of the first cycle. The cycles are repeated until no exchange becomes necessary. Write a script to reorder x in increasing order. Do not use the `sort` command.

(1.15) A matrix m is defined by

$$m = \begin{bmatrix} 1 & 2 & 5 \\ 3 & 1 & 2 \\ 4 & 1 & 3 \end{bmatrix}$$

How do you read m into MATLAB by the `input` statement? Show that your procedure is correct on MATLAB.

(1.16) What is the result of `sum(m)`, `max(m)`, and `min(m)` on MATLAB, where m is the matrix defined in the previous problem?

(1.17) Write an m-file that examines if a positive integer is a prime number or not without using `factor` or `isprime`.

(1.18) Array x is given by x=[1:99]. Remove all prime numbers from x, then calculate the sum.

(1.19) Write a script to compute

$$S = \sum_{n=1}^{10} \frac{n}{n+1}$$

(a) using a `for/end` loop, but not array operators or `sum`.
(b) using array operators and `sum`, but not any `for/end` loop.
What is the value of S?

(1.20) Write a script that converts any element equal to 1 in a matrix to -1. Run the m-file for the 3×3 array (matrix) m defined in Problem 1.15. Print out your script and its results.

(1.21) Define v by

```
v = 'glacier'
```

or

```
v = ['g', 'l', 'a', 'c', 'i', 'e', 'r']
```

Write a script to find the address of i in v.

(1.22) A matrix (or array) generated by `m=rand(4,4)` is an array of random numbers. Write a script that prints out the addresses (row and column numbers) of the numbers that are less than 0.5. Execute your script and make sure it is correct. Print out your script and the answers.

(1.23) Develop a function m-file, `fun_es(x)`, to compute the following function:

$$y = 0.5e^{x/3} - x^2 \sin x$$

The argument must accept a scalar as well as a vector. Test your function by typing the following on MATLAB:

```
fun_es(3)
fun_es([1 2 3])
```

(1.24) Repeat the task of Problem (1.23) for the function:

$$y = \sin(x) \log(1+x) - x^2, \quad x > 0$$

Denote the function `fun_lg(x)`.

(1.25) (a) Write a function m-file that calculates the solution of

$$ax^2 + bx + c = 0$$

Its synopsis is `quad_rt(a,b,c)`, where a, b, and c are allowed to be vectors.
(b) Test the function for a=3, b=1, c=1.
(c) Test the function for a=[3 1 2], b=[1 -4 9], c=[1 3 -5].

(1.26) The reader is assumed to have completed `fun_es` and `fun_lg` developed for Problems 1.23 and 1.24. Now, develop a function, `t_es(x)`, that:
(a) asks for the name of the function to be evaluated
(b) lets the user type the function name
(c) evaluates the function by `feval` and returns the functional values
(d) stops if the choice is neither `fun_es` nor `fun_lg`.

Test your `t_es` by asking to evaluate `fun_es(3)` and `fun_lg(3)`.

(1.27) Two variables, x and y, are saved in the `out_asc.m` file:

```
x = 1:5
y = [-1:-1:-5]'
save out_asc x y -ascii
```

How does the file look when the file is opened as an m-file? Is it possible to read both x and y from the same file? If x and y have to be saved in ASCII format and also have to be loaded later, what should you do?

(1.28) A vector is given:

```
A = [1 2 3 4 5 6 7 8 9 0]
```

Write a script to print out the vector content using the `fprintf` command in a loop such that the printout will look like:

```
Vector A is
[  1, 2, 3, 4, 5, 6, 7, 8, 9, 0]
Print completed.
```

Note that each number except the last is followed by a comma and one blank space. Your script should work for any other definition of vector A.

(1.29) Write an m-file that asks the player to type 0 or 1. If 1, the software finds 10 numbers randomly from 1 through 6. Print out the 10 numbers found in a row vector form. If the player's input is 0, the program is stopped. Obtain a seed random number by `clock` as follows:

```
c = clock;
sdnum = c(1)*c(2)*c(3)*c(4)*c(5)*c(6);
```

(1.30) Develop an m-file named `fun_xa` that evaluates the following series:

$$f(x) = 1 + x + \frac{x^2}{2!} + \frac{x^3}{3!} + .. + \frac{x^n}{n!}$$

The values of x and n are to be given by `input`. Test the function by comparing the result with hand calculations for $x = 1$ and $n = 4$. The foregoing series is a truncated Maclaurin expansion of e^x and converges for $-\infty < x < \infty$. Knowing this, test your function for selected x values, such as $x = 0.5, 3.0$ and -1, with $n = 1, 2, 3, 5, 10$, and compare with e^x.

(1.31) Develop an m-file named `fun_xb` that evaluates the following series:

$$f(x) = x - \frac{x^2}{2} + \frac{x^3}{3} - .. + (-1)^{n+1}\frac{x^n}{n}$$

The values of x and n are to be given by `input`. Test the function by comparing the result with hand calculations for $x = 1$ and $n = 4$. The foregoing series is a truncated Maclaurin expansion of $\log(1+x)$ and converges for $-1 < x < 1$. Knowing this, test your function for selected x value, such as $x = -0.5$ and 0.5, with $n = 1, 2, 3, 5, 10, 20, 50$, and compare with $\log(1+x)$. (Convergence becomes increasingly difficult as x approaches -1 or 1.)

Chapter 2

GRAPHICS WITH MATLAB

Graphics play a central role in the computing environment with MATLAB. Plotting a given data set or the results of computation is possible with very few commands. Yet, MATLAB allows you to finish scientific graphics with the highest possible sophistication and elegance. Readers are encouraged to plot mathematical functions and results of analysis as often as possible. Trying to understand mathematical equations with graphics is an enjoyable and very efficient way of learning mathematics. Indeed, we might say that *unless you understand mathematical equations graphically, you don't understand the equations.* Being able to plot mathematical functions and data freely is the most important step, and this chapter is written to assist you to do just that.

For professional people, the importance of graphics is even more profound. Massive data generated today by computers and experiments, as well as from information source, cannot be expressed in mathematical functions. The only way in many cases to analyze the data is through graphic visualization. This means to plot the data in appropriate forms including one-, two-, and three-dimensional plots, and motion pictures (four-dimensional plots). This is another reason why students are encouraged to learn graphic visualization methods.

Learning graphic commands is similar to learning how to write short sentences in a foreign language, although the former is far easier than the latter. A language cannot be learned by listening to or reading explanations of vocabulary or grammar. Practice is the key. The best way to learn graphic commands is to read a small amount of instructions and then practice on MATLAB, first by typing examples in the command window or executing the script m-files of the book and, second, by changing the m-files in various ways.[1]

---

[1] *Reminder* See "How to obtain the m-file package" in "Preface."

2.1 SIMPLE PLOTTING

plot: Suppose a set of data points, (x_i, y_i), $i = 1, 2, ..., n$, is to be plotted, where x_i is an abscissa value and y_i is an ordinate value. You need to prepare x and y in an identical array form; namely, x and y are both row arrays or column arrays of the same length. Then, the data may be plotted using plot. As an example, $y = \sin(x)\exp(-0.4x)$, $0 \le x \le 10$, is plotted in Figure 2.1 by List 2.1.

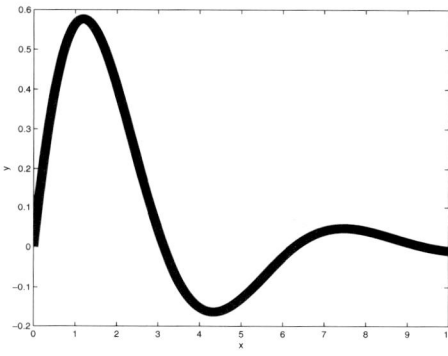

Figure 2.1 Plot by List 2.1 or 2.2.

List 2.1
```
n=201;
delx=10/(n-1);
for k=1:n
  x(k)=(k-1)*delx;
  y(k)=sin(x(k))*exp(-0.4*x(k));
end
%plot(x,y)
plot(x,y, 'linewidth',4)
xlabel('x'); ylabel('y')
```

Notice in the preceding list, x is a row array of 201 abscissa values of 0, 0.05, 0.1, ..., 10, and y is a row array of ordinate values of the same length. Then, plot(x,y, 'linewidth',4) plots the data. The axes are labeled by xlabel('x') and ylabel('y'), explained in more detail later. The value of n is selected arbitrarily. However, if n is too small, the plotted graph will lack smoothness.

The curve plotted in Figure 2.1 is very thick compared with other figures in this book. The thickness of the plotted line or curve is controlled by 'linewidth' and 4 within the plot command.[2] As 4 is replaced by a smaller

---
[2]In earlier versions of MATLAB, the same had to be written in two steps as h=plot(x,y); set(h,'linewidth',4).

number, the thickness goes down; the opposite is also true. The default value is 0.5, and in this case plot(x,y) will suffice as shown after the percent mark in List 2.1.

The foregoing script can be written more compactly, of course, using array expressions as follows:

List 2.2
```
x = 0:0.05:10;
y=sin(x).*exp(-0.4*x);
%plot(x,y)
plot(x,y, 'linewidth',4)
xlabel('x'); ylabel('y')
```

Because sin(x) and exp(-0.4x) are both arrays, the array multiplication operator .* is used in the second line of the preceding list. Arrays x and y can also be column vectors. The two foregoing scripts produce the same graph as in Figure 2.1.

Figure 2.2 is plotted by List 2.3 connecting a series of points on a complex plane.

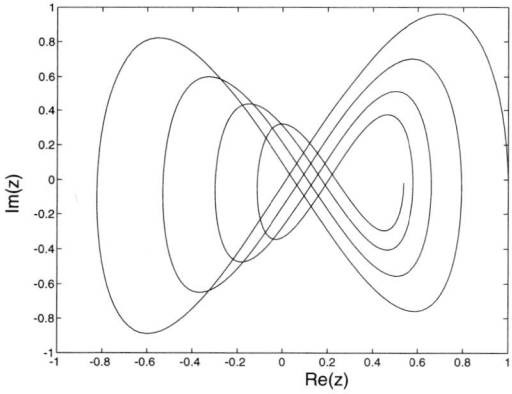

Figure 2.2 Plot by List 2.3.

List 2.3
```
p=0:0.05:8*pi;
z=(cos(p) + i*sin(2*p)).*exp(-0.05*p) + 0.01*p;
plot(real(z), imag(z))
xlabel('Re(z)'); ylabel('Im(z)')
```

plotting by marks only: Data can be plotted by marks only without being connected by lines. Nine types of marks (among many others) are illustrated here.

Section 2.1 Simple Plotting

Mark Type	Symbol
Point	.
Plus	+
Star	*
Diamond	d
Circle	o
Pentagon	p
Square	s
Triangle	^
x-mark	x

To find more marks, type `help plot`. To plot with one type of mark only, place the mark symbol as a string after the coordinates in the arguments of `plot`. The graph produced by List 2.4 is shown in Figure 2.3.

List 2.4
```
x = (0:0.4:10)';
y=sin(x).*exp(-0.4*x);
plot(x,y,'+')
xlabel('x'); ylabel('y')
```

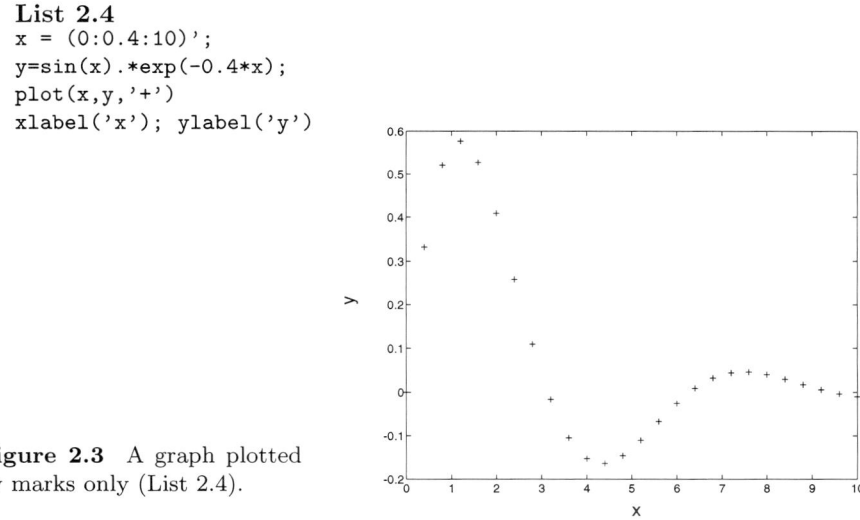

Figure 2.3 A graph plotted by marks only (List 2.4).

plotting a function with both lines and a mark: Plot twice, namely, the first time with lines and the second time with marks only. To plot in this way, the last statement in List 2.4 is changed to `plot(x,y,x,y,'+')`. The `text` command may be used to plot with any mark or letter; however, the location of the mark may be somewhat offset from the actual location of the data point.

line types and line colors: Four line types are available:

Line Type	Symbol
Solid	-
Dash	--
Dotted	:
Dashdot	-.

Default is the solid line type. To plot with a selected line type, specify the line mark after the coordinates; for example,

    `plot(x,y,'--')`

Eight colors, namely, red, yellow, magenta, cyan, green, blue, white, and black, are available for the lines and marks. These colors are specified by letters, `r`, `y`, `m`, `c`, `b`, `w`, and `k`, respectively. Use the color symbol just like the line types in the argument of `plot`, for example:

    `plot(x,y,'g')`

A combination of mark and color is also possible:

    `plot(x,y,'+g')`

plots the data by + marks in green.

clf, cla: `clf` clears everything inside the graphic window, while `cla` clears the plotted curves and redraws the `axes`.

figure: `figure` opens a new graphic window that is numbered consecutively from the previous one, while `figure(n)` opens the figure window specifically numbered n. If multiple figure windows exist, you have to be aware which one is the current figure. This is because all the graphic commands apply to the current figure. The latest window opened is the current window unless you have respecified an older one as current. To make an existing figure window n current, type `figure(n)`.

The size and shape of the window opened by `figure` are determined by default. Often, however, it becomes desirable to change both, particularly if the figure is to be used in another document. In MATLAB-6, the size and shape may be changed by `figure('Position', [pix, piy, pwx, pwy])`[3], where `pix` and `piy` are the horizontal and vertical pixel coordinates, respectively, of the

---

[3]In an earlier version of MATLAB, the same results were achieved by first `h=figure`, and then `set(h,'Position', [pix, piy, pwx, pwy])`.

left bottom corner of the window; pwx is the number of pixels in the width; and pwy is the number of pixels in the height of the window. By specifying [pix, piy, pwx, pwy] appropriately, a desired size and shape may be obtained. The default setting is figure('Position', [232 258 560 420]). The existing (current) figure may also be changed by set(gcf,'Position', [pix, piy, pwx, pwy]).

close: close(n) closes the graphic window n, and close all closes all graphic windows.

implicit function: If a function is given implicitly, for example,

$$y^3 + \exp(y) = \tanh(x)$$

it cannot be expressed by x as a function of y, nor y as a function of x. The curve can be plotted, however, using contour. More details of this approach are discussed in Section 2.4.

axis, axis on, axis off: The minimum and maximum of the coordinates, tic marks, and the coordinate values at the tic marks, are all determined automatically. The shape of the frame, and minimum and maximum of the coordinates, however, may be changed by axis. A figure can be reshaped to a square form by axis square. See Figure 2.4.

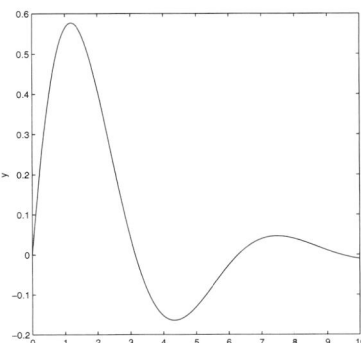

Figure 2.4 A plot with axis square.

The coordinate axes and tic marks can be removed by

    axis off

The axes and tic are reinstated by axis on.

The maximum and minimum of the coordinates on the graph may be specified by

```
axis([x_min, x_max, y_min, y_max])
```

Any lines outside the limits will be clipped. This command is used after `plot` so that the view area can be changed as many times as desired. It is suggested that the reader appends `axis([-2, 6, -0.7, 0.7])` to List 2.4 to test the effect of `axis`.

zoom: This is an interactive way to zoom into a specified part of a figure without using `axis`. Type `zoom` in the command window. Then, on the graphic window, enclose the area to zoom in by moving the mouse while pushing the left button. As soon as the button is released, the zooming occurs. To unzoom, click again on the graphic window.

grid on, grid off: A grid can be added to the graph by `grid on`. On the other hand, `grid off` removes the grid. Simply using `grid` multiple times turns the grid on and off. An example of using `grid on` is illustrated in Figure 2.5 plotted by List 2.5.

List 2.5
```
x = (0:0.2:10)';
y=sin(x).*exp(-0.4*x);
plot(x,y)
grid on
xlabel('x'); ylabel('y')
```

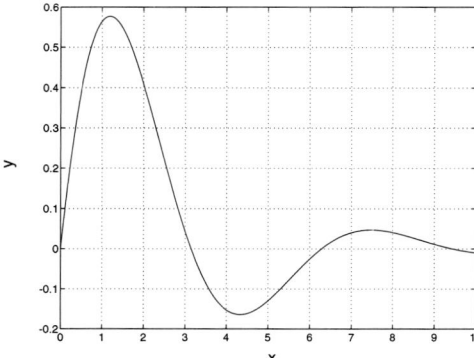

Figure 2.5 A figure with a grid (List 2.5).

polar plot: A function on a polar coordinate can be plotted by `polar`. Figure 2.6 is plotted by List 2.6.

Section 2.1 Simple Plotting

List 2.6

```
t = 0:.05:pi+.01;
y = sin(3*t).*exp(-0.3*t);
polar(t,y)
title('Polar plot')
grid
```

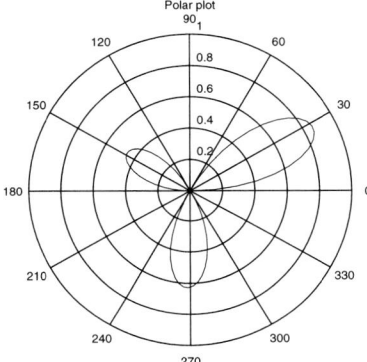

Figure 2.6 Polar plot (List 2.6).

log and semilog plots: A function may be plotted on a log-log scale by `loglog`. (See List 2.7 and Figure 2.7.)

List 2.7

```
t = .1:.1:3;
x = exp(t);
y = exp(t.*sinh(t));
loglog(x,y)
grid
xlabel('x');ylabel('y')
```

A semilog plot with the log scale for y is produced by List 2.8.

List 2.8

```
t = .1:.1:3;
semilogy(t,exp(t.*t))
grid
xlabel('t'); ylabel('exp(t.*t)');
```

Similarly, a semilog plot with the log scale for x is produced by List 2.9.

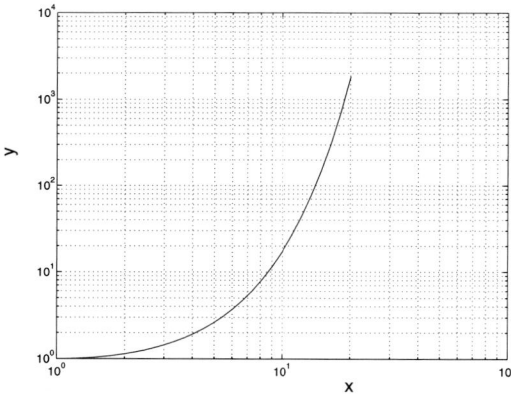

Figure 2.7 A log plot (List 2.7).

List 2.9
```
t = .1:.1:3;
semilogx(t,exp(t.*t))
grid
xlabel('t'); ylabel('exp(t.*t)');
```

multiple curves: To plot two or more curves with a single `plot` command, write all the sets of coordinates repeatedly in the `plot` command:

List 2.10
```
x = 0:0.05:5;
y = sin(x);
z = cos(x);
plot(x,y,x,z)
```

Different line type or color is automatically selected for each curve by default. Line color, line type, or mark, however, may be specified after each pair of coordinates; for example,

```
plot(x,y,'--', x,z, '*')
plot(x,y,':', x,z, '*g')
plot(x,y,'r', x,z, 'y')
```

The following two lists show another way to plot multiple curves by one `plot` command:

List 2.11
```
x = 0:0.05:5;
y(1,:) = sin(x);
y(2,:) = cos(x);
plot(x,y)
```

Section 2.1 Simple Plotting

List 2.12
```
x = (0:0.05:5)';
y(:,1) = sin(x);
y(:,2) = cos(x);
plot(x,y)
```

hold on, hold off: Until now we plotted all the curves at once with a single `plot` command. It often becomes desirable, however, to add a curve to a graph that has already been plotted. Such additional plotting can be done using `hold on` (see Figure 2.8 plotted by List 2.13).

List 2.13
```
x = 0:0.05:5;
y = sin(x);
plot(x,y);
hold on
z = cos(x);
plot(x,z,'--')
xlabel('x');ylabel('y(-) and  z(--) ');
```

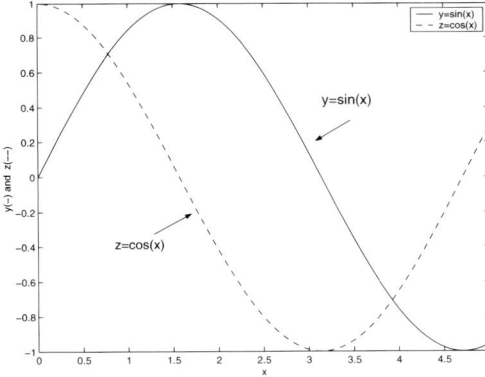

Figure 2.8 Two curves plotted with the `hold on` command (List 2.13). Legend and text with arrow signs were added by manual operation on the figure window as explained in the text.

In Figure 2.8, however, two additional things were added by manual operation after List 2.3 was executed. More details are explained in Section 2.2.

Once the `hold on` command is issued, the graph stays on even when another script is executed. Therefore, it is prudent to place a `hold off` command at the end of the script.

When multiple curves are plotted with `hold on`, it is desirable to specify minimums and maximums of the coordinates on the graphic domain by the axis command. Otherwise, the limits are determined by default based on the first curve, which may cause other curves to be clipped.

The hold on command also becomes important when a time-consuming plot is undertaken for the following reason. The command to change parameters for figures such as axis, color map, view angles, color axis, and other parameters can be changed after a figure is plotted, but each time a new command is issued, the whole figure is replotted. In order to save time, give all the parameter commands before plotting, hold with hold on, and then use plot.

titles, xlabel, ylabel: Coordinate labels and titles may be added to the graph using xlabel, ylabel, and title. The following script uses all three commands:

List 2.14
```
clear,clf,hold off
M = [0: 0.01: 1]';k=1.4;
p0_over_p = (1 + (k-1)/2*M.^2).^(k/(k-1));
plot(M,p0_over_p)
xlabel('M, Mach number')
ylabel('p_o/p')
title('Pressure ratio, p(stagnation)/p(static)','fontsize',14)
```

Figure 2.9 illustrates the graph produced by List 2.15A in which the font size and line width are both increased.

List 2.15A
```
clear,clf,hold off
M = [0: 0.01: 1]';k=1.4;
p0_over_p = (1 + (k-1)/2*M.^2).^(k/(k-1));
plot(M,p0_over_p, 'linewidth', 3)
xlabel('M, Mach number','fontsize',14)
ylabel('p_o/p','fontsize',14)
title('Pressure ratio, p(stagnation)/p(static)','fontsize',14)
```

The argument of xlabel, ylabel, and text can include more than one string, but they must be written in row vector form; for example,

```
title(['string1', 'string2', ...])
```

legend: The legend in a figure can be written by the legend command. The legend in Figure 2.8 is added by legend('y=sin(x)','y=cos(x)'), in which the first argument y=sin(x) refers to the first function plotted and

Section 2.1 Simple Plotting

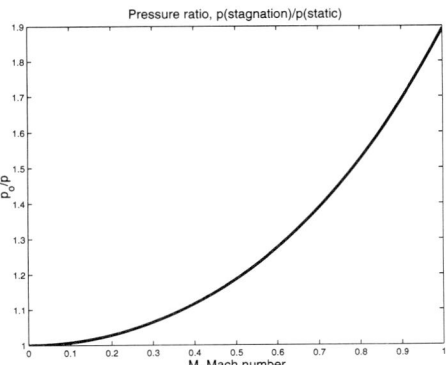

Figure 2.9 Application of `title` command (List 2.15A).

the second y=cos(x) to the second function plotted.

num2str: In writing texts and labels, one may wish to include numerical values in the text. The commands `num2str` and `int2str`, which stand for *number to string* and *integer to string*, respectively, may be used for this purpose; for example,

```
st = num2str(pi)
```

defines `st` as a string containing 3.142. By `int2str`, a real number is converted to a string containing only the integer part of the number. For example, by

```
st = int2str(pi)
```

`st` becomes a string variable containing 3. Once the number is converted to a string, it can be used in the arguments of `title`, `xlabel`, and `ylabel`, or `text`; for example,

```
title([' Case: ', st, ' cm'])
```

or equivalently,

```
kase=' Case: ';
cen=' cm';
title([kase, st, cen])
```

where `kase` and `cen` are used as string variables.

text: Text can be written in a graph by `text` or `gtext`. The former needs three parameters in the argument, namely, `text(x, y, 'string')`. The first two are x and y values of the absolute coordinates where the string starts. The third is a string variable to be printed. The string variable can be a text enclosed by quote signs or a predefined string variable. An example of the command is

```
text( 2, 4, 'Any string you wish.')
```

The foregoing command prints 'Any string you wish.', which starts at (2,4) on the current coordinate system.

List 2.15B illustrates the use of text, and its result is illustrated in Figure 2.10.

List 2.15B
```
set(gcf, 'NumberTitle','off','Name', 'Figure 2.10; List 2.15B')
clear; clf; hold off;
M = [0:0.01:1]';
k=1.4;
p0_over_p = (1 + (k-1)/2*M.^2).^(k/(k-1));
hold on
axis square;                  %makes graph square
plot(M,p0_over_p)
xlabel('Mach number, M','fontsize',14)
ylabel('p0/p','fontsize',14)
title('Pressure ratio, p(stagnation)/p(static)','fontsize',14)
text(0.45, 1.55, 'Compressible','fontsize',14)
Mb= [0: 0.01: 0.7]';
p0_over_pb = 1 + k/2*Mb.^2;
plot(Mb,p0_over_pb,'--')
text(0.5, 1.1, 'Incompressible','fontsize',14)
```

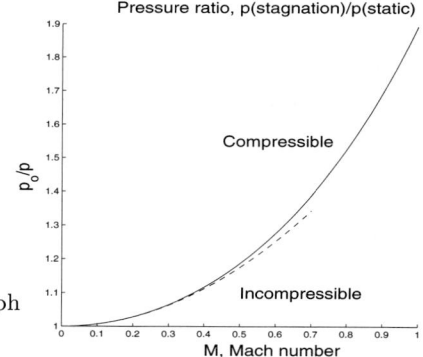

Figure 2.10 A graph with texts (List 2.15B).

If location of a text needs to be determined manually, gtext('string') is useful. When this command is executed, the program waits for a mouse or key to be pressed while the mouse pointer is within the graphic screen. The text is written at any desired location pointed to by the mouse pointer.

While `text` also works in three-dimensional axes, `gtext` works only in two-dimensional axes.

Color and font size of a text in the graph may be changed. For example,

>   text(0.3,0.2,'string','fontsize',18,'Color','r')

will print `string` in red color with font size 18. If a default color is to be changed to blue, for example, use:

>   set(gcf,'DefaultTextColor','blue')

Thereafter, the text will be typed in blue. Color for text may be chosen from red, yellow, green, cyan, blue, and magenta, which can be abbreviated by 'r', 'y', 'g', 'c', 'b', and 'm', respectively. Color may be changed for another text in a similar way as many times as necessary. Availability of font sizes seem to vary depending on the MATLAB edition.

Greek symbols may be typed by `text`. For example,

>   text(2,0,'\alpha \beta \delta \epsilon \gamma \Gamma \Omega')

will print $\alpha\beta\delta\epsilon\gamma\Gamma\Omega$. Other symbols may also be included, all according to the LaTex.[4]

The font size of the axis tic mark values may be changed by the `set` command; for example,

>   set(gca, 'fontsize',18)

will change the font of axis to size 18. In case a text is improperly placed, there is no means to erase it. The only way to correct it is to redraw the whole figure after correcting the script.

Superscript and subscripts may be used in `text`. To type a single character or a group of superscript use the caret symbol ^ followed by the single or group of letters enclosed by {} . For example, `text(2, 4, 'x^{-2}')` will type x^{-2} as text at x=2 and y=4. Subscript is the same as superscript except the ^ is replaced by underscore: for example, `text(2, 4, 's_{i,j}')` will type $s_{i,j}$ as text. Notice that the group of subscripts 'i,j' in the script or command are enclosed in {} .

subplot: With `subplot` one can plot $m\times n$ graphs in a single figure. The synopsis is

---

[4]Shultis, J. K. *Latex Notes, Practical Tips for Preparing Technical Documents*, Prentice Hall, 1994.

```
subplot(m,n,k)
```

where `m`, `n`, and `k` are integers. Here, the pair of `m` and `n` means a m×n array of graphs, and `k` is the sequential number of the graph. For example, `plot` following `subplot(3,2,1)` will plot the first graph in the 3×2 figures. The following script plots four graphs, as illustrated in Figure 2.11:

List 2.16
```
clear;clf
t=0:.1:30;
subplot(2,2,1), plot(t,sin(t)),title('SUBPLOT 2,2,1')
           xlabel('t'); ylabel('sin(t)')
subplot(2,2,2), plot(t,t.*sin(t)),title('SUBPLOT 2,2,2')
           xlabel('t'); ylabel('t.*sin(t)')
subplot(2,2,3), plot(t,t.*sin(t).^2),title('SUBPLOT 2,2,3')
           xlabel('t'); ylabel('t.*sin(t).^2')
subplot(2,2,4), plot(t,t.^2 .*sin(t).^2),title('SUBPLOT 2,2,4')
           xlabel('t'); ylabel('t.^2.*sin(t).^2')
```

A vertical stack of two graphs is plotted by

```
subplot(2,1,1), plot( ..
subplot(2,1,2), plot( ..
```

Likewise, a row of two graphs is plotted by

```
subplot(1,2,1), plot( ..
subplot(1,2,2), plot( ..
```

axes: Advanced users of MATLAB may be interested in `axes` command, which is useful for plotting multiple graphs in one figure window like `subplot`. However, `axes` provides more freedom with respect to locations and sizes of the plots. See Appendix E for more details of `axes`.

properties of figure: Properties of a figure, such as size, location, assigned color map, and so on, may be changed. To know the current property values use `get(gcf)`. One property at a time can be changed by using the `set` command. For example, `set(gcf, 'paperposition',[0.25 2.5 4 3])` sets the lower bottom corner of the figure, when printed, at 0.25in from the left edge, 2.5in above the bottom edge, with figure width 4in and height 3in. For more details, use `help figure`.

3d plot: `plot3` is the three-dimensional version of `plot`. All the rules and commands explained for `plot` apply to `plot3`. A spiral motion of a particle from point A to B in Figure 2.12 is plotted by List 2.17. The view angle may be changed by `view`, as explained in Section 2.6. The `axis` command,

Section 2.2 Interactive Editing of Figures

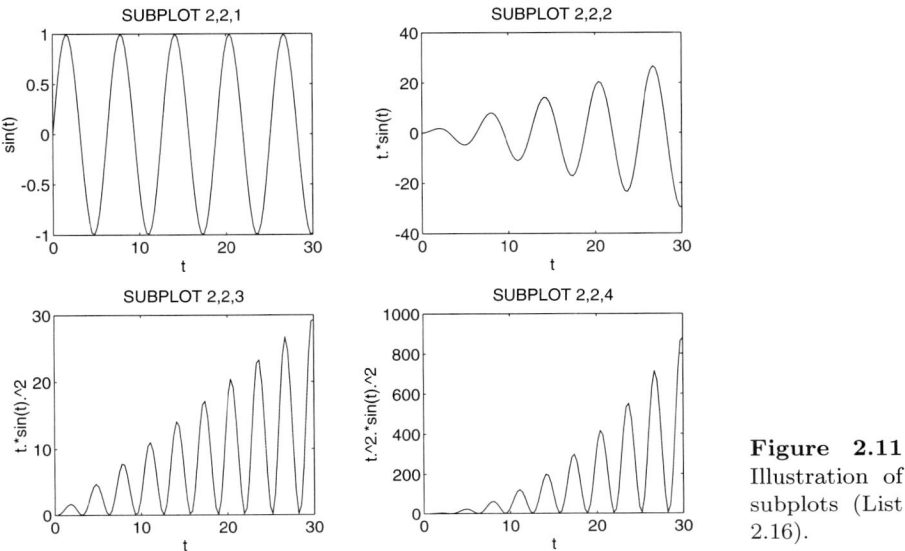

Figure 2.11 Illustration of subplots (List 2.16).

```
axis([x_min, x_max, y_min, y_max, z_min, z_max])
```

may be used to define bounds of the three-dimensional space.

List 2.17
```
clear,clf
t=0:0.1:20;
r= exp(-0.2*t);
th=pi*t*0.5;
z=t;
x=r.*cos(th);
y=r.*sin(th);
plot3(x,y,z)
hold on
plot3([1,1], [-0.5,0], [0,0])
text( 1,-0.7,0, 'A')
n=length(x);
text( x(n),y(n),z(n)+2,'B')
xlabel('X'); ylabel('Y'); zlabel('Z');
```

2.2 INTERACTIVE EDITING OF FIGURES[5]

In MATLAB-6, all editing of a figure, which was performed by commands in the previous section, can be interactively operated in the figure window. In

---

[5]The features explained in this section do not apply to MATLAB-4 and 5.

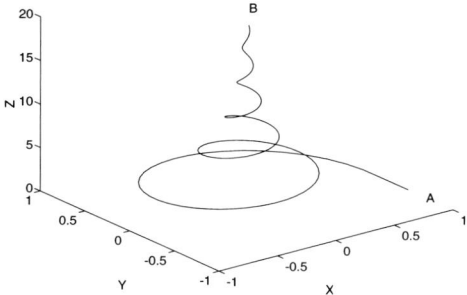

Figure 2.12 Illustration of 3D plot (List 2.17).

addition, arrows and lines that connect captions and texts in the figure can be added interactively. In the following explanations, we will assume that we operate on a figure that already exists.

properties of plotted line: The color, line width, and line style of a plot in a figure can be changed interactively. Click on the button of the arrow sign pointing to the northwest direction on the menu bar. Move the mouse pointer to any point on the curve to be edited and click once. Black spots will appear along the curve. Double-click at the same location, and a *Property Editor* window will open, where the properties of the curve can be changed. If the *Property Editor* does not open at a double-click, go to the *Edit* menu and select *Current Object Properties*.

legend: To interactively add a legend (as illustrated in Figure 2.8), click open *Insert* in the menu bar of the figure window and pull down. Click *Legend*, and a basic legend box will appear at the top right corner in the figure, which can be modified to your satisfaction. To edit the legend, click on the text in the legend box first then go to the *Edit* menu, click and pull down.[6] Select *Current Object Properties*. A *Property Editor* window will open, in which the properties of the legend can be changed, including the text and font sizes. When editing on the *Property Editor* window is finished, click on *Apply* and *OK*.

text: Click on the *Insert* menu and select *Text* or push the button *A* in the menu bar. Move the mouse pointer to the location where the text

---

[6]To open the *Property Editor* window, first click on the arrow sign pointing to the upper left direction in the menu bar, then double-click on the object. The steps of pulling down the *Edit* menu can be omitted. The same applies to interactive editing of other items.

should start, and click. A small text box will appear. You can immediately start writing text like $y = \sin(x)$ in Figure 2.8, for example. To change any property of this text such as the font size, double-click on $y = \sin(x)$ and pull down *Edit* in the menu bar. Select *Current Object Properties*. In this *Property Editor*, we can specify font type, size, or other properties that you wish to change.

x-label, y-labels, and title: The procedure of using these is very similar to `legend` and `text`. Start with the *Insert* menu and select an appropriate item.

arrow: The arrow sign in a figure can be drawn by interactive operation. Like adding text, the operation may be initiated from the *Insert* menu. Select *Arrow* in the pull-down menu. Then move the pointer and click at the location where the arrow sign should start. Drag the mouse to the point where the arrow's head should be located. Release the mouse button. The same applies to a straight line with no arrow head.

axes properties: The line width of the axes and the tic label font size can be changed. Click inside the figure or at the border of the axes. Go to the *Edit* menu and select *Current Object Properties*. The tic label font size and axes line width can be changed in the *Property Editor*.

2.3 HOW TO PRINT OR RECORD GRAPHS

To print the current figure on the screen on the current printer, simply type `print`.

In order to create a file of the figure to be printed out later or used in other documentations, the format must be specified. For example, to create a file in the PostScript format, the command is

```
print -dps filename
```

or

```
print filename.ps
```

This creates a PostScript file `filename.ps`.[7] For the JPEG format, as another example, the command is

---

[7] Most figures in this book were created by MATLAB and saved as PostScript files.

```
print -djpeg filename
```

The foregoing command creates a file named `filename.jpg`, which can be used in Web pages, MS Word, and PowerPoint. The figures in the JPEG format may be converted to the GIF format to produce motion pictures, as described in more detail in Appendix C. To obtain more information about other formats, use `help print`.

size and position of the figure: The size and position of the figure printed on the sheet of paper can be changed by the `set` command. To do this, open the figure window by `h=figure` where `h` is the handle. Then, before or after the `plot` command, use `set(h, 'PaperPosition', [a, b, c, d])` where `a, b, c,` and `d` are numbers in inches; `a` is the left margin, `b` the bottom margin, and `c` and `d` are, respectively, the width and height on the sheet of paper. The default is `[0.25, 2.5, 8, 6]`. Other parameters of the figure may be changed in a similar way. To see what parameters are set for the figure, type `get(h)`. The handle of the current figure is `gcf`.

2.4 PLOT OF TWO-DIMENSIONAL FUNCTIONS

A two-dimensional function $z = f(x, y)$ may be represented approximately with discrete points by

$$z_{i,j} = f(\tilde{x}_i, \tilde{y}_j) \tag{2.4.1}$$

where $\tilde{x}_i$ with $i = 1, 2, ...m$ and $\tilde{y}_j$ with $j = 1, 2, ...n$ are points on the x and y axes in increasing order. The intersections of $x = \tilde{x}_i$ and $y = \tilde{y}_i$ comprise a Cartesian grid, and are called grid points. The grid points may be identified by $(\tilde{x}_i, \tilde{y}_j)$ or, equivalently, by $(x_{i,j}, y_{i,j})$, where $x_{i,j}$ and $y_{i,j}$ are two-dimensional arrays, respectively, defined by

$$x_{i,j} = \tilde{x}_i$$
$$y_{i,j} = \tilde{y}_i$$

and functional values by

Latex, which was used to typeset the book, is capable of including the graphs from PostScript files. To do this, the names of the PostScript files are written in appropriate places in the LaTex manuscript.

Section 2.4   Plotting of Two-Dimensional Functions

$$z_{i,j} = f(x_{i,j}, x_{i,j}) \tag{2.4.2}$$

meshgrid: Two-dimensional arrays, x and y, can be generated from the one-dimensional arrays, x_tilde, y_tilde, by `meshgrid` as

```
[x,y] = meshgrid(x_tilde,y_tilde)
```

where x_tilde and y_tilde are one-dimensional arrays that represent $\tilde{x}_i$ and $\tilde{y}_j$, respectively, and x and y represent $x_{i,j}$ and $y_{i,j}$, respectively. The grid (x,y) itself may be plotted by

```
mesh(x,y,0*x); view([0,0,10000]); xlabel('x'); ylabel('y')
```

mesh: The two-dimensional function $z_{i,j} = f(x_{i,j}, y_{i,j})$, explained earlier, can be plotted by `mesh`. For illustration, let us consider the grid defined by

$$x_{i,j} = \tilde{x}_i = -2 + 0.2(i-1), \quad 1 \le i \le 21$$
$$y_{i,j} = \tilde{y}_j = -2 + 0.2(j-1), \quad 1 \le j \le 21$$

The function defined by

$$z_{i,j} = x_{i,j} \exp(-x_{i,j}^2 - y_{i,j}^2) \tag{2.4.3}$$

is plotted in Figure 2.13 by List 2.18A.

List 2.18A
```
clear, clf
x_tilde = -2:.2:2;
y_tilde = -2:.2:2;
[x,y] = meshgrid(x_tilde,y_tilde);
z = x .* exp(-x.^2 - y.^2);
mesh(x,y,z)
title('This is a 3-D plot of  z = x * exp(-x^2 - y^2)')
xlabel('x'); ylabel('y'); zlabel('z');
```

Although z is defined in a vector form by a single line in the foregoing list, two `for/end` loops become necessary if the function definition needs conditional statements. Let us plot the two-dimensional function given by

$$f(x,y) = \begin{cases} 10 - 1/r, & \text{if } r \ge 1 \\ 9, & \text{otherwise} \end{cases} \tag{2.4.4}$$

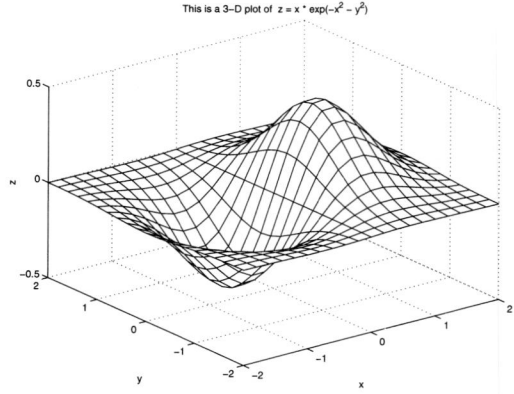

Figure 2.13 Mesh plot (List 2.18A).

where

$$r = \sqrt{(x-1)^2 + (y-1)^2} \qquad (2.4.5)$$

in the domain, $-10 < x < 10$, and $-10 < y < 10$. The script becomes

List 2.18B
```
clear, clf
xa = -10:.1:10;
ya = -10:.1:10;
[x,y] = meshgrid(xa,ya);
r=sqrt((x-1).^2+ (y-1).^2);
for i=1:length(xa)
  for j=1:length(ya)
    if    r(i,j)>1, z(i,j)=10-1/r(i,j);
    else,           z(i,j)=9;
    end
  end
end
mesh(x,y,z)
title ...
('z = 10-1/r if r>1, else z = 9, with r=sqrt((x-1)^2+(y-1)^2)')
xlabel('x'); ylabel('y'); zlabel('z');
```

contour: As an alternative to the `mesh` command, the two-dimensional function can also be plotted by `contour`. Its basic synopsis is

```
contour(x, y, z, level)
```

where `x`, `y`, and `z` are exactly the same as in `mesh`. While `level` is an array of contour levels, it may be replaced by an integer, `m`, which is the number

Section 2.4 Plotting of Two-Dimensional Functions

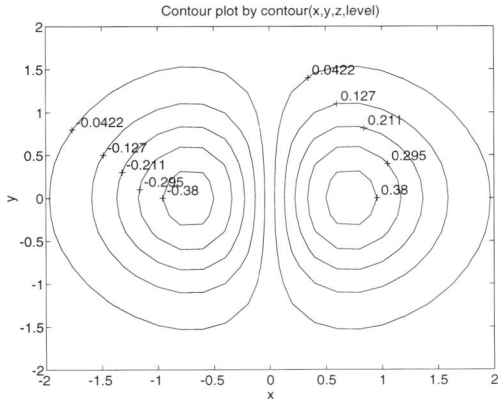

Figure 2.14 Contour plot (List 2.19).

of contour levels. Then, the contour levels are determined by dividing the minimum and maximum values of z into m-1 intervals.

Figure 2.14 shows a contour plot by List 2.19, where the function plotted is defined by Eq.(2.3.1) and the same as for Figure 2.13. The contour values in the figure were annotated by clabel(h,'manual') which allows the user to locate the position of the numbers by use of the mouse. The contour levels can also be automatically annotated by clabel(h). Do not leave a contour plot without contour labels.

List 2.19
```
clear, clc, clf, axis square
xm=-2:.2:2; ym=-2:.2:2;
[x , y ] = meshgrid(xm,ym);
z = x .* exp(-x.^2 - y.^2);
zmax=max(max(z)); zmin=min(min(z));
dz = (zmax-zmin)/10;
level = zmin + 0.5*dz: dz: zmax;
h=contour(x,y,z,level); clabel(h,'manual')
title('Contour plot by contour(x,y,z,level)')
xlabel('x'); ylabel('y')
```

The contour command may be used to plot an implicit function such as

$$y^3 + \exp(y) = \tanh(x)$$

To plot the curve, we rewrite the equation to

$$f(x, y) = y^3 + \exp(y) - \tanh(x)$$

and plot the contour for only one level corresponding to $f = 0$ (see Figure 2.15). The following script illustrates the plotting procedure:

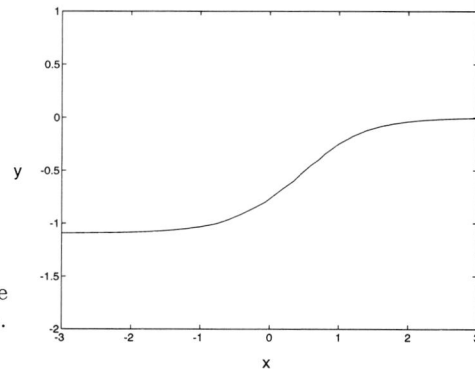

Figure 2.15 Plot of a curve specified by an implicit function.

List 2.20
```
clear, clf
xm = -3:0.2:3;  ym = -2:0.2:1;
[x, y] = meshgrid(xm, ym);
f = y.^3 + exp(y) - tanh(x);
contour(x,y,f,[0,0])
xlabel('x'); ylabel('y')
```

Notice in the foregoing script that the vector [0,0] in the arguments of contour is to specify the level of the contour. The only contour we are interested in is for level 0, but the contour levels must be in a vector form, so we repeat zero twice.

quiver: Data at grid points sometimes involve both magnitude and direction. For example, velocity distribution in a two-dimensional fluid flow may be expressed by a velocity vector at each grid point. The vectors at grid points may be plotted by quiver. The vectors for the grid points need two components, one for the x direction and another for the y direction. Suppose these components are given by u and v, which are both matrices of the same size as x and y. Then, the vectors are plotted by

```
quiver(x,y,u,v,s)
```

where s is a scale factor, that is, a user parameter to adjust the lengths of the vectors in the figure. Figure 2.16 illustrates the plots of velocity vectors in a typical flow problem (called a driven cavity flow). The figure also shows

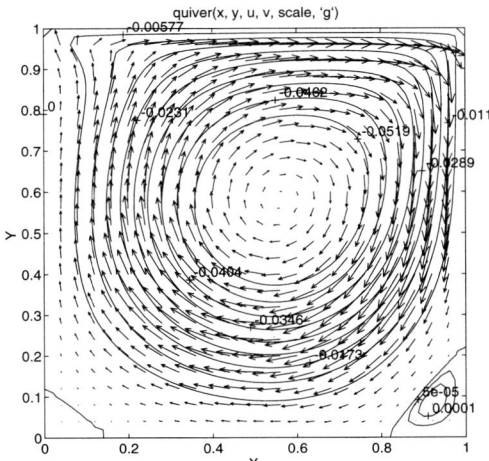

Figure 2.16 Contour and vectors.

plots of stream lines by `contour`. The following script illustrates essential parts of the script to plot Figure 2.16.

```
% (Earlier part of the script to compute x,y,s,u, and v
%  are omitted.)
clf
L=[-0.00577:-0.00577:-0.054,  0, 0.0001, 0.00005];
c=contour(x,y,s,L);     % s=stream function
clabel(c)
title('stream function   Re=400 (grid 51x51)')
xlabel('x    direction')
ylabel('y    direction')
axis square
hold on                 % u and v comprise a vector.
quiver(x(1:2:ni,1:2:ni),y(1:2:ni,1:2:ni), ...
       u(1:2:ni,1:2:ni),v(1:2:ni,1:2:ni),4)
```

In the foregoing list, we assume that x, y, u, and v have been computed earlier, but not shown.

2.5 TRIANGULAR GRID AND CONTOURS

A triangular grid consists of triangular elements and is most often used in finite element or finite volume analysis.

plotting a triangular grid: To plot a triangular grid, the two data files denoted `cell_da` and `point_da` are necessary. The former includes the data of triangular elements, and the latter includes the coordinates of the nodal points. (More details of the files are explained in FM 2-1 of Section 2.10.)

When List 2.21 is executed, two questions are prompted. The first question is whether element numbers are to be annotated. Type 1 for yes, or 0 for no. The second question is whether point numbers are to be annotated. Type 1 for yes, or 0 for no. The first figure of Figure 2.17 shows the plotted grid.

List 2.21
```
%tri_grid_plot
clear,clf
load cell_da
load point_da
tri_grid(cell_da,point_da, 1.8)
```

contour plot on triangular grid: For a discrete function defined at

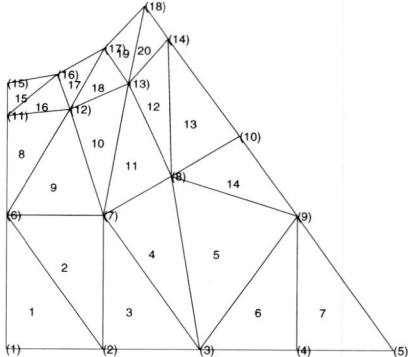

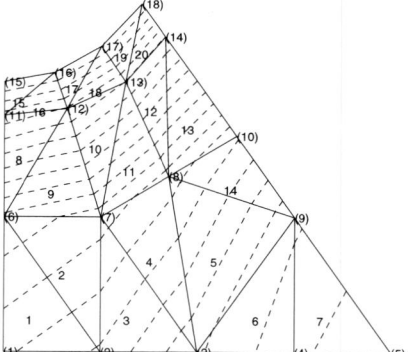

Figure 2.17 Triangular grid, and contour plot.

the nodal points on a triangular grid, contour may be plotted by `tri_cont` in FM 2-2. To run this script, two data files `cell_da` and `point_da` (the same as used in `tri_cont`) and an additional function file `f_da` are necessary. The second figure in Figure 2.17 illustrates the contour plot by List 2.22 using `tri_cont`.

List 2.22

```
%Contour plot on triangular grid
clear,clf
load cell_da
load point_da
load f_da
tri_cont(cell_da,point_da,f_da, 1.8)
```

2.6 CURVILINEAR GRID AND CONTOURS

The rectangular grids discussed in Section 2.3 are called Cartesian grids. When the grid points are on curves, the grid is called a curvilinear grid. For example, the grid based on the polar coordinates shown in Figure 2.18 is a curvilinear gird.

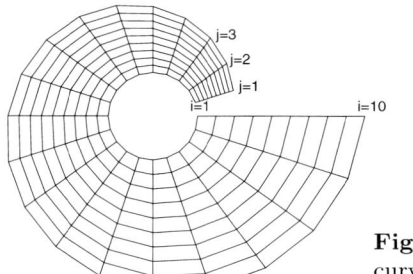

Figure 2.18 Plot of a curvilinear grid.

A function $z(x,y)$ may be represented on the grid points by

$$z_{i,j} = f(x_{i,j}, y_{i,j})$$

where f is a function of x and y, and $x_{i,j}$ and $y_{i,j}$ are coordinates of the curvilinear grid points.

Plotting contour on the curvilinear grid is easy because the contour command works for curvilinear grids, and its synopsis is the same as for the rectangular grid, namely:

```
contour(x, y, z, level)
```

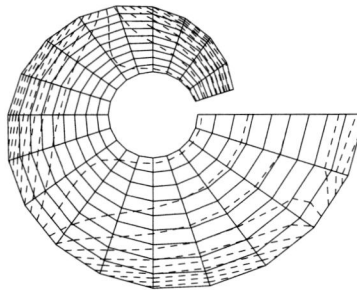

Figure 2.19 A sample of a contour plot.

List 2.23A is used to plot Figures 2.18 and 2.19 (after removing the percent sign before `contour`). The `mesh` command is used to overlay the curvilinear grid. Note that if the order of contour and mesh are switched, a totally different view takes place. `td_data` is a function defined in FM 2-3 of Section 2.10.

List 2.23A
```
clf; clear
[x,y,f]=td_data; ;
%contour(x,y,f); hold on;
mesh(x,y,zeros(size(f))-0.01);
axis equal; xlabel('x'); ylabel('y');
title('Contour plot on a curvilinear grid')
axis([-12 15 -15 10])
```

2.7 PLOTTING CURVED SURFACES

Plotting a curved surface becomes necessary to express a non-flat surface of a structure or to plot a function distributed on a curved surface. Indeed, the contour plot shown in Figure 2.19 can be switched to a mesh plot as illustrated in Figure 2.20. Its script is shown in List 2.23B. Compare this to List 2.23A. Also, `mesh` may be replaced by `surf`.

Section 2.7 Plotting Curved Surfaces

List 2.23B
```
clf; clear
[x,y,f]=td_data; ;
mesh(x,y,f); hold on;
xlabel('x'); ylabel('y');
```

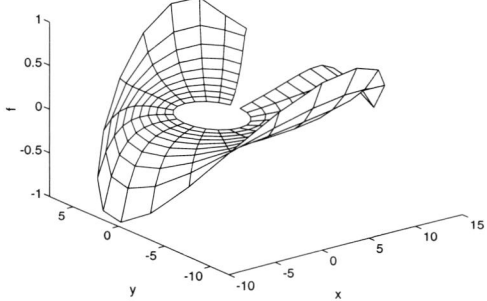

Figure 2.20 Surface plot corresponding to Fig.2.19.

quantity distribution on a curved surface: We now ask how to express a distribution of a quantity such as temperature on the curved surface. This may be achieved by mesh or surf, except that the magnitude of the quantity should be expressed by color, because all the geometrical coordinates, x, y, and z, must be used to express the surface.

default color: On a color screen, the lines connecting the points are colored by the default color map hsv (hue saturation value). Red is assigned for both the lowest and highest values of z(i,j). In between the lowest and highest, the color is determined linearly in order of red, yellow, green, cyan, blue, magenta, and red.

Plot Figure 2.21 in colors on your computer by List 2.24. The lines in Figure 2.21 at the highest elevation (if viewed on a color screen) are purple, and at the lowest elevation are reddish yellow. This is because the color of a line is determined by the average of the z values of the two points connected. For the present mesh plot, the color value of a line at the highest elevation is somewhere close to magenta, while the color value of the line at the lowest elevation is close to yellow. If a much finer mesh is plotted, then the highest and lowest lines both become red.

List 2.24
```
clear, clf
```

```
for i=1:4
  for j=1:7
    z(j,i)=sqrt(i^2 + j^2);
  end
end
mesh(z)
xlabel('x'); ylabel('y'); zlabel('z')
```

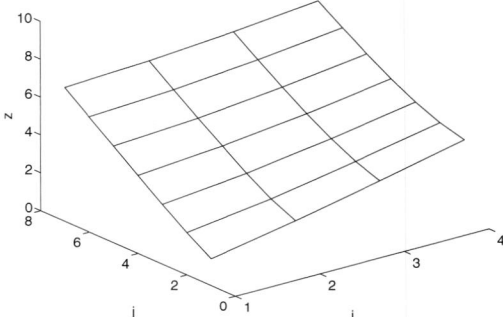

Figure 2.21 Mesh plot of a surface.

axis and labels: The limits of the three-dimensional space in the plot are determined automatically, but may be changed by `axis[xmin, xmax, ymin, ymax, zmin, zmax]` just like its use in two-dimensional plots. The labels for the x-, y-, and z-axis may be added by `xlabel`, `ylabel`, and `zlabel`, respectively.

view: The view angle of a three-dimensional plot may be changed by `view([az, el])` or `view([x, y, z])`. Here, `az` is the azimuthal angle and `el` is the elevation angle. When `az=0` and `el=0`, the viewer's eye position is at the reference view angle that is along the negative y-axis (see Figure 2.22). With this view, the plot becomes a two-dimensional x-z plane with the z-axis vertical and the x-axis stretching horizontally to the right. The `az` rotates the eye position *counterclockwise* by `az` degrees about the z-axis from the reference angle (the same as rotating the plot about the z-axis clockwise by the same degrees). The `el` elevates the eye angle by `el` degrees from the x-y plane. The default values are `az = -37.5` degrees and `el=30` degrees.

When `view` is used with three-dimensional coordinates as `view([x, y, z])`, the viewer's eye is assumed to be along the vector `[x, y, z]` extended from the origin (see Figure 2.23). The `view([0,-1,0])` is equivalent to `view([0,0])` in angles. The relations between angles and triplets are given by

Section 2.7 Plotting Curved Surfaces

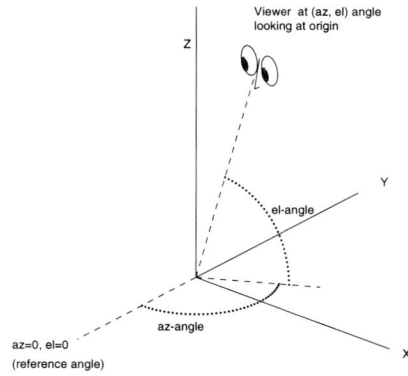

Figure 2.22 Eye position in angles.

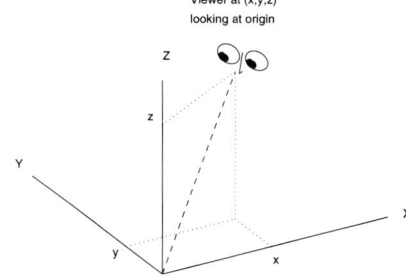

Figure 2.23 Eye position at (x, y, z).

```
az = atan2(x,-y)*180/pi;
el = atan2(z,sqrt(x^2 + y^2))*180/pi
```

Figures 2.24 and 2.25 illustrate different views of a mesh. The mesh plots illustrated in Figure 2.24 are plotted by the following script:

List 2.25
```
clear, clf
yp=1:5; xp=1:4; [x,y]=meshgrid(xp,yp);
z=sqrt(x.^2 + y.^2);
%
subplot(221); mesh(x,y,z); axis([0,5,0,5,0,10])
title('default view');
xlabel('X'); ylabel('Y'); zlabel('Z')
%
subplot(222); mesh(x,y,z); axis([0,5,0,5,0,10])
title('[35,20]')
```

```
view([35,20])
xlabel('X'); ylabel('Y'); zlabel('Z')
%
subplot(223); mesh(x,y,z); axis([0,5,0,5,0,10])
title('[35, -20]')
view([35, -20])
xlabel('X'); ylabel('Y'); zlabel('Z')
%
subplot(224); mesh(x,y,z); axis([0,5,0,5,0,10])
title('[10,90]')
view([10,90])
xlabel('X'); ylabel('Y'); zlabel('Z')
axis square
```

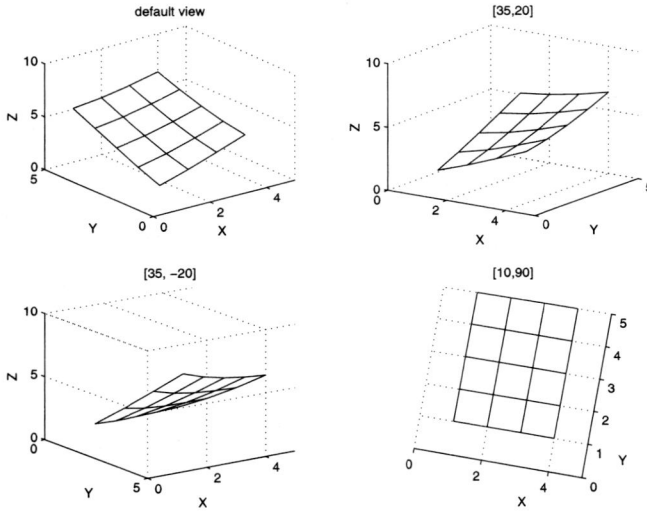

Figure 2.24 Mesh with different views.

contour with mesh: The meshc plots contour of z on the x-y plane in addition to plots by mesh(z). Figure 2.26 is plotted by the following script:

List 2.26
```
clear,clf,hold off
j=1:21; i=1:10;
x = log(i); y = log(j);
[x,y] = meshgrid(x,y);
z=sqrt(0.1*((x-log(5)).^2 + (y-log(5)).^2))+1;
meshc(x,y,z)
xlabel('x'); ylabel('y'); zlabel('z')
```

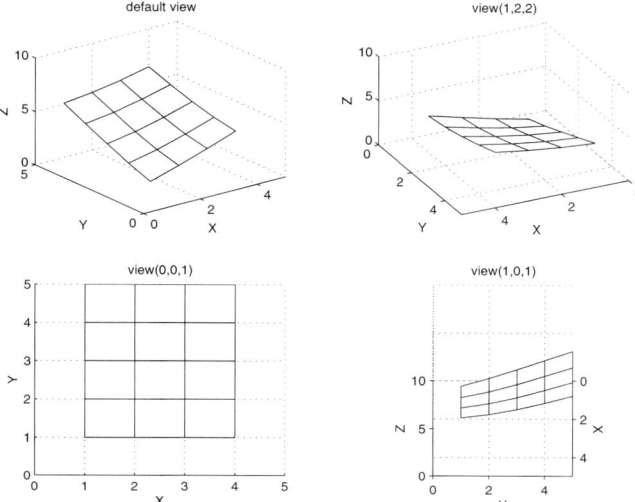

Figure 2.25 Mesh plot with different views.

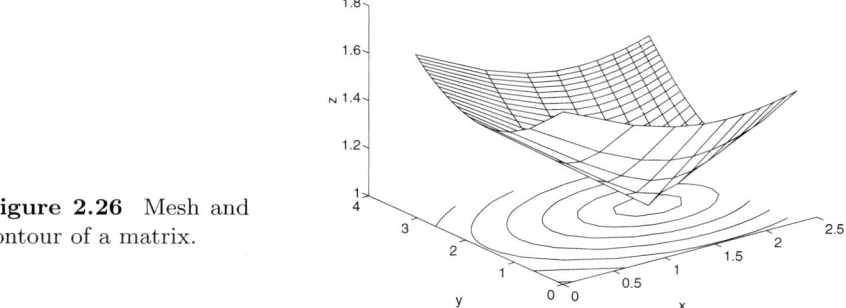

Figure 2.26 Mesh and contour of a matrix.

surface and contour: The surf and surfc commands produce similar plots as mesh and meshc, except surf and surfc paint the inside of each mesh cell with color so that an image of surfaces is created. The color of the cell is determined by the average of z at the four corner points.

surface with lighting: The surf command can be replaced by surfl, but the latter creates a surface object with lighting. The direction of the light sources can also be specified. For example, its basic synopsis is surfl(x,y,z,s) with a default lighting. However, a specific lighting source direction may be specified by surfl(x,y,z,s), where s is a directional vector for the light in the same form as the view angle in degrees. It is recommended that `surfl` be used with `colormap gray` and `shading flat` or `shading interp`. An example of a plot is illustrated in Appendix B (see Figure B.4).

more control of lighting conditions:[8] More lighting control is possible using `surfnorm` and `diffuse` or `specular` in conjunction with `surf`. The `[xn,yn,zn] = surfnorm(x,y,z)` command generates a vector set `[xn,yn,zn]` that represents the normal directions of the surface `(x,y,z)`. Command `r = specular(xn,yn,zn,L)` determines the intensity of light that comes from the surface, where `L` is a directional vector or an angular vector in degrees that defines the direction of the light. Therefore, by using `r` in place of color vector in `surf`, a diffuse lighting image is created. The `diffuse` may be replaced by `specular(xn,yn,zn,L,V)`, where `V` is a directional vector or angular vector that defines the viewer's direction. A sample script is illustrated next. Readers are encouraged to investigate the effects of changing parameters in the script.

```
clear,clf
axis([-1.5, 1.5, -1.5 1.5, -1.3 1.3])
view([1 -0.5 0.31])
caxis([-0.8 1.5])
colormap hot
hold on
L=[0.5,0.3,0.7]; V=[1,1,1];
[x,y,z] = sphere(20);
[xn,yn,zn] = surfnorm(x,y,z);
% r = specular(xn,yn,zn, L,V);
  r = diffuse(xn,yn,zn, L);
surf(x,y,z,r)
shading interp
```

mesh or surface on a curvilinear grid: For a surface on a curvilinear grid, the order of `i` and `j` is of no concern as long as they are used consistently among all arrays involved. For a curvilinear grid, x is an $n \times m$ matrix and its element, `x(i,j)`, is the x-coordinate of point `(i,j)`, while y is the y-coordinate. The first figure in Figure 2.27 displays the surface plot with the nonrectangular grid (see List 2.27).

List 2.27

```
clear,clf,hold off
dth=pi/20
```

---

[8]This is an advanced subject. Beginners are advised to skip this topic.

Section 2.7 Plotting Curved Surfaces

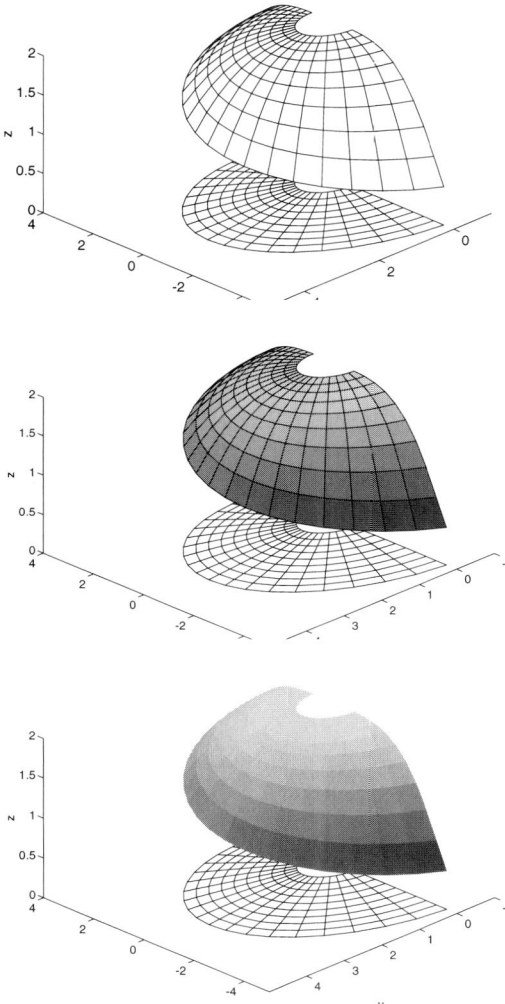

Figure 2.27 Surface on a curvilinear grid.

```
for j=1:21
  for i=1:10
    r=0.5+0.2*i + j*0.01*i;
    th = dth*(j-1);
    x(i,j) = r*cos(th);
    y(i,j)= r*sin(th);
    z=cos(0.1*(x.^2 + y.^2))+1;
```

```
            end
        end
        surf(x,y,z) % plotting a surface
        xlabel('x'); ylabel('y'); zlabel('z')
        axis([-5, 4, -1 , 5 ]);   view([-135,40])
        hold on
        mesh(x,y,zeros(size(x))) % plotting a grid on x-y plane
        colormap hot;   caxis([-0.5,3])
        hold off
        % shading flat    % for the second plot of Fig 2.27
```

Contour cannot be plotted by mesh c and surfc if the grid is not rectangular.

color axis: The control of colors is possible by writing the fourth argument in mesh and surf commands; for example,

```
mesh(x,y,z,c)
```

The fourth argument c is a vector of the same size as z and specifies the color coordinate. When c is omitted, c is assumed to equal z, and the colors of lines and surfaces are determined by the values of z.

Unless the colormap command has been used, the colormap is set to colormap hsv by default. Then, the red color is assigned to the point with the lowest value of c(j,i), as well as to the point with the highest value of c(j,i). The color for c(j,i) in between the lowest and highest is determined linearly in order of red, yellow, green, cyan, blue, magenta, and red. Different color values, however, can be assigned to the mesh points by c defined by the user. The command

```
caxis([0, 100])
```

sets a colormap between 0 and 100. Therefore, if the color matrix elements in c(j,i) are all set near 0, the whole plot becomes reddish, while if the color matrix elements are around 50, the whole plot becomes bluish to purple.

colormap: The definition of colors on the color axis may be changed by colormap. Alternative colormap definitions include colormap(hot), colormap(cold), and colormap(jet) to replace colormap(hsv). Try these commands to alter the color scheme of a mesh or surface plot. More general aspects are described in Appendix A. The argument of colormap may be written without parentheses like colormap hsv.

shading: The objects created by surf consist of quadrilateral tiles which are separated by black lines as illustrated in the second figure in Figure 2.27. This corresponds to the default option of shading, namely, shading faceted. The border lines may be eliminated by shading flat. To both eliminate and make the surface smooth, use shading interp. The second figure in Figure 2.27 is plotted by adding the shading interp command. (See also Figures 5.14 and 9.11.)

hold on revisited: The hold on command becomes very important when a time-consuming plot is undertaken for the following reason: The command to change graphic properties such as axis, color map, view angles, color axis, and other parameters can be specified after a figure is plotted; but each time a new command is issued, the whole figure is replotted. Time can be saved by giving all the property commands before plotting and hold with hold on.

2.8 MATLAB AS A DRAWING BOARD

MATLAB can be used as a drawing board for pictures and diagrams. Unlike ordinary drawing software, mathematical functions may be used to define lines and curves. In this section, we first explain elements of drawing pictures and diagrams with MATLAB, and then introduce a set of drawing tools.

simple picture: The first thing to do before drawing is to determine the area of the drawing on the x-y plane by axis followed by hold on. Then, lines and curves are plotted by plot. The following script draws a happy face as shown in the first picture in Figure 2.28.

List 2.28
```
clear, clf, hold off
dt = pi/20;
t=0:dt:2*pi;
x=cos(t); y=sin(t);
axis([-1 1 -1 1]), hold on
plot( x,y)        % face outline
hold on
for k=0.8:-0.05:0.05
    plot(k*0.1*x-0.3,k*0.15*y+0.1) %  left eye
```

```
        plot(k*0.1*x+0.3,k*0.15*y+0.1) % right eye
    end
    s1 = 3*pi/2-1.1;
    s2 = 3*pi/2+1.1;
    s = s1:dt:s2;
    xs = 0.5*cos(s); ys = 0.5*sin(s);
    plot(xs,ys)            % mouth
    hold off
```

By adding `axis square` and `axis off`, the drawing is completed as the second picture in Figure 2.28.

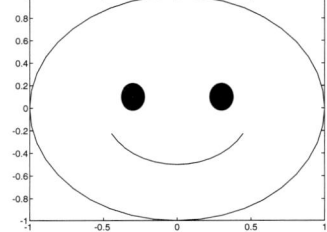
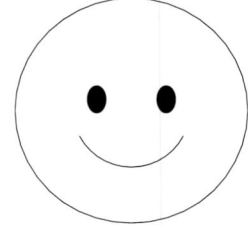

Figure 2.28 Happy face.

Mathematical functions are useful to draw creative figures and patterns. Figure 2.29 illustrates a soap bubble pattern created by randomly drawing circles. The locations and sizes of the bubbles are determined by `rand`. See List 2.29.

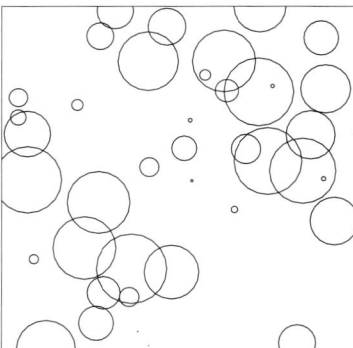

Figure 2.29 Soap bubbles.

List 2.29
```
clear,clf, hold off
axis([-0. 1. -0. 1. ])
axis square
```

```
axis off
hold on
plot([0,1,1,0,0], [0,0,1,1,0])
h=pi/10;
t=0:h:pi*2;
xx = cos(t);
yy = sin(t);
for n=1:40
   r = rand(1)*0.1;
   xc = rand(1);
   yc = rand(1);
x = xx*r + xc;
y = yy*r + yc;
plot (x,y)
end
hold off
```

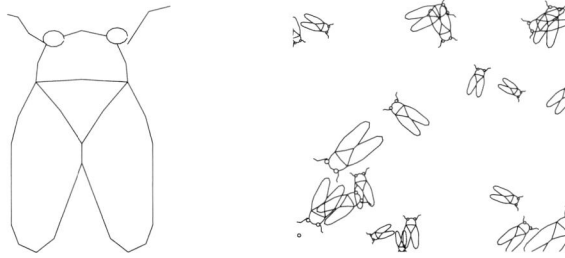

Figure 2.30 An insect and its random pattern.

Figures may be expressed by connecting a series of points. For example, the wings and body of the insect in the first picture of Figure 2.30 are defined by points connected by lines. Function insect_(p1, p2) in FM 2-4 plots one insect placed between two points, p1 and p2, where p1 and p2 are coordinate pairs in vector forms. Function insect_ may be tested by executing insect_t listed after insect_.m. The second picture in Figure 2.30 is created by rotating and translating the insect by the algorithms explained in the next section.

rotation and translation: When you wish to draw a complicated picture or diagram, a number of subfigures may be developed as function m-files. Each subfigure may be developed in a normalized domain such as $-1 \leq x \leq 1, -1 \leq y \leq 1$, or $0 \leq x \leq 1$, $0 \leq y \leq 1$. Then, by translation, rotation, and rescaling, they are placed at desired locations. Figure 2.31 illustrates a coil defined in a unit area, and its replacement after rotation and translation to a location in a larger figure.

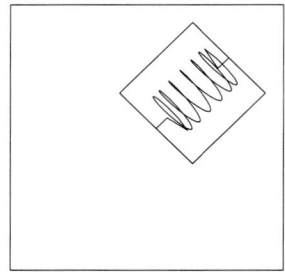

Figure 2.31 Translation and rotation of a figure.

In translation and rotation, we need to specify two reference points in the subfigure and two corresponding points in the whole picture. The coordinates of the two points in the subfigure will be denoted by (x_1, y_1) and (x_2, y_2), while the coordinates of the corresponding points in the whole figure are denoted by (X_1, Y_1) and (X_2, Y_2). In order to keep the shape of the figure the same after rotation and translation, the following relation must be satisfied between the coordinates (x, y) and (X, Y):

$$\begin{aligned} X &= cx - dy + f \\ Y &= dx + cy + g \end{aligned} \qquad (2.8.1)$$

where the coefficients c, d, f, and g are determined by

$$\begin{aligned} X_1 &= cx_1 - dy_1 + f \\ Y_1 &= dx_1 + cy_1 + g \\ X_2 &= cx_2 - dy_2 + f \\ Y_2 &= dx_2 + cy_2 + g \end{aligned} \qquad (2.8.2)$$

Particularly, if $x_1 = -1, x_2 = 1, y_1 = y_2 = 0$, the coefficients become

$$\begin{aligned} c &= 0.5(x_2 - x_1) \\ d &= y_2 - y_1 \\ g &= x_2 + x_1 \\ f &= y_2 + y_1 \end{aligned} \qquad (2.8.3)$$

A subfigure originally developed in an arbitrarily chosen domain may be standardized by the inverse of the foregoing transformation. Suppose that the reference points of the original figures are given by (X_1, Y_1) and (X_2, Y_2). Then, the figure is transformed to the normalized domain of $(x_1 = -1, y_1 = 0)$ and $(x_2 = 1, y_2 = 0)$ by

$$\begin{aligned} x &= CX - DY + F \\ y &= DX + CY + G \end{aligned} \qquad (2.8.4)$$

where the coefficients C, D, F, and G are determined by

$$\begin{aligned} x_1 &= CX_1 - DY_1 + F = -1 \\ y_1 &= DX_1 + CY_1 + G = 0 \\ x_2 &= CX_2 - DY_2 + F = 1 \\ y_2 &= DX_2 + CY_2 + G = 0 \end{aligned} \qquad (2.8.5)$$

The coefficients satisfying the foregoing equations are

$$\begin{aligned} C &= \frac{-2(X_1 - X_2)}{(Y_1 - Y_2)^2 + (X_1 - X_2)^2} \\ D &= \frac{2(Y_1 - Y_2)}{(Y_1 - Y_2)^2 + (X_1 - X_2)^2} \\ F &= 1 - CX_2 + DY_2 \\ G &= -DX_2 - CY_2 \end{aligned} \qquad (2.8.6)$$

drawing diagrams: Table 2.1 is a list of subfigures that can be used to develop diagrams and pictures:

Table 2.1 Commands for Component Pictures and Diagrams

f-name	Synopsis
capacit_	capacit_(u,w,p1,p2)
battery_	battery_(u,w,p1,p2)
circle_	circle_(r,x0,y0)
coil_b	coil_b(n,u,w,p1,p2)
coil_a	coil_a(n,u,w, p1,p2)
damper_	damper_(w,p0,p1)
line_	line_(p1,p2)
arrow_	arrow_(w, p1,p2)
arrow_dot	arrow_dot(w, p1,p2)
resist_	resist_(n,u,w,p1,p2)
spring_	spring_(n,u,w,p1,p2)
switch_	switch_(u,w,p1,p2)
box_	box_(w,p1,p2)
human_	human_(p1,p2, Body, ...

	Rarm1,Rarm2,Larm1,Larm2, ...
	Rleg1,Rleg2,Lleg1,Lleg2)
insect_	insect_(p1,p2)
two_eyes	two_eyes(phi,eyeangle, x0,y0,z0,width)
ellip_	ellip_(x0,y0,rx,ry)

The meanings of arguments in the foregoing table are as follows:

- n: number of oscillations or winding
- u: relative length of the component
- w: relative width of the component
- p1: the x and y values of the left reference point (row vector)
- p2: the x and y values of the right reference point (row vector)
- r: radius of circle
- x0, y0: center of circle
- Body, Rarms1, etc: (see Figure 2.36)
- phi, eyeangle, etc: (see FM 2-4 for two_eyes)
- rx,ry: radii in x and y directions

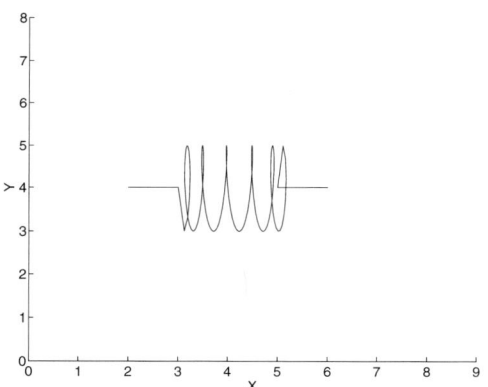

Figure 2.32 A coil.

Each component can be placed at a desired location with a desired amount of rotation in the final drawing by appropriate definitions of p1 and p2. It is important to set axis and hold on before calling the functions. List 2.30 illustrates the use of a component. The figure drawn by List 2.30 is shown in Figure 2.32. Notice that the coil starts at p1 ($x = 2, y = 4$) and ends at p2 ($x = 6$, $y = 4$).

Figures 2.33 illustrates pictures created by human_. The script of human_.m is found in FM 2-5.

List 2.30

```
clear,clf
axis([0,9,0,8])
hold on
p1=[2,4]; p2 =[6,4]
n = 6; u = 0.5, w=0.5;
coil_b(n,u,w, p1,p2)
hold off
```

Seven noisy kids are coming.   They are going back.

Figure 2.33 Noisy kids.

2.9 INTERACTIVE GRAPHICS

The most fundamental element of interactive graphics is the capability of a program to read the coordinates of the mouse pointer at any desired location. This is possible with `ginput` in one of the following formats:

```
[x,y] = ginput
[x,y,button] = ginput
[x,y,button] = ginput(n)
```

Suppose the mouse is clicked at a desired location within a graphic screen. Then, [x,y] = ginput gathers an unlimited number of points until the return key is hit, so x and y become vectors of the length equal to the number of points gathered. [x,y,button] = ginput is the same except that the button numbers of the mouse are also recorded. The button number is 1, 2, or

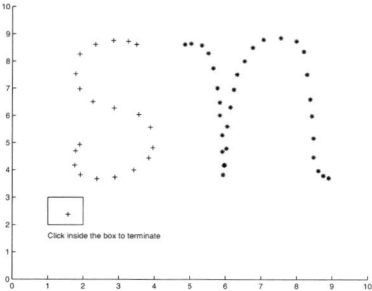

Figure 2.34 MATLAB graffiti.

3, respectively, counted from the left side of the mouse. [x,y,button] = ginput(n) gathers *n* points, but can be terminated by the return key.

List 2.31 illustrates use of ginput. When List 2.31 is executed, the program awaits the mouse to be clicked. If the left button of the mouse is clicked, a '+' mark in red is printed at the location of the pointer. Likewise, if the middle button or right button is clicked, a 'o' mark in yellow, or a '*' in green is printed, respectively. The execution is terminated if the mouse is clicked with cursor inside the box at the left bottom corner of the screen. Figure 2.34 illustrates the marks plotted by List 2.31.

List 2.31
```
clear,clf,hold off
axis([0,10,0,10])
hold on
plot([1,2,2,1,1], [2,2,3,3,2])
text(1,1.6,'Click inside the box to terminate')
while 1
   [x,y,button] = ginput(1)
   if button==1, plot(x,y,'+r'), end
   if button==2, plot(x,y,'oy'), end
   if button==3, plot(x,y,'*g'), end
   if x>1 & x<2 & y>2 & y<3, break;end
end
hold off
```

2.10 M-FILES

FM 2-1. Triangular mesh plot
Purpose: To plot a triangular grid.
Synopsis: tri_grid(data1, data2, y_scale)
 data1: Name of the array that contains the vertex point numbers for each triangular element. Column 1 is the triangle number. Columns

Section 2.10 M-Files   93

         2 through 4 are the vertex numbers for the triangle in the clockwise order. See the sample data file named `cell_da`.

data2: Name of the array that contains coordinates of vertices. The first column is the sequential number of the points, and the next two columns are x and y values of the point. See the file `point_da`.

y_scale: Scale factor for the y-coordinate. If a circle is plotted without adjustment, for example, it becomes an ellipse. An appropriate scale factor can be found by measuring how a square or a circle is distorted when this factor is set to unity.

Example: `tri_grid(cell_da, point_da, y_scale)`

tri_grid.m
```
function tri_grid(tri_d, xy_d, y_scale)
hold off
[n_tr,n] = size(tri_d);
[n_pt,n] = size(xy_d);
nmax=tri_d(1,1);
x=xy_d(:,2);
y=xy_d(:,3)*y_scale;
tri_num_prnt = input('Annotate element numbers ?  1 yes/ 0 no: ');
pnt_num_prnt = input('Annotate grid point numbers ? 1 yes/0 no: ');
xmin =min(x);   xmax =max(x); x_cen = 0.5*(xmin + xmax);
ymin =min(y);   ymax =max(y); y_cen = 0.5*(ymin + ymax);
Dx=xmax-xmin; Dy=ymax-ymin;
if Dx<Dy, xmin = x_cen-Dy/2; xmax = x_cen+Dy/2; end
if Dx>Dy, ymin = y_cen-Dx/2; ymax = y_cen+Dx/2; end
clf;  hold off;   clc;  %axis square
axis([xmin, xmax,ymin,ymax])
xlabel('Plot of triangular grid');   hold on
del_x = 0.1; del_y = 0.1; % Adjust location of element no.
for k=1:n_tr
   for l=1:3
      p=tri_d(k,l+1);
      xx(l)=x(p);  yy(l)=y(p);
   end
   xx(4)=xx(1);  yy(4)=yy(1);
   plot(xx,yy)
   x_cen = sum(xx(1:3))/3;  y_cen = sum(yy(1:3))/3;
   if tri_num_prnt == 1 % if 0, elmnt numbers are not printed.
      text(x_cen - del_x, y_cen - del_y, int2str(k))
   end
end
%plot(x,y,'*')
if pnt_num_prnt == 1   % if 0, point numbers are not printed.
```

```
   for n=1:n_pt
   text(x(n), y(n), ['(',int2str(n),')'])
   end
end
axis off
```

cell_da

1	1	6	2
2	2	6	7
3	3	2	7
4	3	7	8
5	3	8	9
6	3	9	4
7	4	9	5
8	6	11	12
9	7	6	12
10	7	12	13
11	7	13	8
12	8	13	14
13	8	14	10
14	8	10	9
15	11	15	16
16	11	16	12
17	12	16	17
18	12	17	13
19	13	17	18
20	13	18	14

point_da

1	0.0	0.0
2	1.0	0.0
3	2.0	0.0
4	3.0	0.0
5	4.0	0.0
6	0.0	1.0
7	1.0	1.0
8	1.7	1.3
9	3.0	1.0
10	2.4	1.6
11	0.0	1.75
12	0.65	1.8
13	1.25	2.0
14	1.66	2.34
15	0.0	2.0
16	0.518	2.069
17	1.0	2.268
18	1.414	2.586

FM 2-2. Contour plotting on a triangular grid

Purpose: To plot a contour for a function defined on a triangular grid.

Synopsis: tri_cont(data1, data2, data3, y_scale)

    data1: see FM 2-1

    data2: see FM 2-1

    data3: functional values on the grid points. See data named phi_da

    scale: see FM 2-1

Example: tri_cont(cell_da, point_da, phi_da, y_scale)

tri_cont.m
```
function dummy=tri_cont(tri_data,xy_data,f_data,ys)
[n_tr,n] = size(tri_data);
[n_pt,n] = size(xy_data);
nmax=tri_data(1,1);
x=xy_data(:,2);
y=xy_data(:,3);
f = f_data;
tri_num_prnt = input('Annotate element numbers ?  1 yes/ 0 no: ');
pnt_num_prnt = ...
        input('Annotate grid point numbers ? 1 yes/0 no: ');
xmin =min(x);   xmax =max(x); x_cen = 0.5*(xmin + xmax);
ymin =min(y*ys);ymax =max(y*ys);y_cen = 0.5*(ymin + ymax);
fmin =min(f)+0.01;   fmax =max(f)-0.01;
Dx=xmax-xmin; Dy=ymax-ymin;
n_cont=20;
df = (fmax-fmin)/n_cont;kmax=n_cont;
s = fmin:df:fmax;
if Dx<Dy, xmin = x_cen-Dy/2, xmax = x_cen+Dy/2, end
if Dx>Dy, ymin = y_cen-Dx/2, ymax = y_cen+Dx/2, end
clf;   hold off;   clc;   %axis square
axis([xmin, xmax,ymin,ymax]); m=0;
title('Contour Plot');   hold on
del_x = 0.1; del_y = 0.1; % Adjust location of element no.
for k=1:n_tr
  for j=1:3
    p=tri_data(k,j+1);
    xx(j)=x(p);   yy(j)=y(p);
    ff(j) = f(p);
  end
  xx(4)=xx(1);  yy(4)=yy(1); ff(4)=ff(1);
  plot(xx,yy*ys)
  f_min = min([ff(1), ff(2), ff(3)]);
  f_max = max([ff(1), ff(2), ff(3)]);
  for kv = 1:kmax
    if f_min <= s(kv) & s(kv) <= f_max;
      m=0;
```

```
          for i=1:3
            if (s(kv) - ff(i)) * (s(kv) - ff(i+1))<= 0,
              m = m + 1;
              if f(i+1) == f(i),   alph=0.5;end
              if f(i+1) ~= f(i),
                 alph = (s(kv)-ff(i))/(ff(i+1)-ff(i));
              end
              xp(m)= alph*xx(i+1) + (1-alph)*xx(i);
              yp(m)= alph*yy(i+1) + (1-alph)*yy(i);
            end
            if m == 2,
              plot([xp(1),xp(2)],[yp(1)*ys,yp(2)*ys],'--');
              break
            end
          end
        end
      end
    end
    %==
    x_cen = sum(xx(1:3))/3;   y_cen = sum(yy(1:3))/3;
    if tri_num_prnt == 1 % if 0, elmnt numbers are not printed.
       text(x_cen - del_x, (y_cen - del_y)*ys, int2str(k))
    end
end
% plot(x,y*ys,'*')    % Use if points are to be marked by *.
%==================
if pnt_num_prnt == 1    % if 0, point numbers are not printed.
   for n=1:n_pt
   text(x(n), y(n)*ys, ['(',int2str(n),')'])
   end
end
axis off
```

phi_da

3.3744378e+02	3.4924482e+02	3.7328341e+02	3.9020757e+02
4.0131868e+02	3.1453162e+02	3.2645937e+02	3.3443546e+02
3.8200298e+02	3.4679150e+02	2.5358725e+02	2.5990002e+02
2.6843571e+02	2.6889073e+02	2.2356239e+02	2.2439244e+02
2.2498863e+02	2.2577131e+02		

FM 2-3. Function to create sample data of curvilinear grid

Purpose: To generate data for illustration of plotting curvilinear grid and contour.

Synopsis: g_cont(x, y, f, s)

      x: 2-dim. array of x-coordinates

Section 2.10 M-Files 97

  y: 2-dim. array of y-coordinates
  f: 2-dim. array of functional values

td_data.m
```
function [x,y,f] = td_data
ni= 10; nj=20;
  for j=1:nj
    for i=1:ni
      r = 3 + (5+j)*0.05*(i-1) ;
      th = j*pi/10;
      x(i,j) = r*cos(th) ;
      y(i,j) = r*sin(th);
    end
  end
  f=zeros(ni,nj);
  for j=2:nj-1
    f(ni,j)=sin(0.5*j);
  end
  for it = 1:20
    for i=2:ni-1
      f(i,nj) = f(i,nj-1);
      f(i,1) = f(i,2);
    end
    f(ni,nj) = 0.5*(f(ni-1,nj) + f(ni,nj-1));
    f(ni,1) = 0.5*(f(ni,2) + f(ni-1,1));
    for i=2:ni-1
      for j=2:nj-1
        f(i,j) = 0.375*(f(i-1,j)+f(i+1,j)+f(i,j-1)+f(i,j+1)) ...
            - 0.5* f(i,j) ;
      end
    end
  end
```

FM 2-4. Subfigures of pictures and diagrams

Purpose: To draw a component of a picture or diagram at a desired location.
Synopsis: see Table 2.1. (It is important to set axis and hold on before calling the picture and diagram functions listed here.)

capacit_.m   size
```
function y =  capacit_(u,w, p1,p2)
c = (p2(1)-p1(1))/2;   d = (p2(2)-p1(2))/2;
f = (p2(1)+p1(1))/2;   g = (p2(2)+p1(2))/2;
x1 =[-1,-u];  y1 = [0, 0];
x2 = [-u,-u]; y2 = [-1,1]*w;
x3 = [u,u];   y3 = [-1,1]*w;
```

```
x4 =[u,1];     y4 = [0, 0];
 xx1 = c*x1 - d*y1 + f;    yy1 = d*x1 + c*y1 + g;
 xx2 = c*x2 - d*y2 + f;    yy2 = d*x2 + c*y2 + g;
 xx3 = c*x3 - d*y3 + f;    yy3 = d*x3 + c*y3 + g;
 xx4 = c*x4 - d*y4 + f;    yy4 = d*x4 + c*y4 + g;
plot(xx1,yy1)
plot(xx2,yy2)
plot(xx3,yy3)
plot(xx4,yy4)
```

circle_.m

```
function y =  circle_(r,x0,y0)
delt = 2*pi/30;
t = 0:delt:2*pi;
x=r*cos(t)+x0;  y = r*sin(t)+y0;
plot(x,y)
```

coil_b.m

```
function dummy =  coil_b(n,u,w, p1,p2)
c = (p2(1)-p1(1))/2;  d = (p2(2)-p1(2))/2;
f = (p2(1)+p1(1))/2;  g = (p2(2)+p1(2))/2;
k = n*2;
Dx = 2/k/2;
x = -1:0.01:1;
z = k*acos(x);
y = w*sin(z);
x = x + 0.1*(1-cos(z)); %x = [-1,x,1];
x = [-1,-u, u*x,u,1];
y = [0,0,y,0,0];
xx = c*x - d*y + f;
 yy = d*x + c*y + g;
plot(xx,yy)
```

coil_a.m

```
function dummy =  coil_a(n,w, p1,p2)
c = (p2(1)-p1(1))/2;  d = (p2(2)-p1(2))/2;
f = (p2(1)+p1(1))/2;  g = (p2(2)+p1(2))/2;
x = -1:0.01:1;
t =(x+1)*pi*(n+0.5);
y = -w*sin(t);
x = x + 0.15*(1-cos(t));  a=x(1); b=x(length(x));
x = 2*(x-a)/(b-a) - 1;
xx = c*x - d*y + f;
yy = d*x + c*y + g;
plot(xx,yy)
```

damper_.m

```
function y =  damper_(w,p0,p1)
```

Section 2.10 M-Files

```
c = (p1(1)-p0(1))/2;   d = (p1(2)-p0(2))/2;
f = (p1(1)+p0(1))/2;   g = (p1(2)+p0(2))/2;
s = 0.25;
x1 =[-1,-s];   y1 = [0, 0];
x2 = [-s,-s];  y2 = [-1.2,1.2]*w;
x3 = [s,s];    y3 = [-0.7,0.7]*w;
x4 =[s,1];     y4 = [0, 0];
 tx1 = c*x1 - d*y1 + f;   ty1 = d*x1 + c*y1 + g;
 tx2 = c*x2 - d*y2 + f;   ty2 = d*x2 + c*y2 + g;
 tx3 = c*x3 - d*y3 + f;   ty3 = d*x3 + c*y3 + g;
 tx4 = c*x4 - d*y4 + f;   ty4 = d*x4 + c*y4 + g;
plot( tx1, ty1)
plot( tx2, ty2)
plot( tx3, ty3)
plot( tx4, ty4)
x=[-s, 2*s];  y = [1.2,1.2]*w
 tx = c*x - d*y + f;   ty = d*x + c*y + g;
plot( tx, ty)
x=[-s, 2*s];  y = [-1.2,-1.2]*w
 tx = c*x - d*y + f;   ty = d*x + c*y + g;
plot( tx, ty)
```

line_.m

```
function dummy = line_(p1,p2)
plot([p1(1),p2(1)],[p1(2),p2(2)])
```

resistor_.m

```
function dummy =  resist_(n,u,w, p1,p2)
% n: # of turns
% u: length
% w: width
% p1: coordinate pair for starting point
% p2: same for ending point
% Example>> p1 =[1,0]; p2=[2,0]; resist_(5, 0.4, 0.1, p1,p2)
c = (p2(1)-p1(1))/2;   d = (p2(2)-p1(2))/2;
f = (p2(1)+p1(1))/2;   g = (p2(2)+p1(2))/2;
 Dx = 1/(2*n);
x =u*[-1+Dx:2*Dx:1];
[m1,n1]=size(1:length(x));
y = w*[0, (-ones(1,n1-2)).^(1:n1-2),0];
x=[-1,x,1];
y=[0,y,0];
 xx = c*x - d*y + f;
 yy = d*x + c*y + g;
plot(xx,yy)
```

spring_.m

```
function dummy =  spring_(n,u,w, p1,p2)
```

```
% n: # of winding
% u: length of spring
% w: width of spring
% p1: coordinate pair for starting point
% p2: same for ending point
% Example>> p1 =[1,0];    p2=[2,0];
%            spring_(5,0.4, 0.2, p1,p2)
c = (p2(1)-p1(1))/2;   d = (p2(2)-p1(2))/2;
f = (p2(1)+p1(1))/2;   g = (p2(2)+p1(2))/2;
k = 2*n;
x = -1:0.02:1;
z=k*x*2;
y = w*cos(z).*cos(-x*pi/2);
x = x - 0.2*sin(z);
x=[-1,u*x,1]; y=[0,y,0];
xx = c*x - d*y + f;
yy = d*x + c*y + g;
plot(xx,yy)
```

switch_.m

```
function y =  switch_(u, w, p1,p2)
% u: switch size
% w: relative height of switch
% p1: coordinate pair for starting point
% p2: same for ending point
% Example>>
%      p1 =[1,0]; p2=[2,0]; switch_(0.4, 1.2, p1,p2)
c = (p2(1)-p1(1))/2;   d = (p2(2)-p1(2))/2;
f = (p2(1)+p1(1))/2;   g = (p2(2)+p1(2))/2;
x1 =[-1,-0.5*u, 0.5*u];
y1 = w*[0, 0, 0.5*u];
x2 = [0.5*u, 1];
y2 = [0,0];
 x1 = c*x1 - d*y1 + f;
 y1 = d*x1 + c*y1 + g;
 x2 = c*x2 - d*y2 + f;
 y2 = d*x2 + c*y2 + g;
plot( x1, y1)
plot( x2, y2)
```

box_.m

```
function dummy =  box_(hi, p1,p2)
% hi=height of box; p1 and p2 are coordinates of center point
% of the left side of box wall, and p2 the same for the right.
% Example >> p1 = [0,0]; p2 =[1,0]; box_(0.5,p1,p2)
%
c = (p2(1)-p1(1))/2;   d = (p2(2)-p1(2))/2;
f = (p2(1)+p1(1))/2;   g = (p2(2)+p1(2))/2;
```

Section 2.10 M-Files

```
x = [-1 1 1 -1 -1]; y = hi*[-1 -1 1 1 -1];
 xx1 = c*x - d*y + f;   yy1 = d*x + c*y + g;
plot(xx1,yy1)
```

human_.m

```
function y =  human_(p1,p2, Body,    ...
Rarm1,Rarm2,Larm1,Larm2, ...
Rleg1,Rleg2,Lleg1,Lleg2  )
%10,10,30,30,90 30 90 90 20
x0=p1(1);
y0=p1(2);
x1=p2(1);
y1=p2(2);
c = (x1-x0)/2;   d = (y1 - y0)/2;
f = (x1+x0)/2;   g = (y1 + y0)/2;
M = [c,-d; d,c]/3; F = [f,g]';
  thb = Body/180*pi;% body angle
  thrh1=Rarm1/180*pi;% right arm theta-1
  thrh2=Rarm2/180*pi;% right arm theta-2
  thlh1=Larm1/180*pi;% left arm theta-1
  thlh2=Larm2/180*pi;% left arm theta-2
  thrg1=Rleg1/180*pi;% right leg theta-1
  thrg2=Rleg2/180*pi;% right leg theta-2
  thlg1=Lleg1/180*pi;% left leg theta-1
  thlg2=Lleg2/180*pi;% left leg theta-2
  t = 0:0.25:6.3;
% body
  b1=[0,0]';
  b2=b1 + 1.5*[sin(thb), cos(thb)]';
  b3=b1 + 2*[sin(thb), cos(thb)]';
  b=[b1,b2,b3];
  [m,n]=size(b); w=ones(1,n); b = M*b+[f*w;g*w];
  plot(b(1,:), b(2,:))
% head
  b4=b3+1.*[sin(thb), cos(thb)]';
  xHd= 1.*cos(t)+b4(1);
  yHd= 1.*sin(t)+b4(2);
  b = [xHd; yHd];
  w=ones(1,n);
  [m,n]=size(b); w=ones(1,n); b = M*b+[f*w;g*w];
  plot(b(1,:), b(2,:))
%right arm/hand
  rh1=b2;
  rh2=rh1 + 1.5*[cos(thrh1), sin(thrh1)]';
  rh3=rh2 + 1.5*[cos(thrh2), sin(thrh2)]';
  rh4=rh3 + 0.2*[cos(thrh2), sin(thrh2)]';
  b=[rh1,rh2,rh3];
  w=ones(1,n);
```

```
  [m,n]=size(b); w=ones(1,n); b = M*b+[f*w;g*w];
  plot(b(1,:), b(2,:))
  xrp= 0.2*cos(t)+rh4(1);
  yrp= 0.2*sin(t)+rh4(2);
  b=[xrp;yrp];
  w=ones(1,n);
  [m,n]=size(b); w=ones(1,n); b = M*b+[f*w;g*w];
  plot(b(1,:), b(2,:))
%left arm/hand
  lh1=b2;
  lh2=lh1 + 1.5*[-cos(thlh1), sin(thlh1)]';
  lh3=lh2 + 1.5*[-cos(thlh2), sin(thlh2)]';
  lh4=lh3 + 0.2*[-cos(thlh2), sin(thlh2)]';
  b=[lh1,lh2,lh3];
w=ones(1,n);
  [m,n]=size(b); w=ones(1,n); b = M*b+[f*w;g*w] ;
  plot(b(1,:), b(2,:))
  xlp= 0.2*cos(t)+lh4(1);
  ylp= 0.2*sin(t)+lh4(2);
b = [xlp;ylp];
 w=ones(1,n);
  [m,n]=size(b); w=ones(1,n); b = M*b+[f*w;g*w] ;
  plot(b(1,:), b(2,:))
%right leg/foot
  rg1=b1;
  rg2=rg1 + 1*[cos(thrg1), -sin(thrg1)]';
  rg3=rg2 + 1.5*[cos(thrg2), -sin(thrg2)]';
  rg4=rg3 + 0.2*[cos(thrg2), -sin(thrg2)]';
  b=[rg1,rg2,rg3];
  w=ones(1,n);
  [m,n]=size(b); w=ones(1,n); b = M*b+[f*w;g*w];
  plot(b(1,:), b(2,:))
  xrf= 0.2*cos(t)+rg4(1);
  yrf= 0.2*sin(t)+rg4(2);
  b=[ xrf; yrf];
  w=ones(1,n);
  [m,n]=size(b); w=ones(1,n); b = M*b+[f*w;g*w];
  plot(b(1,:), b(2,:))
%left leg/foot
  lg1=b1;
  lg2=lg1 + 1.*[-cos(thlg1), -sin(thlg1)]';
  lg3=lg2 + 1.5*[-cos(thlg2), -sin(thlg2)]';
  lg4=lg3 + 0.2*[-cos(thlg2), -sin(thlg2)]';
  b=[lg1,lg2,lg3];
  w=ones(1,n);
  [m,n]=size(b); w=ones(1,n); b = M*b+[f*w;g*w];
  plot(b(1,:), b(2,:))
```

Section 2.10 M-Files

```
        xlf= 0.2*cos(t)+lg4(1);
        ylf= 0.2*sin(t)+lg4(2);
        b=[xlf;ylf];
        [m,n]=size(b); w=ones(1,n); b = M*b+[f*w;g*w] ;
        plot(b(1,:), b(2,:))
```

two_eyes.m

```
function f=two_eyes(phi,eyeangle, x0,y0,z0,width)
% Sample call statement:
%       clf;hold on; Two_eyes(120,45,0,0,0,0.2);view(120,30)
%       axis([-1 1 -1 1 -1 1]); ylabel('y'); hold off
% phi : direction of face. Degrees.
%       If 0 the face is on the x-z plane toward positive y.
% eyeangle:  direction of eye balls. Degree.
eyr = 0.2;
angle0=eyeangle;
x=[-1,0,1,0,-1]; z=[0, 0.3,0,-0.3, 0]; y=[0,0,0,0,0];
dth=pi/10;  th=0:dth:2*pi;
zc=cos(th)*eyr; xc=sin(th)*eyr; yc=zeros(size(xc));
th=0:dth:10*pi;
ze=cos(th)*eyr.*(1.0- 0.03*th);     %eye ball
xe=sin(th)*eyr.*(1.0- 0.03*th);
angle = angle0/180*pi;
xd=xe/2 + eyr*cos(angle)/2;
zd=ze/2 + eyr*sin(angle)/2;
b = eyr^2 - xd.^2 - zd.^2;
yd=sqrt((eyr+0.01)^2 - xd.^2 - zd.^2);
xcL=xc-0.25; xcR=xc+0.25;
yc=yc;  zc=zc;
xdL=xd-0.25;   xdR=xd+0.25;
yd=yd*0.2; zd=zd;  xdR=xd+0.25;
xns=[0,0,0];  yns=[0, 0.1,0];   zns=[0.1,-0.3,-0.3]; % nose
S=width/0.2/2;   %scale factor
[x1,y1,z1]=rotz_(xcL,yc,zc, phi);
plot3(x1*S+x0,y1*S+y0,z1*S+z0);
[x2,y2,z2]=rotz_(xcR,yc,zc, phi);
plot3(x2*S+x0,y2*S+y0,z2*S+z0);
[x3,y3,z3]=rotz_(xdL,yd,zd, phi);
plot3(x3*S+x0,y3*S+y0,z3*S+z0);
[x4,y4,z4]=rotz_(xdR,yd,zd, phi);
plot3(x4*S+x0,y4*S+y0,z4*S+z0);
[x5,y5,z5]=rotz_(xns,yns,zns, phi);
plot3(x5*S+x0,y5*S+y0,z5*S+z0);
axis off
```

arrow_.m

```
function dummy =  arrow_(w, p1,p2)
%    w width of arrow
```

```
%    p1 and p2:  starting and ending point coordinate pairs
c = (p2(1)-p1(1))/2;   d = (p2(2)-p1(2))/2;
f = (p2(1)+p1(1))/2;   g = (p2(2)+p1(2))/2;
x = [-1 1]; y = [0,0];
xx1 = c*x - d*y + f;   yy1 = d*x + c*y + g;
plot(xx1,yy1)
x = [0.5, 1]; y = w*[0.5,0];
xx1 = c*x - d*y + f;   yy1 = d*x + c*y + g;
plot(xx1,yy1)
x = [0.5, 1]; y = w*[-0.5,0];
xx1 = c*x - d*y + f;   yy1 = d*x + c*y + g;
plot(xx1,yy1)
```

arrow_dot.m

```
function dummy = arrow_dot(w, p1,p2)
%    w width of arrow
%    p1 and p2:  starting and ending point coordinate pairs
c = (p2(1)-p1(1))/2;   d = (p2(2)-p1(2))/2;
f = (p2(1)+p1(1))/2;   g = (p2(2)+p1(2))/2;
x = [-1 1]; y = [0,0];
xx1 = c*x - d*y + f;   yy1 = d*x + c*y + g;
plot(xx1,yy1,':')
x = [0.5, 1]; y = w*[0.5,0];
xx1 = c*x - d*y + f;   yy1 = d*x + c*y + g;
plot(xx1,yy1,':')
x = [0.5, 1]; y = w*[-0.5,0];
xx1 = c*x - d*y + f;   yy1 = d*x + c*y + g;
plot(xx1,yy1,':')
```

insect_.m

```
function y = insect_(p1,p2)
hold on
x0 = p1(1); y0=p1(2);
x1 = p2(1); y1=p2(2);
c = (x1-x0)/2;   d = (y1 - y0)/2;
f = (x1+x0)/2;   g = (y1 + y0)/2;
xwL = [-13  -18 -20 -20 -18 -13 -8 -6  0  0 -6 -13]/50;
ywL = [ 13   0  -10 -40 -47 -50 -45 -38 -17 -10 2 13]/50;
xx = c*xwL - d*ywL + f;
yy = d*xwL + c*ywL + g;
xxb = -c*xwL - d*ywL + f;
yyb = -d*xwL + c*ywL + g;
plot(xx,yy); plot( xxb,yyb)
xneck = [-13   0   13]/50;
yneck = [ 13  14   13]/50;
xx = c*xneck - d*yneck + f;
```

```
yy = d*xneck + c*yneck + g;
plot(xx,yy)
xhL = [ -13 -12.5 -10]/50;
yhL = [13 20 27]/50;
xx = c*xhL - d*yhL + f;
yy = d*xhL + c*yhL + g;   plot(xx,yy)
xx = -c*xhL - d*yhL + f;
yy = -d*xhL + c*yhL + g;   plot(xx,yy)
xtop = [-5 0 7]/50;
ytop = [30 32 30]/50;
xx = c*xtop - d*ytop + f;
yy = d*xtop + c*ytop + g;   plot(xx,yy)
t = 0:0.5:pi*2;
xeyeL =( -.08 + .03*cos(t))*2;
yeyeL =( .29 + .03*sin(t))*2;
xx = c*xeyeL - d*yeyeL + f;
yy = d*xeyeL + c*yeyeL + g;   plot(xx,yy)
xeyeR = (.10 + .03*cos(t))*2;
yeyeR = (.30 + .03*sin(t))*2;
xx = c*xeyeR - d*yeyeR + f;
yy = d*xeyeR + c*yeyeR + g;   plot(xx,yy)
plot (xeyeR, yeyeR)
xantL=[-10 -15 -18 -21]/50;
yantL=[27 31 37 38]/50;
xx = c*xantL - d*yantL + f;
yy = d*xantL + c*yantL + g;   plot(xx,yy)
xantR=[25 19 13]/50;
yantR=[41 39 27]/50;
xx = c*xantR - d*yantR + f;
yy = d*xantR + c*yantR + g;   plot(xx,yy)
hold off
```

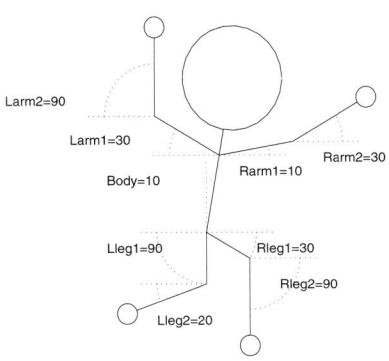

Figure 2.35 Explanation of arguments in human.

FM 2-5. Illustration of a picture drawing
Purpose: To draw Figure 2.33.

Synopsis: kids1

kids1.m
```
hold off, clear, clf
axis([-5 14 -5 14])
hold on
axis square
axis off
x0=-1;x1=2;y0=2;y1=2;
Body=10 ;              % body angle.  See Figure 2.35.
Rarm1=10; Rarm2=30;
Larm1=30; Larm2=90;
Rleg1=30; Rleg2=90;
Lleg1=90; Lleg2=20;
human_([x0,y0],[x1,y1], Body, Rarm1,Rarm2,Larm1,Larm2, ...
                       Rleg1,Rleg2,Lleg1,Lleg2  )
human_([2,0],[5,1], Body, Rarm1,Rarm2,Larm1,Larm2, ...
                       Rleg1,Rleg2,Lleg1,Lleg2  )
human_([3,1],[6,1], -Body, Rarm1,Rarm2,Larm1,Larm2, ...
                       Rleg1,Rleg2,Lleg1,Lleg2  )
human_([-3,1],[-1.,1], Body*1.1,-Rarm1,Rarm2,Larm1,Larm2, ...
                       Rleg1,Rleg2,Lleg1,Lleg2  )
human_([-4,4],[-2.,4], Body, Rarm1,Rarm2,Larm1,Larm2, ...
                       Rleg1,Rleg2,Lleg1,Lleg2  )
human_([7,0.5],[10.5,0.5], Body, -Rarm1,Rarm2*2,Larm1,Larm2, ...
human_([9.5,-2],[13,-2], 2*Body, -Rarm1,-Rarm2,Larm1,Larm2, ...
                       Rleg1,Rleg2,Lleg1,Lleg2  )
xlabel('Seven noisy kids are coming.')
```

FM 2-6. Demonstration of an insect drawing
Purpose: To illustrate drawing insect patterns.

Synopsis: insect_t

insect_t.m
```
%insect_test
clear, clf, hold on
axis([-0, 10, -0, 10])
axis square
for k=1:20
  r   = rand(size(1:6));
  r(1:4)=r(1:4)*10;
  p1 = [r(1), r(2)];
  p2 = [r(1)+(2*r(5)-1)*2, r(2)+(2*r(6)-1)*2];
  insect_(p1,p2)*2;
end
axis off
```

PROBLEMS

The figures you produce in the following assignments must include the title of the figure, axis labels, and legends to explain the meaning of each curve if there are multiple curves. (Use xlabel, ylabel, title, text, gtext.) Plotting a figure is by no means easy. Always try to achieve two things: first, understand the function being plotted completely by repeated plotting in different ways and second, make the figure understandable to other people without ambiguity.

(2.1) Replot Figure 2.3 by replacing the + symbols by the * symbols.

(2.2) Replot Figure 2.3 by connecting data points by red lines with no + symbols.

(2.3) Replot Figure 2.3 by connecting data points by red lines without removing the + symbols.

(2.4) Rewrite List 2.4 without using the array arithmetic operators such as .* and .^. (Hint: use for/end loop.) Compare the result with that of List 2.4.

(2.5) Plot each of the following functions separately in the indicated domain:
(a) first without using the array arithmetic operators and then, (b) using the array arithmetic operators:

$$y = \frac{\sin(x)}{1+\cos(x)}, \quad 0 \leq x \leq 4\pi$$

$$y = \frac{1}{1+(x-2)^2}, \quad 0 \leq x \leq 4$$

$$y = \exp(-x)x^2, \quad 0 \leq x \leq 10$$

(c) Plot all three functions together in a single figure. Indicate the meaning of each curve by legends.

(2.6) Plot $y = \tan(x)$ in the graphic domain, $0 \leq x \leq 10, -10 \leq y \leq 10$, as accurately as possible. Explain what special effort is necessary to do this.

(2.7) Plot the following two functions on the same graph by a single use of plot:

$$y = \frac{(x-1)(x-2)(x-4)(x-5)}{(3-1)(3-2)(3-4)(3-5)}, \quad 0 \leq x \leq 6$$

$$y = \frac{(x-2)(x-3)(x-4)(x-5)}{(1-2)(1-3)(1-4)(1-5)}, \quad 0 \leq x \leq 6$$

Repeat the same using the plot command two times and hold on.

(2.8) Plot the following function by a smooth curve in the range, $0 \leq x \leq 2\pi$:

$$y(x) = \begin{cases} \sin(x), & \text{for } x \leq \pi \\ 2\sin(x), & \text{for } x > \pi \end{cases} \quad (2.10.1)$$

(2.9) Plot the following function by a smooth curve in the range, $0 \le x \le 6\pi$:

$$y(x) = \begin{cases} 1 - x/\pi, & \text{for } 0 \le x \le \pi \\ x/\pi - 2, & \text{for } \pi \le x < \pi \\ 3 - x/\pi, & \text{for } 2\pi \le x \le 3\pi \\ x/\pi - 3, & \text{for } 3\pi \le x < 4\pi, \end{cases} \quad (2.10.2)$$

(2.10) Plot $y = \cos(m \cos^{-1}(x))$, named Chebyshev polynomials, for each of m = 1, 2, ... 8 in $-1 \le x \le 1$ in two sets of four graphs using `subplot`.

(2.11) The following functions have singularities. Plot each of the following functions separately in the indicated domain:

$$y = \tan(x)/x^{0.3}, \quad 0 < x \le 5$$
$$y = \frac{\exp(x)}{\sqrt{1-x^2}}, \quad 0 < x \le 1$$
$$y = x^{-x}, \quad 0 < x \le 2$$

(2.12) A curve is expressed by

$$x = \sin(-t) + t, \quad y = 1 - \cos(-t)$$

Plot the curve on the x-y plane for $0 \le t \le 4\pi$.

(2.13) Suppose $z = x + iy$ is a line on the complex domain, where $i = \sqrt{-1}$. Show graphically that $w = 1/z$ becomes a circle for any line. Hint: Plot w for $y = ax + b$ with three sets of values of a and b:

$a = 0, b = 1$
$a = 1, b = 1$
$a = 100, b = 0$

(2.14) Plot the following function by `mesh`:

$$f(x,y) = 0.2 \cos x + y \exp(-x^2 - y^2), \quad -3 \le x \le 3, -3 \le y \le 3$$

(2.15) Using `contour`, plot the implicit function $f(x,y) = 0$ where

$$f(x,y) = y^2 + x \exp(y) - \tanh(x), \quad 0 \le x \le 5$$

(2.16) Plot the ellipse given by the following equation in two different ways:

$$(x-2)^2 + 2(y - x - 1)^2 = 3$$

(a) Solve the equation for y as a function of x. You will get two equations, one for the top part of the ellipse, and another for the lower part. Plot both as functins of x.

(b) Plot the ellipse as an implicit function.

If there is any abnormality in the plot by (a), investigate and correct.

(2.17) An ellipse is given by

$$2(2y+x)^2 + (y-x-1)^2 = 4$$

Plot the ellipse. The method of plotting is left up to the reader.

(2.18) Two design parameters are bounded by $0 < x < 5$, and $0 < y < 5$. The cost of the product is

$$f = x^2 - 8x + y^2 - 6y - 0.1xy + 50$$

Using the mesh plot, find the approximate optimum parameters to minimize the cost, and the minimum cost.

(2.19) Repeat Problem (2.18) by `contour`.

(2.20) Draw your own happy face with nose and hair.

(2.21) Using the commands in Table 2.1, draw an electrical diagram of Figure 10.1 or Figure 10.6.

(2.22) Draw a random pattern of ten insects by `insect_` with heads up.

(2.23) Draw two persons boxing by `human_`.

(2.24) Draw a bicycle with a rider by `human_`.

(2.25) Develop an interactive graphic program by modifying the script in List 2.31 such that: (a) multiple points are collected by clicking the left the mouse button until the middle button is hit, and (b) as points are collected they are marked on the screen by 'x' marks and connected by lines. The graph is shown until the mouse is clicked inside the box at the left bottom corner.

Chapter 3

LINEAR ALGEBRA

There are two primary reasons why it is advantageous to learn linear algebra at this early stage of the numerical methods study. First, linear algebra is fundamental in numerical methods, so the sooner we learn it the easier the remainder of study of numerical methods will be. Second, MATLAB capabilities are built upon the matrix and vector operations. Therefore, proficiency on MATLAB will be significantly enhanced by learning linear algebra.

The objective of this chapter is to understand the fundamentals of linear algebra and become able to solve linear equations, particularly with MATLAB. This, however, requires at least four areas of study. First, we have to understand how to express linear equations and basic operations of equations in matrix and vector notations. Second, we have to understand MATLAB commands to operate linear equations in the matrix notations. Third, we have to understand problems that are difficult or impossible to solve. The fourth area includes additional topics that enhance understanding as well as help apply linear algebra.

3.1 MATRICES AND VECTORS

In mathematical notation, matrices are enclosed in a pair of parentheses or square brackets and follow certain mathematical rules. In MATLAB, matrices are printed out without parentheses or brackets. Although *matrix* and *array* are synonymous in MATLAB, one should be aware of whether an array is being used for a matrix in mathematics, or simply as an array variable. In this chapter, we discuss matrices and vectors in the former sense.

A matrix is a rectangular array of numbers enclosed in a pair of brackets or parentheses:

Section 3.1 Matrices and Vectors

$$\begin{bmatrix} b_{1,1} & b_{1,2} & . & b_{1,n} \\ b_{2,1} & b_{2,2} & . & b_{2,n} \\ . & . & . & . \\ b_{m,1} & b_{m,2} & . & b_{m,n} \end{bmatrix} \tag{3.1.1}$$

The foregoing matrix is called an $m \times n$ matrix. Notice that the first subscript in a matrix changes in the vertical direction and the second subscript changes in the horizontal direction. A matrix is represented by a symbol; for example,

$$B = \begin{bmatrix} b_{1,1} & b_{1,2} & . & b_{1,n} \\ b_{2,1} & b_{2,2} & . & b_{2,n} \\ . & . & . & . \\ b_{m,1} & b_{m,2} & . & b_{m,n} \end{bmatrix} \tag{3.1.2}$$

Once B is defined as Eq.(3.1.2), mathematical equations can be expressed in terms of B rather than writing the whole matrix. The definition may be abbreviated by

$$B = [b_{i,j}]$$

Vectors are special forms of matrices. If $m > 1$ but $n=1$, B becomes

$$B = \begin{bmatrix} b_{1,1} \\ b_{2,1} \\ . \\ b_{m,1} \end{bmatrix}$$

with only one column, which is called a column vector. On the other hand, if $m = 1$ and $n > 1$, the matrix becomes

$$B = \begin{bmatrix} b_{1,1} & b_{1,2} & . & b_{1,n} \end{bmatrix}$$

which has only one row, and is called a row vector. When the number of columns or rows is only one, it is not necessary to use two subscripts. Indeed, the second index of the elements in the column vector and the first subscript of the elements in the row vector are omitted, so the column and row vectors are written as

$$B = \begin{bmatrix} b_1 \\ b_2 \\ . \\ b_m \end{bmatrix} \tag{3.1.3}$$

and

$$B = \begin{bmatrix} b_1 & b_2 & . & b_n \end{bmatrix} \qquad (3.1.4)$$

respectively.

In another special case of $m = n = 1$, B is a 1×1 matrix and may be written as

$$B = [b_{1,1}]$$

or simply

$$B = [b]$$

The 1×1 matrix B is called a scalar, and the same as $B = b$.

Names of some special matrices and vectors are defined next.

SQUARE MATRIX: a matrix with $m = n$.

NULL MATRIX: elements of the null matrix are all zero:

$$A = \begin{bmatrix} 0 & 0 & 0 \\ 0 & 0 & 0 \\ 0 & 0 & 0 \end{bmatrix} \qquad (3.1.5)$$

A null matrix is defined in MATLAB by `zeros`. By `A = zeros(m,n)`, `A` becomes an $m \times n$ null matrix. An $n \times n$ null matrix is returned by `A = zeros(n)`.

IDENTITY MATRIX: a square matrix in which all the diagonal elements are unity but all other elements are zero. An identity matrix is denoted by I, namely

$$I = \begin{bmatrix} 1 & 0 & 0 \\ 0 & 1 & 0 \\ 0 & 0 & 1 \end{bmatrix} \qquad (3.1.6)$$

The MATLAB command to define an identity matrix is `eye`. By `A = eye(n)`, `A` becomes an $n \times n$ identity matrix.

TRANSPOSED MATRIX: the transpose of matrix $A = [a_{i,j}]$ is $A^t = [a_{j,i}]$ (i and j are interchanged). For example:

$$A = \begin{bmatrix} 2 & 3 \\ 0 & 5 \end{bmatrix}, \qquad A^t = \begin{bmatrix} 2 & 0 \\ 3 & 5 \end{bmatrix} \qquad (3.1.7)$$

$$B = \begin{bmatrix} 1 \\ 7 \end{bmatrix}, \qquad B^t = \begin{bmatrix} 1 & 7 \end{bmatrix} \qquad (3.1.8)$$

Section 3.1 Matrices and Vectors 113

The transpose of a matrix is defined in MATLAB with the prime operator.

PERMUTATION MATRIX: a matrix that is obtained by exchanging rows of Eq.(3.1.6), a permutation matrix is obtained:

$$A = \begin{bmatrix} 0 & 0 & 1 \\ 0 & 1 & 0 \\ 1 & 0 & 0 \end{bmatrix} \qquad (3.1.9)$$

addition and subtraction of matrices: A matrix may be added to or subtracted from another matrix if the matrices have the same size (same numbers of columns and rows). Because vectors are a special form of matrices, the same rules apply to vectors. Addition and subtraction of two matrices

$$A = [a_{i,j}], \quad B = [b_{i,j}]$$

of the same size are defined by

$$C = A \pm B \qquad (3.1.10)$$

where $C = [c_{i,j}]$ is a matrix with

$$c_{i,j} = a_{i,j} \pm b_{i,j}$$

Example 3.1

Two square matrices and two vectors are defined by

$$A = \begin{bmatrix} 1 & 2 & 4 \\ 3 & 1 & 2 \\ 4 & 1 & 3 \end{bmatrix}, \qquad B = \begin{bmatrix} 7 & 3 & 1 \\ 2 & 3 & 5 \\ 8 & 1 & 6 \end{bmatrix}$$

$$x = \begin{bmatrix} 1 \\ 4 \\ 2 \end{bmatrix}, \qquad y = \begin{bmatrix} 3 \\ 9 \\ 4 \end{bmatrix}$$

Calculate $A + B$, $B - A$, $x + y$, and $x - y$.

Solution

The calculations are shown here:

$$A + B = \begin{bmatrix} 1+7 & 2+3 & 4+1 \\ 3+2 & 1+3 & 2+5 \\ 4+8 & 1+1 & 3+6 \end{bmatrix} = \begin{bmatrix} 8 & 5 & 5 \\ 5 & 4 & 7 \\ 12 & 2 & 9 \end{bmatrix}$$

$$A - B = \begin{bmatrix} 1-7 & 2-3 & 4-1 \\ 3-2 & 1-3 & 2-5 \\ 4-8 & 1-1 & 3-6 \end{bmatrix} = \begin{bmatrix} -6 & -1 & 3 \\ 1 & -2 & -3 \\ -4 & 0 & -3 \end{bmatrix}$$

$$x + y = \begin{bmatrix} 1+3 \\ 4+9 \\ 2+4 \end{bmatrix} = \begin{bmatrix} 4 \\ 13 \\ 6 \end{bmatrix}$$

$$x - y = \begin{bmatrix} 1-3 \\ 4-9 \\ 2-4 \end{bmatrix} = \begin{bmatrix} -2 \\ -5 \\ -2 \end{bmatrix}$$

multiplication: Suppose B and C are matrices. When the number of columns of A and the number of rows of B are identical, they can be multiplied as

$$C = AB$$

where $C = [c_{i,j}]$ is a matrix representing the result of the multiplication. The elements of C are related to those of A and B by

$$c_{i,j} = \sum_k a_{i,k}\, b_{k,j} \qquad (3.1.11)$$

The number of rows of C equals that of A, and the number of columns of C equals that of B. In other words, if A is a $p \times q$ matrix and B is a $q \times r$ matrix, then C is a $p \times r$ matrix. Obviously, if A and B are square matrices of the same size, then C also becomes a square matrix of the same size.

The product AB is not equal to BA in general. If $AB = BA$, then matrices A and B are said to commute.

division: Division of a vector by a matrix is related to finding the solution of a linear equation in a matrix form. More details are explained in Section 3.4.

Example 3.2

Calculate the following products:

(a)
$$\begin{bmatrix} 1 & 2 \\ 4 & 3 \\ 0 & 2 \end{bmatrix} \begin{bmatrix} 5 \\ 1 \end{bmatrix}$$

(b)
$$\begin{bmatrix} 2 & 1 & 7 \end{bmatrix} \begin{bmatrix} 1 & 2 \\ 4 & 3 \\ 0 & 2 \end{bmatrix}$$

(c)
$$\begin{bmatrix} 8 & 1 & 3 \\ 1 & 5 & 2 \end{bmatrix} \begin{bmatrix} 1 & 2 \\ 4 & 3 \\ 0 & 2 \end{bmatrix}$$

(d)
$$\begin{bmatrix} 1 & 2 \\ 4 & 3 \\ 0 & 2 \end{bmatrix} \begin{bmatrix} 8 & 1 & 3 \\ 1 & 5 & 2 \end{bmatrix}$$

Solution

(a)
$$\begin{bmatrix} 1 & 2 \\ 4 & 3 \\ 0 & 2 \end{bmatrix} \begin{bmatrix} 5 \\ 1 \end{bmatrix} = \begin{bmatrix} 1 \times 5 + 2 \times 1 \\ 4 \times 5 + 3 \times 1 \\ 0 \times 5 + 2 \times 1 \end{bmatrix} = \begin{bmatrix} 7 \\ 23 \\ 2 \end{bmatrix}$$

(b)
$$\begin{bmatrix} 2 & 1 & 7 \end{bmatrix} \begin{bmatrix} 1 & 2 \\ 4 & 3 \\ 0 & 2 \end{bmatrix} = \begin{bmatrix} 2 \times 1 + 1 \times 4 + 7 \times 0 & 2 \times 2 + 1 \times 3 + 7 \times 2 \end{bmatrix}$$
$$= \begin{bmatrix} 6 & 21 \end{bmatrix}$$

(c)
$$\begin{bmatrix} 8 & 1 & 3 \\ 1 & 5 & 2 \end{bmatrix} \begin{bmatrix} 1 & 2 \\ 4 & 3 \\ 0 & 2 \end{bmatrix} = \begin{bmatrix} 8 \times 1 + 1 \times 4 + 3 \times 0 & 8 \times 2 + 1 \times 3 + 3 \times 2 \\ 1 \times 1 + 5 \times 4 + 2 \times 0 & 1 \times 2 + 5 \times 3 + 2 \times 2 \end{bmatrix}$$
$$= \begin{bmatrix} 12 & 25 \\ 21 & 21 \end{bmatrix}$$

(d)

$$\begin{bmatrix} 1 & 2 \\ 4 & 3 \\ 0 & 2 \end{bmatrix} \begin{bmatrix} 8 & 1 & 3 \\ 1 & 5 & 2 \end{bmatrix} = \begin{bmatrix} 1 \times 8 + 2 \times 1 & 1 \times 1 + 2 \times 5 & 1 \times 3 + 2 \times 2 \\ 4 \times 8 + 3 \times 1 & 4 \times 1 + 3 \times 5 & 4 \times 3 + 3 \times 2 \\ 0 \times 8 + 2 \times 1 & 0 \times 1 + 2 \times 5 & 0 \times 3 + 2 \times 2 \end{bmatrix}$$

$$= \begin{bmatrix} 10 & 11 & 7 \\ 35 & 19 & 18 \\ 2 & 10 & 4 \end{bmatrix}$$

Example 3.3

Calculate AB, BA, Ax, and $x^t A^t$ using the definitions of the matrices and vectors given in Example 3.1.

Solution

The calculations are shown here:

$$AB = \begin{bmatrix} 1 & 2 & 4 \\ 3 & 1 & 2 \\ 4 & 1 & 3 \end{bmatrix} \begin{bmatrix} 7 & 3 & 1 \\ 2 & 3 & 5 \\ 8 & 1 & 6 \end{bmatrix}$$

$$= \begin{bmatrix} 1 \times 7 + 2 \times 2 + 4 \times 8 & 1 \times 3 + 2 \times 3 + 4 \times 1 & 1 \times 1 + 2 \times 5 + 4 \times 6 \\ 3 \times 7 + 1 \times 2 + 2 \times 8 & 3 \times 3 + 1 \times 3 + 2 \times 1 & 3 \times 1 + 1 \times 5 + 2 \times 6 \\ 4 \times 7 + 1 \times 2 + 3 \times 8 & 4 \times 3 + 1 \times 3 + 3 \times 1 & 4 \times 1 + 1 \times 5 + 3 \times 6 \end{bmatrix}$$

$$= \begin{bmatrix} 43 & 13 & 35 \\ 39 & 14 & 20 \\ 54 & 18 & 27 \end{bmatrix}$$

$$BA = \begin{bmatrix} 7 & 3 & 1 \\ 2 & 3 & 5 \\ 8 & 1 & 6 \end{bmatrix} \begin{bmatrix} 1 & 2 & 4 \\ 3 & 1 & 2 \\ 4 & 1 & 3 \end{bmatrix} = \begin{bmatrix} 20 & 18 & 37 \\ 31 & 12 & 29 \\ 35 & 23 & 52 \end{bmatrix}$$

(Notice that AB is not equal to BA.)

$$Ax = \begin{bmatrix} 1 & 2 & 4 \\ 3 & 1 & 2 \\ 4 & 1 & 3 \end{bmatrix} \begin{bmatrix} 1 \\ 4 \\ 2 \end{bmatrix} = \begin{bmatrix} 1 \times 1 + 2 \times 4 + 4 \times 2 \\ 3 \times 1 + 1 \times 4 + 2 \times 2 \\ 4 \times 1 + 1 \times 4 + 3 \times 2 \end{bmatrix} = \begin{bmatrix} 17 \\ 11 \\ 11 \end{bmatrix}$$

$$x^t A^t = \begin{bmatrix} 1 & 4 & 2 \end{bmatrix} \begin{bmatrix} 1 & 3 & 4 \\ 2 & 1 & 1 \\ 4 & 2 & 3 \end{bmatrix}$$

$$= \begin{bmatrix} 1 \times 1 + 4 \times 2 + 2 \times 4 & 1 \times 3 + 4 \times 1 + 2 \times 2 & 1 \times 4 + 4 \times 1 + 2 \times 3 \end{bmatrix}$$

$$= \begin{bmatrix} 17 & 11 & 11 \end{bmatrix}$$

transpose of a product of matrices: The transpose of a product of matrices becomes a product of the transpose of each matrix in the reversed order. For example, $(AB)^t = B^t A^t$, and $(AB..G)^t = G^t..B^t A^t$.

3.2 MATRIX AND VECTOR OPERATIONS IN MATLAB

In MATLAB, matrix, column vector, and row vector are entered by the same rule as arrays, as explained in Chapter 1, "MATLAB Primer." For example, the matrix

$$b = \begin{bmatrix} 1 & 6 \\ 5 & 2 \end{bmatrix}$$

is entered into MATLAB by

```
b = [1, 6; 5, 2];
```

A column or a row vector may be defined as a matrix of one column or one row, respectively; for example,

```
c = [1, 2];  (row vector)
d = [1; 7];  (column vector)
```

A matrix may be transposed in MATLAB by placing a prime after the matrix; for example, by

```
e = b'
```

matrix e becomes the transpose of matrix b.

An $m \times m$ identity matrix is generated by

```
s = eye(m)
```

Similarly, an $m \times m$ null matrix is

```
s = zeros(m)
```

An $m \times n$ null matrix is generated by `s = zeros(m,n)`. An $m \times n$ matrix consisting of unity only is written as

```
w = ones(m,n)
```

If a is an already existing matrix, zeros(size(a)) and ones(size(a)) become, respectively, the null matrix and the unity matrix of the same size as a. An $m \times n$ random matrix is generated by rand(m,n) (see more details of random numbers in Section 1.5). A special matrix named the *Hilbert matrix* is generated by hilb(m) (see Example 3.6).

Multiplication of matrices in MATLAB is expressed by the multiplication operator; for example,

```
b = [1 2; 4 3; 0 2];
d = [5; 1];
g = b*d
```

yields

```
g =
    7
   23
    2
```

which corresponds to (a) in Example 3.2. Additions and subtractions of matrices are the same as for two-dimensional arrays.

3.3 INVERSE MATRIX

Having learned how to multiply matrices by both hand calculations and MATLAB, we can now study the concept of inverse matrices. When two square matrices A and B satisfy

$$AB = I \quad \text{or} \quad BA = I \tag{3.3.1}$$

where I is an identity matrix, then A and B are in the inverse relation. That is, A is the inverse of B, and B is the inverse of A; for example,

$$A = \begin{bmatrix} 1 & 6 \\ 5 & 2 \end{bmatrix}, \; B = \begin{bmatrix} -0.0714 & 0.2143 \\ 0.1786 & -0.0357 \end{bmatrix}$$

are in the inverse relation to each other, because

$$AB = \begin{bmatrix} 1 & 6 \\ 5 & 2 \end{bmatrix} \begin{bmatrix} -0.0714 & 0.2143 \\ 0.1786 & -0.0357 \end{bmatrix} = \begin{bmatrix} 1 & 0 \\ 0 & 1 \end{bmatrix}$$

and

$$BA = \begin{bmatrix} -0.0714 & 0.2143 \\ 0.1786 & -0.0357 \end{bmatrix} \begin{bmatrix} 1 & 6 \\ 5 & 2 \end{bmatrix} = \begin{bmatrix} 1 & 0 \\ 0 & 1 \end{bmatrix}$$

Section 3.3 Inverse Matrix

The inverse of a matrix M is written as M^{-1}. Therefore, the foregoing relation between A and B may be written as $A = B^{-1}$ and $B = A^{-1}$. Thus, Eq.(3.3.1) may be written as

$$AA^{-1} = I \quad \text{and} \quad A^{-1}A = I \quad (3.3.2)$$

Inverse exists only for square matrices.

The inverse of a product of matrices is equal to the product of the inverse of the matrices in the reversed order. For example, if $W = ABC...G$, where $A, B, ... G$ are square matrices, then

$$W^{-1} = G^{-1}...C^{-1}B^{-1}A^{-1} \quad (3.3.3)$$

In MATLAB, the inverse of M is computed by inv(M). For example, let

```
A = [1 6; 5 2]
```

then,

```
B = inv(A)
```

yields

```
B =
    -0.0714    0.2143
     0.1786   -0.0357
```

To make sure B is the inverse of A, we compute both AB and BA as follows:

```
A*B
ans =
    1.0000    0.0000
    0.0000    1.0000

B*A
ans =
    1.0000    0.0
    0.0000    1.0000
```

The inv command will compute the inverse of any square matrix except when it is singular. If MATLAB refuses to compute the inverse of a square matrix, we find that the matrix is singular. It is worthwhile, however, to learn how to make an example of a singular matrix. A singular matrix is such that at least one row (or column) can be expressed by subtracting or adding a multiple of other rows (or columns). This includes the case that one row equals another row or a multiple of another row. Therefore, in order to make a 3×3 singular matrix, write the first and second rows by arbitrarily choosing numbers, but write the third row by copying the first or second row, or a multiple of each case, or as a constant times the first row, plus another constant times the second row. Then, the matrix is singular. If no row (or column) can be expressed by adding or subtracting other rows (or columns), all the rows (or columns) are linearly independent and the matrix is nonsingular.

3.4 LINEAR EQUATIONS

We consider a set of m equations with n unknowns given by

$$\begin{aligned}
a_{1,1}x_1 + a_{1,2}x_2 + a_{1,3}x_3 + \cdots + a_{1,n}x_n &= y_1 \\
a_{2,1}x_1 + a_{2,2}x_2 + a_{2,3}x_3 + \cdots + a_{2,n}x_n &= y_2 \\
&\cdots \\
a_{m,1}x_1 + a_{m,2}x_2 + a_{m,3}x_3 + \cdots + a_{m,n}x_n &= y_m
\end{aligned} \qquad (3.4.1)$$

where $a_{i,j}$ are known coefficients, x_i are unknowns, and y_i are known terms which are named inhomogeneous terms (or source terms).

The foregoing linear equations may be expressed compactly by

$$Ax = y \qquad (3.4.2)$$

where A, x, and y are, respectively, defined by

$$A = \begin{bmatrix} a_{1,1} & \cdots & a_{1,n} \\ \vdots & & \\ a_{m,1} & & a_{m,n} \end{bmatrix}$$

$$x = \begin{bmatrix} x_1 \\ \vdots \\ x_n \end{bmatrix}$$

$$y = \begin{bmatrix} y_1 \\ \cdot \\ \cdot \\ y_n \end{bmatrix}$$

Eq.(3.4.2) may also be expressed in the form,

$$x^t A^t = y^t \tag{3.4.3}$$

where A^t is an $n \times m$ matrix, and x^t and y^t are row vectors.

Linear equations expressed by Eq.(3.4.2) may be classified into the following three cases:

Case 1: $m=n$
Case 2: $m < n$ (underdetermined equation)
Case 3: $m > n$ (overdetermined equation)

Case 1 is the most usual case in that the number of equations is equal to the number of unknowns. In Case 2, the number of equations is less than the number of unknowns, which is called an underdetermined problem. In Case 3, the number of equations is greater than the number of unknowns, which is called an overdetermined problem. This occurs in curve fitting and will be further discussed in Chapter 8, "Curve Fitting to Measured Data."

In Case 1, the matrix is square. To find the solution by MATLAB, write

```
x = A\y
```

Another equivalent method is

```
x = inv(A)*y
```

The first example, however, is more efficient computationally (the computational time in MATLAB for the second example is approximately 50 percent longer than that for the former).

When the equation is written in the form of Eq.(3.4.3), the MATLAB solution is obtained by

```
z = y'/A'
```

where y' is a row vector and z also becomes a row vector. The following commands all yield the same result:

```
A\y
inv(A)*y
A^(-1)*y
y'*inv(A')
y'/A'
```

The results of the first three are in the column vector form while those of the last two are in the row vector form.

Example 3.4

Using MATLAB, find the solution of
$$Ax = y$$
where
$$A = \begin{bmatrix} 3 & 2 \\ 1 & -1 \end{bmatrix}, \quad y = \begin{bmatrix} -1 \\ 1 \end{bmatrix}$$

Solution

Set
```
A = [ 3   2;  1  -1];
y = [-1,  1]';
```
Then,
```
x = A\y
```
yields
```
x =
    0.2000
   -0.8000
```
Also, if we write
```
z = y'/A'
```
the same answer comes back in a row vector form as
```
z =
    0.2000   -0.8000
```

Example 3.5

Shown in Figure 3.1(upper) is an electric network connected to three terminals with known voltages. Find the voltages of the nodes a, b, and c.

Section 3.4 Linear Equations

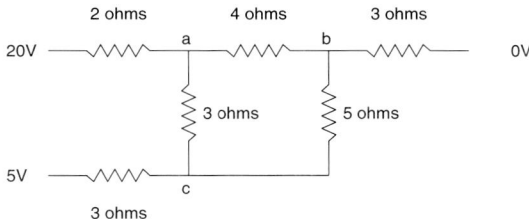

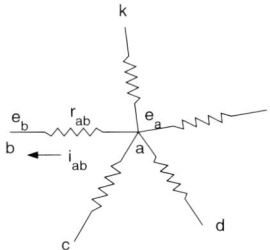

Figure 3.1 Electric networks.

Solution

We first refer to a hypothetical node a that is connected to b, c, $\cdots$, k shown in Figure 3.1(lower). The electric current i from node a to b, denoted by i_{ab}, is related to voltages by

$$i_{ab} = \frac{e_a - e_b}{r_{ab}} \tag{A}$$

where r_{ab} is the resistance between a and b, and e_a and e_b are voltages. The total of the currents leaving node a must be zero:

$$\sum_{j=b,c,..k} i_{aj} = 0 \tag{B}$$

or equivalently, by introducing the relations between current and voltages as in Eq.(A),

$$\sum_{j=b,c,..k} \frac{e_a - e_j}{r_{aj}} = 0 \tag{C}$$

The foregoing equation applies to each node of an unknown voltage. For the network of Figure 3.1(i), three equations are written as

$$\frac{e_a - 20}{2} + \frac{e_a - e_b}{4} + \frac{e_a - e_c}{3} = 0$$

$$\frac{e_b - e_a}{4} + \frac{e_b - 0}{3} + \frac{e_b - e_c}{5} = 0$$

$$\frac{e_c - 5}{3} + \frac{e_c - e_a}{3} + \frac{e_c - e_b}{5} = 0$$

or equivalently

$$\left(\frac{1}{2} + \frac{1}{4} + \frac{1}{3}\right)e_a - \frac{1}{4}e_b - \frac{1}{3}e_c = \frac{20}{2}$$

$$-\frac{1}{4}e_a + \left(\frac{1}{4} + \frac{1}{3} + \frac{1}{5}\right)e_b - \frac{1}{5}e_c = 0$$

$$-\frac{1}{3}e_a - \frac{1}{5}e_b + \left(\frac{1}{3} + \frac{1}{3} + \frac{1}{5}\right)e_c = \frac{5}{3}$$

The MATLAB solution of the equations is as follows:

List 3.1
```
clear
a = [1/2 + 1/4 + 1/3, -1/4,              -1/3;      ...
     0,                1/4 + 1/3 + 1/5,  -1/5;      ...
     0,                0,                1/3 + 1/3 + 1/5];
a(2,1) = a(1,2);
a(3,1) = a(1,3);
a(3,2) = a(2,3);
y=[20/2; 0; 5/3];
x = a\y;
x' =
     13.3453    6.4401    8.5420
```

In the foregoing results, the values are, respectively, e_a, e_b, and e_c in voltages.

3.5 UNSOLVABLE PROBLEMS

A set of linear equations is not always numerically solvable. The following three sets of equations are simple but important examples:

Section 3.5 Unsolvable Problems

(A)
$$\begin{aligned} -x_1 + x_2 &= 1 \\ -2x_1 + 2x_2 &= 2 \end{aligned} \qquad (3.5.1)$$

(B)
$$\begin{aligned} -x_1 + x_2 &= 1 \\ -x_1 + x_2 &= 0 \end{aligned} \qquad (3.5.2)$$

(C)
$$\begin{aligned} x_1 + 2x_2 &= -2 \\ -x_1 + x_2 &= 1 \\ 2x_1 - x_2 &= 0 \end{aligned} \qquad (3.5.3)$$

The equations in each set are plotted in Figure 3.2.

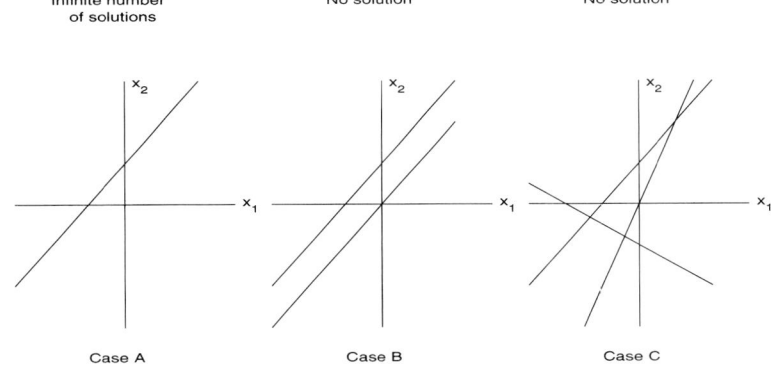

Figure 3.2 Three unsolvable sets of linear equations.

In (A), the second equation is two times the first equation, so they are mathematically identical. Any point (x_1, x_2) satisfying one equation also satisfies the other. Therefore, the number of solutions is infinite. In more general terms, if one equation is a multiple of another or can be obtained by adding or subtracting other equations, that equation is said to be linearly dependent. If none of the equations is linearly dependent, the equations are linearly independent.

In (B), the two equations are parallel lines which never intersect, so there is no solution. Such a system is called an *inconsistent system*. A set of equations is inconsistent if the left side of at least one equation can be completely eliminated by adding or subtracting other equations, while the right side still remains nonzero.

In (C), there are three independent equations for two unknowns. As seen in Figure 3.2, these three equations can never be simultaneously satisfied.

Let us apply MATLAB to these cases to see what happens:

(A): The MATLAB command to get the solution is

```
[-1, 1; -2, 2]\[1;2]
```

The MATLAB response is

```
Warning:  Matrix is singular to working precision.
ans =
        ∞   ∞
```

If we try, however, to solve only the first equation by

```
[-1, 1]\[1]
```

then the MATLAB response is

```
ans =
        -1
         0
```

(B): The MATLAB command is

```
[-1, 1; -1, 1]\[1;0]
```

then the MATLAB response is

```
Warning:  Matrix is singular to working precision.
ans =
        ∞   ∞
```

which is the same as for (A).

(C): The MATLAB command is

```
[1, 2; -1, 1; 2, -1]\[-2; 1; 0]
```

which is responded to without any complaints by

```
ans =
        -0.6
        -0.6
```

Notice, however, the foregoing solution does not satisfy any of the equations in (C). How can this be true?

We now review what happened to the MATLAB answers. The answer for Eq.(3.5.1) is reasonable and consistent with what we pointed out. That is, (A) has an infinite number of solutions but no unique solution. MATLAB, however, determines that the coefficient matrix is singular, so the problem cannot be solved. The printout, $x_1 = x_2 = \infty$, indicates that there is no unique solution or no solution at all. It is interesting that if only one equation is solved, MATLAB finds a solution. The solution $x_1 = $ -1 and $x_2 = 0$ is a solution among an infinite number of possible solutions. MATLAB finds one answer of an underdetermined equation if equations are linearly independent. The answer for (B) is exactly the same as for (A). MATLAB does not comment on the inconsistency of the equations. (C) needs serious attention because, as stated earlier, there is no solution, but MATLAB prints out a solution. What happened is that MATLAB solves (C) as overdetermined equations and prints out the solution of

$$A^t A x = A^t y \tag{3.5.4}$$

The foregoing equation may be derived by the least-square method. The solution does not exactly satisfy the original equation when overdetermined, but the total of the square of the residual of each equation, namely,

$$R \equiv (x_1 + 2x_2 + 2)^2 + (-x_1 + x_2 - 1)^2 + (2x_1 - x_2)^2 \tag{3.5.5}$$

is minimized (residual is the left side minus the right side of each equation). Equation (3.5.4) is obtained by

$$\frac{\partial R}{\partial x_1} = 0, \ \frac{\partial R}{\partial x_2} = 0 \tag{3.5.6}$$

3.6 THE DETERMINANT

The determinant is an important quantity associated with a square matrix. Indeed, an inhomogeneous set of linear equations cannot be uniquely solved if the determinant of the coefficient matrix is zero. This is because, if at least one equation in a set of linear equations is not linearly independent, the determinant becomes zero.[1] If the value of the determinant is extremely

---
[1] If the determinant is zero, the matrix is said to be a singular matrix. For a singular matrix, there is no inverse. Remember that I wrote earlier how to write an example of a singular matrix.

small or large, it is indicative of possibly large errors in the solution of the equations. The determinant of a matrix plays an important role also when eigenvalues of a matrix are computed.

The determinant of matrix A is expressed by $\det(A)$ or $|A|$. For a 2×2 matrix, the determinant of matrix A is calculated as

$$\det(A) = \begin{bmatrix} a_{1,1} & a_{1,2} \\ a_{2,1} & a_{2,2} \end{bmatrix} = a_{1,1}a_{2,2} - a_{2,1}a_{1,2} \qquad (3.6.1)$$

For a 3×3 matrix, the determinant is

$$\begin{aligned}\det(A) = \det\begin{bmatrix} a_{1,1} & a_{1,2} & a_{1,3} \\ a_{2,1} & a_{2,2} & a_{2,3} \\ a_{3,1} & a_{3,2} & a_{3,3} \end{bmatrix} \\ = a_{1,1}a_{2,2}a_{3,3} + a_{2,1}a_{3,2}a_{1,3} + a_{3,1}a_{1,2}a_{2,3} \\ - a_{1,1}a_{3,2}a_{2,3} - a_{2,1}a_{1,2}a_{3,3} - a_{3,1}a_{2,2}a_{1,3} \qquad (3.6.2)\end{aligned}$$

We may easily memorize the rule for a 3×3 matrix as the *spaghetti rule*. In Figure 3.3, each of three solid lines connects three numbers. The products along the solid lines have positive signs in Eq.(3.6.2). The products of three numbers along dotted lines have negative signs in Eq.(3.6.2). The spaghetti rule can't be extended to a matrix of 4×4 or greater, however.

A formal definition of the determinant of a matrix A of order n is given by

$$\det(A) = \sum_{(i,j,k\ ...\ r)} (\pm) a_{i,1} a_{j,2}\ a_{k,3} ... a_{r,n} \qquad (3.6.3)$$

where the summation is extended over all permutations of the first subscript of a, and $(\pm)$ takes $+$ if the permutation is even and $-$ if it is odd.[2] Equations (3.6.1) and (3.6.2) are in accordance with Eq.(3.6.3).

In case the matrix is a lower triangular matrix, an upper triangular matrix, or a diagonal matrix, the computation of Eq.(3.6.3) becomes very simple. The lower triangular matrix is a matrix in which all the elements

---

[2] The sequence of the first subscript $(i, j, k, \cdots, r)$ is called "permutation." A permutation is odd or even if $(i, j, k, \cdots, r)$ is obtained by changing the order of any two consecutive numbers in (1,2,3,...,n) an odd or even number of times, respectively. For example, (3,2,1,4,...,n) is obtained through exchanges of the first three numbers as 123 → 213 → 231 → 321, (namely, three times). So, the permutation of (3,2,1,4,...,n) is odd. It turns out, however, that the exchanges of two numbers do not have to be between two consecutive numbers, but can be done between any pair of numbers. In the present example, (3,2,1,4,...,n) is obtained by exchanging 1 and 3 in (1,2,3,...,n). The number of exchanges is one, so the permutation (3,2,1,4,...,n) is odd.

Section 3.6 The Determinant

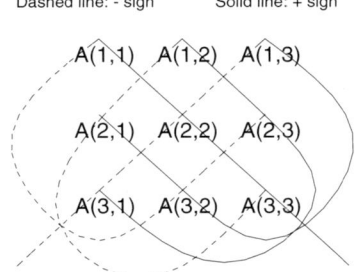

Figure 3.3 The Spaghetti rule to calculate the determinant of a 3×3 matrix.

above the diagonal line are zero. The upper triangular matrix is a matrix in which all the elements below the diagonal line are zero. The diagonal matrix is a special case of the upper triangular or lower triangular matrix. For these matrices, Eq.(3.6.3) reduces to

$$\det(A) = a_{1,1} a_{2,2}\, a_{3,3}...a_{n,n} \qquad (3.6.4)$$

that is, the determinant equals the product of all the diagonal elements. For example,

$$\det \begin{bmatrix} 1 & 5 & 3 \\ 0 & 4 & 6 \\ 0 & 0 & 2 \end{bmatrix} = (1)(4)(2) = 8 \qquad (3.6.5)$$

$$\det \begin{bmatrix} -9 & 0 & 0 \\ 1 & 7 & 0 \\ 6 & 2 & 3 \end{bmatrix} = (-9)(7)(3) = -189 \qquad (3.6.6)$$

$$\det \begin{bmatrix} 4 & 0 & 0 \\ 0 & 1 & 0 \\ 0 & 0 & -4 \end{bmatrix} = (4)(1)(-4) = -16 \qquad (3.6.7)$$

If a matrix is expressed as a product of matrices like $M = ABC...K$, the determinant of M equals the product of the determinants of the matrices, namely

$$\det(M) = \det(A) \det(B) \det(C)... \det(K) \qquad (3.6.8)$$

Therefore, when the determinant of a matrix needs to be evaluated, often the matrix is transformed to a product of the matrices for which the evaluation of the determinant is easy. For example, if a matrix M is decomposed to the product of L and U, where L is a lower triangular matrix and U is an upper triangular matrix, $\det(A)$ equals $\det(L)\det(U)$. More details of the L and U matrices are described in Section 3.10.

Another alternative of computing the determinant of a matrix is to use the forward elimination of the Gauss elimination. More details are described in Section 3.8.

To compute the determinant in MATLAB, use det(A) where A is a square matrix. The following illustration shows a calculation of the determinant of a 3×3 matrix:

```
A = [3, 4, 1; 0, 2, 7; 5, -1, 2];
d = det(A)
d =
      163
```

3.7 ILL-CONDITIONED PROBLEMS

There are a number of linear equations that are solvable yet whose solutions become inaccurate because of severe rounding errors. Problems of this type are named ill-conditioned problems.

Small rounding errors during computation or small changes in coefficients can cause significant errors in solving an ill-conditioned problem. The effect of rounding errors can be illustrated with two equations:

$$\begin{array}{ll}(A) & 0.12065x + 0.98775y = 2.01045 \\ (B) & 0.12032x + 0.98755y = 2.00555\end{array} \qquad (3.7.1)$$

where the two equations are very close to each other. The solution will be denoted by (x_1, y_1), which is

$$x_1 = 14.7403$$
$$y_1 = 0.23942$$

To illustrate the effect of an error in the coefficients, we artificially increase the inhomogeneous term of the first equation (A) by 0.001, so Eq.(3.7.1) is now altered to

$$\begin{array}{ll}(C) & 0.12065x + 0.98775y = 2.01145 \\ (B) & 0.12032x + 0.98755y = 2.00555\end{array} \qquad (3.7.2)$$

The solution of Eq.(3.7.2) denoted by (x_2, y_2) becomes

$$x_2 = 17.9756$$
$$y_2 = -0.15928$$

The amounts of differences between (x_1, y_1) and (x_2, y_2) are significant, particularly when compared to the amount of the change made in the inhomogeneous term of the first equation. Small changes in other coefficients can cause similar effects. Errors in the coefficients can occur by rounding in the process of solving the equation.

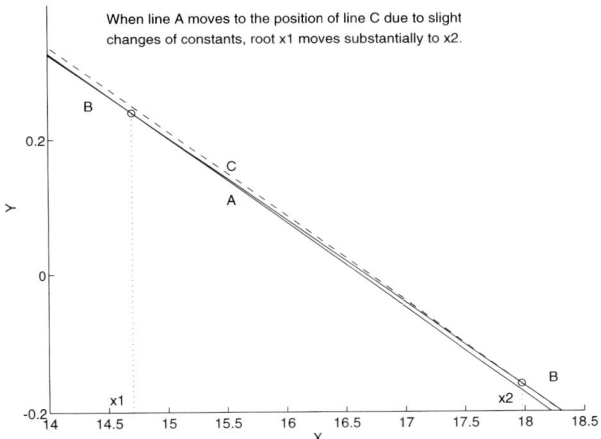

Figure 3.4 Ill-conditioned problem.

In Figure 3.4, the two equations in Eq.(3.7.1) and the first equation in Eq.(3.7.2) are shown as A, B, and C, respectively. Line A intersects with B at a very acute angle (a characteristic symptom of the ill-conditioned problem). Line C is parallel to A but slightly higher than A. Since gradients of Lines A and B are very close, any small change in the gradient or height of one of the lines causes a serious shift in the location of the intersection of the two lines. Although a set of only two equations is used in the preceding illustration, similar effects occur for a larger set of ill-conditioned equations. The reader might graphically explain how the solution of an ill-conditioned set of three linear equations can be affected by errors in the coefficients. The effect of rounding errors becomes more pronounced as the number of equations increases.

When a matrix is poorly conditioned, its determinant tends to be very small.

Another indicator for an ill-conditioned matrix is the *condition number*. To understand it, we have to start the definition of *2-norm*. The 2-norm of matrix A is defined by

$$||A|| = \left(\sum_{i,j} |a_{i,j}|^2\right)^{1/2} \tag{3.7.3}$$

where $A = [a_{i,j}]$. The condition number of matrix A, denoted by $\mathrm{Cond}(A)$, is defined by

$$\mathrm{Cond}(A) = ||A|| \times ||A^{-1}||$$

The condition number always satisfies

$$\mathrm{Cond}(A) \geq 1$$

The condition number tends to be large when the matrix is ill-conditioned, but does not give a direct measure of the error of the solution. In MATLAB, the condition number can be calculated by

```
cond(A)
```

For example, the condition number for Eq.(3.7.1) is calculated as

```
cond([0.12065, 0.98775; 0.12032, 0.98755])
ans =
       6.5598e+3
```

In order to accurately compute the solution of an ill-conditioned problem, the precision of the computing should be high. For mildly ill-conditioned problems, double precision eliminates the difficulty. Severely ill-conditioned problems may need much higher precision, such as quadruple precision.[3]

The computed inverse and determinant both become inaccurate if the matrix is ill-conditioned. Therefore, ill-conditioned problems may be detected by one of the following symptoms:

(a) Computed $\det(A)\det(A^{-1})$ deviates from 1.

(b) Computed $\mathrm{inv}(\mathrm{inv}(A))$ becomes different from A.

---

[3]Not possible with MATLAB.

Section 3.7 Ill-conditioned Problems

(c) Computed $A * \text{inv}(A)$ deviates from the identity matrix.[4]

(d) Deviation of $\text{cond}(A * \text{inv}(A))$ from unity is an accurate measure of deviation of $A * \text{inv}(A)$ from the identity matrix.

The severeness of errors in the solution of a linear equation set also depends on the precision of the computing environment. The condition number and the determinant are independent of the computing environment, so a large condition number or a very small determinant do not necessarily mean that the solution of the linear equation is inaccurate immediately. It indicates the potential of very poor accuracy, but the solution can be accurate if double or quadruple precision is used. On the other hand, the four tests described in the foregoing paragraph using A^{-1} are dependent on the precision of the computing environment and therefore can be used as direct measures of errors in the solution under the current precision.

Example 3.6

Hilbert matrices are notoriously ill-conditioned. They are defined by

$$A = [a_{i,j}]$$

where

$$a_{i,j} = \frac{1}{i + j - 1}$$

Compute the condition number, determinant, and $\det(A)\det(A^{-1})$ for the 5×5 through 14×14 Hilbert matrices.

Solution

Both answers are computed by the following script:

List 3.2
```
clear
for n=5:14
   for i=1:n
      for j=1:n
         a(i,j) = 1/(i+j-1);
      end
```

---

[4]Computed $A^{-1}(A^{-1})^{-1}$ deviates from the identity matrix more significantly than AA^{-1}.

```
        end
        c = cond(a);
        d=det(a);
        dd = det(a)*det(a^(-1));
        fprintf('n=%3.0f cond(a)=%e,det=%e,det*det=%4.2f\n',n,c,d,dd)
    end
```

The output is:

```
    n=  5 cond(a)=4.766073e+005, det=3.749295e-012,  det*det= 1.00
    n=  6 cond(a)=1.495106e+007, det=5.367300e-018,  det*det= 1.00
    n=  7 cond(a)=4.753674e+008, det=4.835803e-025,  det*det= 1.00
    n=  8 cond(a)=1.525758e+010, det=2.737050e-033,  det*det= 1.00
    n=  9 cond(a)=4.931544e+011, det=9.720265e-043,  det*det= 1.00
    n= 10 cond(a)=1.602529e+013, det=2.164406e-053,  det*det= 1.00
    n= 11 cond(a)=5.223946e+014, det=3.027283e-065,  det*det= 1.00
    n= 12 cond(a)=1.794510e+016, det=2.857325e-078,  det*det= 0.94
    n= 13 cond(a)=3.754394e+018, det=4.464959e-092,  det*det= 0.84
    n= 14 cond(a)=4.074634e+017, det=-3.23610e-107,  det*det=-0.33
```

During the execution, a message similar to the following is printed out for each of $n = 11$ through $n = 14$:

```
    Warning: Matrix is close to singular or badly scaled.
             Results may be inaccurate. RCOND = 2.48e-17
```

The condition number is already huge for $n = 5$, and it increases rapidly as n increases. However, such a huge condition number does not necessarily indicate immediate errors when a linear equation is solved. The values of det*det, which indicates $det(A) * det(A^{-1})$, are sensitive to the rounding errors that are dependent on the computer or computing environment. Therefore, the reader may not get exactly the same values as above. In other words, a deviation of det*det from unity indicates that the inverse of the matrix is not accurate in the current computing environment. The det*det starts to seriously deviate from unity at n=12 in the present example.

Example 3.7

Compute AA^{-1} and print out the product where A is the 11×11 Hilbert matrix.

Solution

The product of the matrices is computed by the following script:

List 3.3
```
clear
for n=11:11
   for i=1:n
      for j=1:n
         a(i,j) = 1/(i+j-1);
      end
   end
   a_inv = a*inv(a);
   for j=1:n;
      for i=1:n
      fprintf(' %7.4f', a_inv(i,j))
      end
      fprintf(' \n')
   end
end
```

The product of the matrices must become exactly an identity matrix if computation is precise. The output shown next, however, demonstrates a significant deviation from the identity matrix:

```
 0.9998 -0.0001 -0.0001 -0.0001 -0.0001 -0.0001 -0.0001 -0.0001 -0.0001 -0.0001 -0.0001
-0.0001  0.9999 -0.0001 -0.0001 -0.0000 -0.0000 -0.0000 -0.0000 -0.0000 -0.0000 -0.0000
 0.0014  0.0012  1.0010  0.0009  0.0008  0.0008  0.0007  0.0006  0.0006  0.0006  0.0005
-0.0006 -0.0005 -0.0004  0.9997 -0.0003 -0.0003 -0.0002 -0.0002 -0.0002 -0.0002 -0.0002
 0.0029  0.0022  0.0016  0.0014  1.0012  0.0011  0.0009  0.0008  0.0007  0.0006  0.0006
-0.0103 -0.0072 -0.0059 -0.0049 -0.0039  0.9962 -0.0030 -0.0028 -0.0024 -0.0025 -0.0018
 0.0241  0.0176  0.0140  0.0118  0.0093  0.0089  1.0074  0.0075  0.0062  0.0053  0.0043
-0.0354 -0.0269 -0.0226 -0.0186 -0.0155 -0.0135 -0.0114  0.9890 -0.0101 -0.0094 -0.0080
 0.0291  0.0224  0.0166  0.0151  0.0117  0.0112  0.0090  0.0091  1.0077  0.0072  0.0061
-0.0129 -0.0096 -0.0074 -0.0062 -0.0052 -0.0049 -0.0037 -0.0038 -0.0031  0.9969 -0.0023
 0.0020  0.0013  0.0010  0.0008  0.0006  0.0005  0.0004  0.0004  0.0003  0.0003  1.0002
```

3.8 GAUSS ELIMINATION

Gauss elimination consists of both forward elimination and backward substitution. For Eq.(3.4.1) with $m = n$, the forward elimination proceeds as follows: The first equation times $a_{2,1}/a_{1,1}$ is subtracted from the second equation to eliminate the first term of the second equation. Likewise, the first term of every equation thereafter, $i > 2$, is eliminated by subtracting the first equation times $a_{i,1}/a_{1,1}$. Then, the equations should look like

$$a_{1,1}x_1 + a_{1,2}x_2 + a_{1,3}x_3 + \cdots + a_{1,n}x_n = y_1$$
$$a'_{2,2}x_2 + a'_{2,3}x_3 + \cdots + a'_{2,n}x_n = y'_2$$
$$\cdots$$

$$a'_{n,2}x_2 + a'_{n,3}x_3 + \cdots + a'_{n,n}x_n = y'_n \qquad (3.8.1)$$

where

$$a'_{i,j} = a_{i,j} - (a_{i,1}/a_{1,1})a_{1,j}$$
$$y'_i = y_i - (a_{i,1}/a_{1,1})y_1$$

Notice that the first equation is unchanged.

Next, the leading term of every equation in the third through the last equation, $i > 2$, is eliminated by subtracting the second equation times $a'_{i,2}/a'_{2,2}$. After this step is completed, the leading terms of the fourth through the last equations are eliminated, and so on. When the forward elimination process is finished, the set of the equations will be in the form

$$\begin{aligned} a_{1,1}x_1 + a_{1,2}x_2 + a_{1,3}x_3 + \cdots + a_{1,n}x_n &= y_1 \\ a'_{2,2}x_2 + a'_{2,3}x_3 + \cdots + a'_{2,n}x_n &= y'_2 \\ a''_{3,3}x_3 + \cdots + a''_{3,n}x_n &= y''_3 \\ &\cdots \\ a^{(n-1)}_{n,n}x_n &= y^{(n-1)}_n \end{aligned} \qquad (3.8.2)$$

The leading term in each equation in Eq.(3.8.2) is the diagonal element. Each equation could have been normalized by dividing through by the leading coefficient, but no normalization is used in Gauss elimination. The primary reason is that normalization of the equations increases the overall computing time, but also the computation of the determinant during Gauss elimination is easier without normalization.

The backward substitution procedure starts with the last equation. The solution for x_n is obtained from the last equation by

$$x_n = y_n^{(n-1)}/a_{n,n}^{(n-1)} \qquad (3.8.3)$$

Subsequently,

$$x_{n-1} = \left(y_{n-1}^{(n-2)} - a_{n-1,n}^{(n-2)}x_n\right)/a_{n-1,n-1}^{(n-2)} \qquad (3.8.4)$$

$$\cdots$$

$$x_1 = \left(y_1 - \sum_{i=2}^{n} a_{1,i}x_i\right)/a_{1,1} \qquad (3.8.5)$$

Thus, Gauss elimination is completed.

Section 3.8 Gauss Elimination

So far we assumed an ideally simple situation where no diagonal element (or diagonal coefficient), $a_{i,i}$, becomes zero. If any diagonal element becomes zero in the process of the solution, however, the forward elimination process cannot proceed. Pivoting helps to prevent this, but it also helps increase accuracy of the solution even when the diagonal coefficients, $a_{i,i}$, are all nonzero.

Pivoting exchanges the order of equations so that the diagonal element coefficient $a_{i,i}$ becomes larger in magnitude than any other coefficients to be eliminated in the same column. For example, look at Eq.(3.4.1) before elimination starts, assuming $m = n$. The first diagonal element $a_{1,1}$ is compared with leading coefficients of each equation below it. If $|a_{1,1}| \geq |a_{i,1}|$ for $i > 1$, no pivoting is necessary. Otherwise, the first equation is exchanged with the one with the largest $|a_{i,1}|$. The second pivoting may take place before the second elimination process starts, when the equation is in the form of Eq.(3.8.1). That is, $|a'_{2,2}|$ is compared with $|a'_{i,2}|$ of each equation below it. If $|a'_{2,2}| \geq |a'_{i,2}|$ is not satisfied, then the equation is exchanged so that the diagonal element becomes the largest in magnitude before elimination starts. The same is repeated for every diagonal element until the forward elimination is completed. Gauss elimination with pivoting is illustrated in Example 3.8, and the effect of pivoting on the accuracy of the solution is illustrated in Example 3.9.

Example 3.8

Solve the following equation step×step by Gauss elimination on MATLAB:

$$\begin{bmatrix} -0.04 & 0.04 & 0.12 \\ 0.56 & -1.56 & 0.32 \\ -0.24 & 1.24 & -0.28 \end{bmatrix} \begin{bmatrix} x_1 \\ x_2 \\ x_3 \end{bmatrix} = \begin{bmatrix} 3 \\ 1 \\ 0 \end{bmatrix} \quad (A)$$

Solution

We define an augmented matrix by

```
a = [-0.04  0.04  0.12   3; ...
      0.56 -1.56  0.32   1; ...
     -0.24  1.24 -0.28   0]
```

where the first three columns are the coefficient matrix and the last column is the right side of Eq.(A).

First pivoting (rows 1 and 2 are exchanged):

```
tempo = a(2,:); a(2,:) = a(1,:); a(1,:) = tempo;
```
Then,
```
a =
    0.5600   -1.5600    0.3200    1.0000
   -0.0400    0.0400    0.1200    3.0000
   -0.2400    1.2400   -0.2800         0
```
Elimination of numbers below the first diagonal element by
```
a(2,:) = a(2,:) - a(1,:)*a(2,1)/a(1,1);
a(3,:) = a(3,:) - a(1,:)*a(3,1)/a(1,1);
```
yields
```
a =
    0.5600   -1.5600    0.3200    1.0000
         0   -0.0714    0.1429    3.0714
         0    0.5714   -0.1429    0.4286
```
Since the absolute value of the second diagonal element is less than that of the number below, second pivoting is necessary:
```
tempo = a(3,:); a(3,:) = a(2,:); a(2,:) = tempo;
```
Then,
```
a =
    0.5600   -1.5600    0.3200    1.0000
         0    0.5714   -0.1429    0.4286
         0   -0.0714    0.1429    3.0714
```
Eliminating the number below the second diagonal element by
```
a(3,:) = a(3,:) - a(2,:)*a(3,2)/a(2,2);
```
yields
```
a =
    0.5600   -1.5600    0.3200    1.0000
         0    0.5714   -0.1429    0.4286
         0         0    0.1250    3.1250
```
The forward elimination is completed. Backward substitution is
```
x(3) = a(3,4)/a(3,3);
x(2) = (a(2,4) - a(2,3)*x(3))/a(2,2);
x(1) = (a(1,4) - a(1,2:3)*x(2:3))/a(1,1);
```
The solution becomes
```
x =
    7.0000
```

```
            7.0000
           25.0000
```

The entire script for the foregoing computation is shown here.

List 3.4
```
clear
a = [-0.04 0.04 0.12 3; 0.56 -1.56 0.32 1; -0.24 1.24 -0.28 0]
x = [0,0,0]';   % x is initialized as a column vector
% First pivoting (Rows 1 and 2 are exchanged)
tempo = a(2,:);   a(2,:) = a(1,:); a(1,:)=tempo;a
% Elimination of elements below the first pivot.
a(2,:) = a(2,:) - a(1,:)*a(2,1)/a(1,1);
a(3,:) = a(3,:) - a(1,:)*a(3,1)/a(1,1);a
% Second pivoting (Rows 2 and 3 are exchanged)
tempo = a(3,:);   a(3,:) = a(2,:); a(2,:)=tempo;a
% Eliminating the elements below the second pivot.
a(3,:) = a(3,:) - a(2,:)*a(3,2)/a(2,2);a
x(3) = a(3,4)/a(3,3);
x(2) = (a(2,4) - a(2,3)*x(3))/a(2,2);
x(1) = (a(1,4) - a(1,2:3)*x(2:3))/a(1,1);x
```

Example 3.9

The following array represents a linear equation set with four equations and four unknowns. The exact solution is unity for all the unknowns, because each inhomogeneous term (last column) equals the summation of the coefficients on the same line:

```
1.334-4   4.123+1   7.912+2   -1.544+3   -711.5698662
1.777     2.367-5   2.070+1   -9.035+1    -67.87297633
9.188     0        -1.015+1    1.988-4     -0.961801200
1.002+2   1.442+4  -7.014+2    5.321     13824.12100
```

(i) Solve the equations without pivoting, and then with pivoting, using single precision in Fortran or C.

(ii) Repeat the same using double precision.

(iii) Repeat the same by MATLAB.

Solution

The solutions for (i) and (ii) were obtained by Fortran.

(i) Single precision:

	Without Pivoting	With Pivoting
i	x_i	x_i
1	0.95506	0.99998
2	1.00816	1
3	0.96741	1
4	0.98352	1

The results in single precision without pivoting are very poor, but pivoting improves accuracy significantly.

(ii) Double precision:

	Without Pivoting	With Pivoting
i	x_i	x_i
1	0.9999 9999 9861 473	1.0000 0000 0000 002
2	1.0000 0000 0000 784	1.0000 0000 0000 000
3	0.9999 9999 9984 678	1.0000 0000 0000 000
4	0.9999 9999 9921 696	1.0000 0000 0000 000

Double precision improves the accuracy significantly, but the best result is obtained when both double precision and pivoting are applied.

(iii) MATLAB:

The solution was obtained by the following script:

List 3.5
```
clear
a = [ 1.3340e-04  4.1230e+01  7.9120e+02 -1.5440e+03;
      1.7770e+00  2.3670e-05  2.0700e+01 -9.0350e+01;
      9.1880e+00           0 -1.0150e+01  1.9880e-04;
      1.0020e+02  1.4420e+04 -7.0140e+02  5.3210e+00]
y=sum(a')';
format long e
x=a\y
```

The results are

```
x =
       1.0000 0000 0000 007
       1.0000 0000 0000 000
       1.0000 0000 0000 000
       1.0000 0000 0000 000
```

The result of MATLAB is equivalent to the solution with Fortran or C in double precision on an IBM PC or a workstation.

Using Gauss elimination, the determinant of the matrix may be easily and efficiently computed. Indeed, when the forward elimination of Gauss elimination is completed, the determinant equals the product of all the diagonal elements (terms along the diagonal line), times 1 or -1, depending upon whether the number of pivoting operations is even or odd, respectively.

3.9 GAUSS-JORDAN ELIMINATION AND MATRIX INVERSION

Gauss-Jordan elimination is a variation of Gauss elimination. The Gauss-Jordan elimination eliminates the numbers above and below a diagonal element without distinguishing the forward elimination and backward substitution separately. Pivoting is necessary, however, for the same reason as for Gauss elimination.

In this section, we first illustrate a solution of a linear equation by Gauss-Jordan elimination, and then apply it to invert a matrix. A benefit of Gauss-Jordan elimination is that the explanation of the algorithm to compute inverse of a matrix becomes simple.

Example 3.10

Solve the same problem of Example 3.8 by Gauss-Jordan elimination.

Solution

We start with the same augmented matrix as in Example 3.8. The procedure for the first pivoting is the same as in Example 3.8. After the first pivoting, however, the first row is normalized by dividing through by the diagonal element:

```
a =
    1.0000   -2.7857    0.5714    1.7857
   -0.0400    0.0400    0.1200    3.0000
   -0.2400    1.2400   -0.2800         0
```

All the elements below the first diagonal element are then eliminated by subtracting (or adding) a multiple of the first row:

```
a =
```

$$a = \begin{matrix} 1.0000 & -2.7857 & 0.5714 & 1.7857 \\ 0 & -0.0714 & 0.1429 & 3.0714 \\ 0 & 0.5714 & -0.1429 & 0.4286 \end{matrix}$$

The second diagonal element is compared with the elements below it. Since the second diagonal element is smaller in magnitude than the element below, pivoting is necessary. Then, the second row is divided by its own diagonal element:

$$a = \begin{matrix} 1.0000 & -2.7857 & 0.5714 & 1.7857 \\ 0 & 1.0000 & -0.2500 & 0.7500 \\ 0 & -0.0714 & 0.1429 & 3.0714 \end{matrix}$$

All the elements above and below the second diagonal element are eliminated by subtracting (or adding) a multiple of the second row:

$$a = \begin{matrix} 1.0000 & 0 & -0.1250 & 3.8750 \\ 0 & 1.0000 & -0.2500 & 0.7500 \\ 0 & 0 & 0.1250 & 3.1250 \end{matrix}$$

The third row is now normalized by dividing by its own diagonal element:

$$a = \begin{matrix} 1.0000 & 0 & -0.1250 & 3.8750 \\ 0 & 1.0000 & -0.2500 & 0.7500 \\ 0 & 0 & 1.0000 & 25.0000 \end{matrix}$$

The elements above the third diagonal element are eliminated by subtracting (or adding) the third row times the number to be eliminated. Now, the augmented matrix is

$$a = \begin{matrix} 1.0000 & 0 & 0 & 7.0000 \\ 0 & 1.0000 & 0 & 7.0000 \\ 0 & 0 & 1.0000 & 25.0000 \end{matrix}$$

Here, the first three columns comprise an identity matrix, while the last column is the solution.

Example 3.11

Find the inverse of the matrix in Example 3.10.

Section 3.9 Gauss-Jordan Elimination and Matrix Inversion

Solution
As mentioned earlier, Gauss-Jordan elimination may be used to find the inverse of a matrix. To do this, an augmented matrix is written in which the first three columns are the original matrix A, and the next three columns are the identity matrix:

$$a = \begin{matrix} -0.0400 & 0.0400 & 0.1200 & 1.0000 & 0 & 0 \\ 0.5600 & -1.5600 & 0.3200 & 0 & 1.0000 & 0 \\ -0.2400 & 1.2400 & -0.2800 & 0 & 0 & 1.0000 \end{matrix}$$

The remainder of the operation is exactly the same as in Example 3.10. After the pivoting, the first row is normalized.

$$a = \begin{matrix} 1.0000 & -2.7857 & 0.5714 & 0 & 1.7857 & 0 \\ -0.0400 & 0.0400 & 0.1200 & 1.0000 & 0 & 0 \\ -0.2400 & 1.2400 & -0.2800 & 0 & 0 & 1.0000 \end{matrix}$$

The elements below the first diagonal element are eliminated by subtracting the first row times the number to be eliminated:

$$a = \begin{matrix} 1.0000 & -2.7857 & 0.5714 & 0 & 1.7857 & 0 \\ & -0.0714 & 0.1429 & 1.0000 & 0.0714 & 0 \\ 0 & 0.5714 & -0.1429 & 0 & 0.4286 & 1.0000 \end{matrix}$$

Second pivoting yields

$$\begin{matrix} 1.0000 & -2.7857 & 0.5714 & 0 & 1.7857 & 0 \\ 0 & 0.5714 & -0.1429 & 0 & 0.4286 & 1.0000 \\ 0 & -0.0714 & 0.1429 & 1.0000 & 0.0714 & 0 \end{matrix}$$

The second row is normalized by dividing by its own diagonal element:

$$a = \begin{matrix} 1.0000 & -2.7857 & 0.5714 & 0 & 1.7857 & 0 \\ 0 & 1.0000 & -0.2500 & 0 & 0.7500 & 1.7500 \\ 0 & -0.0714 & 0.1429 & 1.0000 & 0.0714 & 0 \end{matrix}$$

The elements above and below the second diagonal element are eliminated by subtracting the second row times the number to be eliminated:

$$a = \begin{matrix} 1.0000 & 0 & -0.1250 & 0 & 3.8750 & 4.8750 \\ 0 & 1.0000 & -0.2500 & 0 & 0.7500 & 1.7500 \\ 0 & 0 & 0.1250 & 1.0000 & 0.1250 & 0.1250 \end{matrix}$$

The third row is normalized and then the numbers above the third diagonal element are eliminated by subtracting the third row times the number to be eliminated:

```
a =
    1.0000         0         0   1.0000   4.0000   5.0000
         0    1.0000         0   2.0000   1.0000   2.0000
         0         0    1.0000   8.0000   1.0000   1.0000
```

Now, the first three columns are an identity matrix, and the last three columns are the inverse of A. We denote the inverse by A_inv:

```
A_inv =
    1.0000   4.0000   5.0000
    2.0000   1.0000   2.0000
    8.0000   1.0000   1.0000
```

To check, we calculate A*A_inv and find

```
A*A_inv
ans =
    1.0000        0        0
         0   1.0000        0
         0        0   1.0000
```

A script to perform the foregoing computation is shown:

List 3.6
```
clear
A = [-0.04 0.04 0.12 ; 0.56 -1.56 0.32 ...
; -0.24 1.24 -0.28]
a=[A,eye(3)];
% First pivoting (Rows 1 and 3 are exchanged)
tempo = a(2,:);  a(2,:) = a(1,:); a(1,:)=tempo;
% Fist row is divided by its pivot:
a(1,:) = a(1,:)/a(1,1)
% The elements below a(1,1) are all eliminated.
for i=2:3;  a(i,:)=a(i,:) - a(i,1)*a(1,:);  end;a
% Eliminates all the elements above and
%                          below the second pivot.
% Second pivoting
tempo = a(3,:);   a(3,:) = a(2,:); a(2,:)=tempo;a
% Normalization of second row
a(2,:)=a(2,:)/a(2,2);a
for i=1:3; if i~=2, a(i,:)=a(i,:)-a(i,2)*a(2,:); end;
end;a
% Eliminate all the elements above the third pivot.
```

```
a(3,:)=a(3,:)/a(3,3)
for i=1:3; if i~=3, a(i,:)=a(i,:)-a(i,3)*a(3,:); end;
end;a
A_inv = a(:,4:6)
A*A_inv
```

3.10 LU DECOMPOSITION

The LU decomposition scheme transforms a matrix A to a product of two matrices,
$$A = LU \tag{3.10.1}$$
where L is a lower triangular matrix and U is an upper triangular matrix. With $A = LU$, the equation $Ax = y$ is written equivalently as
$$LUx = y \tag{3.10.2}$$
The foregoing equation is solved as follows. By setting
$$Ux = z \tag{3.10.3}$$
Eq.(3.10.2) becomes
$$Lz = y \tag{3.10.4}$$
The solution of Eq.(3.10.4) proceeds first, which is easy because of the triangular form of L. Once z is obtained, Eq.(3.10.3) is solved for x.

When solving the same linear equation sets with different inhomogeneous (right-side) terms many times, the LU decomposition is significantly more efficient than solving each by Gauss elimination.

Example 3.12

By LU decomposition, solve the linear equation
$$Ax = y$$
where
$$A = \begin{bmatrix} 2 & 1 & -3 \\ -1 & 3 & 2 \\ 3 & 1 & -3 \end{bmatrix}, \quad y = \begin{bmatrix} 2 \\ 0 \\ 1 \end{bmatrix}$$
Here, L and U satisfy $A = LU$, and are given

$$L = \begin{bmatrix} 1 & 0 & 0 \\ -0.5 & 1 & 0 \\ 1.5 & -0.1428 & 1 \end{bmatrix}, \quad U = \begin{bmatrix} 2 & 1 & -3 \\ 0 & 3.5 & 0.5 \\ 0 & 0 & 1.5714 \end{bmatrix}$$

Solution

We first solve $Lz = y$:

$$\begin{bmatrix} 1 & 0 & 0 \\ -0.5 & 1 & 0 \\ 1.5 & -0.1428 & 1 \end{bmatrix} \begin{bmatrix} z_1 \\ z_2 \\ z_3 \end{bmatrix} = \begin{bmatrix} 2 \\ 0 \\ 1 \end{bmatrix}$$

The solution is $z_1 = 2$, $z_2 = 0 - 2(-0.5) = 1$ and $z_3 = 1 - 2(1.5) - (-0.1428) = -1.8572$. Then, $Ux = z$ becomes

$$\begin{bmatrix} 2 & 1 & -3 \\ 0 & 3.5 & 0.5 \\ 0 & 0 & 1.5714 \end{bmatrix} \begin{bmatrix} x_1 \\ x_2 \\ x_3 \end{bmatrix} = \begin{bmatrix} 2 \\ 1 \\ -1.8572 \end{bmatrix}$$

The solution is

$$x_3 = -1.8572/1.5714 = -1.1818$$
$$x_2 = (1 - 0.5x_3)/3.5 = 0.4545$$
$$x_1 = (2 - x_2 + 3x_3)/2 = -1$$

A matrix may be decomposed to L and U using Gauss elimination. Indeed, the matrix after the forward elimination is the U matrix. We first assume that no pivoting is necessary. The forward elimination may be regarded as a transformation of matrix A to U, and the transformation is represented equivalently by the premultiplication of a matrix F:

$$FA = U \tag{3.10.5}$$

The matrix F can be found if we apply the same operation of the forward elimination to an identity matrix. To illustrate the point, we first write matrix A of Example 3.12 and an identity matrix next to each other:

$$\begin{bmatrix} 2 & 1 & -3 \\ -1 & 3 & 2 \\ 3 & 1 & -3 \end{bmatrix}, \quad \begin{bmatrix} 1 & 0 & 0 \\ 0 & 1 & 0 \\ 0 & 0 & 1 \end{bmatrix} \tag{3.10.6}$$

Section 3.10 LU Decomposition

If we apply the forward elimination to the first matrix and perform the same operation to the identity matrix, the results are

$$\begin{bmatrix} 2 & 1 & -3 \\ 0 & 3.5 & 0.5 \\ 0 & 0 & 1.5714 \end{bmatrix}, \quad \begin{bmatrix} 1 & 0 & 0 \\ 0.5 & 1 & 0 \\ -1.4286 & 0.1428 & 1 \end{bmatrix} \quad (3.10.7)$$

The first matrix is $FA = U$. The second matrix is the result of F times an identity matrix, I, which equals F itself. $FA = U$ can be written as

$$A = F^{-1}U \quad (3.10.8)$$

By comparing the foregoing equation to Eq.(3.10.1), F must equal the inverse of L, namely $F = L^{-1}$. In other words, L can be obtained by taking the inverse of F. Inverse of a triangular matrix is easy and fast. Inverse of a lower triangular matrix is always a lower triangular matrix.

We now ask how pivoting affects L and U matrices. Remember that in Gauss elimination, the order of rows is changed by pivoting. Although the changes of the order are not known prior to Gauss elimination, the effects of changes may be expressed by an operator P, where P is a permutation matrix. Premultiplying the original equation $Ax = y$ by P yields

$$PAx = Py$$

or equivalently

$$\widetilde{A}x = \widetilde{y} \quad (3.10.9)$$

where $\widetilde{A} = PA$ and $\widetilde{y} = Py$. If we apply Gauss elimination to the foregoing $\widetilde{A}$, no pivoting will be necessary. Likewise, if $\widetilde{A}$ is decomposed to L and U, no further pivoting is necessary. In Gauss elimination with pivoting, the matrix after the forward elimination is the U matrix for $\widetilde{A}$.

The P matrix may be obtained by applying the pivoting to an identity matrix in the same way as performed in the Gauss elimination.

The LU decomposition may be performed by lu in MATLAB. There are two formats in writing the command. The first format is

```
[l,u,p] = lu(A)
```

where A is the matrix to be decomposed; l, u, and p, respectively, correspond to L, U, and P in the foregoing discussions. For example, if we write:

```
A = [2 1 -3; -1 3 2; 3 1 -3];
[l, u, p] = lu(A)
```

then the answer is

```
l =
    1.0000         0         0
   -0.3333    1.0000         0
    0.6667    0.1000    1.0000

u =
    3.0000    1.0000   -3.0000
         0    3.3333    1.0000
         0         0   -1.1000

p =
     0     0     1
     0     1     0
     1     0     0
```

Here, l is the lower triangular matrix, u is the upper triangular matrix, and p is the permutation matrix representing the pivoting. The L and U matrices thus obtained satisfy

$$PA = LU \qquad (3.10.10)$$

That is, LU is the decomposition of PA rather than A. Therefore, the original linear equation is written first as

$$PAx = Py \qquad (3.10.11)$$

and then

$$LUx = Py \qquad (3.10.12)$$

The original matrix A may be recovered from L, U, and P by $P^{-1}LU$. In MATLAB, we type

```
p^(-1)*l*u
```

then the response is

```
ans =
     2     1    -3
    -1     3     2
     3     1    -3
```

The second format is

```
[l,u] = lu(A)
```

which yields

```
l =
    0.6667    0.1000    1.0000
   -0.3333    1.0000         0
    1.0000         0         0

u =
    3.0000    1.0000   -3.0000
         0    3.3333    1.0000
         0         0   -1.1000
```

where l equals $P^{-1}L$ and u equals U, so $(P^{-1}L)U = A$.

3.11 ITERATIVE SOLUTION

The iterative solution of linear equations is not applicable to every problem, but it is useful to solve certain types of problems. When the number of unknowns is very large but the coefficient matrix is sparse, Gauss elimination becomes inefficient and sometimes inapplicable if the memory requirement exceeds the limit. For such problems, iterative methods are preferred. Additional advantages of iterative methods are simple programming and easy application when coefficients are nonlinear. Although there are many versions of iterative schemes, we introduce three iterative methods here: Jacobi iterative, Gauss-Seidel, and successive-over-relaxation (SOR) methods. Consider a linear equation,

$$Ax = y \qquad (3.11.1)$$

where A is a square matrix, x is an unknown vector, and y is a known vector. All iterative schemes need an initial guess for iteration to get started, which will be denoted by $x^{(0)}$. The initial guess can be any arbitrary vector, including a null vector. If a good guess is available, convergence of the iterative solution becomes fast; if not, the initial guess may be set to a null vector (all elements are zero). In most cases, however, an attempt to find a good guess is not worth time because the gain is not substantial. The only exception is that, when very similar problems are solved consecutively, the solution for previous problem may be a good initial guess.

A sufficient condition for the iterative solution to converge is:[5]

$$|a_{i,i}| > \sum_{j=1, j \neq i}^{n} |a_{i,j}|, \quad \text{for all } i \qquad (3.11.2)$$

If A is irreducible, however, (that is, if no part of the equation can be solved independently of the rest), a sufficient condition is

$$|a_{i,i}| \geq \sum_{j=1, j \neq i}^{n} |a_{i,j}|, \quad \text{for all } i \qquad (3.11.3)$$

with strict inequality for at least one i.

The linear equations arising from (but not limited to) the following problems are known to satisfy one or both of the foregoing conditions:

(a) Electric network consisting of resistors
(b) Heat-conduction problems
(c) Particle diffusion
(d) Certain stress-strain problems
(e) Fluid, magnetic, or electric potential

The Jacobi iterative method is written as

$$x_i^{(t)} = \left(y_i - \sum_{j=1, j \neq i}^{n} a_{i,j} x_j^{(t-1)} \right) / a_{i,i} \qquad (3.11.4)$$

where superscript t is the iteration count. When $t = 1$ in the foregoing equation, x on the right side has superscript 0, which means that the value is an initial guess. In each iteration cycle, x_i is evaluated in increasing order of i.

The Gauss-Seidel method is slightly different from the Jacobi iterative scheme and is written as

$$x_i^{(t)} = \left(y_i - \sum_{j=1}^{i-1} a_{i,j} x_j^{(t)} - \sum_{j=i+1}^{n} a_{i,j} x_j^{(t-1)} \right) / a_{i,i} \qquad (3.11.5)$$

This scheme is related to the Jacobi iterative method as follows: In Eq.(3.11.5), x_j for $j < i$ has superscript (t) rather than $(t-1)$. That is, whenever updated

---

[5]For a nonsingular matrix, the iterative solution described in this section unconditionally converges if applied after premultiplying the equation $Ax = y$ by A^t.

values of iteratives are available, they are used. This helps accelerate convergence and also simplifies programming as the new values can be written over the old values.

The successive-over-relaxation (SOR) method is a further improvement of the Gauss-Seidel scheme, and is written as

$$x_i^{(t)} = \omega \left(y_i - \sum_{j=1}^{i-1} a_{i,j} x_j^{(t)} - \sum_{j=i+1}^{n} a_{i,j} x_j^{(t-1)} \right) / a_{i,i} + (1-\omega) x_i^{(t-1)} \quad (3.11.6)$$

where ω is an over-relaxation parameter satisfying

$$1 \leq \omega < 2$$

The SOR reduces to the Gauss-Seidel method when $\omega = 1$.

Example 3.13

Solve the linear equation in Example 3.5 by SOR.

Solution

A script to solve the equation by SOR is given here:

List 3.7
```
clear
a(1,1) = 1/2 + 1/4 + 1/3; a(1,2) = -1/4; a(1,3) = -1/3;
a(2,1) = a(1,2); a(2,2) = 1/4 + 1/3 + 1/5; a(2,3) = -1/5;
a(3,1) = a(1,3); a(3,2) = a(2,3); a(3,3) = 1/3 + 1/5 + 1/3;
y(1) = 20/2; y(2) = 0; y(3) = 5/3;
x = zeros(1,3);
w=1.2;
for it=1:50
    error = 0;
    for i=1:3
        s=0; xb = x(i);
        for j=1:3
            if i~=j, s = s + a(i,j)*x(j); end
        end
        x(i) = w*(y(i) -s)/a(i,i) + (1-w)*x(i);
        error = error + abs(x(i) - xb);
    end
    fprintf(' It. no. = %3.0f, error = %7.2e\n', ...
            it, error)
```

```
            if error/3 < 0.0001, break; end
    end
x
```

The result is:
```
    It. no. =   1, error = 2.39e+01
    It. no. =   2, error = 4.75e+00
    It. no. =   3, error = 7.24e-01
    It. no. =   4, error = 2.64e-01
    It. no. =   5, error = 5.03e-02
    It. no. =   6, error = 1.36e-02
    It. no. =   7, error = 4.39e-03
    It. no. =   8, error = 1.16e-03
    It. no. =   9, error = 3.03e-04
    It. no. =  10, error = 8.55e-05
x =
    13.3453      6.4401      8.5420
```

3.12 MATRIX EIGENVALUES

Suppose A is an $n \times n$ matrix. Then, the function defined by

$$f(\lambda) = \det[A - \lambda I] \qquad (3.12.1)$$

is called the characteristic polynomial of matrix A. The function $f(\lambda)$ is a polynomial of λ of order n. For example, for

$$A = \begin{bmatrix} 1 & 3 \\ -1 & 2 \end{bmatrix} \qquad (3.12.2)$$

$f(x)$ becomes

$$\begin{aligned} \det[A - \lambda I] &= (1 - \lambda)(2 - \lambda) + 3 \\ &= \lambda^2 - 3\lambda + 5 \end{aligned} \qquad (3.12.3)$$

Therefore, Eq.(3.12.1) is reduced to

$$f(\lambda) = \lambda^2 - 3\lambda + 5 \qquad (3.12.4)$$

The solutions of $f(\lambda) = 0$ are called characteristic values and are the same as the eigenvalues of matrix A.

In MATLAB, the coefficients of the characteristic polynomial are computed by

Section 3.12 Matrix Eigenvalues

```
c = poly(A)
```

where A is the matrix and c is an array of polynomial coefficients. The characteristic values are then computed by

```
roots(c)
```

Eigenvalues of matrix A may be more directly computed by

```
eig(A)
```

Of course, the answers of roots(c) and eig(A) are identical.

Example 3.14

Matrix A is given by

$$A = \begin{bmatrix} 3 & 4 & -2 \\ 3 & -1 & 1 \\ 2 & 0 & 5 \end{bmatrix} \tag{A}$$

Find eigenvalues directly by eig. Also, find the characteristic polynomial and then calculate the roots of the characteristic polynomial.

Solution

Matrix A is entered by

```
A = [3 4 -2;  3 -1 1;  2 0 5]
```

Then, eigenvalues are computed as

```
eig(A)
ans =
  -2.7503
   4.8751 + 1.4314i
   4.8751 - 1.4314i
```

The command, c=poly(A), will compute coefficients of the characteristic polynomial:

```
c =
      1.0000   -7.0000   -1.0000   71.0000
```

which indicates that the characteristic equation is

$$f(\lambda) = \det(A - \lambda I) = \lambda^3 - 7\lambda^3 - \lambda + 71 \tag{B}$$

The roots of a polynomial can be computed by root:

```
roots(c)
ans =
   4.8751 + 1.4314i
   4.8751 - 1.4314i
  -2.7503
```

The roots of the characteristic equations are identical to the eigenvalues computed directly by the `eig` command.

Example 3.15

Consider a system consisting of masses and springs as shown in Figure 3.5. The equations for the displacements are given by

$$m_1 \frac{d^2}{dt^2} y_1(t) = -(k_{01} + k_{12})y_1 + k_{12}y_2 \tag{A}$$

$$m_2 \frac{d^2}{dt^2} y_2(t) = k_{12}y_1 - k_{12}y_2$$

where y_1 and y_2 are displacements of m_1 and m_2 (downward positive), respectively, and

$$k_{01} = 0.3 \text{ N/m}, \quad k_{12} = 0.1 \text{ N/m} \quad \text{(spring constants)}$$
$$m_1 = 0.1 \text{ kg}, \quad m_2 = 0.2 \text{ kg} \quad \text{(masses)}$$

Find the frequencies of harmonic oscillations.

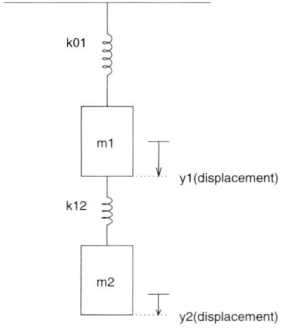

Figure 3.5 A spring-mass system.

Solution

For a harmonic oscillation, the solution may be found in the form

$$y_k(t) = e^{2\pi j \lambda t} f_k, \quad k = 1, 2 \tag{B}$$

where λ is the frequency, $j = \sqrt{-1}$, and f_k is the unknown amplitude. Introducing Eq.(B) into Eq.(A) yields

$$-\gamma f_1 = -\frac{k_{01} + k_{12}}{m_1} f_1 + \frac{k_{12}}{m_1} f_2$$

$$-\gamma f_2 = \frac{k_{12}}{m_2} f_1 - \frac{k_{12}}{m_2} f_2$$

(C)

where $\gamma = (2\pi\lambda)^2$. The foregoing two equations may be written in a matrix form as

$$(A - \gamma I)f = 0 \qquad (D)$$

with

$$A = \begin{bmatrix} (k_{01} + k_{12})/m_1 & -k_{12}/m_1 \\ -k_{12}/m_2 & k_{12}/m_2 \end{bmatrix} = \begin{bmatrix} 4 & -1 \\ -0.5 & 0.5 \end{bmatrix}$$

$$f = \begin{bmatrix} f_1 \\ f_2 \end{bmatrix}$$

We now find eigenvalues of A by

```
eig([4, -1; -0.5, 0.5])
```

which yields

```
ans =
    4.1375
    0.3625
```

Using the earlier definition, $\gamma = (2\pi\lambda)^2$, the frequencies are $\lambda = \sqrt{\gamma}/(2\pi) = 0.3237$ and 0.0958Hz.

PROBLEMS

(3.1) Calculate $C = A + B$, $D = A - B$, and $E = AB$ where

$$A = \begin{bmatrix} 1 & 2 & 3 \\ 0 & 1 & 4 \\ 3 & 0 & 2 \end{bmatrix}, \quad B = \begin{bmatrix} 4 & 1 & 2 \\ 3 & 2 & 1 \\ 0 & 1 & 2 \end{bmatrix}$$

(3.2) Calculate $B^t A^t$ and $(AB)^t$ where A and B are defined in the previous problem and show that the results are identical.

(3.3) Calculate $E = AB$ where

$$A = \begin{bmatrix} 1 & 2 & 3 \\ 0 & 1 & 4 \\ 3 & 0 & 2 \end{bmatrix}$$

$$B = \begin{bmatrix} 3 \\ 5 \\ 1 \end{bmatrix}$$

(3.4) Calculate $D = A + E$, $E = A - E$, $F = AB$, $G = BA$, and $H = BC$ where

$$A = \begin{bmatrix} 1 & 2 & 3 & 1 \\ 0 & 1 & 4 & 2 \\ 3 & 0 & 2 & 3 \end{bmatrix}, \quad E = \begin{bmatrix} 2 & 3 & 0 & 1 \\ 0 & 1 & 0 & 1 \\ 2 & 1 & 5 & 0 \end{bmatrix}$$

$$B = \begin{bmatrix} 4 & 1 & 2 \\ 3 & 2 & 1 \\ 0 & 1 & 2 \\ 3 & 1 & 0 \end{bmatrix}$$

$$C = \begin{bmatrix} 7 \\ 1 \\ 4 \end{bmatrix}$$

(3.5) Compute $E = B + CD$ where

$$B = \begin{bmatrix} 3 & 2 & 1 \\ 0 & 4 & 3 \\ 0 & 0 & 6 \end{bmatrix}, \quad C = \begin{bmatrix} 1 & 0 & 2 \\ -1 & 1 & 0 \\ 0 & 3 & 2 \end{bmatrix}, \quad D = \begin{bmatrix} 1 & 0 & 0 \\ -2 & 1 & 0 \\ 5 & 2 & 7 \end{bmatrix}$$

(3.6) Solve the following equations by MATLAB and verify the results by hand calculations.

$$\begin{bmatrix} 2 & 1 & -3 \\ -1 & 3 & 2 \\ 3 & 1 & -3 \end{bmatrix} \begin{bmatrix} x_1 \\ x_2 \\ x_3 \end{bmatrix} = \begin{bmatrix} -1 \\ 12 \\ 0 \end{bmatrix} \quad (a)$$

$$\begin{bmatrix} 0.1 & -0.6 & 1 \\ -2 & 8 & 0.3 \\ 1 & 6 & 4 \end{bmatrix} \begin{bmatrix} x_1 \\ x_2 \\ x_3 \end{bmatrix} = \begin{bmatrix} 0 \\ 1 \\ 2 \end{bmatrix} \quad (b)$$

(3.7) Solve the following equations by Gauss-Jordan elimination:

$$\begin{bmatrix} 4 & 1 & -1 \\ 3 & 2 & -6 \\ 1 & -5 & 3 \end{bmatrix} \begin{bmatrix} x_1 \\ x_2 \\ x_3 \end{bmatrix} = \begin{bmatrix} 9 \\ -2 \\ 1 \end{bmatrix} \quad (a)$$

$$\begin{bmatrix} 1 & 1 & 0 \\ -1 & 2 & -1 \\ 0 & -1 & 1.1 \end{bmatrix} \begin{bmatrix} x_1 \\ x_2 \\ x_3 \end{bmatrix} = \begin{bmatrix} 0 \\ 1 \\ 0 \end{bmatrix} \quad (b)$$

(3.8) The following linear equations have common coefficients but different right-side terms

$$\begin{bmatrix} 1 & 1 & 1 \\ 2 & -1 & 3 \\ 3 & 2 & -2 \end{bmatrix} \begin{bmatrix} x_1 \\ x_2 \\ x_3 \end{bmatrix} = \begin{bmatrix} 1 \\ 4 \\ -2 \end{bmatrix} \quad (a)$$

$$\begin{bmatrix} 1 & 1 & 1 \\ 2 & -1 & 3 \\ 3 & 2 & -2 \end{bmatrix} \begin{bmatrix} x_1 \\ x_2 \\ x_3 \end{bmatrix} = \begin{bmatrix} -2 \\ 5 \\ 1 \end{bmatrix} \quad (b)$$

$$\begin{bmatrix} 1 & 1 & 1 \\ 2 & -1 & 3 \\ 3 & 2 & -2 \end{bmatrix} \begin{bmatrix} x_1 \\ x_2 \\ x_3 \end{bmatrix} = \begin{bmatrix} 2 \\ -1 \\ 4 \end{bmatrix} \quad (c)$$

The coefficients and the three sets of right-side terms may be combined into an array

$$\begin{bmatrix} 1 & 1 & 1 & 1 & -2 & 2 \\ 2 & -1 & 3 & 4 & 5 & -1 \\ 3 & 2 & -2 & -2 & 1 & 4 \end{bmatrix}$$

If we apply the Gauss-Jordan scheme to the foregoing array and reduce the first three columns to the unit matrix form, then the solutions for the three problems are automatically obtained in the fourth, fifth, and sixth columns when the elimination is completed. Calculate the solution step×step in this way by MATLAB.

(3.9) Calculate the inverse of

$$A = \begin{bmatrix} 7 & 1 \\ 4 & 5 \end{bmatrix}$$

by MATLAB, and then verify that $AA^{-1} = I$ and $A^{-1}A = I$.

(3.10) By MATLAB, calculate the inverse of

$$A = \begin{bmatrix} 4 & 3 & 2 & 1 \\ 3 & 3 & 2 & 1 \\ 2 & 2 & 2 & 1 \\ 1 & 1 & 1 & 1 \end{bmatrix}$$

$$B = \begin{bmatrix} 1 & 4 & 5 \\ 2 & 1 & 2 \\ 8 & 1 & 1 \end{bmatrix}$$

(3.11) By MATLAB find the inverse of

$$M = \begin{bmatrix} 3 & 1 & 0 \\ 1 & 2 & 1 \\ 0 & 1 & 1 \end{bmatrix}$$

(3.12) Find the inverse of

$$M = \begin{bmatrix} 0 & 5 & 1 \\ -1 & 6 & 3 \\ 3 & -9 & 5 \end{bmatrix}$$

by writing an m-file for the Gauss-Jordan method on MATLAB. Use pivoting.

(3.13) Decompose the following matrices into L and U matrices step×step by MATLAB, then verify the decomposition by calculating the product LU.

$$A = \begin{bmatrix} 2 & -1 & 0 \\ -1 & 2 & -1 \\ 0 & -1 & 2 \end{bmatrix} \quad (a)$$

$$B = \begin{bmatrix} 2 & -1 & 0 \\ -3 & 4 & -1 \\ 0 & -1 & 2 \end{bmatrix} \quad (b)$$

(3.14) Solve the following equations using LU decomposition:

$$\begin{bmatrix} 2 & -1 & 0 \\ -1 & 2 & -1 \\ 0 & -1 & 2 \end{bmatrix} \begin{bmatrix} x_1 \\ x_2 \\ x_3 \end{bmatrix} = \begin{bmatrix} 1 \\ 2 \\ 3 \end{bmatrix} \quad (a)$$

$$\begin{bmatrix} 2 & -1 & 1 \\ -3 & 4 & -1 \\ 1 & -1 & 1 \end{bmatrix} \begin{bmatrix} x_1 \\ x_2 \\ x_3 \end{bmatrix} = \begin{bmatrix} 4 \\ 5 \\ 6 \end{bmatrix} \quad (b)$$

(3.15) Find the determinant of the following matrices by forward elimination of the Gauss elimination method:

$$A = \begin{bmatrix} 1 & 4 \\ 3 & 2 \end{bmatrix}$$

$$B = \begin{bmatrix} 3 & 2 \\ 1 & 3 \end{bmatrix}$$

$$C = \begin{bmatrix} 4 & -1 & 2 \\ 1 & 2 & -3 \\ 0 & 3 & 1 \end{bmatrix}$$

$$D = \begin{bmatrix} -1 & 1 & 2 & -3 \\ 2 & -1 & 3 & 2 \\ 0 & 2 & 4 & 1 \\ 5 & 1 & 1 & -1 \end{bmatrix}$$

(3.16) By hand calculation, calculate the determinant of

$$A = \begin{bmatrix} 8 & 2 & 1 & 1 \\ 1 & 9 & 3 & 0 \\ 3 & -1 & 2 & 6 \\ 2 & -2 & -1 & 4 \end{bmatrix}$$

which may be decomposed to the product of

$$L = \begin{bmatrix} 8 & 0 & 0 & 0 \\ 1 & 8.75 & 0 & 0 \\ 3 & -1.75 & 2.2 & 0 \\ 2 & -2.5 & -0.4285 & 4.8052 \end{bmatrix}$$

$$U = \begin{bmatrix} 1 & 0.25 & 0.125 & 0.125 \\ 0 & 1 & 0.3286 & -0.0143 \\ 0 & 0 & 1 & 2.545 \\ 0 & 0 & 0 & 1 \end{bmatrix}$$

(3.17) (a) Develop an example of a 3×3 matrix which is singular, (b) try to find the inverse of the matrix, (c) try to find the determinant of the matrix, and (d) try to decompose the matrix to L and U matrices.

(3.18) Evaluate the determinant of B, C, and D first by hand calculation, and calculate A^{-1} using the determinants of B, C, and D where

$$A = BCD$$

and

$$B = \begin{bmatrix} 3 & 2 & 1 \\ 0 & 4 & 3 \\ 0 & 0 & 6 \end{bmatrix}, \quad C = \begin{bmatrix} 1 & 0 & 2 \\ -1 & 1 & 0 \\ 0 & 3 & 2 \end{bmatrix}, \quad D = \begin{bmatrix} 1 & 0 & 0 \\ -2 & 1 & 0 \\ 5 & 2 & 7 \end{bmatrix}$$

(3.19) Evaluate the determinant of the transpose of the matrices of the previous problem and show that the determinant of A equals the determinant of A^t. Do this first by hand calculation, and then verify by MATLAB.

(3.20) Matrix A is $n \times n$ Hilbert matrix given by

$$A = [a_{i,j}]$$

where $a_{i,j} = 1/(i+j-1)$. For each of $n = 5$ and $n = 12$, compute (a) determinants of $A^{-1}A$ and $(A^{-1})^{-1}A^{-1}$, (b) the condition numbers of $A^{-1}A$ and $(A^{-1})^{-1}A^{-1}$, (c) print out both $A^{-1}A$ and $(A^{-1})^{-1}A^{-1}$, and (d) observe pathological features if any.

(3.21) Develop your own script to solve a linear equation of any size (square matrix) by Gauss elimination. The script should include computation of the determinant.

(3.22) Develop your own script to compute the inverse of any square matrix by the Gauss-Jordan method.

(3.23) Expand the determinant of the following matrix into a polynomial form by using (a) Spaghetti rule, and (b) `poly`:

$$A = \begin{bmatrix} 2-s & 4 & 6 \\ 1 & -1-s & 5 \\ 2 & 0 & 1-s \end{bmatrix}$$

Chapter 4

POLYNOMIALS AND INTERPOLATION

The main purpose of polynomial interpolation is to fit a polynomial to values of a function at discrete points so that the functional values between these data points can be estimated. This basic purpose, however, is extended and polyomial interpolations are applied in many different ways in deriving other numerical methods. For example, numerical integration schemes are derived by integrating interpolation polynomials. Finite difference approximations are derivatives of interpolation polynomials. For this reason, it is essential to study expressions of interpolation polynomials, their accuracy, and the effects of selecting data points. Although there are alternative ways of expressing the interpolation polynomials, we focus on power series and Lagrange interpolation forms. We also study differentiation and integration of interpolation polynomials. Interpolation polynomials using nonequispaced points are introduced in conjunction with Chebyshev points. For two dimensions, double Lagrange interpolation and transfinite interpolation are introduced.

4.1 MATLAB COMMANDS FOR POLYNOMIALS

We express the power series form of a polynomial by

$$y = c_1 x^n + c_2 x^{n-1} + ... + c_n x + c_{n+1} \qquad (4.1.1)$$

where n is the order of the polynomial and c_is are coefficients. The polynomial may also be expressed in the clustered form

$$y = ((..((c_1 x + c_2)x + c_3)x ... + c_n)x + c_{n+1}) \qquad (4.1.2)$$

or in the factorized form

$$y = c_1(x - r_1)(x - r_2)...(x - r_n) \tag{4.1.3}$$

where r_is are roots of the polynomial. For example, the polynomial

$$y = x^4 + 2x^3 - 7x^2 - 8x + 12 \tag{4.1.4}$$

may be written equivalently as

$$y = ((((x+2)x - 7)x - 8)x + 12) \tag{4.1.5}$$

or

$$y = (x-1)(x-2)(x+2)(x+3) \tag{4.1.6}$$

A polynomial of order n has n roots, some of which may be multiple or complex values. If all the coefficients are real, all the complex roots are found in complex conjugate pairs.

power coefficients: In MATLAB, a polynomial is represented by a row vector containing the coefficients of powers in descending order. For example, the polynomial

$$y = 2x^3 + x^2 + 4x + 5 \tag{4.1.7}$$

is represented by

```
p = [2   1   4   5]
```

roots: The roots of a polynomial are found by the `roots` command. For example, for the polynomial given by Eq.(4.1.7),

```
r = roots(p)
```

yields

```
r =
    0.2500 + 1.5612i
    0.2500 - 1.5612i
   -1.0000
```

Here, the roots are given in a column vector form.

When all the roots are known, can we recover the original polynomial? The answer is yes to some extent, but not entirely positive. The `poly` command detemines the coefficients of the original polynomial except for a constant multiplier. Let us see how it works. For example,

```
poly(r)
```

yields

```
ans =
   1.0000   0.5000   2.0000   2.5000
```

Notice, however, that all the coefficients are half the original coefficients of Eq.(4.1.7). All the polynomial determined by `poly` times any constant multiplier has the same roots. The polynomial given by `poly` is normalized so that the leading coefficient becomes unity.

In order to determine a polynomial of order n, $n+1$ conditions (or pieces of information) are necessary, but the number of information used in `poly` is just n. That is, one condition is still missing to determine the polynomial completely. That one condition can be the coordinates pair of one point that the original polynomial passes through. For example, y of the original polynomial for x is $y(0) = 5$, while $y(0)$ of the polynomial determined by the roots alone is 2.5, so the constant multiplier is $5/2.5 = 2$. Of course, this number equals the leading coefficient of the original polynomial. So the leading coefficient, if known, is enough as the additional condition.

Although conversions from coefficients to roots and back from roots to coefficients are easy with MATLAB, you should be cautious about the accuracy of the computations. The conversion tends to be less accurate if there are multiple roots.[1] For an example of poor accuracy, consider

$$y = (x-1)^6$$
$$= x^6 - 6x^5 + 15x^4 - 20x^3 + 15x^2 - 6x + 1 \quad (4.1.8)$$

which has sextuple roots of $x = 1$. If we try to compute the roots by `roots`, the answers are

```
r = roots([1 -6 15 -20 15 -6 1])
r =
```

---

[1] Computing a highly multiple root is one of the most difficult problems for numerical methods.

```
1.0042 + 0.0025i
1.0042 - 0.0025i
1.0000 + 0.0049i
1.0000 - 0.0049i
0.9958 + 0.0024i
0.9958 - 0.0024i
```

which deviate from unity. The discrepancy of each root from unity is due to rounding errors in computation, and depends on the computer used. On a different computer, the discrepancies may change.[2]

polyval: Polynomials can be evaluated by the `polyval` command. As an example, for the polynomial

$$y = 3x^4 - 7x^3 + 2x^2 + x + 1 \qquad (4.1.9)$$

the following commands compute the value of $y(2.5)$:

```
c = [3, -7, 2, 1, 1];
xi = 2.5;
yi = polyval(c, xi)
```

If `xi` is an array of multiple values of abscissa, `yi` becomes a vector of the answers with the same length as `xi`.

polyfit: A polynomial of order n is determined uniquely if $n+1$ points are given. In other words, the polynomial of order n fitted to $n+1$ data points, (x_i, y_i), $i = 1, 2, ..., n+1$, is unique. The coefficients of the polynomial can be determined easily by `polyfit`. Suppose a data set is given by

```
x = [1.1,    2.3,    3.9,    5.1]
y = [3.887, 4.276, 4.651, 2.117]
```

Then

```
a = polyfit(x,y,length(x)-1)
```

yields

```
a =
    -0.2015    1.4385    -2.7477    5.4370
```

---

[2]The roots here were calculated by MATLAB-6 on PC. The roots calculated by MATLAB-4 on SGI were slightly different. At any rate, the multiple roots computed are very inaccurate but sensitive to rounding off errors.

Section 4.1   MATLAB Commands for Polynomials

which is an array of the coefficients of the polynomial. The third argument in `polyfit` is the order of the polynomial, which is set to `length(x)-1` because the order of the polynomial equals the number of data points minus one. The polynomial determined here is

$$y = -0.2015x^3 + 1.4385x^2 - 2.7477x + 5.4370 \quad (4.1.10)$$

The roots of the polynomial can be used as data points in `polyfit`, but one more data point is necessary because the number of roots of an nth-order polynomial is n while the number of data points required is $n+1$. The additional point can be the y value for $x = 0$ unless $x = 0$ is a root.

differentiation and integration: Integration of the polynomial given by Eq.(4.1.1) is

$$Y = \int y dx = \frac{c_1}{n+1}x^{n+1} + \frac{c_2}{n}x^n + \ldots + \frac{c_n}{2}x^2 + c_{n+1}x + c_{n+2} \quad (4.1.11)$$

where c_{n+2} is an integrating constant. If the coefficients of Eq.(4.1.11) are given by a row vector c, the coefficients of Y may be computed by the `poly_itg` listed in FM 4-1. Its synopsis is as follows:

   d = poly_itg(c)

where c is the coefficient of the polynomial y and d is the coefficient after integration, which equals

$$[\frac{c_1}{n+1}, \frac{c_2}{n}, \ldots, c_{n+1}] \quad (4.1.12)$$

Notice, however, the integrating constant c_{n+2} is not included.

The first derivative of Eq.(4.1.1) is

$$y' = nc_1 x^{n-1} + (n-1)c_2 x^{n-2} + \ldots + c_n \quad (4.1.13)$$

The coefficients of the first derivative may be computed by `polyder`. Its synopsis is

   b = polyder(c)

where c is the same as before, while b is the coefficient after differentiation, given by

$$[nc_1, (n-1)c_2, \ldots, c_n] \quad (4.1.14)$$

We define two polynomials:

$$y_a = a_1 x^m + a_2 x^{m-1} + \ldots + a_m x + a_{m+1}$$
$$y_b = b_1 x^n + b_2 x^{n-1} + \ldots + b_n x + b_{n+1}$$

and assume that their coefficient vectors are `a` and `b`, respectively. The command `poly_add` (FM 4-2) may be used to do this chore. The synopsis is

```
c = poly_add(a,b)
```

For the subtraction of polynomial `b` from `a`:

```
c = poly_add(a,-b)
```

The product of two polynomials, one of order m and the other of order n, becomes a polynomial of order $d = m + n$:

$$y_c = y_a y_b = c_1 x^d + c_2 x^{d-1} + \ldots + c_d x + c_{d+1} \tag{4.1.15}$$

The MATLAB command to find the coefficients of y_c is

```
c = conv(a,b)
```

Division of a polynomial y_a by another polynomial y_b satisfies

$$y_a = y_q y_b + y_r$$

where y_q is the quotient and y_r is the remainder upon division. The polynomials y_q and y_r are computed by `deconv` as

```
[q,r] = deconv[a,b]
```

where `q` and `r` represent coefficients of y_q and y_r, respectively.

4.2 LINEAR INTERPOLATION

Linear interpolation is a basis for many numerical schemes. For example, by integrating the linear interpolation, the integration scheme called the trapezoidal rule is derived. As another example, the gradient of the linear interpolation is used as an approximation for the first derivative of the function.

Section 4.2 Linear Interpolation

The linear interpolation is a line fitted to two data points (see Figure 4.1) and is given by

$$g(x) = \frac{b-x}{b-a} f(a) + \frac{x-a}{b-a} f(b) \qquad (4.2.1)$$

or equivalently

$$g(x) = \frac{f(b)-f(a)}{b-a}(x-a) + f(a)$$

where $f(a)$ and $f(b)$ are known values of $f(x)$ at $x = a$ and $x = b$, respectively.

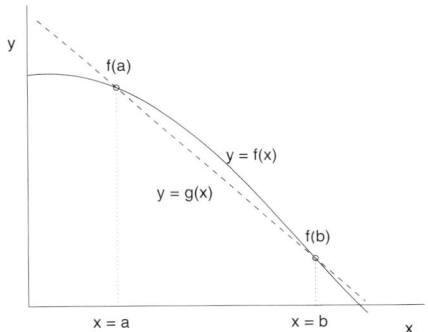

Figure 4.1 Linear interpolation.

An error of the linear interpolation may be expressed in the form

$$e(x) = 0.5(x-a)(x-b) f''(\xi), \quad a \le x \le b, \quad a \le \xi \le b \qquad (4.2.2)$$

where ξ (pronounced "xi") is dependent on x but somewhere between a and b. Equation (4.2.2) is an awkward function because we have no means to evaluate ξ exactly. From Eq.(4.2.2), however, we can say that $|e(x)|$ is bounded by

$$|e(x)| \le 0.5 |(x-a)(x-b)| \max_{a \le x \le b} \left| f''(\xi) \right| \qquad (4.2.3)$$

It is seen that the error is a function of x, which vanishes at $x = a$ and $x = b$. The peak of the error occurs approximately at the midpoint, $x_m = 0.5(a+b)$.

When $f''(x)$ is nearly constant in the interval, $f''(\xi)$ in Eq.(4.2.2) may be approximated by $f''(x_m)$.

A command for linear interpolation is available in MATLAB. The `interp1` command determines the functional value for a specified abscissa denoted by `xi` by linearly interpolating from the function table. With `interp1`, linear interpolation is applied to each data interval. The `xi` may also be a vector of specified x values. Its synopsis is

```
yi = interp1(x, y, xi)
```

Here, `x` is a column array of the x values of the data; `y` is a column array of the y values of the data. Both arrays, `x` and `y`, must have the same length; however, `y` can have more than one column. `xi` is a scalar or an array of x values for which y values are to be evaluated by linear interpolation. Alternatively, in the second format, the method of interpolation can be chosen from (i) linear interpolation, (ii) cubic spline, (iii) cubic interpolation, among a few others. For example:

```
yi = interp1(x, y, xi, 'linear')
yi = interp1(x, y, xi, 'spline')
yi = interp1(x, y, xi, 'cubic')
```

In any case, x should be monotonic. The cubic interpolation requires that x be equispaced. More details of cubic and spline interpolation are described in Chapter 9, "Spline Functions and Nonlinear Interpolation."

Example 4.1

Two material properties of carbon monoxide gas are given in the following table:

T	Beta	Alpha
300	3.33e3	0.2128e4
400	2.50e3	0.3605e4
500	2.00e3	0.5324e4
600	1.67e3	0.7190e4

where T is the temperature in Kelvin, Beta (or β) is the thermal expansion coefficient (1/K), and Alpha (or α) is the thermal diffusivity (m^2/s). Using MATLAB find the properties for T= 321, 440, and 571, respectively.

Solution

The following script will answer the question:

Section 4.2 Linear Interpolation

```
Temp = [300, 400, 500, 600]';
Beta = 1000*[3.33, 2.50, 2.00, 1.67]';
Alpha= 10000*[ 0.2128, 0.3605, 0.5324, 0.7190]';
Ti=[321, 440, 571]';
Propty = interp1(Temp, [Beta, Alpha], Ti, 'linear');
[Ti, Propty]
```

The results are

```
ans =
   1.0e+03 *
    0.3210    3.1557    2.4382
    0.4400    2.3000    4.2926
    0.5710    1.7657    6.6489
```

where the first column is temperature, the second is Beta, and the third is Alpha.

Example 4.2

Suppose a functional relation $y = y(x)$ is given in a tabular form as in

```
x    y
0    0.9162
0.25 0.8109
0.50 0.6931
0.75 0.5596
1.00 0.4055
```

where $y(x)$ is a monotonically decreasing function of x. Find the values of x that satisfy $y = 0.9, 0.7, 0.6$, and 0.5, respectively, using MATLAB.

Solution

This is an inverse problem; that is, x is considered to be a function of y, namely, $x = f(y)$. The solution is computed by the following script:

```
x = [0.0, 0.25, 0.5, 0.75, 1.0]';
y = [0.9162, 0.8109, 0.6931, 0.5596, 0.4055]';
yi = [0.9, 0.7, 0.6, 0.5]';
xi = interp1(y, x, yi, 'linear');
[yi, xi]
```

The results are

```
ans =
    0.9000    0.0385
```

0.7000	0.4854
0.6000	0.6743
0.5000	0.8467

where the first column is for y values, and the second is for x values.

4.3 POLYNOMIAL INTERPOLATION WITH POWER SERIES

Although we studied how to fit a polynomial to a set of data points by `polyfit`, we revisit the subject from a more fundamental point of view in this section.

An interpolation polynomial may be expressed in various alternative forms, which can be transformed from one to another. Among them are power series, Lagrange interpolation, Newton forward interpolation, and Newton backward interpolation. Regardless of the formula of expression, all polynomial interpolation formulas fitted to the same data are mathematically equivalent.

Suppose $n+1$ data points are given as

x_1	x_2	...	x_{n+1}
y_1	y_2	...	y_{n+1}

where x_1, x_2 ... are abscissas of the data points and assumed to be in increasing order. The increment between two consecutive x values is arbitrary. The polynomial of order n passing through the $n+1$ data points may be written in a power series such as

$$g(x) = c_1 x^n + c_2 x^{n-1} + \ ... \ + c_{n+1} \qquad (4.3.1)$$

where c_is are coefficients. Setting $g(x_i) = y_i$ for each of the $n+1$ data points yields $n+1$ linear equations, which are expressed in matrix notation by

$$Ac = y \qquad (4.3.2)$$

where

$$A = \begin{bmatrix} x_1^n & x_1^{n-1} & .. & x_1 & 1 \\ x_2^n & x_2^{n-1} & .. & x_2 & 1 \\ . & . & .. & . & 1 \\ x_{n+1}^n & x_{n+1}^{n-1} & .. & x_{n+1} & 1 \end{bmatrix}, \ c = \begin{bmatrix} c_1 \\ c_2 \\ . \\ c_{n+1} \end{bmatrix}, \ y = \begin{bmatrix} y_1 \\ y_2 \\ . \\ y_{n+1} \end{bmatrix} \qquad (4.3.3)$$

By solving Eq.(4.3.2), the coefficients are determined. The coefficients can also be determined by `polyfit(x,y,n)`, as described in Section 4.1. Figure

4.2 illustrates a polynomial fitted to four data points taken from a function $y(x)$.

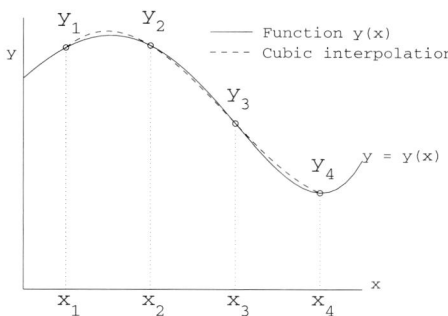

Figure 4.2 Polynomial of order three fitted to four data points.

Example 4.3

Determine the polynomial that passes through the three data points: (0, 1), (1, 0.75), and (2, 0), where the first number in the parentheses is for the x value and the second is for the y value of each data point.

Solution

The order of a polynomial that fits to three data points is 2, so we first write the second-order polynomial as

$$g(x) = c_1 x^2 + c_2 x + c_3$$

By setting the polynomial to each data point, we get

$$c_1(0)^2 + c_2(0) + c_3 = 1$$
$$c_1(1)^2 + c_2(1) + c_3 = 0.75$$
$$c_1(2)^2 + c_2(2) + c_3 = 0$$

From the first equation, we get $c_3 = 1$. From the second and third equations, we find $c_2 = 0$ and $c_1 = -0.25$. Therefore, the polynomial is

$$g(x) = -0.25x^2 + 1$$

Example 4.4

A set of four data points is given by

$$x = [1.1, \quad 2.3, \quad 3.9, \quad 5.1]$$
$$y = [3.887, 4.276, 4.651, 2.117]$$

Find the coefficients of the interpolation polynomial fitted to the data set by solving Eq.(4.3.2), and then determine the value of y for $x = 2.101$ and 4.234 by the interpolation formula. Plot the polynomial along with the data points.

Solution

A MATLAB script is shown next:

List 4.1
```
clear,clf,hold off
x = [1.1,   2.3,   3.9,   5.1]';
y = [3.887, 4.276, 4.651, 2.117]' ;
n=length(x)-1 ;
a(:,n+1)=ones(x);
a(:,n)=x;
for j=n-1:-1:1
   a(:,j)=a(:,j+1).*x;
end
%Solution of linear equation.
coeff=a\y
xi=[2.101, 4.234];
yi=zeros(size(xi))
for k=1:n+1
   yi = yi + coeff(k)*xi.^(n+1-k)
end
yi
%   plotting
xp=1.1:0.05:5.1;
yp=zeros(size(xp));
for k=1:n+1
   yp = yp + coeff(k)*xp.^(n+1-k);
end
plot(xp,yp, x,y,'o')
xlabel('x')
ylabel('g(x):-,  data points: o')
```

The answer is

```
coef =
    -0.2015    1.4385   -2.7477    5.4370
ans =
     4.1457    4.3007
```

The interpolation polynomial determined is plotted in Figure 4.3. The foregoing script may be much more compactly written using `polyfit` and `polyval` or `Lagran_`.

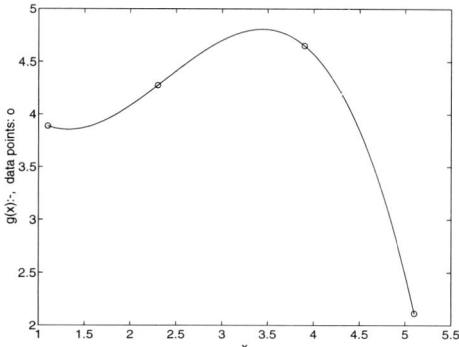

Figure 4.3 Plot of the interpolation polynomial.

The uniqueness of the interpolation polynomial of order n fitted to $n+1$ data points may be proved as follows: Assume the contrary by hypothesis that the interpolation $g(x)$ is not unique. If so, there must be another polynomial $k(x)$ of order n that passes through the same $n+1$ data points. The difference between the interpolation polynomials $g(x)$ and $k(x)$ is defined by

$$r(x) = g(x) - k(x)$$

which must be a polynomial of order n or less because $g(x)$ and $k(x)$ are both polynomials of order n. On the other hand, since $g(x)$ and $k(x)$ both agree at the $n+1$ data points, $r(x)$ must become zero at the $n+1$ data points. It means that $r(x)$ has $n+1$ zeros, so $r(x)$ must be a polynomial of order $n+1$. This is contradictory to the hypothesis that $r(x)$ is a polynomial of order n or less, and proves that the hypothesis is incorrect.

4.4 LAGRANGE INTERPOLATION POLYNOMIAL

The Lagrange interpolation formula is an alternative to the power series form of an interpolation polynomial. It has the following two major advantages: (1) with the Lagrange interpolation formula, there is no need to solve linear equations, and (2) the Lagrange interpolation formulas allow interpolation even when functional values are expressed by symbols but no numerical values are known. Because of (1), the computational efficiency of Lagrange interpolation is higher than the power series form, particularly when the number of data points is large. Furthermore, it is less susceptible to the rounding error effects. Because of (2), it becomes possible to express a polynomial in terms of undetermined ordinates of data points.

We consider a polynomial interpolation formula that passes through the data points:

$$\begin{array}{cccc} x_1 & x_2 & \cdots & x_{n+1} \\ y_1 & y_2 & \cdots & y_{n+1} \end{array}$$

To introduce the basic principle of the Lagrange formula, consider the product of factors

$$u_1(x) = (x - x_2)(x - x_3)...(x - x_{n+1}) \qquad (4.4.1)$$

which is related to the $n+1$ data points shown in the previous section. The function u_1 is an nth-order polynomial of x, and becomes zero at $x = x_2, x_3, ..., x_{n+1}$ but not zero for $x = x_1$. If we divide $u_1(x)$ by $u_1(x_1)$, the resulting function

$$v_1(x) = \frac{u_1(x)}{u_1(x_1)} = \frac{(x - x_2)(x - x_3)...(x - x_{n+1})}{(x_1 - x_2)(x_1 - x_3)...(x_1 - x_{n+1})} \qquad (4.4.2)$$

satisfies $v_1(x_1) = 1$ and $v_1(x_i) = 0$ for $i = 2, 3, ..., n + 1$. Similarly,

$$v_2(x) = \frac{u_2(x)}{u_2(x_2)} = \frac{(x - x_1)(x - x_3)...(x - x_{n+1})}{(x_2 - x_1)(x_2 - x_3)...(x_2 - x_{n+1})}$$

satisfies $v_2(x_2) = 1$, and $v_2(x_i) = 0$ for all i, except for $i = 2$. In more general terms, we can write v_i by

$$v_i(x) = \frac{u_i(x)}{u_i(x_i)} = \prod_{j=1, j \neq i}^{n+1} \frac{(x - x_j)}{(x_i - x_j)} \qquad (4.4.3)$$

The function $v_i(x)$ is an nth-order polynomial which satisfies $v_i(x_i) = 1$ and $v_i(x_j) = 0$ for all $j \neq i$. We call $v_i(x)$ a coefficient polynomial or shape function. The shape functions are illustrated in Figure 4.4, where $n = 7$ and the spacing of the abscissas is assumed to be unity.

Section 4.4 Lagrange Interpolation Polynomial

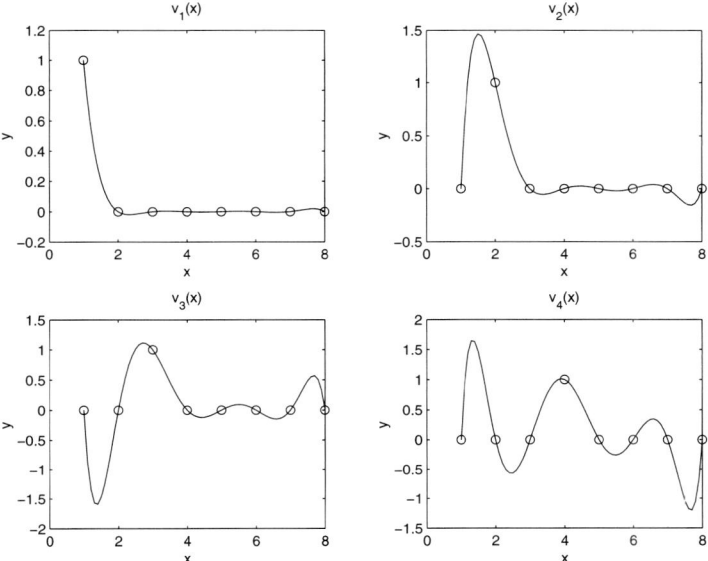

Figure 4.4 Illustration of shape functions.

If we multiply $v_1(x)$, $v_2(x)$, ...$v_{n+1}(x)$ by y_1, y_2, ..., y_{n+1}, respectively, and add them together, the summation becomes a polynomial of order n again, and equals y_i for each $x = x_i$. The $v_i(x)$ functions are illustrated in Figure 4.4. The Lagrange interpolation formula of order n is written by

$$g(x) = \sum_{i=1}^{n+1} v_i(x) y_i \qquad (4.4.4)$$

For $n = 3$ as an example, the foregoing equation is written more explicitly as

$$\begin{aligned}
g(x) &= \frac{(x-x_2)(x-x_3)(x-x_4)}{(x_1-x_2)(x_1-x_3)(x_1-x_4)} y_1 \\
&+ \frac{(x-x_1)(x-x_3)(x-x_4)}{(x_2-x_1)(x_2-x_3)(x_2-x_4)} y_2 \\
&+ \frac{(x-x_1)(x-x_2)(x-x_4)}{(x_3-x_1)(x_3-x_2)(x_3-x_4)} y_3
\end{aligned}$$

$$+ \frac{(x-x_1)(x-x_2)(x-x_3)}{(x_4-x_1)(x_4-x_2)(x_4-x_3)} y_4$$

Example 4.5

(a) Densities of sodium for three temperatures are given as follows:

i	Temperature T_i	Density ρ_i
1	94°C	929kg/m^3
2	205	902
3	371	860

Write the Lagrange interpolation formula that fits the three data points. (b) Find the density for $T = 251°C$ by the Lagrange interpolation.

Solution

(a) Since the number of data points is three, the order of the Lagrange interpolation formula is 2. The Lagrange interpolation becomes

$$\rho(T) = \frac{(T-205)(T-371)}{(94-205)(94-371)}(929) + \frac{(T-94)(T-371)}{(205-94)(205-371)}(902) + \frac{(T-94)(T-205)}{(371-94)(371-205)}(860)$$

(b) By setting $T = 251°C$ in the equation above, we obtain

$$g(251) = 890.5 \text{kg/m}^3$$

The function `Lagran_` in FM 4-4 performs Lagrange interpolation. Its synopsis is

    yi = Lagran_(x, y, xi)

where x and y are, respectively, arrays of abscissas and ordinates of the data set; xi is the array of x values for which y values are to be evaluated by interpolation; and yi is the result of interpolation. List 4.2 illustrates the application of the `Lagran_` function with the data in Example 4.4.

List 4.2
```
clear
x = [1.1, 2.3, 3.9, 5.1];
y=[3.887, 4.276, 4.651, 2.117];
xi = [2.101, 4.234];
yi = Lagran_(x, y, xi)
```

The results are:
```
yi =
    4.1457    4.3007
```

4.5 ERROR OF INTERPOLATION POLYNOMIALS

To show how an error occurs in polynomial interpolation, let us write an interpolation approximation for $y = \sin(x)$ in $0 \le x \le \pi$ with five equispaced points. The interpolation polynomial is a fourth-order polynomial passing through the data points given by

$$x = [0, \frac{\pi}{4}, \frac{\pi}{2}, \frac{3\pi}{4}, \pi]$$
$$y = [0, \sin(\frac{\pi}{4}), \sin(\frac{\pi}{2}), \sin(\frac{3\pi}{4}), \sin(\pi)]$$

The error is defined by

$$e(x) = \sin(x) - g(x)$$

where g is the interpolation polynomial fitted to the five data points. The error times 100 and the $\sin(x)$ function are plotted in Figure 4.5. We can observe that the error oscillates and its magnitude becomes greatest in the intervals near the endpoints. This behavior of the error is typical of any polynomial interpolation with equispaced points, although the actual shape of the error distribution changes depending on the function being interpolated and the size of the interpolation range, $|b - a|$.

In order to analyze the error of interpolations, we need to express it in a more systematic form. Indeed, the error of a polynomial interpolation formula (for both power series and Lagrange interpolation forms) is given by

$$e(x) = f(x) - g(x) = L(x)f^{(n+1)}(\xi) \tag{4.5.1}$$

$$x_1 = a \le \xi \le b = x_{n+1} \tag{4.5.2}$$

where $n+1$ is the number of data points, and $f^{(n+1)}$ is the $(n+1)$th derivative of $f(x)$ and

$$L(x) = \frac{(x-x_1)(x-x_2)...(x-x_n)(x-x_{n+1})}{(n+1)!} \qquad (4.5.3)$$

In Eq.(4.5.1) ξ depends on x but it is between a and b. If $f(x)$ is a polynomial of order n or less, the $(n+1)$th derivative of $f(x)$ vanishes, so the error becomes zero. When the error does not vanish, we have the same difficulty we had for Eq.(4.2.2) because ξ is dependent on x but not known. From Eq.(4.5.1), however, we can write

$$|e(x)| \leq |L(x)| \max_{a \leq \xi \leq b} |f^{(n+1)}(\xi)| \qquad (4.5.4)$$

The right side of Eq.(4.5.4) gives an upper estimate of the error at any value of x. The second term is a constant for the whole domain, so the distribution of the right side is determined by $L(x)$. Figure 4.6(a) shows a plot of $L(x)$ for the interpolation with five equispaced points. By comparison of Figure 4.6(a) to Figure 4.5, we can find that the peaks of errors in the intervals near the endpoints (in Figure 4.5) are due to local peaks of $|L(x)|$ near the endpoints.

Naturally, we are curious as to how the errors of interpolation polynomials can be decreased. Two immediate answers can be drawn from an analysis of $L(x)$. The first is to decrease the domain of interpolation, namely $b-a$. For example, by reducing the range of interpolation to one half, namely $0 \leq x \leq 0.5\pi$, $L(x)$ becomes approximately $1/30$, as plotted in Figure 4.6(b). The second is to increase the number of points. Figure 4.6(c) shows a plot of $L(x)$ with seven points for the original range of $0 \leq x \leq \pi$. Compared

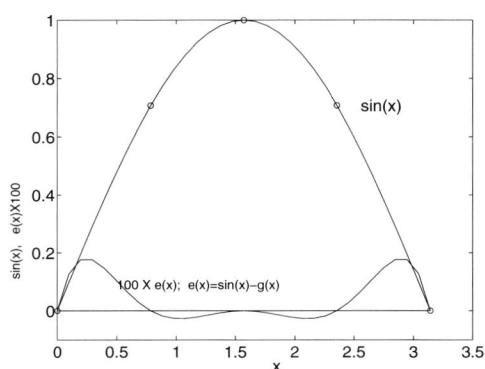

Figure 4.5 Interpolating approximation of the sine function.

to Figure 4.6(a), the error has decreased to approximately 1/40. An additional means of reducing errors of interpolation is to use variably spaced data points, as illustrated in Figure 4.6(d), where the Chebyshev points described in more detail in Section 4.7 are used.

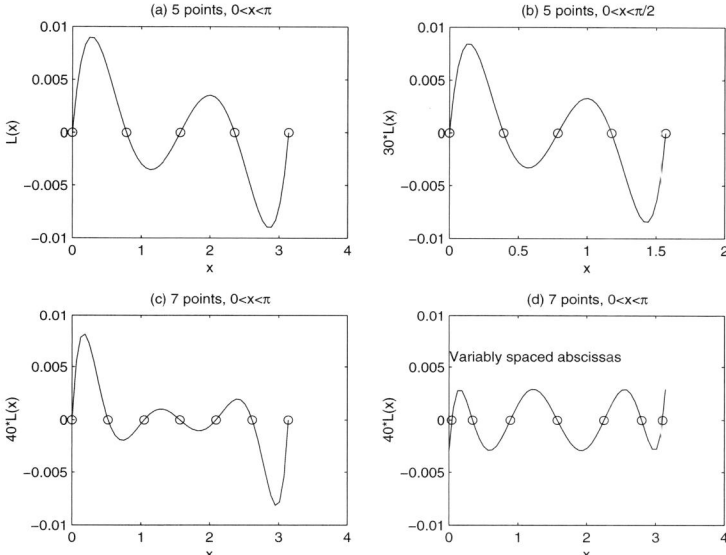

Figure 4.6 L(x) and effects of $|b - a|$ and number of points: (a) 5 points, (b) 5 points for half the width, (c) 7 points, and (d) 7 with variable spacing.

Although the reduction of errors by an increase in the number of data points is remarkable, as shown in the preceding paragraph, it should not be overdone. The reason for this precaution is that, if the ordinates of data points have errors or uncertainties, the error of the interpolation polynomial becomes large, and it increases rapidly as the number of points increases. In other words, if the data has errors, accuracy becomes worse as the number of points increases. The errors of data can come from many different sources, including human errors, rounding errors, and experimental errors.

We will show the effect of the data errors. Suppose the data is expressed by
$$f_i = f_{i,exact} + e_i$$
where $f_{i,exact}$ is the exact value of f_i and e_i is an error. Then the error of the Lagrange interpolation due to the data error is given by

$$e_d(x) = \sum_{i=1}^{n+1} v_i(x) e_i \qquad (4.5.5)$$

which is in the same form as Eq.(4.4.4) except g is replaced by e_d and y_i is replaced by e_i. For illustration purposes, we consider interpolation of the $\sin(x)$ function in $0 \leq x \leq \pi$ as before, with various numbers of points. Suppose all the data are exact except that the midpoint in each data set has one percent error, namely, $e_i = 0$ except $e_m = 1$ percent error, where m is the index of the midpoint. Then Eq.(4.5.5) becomes

$$e_d(x) = v_m(x) \quad \% \qquad (4.5.6)$$

Figure 4.7 shows a plot of the foregoing equation. The errors with five and seven points (see Figures 4.7(a) and 4.7(b)) are comparable to the error at the midpoint. The error with 11 points, however, (see Figure 4.7(c)) is amplified by a factor of approximately 5 in the first and last intervals, and the error with 21 points (see Figure 4.7(d)) is amplified by a factor of approximately 1250.

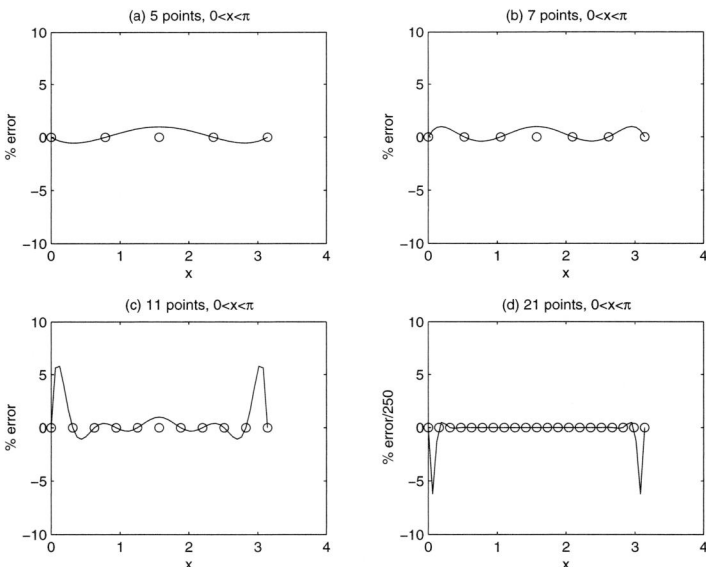

Figure 4.7 Effects of data error: (a) 5 points, (b) 7 points, (c) 11 points, and (d) 21 points.

To summarize, (1) the use of interpolation polynomial is recommended in as small a domain as possible, (2) the accuracy of interpolation increases with an increase in the number of data points only up to a certain number.

4.6 DIFFERENTIATION AND INTEGRATION OF LAGRANGE INTERPOLATION FORMULA

While a function is approximated by an interpolation polynomial, the derivative and integration of the function may also be approximated by the derivative and integration, respectively, of the interpolation polynomial. Indeed, this is the basic principle in deriving numerical differentiation and integration methods. In this section, we do not look into the details of the numerical differentiation or integration (we cover this in Chapters 5 and 6, "Numerical Integration" and "Numerical Differentiation"). We do discuss, however, how to evaluate derivative and integration of an interpolation polynomial, particularly the Lagrange interpolation formula.

By differentiating Eq.(4.4.4), the first derivative of the Lagrange interpolation is written as

$$g'(x) = \sum_{i=1}^{n+1} v_i'(x) y_i \qquad (4.6.1)$$

The shape function v_i is given by Eq.(4.4.3) in a factorized form. In order to evaluate v_i', we express it in a power series form first.

Recognize that v_1 in Eq.(4.4.3) is a polynomial of order n fitted to the data points:

$$x = [x_1, x_2, ... x_{n+1}]$$
$$y = [1, 0, ..., 0]$$

Similarly, v_2 is for

$$x = [x_1, x_2, ..., x_{n+1}]$$
$$y = [0, 1, 0, .., 0]$$

and, in more general terms, v_i is for

$$x = [x_j]$$
$$y = [y_j], \text{ with } y_j = 0 \text{ except } y_i = 1$$

Therefore, the polynomial v_i may be expressed in a power series form by fitting a polynomial of order n to the data.

The power series form of $v_i(x)$ for all i may be computed by shape_pw listed in FM 4-6. Its synopsis is

```
p = shape_pw(x):
```

where x is an array of abscissa points, and p is a matrix in which the ith row represents the power coefficients for $v_i(x)$.

To verify shape_pw, a script to evaluate the Lagrange interpolation for x_i is shown in List 4.3:

List 4.3
```
clear
x = [1.1,   2.3,   3.9,   5.1];
y = [3.887, 4.276, 4.651, 2.117];
xi = [2.101, 4.234];
np = length(x)
p=shape_pw(x)
for inp=1:2
  for i=1:np
    Temp = polyval(p(i,:),xi(inp))
    v(i) = Temp
  end
  yi(inp)=v*y';
end
yi
```

The answer is:

```
yi =
     4.1457    4.3007
```

The solution above agrees with that of Example 4.4.

To compute the first derivative of the Lagrange interpolation polynomial, each row of p is converted to the array of coefficients of the first derivative using polyder. The following script shows the computation of the first derivative at the abscissa points of the data set in Example 4.4:

List 4.4
```
clear
x = [1.1,   2.3,   3.9,   5.1];
y = [3.887, 4.276, 4.651, 2.117];
xi = [2.101, 4.234];
np = length(x);
p=shape_pw(x);
for i=1:np
    pd(i,:) = polyder(p(i,:));
end
for inp=1:length(xi)
```

```
      for i=1:np
        vd(i) = polyval(pd(i,:),xi(inp));
      end
      yi(inp)=vd*y';
    end
    yi
```

The answer is:

```
    yi =
        0.6292    -1.4004
```

In the foregoing script, `p(i,:)` is the ith row of `p` and the power coefficients of $v_i(x)$, and `pd(i,:)` is the power coefficient of $v'_i(x)$. The values of `yi` are the first derivative values of the Lagrange interpolation evaluated for $x = 2.101$ and 4.234, respectively.[3]

4.7 INTERPOLATION WITH CHEBYSHEV POINTS

From Figure 4.6(a-c), we learned that local peaks of errors of the Lagrange interpolation using equispaced points become smallest in the middle, but increase toward the edges of the domain. The question is how to reduce the maximum error of an interpolation. The answer is to redistribute the points by increasing the interval size in the middle, but decreasing the interval size toward the endpoints. The optimal distribution of points, however, depends on the purpose of the interpolation polynomial.

If the interpolation is to approximate a function, the points determined by a Chebyshev polynomial is optimal, because the $L(x)$ distribution becomes most evenly distributed. Another advantage is that errors in data are not spread or amplified as with equispaced points.

Chebyshev polynomials and Chebyshev points: Chebyshev polynomials are given by

$$T_0(x) = 1$$
$$T_1(x) = x - 1$$
$$T_2(x) = 2x^2 - 1$$
$$T_3(x) = 4x^3 - 3x$$

---

[3] An alternative way to get the former is to find the element before the last of the vector returned by `c=polyfit(x-2.101, y, length(x)-1)`. Likewise, the latter is the same for `c=polyfit(x-4.234, y, length(x)-1)`. For more details, see Section 6.1.

$$T_k(x) = 2xT_{k-1}(x) - T_{k-2}(x) \qquad (4.7.1)$$

The Chebyshev polynomials are plotted in Figure 4.8 for $n = 0, 1, 2, 3, 5$, and 8.

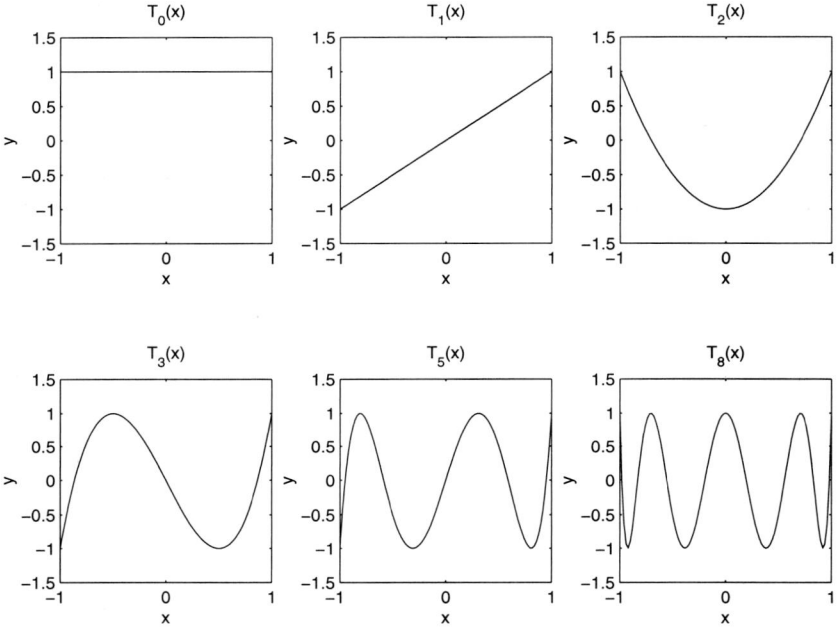

Figure 4.8 Plot of Chebyshev polynomials.

The coefficients of a Chebyshev polynomial in power series form may be computed by function `Cheby_pw` listed in FM 4-5. Its synopsis is

```
p = Cheby_pw(n)
```

where n is the order of the Chebyshev polynomial, and p is a row array of the coefficients.

Chebyshev roots may be computed by

```
sort(roots(Cheby_pw(n)))
```

where `sort` is used to list the roots in ascending order. If $n = 5$, for example, the foregoing command yields:

```
sort(roots(Cheby_pw(5)))
```

Section 4.7 Interpolation with Chebyshev Points

```
ans =
   -0.95105651629515
   -0.58778525229247
                   0
    0.58778525229247
    0.95105651629515
```

The Chebyshev polynomial of order k can be alternatively written by

$$T_k(x) = \cos(k\cos^{-1}(x)), \quad -1 \le x \le 1 \tag{4.7.2}$$

Equation (4.7.2) has k roots, all of which are in $[-1, 1]$. The roots can also be computed by

$$x_i = \cos(\frac{k + 0.5 - i}{k}\pi), \quad i = 1, 2, ...k \tag{4.7.3}$$

which yields identical results as roots(Cheby_pw(n)). If the range of interpolation is $[a, b]$, the roots given by Eq.(4.7.3) are mapped to the range $[a, b]$ by

$$x_i = \frac{1}{2}[(b - a)\cos(\frac{k + 0.5 - i}{k}\pi) + a + b], \quad i = 1, 2, ...k \tag{4.7.4}$$

Figure 4.9 shows the distribution of $L(x)$ with nine Chebyshev points and the same with equispaced points for the range of interpolation, $0 \le x \le 5$. The heights of local peaks of $L(x)$ are uniform, and the maximum value of $|L(x)|$ is approximately one-fifth of that with the equispaced points.

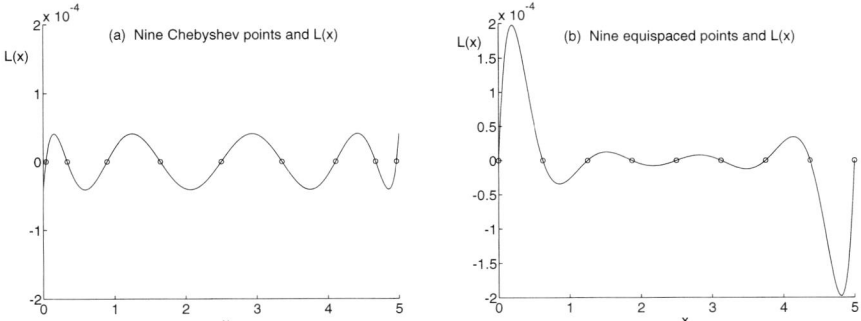

Figure 4.9 $L(x)$ of Chebyshev points (left) and that of equispaced points (right).

Besides the reduction of the peak error by the Chebyshev points, another significant advantage is that the data error is not amplified as with the equispaced points. In Figure 4.10, we plot the percentage error of the interpolation due to the data error of one percent at the middle data point. Comparing Figure 4.10 to each part of Figure 4.7, we can see that the influence of the data error is confined in the vicinity of that data point. Although we illustrated the effect of data error at the center point, the same conclusion can be drawn for data errors at different points.

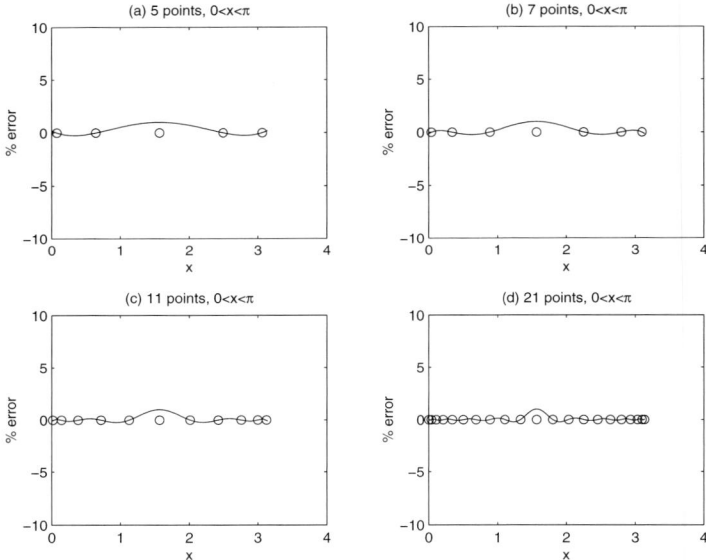

Figure 4.10 Effects of data error with Chebyshev points.

Lobatto points: Lobatto points are roots of the first derivative of a Chebyshev polynomial plus $x = -1$ and $x = 1$. For an interval $[a, b]$, the Chebyshev polynomial of order k generates $k+1$ Lobatto points, namely

$$x_i = \frac{1}{2}[(b-a)\cos(\frac{k-i}{k}\pi) + a + b], \quad i = 0, 1, ...k \qquad (4.7.5)$$

Lobatto points, and $L(x)$ based on them are plotted in Figure 4.11. The peak value of $L(x)$ in Figure 4.11 is higher than with the Chebyshev points in Figure 4.9(a) but significantly smaller than with equispaced points as in

Figure 4.9(b).

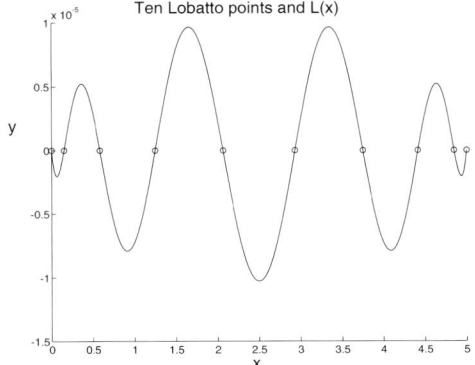

Figure 4.11 $L(x)$ with Lobatto points: (a) 5 points, (b) 7 points, (c) 11 points, and (d) 21 points.

Legendre points: The Legendre points are seldom used for mere interpolation purposes, but they are important because the numerical integration method, named *Gauss-Legendre* quadrature (see Section 5.3), is based on the integration of the interpolation polynomial using the Legendre points.

The Legendre polynomials are given by

$$P_0(x) = 1$$
$$P_1(x) = x$$
$$P_2(x) = \frac{1}{2}(3x^2 - 1)$$
$$P_3(x) = \frac{1}{2}(5x^3 - 3x)$$
$$\cdots$$
$$P_j(x) = \frac{1}{j}[(2j-1)xP_{j-1}(x) - (j-1)P_{j-2}(x)]$$

The coefficients of the Legendre polynomial of order n may be computed by Legen_pw; for example,

```
p = Legen_pw(6)
```

yields

```
p =
     14.4375, 0, -19.6875, 0, 6.5625, 0, -0.3121
```

The roots of a Legendre polynomial may be computed using roots. Let us use $n = 6$ as an example:

```
sort(roots(Legen_pw(6)))
ans =
     -9.324695142031516e-01
     -6.612093864662646e-01
     -2.386191860831969e-01
      2.386191860831969e-01
      6.612093864662645e-01
      9.324695142031515e-01
```

where `sort` is used to list the points in ascending order.

4.8 CUBIC HERMITE INTERPOLATION

A polynomial can be fitted not only to functional values but also to derivatives. The polynomials fitted to both functional and derivative values are named *Hermite interpolation* polynomials or *osculating* polynomials. We consider here the cubic Hermite polynomial,

$$f(s) = c_1 s^3 + c_2 s^2 + c_3 s + c_4 \qquad (4.8.1)$$

which is fitted to two functional values and two derivatives. Consider the interval between two points, s_1, s_2, and assume the functional values and first derivatives are specified at both points (see Figure 4.12). The four equations are written as

$$\begin{aligned} f(s_1) &= c_1 s_1^3 + c_2 s_1^2 + c_3 s_1 + c_4 = f_1 \\ f'(s_1) &= 3 c_1 s_1^2 + 2 c_2 s_1 + c_3 = f_1' \\ f(s_2) &= c_1 s_2^3 + c_2 s_2^2 + c_3 s_2 + c_4 = f_2 \\ f'(s_2) &= 3 c_1 s_2^2 + 2 c_2 s_2 + c_3 = f_2' \end{aligned} \qquad (4.8.2)$$

Equation (4.8.2) has four linear equations with four coefficients to be determined.

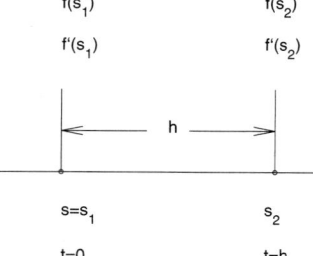

Figure 4.12 Interval for cubic Hermite interpolation.

Example 4.6

Determine a curve that passes through point A and point B on the x-y coordinates (see Figure 4.13) with the following conditions:

(i) $x = 1$, $y = 1$, $dy/dx = 0$
(ii) $x = 4$, $y = 2$, $dx/dy = 0$

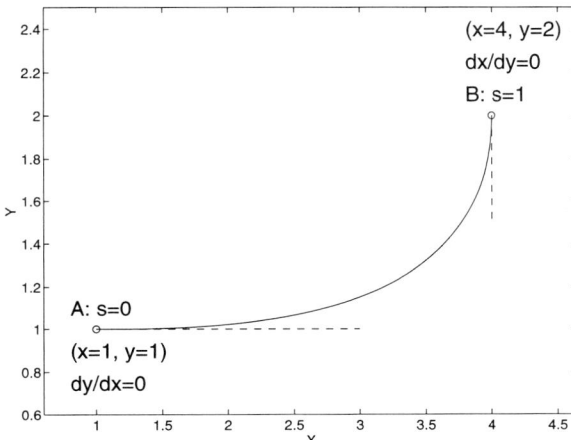

Figure 4.13 Conditions for the curve desired.

Solution

Because both $y(x)$ and $x(y)$ become singular at one of the endpoints, it is not possible to fit y as a function of x, or x as a function of y. In fitting a geometric curve, as in this example, it is common to introduce a parameter s, and express each of x and y as $x(s)$ and $y(s)$. We assume $s = 0$ at point A and $s = 1$ at point B. Each of x and y will be expressed as a cubic polynomial of s as

$$x = x(s) = c_1 s^3 + c_2 s^2 + c_3 s + c_4 \qquad (A)$$

$$y = y(s) = d_1 s^3 + d_2 s^2 + d_3 s + d_4 \qquad (B)$$

The boundary conditions for $x(s)$ and $y(s)$ may be written as

$$s = 0: \quad x(0) = 1, dx/ds = a; \quad y(0) = 1, dy/ds = 0 \qquad (C)$$

$$s = 1: \quad x(1) = 4, dx/ds = 0; \quad y(1) = 2, dy/ds = b \qquad (D)$$

where a and b are arbitrary parameters. By eliminating ds, the original end conditions

$$s = 0 : dy/dx = 0$$

$$s = 1 : dx/dy = 0$$

are satisfied.

Introducing Eqs.(A) and (B) into (C) and (D), respectively, yields

$$c_4 = 1$$
$$c_3 = a$$
$$c_1 + c_2 + c_3 + c_4 = 4$$
$$3c_1 + 2c_2 + c_3 = 0$$

$$d_4 = 1$$
$$d_3 = 0$$
$$d_1 + d_2 + d_3 + d_4 = 2$$
$$3d_1 + 2d_2 + d_3 = b$$

The constants a and b are arbitrary, but they affect the shape of the curve to some extent. After a few trials, we choose the following values: $a = b = 3$. A script to determine the coefficients by solving the foregoing equations is

```
a = 3;
b = 3;
c = [0,0,0,1; 0,0,1,0; 1,1,1,1; 3,2,1,0]\[1; a; 4; 0]
d = [0,0,0,1; 0,0,1,0; 1,1,1,1; 3,2,1,0]\[1; 0; 2; b]
s = 0:0.01:1;
x = polyval(c,s); y = polyval(d,s);   plot(x,y)
```

The result is

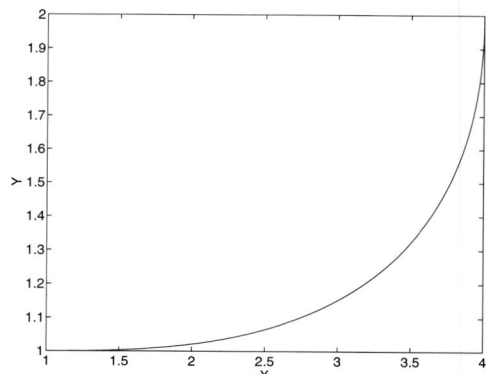

Figure 4.14 Curve determined by Hermite interpolation.

Section 4.8 Cubic Hermite Interpolation

```
c =
    -3.0000
     3.0000
     3.0000
     1.0000

d =
     1
     0
     0
     1
```

A plot of the cubic Hermite interpolation curve is shown in Figure 4.14.

Implementation of cubic Hermite interpolation can be simplified if the derivative boundary conditions are represented by a finite difference approximation, because then the Hermite interpolation can be implemented by means of the Lagrange interpolation. This approach is only an approximation, but the amount of error can be, practically, negligible. The boundary conditions given by Eq.(4.8.2) may be approximated by

$$\begin{aligned} f(s_1) &= f_1 \\ f(s_1 + \zeta) &\approx f_1 + \zeta f_1' \\ f(s_2) &= f_2 \\ f(s_2 - \zeta) &\approx f_2 - \zeta f_2' \end{aligned} \quad (4.8.3)$$

where ζ is an arbitrarily chosen parameter satisfying $\zeta \ll s_2 - s_1$. Then, a third-order polynomial can be determined to fit to the conditions of Eq.(4.8.3) by the Lagrange interpolation.

Example 4.7

Repeat the task of Example 4.6 by `polyfit`.

Solution

By applying Eq.(4.8.3), we set four data points as follows:

$$\begin{aligned} s = 0 &: \quad x = 1, \ y = 1 \\ s = \zeta &: \quad x = 1 + a\zeta, \ y = 0 \\ s = 1 - b\zeta &: \quad x = 4, \ y = 2 - b\zeta \\ s = 1 &: \quad x = 4, \ y = 2 \end{aligned}$$

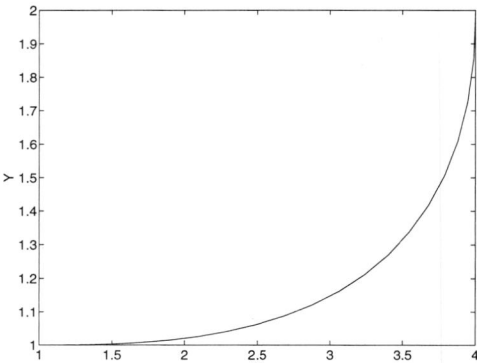

Figure 4.15 Hermite curve determined approximately by Lagrange interpolation.

The value ζ is an arbitrarily small positive quantity, so we set to $\zeta = 0.01$. If it is too small, however, rounding errors occur in determining the coefficients. The parameters a and b in the foregoing equations have similar roles to those they have in Example 4.6.

List 4.5 is a script to determine coefficients of cubic polynomials.

List 4.5
```
clear,clf,hold off
z=0.01; a=3; b=3;
s(1) = 0;         x(1) = 1;         y(1) = 1;
s(2) = z;         x(2) = 1+z*a;     y(2) = 1;
s(3) = 1 - z;     x(3) = 4;         y(3) = 2 - z*b;
s(4) = 1;         x(4) = 4;         y(4) = 2;
c=polyfit(s,x,length(s)-1)
d=polyfit(s,y,length(s)-1)
ss=0:0.1:1;
xp = polyval(c,ss);
yp = polyval(d,ss);
plot(xp,yp)
```

The result is:

```
c =
    -3.0921    3.1231    2.9691    1.0000
d =
     1.0307   -0.0309    0.0002    1.0000
```

These values are close to the coefficients determined in Example 4.6. The plot of the curve shown in Figure 4.15 agrees well with that of Figure 4.14.

4.9 TWO-DIMENSIONAL INTERPOLATION

bilinear interpolation: Data in a two-dimensional function table can be interpolated using linear interpolation twice.

The two-dimensional function table is an array of functional values $f_{i,j} = f(x_i, y_j)$ on a rectangular grid, (x_i, y_j). Suppose we have to estimate the functional value at a point located in a rectangular domain defined by $x_{i-1} \leq x \leq x_i$ and $y_{j-1} \leq y \leq y_j$, as shown in Figure 4.16. By linear interpolation in the y-direction, the values at E and F are found, respectively, as

$$f_E = \frac{y_j - y}{y_j - y_{j-1}} f_{i-1,j-1} + \frac{y - y_{j-1}}{y_j - y_{j-1}} f_{i-1,j}$$

$$f_F = \frac{y_j - y}{y_j - y_{j-1}} f_{i,j-1} + \frac{y - y_{j-1}}{y_j - y_{j-1}} f_{i,j}$$
(4.9.1)

Linear interpolation of f_E and f_F then yields

$$g(x,y) = \frac{x_i - x}{x_i - x_{i-1}} f_E + \frac{x - x_{i-1}}{x_i - x_{i-1}} f_F \quad (4.9.2)$$

Combining the two steps into one equation, the bilinear interpolation can be written as

$$g(x,y) = \frac{1}{(x_i - x_{i-1})(y_j - y_{j-1})} \times$$
$$[(x_i - x)(y_j - y)f_{i-1,j-1} + (x_i - x)(y - y_{j-1})f_{i-1,j}$$
$$+ (x - x_{i-1})(y_j - y)f_{i,j-1} + (x - x_{i-1})(y - y_{j-1})f_{i,j}](4.9.3)$$

In MATLAB, bilinear interpolation is performed by `table2`. Its synopsis is as follows:

```
g =table2(tab,x,y)
```

Here, g represents $g(x, y)$ of Eq.(4.9.3); `tab` is a two-dimensional data table. The first column of `tab` is the array of x_i values and the first row is the array of y_j values, both in increasing order. The remainder of columns and rows are occupied by $f_{i,j}$. The x and y are coordinates for which the interpolation is to be evaluated, and can be scalar, vector, or matrix.

double Lagrange interpolation: Double Lagrange interpolation is to apply the Lagrange interpolation method twice in two dimensions. Therefore, the interpolation uses all the data points in the table. Suppose the

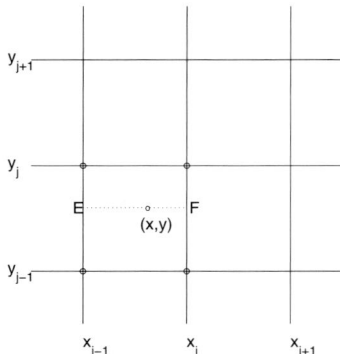

Figure 4.16 Bilinear interpolation in a two-dimensional domain.

function table has M columns and N rows. The coordinates of the points are denoted by (x_m, y_n), and the functional values by $f_{m,n}$. Then, double Lagrange interpolation is given by

$$g(x,y) = \sum_{m=1}^{M} \sum_{n=1}^{N} \phi_m(x)\psi_n(y) f_{m,n} \qquad (4.9.4)$$

where ϕ_m and ψ_n are shape functions given by

$$\phi_m(x) = \prod_{k=1, k \neq m}^{M} \frac{x - x_k}{x_m - x_k}$$

$$\psi_n(y) = \prod_{k=1, k \neq n}^{N} \frac{y - y_k}{y_n - y_k} \qquad (4.9.5)$$

Recognize that $\phi_m(x)\psi_n(y)$ is a two-dimensional shape function that becomes zero at all the data points except at (x_m, y_n). When $M = N = 2$, Eq.(4.9.4) reduces to the bilinear interpolation, Eq.(4.9.3). The Chebyshev or Lobatto points may be used to select x_m and y_n.

4.10 TRANSFINITE INTERPOLATION

Transfinite interpolation is an interpolation method for a two-dimensional space where the functional values along the external boundaries, as well as along the vertical and horizontal lines inside the boundaries, are known. The double interpolation method of Section 4.9 applies when functional values are

Section 4.10 Transfinite Interpolation

known only at the intersections of vertical and horizontal lines. In contrast to double interpolation, transfinite interpolation fits to continuous functions specified along the horizontal and vertical lines.

To illustrate an application of transfinite interpolation, imagine an architect designing a curved roof on a rectangular building, the top view of which satisfies

$$x_1 \leq x \leq x_2, \ y_1 \leq y \leq y_2$$

His client has specified the shape of the roof line along the four edges, which are four analytical functions expressing the height of the roof along the edges. These four functions are continuous through the corners, so no sudden change of height occurs at any corner of the roof. The architect needs to create a smooth surface that fits the edge heights of his client.

The task can be restated as follows: Determine a smooth function $g(x,y)$ that satisfies the boundary conditions given by

$$\begin{aligned} g(x_1, y) &= f_W(y) \\ g(x_2, y) &= f_E(y) \\ g(x, y_1) &= f_S(x) \\ g(x, y_2) &= f_N(x) \end{aligned} \tag{4.10.1}$$

where the right side of each equation is an analytical function that the client has given to the architect. We recognize that no unique solution exists to this problem since there is no unique way of interpolating given data. There are several possible ways to find such a function, however, among which are (1) to solve a Laplace equation

$$\nabla^2 g(x,y) = 0 \tag{4.10.2}$$

with the boundary conditions, and (2) transfinite interpolation.

The transfinite interpolation for this problem can be written as

$$g(x,y) = \sum_{m=1}^{2} \phi_m(x) f(x_m, y) + \sum_{n=1}^{2} \psi_n(y) f(x, y_n) \\ - \sum_{m=1}^{2} \sum_{n=1}^{2} \phi_m(x) \psi_n(y) f(x_m, y_n) \tag{4.10.3}$$

where

$$\phi_1(x) = \frac{x_2 - x}{x_2 - x_1}$$

$$\phi_2(x) = \frac{x - x_1}{x_2 - x_1}$$

$$\psi_1(y) = \frac{y_2 - y}{y_2 - y_1}$$

$$\psi_2(y) = \frac{y - y_1}{y_2 - y_1}$$

The transfinite interpolation is smooth and satisfies the boundary conditions.

The foregoing transfinite interpolation can be generalized to include the functions specified along multiple lines. Consider a rectangular domain divided by vertical and horizontal lines, as shown in Figure 4.17. The leftmost vertical line is the left boundary and the rightmost vertical line is the right boundary. The vertical lines are indexed by m, where the leftmost vertical lines are indexed by $m = 1$, while the last one is indexed by $m = M$. Likewise, the horizontal lines are indexed by n, where $n = 1$ is the bottom boundary and $n = N$ is the top boundary. Suppose the values of $f(x,y)$ are known along all the horizontal and vertical lines. The function given along the mth vertical line, $f(x_m, y)$, is set to the known function; that along the nth horizontal line, $f(x, y_n)$, is also set to the corresponding known function.

Then, finding $g(x,y)$ satisfying these conditions along the vertical and horizontal lines is the task. This problem can be restated as: find a smooth function $g(x,y)$ that satisfies

$$\begin{aligned} g(x,y) &= f(x_m, y), \quad \text{along } x = x_m \quad (m\text{th vertical line}) \\ g(x,y) &= f(x, y_n), \quad \text{along } y = y_n \quad (n\text{th horizontal line}) \end{aligned} \quad (4.10.4)$$

The transfinite interpolation satisfying the given conditions is

$$\begin{aligned} g(x,y) = &\sum_{m=1}^{M} \phi_m(x) f(x_m, y) + \sum_{n=1}^{N} \psi_n(y) f(x, y_n) \\ &- \sum_{m=1}^{M} \sum_{n=1}^{N} \phi_m(x) \psi_n(y) f(x_m, y_n) \end{aligned} \quad (4.10.5)$$

where

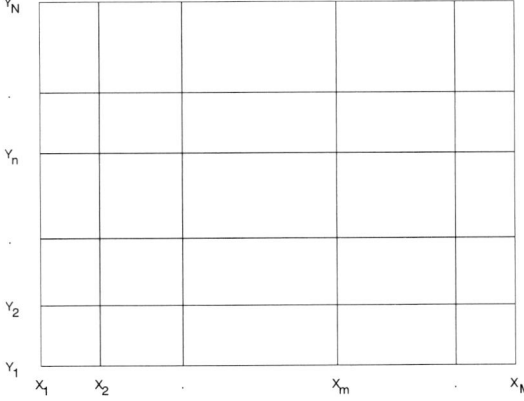

Figure 4.17 Domain for transfinite interpolations.

$$\begin{aligned}\phi_m(x) &= \prod_{k=1, k\neq m}^{M} \frac{x - x_k}{x_m - x_k} \\ \psi_n(y) &= \prod_{k=1, k\neq n}^{N} \frac{y - y_k}{y_n - y_k}\end{aligned} \qquad (4.10.6)$$

One can see that the first term of Eq.(4.10.5) is the Lagrange interpolation on the x-coordinate of the vertical lines, while the second term is the Lagrange interpolation on the y-coordinate of the functions given along the horizontal lines. The third term is a double Lagrange interpolation given by Eq.(4.9.4). The transfinite interpolation satisfies all the boundary conditions at the external boundaries as well as along the internal boundaries.

To clarify the relation between the transfinite interpolation method and the double Lagrange interpolation, assume that f values are known only at intersections (m, n). In this case, $g(x, y_n)$ and $g(x_m, y)$ can be expressed by Lagrange interpolation as follows:

$$\begin{aligned}g(x, y_n) &= \sum_{m=1}^{M} \phi_m(x) f(x_m, y_n) \\ g(x_m, y) &= \sum_{n=0}^{N} \psi_n(y) f(x_m, y_n)\end{aligned} \qquad (4.10.7)$$

When the foregoing equations are introduced into Eq.(4.10.5), all three terms on the right side become identical except for signs, so two of them cancel and the transfinite interpolation reduces to the double Lagrange interpolation given by Eq.(4.9.4) with $f_{m,n} = f(x_m, y_n)$.

Although we have assumed that the functions along the vertical and horizontal lines are analytical functions, a discretely defined function may be used instead, as illustrated in Example 4.8.

Example 4.8

In Table 4.1, the functional values are given along certain columns and rows. Fill in the blanks by transfinite interpolation.

Table 4.1 A Data Table Given for $F(x_i, y_j)$

j	i=1	2	3	4	5	6	7	8	9	10	11
1	0.2955	0.3894	0.4794	0.5646	0.6442	0.7174	0.7833	0.8415	0.8912	0.9320	0.9636
2	0.4794					0.8415					0.9975
3	0.6442					0.9320					0.9917
4	0.7833	0.8415	0.8912	0.9320	0.9636	0.9854	0.9975	0.9996	0.9917	0.9738	0.9463
5	0.8912					0.9996					0.8632
6	0.9636					0.9738					0.7457
7	0.9975	0.9996	0.9917	0.9738	0.9463	0.9093	0.8632	0.8085	0.7457	0.6755	0.5985

Solution

The table filled with the transfinite interpolation is shown in Table 4.2.

Table 4.2 Results of transfinite interpolation, $A(i,j)$

j	i=1	2	3	4	5	6	7	8	9	10	11
1	0.2955	0.3894	0.4794	0.5646	0.6442	0.7174	0.7833	0.8415	0.8912	0.9320	0.9636
2	0.4794	0.5647	0.6443	0.7174	0.7834	0.8415	0.8912	0.9320	0.9635	0.9854	0.9975
3	0.6442	0.7174	0.7834	0.8415	0.8912	0.9320	0.9635	0.9854	0.9974	0.9995	0.9917
4	0.7833	0.8415	0.8912	0.9320	0.9636	0.9854	0.9975	0.9996	0.9917	0.9738	0.9463
5	0.8912	0.9320	0.9635	0.9854	0.9975	0.9996	0.9917	0.9739	0.9464	0.9094	0.8632
6	0.9636	0.9854	0.9974	0.9995	0.9916	0.9738	0.9464	0.9094	0.8633	0.8086	0.7457
7	0.9975	0.9996	0.9917	0.9738	0.9463	0.9093	0.8632	0.8085	0.7457	0.6755	0.5985

4.11 M-FILES

FM 4-1. Integration of a polynomial
Purpose: Finding the coefficients of the integrated polynomial.
Synopsis: py = poly_itg(p)
        p: coefficients of the polynomial to be integrated.
        py: coefficients of the polynomial after integration.

poly_itg.m
```
function py = poly_itg(p)
n=length(p)
py = [p.*[n:-1:1].^(-1),0]
```

FM 4-2. Adding two polynomials
Purpose: Adding two polynomials.
Synopsis: b = poly_add(p1,p2)
        p1, p2: arrays of coefficients of the two polynomials.
        b : array of coefficients after addition.

poly_add.m
```
function p3 = poly_add(p1,p2)
n1=length(p1); n2 = length(p2);
if n1==n2 p3 = p1 + p2; end
if n1>n2  p3 = p1 + [zeros(1,n1-n2) ,p2];end
if n1<n2  p3 = [zeros(1,n2-n1) ,p1] + p2; end
```

FM 4-3. Lagrange interpolation
Purpose: To interpolate data by Lagrange interpolation.
Synopsis: yi = Lagran_(x,y,xi)
        x, y: data table in array form.
        xi : array of abscissas for which y values are to be computed.
        yi : array of y values computed by Lagrange interpolation.

Lagran_.m
```
function fi = Lagran_(x, f, xi)
fi=zeros(size(xi));
np1=length(f);
for i=1:np1
  z=ones(size(xi));
  for j=1:np1
    if i~=j, z = z.*(xi - x(j))/(x(i)-x(j));end
```

```
    end
    fi=fi+z*f(i);
end
return
```

FM 4-4. Shape function in power series form
Purpose: To expand Lagrange interpolation into power series.
Synopsis: c = shape_pw(x)
      c: power coefficients of all the shape functions. The jth row becomes the power coefficients of the jth shape function.
      x: abscissas of data table in array form.

shape_pw.m
```
function p = shape_pw(x)
np = length(x);
for j=1:np
    y = zeros(1,np); y(j) = 1;
    p(j,:)=polyfit(x,y,np-1);
end
```

FM 4-5. Chebyshev polynomial in power series form
Purpose: To expand the power coefficients of a Chebyshev polynomial.
Synopsis: c = Cheby_pw
      c: power coefficients in array form.
      n: order of Chebyshev polynomial.

Cheby_pw.m
```
function pn = Cheby_pw(n)
pbb=[1];   if n==0, pn=pbb; break; end
pb=[1 0];  if n==1, pn=pb;  break; end
for i=2:n;
    pn=   2*[pb,0] - [0, 0, pbb] ;
    pbb=pb; pb=pn;
end
```

FM 4-6. Legendre polynomial in power series form
Purpose: To find power coefficients of a Legendre polynomial.
Synopsis: c = Legen_pw(n)
      c: power coefficients in array form.
      n: order of Chebyshev polynomial.

Legen_pw.m
```
function pn = Legen_pw(n)
pbb=[1];   if n==0, pn=pbb; break; end
pb=[1 0];  if n==1, pn=pb;  break; end
for i=2:n;
   pn=  ( (2*i-1)*[pb,0] - (i-1)*[0, 0, pbb] )/i;
   pbb=pb; pb=pn;
end
```

PROBLEMS

(4.1) Rewrite the following polynomials into the clustered form:
$$y = x^4 - 3x^3 + 2x^2 + x + 2$$
$$y = 3x^5 + 2x^3 + x^2 + 7$$

(4.2) Rewrite the polynomials of Problem 4.1 into the factorized form.

(4.3) Rewrite the following polynomials into the power series form using (a) `poly`, and (b) `polyfit`:
$$y = 5(x-3)(x-4)(x+1)(x+3)$$
$$y = 4x(x-2)(x-1)(x+3)(x+5)$$

(4.4) (a) Find the polynomial fitted to data points 2, 3, 4, and 5 of the following data:

k	x_k	$f(x_k)$
1	0	0.9162
2	0.25	0.8109
3	0.5	0.6931
4	0.75	0.5596
5	1.0	0.4055

(b) Transform the polynomial to the clustered form. (c) Transform the polynomial to the factorized form.

(4.5) Convert the following polynomial to the power series form using `polyfit`:
$$v(x) = \frac{(x-1)(x-2.5)(x-4)(x-6.1)(x-7.2)(x-10)}{(5-1)(5-2.5)(5-4)(5-6.1)(5-7.2)(5-10)}$$

(4.6) Repeat Problem 4.5 using `poly`.

(4.7) A polynomial has three roots: -2, 1, and 2. If the polynomial y becomes $y(0) = 1$, determine the polynomial in the power series form.

(4.8) Determine the polynomial in the power series form that passes through each of the following data sets:

    (a)   (0,1), (2,0)

    (b)   (1,1), (2,0), (4,2)

    (c)   (−1,2), (0,2.5), (1,1), (2,−1)

Work with Eq.(4.3.3) first, and then verify the results by `polyfit`.

(4.9) Determine the polynomial in the power series form that passes through each of the following data sets:

    (a)   (−1,1), (1,4)

    (b)   (−2,2), (0,−1), (2,1)

    (c)   (−1,−1), (0,0), (1,2), (2,5)

Work with Eq.(4.3.3) first, and then verify the results by `polyfit`.

(4.10) Write a linear interpolation formula that approximates $\sin(x)$ in the interval of $0 \leq x \leq \pi/4$ using the values at $x = 0$ and $x = \pi/4$. Find the maximum error of the interpolation and at what x it occurs by plotting the error.

(4.11) Knowing that $\max|f''| \approx 0.3827$ in $0 \leq x \leq \pi/4$, predict the maximum possible error of the linear interpolation determined in Problem 4.10, using Eq.(4.2.3).

(4.12) (a) Find the polynomial in the power series form fitted to the data points, $k = 2$, 3, and 4, given in the following table:

k	x_k	$f(x_k)$
1	0	0.9162
2	0.25	0.8109
3	0.5	0.6931
4	0.75	0.5596
5	1.0	0.4055

    (b) Evaluate the polynomial for $x = 0.6$.

(4.13) Find the polynomial fitted to data points 2, 3, 4, and 5 of Problem 4.12 in the power series form.

(4.14) Using the data table given in Problem 4.12, estimate the x values that satisfy $f(x) = 0.4137, 0.7233$, and 0.8501, using `interp1` for linear interpolations.

(4.15) (a) Write the polynomial $y(x)$ in the power series fitted to the following data points:

k	x_k	$f(x_k)$
1	0	1.21
2	0.5	1.32
3	2.0	1.05
4	2.5	0.97

(b) Evaluate its value and the first derivative of the polynomial at $x = 1.75$.

(4.16) (a) Write the Lagrange interpolation that passes through the following data points:

x	0	0.4	0.8	1.2
f	1.0	1.491	2.225	3.320

(b) Knowing $f''''(0.6) = 1.822$, estimate the error at $x = 0.2$, 0.6, and 1.0 by Eq.(4.5.4) with $\xi_i = x_m$. (In case f'''' is not known, an approximation for f'''' may be calculated by a difference approximation if one more data point is available from the functional table.)

(c) Given the fact that the data table has been obtained from $f(x) = \exp(x)$, evaluate the error of the interpolation formula at $x = 0.2$, 0.6, and 1.0 by $e(x) = f(x) - g(x) = \exp(x) - g(x)$.

(4.17) Repeat Problem 4.15 by the Lagrange interpolation fitted to all the data points.

(4.18) Fit $x\sin(x)$ in $0 \le x \le \pi/2$ with the Lagrange interpolation polynomial of order 4, using equispaced points. Calculate the error of each interpolation formula at every increment of $\pi/16$, and plot.

(4.19) (a) Write a program to evaluate the Lagrange interpolation for $y = x\cos(x)$ in $0 \le x \le 2$ with six equally spaced grid points with $h = 0.4$.

(b) Calculate the error of the interpolating polynomial at each increment of 0.1 of x. Plot the error distribution.

(4.20) Fit $\sin(x)$ in $0 \le x \le 2\pi$ by the Lagrange interpolation polynomial of order 4 and 8 using equispaced points (5 and 9 points, respectively). Plot the interpolating polynomials together with $\sin(x)$, and the error distributions.

(4.21) (a) Write the Lagrange interpolation formula fitted to:

x	0.5	1.0	1.5	2.0
y	y_1	y_2	y_3	y_4

where y_k are unknown values. (b) Convert the interpolation formula to the power series form. (c) Derive the first derivative of the polynomial.

(4.22) Approximate
$$y = \frac{1+x}{1+2x+3x^2}$$
in $0 \le x \le 5$ by the Lagrange interpolation of order 4, and evaluate the error by $e(x) = y - g(x)$. Work according to the following steps: (a) determine the points, (b) write the Lagrange interpolation, (c) calculate the error for each increment of 0.2 in x, and (d) plot the error distribution.

(4.23) If a Lagrange interpolation is fitted to four data points at $x_i = 1, 2, 3$, and 4, the following cubic polynomials appear in the Lagrange interpolation formula:

$$\frac{(x-2)(x-3)(x-4)}{(1-2)(1-3)(1-4)}$$

$$\frac{(x-1)(x-3)(x-4)}{(2-1)(2-3)(2-4)}$$

$$\frac{(x-1)(x-2)(x-4)}{(3-1)(3-2)(3-4)}$$

$$\frac{(x-1)(x-2)(x-3)}{(4-1)(4-2)(4-3)}$$

Plot the four functions above and discuss implications of the shape of each.

(4.24) The Lagrange interpolation of order N fitted to $N+1$ points of a function $f(x)$ becomes exact if $f(x)$ is a polynomial of order N or less. Explain the reason in two different ways.

(4.25) Using Eq.(4.7.1), derive the following Chebyshev polynomials and plot: T_4, T_5, T_6.

(4.26) (a) Develop a Lagrange interpolation approximation for $\log_e(x)$ in $1 \le x \le 2$ using four Chebyshev points. (b) Calculate actual error by $e(x) = \log_e(x) - g(x)$ and plot for $x = 1, 1.2, 1.3,...$ 1.9, and 2.0.

(4.27) The Legendre polynomials satisfy the orthogonality relation:

$$\int_{-1}^{1} P_m(x) P_n(x) dx = \begin{Bmatrix} 0, & \text{if } m \ne n \\ \dfrac{2}{2n+1}, & \text{if } m = n \end{Bmatrix}$$

Verify the foregoing relation by computing

$$a_{m,n} = \int_{-1}^{1} P_m(x) P_n(x) dx$$

for $m = 1$ through 5 and n=1 through 5. Hint : use `poly_itg` explained in Section 4.1. Organize the results in a tabular form.

Chapter 5

NUMERICAL INTEGRATION

Numerical integration schemes allow integration of functions that are analytically defined or given in a tabular form. The basic principle of numerical integration schemes is to fit a polynomial to functional data points and then integrate it. Therefore, by changing the distribution of the abscissas of the data points, many different integration schemes can be derived. In this chapter, we will start with two simple but most frequently used methods, namely, trapezoidal and Simpson's rules, followed by a more general derivation of the Newton-Cotes closed formulas and Gauss quadrature. We will also study numerical computations of improper integrals and double integrals.

5.1 TRAPEZOIDAL RULE

The trapezoidal rule is a numerical integration method derived by integrating the linear interpolation formula. Suppose we evaluate

$$I = \int_a^b f(x)dx \qquad (5.1.1)$$

We approximate $f(x)$ by a linear interpolation

$$g(x) = \frac{b-x}{b-a}f_1 + \frac{x-a}{b-a}f_2 \qquad (5.1.2)$$

where

$$f_1 = f(a)$$
$$f_2 = f(b)$$

Then, Eq.(5.1.1) becomes

$$I = \int_a^b f(x)dx \approx \int_a^b g(x)dx = \frac{h}{2}(f_1 + f_2) \qquad (5.1.3)$$

with

$$h = b - a \tag{5.1.4}$$

Equation (5.1.3) is the trapezoidal rule. We can rewrite it as

$$I = \int_a^b f(x)dx = \frac{h}{2}(f_1 + f_2) + E \tag{5.1.5}$$

where E represents the truncation error. The trapezoidal rule is graphically illustrated in Figure 5.1. The area under the line interpolation, $g(x)$, equals the integral computed by the trapezoidal rule, while the area under $y = f(x)$ is the exact value. The error of Eq.(5.1.3), therefore, is equal to the area between $g(x)$ and $f(x)$, and is approximately,

$$E \approx -\frac{1}{12}h^3 f'' \tag{5.1.6}$$

where f'' is the second derivative of $f(x)$, crudely somewhere in $a \leq x \leq b$. This equation indicates that the error decreases in proportion to h^3 as h is decreased, but is seldom used to estimate the actual error.

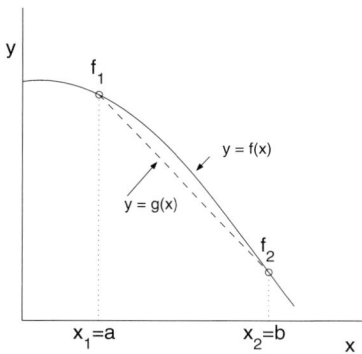

Figure 5.1 Trapezoidal rule.

Equation (5.1.6) may be verified easily as follows: First, expand $f(x)$ into the Taylor expansion about a selected point, say $x = a$. By integrating the Taylor expansion, the exact integral is expressed in power series form. On the other hand, the result of the trapezoidal rule may also be expressed in power series form by expanding f_2 into the Taylor series about the same point $x = a$. By subtracting the latter from the former and keeping the leading term, Eq.(5.1.6) is obtained.

The trapezoidal rule can be extended to multiple intervals. If the function integrated is represented by $n + 1$ data with equally spaced abscissa points,

Eq.(5.1.5) is applied repeatedly to each interval, as illustrated in Figure 5.2. The equation thus obtained is the extended trapezoidal rule and is written as

$$I = \int_a^b f(x)dx = \frac{h}{2}(f_1 + 2f_2 + ... + 2f_n + f_{n+1}) + E \qquad (5.1.7)$$

with

$$h = (b-a)/n$$
$$x_i = a + (i-1)h$$
$$f_i = f(x_i)$$
$$i = 1, 2, .., n+1$$

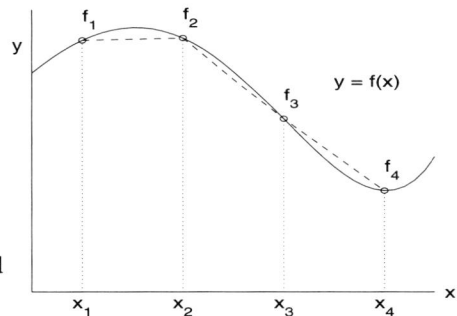

Figure 5.2 Extended trapezoidal rule.

The error term of the extended trapezoidal rule is given by

$$E \approx -\frac{b-a}{12}h^2 \overline{f''} \qquad (5.1.8)$$

or equivalently

$$E \approx -\frac{(b-a)^3}{12n^2}\overline{f''} \qquad (5.1.9)$$

where $\overline{f''}$ is the average of $f''(x)$ in $a < x < b$. The foregoing equation indicates that the error is inversely proportional to n^2.

Suppose f is an array of f_i for equispaced abscissa points with an interval size h. The extended trapezoidal rule may be written in MATLAB as

```
I = h*(sum(f) - 0.5*(f(1) + f(length(f))))
```

A more convenient way of applying the trapezoidal rule is to use `trapez_v`, `trapez_n`, or `trapez_g` listed in Section 5.7, although these m-files must have been installed in your working directory.[1] Its synopsis of `trapez_v` is

```
I = trapez_v(f, h)
```

where `f` is a vector of the ordinates of the integrand and `h` is the interval size. Synopses of `trapez_n` and `trapez_g` are

```
I = trapez_n('f_name', a, b, n)
I = trapez_g('f_name', a, b, n)
```

where `f_name` is the name of the function to be integrated, `a` and `b` are limits of integration, and `n` is the number of intervals used in the extended trapezoidal rule. The name of a user-defined function m-file may be used for `f_name`.

Example 5.1

An automobile of mass $M = 2000$kg is cruising at a speed of 30m/s. The engine is suddenly disengaged at $t = 0$s. Assume that the equation of cruising after $t = 0$ is given by

$$2000\, u\frac{du}{dx} = -8.1u^2 - 1200 \tag{A}$$

where u is the velocity and x is the linear distance of the car measured from the location at $t = 0$. The left side is the force of acceleration, the first term on the right side is the aerodynamic resistance, and the second term is the rolling resistance. Calculate how far the car moves before the speed reduces to 15m/s.

Solution

We rewrite Eq.(A) to

$$\frac{2000\, udu}{-8.1u^2 - 1200} = dx$$

Integrating yields

$$\int_{15}^{30} \frac{2000\, udu}{8.1u^2 + 1200} = \int_0^x dx' = x \tag{B}$$

---

[1] *Reminder* See "How to obtain the m-file package" in the "Preface."

where the sign on the left side of Eq.(B) has been changed by switching the limits of integration. To evaluate the integral on the left side, we use the extended trapezoidal rule. If we use 15 intervals (or 16 data points), u_i is first set to

$$u_i = 15 + (i-1)\Delta u, \quad i = 1, 2, ..., 16$$

where $\Delta u = (30-15)/15 = 1$. By defining

$$f_i = \frac{200 \, u_i}{8.1 u_i^2 + 1200}$$

and applying the trapezoidal integration, Eq.(A) becomes

$$x \approx \Delta u \left[\sum_{i=1}^{16} f_i - 0.5(f_1 + f_{16}) \right]$$

A script to compute the foregoing equation follows:

List 5.1
```
clear
n_points=16 ; i = 1:n_points;
h=(30-15)/(n_points-1); u = 15 + (i-1)*h;
f = 2000*u./(8.1*u.^2 + 1200);
x = h*(sum(f) - 0.5*(f(1) + f(length(f))))
```

The result is

```
x =
    127.50
```

Compare this to the exact solution, 127.51m (the error is 0.005%).

Example 5.2

Knowing that the exact answer is $I = 4.006994$, analyze the effect of the number of intervals, n, on the errors of the trapezoidal rule applied to the following integral:

$$I = \int_0^2 \sqrt{1 + \exp(x)} \, dx$$

Solution

The following script is written to answer the question:

List 5.2
```
clear;   Iexact = 4.006994;
a = 0; b=2;
fprintf('\n Extended Trapezoidal Rule\n');
fprintf('\n   n           I             Error\n');
n = 1;
for k=1:6
   n = 2*n;
   h = (b-a)/n;    i = 1:n+1;
   x = a + (i-1)*h;    f = sqrt(1 + exp(x));
   I = trapez_v(f,h);
   fprintf('     %3.0f    %10.5f    %10.5f\n', ...
                       n,        I,    Iexact - I);
end
```

The result is:

```
Extended Trapezoidal Rule
    n        I         Error
    2     4.08358     0.07659
    4     4.02619     0.01919
    8     4.01180     0.00480
   16     4.00819     0.00120
   32     4.00729     0.00030
   64     4.00707     0.00008
```

As n is doubled, the error decreases approximately by a factor of 4 (see Eq.(5.1.9)).

Example 5.2 indicates that errors of the extended trapezoidal rule decrease to approximately one-fourth whenever the number of intervals is doubled. The trend can be verified by Eq.(5.1.8). Knowing this behavior, we can eliminate at least a major part of the errors. If we denote the result of the extended trapezoidal rule with n intervals by I_n and that with $2n$ by I_{2n}, then $I_n - I_{2n}$ must equal approximately three times the error of I_{2n}. Subtracting the error thus estimated, the result should become significantly more accurate. The formula based on this principle is named Romberg integration, and written as

$$I = I_{2n} - \frac{1}{3}(I_n - I_{2n}) \qquad (5.1.10)$$

The result, however, becomes identical to the Simpson's 1/3 rule using $2n$ intervals (see Section 5.2).

5.2 SIMPSON'S RULES

There are two Simpson's rules; namely, the 1/3 and 3/8 rules, which are complementary to each other. Considering evaluation of Eq.(5.1.1) again, a quadratic (second order) interpolation polynomial may be determined with three data points at $x_1 = a$, $x_2 = (a+b)/2$, and $x_3 = b$. We denote the functional values at the data points by f_1, f_2, and f_3 as shown in Figure 5.3. Simpson's 1/3 rule is derived by substituting this quadratic polynomial to $f(x)$ in Eq.(5.1.1):

$$I \approx \frac{h}{3}(f_1 + 4f_2 + f_3) \tag{5.2.1}$$

where

$$h = (b-a)/2$$

Including the error term, Eq.(5.2.1) may be written as

$$I = \frac{h}{3}(f_1 + 4f_2 + f_3) + E \tag{5.2.2}$$

where E is the error term given by

$$E \approx -\frac{h^5}{90} f'''' \tag{5.2.3}$$

which indicates that the error is proportional to h^5. The error vanishes if $f(x)$ happens to be a polynomial of order 3 or less. Equation (5.2.3) may be verified as follows. The exact integral may be expressed in a power series form by integrating the Taylor expansion of $f(x)$ about $x = a$. On the other hand, f_2 and f_3 in Eq.(5.2.1) may be expanded into Taylor series about

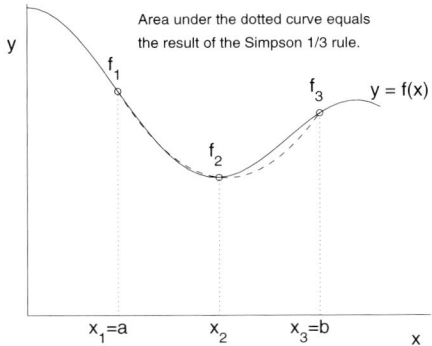

Figure 5.3 Simpson's 1/3 rule uses three points fitted by a quadratic polynomial.

$x = a$. After expressing both the exact integral and Simpson's 1/3 rule in power series forms, we subtract the latter from the former, and keep only the leading term.

The extended Simpson's 1/3 rule is a repeated application of Eq.(5.2.1) for a domain divided into an even number of intervals. Denoting the total number of intervals by n(even), the extended Simpson's 1/3 rule is written as

$$I = \int_a^b f(x)dx$$
$$= \frac{h}{3}(f_1 + 4f_2 + 2f_3 + 4f_4 + \ldots + 2f_{n-1} + 4f_n + f_{n+1}) + E \quad (5.2.4)$$

where

$$f_i = f(a + (i-1)h) \quad (5.2.5)$$

with

$$h = (b-a)/n \quad (5.2.6)$$

The error term is given by

$$E \approx -(b-a)\frac{h^4}{180}\overline{f''''} \quad (5.2.7)$$

where $\overline{f''''}$ is the average of f'''' in $a < x < b$.

Example 5.3

Evaluate the integral in Example 5.2 again by the extended Simpson's 1/3 rule with $n = 2, 4, 8,$ and 16.

Solution

The question is answered by the following script:

```
List 5.3
clear
Iexact = 4.006994;
a = 0; b=2;
fprintf('\n Extended Simpson 1/3 Rule\n');
fprintf('n              I              Error\n');
n = 1;
for k=1:4,    n = 2*n;
   h = (b-a)/n;    i = 1:n+1;
```

Section 5.2 Simpson's Rules

```
        x = a + (i-1)*h;   f = sqrt(1 + exp(x));
        I =   (h/3)*( f(1)+ 4*sum(f(2:2:n)) + f(n+1));
        if n>2, I = I+ (h/3)*2*sum(f(3:2:n)); end
        fprintf('%3.0f %10.5f    %10.5f\n', n,I,Iexact-I);
    end
```

The results are:

```
Extended Simpson 1/3 Rule
    n       I           Error
    2     4.00791     0.00092
    4     4.00705     0.00006
    8     4.00700     0.00000
   16     4.00699     0.00000
```

Simpson's 3/8 rule uses three intervals rather than two. It is based on the third-order interpolation polynomial and is given by

$$I = \frac{3h}{8}(f_1 + 3f_2 + 3f_3 + f_4) + E \tag{5.2.8}$$

where $h = (b-a)/3$, $f_i = f(a + (i-1)h)$, and E represents the error. The error term is given by

$$E \approx -\frac{3h^5}{80} f'''' \tag{5.2.9}$$

The foregoing expression for the error can be derived by the Taylor expansion in a manner similar to that described for Simpson's 1/3 rule.

The 3/8 rule may be extended but its extension is applicable only to a multiple of three intervals. It is often used as a complement to the 1/3 rule as follows: The extended Simpson's 1/3 rule is not applicable if the number of intervals is odd. In this case, the 3/8 rule is applied to the first or last three intervals, and then the extended 1/3 rule is applied to the remainder of the intervals. Since the order of error of the 3/8 rule is the same as that of the 1/3 rule, the two rules blend well without losing their order of accuracy.[2]

Two functions, Simps_v and Simps_n included in the M-files Package, may be used to integrate a function. The synopsis of the former is

```
    I = Simps_v(f,h)
```

---

[2] If Simpson's rule is blended with the trapezoidal rule, the order of accuracy of the combined scheme becomes that of the trapezoidal rule.

where `f` is the vector containing the ordinates of the integrand with an equispaced interval size `h`. The number of the intervals is arbitrary, except that it must be at least 2. If the number of intervals is odd, the 3/8 rule is applied first, and then the 1/3 rule is applied to the remainder of intervals, as explained in the preceding paragraphs. The synopsis of `Simps_n` is

```
I = Simps_n('f_name', a, b, n)
```

where `f_name` is the name of the function (or function m-file name), `a` and `b` are limits of integration, and `n` is the number of intervals used in the extended trapezoidal rule. More details of the functions are explained in Section 5.7.

Example 5.4

A spherical water reservoir of radius 5m is full to the top. Water is to be drained from the hole of radius $b = 0.1$m at the bottom, starting at $t = 0$s. If there is no friction, how much time does it take to drain the water until the water level reaches 0.5m measured from the bottom?

Solution

The velocity of the water draining from the hole is determined by the energy equation:

$$g(z + R) = \frac{u^2}{2} \tag{A}$$

where u is the velocity, z is the level of water measured from the horizontal line passing through the spherical center, R is the radius of the tank, and g is the gravity acceleration that equals 9.81m/s^2. Consider the change of the water level dz during time interval dt. The volume of water in dz equals $\pi x^2 dz$, where x is the radius of the circular water surface at elevation z. The flow continuity relation can be written:

$$uA dt = -\pi x^2 dz \tag{B}$$

where A is the cross-sectional area of the exit hole given by

$$A = \pi b^2 \tag{C}$$

The radius of the water surface r is related to z by

$$R^2 = z^2 + r^2 \tag{D}$$

Eliminating u, r, and A from Eq.(B) by Eqs.(A), (C), and (D) yields

$$dt = -\frac{R^2 - z^2}{b^2\sqrt{2g(z+R)}}dz$$

Notice that the level of water at the top of the tank is $z = R$, while that at 0.5m from the bottom is $z = -0.9R$. By integrating from $z = R$ to $-0.9R$, we get

$$t = -\int_R^{-0.9R} \frac{R^2 - z^2}{b^2\sqrt{2g(z+R)}}dz = \int_{-0.9R}^R \frac{R^2 - z^2}{b^2\sqrt{2g(z+R)}}dz$$

where the lower and upper limits of integration have been interchanged. Now we evaluate the foregoing equation by the extended Simpson's rule:

```
clear
R = 5;  g= 9.81;  b = 0.1;
z1=-R*0.90;  z2 = R;   h = (z2 - z1)/20;
z= z1:h:z2;
f = (R^2 - z.^2)./( b^2*sqrt(2*g*(z+R)));
I = Simps_v(f,h)/3600
```

The result is

```
0.5145   hour
```

5.3 OTHER QUADRATURES

As we pointed out previously, many other numerical quadratures are derived by integrating different interpolation polynomials. We explain a few of them here.

Newton-Cotes closed formulas: The Newton-Cotes closed formula of order n uses $n + 1$ data points with equispaced intervals. The abscissas of data points are

$$x_i = \frac{b-a}{n}(i-1) + a, \quad i = 1, 2, ..., n+1 \tag{5.3.1}$$

and ordinates of the data points are $f_i = f(x_i)$. Then, the Newton-Cotes closed formulas may be written as

$$I = \int_a^b f(x)dx \approx h \sum_{i=1}^{n+1} w_i f_i \tag{5.3.2}$$

where $n+1$ is the total number of points, w_is are weights given in Table 5.1, and

$$h = \frac{b-a}{n}$$

For $n = 1$, 2, and 3, Eq.(5.3.2) becomes the trapezoidal rule, Simpson's 1/3 rule, and Simpson's 3/8 rule, respectively.

Table 5.1 Weights of Newton-Cotes Closed Formulas

$n=1$	i:	0	1		
	w:	0.5000,0000	0.5000,0000		
$n=2$	i:	0	1	2	
	w:	0.3333,3333	1.3333,3333	0.3333,3333	
$n=3$	i:	0	1	2	3
	w:	0.3750,0000	1.1250,0000	1.1250,0000	0.3750,0000
$n=4$	i:	0 4	1	2	3
	w:	0.3111,1111 0.3111,1111	1.4222,2222	0.5333,3333	1.4222,2222
$n=5$	i:	0 4	1 5	2	3
	w:	0.3298,6111 1.3020,8333	1.3020,8333 0.3298,6111	0.8680,5555	0.8680,5555
$n=6$	i:	0 4	1 5	2 6	3
	w:	0.2928,5714 0.1928,5714	1.5428,5714 1.5428,5714	0.1928,5714 0.2928,5714	1.9428,5714
$n=7$	i:	0 4	1 5	2 6	3 7
	w:	0.3042,2453 1.2108,2175	1.4490,1620 0.5359,3749	0.5359,3749 1.4490,1620	1.2108,2175 0.3042,2453
$n=8$	i:	0 4 8	1 5	2 6	3 7
	w:	0.2790,8289 -1.2811,2874 0.2790,8289	1.6615,1675 2.9618,3421	-0.2618,6948 -0.2618,6948	2.9618,3421 1.6615,1675

To show how to derive Eq.(5.3.2), we write the Lagrange interpolation formula fitted to $f(x)$ in $a \leq x \leq b$ with equispaced points x_i as

$$g(x) = \sum_{i=1}^{n+1} v_i(x) f_i \tag{5.3.3}$$

where

$$v_i(x) = \prod_{j=1, j \neq i}^{n+1} \frac{(x - x_j)}{(x_i - x_j)} \tag{5.3.4}$$

Approximating $f(x)$ by $g(x)$ in Eq.(5.3.2) yields

$$I = \int_a^b f(x) dx \approx \int_a^b g(x) dx = \sum_{i=1}^{n+1} \gamma_i f_i \tag{5.3.5}$$

where

$$\gamma_i = \int_a^b v_i(x) dx = \int_a^b \prod_{j=1, j \neq i}^{n+1} \frac{(x - x_j)}{(x_i - x_j)} dx \tag{5.3.6}$$

To evaluate (5.3.6), we define a new variable by

$$s = \frac{x - a}{h} + 1 \tag{5.3.7}$$

where $h = (b - a)/n$ as mentioned before. In terms of s, Eq.(5.3.6) becomes

$$\gamma_i = h \int_1^{n+1} \prod_{j=1, j \neq i}^{n+1} \frac{(s - j)}{(i - j)} ds \tag{5.3.8}$$

or equivalently

$$\gamma_i = h w_i \tag{5.3.9}$$

with

$$w_i = \int_1^{n+1} \prod_{j=1, j \neq i}^{n+1} \frac{(s - j)}{(i - j)} ds \tag{5.3.10}$$

Notice in Eq.(5.3.10) that w_i is determined by i and n only. We convert the integrand of Eq.(5.3.10) to a power series form,

$$\prod_{j=1, j \neq i}^{n+1} \frac{(s - j)}{(i - j)} = \sum_{k=1}^{n+1} a_{i,k} s^{n+1-k} \tag{5.3.11}$$

The left side of Eq.(5.3.11) is a polynomial passing through the points

$$s = [1, 2, 3, ..., n+1]$$
$$y = [0, 0, ...1, ...0]$$

where the elements of y are all zero except that the i-th element is unity. The power coefficients $a_{i,k}$s are obtained by `polyfit` as

```
s = 1:n+1;
y = eye(n+1);
for i=1:n+1
    a(i,:) = polyfit(s,y(i,:))
end
```

where the i-th row of a contains the power coefficients, $a_{i,j}$s, for $i = 1, 2, ..n+1$. Introducing Eq.(5.3.11) into Eq.(5.3.10) yields

$$\begin{aligned} w_i &= \int_1^{n+1} \left(\sum_{k=1}^{n+1} a_{i,k} s^{n+1-k} \right) ds \\ &= \sum_{k=1}^{n+1} a_{i,k} \int_1^{n+1} s^{n+1-k} ds \\ &= \sum_{k=1}^{n+1} a_{i,k} \left[\frac{s^{n+2-k}}{n+2-k} \right]_{s=1}^{s=n+1} \\ &= \sum_{k=1}^{n+1} a_{i,k} \frac{(n+1)^{n+2-k} - 1}{n+2-k} \end{aligned} \quad (5.3.12)$$

Thus, the weights of the Newton-Cotes quadrature listed in Table 5.1 are computed by Eq.(5.3.12).

An analytical function may be integrated by `Newt_itg`. Its synopsis is

```
I = Newt_itg('f_name', a, b, n)
```

where `f_name` is the name of a function m-file that defines the integrand; `a` and `b` are lower and upper limits, respectively; and `n` is the number of equispaced intervals between the two integrating limits.

Gauss-Legendre quadrature: The accuracy of integration can be significantly increased using nonequispaced points. The Gauss-Legendre quadrature uses roots of a Legendre polynomial. Its order of accuracy becomes twice as high as the Newton-Cotes formula using the same number of points.

The Legendre polynomials are given by

$$P_0(x) = 1$$
$$P_1(x) = x$$
$$P_2(x) = \frac{1}{2}(3x^2 - 1)$$
$$P_3(x) = \frac{1}{2}(5x^3 - 3x) \quad (5.3.13)$$
$$\cdots$$
$$P_n(x) = \frac{2n-1}{n}xP_{n-1}(x) - \frac{n-1}{n}P_{n-2}(x)$$

The coefficients of a Legendre polynomial in the power form,

$$P_n(x) = c_1 x^n + c_2 x^{n-1} + \ldots + c_{n+1} \quad (5.3.14)$$

can be obtained by Legen_pw(n) (listed in FM 5-5), which will return the coefficients in an array where n is the order of the Legendre polynomial. The roots of the Legendre polynomial of order n has n roots that are all between -1 and 1, as illustrated in Figure 5.4 for $n = 7$. Notice that no roots are located at the endpoints, and that the interval size decreases toward the edges.

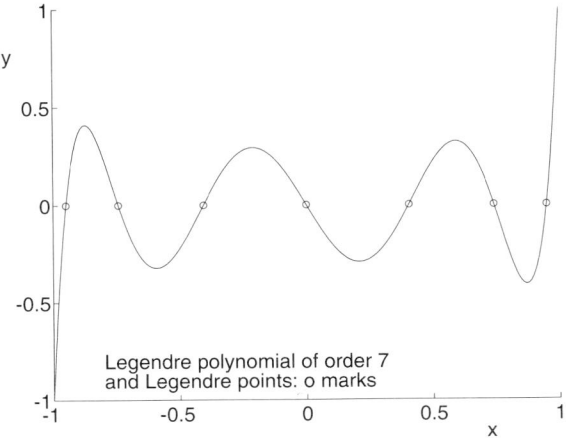

Figure 5.4 Legendre polynomial of order 7 and its roots.

We will first consider evaluation of the integral extended from $x = -1$ to $x = 1$:

$$I = \int_{-1}^{1} f(x)dx \tag{5.3.15}$$

The Gauss-Legendre quadrature of order n to evaluate Eq.(5.3.15) may be stated as follows: The integrand is approximated by an interpolation polynomial fitted at the roots of the nth-order Legendre polynomial, which is then integrated. The Gauss-Legendre quadrature is written as

$$I \approx \int_{-1}^{1} g(x)dx = \sum_{i=1}^{n} w_i f(x_i) \tag{5.3.16}$$

with

$$w_i = \int_{-1}^{1} v_i(x)dx = \int_{-1}^{1} \prod_{j=1, j \neq i}^{n} \frac{(x - x_j)}{(x_i - x_j)} dx \tag{5.3.17}$$

where x_is are the roots of the Legendre polynomial of order n. The values of w_i and x_i are tabulated in Table 5.2.

When the integrating limits are not -1 and 1, the roots between -1 and 1 are mapped between the actual limits, a and b, by a coordinate transformation. For an integral,

$$I = \int_{a}^{b} f(z)dz \tag{5.3.18}$$

the Gauss-Legendre quadrature is written as

$$I \approx \frac{b-a}{2} \sum_{i=1}^{n} w_i f(z_i) \tag{5.3.19}$$

where z_i is given by the transformation:

$$z_i = \frac{(b-a)x_i + a + b}{2} \tag{5.3.20}$$

and satisfies $a < z_i < b$.

The roots of a Legendre polynomial of order n may be found by first obtaining the coefficients by `c=Legen_pw(n)` and then `roots(c)`. The Gauss-Legendre quadrature may be applied by `Gauss_q`. Its synopsis is

   `Gauss_q('f_name', a, b, n_points)`

where `f_name` is the name of a function m-file that defines the integrand; `a` and `b` are lower and upper limits, respectively; and `n_points` is the number of points that equals the order of the Legendre polynomial.

Table 5.2 Weights of Gauss-Legendre Quadrature

$n=2$	x:	-0.5773,5027	0.5773,5027		
	w:	1.0000,0000	1.0000,0000		
$n=3$	x:	-0.7745,9667	0.0000,0000	0.7745,9667	
	w:	0.5555,5556	0.8888,8889	0.5555,5556	
$n=4$	x:	-0.8611,3631	-0.3399,8104	0.3399,8104	0.8611,3631
	w:	0.3478,5485	0.6521,4515	0.6521,4515	0.3478,5485
$n=5$	x:	-0.9061,7985 0.9061,7985	-0.5384,6931	0.0000,0000	0.5384,6931
	w:	0.2369,2689 0.2369,2689	0.4786,2867	0.5688,8889	0.4786,2867
$n=6$	x:	-0.9324,6951 0.6612,0939	-0.6612,0939 0.9324,6951	-0.2386,1919	0.2386,1919
	w:	0.1713,2449 0.3607,6157	0.3607,6157 0.1713,2449	0.4679,1393	0.4679,1393
$n=7$	x:	-0.9491,0791 0.4058,4515	-0.7415,3119 0.7415,3119	-0.4058,4515 0.9491,0791	0.0000,0000
	w:	0.1294,8497 0.3818,3005	0.2797,0539 0.2797,0539	0.3818,3005 0.1294,8497	0.4179,5918
$n=8$	x:	-0.9602,8986 0.1834,3464	-0.7966,6648 0.5255,3241	-0.5255,3241 0.7966,6648	-0.1834,3464 0.9602,8986
	w:	0.1012,2854 0.3626,8378	0.2223,8103 0.3137,0665	0.3137,0665 0.2223,8103	0.3626,8378 0.1012,2854
$n=9$	x:	-0.9681,6024 0.0000,0000 0.9681,6024	0.8360,3111 0.3242,5342	0.6133,7143 0.6133,7143	-0.3242,5342 0.8360,3111
	w:	0.0812,7439 0.3302,3936 0.0812,7439	0.1806,4816 0.3123,4708	0.2606,1070 0.2606,1070	0.3123,4708 0.1806,4816

5.4 NUMERICAL INTEGRATION WITH INFINITE LIMITS OR SINGULARITIES

In this section, we study two kinds of integrals that need special attention; for example,

$$I = \int_{-\infty}^{\infty} \exp(-x^2) dx \tag{5.4.1}$$

$$I = \int_{0}^{1} \frac{1}{\sqrt{x}(\exp(x)+1)} dx \tag{5.4.2}$$

$$I = \int_0^1 x^{0.7} \cos(x) dx \tag{5.4.3}$$

The integration of Eq.(5.4.1) is extended over an infinite domain. Equations (5.4.2) and (5.4.3) involve a singularity of the integrand at $x = 0$ (the function approaches infinity as x approaches 0). Equation (5.4.3) does not seem difficult at a glance, but it is not a trivial problem for any numerical integration method described earlier. Indeed, if the extended trapezoidal rule or Simpson's rule is applied, the answer keeps changing as the number of intervals is doubled. The reason is that the function is not analytic at $x = 0$.

A function is integrable in an infinite or semi-infinite domain only if the function is significantly different from zero only in a small domain, while the function approaches zero as x approaches ∞ or $-\infty$. The first step of evaluating

$$I = \int_{-\infty}^{\infty} f(x) dx \tag{5.4.4}$$

is to replace the infinite limits by finite limits as

$$I = \int_{-X}^{X} f(x) dx \tag{5.4.5}$$

where X is a sufficiently large value such that the contribution from outside of $-X < x < X$ is negligibly small (see Figure 5.5).

5.4.1 Use of the Extended Trapezoidal Rule

The most efficient method for numerical integration for Eq.(5.4.5) is the extended trapezoidal rule,[3] which can be written as

$$I \approx h \left(\sum_{i=-n}^{n} g_i - 0.5(g_{-n} + g_n) \right) \tag{5.4.6}$$

where $x_i = ih$ and $nh = X$. Indeed, the following example shows that the extended trapezoidal rule gives highly accurate results with a relatively small number of points:

---

[3]M. Mori and R. Piessens, ed. *Numerical Quadrature*, North-Holland, 1987.

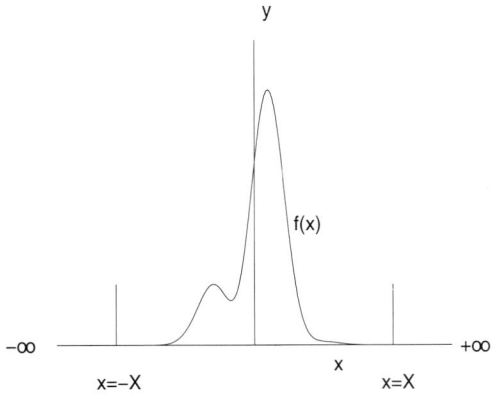

Figure 5.5 Sketch of a function integrable from $-\infty$ to ∞, and artificial limits for numerical integration.

Example 5.5

Evaluate

$$I = \frac{1}{\sqrt{\pi}} \int_{-\infty}^{\infty} \exp(-x^2)\, dx$$

by the extended trapezoidal rule.

Solution

We replace the limits of integration by -10 and 10 as sufficiently large values for the present problem:

$$I = \frac{1}{\sqrt{\pi}} \int_{-10}^{10} \exp(-x^2)\, dx$$

The foregoing integral evaluated by trapez_v, with $n = 10$ and 20, for example, becomes

h	n	I
1	10	1.00010344
0.5	20	1.00000000

The exact value is 1, so the result using $n = 20$ is perfect to the eighth decimal place.

Until now, we assumed we knew an appropriate value for X. In general, however, it is not known a priori, so a few trials to find $\bar{X}$ are necessary.

If X is too large, not only is the computational time wasted, but there is also a danger of causing overflow or underflow in the computations. On the other hand, if X is too small, the result of integration will be inaccurate. An optimum value of X is such that I will be affected if X is decreased by a factor of, say, 1.5, but will not change if X is increased. In order to determine an appropriate value for X, first fix h at a reasonable value. Then, evaluate Eq.(5.4.6) with varying values of n; and increase n by approximately a factor of 1.5 after each trial (each time X increases by the same factor). When the computed value of I does not change at all for the increased n, fix X to the final value. After X is fixed, the sensitivity of I on h should be examined by doubling n with $h = X/n$ and computing I until I does not change any longer. Although determining both X and n by trials may seem cumbersome, the whole procedure does not take more than 10 trials.

5.4.2 Exponential Transformation

Next, we consider integrating a function that is singular at one or both of the finite limits (see Eqs.(5.4.2) and (5.4.3), for example). The finite domain of integration, say $[a, b]$, can be transformed to $[-\infty, \infty]$ by a coordinate transformation. Once it is reduced to the form of Eq.(5.4.4), the extended trapezoidal rule is applied.[4]

Consider

$$I = \int_a^b f(x)dx \qquad (5.4.7)$$

where a and b are finite limits. The mapping may be written by

$$z = z(x)$$

or equivalently

$$x = x(z) \qquad (5.4.8)$$

such that

$$z(a) = -\infty, \ z(b) = \infty$$

---

[4]References: [1] M. Mori, "Quadrature Formulas Obtained by Variable Transformation and DE-rule." *J. Comp. Appl. Math.* Vol. 12-13, p. 119-130, 1980. [2] M. Mori and R. Piessens, ed. *Numerical Quadrature*, North-Holland, 1987.

Equation (5.4.7) can then be written as

$$I = \int_{-\infty}^{\infty} f(x(z)) \frac{dx}{dz} dz \qquad (5.4.9)$$

An example for such transformation is the exponential transformation given by

$$x = \frac{a + b + (b - a)\tanh(z)}{2} \qquad (5.4.10)$$

or equivalently

$$z = \tanh^{-1}(\frac{2x - a - b}{b - a}) \qquad (5.4.11)$$

The first derivative of Eq.(5.4.10) is given by

$$\frac{dx}{dz} = \frac{b - a}{2\cosh^2(z)} \qquad (5.4.12)$$

Example 5.6

(1) Evaluate

$$I = \int_0^1 f(x) dx \qquad \text{(A)}$$

where

$$f(x) = \frac{\exp(-x^2)}{\sqrt{1 - x^2}}$$

by the extended trapezoidal rule after the exponential transformation using Eq.(5.4.10). Set the limits of integration on the z axis to ± 6 and $h = 0.1$.

(2) Graphically illustrate the transformation between the x and z coordinates.

(3) Plot the integrand $f(x)$ on the x-y coordinates with the data points used in the numerical integration.

(4) Plot the integrand, $g(z) = f(x)dx/dz$, on the z-x domain.

Solution

With $a = 0$ and $b = 1$, the transformation Eq.(5.4.10) becomes

$$x = \frac{1 + \tanh(z)}{2}$$

(1) By dividing the domain, $-6 \leq z \leq 6$, into equispaced intervals of $h = 0.2$, the z values of the points are

$$z_i = ih, \qquad i = -30, ..., 30 \tag{B}$$

We now approximate Eq.(A) by

$$I = \int_0^1 f(x)dx = \int_{-\infty}^{+\infty} f(x)\frac{dx}{dz}dz \approx \int_{-6}^{+6} g(z)dz \approx h \sum_{i=-30}^{30} g(z_i) \tag{C}$$

with

$$g(z) = f(x(z))\frac{dx}{dz} \tag{D}$$

The g_i values on the equispaced data points are computed by

$$g_i = g(z_i) = \frac{\exp(-x_i^2)}{\sqrt{1 - x_i^2}} \frac{1}{2\cosh^2(z_i)} \tag{E}$$

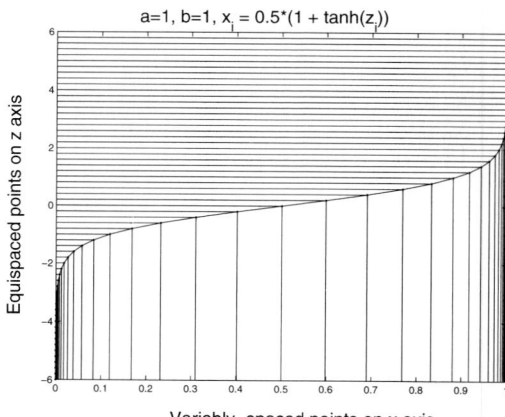

Figure 5.6 Transformation of equispaced points on the z-axis to the x-axis.

Section 5.4 Numerical Integration with Infinite Limits or Singularities 227

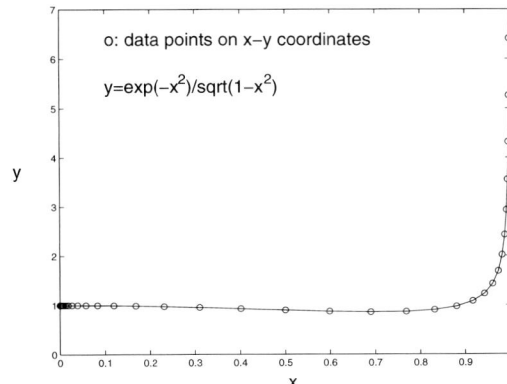

Figure 5.7 Integrand and data points along the x-axis.

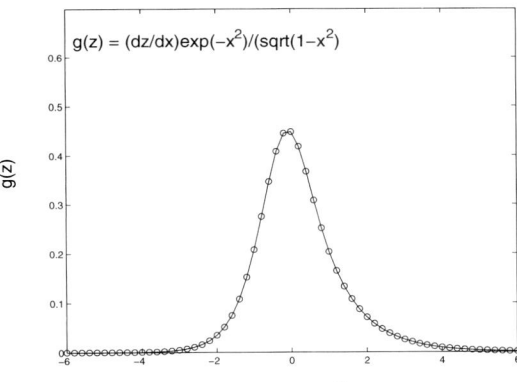

Figure 5.8 Integrand and data points on the z-axis.

where x_i are the points corresponding to z_i given by

$$x_i = \frac{1 + \tanh(z_i)}{2} \tag{F}$$

Then, the numerical result becomes

$$I \approx h \left(\sum_{i=-30}^{30} g_i - 0.5(g_{-30} + g_{30}) \right) = 1.0120$$

The foregoing computation may be evaluated by `trapez_v`.

(2) Figure 5.6 shows the transformation of the equispaced points onto the x axis.
(3) Figure 5.7 shows the data points along the integrand.

(4) Figure 5.8 shows the distribution of $g(z)$ and the data points used in the trapezoidal rule computation.

5.4.3 Double-Exponential Transformation

Accuracy of the numerical integration is affected by the choice of the transformation. The double-exponential transformation given by

$$x = \frac{a + b + (b-a)\tanh(\frac{\pi}{2}\sinh(z))}{2} \tag{5.4.13}$$

has been proposed as an alternative to Eq.(5.4.10).[5] With this choice dx/dz becomes

$$\frac{dx}{dz} = \frac{\pi}{4}\frac{(b-a)\cosh(z)}{\cosh^2\left(\frac{\pi}{2}\sinh(z)\right)} \tag{5.4.14}$$

We introduce Eqs.(5.4.13) and (5.4.14) into Eq.(5.4.9) and apply the extended trapezoidal rule. Here, the infinite limits in Eq.(5.4.9) are replaced by finite limits $-Z$ and Z. Then, the extended trapezoidal rule is applied:

$$I = h \sum_{k=-n}^{n} f(x_k)\left(\frac{dx}{dz}\right)_k \tag{5.4.15}$$

where $h = Z/n$, and

$$-Z \leq z_k = kh \leq Z \tag{5.4.16}$$

$$x_k = \frac{1}{2}\left[a + b + (b-a)\tanh\left(\frac{\pi}{2}\sinh(z_k)\right)\right] \tag{5.4.17}$$

$$\left(\frac{dx}{dz}\right)_k = \frac{\pi}{4}\frac{(b-a)\cosh(z_k)}{\cosh^2\left(\frac{\pi}{2}\sinh(z_k)\right)} \tag{5.4.18}$$

In Eq.(5.4.16), the question is how large the value of Z should be. This may be answered by examining the denominator of Eq.(5.4.18). When z_k increases, it approaches

---

[5]Reference: H. Takahashi and M. Mori, "Double Exponential Formlas for Numerical Integration," *Publ. RIMS*, Kyoto University, Vol. 9, No. 3, Kyoto, Japan, 1974.

$$\cosh^2\left(\frac{\pi}{2}\sinh(z_k)\right) \longrightarrow \frac{1}{4}\exp\left[\frac{\pi}{2}\exp(z_k)\right] \qquad (5.4.19)$$

This term increases double-exponentially, and may cause an overflow. With single precision in Fortran or C on typical workstations, it occurs when

$$\frac{1}{4}\exp\left(\frac{\pi}{2}\exp(z_k)\right) > 2 \times 10^{38} \qquad (5.4.20)$$

or, equivalently, if z_k is greater than approximately 4.0. This criterion determines the maximum possible Z. That is

$$Z = nh < 4 \qquad (5.4.21)$$

In MATLAB, the highest floating value is approximately +9.9e307, so that the criterion for Z is

$$Z = nh < 6.1 \qquad (5.4.22)$$

Another problem is the rounding error in Eq.(5.4.17) that occurs when the hyperbolic tangent term becomes very close to -1 or 1. To avoid this, we first recognize that the hyperbolic tangent term can be written as

$$\tanh(p) = (s - 1/s)/(s + 1/s) \qquad (5.4.23)$$

where $s = \exp(p)$. Using Eq.(4.2.23), Eq.(5.4.17) is written as

$$x_k = \left(bs_k + \frac{a}{s_k}\right) / \left(s_k + \frac{1}{s_k}\right) \qquad (5.4.24)$$

where

$$s_k = \exp\left(\frac{\pi}{2}\sinh(z_k)\right)$$

Since Eq.(5.4.24) has no subtraction operation, a major source of a rounding error has been eliminated.

The numerical scheme with the double-exponential transformation is implemented in `double_exp`. Its synopsis is

```
I = dbl_exp('f_name', a, b, n)
```

where arguments have the same meanings as for `Gauss_q`. See Section 5.7 for more details.

Example 5.7

The length of the curve of $y = g(x)$, $a < x < b$, can be computed by

$$I = \int_a^b \sqrt{1 + (g'(x))^2}\,dx \tag{A}$$

Calculate the length of the parabolic arc, $y^2 = 4x$, satisfying $0 < x < 2$.

Solution

Since $g(x) = 2\sqrt{x}$, its derivative is $g'(x) = 1/\sqrt{x}$. The integral becomes

$$I = \int_0^2 \sqrt{1 + \frac{1}{x}}\,dx \tag{B}$$

The integrand in the foregoing equation is singular at $x = 0$.

The computation is performed by `dbl_exp`. The limits of integration on the transformed coordinate are set to $Z = -4$ and $Z = 4$. The computed results are:

n	I
10	3.600710
20	3.595706
30	3.595706

5.5 MATLAB COMMANDS FOR INTEGRATIONS

The MATLAB toolbox has `quad` and `quad8`. Function `quad` uses a recursive Simpson's rule, and `quad8` uses a recursive Newton-Cotes quadrature of order 8. The synopsis of `quad` includes the following three forms:

```
quad('f_name', a, b)
quad('f_name', a, b, tol)
quad('f_name', a, b, tol, trace)
```

In the first form, the tolerance `tol` is set to a default value, 0.001. The quadrature computation is iterated until the tolerance is satisfied. If the third form is used with a nonzero value for `trace`, a graph showing progress of integration is plotted on the screen. The synopsis of `quad8` is the same except that `quad` is replaced by `quad8`.

5.6 NUMERICAL INTEGRATION ON A TWO-DIMENSIONAL DOMAIN

Let us consider a domain illustrated in Figure 5.9, where the left and right boundaries are vertical lines, and the top and bottom boundaries are given by analytical functions. The integral of $f(x,y)$ extended over this domain is written as

$$I = \int_a^b \int_{c(x)}^{d(x)} f(x,y) dy\ dx \qquad (5.6.1)$$

Equation (5.6.1) is often written in a different form, such as

$$I = \int_a^b dx \int_{c(x)}^{d(x)} dy\ f(x,y)$$

or

$$I = \int \int_A f(x,y) dx\ dy$$

where A is meant by the domain. In any case, the problem should be rewritten in the form of Eq.(5.6.1) before proceeding with numerical integrations. Exchange the order of integrations if necessary.

The general principle of the numerical integration of Eq.(5.6.1) is to reduce it to a combination of one-dimensional problems. If we define

$$G(x) = \int_{c(x)}^{d(x)} f(x,y)\ dy \qquad (5.6.2)$$

then, Eq.(5.6.1) becomes

$$I = \int_a^b G(x)\ dx \qquad (5.6.3)$$

for which any numerical integration method described earlier is applicable. A numerical approximation for Eq.(5.6.3) may be written in the form:

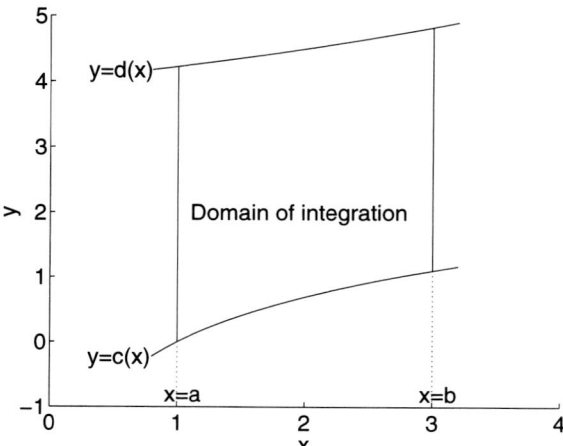

Figure 5.9 A two-dimensional domain for double integration.

$$I \approx \sum_{i=1}^{n+1} w_i G(x_i) \qquad (5.6.4)$$

where w_is are weights and x_is are points of the particular method chosen. Setting $x = x_i$, Eq.(5.6.2) becomes

$$G(x_i) = \int_{c(x_i)}^{d(x_i)} f(x_i, y) \, dy \qquad (5.6.5)$$

which is a one-dimensional problem because the only variable of the integrand is y. Equation (5.6.5) is also evaluated by a numerical integration scheme.

Example 5.8

By the Simpson's 1/3 rule, evaluate the double integral

$$I = \int_a^b \left(\int_{c(x)}^{d(x)} \sin(x+y) dy \right) dx \qquad (A)$$

where the limits of integrations are

$$a = 1$$
$$b = 3$$
$$c(x) = \ln(x)$$
$$d(x) = 3 + \exp(x/5)$$

Section 5.6 Numerical Integration on a Two-Dimensional Domain

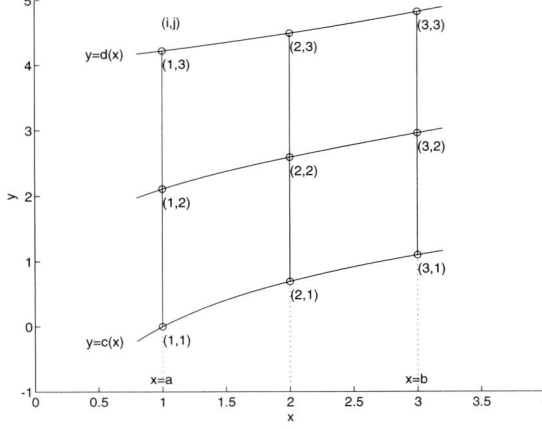

Figure 5.10 A grid for double integration.

Solution

For the Simpson's 1/3 rule, the grid points on the x-axis are

$$x_1 = 1, x_2 = 2, \text{ and } x_3 = 3$$

See Figure 5.10 for the domain of integration and points. Applying Simpson's 1/3 rule to the first integral yields

$$I \approx \frac{h_x}{3}[G(x_1) + 4G(x_2) + G(x_3)] \tag{B}$$

where

$$h_x = (b-a)/2 = 1$$

and

$$G(x_i) = \int_{\ln(x_i)}^{3+\exp(x_i/5)} \sin(x_i + y) \, dy \tag{C}$$

The whole procedure may be written more explicitly as

$$I = \int_1^3 \left(\int_{\ln(x)}^{3+\exp(x/5)} \sin(x+y) \, dy \right) dx$$

$$\approx \frac{h_x}{3} \left[\int_{\ln(1)}^{3+\exp(1/5)} \sin(1+y) \, dy + 4 \int_{\ln(2)}^{3+\exp(2/5)} \sin(2+y) \, dy \right.$$

$$\left. + \int_{\ln(3)}^{3+\exp(3/5)} \sin(3+y) \, dy \right]$$

$$= \frac{h_x}{3} \left[\int_0^{4.2214} \sin(1+y) \, dy + 4 \int_{0.6931}^{4.4918} \sin(2+y) \, dy \right.$$
$$\left. + \int_{1.0986}^{4.8221} \sin(3+y) \, dy \right]$$
(D)

With Simpson's 1/3 rule, the first integral becomes

$$\int_0^{4.2214} \sin(1+y) \, dy$$

$$\approx \frac{2.11070}{3} \left[\sin(1+0) + 4 \sin(1+2.11070) + \sin(1+4.2214) \right]$$

$$= (2.11070/3) \left[0.84147 + (4)(0.03088) + (-0.87322) \right]$$

$$= 0.064581 \tag{E}$$

Similar computations yield

$$\int_{0.6931}^{4.4918} \sin(2+y) \, dy \approx -2.1086$$

$$\int_{1.0986}^{4.8221} \sin(3+y) \, dy \approx -0.67454$$

Thus, the final value of the double integration becomes

$$I \approx (1/3)[0.064581 + (4)(-2.1086) - 0.67454] = -0.30148$$

Section 5.6 Numerical Integration on a Two-Dimensional Domain

The double integration scheme is implemented in dbl_itg. Its synopsis is as follows:

```
I = dbl_itg('f_name', 'lower_limit', ...
            'upper_limit', a, b, m, n)
```

where f_name is the function m-file name of the integrand, lower_limit is the function m-file name that defines $c(x)$, upper_limit is the function m-file name that defines $d(x)$, a and b are lower and upper limits of x, and m and n are the number of intervals in the x and y directions, respectively. Function dbl_itg calls Simps_v so the number of intervals can be any number that equals 2 or greater.

The boundaries for some domains, such as Figure 5.11, may not be expressed by two curves and two vertical lines. For such a domain, a coordinate transformation is necessary. New coordinates (ξ, η) are related to (x, y) by

$$\begin{aligned} x &= x(\xi, \eta) \\ y &= y(\xi, \eta) \end{aligned} \qquad (5.6.6)$$

Then, the double integral on the x-y domain becomes

$$\int\int_D f(x,y)\, dydx = \int\int_\Gamma f(\xi,\eta) J d\eta d\xi \qquad (5.6.7)$$

where Γ is the domain of integration on the ξ-η plane, and

$$J = \frac{\partial(x,y)}{\partial(\xi,\eta)} = x_\xi y_\eta - x_\eta y_\xi \qquad (5.6.8)$$

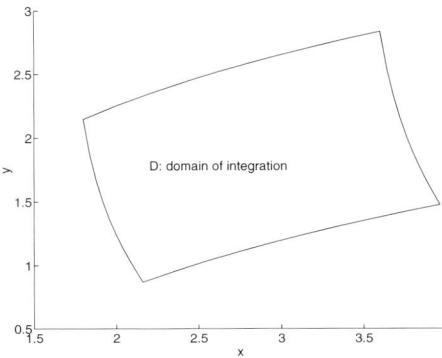

Figure 5.11 A domain of integration.

Suppose the domain is covered by a curvilinear grid, as illustrated in Figure 5.11. If the domain is simple, a curvilinear grid may be easily generated. Otherwise, a numerical grid generation method[6] may be used. With a coordinate transformation, the curved geometry is mapped onto a rectangular domain on the ξ-η coordinates. The grid lines are denoted by indices i and j (see Figure 5.12). The grid line i corresponds to $\xi = i$, and the grid line j corresponds to $\eta = j$ on the domain illustrated in Figure 5.13. The grid on the ξ-η domain is rectangular and equispaced.

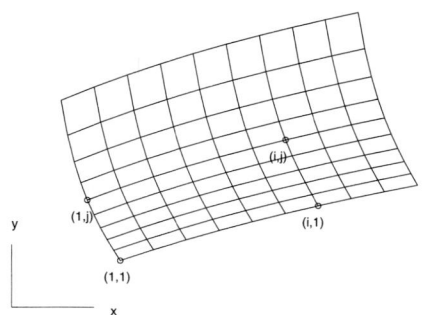

Figure 5.12 Grid on the domain of integration.

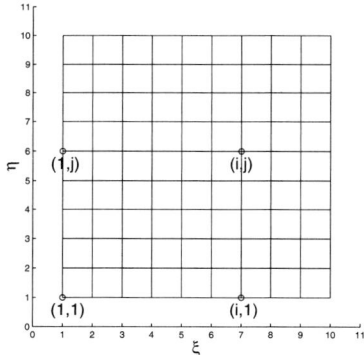

Figure 5.13 Grid on the computational domain.

On the rectangular ξ-η domain, Eq.(5.6.7) becomes

---

[1] J.F. Thompson, "Grid Generation" in *Handbook of Numerical Heat Transfer*, W.J. Minkowycz, et al. ed., Wiley Interscience, 1988. [2] S. Nakamura, "Coordinate Transformation and Structured Grid Generation," in *Handbook of Fluid and Fluid Machinery*, J. A. Schetz, et al. ed., John Wiley, forthcoming. [3] P. Knupp and S. Stenberg, *Fundamentals of Grid Generation*, CRC Press, 1993.

$$\int\int_D f(x,y)dydx = \int_1^m \int_1^n G(\xi,\eta)d\eta d\xi \qquad (5.6.9)$$

where

$$G(\xi,\eta) = f(\xi,\eta)J \qquad (5.6.10)$$

Numerical integration on the right side of Eq.(5.6.9) is performed using the grid on the ξ-η domain illustrated in Figure 5.13. The principle of numerical integration on the ξ-η coordinates is the same as for the double integration on the x-y coordinates. The values of $G_{i,j}$ are computed by

$$G_{i,j} = G(\xi_i,\eta_j) = f(\xi_i,\eta_j)J_{i,j} \qquad (5.6.11)$$

The partial derivatives of x at the grid points are evaluated by the following difference approximations:

$$\begin{aligned}
(x_\xi)_{1,j} &= (-x_{3,j} + 4x_{2,j} - 3x_{1,j})/2 \\
(x_\xi)_{i,j} &= (x_{i+1,j} - x_{i-1,j})/2, \quad 1 < i < m \\
(x_\xi)_{m,j} &= (3x_{m,j} - 4x_{m-1,j} + x_{m-2,j})/2 \\
(x_\eta)_{i,1} &= (-x_{i,3} + 4x_{i,2} - 3x_{i,1})/2 \\
(x_\eta)_{i,j} &= (x_{i,j+1} - x_{i,j-1})/2, \quad 1 < j < n \\
(x_\eta)_{i,n} &= (3x_{i,n} - 4x_{i,n-1} + x_{i,n-2})/2
\end{aligned} \qquad (5.6.12)$$

where m and n are maximum values of i and j, respectively, ($m = n = 10$ in Figure 5.13). The partial derivatives of y are the same as in Eq.(5.6.12) except x is replaced by y.

5.7 M-FILES

FM 5-1. Extended trapezoidal rule (1)
Purpose: Integration of a function by the extended trapezoidal rule.
Synopsis: I = trapez_v(f,h)
    f: array of the data on equispaced points. Vector length of f
      is arbitrary, but must be greater than 1.
    h: interval size
Example: x=0:0.1:5; y=sin(x);I = trapez_v(y,0.1)

trapez_v.m

```
function I = trapez_v(f, h)
I = h*(sum(f) - (f(1) + f(length(f)))/2);
```

FM 5-2. Extended trapezoidal rule (2)
Purpose: Integration of a function by extended trapezoidal rule. Function trapez_n uses the extended trapezoidal rule but does not plot any graph, while trapez_g does plotting.
Synopsis: trapez_n('f_name', a, b, n) or trapez_g('f_name', a, b, n)
    f_name: function m-file name of the integrand, $f(x)$
    a: lower limit of x
    b: upper limit of x
    n: number of intervals
Example: trapez_n('sin', 0, pi, 20)

trapez_n.m
```
function I = trapez_n(f_name, a, b, n)
h = (b-a)/n;
x = a+(0:n)*h;  f = feval(f_name, x);
I =   trapez_v(f,h);
```

trapez_g.m
```
function I = trapez_g(f_name, a, b, n)
n=n;hold off
h = (b-a)/n;
x = a+(0:n)*h;  f = feval(f_name, x);
I = h/2*(f(1) + f(n+1));
if n>1 I = I +  h*sum(f(2:n));end
h2 = (b-a)/100;
xc = a+(0:100)*h2;  fc = feval(f_name, xc);
plot(xc,fc,'r'); hold on
title('Trapezoidal Rule'); xlabel('x');ylabel('y');
plot(x,f);
plot(x,zeros(size(x)))
for i=1:n; plot([x(i),x(i)], [0,f(i)]); end
```

FM 5-3. Extended Simpson's rule
Purpose: Integration of a function in a tabular form by the extended Simpson's rule.
Synopsis: I = Simps_v(f,h) or I = Simps_n('f_name', a, b, n)
    f_name: function m-file name of the integrand, $f(x)$

f: functional data on equispaced abscissa. Number of data points is arbitrary, but must be greater than 3.

h: interval size of the abscissa

Simps_v.m
```
function I = Simps_v(f,h)
n=length(f)-1;
if n==1, ...
  fprintf('Data has only one interval'),return;
  end
if n==2, ...
  I = h/3*(f(1) + 4*f(2) + f(3));
  return;end
if n==3, ...
  I = 3/8*h*(f(1) + 3*f(2) + 3*f(3) + f(4));
  return;end
I=0;
if  2*floor(n/2)~=n,
   I = 3/8*h*(f(n -2) + 3*f(n -1)   ...
       + 3*f(n) + f(n+1));
   m=n -3
else
   m=n;
end
I = I+ (h/3)*( f(1)+ 4*sum(f(2:2:m)) + f(m+1));
if m>2, I = I+ (h/3)*2*sum(f(3:2:m));
end
```

Simps_n.m
```
function I = Simps_n(f_name, a, b, n)
   h = (b-a)/n;
   x = a+(0:n)*h;   f = feval(f_name, x);
   I =  Simps_v(f,h)
```

FM 5-4. Newton-Cotes closed formula

Purpose: Integration of a function by the Newton-Cotes closed formula. The weights are automatically computed.

Synopsis: Newt_itg('f_name', a, b, n)

f_name: name of a function m-file that defines the integrand

a, b: lower and upper limits, respectively

n: number of equispaced intervals between the two integrating limits

Example: Newt_itg('sin', 0, pi, 4)

Newt_itg.m
```
function I = Newt_itg(f_name, a, b, n)
npt=n+1;
if npt<0, break; end
en = npt:-1:1;
x = 1:npt;
for i=1:npt
      power_2(i)  = npt^en(i); power_1(i) = 1^en(i);
end
for j=1:npt
      z = zeros(1,npt) ;   z(j)=1;
      a1 = polyfit(x, z,npt-1);
      w(j) = sum(a1.*(power_2 - power_1)./en);
%       fprintf(' j=%3.0f       w=%12.8f\n', j, w)
end
x=a:(b-a)/(npt-1):b;
y=feval(f_name,x);
I = sum(w.*y)*(b-a)/(npt-1);
fprintf('\n     x             y              w \n')
for j=1:npt
fprintf('%e %e %e\n', x(j),y(j), w(j))
end
```

FM 5-5. Gauss-Legendre quadrature

Purpose: Integration of a function by the Gauss-Legendere quadrature. The Legendre points and weights are automatically computed.

Synopsis: Gauss_q('f_name', a, b, n)
    f_name: function m-file name of the integrand, $f(x)$
    a: lower limit of x
    b: upper limit of x
    n: number of Legendre points

Example: Gauss_q('sin', 0, pi, 8)

Gauss_q.m
```
function I = Gauss_q(f_name, a, b, n)
p=Legen_pw(n);
x = roots(p)';x = sort(x);
for j=1:n
   y = zeros(1,n); y(j)=1;
   p = polyfit(x,y,n-1);
   P = poly_itg(p);
   w(j) = polyval(P,1) - polyval(P,-1);
```

```
end
x = 0.5*((b-a)*x + a + b);
y=feval(f_name, x);
I = sum(w.*y)*(b-a)/2;
fprintf('\n       x              y              w \n')
for j=1:n
fprintf('%e %e %e\n', x(j),y(j), w(j))
end
```

Legen_pw.m
```
function pn = Legen_p(n)
pbb=[1];   if n==0, pn=pbb; break; end
pb=[1 0];  if n==1, pn=pb;  break; end
for i=2:n;
   pn=  ( (2*i-1)*[pb,0] - (i-1)*[0, 0, pbb] )/i;
   pbb=pb; pb=pn;
end
```

FM 5-6. Integration by double-exponential transformation

Purpose: Integration of a function by double-exponential transformation.
Synopsis: `dbl_exp('f_name',a,b,n)`

fun_name: function m-file name of the integrand, $f(x)$

a: lower limit of x

b: upper limit of x

n: number of intervals

Example: `dbl_exp('fun_dbx',0, 2, 200)`

dbl_exp.m
```
function I=dbl_exp(f_name,a,b,n)
%          a : lower limit of integration
%          b : upper limit of integration
%          h : grid interval
%          n : number of intervals
%          dxdz : dx/dz
%          hcos : hyperbolic cosine
%          hsin : hyperbolic sine
%          I : result of integration
zmax=3.; h = 2*zmax/n;
z = -zmax:h:zmax;   exz = exp( z ); exzi=exz.^(-1);
hcos = (exz + exzi)/2.;   hsin = (exz - exzi)/2.;
s = exp( pi*0.5*hsin );  si=s.^(-1);
```

```
x = (b*s + a*si).*(s + si).^(-1);
p = pi*hsin/2;   w = exp( p );
dxdz = (b - a)*pi*hcos.*((w + w.^(-1))/2.0).^(-2)/4;
g = feval(f_name,x).*dxdz;
I = trapez_v(g,h);
```

fun_dbx.m
```
function y = fun_dbx(x)
y = sin(x)/sqrt(x);
```

FM 5-7. Double integration

Purpose: Double integration of a two-dimensional function, $f(x,y)$.

Synopsis: dbl_itg('fun_name','c_lo','c_hi',a,b,m,n)

    fun_name: function m-file name of the integrand, $f(x,y)$
    c_lo: function m-file name of the lower limit of y, $c(x)$
    c_hi: function m-file name of the upper limit of y, $d(x)$
    a: lower limit of x
    b: upper limit of x
    m: number of intervals in the x direction (must be even)
    n: number of intervals in the y direction (must be even)

Example: dbl_itg('fun_dbl','low_lim','upp_lim',1,3,6,6)

The function m-file samples are listed after dbl_itg in the following list:

dbl_itg.m
```
function I=dbl_itg(f_name,c_lo,c_hi,a,b,m,n)
%     Double Integration by Simpson's Rule
%       a :lower limit of integration over x
%       b :upper limit of integration over x
%    c_lo :function name for lower bound curve
%          (function of x),c(x)
%    d_hi :  function name for upper bound curve
%          (function of x), d(x)
% f_name : function name for integrand
% hx, hy : interval sizes
%       I : result of integration
%     m,n: number of intervals in x and y directions, resp.
if    m<2  | n<2
      fprintf( 'Number of intervals invalid \n' ); return
end
mpt=m+1;npt=n+1;    %number of intervals
hx = (b - a)/m ;  x =a+(0:m)*hx;
for i=1:mpt
```

```
        ylo= feval(c_lo,x(i));
        yhi = feval(c_hi, x(i));
        hy=(yhi-ylo)/n;
        y(i,:)=ylo+ (0:n)*hy;
        f(i,:)=feval(f_name,x(i),y(i,:));
        G(i) = Simps_v(f(i,:),hy);
end
I = Simps_v(G,hx);
```

fun_dbl.m
```
function y= fun_dbl( x, y)
y = sin( x + y );
```

low_lim.m
```
function y =low_lim( x)
y = log( x );
```

upp_lim.m
```
function y = upp_lim( x)
  y = 3 + exp( x/5 );
```

PROBLEMS

In answering the questions that require repeated calculations for different values of a parameter such as the number of the data points or intervals, always organize the results in a tabular form.

(5.1) Evaluate the following integral by the extended trapezoidal rule with $n = 2$, 4, 8, and 16 intervals:

(a) $\int_0^{\pi/4} \tan(x)\, dx$

(b) $\int_0^1 \exp(x)\, dx$

(c) $\int_0^1 \frac{1}{2+x}\, dx$

(5.2) Evaluate

$$\int_0^{\pi/2} \sin(x)\, dx$$

by the extended trapezoidal rule with $n = 2, 4, 8, 25$, and 100 intervals. Then, find the error of the numerical results by comparison to the exact value that is 1.

(5.3) A spherical water reservoir of radius 20m is located 40m above the ground. A straight vertical drain pipe of radius $b = 0.2$m and length 40m is connected to the bottom of the tank to drain the water to ground level. The friction factor of the pipe is $f = 0.0016$. The tank is full to the top and draining starts at $t = 0$. How much time is needed to drain the water?

Hint: The energy equation to determine the velocity of the water in the pipe is given by

$$gz = \frac{u^2}{2} + f\frac{L}{2b}\frac{u^2}{2}$$

where the first term on the right side is the kinetic energy of water leaving the pipe and the second term is the friction loss effect. Use 20 intervals.

(5.4) With the function table given below, evaluate

$$\int_0^{0.8} f(x)\, dx$$

by the extended trapezoidal rule with $h = 0.4$, $h = 0.2$, and $h = 0.1$.

x	f(x)
0.0	0
0.1	2.1220
0.2	3.0244
0.3	3.2568
0.4	3.1399
0.5	2.8579
0.6	2.5140
0.7	2.1639
0.8	1.8358

(5.5) The bottom of a circular cylinder has a radius of 0.5m and is perpendicular to the axis, but the top is at a $45°$ angle to the axis, as shown in Figure 5.14. Find the volume by the trapezoidal rule with 20 intervals.

(5.6) By applying the Romberg integral to the results of the trapezoidal rule with $h = 0.1$ and $h = 0.2$ for Problem 5.4, estimate a more accurate integral.

(5.7) A function table is given below.

i	x_i	$f(x_i)$
1	0	0.9162
2	0.25	0.8109
3	0.5	0.6931
4	0.75	0.5596
5	1.0	0.4055

Problems

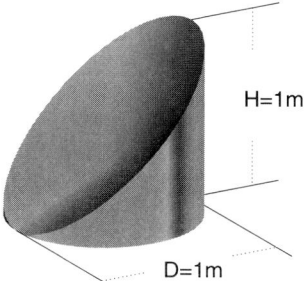

Figure 5.14 A cylinder.

(a) Calculate

$$I = \int_0^1 f(x)\, dx$$

by the extended trapezoidal rule with $h = 0.25$ and $h = 0.5$.

(b) Estimate a more accurate value of I by applying Romberg integration to the results for question (a).

(5.8) Consider three data points, $(-1, f_1)$, $(0, f_2)$, and $(1, f_3)$. Fit the data set by the Lagrange interpolation formula. By integrating the Lagrange interpolation formula, show that the Simpson's 1/3 rule is obtained.

Hint: Transform the shape functions to the power series by `polyfit`. Once the power coefficients are obtained, integrate the polynomial by `poly_itg`.

(5.9) Simpson's 1/3 rule is exact if a polynomial of order 3 or less is integrated. Verify this by integrating

$$I = \int_0^3 x^3 dx$$

by Simpson's 1/3 rule, and analytically. Repeat the same for the Simpson's 3/8 rule.

(5.10) Repeat Problem (5.1) using Simpson's 1/3 method.

(5.11) Evaluate the following integrals by the extended Simpson's 1/3 rule using 2, 4, 8, 16, and 32 intervals:

(a) $\int_0^\pi \dfrac{dx}{2 + \cos(x)}$

(b) $\int_1^2 \dfrac{\log(1 + x)}{x} dx$

(c) $\int_0^{\frac{\pi}{2}} \dfrac{dx}{1+\sin^2(x)}$

(5.12) Evaluate the following integral by the extended Simpson's 1/3 rule using 2, 4, 8, 16, and 32 intervals:

(a) $\int_0^1 x \exp(2x)\,dx$

(b) $\int_0^1 x^{-x}\,dx$

(c) $\int_0^{2\pi} \exp(2x)\sin^2(x)\,dx$

(5.13) Suppose you are an architect planning to use a large arch of the parabolic shape given by

$$y = 0.1x(30 - x) \text{ meters}$$

where y is the height above the ground and x is in meters. Calculate the total length of the arch by the extended Simpson's rule. (Divide the domain from $x = 0$ to $x = 30$m into 10 equally spaced intervals.)

$$L = \int_0^{30} \sqrt{1 + \left(\dfrac{dy}{dx}\right)^2}\, dx$$

(5.14) An automobile of mass $M = 5400$kg is cruising at a speed of 30m/s. The engine is disengaged suddenly at $t = 0$s. Assume that the equation of coasting after $t = 0$ is given by

$$5400 \dfrac{dv}{dt} = -8.276v^2 - 2000$$

where $v = v(t)$ is the speed (m/s) of the car at t. Using $dx/dt = v$, the left side can be written as $Mv(dv/dx)$. The first term on the right side is the aerodynamic drag, and the second term is the rolling resistance of the tires. Calculate how far the car travels until the speed reduces to 15m/s. *Hint*: The equation of motion may be integrated as

$$\int_{15}^{30} \dfrac{5400}{8.276v^2 + 2000} v\,dv = \int_0^x dx' = x$$

Evaluate the equation above using Simpson's 1/3 rule.

(5.15) (a) If $f(x)$ is a polynomial of order n or less, the Newton-Cotes closed formula of order n (using $n+1$ points) becomes exact. Explain the reason. (b) Newton-Cotes closed formula of an even order n becomes exact if f is of order $n + 1$. Explain why.

Problems

(5.16) The length of a curve defined by $x = \phi(t)$, $y = \psi(t)$, $a < t < b$, is given by

$$s = \int_a^b \sqrt{[\phi'(t)]^2 + [\psi'(t)]^2} \, dt$$

Using the Gauss quadrature of 2, 4, and 6 points, find the length of the cycloid defined by

$$x = 3[t - \sin(t)], \quad y = 2 - 2\cos(t), \quad 0 < t < 2\pi$$

(5.17) Repeat Problem (5.1) by Gauss quadrature of 2, 3, 4, 6, and 8 points.

(5.18) If $f(x)$ is a polynomial of order $2n - 1$ or less, the Gauss quadrature using n Legendre points becomes exact. Verify this by computing the following integral by the Gauss quadrature of order 3 (3 Legendre points):

$$y = x^5 + 3x^2$$

(5.19) Evaluate the following improper integral accurately up to the sixth decimal place by the extended trapezoidal rule:

$$\int_{-\infty}^{\infty} \frac{\exp(-x^2)}{1 + x^2} \, dx$$

(5.20) Calculate the following integrals by the Gauss quadrature of 6 points:

(a) $\int_0^\pi \dfrac{1}{2 + \cos(x)} \, dx$

(b) $\int_1^2 \dfrac{\log(1 + x)}{x} \, dx$

(c) $\int_0^1 x \exp(2x) \, dx$

(d) $\int_0^1 \sin(x) \log(x) \, dx$

(e) $\int_{0.5}^2 \log(x) \, dx$

(5.21) Evaluate the following improper integrals accurately up to the sixth decimal place by the extended trapezoidal rule, with the exponential transformation given by Eq.(5.4.10):

(a) $\int_0^1 \dfrac{\tan(x)}{x^{0.7}} \, dx$

(b) $\int_0^1 \dfrac{\exp(x)}{\sqrt{1 - x^2}}$

(5.22) Calculate the following integral by the extended trapezoidal rule for each axis:

$$I = \int_1^2 \int_0^1 \sin(x+y)\, dydx$$

(Use only two intervals for each axis; the sine function is in radians.)

(5.23) Evaluate the following integral by Simpson's 1/3 rule (not the extended Simpson's rule):

$$I = \int_0^1 \int_0^x \sqrt{x+y}\, dydx$$

(5.24) The area of a unit circle is π. Accuracy of a numerical scheme for double integration may be tested by the problem:

$$I = \int\int_D dydx$$

where D means that the integration is extended over the interior of

$$x^2 + y^2 \leq 2x$$

which is a unit circle. Perform the numerical evaluation of the preceding double integration by the extended Simpson's rule in both directions with 2×2, 4×4, 8×8, 16×16, 32×32, and 64×64 intervals.

(5.25) Repeat Problem (5.24) using the double-exponential transformation.

(5.26) By the extended Simpson's rule with 10 intervals in each direction, evaluate the double integral

$$I = \int_0^\pi \int_0^{\sin(x)} \exp(-x^2 - y^2) dydx$$

(5.27) Evaluate the following double integral by Simpson's 1/3 rule:

$$I = \int_1^2 \int_0^{2-0.5x} \sqrt{x+y}\, dydx$$

(5.28) Repeat the problem in Example 5.8 by the Gauss-quadrature of 4 points.

(5.29) The Chebyshev polynomials satisfy the orthogonality relation:

$$\int_{-1}^1 T_{m-1}(x) T_{n-1}(x) \frac{dx}{\sqrt{1-x^2}} = \begin{cases} 0, & \text{if } m \neq n \\ \pi/2, & \text{if } m = n > 1 \\ \pi, & \text{if } m = n = 0 \end{cases}$$

Problems

Verify the foregoing relation for the combination of $m = 1$ through 7, and $n = 1$ through 7. Use the double-exponential transformation for integration. Show the results in the 7×7 matrix $A = [a_{m,n}]$ where

$$a_{m,n} = \int_{-1}^{1} T_{m-1}(x) T_{n-1}(x) \frac{dx}{\sqrt{1-x^2}}$$

Chapter 6

NUMERICAL DIFFERENTIATION

Numerical differentiation helps to evaluate derivatives of a function without analytically differentiating the function. There are two possible reasons why numerical differentiation would become necessary. First, the functional values may be known only on discrete points, or in a tabular form. In these cases, analytical differentiation is not possible. Second, even when the function is given analytically that can be differentiated, the derivation or calculation of derivatives may be cumbersome.

In this chapter two numerical differentiation methods are introduced. The first is difference approximations that evaluate the derivatives using the functional values known at discrete points. The second is application of the Cauchy integral which is useful in evaluation of derivatives of an analytical function.

6.1 DERIVATIVES OF INTERPOLATION POLYNOMIALS

The basic principle of deriving the difference formulas is to fit the discrete functional values by a polynomial and then differentiate the polynomial. When the functional values are known at discrete points, the function can be expressed approximately by an interpolation polynomial. By differentiating the interpolation polynomial, we can evaluate the derivatives.

Suppose we are interested in knowing, at least approximately, the value of the first derivative of a function $y(x)$ at $x = 0$, but assume that $y(x)$ is known only at discrete points, x_i. We now pick up a small number of points around $x = 0$, namely

$$(x_i, y_i), i = 1, 2, ...n + 1$$

where $n + 1$ is the number of the points picked up, and fit them by an interpolation polynomial in power series form as described in Chapter 4, "Polynomial and Interpolation"

$$g(x) = c_1 x^n + c_2 x^{n-1} + ... + c_n x + c_{n+1} \qquad (6.1.1)$$

The first derivative of $g(x)$ for $x = 0$ can be found by differentiating $g(x)$ and setting $x = 0$. The result is $g'(0) = c_n$, which is an approximation for $y'(0)$.

Likewise, the second derivative for $x = 0$ is $g'' = 2c_{n-1}$. In more general terms, since $g(x)$ can be differentiated up to n times, the kth derivatives are

$$g^{(k)}(0) = c_{n+1-k} k!, \quad k = 0, 1, 2, ...n \qquad (6.1.2)$$

which are approximations for $g^{(k)}(0), k = 0, 1, 2, ...n$. It is important to notice that, with $n + 1$ data points, the derivatives up to order n can be approximately evaluated.

The foregoing relations may be applied to the computation of derivatives for any value of x by translating the coordinate. Suppose derivatives of $g(x)$ at $x = a$ are desired. Then, with the coordinate transformation,

$$z = x - a$$

$g(x)$ may be written in terms of z as

$$g(x) = \overline{g}(z) = d_1 z^n + d_2 z^{n-1} + ...d_n z + d_{n+1} \qquad (6.1.4)$$

Therefore, derivatives $g^{(k)}(a)$ are given by

$$g^k(a) = \overline{g}^k(0) = d_{n+1-k} k!, \quad k = 0, 1, 2, ...n \qquad (6.1.5)$$

Coefficients d_i may be obtained directly by fitting $\overline{g}(z)$ to data set $(x_i - a, y_i), i = 1, 2, ..n + 1$ with MATLAB, namely

```
d = polyfit(x-a, y, length(xd)-1)
```

where x is a vector of $x_i, i = 1, 2, ..n+1$ and y is a vector of $y_i, i = 1, 2, ..n+1$. All the derivatives of an interpolation polynomial fitted to a data set may be computed by `poly_drv` listed as FM 6-3 in Section 6.7.

Example 6.1

A data set is given by

```
xd:  0        0.2000   0.4000   0.6000   0.8000   1.0000
yd:  0.3927   0.5672   0.6982   0.7941   0.8614   0.9053
```

Estimate all the derivatives for $x = a = 0.3$.

Solution

We transform x-coordinate to z by $z = x - a$, where $a = 3$. Because there are six data points, a fifth-order polynomial will be used. The power coefficients of the interpolation polynomial are obtained by

```
xd = [0        0.2000   0.4000   0.6000   0.8000   1.0000]
yd = [0.3927   0.5672   0.6982   0.7941   0.8614   0.9053]
a=0.3; L=length(xd);
d = polyfit(xd-a,yd,L-1); fact=[1];
for k=1:L-1; fact=[factorial(k),fact]; end
deriv = d.*fact
```

The results are in decreasing order of derivatives, with the last number being the functional value:

```
1.8750    -1.3750    1.0406    -0.9710    0.6533    0.6376
```

An alternative way is

```
d = polyfit(xd-a,yd,length(xd)-1);
deriv=polyval(d,0);
for n=1:length(xd)-1; d = polyder(d);
    deriv=[polyval(d,0),deriv];
end
deriv
```

6.2 DIFFERENCE APPROXIMATIONS

In the preceding section, we showed that all derivatives of a polynomial fitted to a data set can be easily evaluated. In usual practical numerical analyses, however, not all derivatives are necessary, but rather one or two derivatives of a low order are most frequently required. The formulas to approximate derivatives are difference approximations. In the present section, we derive difference approximations by polynomial interpolation.

To illustrate derivation of difference approximations, we consider a function $f(x)$ as depicted in Figure 6.1, and assume that the first derivative of $f(x)$ at $x = x_0$ is to be evaluated. If the values of $f_{-1} = f(x_0 - h)$, $f_0 = f(x_0)$, and $f_1 = f(x_0 + h)$ are given, where h is an interval between two consecutive points on the x-axis, then $f'_0 = f'(x_0)$ may be approximated by the gradient of linear interpolation A, B, or C depicted in Figure 6.1. The meanings of x_{-1} and x_1 are, respectively, $x_{-1} = x_0 - h$ and $x_1 = x_0 + h$. These three approximations using the gradient of lines A, B, and C are called, respectively, forward, backward, and central difference approximations. Their mathematical formulas are as follows:

(a) Approximation using A (forward difference approximation)

$$f'_0 \approx \frac{f_1 - f_0}{h} \qquad (6.2.1)$$

(b) Approximation using B (backward difference approximation)

$$f'_0 \approx \frac{f_0 - f_{-1}}{h} \qquad (6.2.2)$$

(c) Approximation using C (central difference approximation)

$$f'_0 \approx \frac{f_1 - f_{-1}}{2h} \qquad (6.2.3)$$

Difference approximations are closely related to interpolation polynomials. Let us consider $p+1$ abscissa points, $x_a, x_b, \ldots x_g$, and the corresponding ordinates, $f_a, f_b, \ldots f_g$. The interpolation polynomial fitted to these data points can be expressed by the Lagrange interpolation. The interpolation

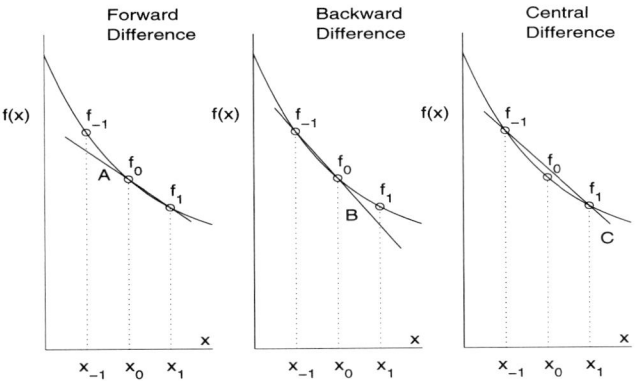

Figure 6.1 Graphic explanation of difference approximations for $f'(x_0)$.

polynomial fitted to $p+1$ points is of order p at most. Therefore, a derivative of up to the pth order can be evaluated. The derivative of the interpolation polynomial at points a, b, ... g are named difference approximations. Depending on which of x_a, x_b, ... x_g the derivative is evaluated for and the order of the derivative, many different approximation formulas can be obtained.

Example 6.2

(a) Write the Lagrange interpolation polynomial that passes through data points $x_0 = 0$, $x_1 = h$, and $x_2 = 2h$, with ordinates f_0, f_1, and f_2, respectively. Derive the difference approximation for $f'(0)$ by differentiating the interpolation formula once and setting $x = 0$. Derive also the difference approximation for $f''(0)$ by differentiating the interpolation formula twice and setting $x = 0$.

(b) Write the Lagrange interpolation polynomial that passes through $x_{-1} = -h$, $x_0 = 0$, and $x_1 = h$ with ordinates f_{-1}, f_0, and f_1, respectively. By differentiating the interpolation formula, derive the difference approximation for $f'_0 = f'(x_0)$. Derive also the difference approximation for $f''_0 = f''(x_0)$.

(c) Repeat the same for the points x_{-2}, x_{-1}, and x_0.

Solution

(a) We approximate $f(x)$ by the Lagrange interpolation polynomial passing through points $i = 0$, 1, and 2:

$$f(x) \approx g(x)$$
$$= \frac{(x-x_1)(x-x_2)}{(x_0-x_1)(x_0-x_2)} f_0 + \frac{(x-x_0)(x-x_2)}{(x_1-x_0)(x_1-x_2)} f_1$$
$$+ \frac{(x-x_0)(x-x_1)}{(x_2-x_0)(x_2-x_1)} f_2$$

Differentiating once and setting $x = 0$, we get

$$f'_0 \approx \frac{-f_2 + 4f_1 - 3f_0}{2h} \tag{A}$$

Differentiating twice and setting $x = 0$ yield

$$f''_0 \approx \frac{f_2 - 2f_1 + f_0}{h^2} \tag{B}$$

Section 6.2 Difference Approximations 255

An alternative approach is as follows. If we define $z = x/h$, the Lagrange interpolation formula can be written as

$$g(x) = \frac{(z-1)(z-2)}{(0-1)(0-2)}f_0 + \frac{(z-0)(z-2)}{(1-0)(1-2)}f_1 + \frac{(z-0)(z-1)}{(2-0)(2-1)}f_2$$

In differentiating the foregoing equation, use the identity

$$\frac{d}{dx} = \frac{1}{h}\frac{d}{dz}$$

MATLAB may be used to evaluate the derivative of the coefficient polynomials. In the case of the coefficient of f_0, for example, recognize that the polynomial is the quadratic polynomial passing through x=[0 1 2], y=[1 0 0], so the power coefficients can be obtained by the `polyfit` command, namely, stt c=polyfit([0 1 2], [1 0 0],2). The power coefficients can also be obtained by the `polyder` command: cd=polyder(c). The derivative value for $z = 0$ can be calculated by polyval(cd,0). The present approach can be easily adapted in (b) and (c) that follow.

(b) The Lagrange interpolation passing through points $i = -1, 0$, and 1 is

$$f(x) \approx g(x)$$
$$= \frac{(x-x_0)(x-x_1)}{(x_{-1}-x_0)(x_{-1}-x_1)}f_{-1} + \frac{(x-x_{-1})(x-x_1)}{(x_0-x_{-1})(x_0-x_1)}f_0$$
$$+ \frac{(x-x_{-1})(x-x_0)}{(x_1-x_{-1})(x_1-x_0)}f_1$$

Differentiating once and twice, respectively, and setting $x = 0$ yield

$$f_0' \approx \frac{f_1 - f_{-1}}{2h} \tag{C}$$

$$f_0'' \approx \frac{f_{+1} - 2f_0 + f_{-1}}{h^2} \tag{D}$$

(c) The Lagrange interpolation passing through points at $i = -2, -1$, and 0 is

$$f(x) \approx g(x)$$
$$= \frac{(x-x_{-1})(x-x_0)}{(x_{-2}-x_{-1})(x_{-2}-x_0)}f_{-2} + \frac{(x-x_{-2})(x-x_0)}{(x_{-1}-x_{-2})(x_{-1}-x_0)}f_{-1}$$
$$+ \frac{(x-x_{-2})(x-x_{-1})}{(x_0-x_{-2})(x_0-x_{-1})}f_0$$

Differentiating once and twice, respectively, and setting $x = 0$ yield

$$f'_0 \approx \frac{3f_0 - 4f_{-1} + f_{-2}}{2h} \tag{E}$$

$$f''_0 \approx \frac{f_0 - 2f_{-1} + f_{-2}}{h^2} \tag{F}$$

Comments: (1) Equations (A), (C), and (E) are all approximations for $f'(0)$, but use different data points. When the accuracy of difference approximation is in question, the general information of the error's behavior of the Lagrange interpolation is helpful. As discussed in Section 4.3, the accuracy of a Lagrange interpolation with equispaced points is best about the center point. This indicates that Eq.(C), which is obtained by evaluating the derivative of the interpolation formula for the center point, is most accurate. The other two equations, (A) and (E), obtained by the derivative evaluated at the leftmost and rightmost points, respectively, are less accurate. (2) Equation (C) is identical to Eq.(6.2.3) that is derived by differentiating the linear interpolation through the two points, $i = -1$ and 1.

Example 6.3

Calculate the first derivative of $\tan(x)$ at $x = 1$ by the five difference approximations derived in this section, Eqs.(6.2.2), (6.2.1), (6.2.3), and Eqs.(E) and(A) in Example 6.2, using $h = 0.1, 0.05,$ and 0.02. Then evaluate the percent error of each approximation by comparison with the exact value.

Solution

By introducing $f_i = f(1 + ih) = \tan(1 + ih)$ into the five equations, the results in Table 6.1 are obtained. The numbers in parentheses are percent errors. Notice that the errors of the first two approximations decrease in proportion to h, while errors of the last three approximations decrease in proportion to h^2 approximately. Clearly, the rate of reduction of error becomes faster as the order of accuracy becomes higher.

Table 6.1 Results of Calculations

	$h = 0.1$	$h = 0.05$	$h = 0.02$
$[f(1) - f(1-h)]/h$	2.9724 (13.2)	3.1805 (7.1)	3.3224 (3.0)
$[f(1+h) - f(1)]/h$	4.0735 (−18.9)	3.7181 (−8.5)	3.5361 (−3.2)
$[f(1+h) - f(1-h)]/2h$	3.5230 (−2.8)	3.4493 (−0.69)	3.4293 (−0.11)
$[3f(1) - 4f(1-h) + f(1-2h)]/2h$	3.3061 (3.5)	3.3885 (1.08)	3.4186 (0.20)
$[-f(1+2h) + 4f(1+h) - 3f(1)]/2h$	3.0733 (10.3)	3.3627 (1.83)	3.4170 (0.25)

6.3 TAYLOR EXPANSION METHOD

The Taylor expansion method is an alternative way of deriving difference approximations. It not only derives the difference formulas systematically, but also derives the error terms. The difference approximation derived by the Taylor expansion is identical to that derived by differentiating the polynomial interpolation when the same data points are used.

For a derivative of order p, the minimum number of data points necessary to derive a difference approximation is $p + 1$. For example, a difference approximation for the first derivative of a function needs at least two points.

Let us consider the derivation of difference approximation for $f'_i = f'(x_i)$ in terms of $f_i = f(x_i)$ and $f_{i+1} = f(x_{i+1})$. The Taylor expansion of f_{i+1} about x_i is

$$f_{i+1} = f_i + hf'_i + \frac{h^2}{2}f''_i + \frac{h^3}{6}f'''_i + \frac{h^4}{24}f''''_i + \ldots \quad (6.3.1)$$

Solving Eq.(6.3.1) for f'_i yields

$$f'_i = \frac{f_{i+1} - f_i}{h} - \frac{h}{2}f''_i - \frac{h^2}{6}f'''_i - \ldots \quad (6.3.2)$$

If we ignore all the terms except the first term on the right side, the forward difference approximation is obtained; it is already shown as Eq.(6.2.1). The terms ignored constitute the truncation error, which is represented by the leading term, $-(h/2)f_i''$. Other terms vanish more rapidly than the leading term when h is decreased. The forward difference approximation is expressed, including the truncation error, as

$$f_i' = \frac{f_{i+1} - f_i}{h} + E \qquad (6.3.3)$$

where

$$E \approx -\frac{h}{2} f_i''$$

The term E indicates that the error is approximately proportional to the grid interval h. The error is also proportional to the second derivative f''.

The backward difference approximation for the first derivative using f_{i-1} and f_i is obtained in a similar manner. The Taylor expansion of f_{i-1} is

$$f_{i-1} = f_i - h f_i' + \frac{h^2}{2} f_i'' - \frac{h^3}{6} f_i''' + \frac{h^4}{24} f_i'''' + \ldots \qquad (6.3.4)$$

Solving Eq.(6.3.4) for f_i', the backward difference approximation is obtained as

$$f_i' = \frac{f_i - f_{i-1}}{h} + E \qquad (6.3.5)$$

where

$$E \approx \frac{h}{2} f_i''$$

The central difference approximation using f_{i+1} and f_{i-1} may be derived by Taylor expansions of f_{i+1} and f_{i-1}, already given as Eqs.(6.3.1) and (6.3.4), respectively. Subtracting the latter from the former yields

$$f_{i+1} - f_{i-1} = 2h f_i' + \frac{1}{3} h^3 f_i''' + \ldots \qquad (6.3.6)$$

where the f_i'' term has disappeared by cancellation. By solving for f_i' we get

$$f_i' = \frac{f_{i+1} - f_{i-1}}{2h} - \frac{1}{6} h^2 f_i''' + \ldots \qquad (6.3.7)$$

Including the error term, the central difference approximation is expressed

as
$$f'_i = \frac{f_{i+1} - f_{i-1}}{2h} + E \qquad (6.3.8)$$

where
$$E \approx -\frac{h^2}{6} f'''_i$$

It is remarkable that, because of the cancellation of the f'' term, the error of the central difference approximation is proportional to h^2 rather than h. When h is decreased, the error decreases more quickly than with the other two approximations.

As explained before, a difference approximation for $f_i^{(p)}$ needs at least $p+1$ data points. As the number of data points increases, a more accurate difference approximation can be obtained. To illustrate the point, we derive a difference approximation for f'_i using f_i, f_{i+1}, and f_{i+2}. Since the minimum number of data points for f' is two, we have one extra point than the minimum required. Expansions of f_{i+1} and f_{i+2} are written as

$$f_{i+1} = f_i + h f'_i + \frac{h^2}{2} f''_i + \frac{h^3}{6} f'''_i + \frac{h^4}{24} f''''_i + \ldots \qquad (6.3.9)$$

$$f_{i+2} = f_i + 2h f'_i + \frac{4h^2}{2} f''_i + \frac{8h^3}{6} f'''_i + \frac{16h^4}{24} f''''_i + \ldots \qquad (6.3.10)$$

With these two equations, it is possible to eliminate the second derivative term, so that the leading term of the truncation errors becomes the third-order derivative term. On the other hand, if the third derivative term in Eqs.(6.3.9) and (6.3.10) were eliminated instead of the second derivative term, the difference approximation obtained would become less accurate because the leading error term becomes one order lower.

By subtracting Eq.(6.3.10) from 4 times Eq.(6.3.9), we obtain

$$4 f_{i+1} - f_{i+2} = 3 f_i + 2 h f'_i + \frac{2h^3}{3} f'''_i + \ldots \qquad (6.3.11)$$

Solving the foregoing equation for f'_i yields

$$f'_i = \frac{-f_{i+2} + 4 f_{i+1} - 3 f_i}{2h} + E \qquad (6.3.12)$$

where the error term is given by
$$E \approx \frac{h^2}{3} f'''_i$$

Equation (6.3.12) is the three-point forward difference approximation, which is the same as Eq.(A) in Example 6.2. Its error is of the same order as the central difference approximation.

Similarly, the three-point backward difference approximation may be derived using f_i, f_{i-1}, and f_{i-2}:

$$f'_i = \frac{3f_i - 4f_{i-1} + f_{i-2}}{2h} + E \qquad (6.3.13)$$

where

$$E \approx \frac{h^2}{3} f'''_i$$

Difference approximations for the second derivative are obtained in a similar manner. The basic principle is to eliminate the first derivative plus as many derivatives of order 3 or higher as possible.

For illustration, we derive the difference approximation for f''_i in terms of f_{i+1}, f_i and f_{i-1}. Taylor expansions of f_{i+1} and f_{i-1} are given by Eqs.(6.3.1) and (6.3.4). By adding the two, we get

$$f_{i+1} + f_{i-1} = 2f_i + h^2 f''_i + \frac{h^4}{12} f''''_i + \ldots$$

or equivalently

$$f_{i+1} - 2f_i + f_{i-1} = h^2 f''_i + \frac{h^4}{12} f''''_i + \ldots$$

Then, truncating after the f'' term and rewriting yield

$$f''_i = \frac{f_{i+1} - 2f_i + f_{i-1}}{h^2} + E \qquad (6.3.14)$$

The foregoing equation is the central difference approximation for f'', which is the same as Eq.(D) in Example 6.2. The error is represented by

$$E \approx -\frac{h^2}{12} f''''_i$$

Another difference approximation for f''_i may be derived in terms of f_i, f_{i-1}, and f_{i-2} (the minimum number of data points for $p = 2$ is 3). Subtracting 2 times the Taylor expansion of f_{i-1} from that of f_{i-2} results in

$$f_{i-2} - 2f_{i-1} = -f_i + h^2 f''_i - h^3 f'''_i + \ldots$$

Solving the foregoing equation for f_i'' yields

$$f_i'' = \frac{f_{i-2} - 2f_{i-1} + f_i}{h^2} + E \qquad (6.3.15)$$

with

$$E \approx hf_i'''$$

Equation (6.3.15) is the backward difference approximation for f_i'', which was already derived in Example 6.1. The order of its truncation error is lower than the central difference approximation given by Eq.(6.3.14). The higher accuracy of the central difference approximation is what we predicted in Section 6.2 from the fact that the accuracy of the Lagrange interpolation is the best at the center.

Difference approximations for even higher derivatives can be obtained in a similar way, but derivation becomes increasingly more cumbersome as both the number of terms and the order of the derivative increase. For this reason, a computer program that automatically finds the difference approximation for a given set of data will be useful. Its algorithm is described in Section 6.3.

The difference approximations that are frequently used are listed in Table 6.2.

Table 6.2 Difference Approximations

First derivative

(a) Forward difference approximations:

$$f_i' = \frac{f_{i+1} - f_i}{h} + E, \quad E \approx -\frac{1}{2}hf_i''$$

$$f_i' = \frac{-f_{i+2} + 4f_{i+1} - 3f_i}{2h} + E, \quad E \approx \frac{1}{3}h^2 f_i'''$$

$$f_i' = \frac{2f_{i+3} - 9f_{i+2} + 18f_{i+1} - 11f_i}{6h} + E, \quad E \approx -\frac{1}{4}h^3 f_i''''$$

(b) Backward difference approximations:

$$f_i' = \frac{f_i - f_{i-1}}{h} + E, \quad E \approx \frac{1}{2}hf_i''$$

$$f'_i = \frac{3f_i - 4f_{i-1} + f_{i-2}}{2h} + E, \quad E \approx \frac{1}{3}h^2 f'''_i$$

$$f'_i = \frac{11f_i - 18f_{i-1} + 9f_{i-2} - 2f_{i-3}}{6h} + E, \quad E \approx \frac{1}{4}h^3 f''''_i$$

(c) Central difference approximations:

$$f'_i = \frac{f_{i+1} - f_{i-1}}{2h} + E, \quad E \approx -\frac{h^2}{6} f'''_i$$

$$f'_i = \frac{-f_{i+2} + 8f_{i+1} - 8f_{i-1} + f_{i-2}}{12h} + E, \quad E \approx \frac{1}{30}h^4 f^{(v)}_i$$

Second derivative

(d) Forward difference approximations:

$$f''_i = \frac{f_{i+2} - 2f_{i+1} + f_i}{h^2} + E, \quad E \approx -h f'''_i$$

$$f''_i = \frac{-f_{i+3} + 4f_{i+2} - 5f_{i+1} + 2f_i}{h^2} + E, \quad E \approx \frac{11}{12}h^2 f''''_i$$

(e) Backward difference approximations:

$$f''_i = \frac{f_i - 2f_{i-1} + f_{i-2}}{h^2} + E, \quad E \approx h f'''_i$$

$$f''_i = \frac{2f_i - 5f_{i-1} + 4f_{i-1} - f_{i-3}}{h^2} + E, \quad E \approx \frac{11}{12}h^2 f''''_i$$

(f) Central difference approximations:

$$f''_i = \frac{f_{i+1} - 2f_i + f_{i-1}}{h^2} + E, \quad E \approx -\frac{1}{12}h^2 f''''_i$$

$$f''_i = \frac{-f_{i+2} + 16f_{i+1} - 30f_i + 16f_{i-1} - f_{i-2}}{12h^2} + E, \quad E \approx \frac{1}{90}h^4 f^{(vi)}_i$$

Third derivative

(g) Forward difference approximation:

$$f'''_i = \frac{f_{i+3} - 3f_{i+2} + 3f_{i+1} - f_i}{h^3} + E, \quad E \approx -\frac{3}{2}h f''''_i$$

(h) Backward difference approximation:

$$f''_i = \frac{f_i - 3f_{i-1} + 3f_{i-2} - f_{i-3}}{h^3} + E, \quad E \approx \frac{3}{2}h f''''_i$$

(i) Central difference approximation:
$$f_i'' = \frac{f_{i+2} - 2f_{i+1} + 2f_{i-1} - f_{i-2}}{2h^3} + E, \quad E \approx -\frac{1}{4}h^2 f_i^{(v)}$$

6.4 ALGORITHMS TO AUTOMATE DERIVATIONS

The objective of this section is to describe two algorithms to automatically derive the difference approximation using a given set of data points. The first is based on differentiation of the Lagrange interpolation formula, and the second is based on the Taylor expansion.

Suppose that L data points are used and they are numbered as $i = \alpha, \beta, ..., \lambda$, as shown in Figure 6.2. We assume $L \geq p+1$ where p is the order of the derivative. The abscissas of the data points are $x_i = \alpha h, \beta h, ..., \lambda h$ with $i = \alpha, \beta, ..., \lambda$, where h is a given constant. If $i = \alpha, \beta, ..., \lambda$ are consecutive integers, h becomes the interval size between two consecutive points. In general, $i = \alpha, \beta, ...$ have to be in increasing order but do not have to be integers.

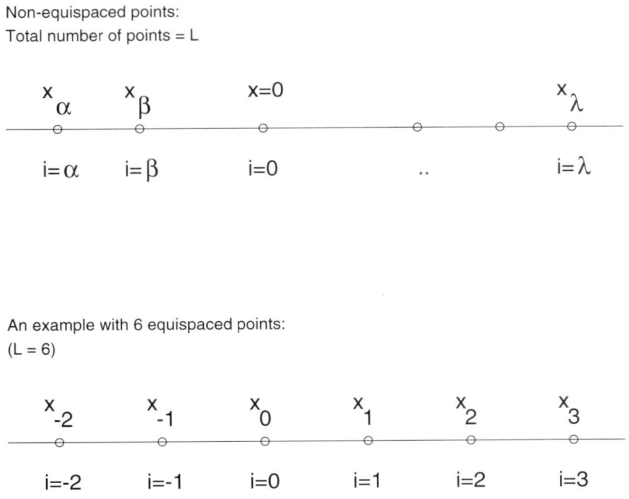

Figure 6.2 Illustration of grid points.

6.4.1 Algorithm 1

The algorithm works easily on MATLAB using `shape_pw` and `polyder`, described in Section 4.6. The Lagrange interpolation fitted at data points x_α, x_β, ..., x_λ, with corresponding functional values f_α, f_β, ..., f_λ, is

$$g(x) = \sum_{i=\alpha,\beta,...,\lambda} v_i(x) f_i \qquad (6.4.1)$$

where v_i is a polynomial of x given by

$$v_i(x) = \prod_{\substack{j=\alpha,\beta,...,\lambda \\ j \neq i}} \frac{(x-x_j)}{(x_i-x_j)}, \quad \text{for } i = \alpha, \beta, ..., \lambda \qquad (6.4.2)$$

The pth derivative of $g(x)$ is written as

$$g^{(p)}(x) = \sum_{i=\alpha,\beta,...,\lambda} v_i^{(p)}(x) f_i \qquad (6.4.3)$$

A difference approximation formula may be obtained by setting x to one of $x_i = x_\alpha, x_\beta, ..., x_\lambda$ in Eq.(6.4.3). See Section 4.6 for evaluation of $v_i^{(p)}$.

In the foregoing approach, the values of x_i, and accordingly their increments, are numerically specified. It is more desirable, however, to be able to change the actual increments while the relative values of the increments are fixed. This becomes possible if we express x_i by $x_i = h\alpha, h\beta, ..., h\lambda$ where h is a parameter to be fixed later, and $\alpha, \beta, ..., \lambda$ are reference (or relative) abscissas of the data points. We also transform x to z by $x = hz$. Then, Eq.(6.4.2) can be written as

$$v_i(z) = \prod_{\substack{j=\alpha,\beta,...,\lambda \\ j \neq i}} \frac{(z-j)}{(i-j)}, \quad \text{for } i = \alpha, \beta, ..., \lambda \qquad (6.4.4)$$

Using the identity

$$\frac{d}{dx} = \frac{1}{h}\frac{d}{dz}$$

Equation(6.4.3) may also be written as

$$g^{(p)}(x) = \frac{1}{h^p}\left(\frac{d}{dz}\right)^p g(x) = \frac{1}{h^p} \sum_{i=\alpha,\beta,...,\lambda} \left(\frac{d}{dz}\right)^p v_i(z) f_i \qquad (6.4.5)$$

The derivatives of $v_i(z)$ with respect to z can be evaluated numerically as follows. Let us consider $v_\alpha(z)$ in detail, because the evaluation of other $v_i(z)$ will be essentially the same. Recognize that $v_1(z)$ is a polynomial passing through $z = [\alpha, \beta, ..., \lambda]$, $g = [1, 0, 0, ..., 0]$, so its power series form can be obtained easily by the `polyfit` command. Its first derivative can be evaluated by differentiating using the `polyder` command, and then `polval` for z=0. For a pth derivative, use `polyder` p times repeatedly before applying `polval`.

6.4.2 Algorithm 2

The difference approximation for the pth derivative of $f(x)$ in terms of f_α, f_β, .. and f_λ may be written in the form:

$$f_0^{(p)} = \frac{a_\alpha f_\alpha + a_\beta f_\beta + ... + a_\lambda f_\lambda}{h^p} + E \tag{6.4.6}$$

where a_α through a_λ are L undetermined coefficients, $f_\alpha = f(x_\alpha)$ through $f_\lambda = f(x_\lambda)$ are ordinates of the data to be used, and E is the error written by

$$E \approx c_1 h^{L-p} f_0^{(L)} + c_2 h^{L-p+1} f_0^{(L+1)} \tag{6.4.7}$$

In Eq.(6.4.7), the second term is ignored if the first coefficient c_1 is not zero. If it is, the error is represented by the second term.

The essence of the algorithm is to introduce the Taylor expansions of f_i into Eq.(6.4.6) and determine the undetermined coefficients so the error is minimized, or equivalently, the order of E becomes the highest possible.

For the simplicity of further explanation, let us assume $p = 1$, $L = 3$, $\alpha = 0$, $\beta = 1$, and $\gamma = 2$. Then, Eq.(6.4.6) becomes

$$f_0' = \frac{a_0 f_0 + a_1 f_1 + a_2 f_2}{h} + E \tag{6.4.8}$$

where a_0, a_1, and a_2 are three undetermined coefficients, and $x_0 = 0$, $x_1 = h$, and $x_2 = 2h$ are abscissas of the data points. Introducing the Taylor expansions of f_1 and f_2 about $x = 0$ into Eq.(6.4.8) yields

$$f_0' = \frac{a_0}{h} f_0$$
$$+ \frac{a_1}{h} [f_0 + h f_0' + \frac{h^2}{2} f_0'' + \frac{h^3}{6} f_0''' + ...]$$

$$+\frac{a_2}{h}[f_0 + 2hf_0' + \frac{4h^2}{2}f_0'' + \frac{8h^3}{6}f_0''' + ...\ ] + E$$

or, after reorganizing terms,

$$\begin{aligned}f_0' &= f_0[a_0 + a_1 + a_2]\frac{1}{h} \\ &+ f_0'[0 + a_1 + 2a_2] \\ &+ f_0''[0 + a_1 + 4a_2]\frac{h}{2} \\ &+ f_0'''[0 + a_1 + 8a_2]\frac{h^2}{6} \\ &+ f_0''''[0 + a_1 + 16a_2]\frac{h^3}{24} \\ &+ ... + E\end{aligned} \qquad (6.4.9)$$

The foregoing equation has three undetermined coefficients which can be determined by imposing three conditions. To minimize the error, we set the coefficients of f_0, f_0', and f_0'' to 0, 1, and 0, respectively:

$$\begin{aligned}a_0 + a_1 + a_2 &= 0 \\ 0 + a_1 + 2a_2 &= 1 \\ 0 + a_1 + 4a_2 &= 0\end{aligned} \qquad (6.4.10)$$

By solving the foregoing equations, the three undetermined coefficients become $a_0 = -3/2$, $a_1 = 2$, and $a_2 = -1/2$.

The higher-order terms in Eq.(6.4.9) that do not vanish constitute the error, namely

$$E \approx -f_0'''(0 + a_1 + 8a_2)\frac{h^2}{6} - f_0''''(0 + a_1 + 16a_2)\frac{h^3}{24} + ... \qquad (6.4.11)$$

By comparing Eq.(6.4.11) to Eq.(6.4.7), and remembering that $L = 3$ and $p = 1$, c_1 and c_2 in the latter are found to be

$$c_1 = -(a_1 + 8a_2)\frac{1}{6}$$
$$c_2 = -(a_1 + 16a_2)\frac{1}{24}$$

which, by introducing $a_1 = 2$ and $a_2 = -1/2$, become

$$c_1 = -(2 - \frac{8}{2})\frac{1}{6} = \frac{1}{3}$$
$$c_2 = -(2 - \frac{16}{2})\frac{1}{24} = \frac{1}{4}$$

Since the first term of Eq.(6.4.7) is not zero, we ignore the second term and write the error term as

$$E \approx \frac{1}{3} h^2 f_0''' \qquad (6.4.12)$$

If the first term of Eq.(6.4.7) becomes zero, the second term would represent the error.

The final result of the present derivation is

$$f_0' = \frac{-3f_0 + 4f_1 - f_2}{2h} + E \qquad (6.4.13)$$

where E has been given by Eq.(6.4.12).

In more general terms, by using L data points we can determine the L undetermined coefficients in Eq.(6.4.6). Thus, the error term becomes proportional to the $(L+1)$th term or, equivalently, the Lth derivative, provided that its coefficient is not zero. If it is zero, the error term becomes one order higher.

The present algorithm works even when the grid indices, α, β, ... are not integers. This means that difference approximation on a nonequispaced grid may be derived by the present algorithm. The algorithm is implemented in diff_fnd (see FM 6-1 in Section 6.7).

6.5 DIFFERENCE APPROXIMATION FOR PARTIAL DERIVATIVES

Difference approximation formulas for partial derivatives of multidimensional functions are essentially the same as the numerical differentiation of one-dimensional functions.

Consider a two-dimensional function $f(x, y)$. The difference approximation for the partial derivative with respect to x, for example, can be derived by fixing y to a constant y_0 and considering $f(x, y_0)$ as a one-dimensional function. Therefore, the forward, central, and backward difference approximations for the preceding partial derivatives may be written, respectively, as

$$f_x \approx \frac{f(x_0 + \Delta x, y_0) - f(x_0, y_0)}{\Delta x}$$
$$f_x \approx \frac{f(x_0 + \Delta x, y_0) - f(x_0 - \Delta x, y_0)}{2\Delta x} \qquad (6.5.1)$$
$$f_x \approx \frac{f(x_0, y_0) - f(x_0 - \Delta x, y_0)}{\Delta x}$$

where f_x means the partial derivative of f with respect to x, or equivalently

$$f_x = \frac{\partial f}{\partial x} \qquad (6.5.2)$$

The central difference approximations for the second derivatives of $f(x,y)$ at (x_0, y_0) are illustrated as

$$f_{xx} \approx \frac{f(x_0 + \Delta x, y_0) - 2f(x_0, y_0) + f(x_0 - \Delta x, y_0)}{\Delta x^2}$$
$$f_{yy} \approx \frac{f(x_0, y_0 + \Delta y) - 2f(x_0, y_0) + f(x_0, y_0 - \Delta y)}{\Delta y^2} \qquad (6.5.3)$$
$$f_{xy} \approx \frac{f(x_0 + \Delta x, y_0 + \Delta y) - f(x_0 - \Delta x, y_0 + \Delta y)}{\Delta x \Delta y}$$
$$+ \frac{-f(x_0 + \Delta x, y_0 - \Delta y) + f(x_0 - \Delta x, y_0 - \Delta y)}{\Delta x \Delta y}$$

where f_{xx}, f_{yy}, and f_{xy} are shorthand notations for

$$\frac{\partial^2 f}{\partial x^2}, \quad \frac{\partial^2 f}{\partial y^2}, \quad \text{and} \quad \frac{\partial^2 f}{\partial x \partial y}$$

respectively.

6.6 NUMERICAL EVALUATION OF HIGH-ORDER DERIVATIVES

The difference approximations discussed in the previous sections are useful to evaluate derivatives of a low order. As the order of derivative becomes higher, accuracy of the difference approximations deteriorates quickly because of both truncation and rounding errors.

For high-order derivatives of an analytical function, the Cauchy integral may become useful; it works accurately for low-order derivatives as well. The Cauchy integral is given by

Section 6.6 Numerical Evaluation of High-Order Derivatives

$$f^{(k)}(z_0) = \frac{k!}{2\pi i} \int_C \frac{f(z)}{(z-z_0)^{k+1}}\, dz \tag{6.6.1}$$

where z is a complex variable. The integral is along a closed curve C on the complex plane, in which $f(z)$ is analytic and z_0 is contained. The integration along C is in the counterclockwise direction. Integration on the complex plane is easy with MATLAB. The shape of the curve C is arbitrary, so the most convenient shape is a circle.

The circle centered at z_0 with radius r on the complex plane is

$$z = re^{i\theta} + z_0, \quad 0 \le \theta < 2\pi \tag{6.6.2}$$

where θ is the angle. Substituting Eq.(6.6.2) into Eq.(6.6.1) yields

$$f^{(k)}(z_0) = \frac{k!}{2\pi i} \int_0^{2\pi} \frac{f(re^{i\theta}+z_0)}{r^{k+1}e^{i(k+1)\theta}}\, ire^{i\theta}d\theta \tag{6.6.3}$$

Applying the trapezoidal rule, a numerical integration for Eq.(6.6.3) becomes

$$f^{(k)}(z_0) \approx \frac{k!}{2\pi}\Delta\theta \sum_{n=1}^{N} \frac{f(re^{i\theta_n}+z_0)}{r^k e^{ik\theta_n}} \tag{6.6.4}$$

where $\Delta\theta = 2\pi/N$, $\theta_n = n\Delta\theta$, and N is the number of intervals chosen for the numerical integration along the circle. Equation (6.6.4) may be evaluated by Cauchy_d. Its synopsis is

```
y = Cauchy_d('f_name', z0, k)
```

where 'f_name' is the function name or the m-file name that defines the function to be differentiated, z0 is z_0, and k is the order of the derivative. The values of r and N are selected by default.

We first test Cauchy_d for 1st through 15th derivatives of $\sin(x)$ for $x=0$ by the following script:

```
for k=1:15
  fd = Cauchy_d('sin', 0, k);
  fprintf(' k = %2d, real(fd)=%12.5e, imag(fd)=%12.5e\n', ...
              k, real(fd), imag(fd))
end
```

The results are:

```
k =  1, real(fd)= 1.00000e+000, imag(fd)= 1.98159e-017
k =  2, real(fd)=-1.88294e-017, imag(fd)=-8.48939e-018
k =  3, real(fd)=-1.00000e+000, imag(fd)=-2.35556e-017
k =  4, real(fd)= 1.89267e-016, imag(fd)= 2.30611e-016
k =  5, real(fd)= 1.00000e+000, imag(fd)= 8.57269e-016
k =  6, real(fd)=-1.32367e-013, imag(fd)=-1.43143e-014
k =  7, real(fd)=-1.00000e+000, imag(fd)=-9.26930e-014
k =  8, real(fd)=-1.80456e-012, imag(fd)= 1.56229e-012
k =  9, real(fd)= 1.00000e+000, imag(fd)= 3.19010e-012
k = 10, real(fd)= 4.49412e-010, imag(fd)= 9.85870e-011
k = 11, real(fd)=-1.00000e+000, imag(fd)= 2.96538e-009
k = 12, real(fd)=-4.86800e-009, imag(fd)= 2.69223e-008
k = 13, real(fd)= 1.00000e+000, imag(fd)=-2.12625e-007
k = 14, real(fd)=-6.35398e-007, imag(fd)= 1.37088e-006
k = 15, real(fd)=-1.00013e+000, imag(fd)=-1.59137e-005
```

where `real(fd)` and `imag(fd)` are real and imaginary parts of the derivative, respectively, the latter of which must be zero if the error of the computation is zero. For $k = 1$, the computed derivative is correct. Although the imaginary part computed is not zero, it is a negligibly small rounding error. For order 2, the exact value of the derivative of the sine function is zero. The computed value is within a rounding error. By continuing our evaluation similarly, we find that computed derivative values are good up to order 14. Beyond 14, however, errors seem to pile up rapidly as the order is increased.

The accuracy of the Cauchy integral is affected by the choice of r and the number of points (in the trapezoidal rule), both of which are fixed in `Cauchy_d`. Readers are encouraged to investigate its effect, particularly if a very high derivative is computed; also the Cauchy integral is not valid if a singularity exists within the circle.

Example 6.4

The Taylor expansions of $\tan(x)$ about $x = a$ are written as:

$$\tan(x) = \tan(a) + h\tan'(a) + \frac{h^2}{2}\tan''(a) + \frac{h^3}{6}\tan'''(a) + ... \frac{h^n}{n!}\tan^{(n)}(a) + ...$$

The truncated Taylor series

$$g_k(x) = \tan(a) + x\tan'(a) + \frac{x^2}{2}\tan''(a) + \frac{x^3}{6}\tan'''(a) + ... \frac{x^k}{k!}\tan^{(k)}(a)$$

is called a Taylor polynomial of order k. In order to investigate the convergence of the Taylor polynomials, set $a = 0$ and plot the series for $k = 4$, 6, and 8, for the interval of $-\pi/2 < x < \pi/2$. Plot also $e(x) = \tan(x) - g_k(x)$ in $0 < x < \pi/2$.

Solution

By Cauchy_d we find derivatives of $\tan(x)$ for $x = 0$:

Order of derivative	Derivative for x=0
0	0
1	1
2	0
3	2
4	0
5	16
6	0
7	272
8	0
9	7936
10	0

Figure 6.3 illustrates the error of the truncated Taylor series with k = 4, 6, and 8.

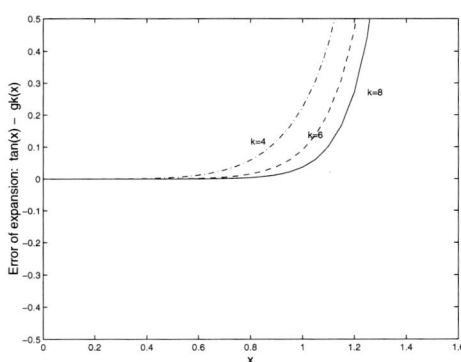

Figure 6.3 Error of truncated Taylor series.

6.7 M-FILES

FM 6-1. Difference approximation finder
Purpose: To find a difference approximation formula.

Synopsis: `diff_fnd`
All input data is prompted by the program.

diff_fnd.m

```
% diff_fnd is a difference approximation finder.
% All inputs are prompted by the program.
while 1
clear
   fprintf( '\n===========================================\n' );
   fprintf( ' Difference Approximation Finder  \n' );
   while 1
      km = input( '** Number of points ?  ' );
      if km>1 break; end
      fprintf(' Input is invalid: Repeat.\n')
   end
%
   while 1
      fprintf( '\nInput the point indices in row vector form ')
      fprintf( '\nlike [x x ... x]\n');   el = input('');
      if length(el) == km;  break; end
      fprintf( ' Number of points do not match with indices')
      fprintf( ' Repeat your input for indices.\n')
   end
   kdr = input('** Order of difference scheme to be derived ?   ' );
   z = 1.0; for  i = 1:kdr;  z = z*i; end
   for k = 1:km+2;    a(k,:) = el.^(k-1); end
   M = a(1:km, 1:km);
   rs = zeros(km,1);   rs(kdr+1) = z;
%  kmp2 = km + 2;
   y = M^(-1)*rs;
   c = a*y;
   u = abs(y);
   for k = 1:km+2
      if k<=km; if u(k)<0.000001, u(k) = 1000;end; end
      if( abs( c(k) ) < 0.00000001 ) c(k) = 0;end
   end
   f_min = min(u);
   cf = y/f_min;
   fprintf( '\nDifference scheme:\n' );
   for  k = 1:km
      finv = 1.0/f_min;
      fprintf( ' +(%8.5f/( %8.5f h^%1.0f))*', cf(k),finv, kdr)
      fprintf(   'f( %3.1fh ) \n',  el(k) );
   end
   fprintf('\nError term\n');
   dd = 1.0;
   for k = 1:km
        dd = dd*k;
```

Section 6.7 M-Files

```
      end
   for k = km+1:km+2,
      cm = -c(k);
      %km1 = k - 1;
      nh = k-1-kdr;
      if( k == km+1 & cm ~= 0 )
            fprintf( '     (%7.3f/%7.3f)h^%1.0f f', cm, dd, nh );
            for (i=1:k-1)   fprintf( '`' );
            end
            break
      end
      if( k == km + 2 ),
         fprintf( '\n    +(%7.3f/%7.3f)h^%1.0f f', cm, dd, nh );
            for i=1:k-1
               fprintf( '`' );
            end
      end
      dd = dd*k ;
   end
   fprintf('\n=============================================\n')
   kont = input( 'Type 1 to continue, or 0 to stop:' );
   if kont ==0, break; end
end
```

FM 6-2. Differentiation by Cauchy integral

Purpose: To compute derivative values of a function.

Synopsis: Cauchy_d('f_name', x, k)

        f_name: name of the function to be differentiated

        x: the abscissa of the function

        k: order of derivative

Cauchy_d.m

```
function f_d = Cauchy_d(f_name, z0, k)
N=2480 + k*10;   r=1;
dth = 2*pi/N;
th=0:dth:2*pi-dth;
z = r*exp(i*th)+ z0;
kf=1; for m=1:k, kf=kf*m; end
f_d = kf/(2*pi)*dth*sum( feval(f_name, z)./(r^k*exp(i*k*th)) );
```

FM 6-3. All derivatives of a polynomial interpolation

Purpose: To compute all derivatives of a polynomial interpolation.

Synopsis: poly_drv(xd,yd,a)

        xd: the abscissas of data points fitted by interpolation

        yd: the ordinates of data points fitted by interpolation

a: x=a at which derivatives are to be evaluated

poly_drv.m
```
function der = poly_drv(xd,yd,a)
m = length(xd)-1;
d = polyfit(xd-a, yd, m);
c = d(m:-1:1);
fact(1)=1; for i=2:m; fact(i)=i*fact(i-1);end
der = c.*fact;
```

PROBLEMS

(6.1) A table of data points for a function $y(x)$ is given:

i	x_i m	y_i m
0	0.0	0.0000
1	0.2	8.6964
2	0.4	10.6800
3	0.6	8.7440
4	0.8	4.7727
5	1.0	0.0000

Evaluate all the derivatives possible at $x = 0$ and $x = 0.5$.

(6.2) The velocity distribution of a fluid near a flat surface is given by

i	y_i mm	u_i mm
0	0	0.0000
1	2	9.8853
2	4	15.4917
3	6	18.2075
4	8	19.0210

Evaluate all the derivatives of $u(y)$ possible at $y = 0$.

(6.3) Evaluate the first derivative of $y(x) = \sin(x)$ for $x = 1$ by the three different schemes:

(a) $y'(1) \approx [y(1+h) - y(1)]/h$

(b) $y'(1) \approx [y(1) - y(1-h)]/h$

(c) $y'(1) \approx [y(1+h) - y(1-h)]/2h$

Evaluate the errors for each of $h = 0.1, 0.05, 0.01, 0.005$, and 0.001 by comparison with the exact values.

(6.4) Calculate $df(x)/dx$, where $f(x) = \sqrt{x}$, for $x = 1$ by the forward, backward, and central difference approximations with $h = 0.1, 0.05$, and 0.025. Evaluate the error of each result by (a) comparison with the exact value, and (b) using the error term shown in Table 6.2, namely, $-(1/2)hf''$, $(1/2)hf''$, and $-(1/6)h^2 f'''$, respectively.

(6.5) A difference approximation formula may be derived by differentiating a Lagrange interpolation formula, as described in Section 6.2. Suppose we have the values of f_{-2}, f_{-1}, and f_0 with an equispaced interval h. Develop a script in MATLAB that finds the coefficients in the difference approximation. Assume that the interval size between two consecutive points equals h. *Hint*: Transform x to z by $x = hz$. Work on the z coordinate. Each term of the Lagrange interpolation may be transformed to a power series form by the `polyfit` command. Then, find the coefficients of the derivative of the polynomial. The derivative on z is then transformed back to the x coordinate by $d/dx = (1/h)d/dz$.

(6.6) Derive a difference approximation and the error term for f'_i in terms of (a) f_{i-1} and f_{i+2}, (b) f_{i-1}, f_i and f_{i+2}, and (c) f_{i-2} and f_{i+2}. Assume grid points are equispaced.

(6.7) Derive a difference approximation and the error term for f''_i in terms of f_i, f_{i-1}, and f_{i-2} (three-point backward difference approximation for f''_i).

(6.8) Repeat Problem 6.4 with the second-order-accurate forward and backward difference approximations:

(a) $f'(1) \approx [-f(1+2h) + 4f(1+h) - 3f(1)]/2h$

(b) $f'(1) \approx [3f(1) - 4f(1-h) + f(1-2h)]/2h$

and evaluate the errors by comparison with the exact value of $f'(1)$.

(6.9) Calculate the first derivative $f'(1)$ for $f(x) = \sin(x)$ by the second-order-accurate forward and backward difference approximations used in Problem 6.8 for $h = 0.1, 0.05, 0.025$, and 0.001. Then, evaluate the error of each numerical approximation by comparison with the exact value. Plot the result. If an increase of error with reduction of h is observed, explain the reason.

(6.10) A difference approximation for f''' is to be derived in terms of f_{-2}, f_{-1}, f_0, f_1, and f_2 by differentiating the Lagrange interpolation formula. Develop a script in MATLAB that answers the question. (Each term of the Lagrange interpolation may be transformed to a power series form by `polyfit`. Then find the coefficients of the derivative of the polynomial.)

(6.11) Evaluate the second derivative of $\tan(x)$ at $x = 1$ by the central difference formula using $h = 0.1$, 0.05, and 0.02. Evaluate the error by comparison with the exact value and show that the error is proportional to h^2.

(6.12) (a) Knowing the error term of

$$f'_i \approx (f_i - f_{i-1})/h$$

estimate the error term for

$$f'_i \approx (f_i - f_{i-2})/2h$$

(b) The accuracy of a difference approximation can be improved by a linear combination of two difference approximations so the lowest-order truncation error of each approximation is cancelled. Determine α of the following approximation so the accuracy is optimized:

$$f'_i \approx \alpha(f_i - f_{i-1})/h + (1-\alpha)(f_i - f_{i-2})/2h$$

(6.13) Determine the optimum value of α for the following equation:

$$f''_i \approx \alpha(f_{i+1} - 2f_i + f_{i-1})/h^2 + (1-\alpha)(f_{i+2} - 2f_i + f_{i-2})/(2h)^2$$

Hint: Eliminate the leading error of both

$$(f_{i+1} - 2f_i + f_{i-1})/h^2$$

and

$$(f_{i+2} - 2f_i + f_{i-2})/(2h)^2$$

(6.14) Derive the most accurate difference approximations for f'_i and f''_i in terms of f_{i-2}, f_{i-1}, f_i, f_{i+1}, and f_{i+2}. Assume that the data points are equispaced.

(6.15) By applying Taylor expansion, derive the difference approximations for f'_i and f''_i in terms of f_i, f_{i+1}, f_{i+2}, and f_{i+3} with the highest possible accuracy for each. Assume that the grid spacing is constant.

(6.16) A function table is given by

x	f
-0.1	4.157
0	4.020
0.2	4.441

(a) Derive the best difference approximation to calculate $f'(0)$ with the data given above.

(b) What is the error term for the difference approximation?

(c) Calculate $f'(0)$ by the formula you derived.

(6.17) Derive the error term of the following difference formula:

$$f_i'(x) \approx (-f_{i+3} + 9f_{i+1} - 8f_i)/6h$$

(6.18) Two difference approximations for the 4th derivative are given by

$$f_i'''' = \frac{f_{i+4} - 4f_{i+3} + 6f_{i+2} - 4f_{i+1} + f_i}{h^4} + O(h)$$

$$f_i'''' = \frac{f_{i+2} - 4f_{i+1} + 6f_i - 4f_{i-1} + f_{i-2}}{h^4} + O(h^2)$$

By the Taylor expansion, find the error terms.

(6.19) The velocity distribution of a fluid near a flat surface is given by

i	y_i (m)	u_i (m/s)
0	0.0	0.0
1	0.001	0.4171
2	0.003	0.9080
3	0.006	1.6180

where y is the distance from the surface and u is the velocity. Assuming that the flow is laminar and $\mu = 0.001 \text{Ns/m}^2$, calculate the shear stress at $y = 0$ using data at the following points:

(a) $i = 0$ and 1
(b) $i = 0, 1,$ and 2

(6.20) The function table for $f(x, y)$ is given below:

y/x	0.0	0.5	1.0	1.5	2.0
0.0	0.0775	0.1573	0.2412	0.3309	0.4274
0.5	0.1528	0.3104	0.4767	0.6552	0.8478
1.0	0.2235	0.4547	0.7002	0.9653	1.2533
1.5	0.2866	0.5846	0.9040	1.2525	1.6348

(a) Evaluate $\partial f/\partial y$ at $x = 1.0$ and $y = 0$ using the forward difference approximation with an error of order h^2 where $h = 0.5$.

(b) Evaluate $\partial^2 f/\partial x^2$ at $x = 1.0$ and $y = 1.0$ using the central difference approximation with an error of order h^2 where $h = 0.5$.

(c) Evaluate $\partial^2 f/\partial x \partial y$ at $x = 0$ and $y = 0$ using the forward difference approximation with an error of order h^2 where $h = 0.5$.

Chapter 7

ROOTS OF NONLINEAR EQUATIONS

Solutions of the nonlinear equation, $f(x) = 0$, whether it is a scalar equation or a set of simultaneous equations, are called zeros or roots of $f(x)$. In this section, we study the methods, such as the graphic, bisection, Newton iteration, secant, and successive substitution methods, to find the real roots of scalar nonlinear equations. Those who are limited in time are suggested to study the first three methods first. If $f(x)$ is a polynomial, we may use roots, as explained in Chapter 4, "Polynomials and Interpolation."

We also study the application of successive substitution and Newton iteration to simultaneous nonlinear equations.

7.1 GRAPHICAL METHOD

Suppose we wish to find a positive root of

$$f(x) = 0 \qquad (7.1.1)$$

where

$$f(x) = x\sin(1/x) - 0.2\exp(-x) \qquad (7.1.2)$$

If you ask a mathematician to find the solution immediately, he will perhaps look at the equation for a minute. After figuring out that as x approaches 0 from the positive side of x, $\sin(1/x)$ oscillates with an increasing frequency and becomes singular at $x = 0$, he would start sketching $x\sin(1/x)$ and $0.2\exp(-x)$. After a few trials, a neat graph would be drawn, done by hand on a piece of scratch paper. From the figure, it would be found that there is only one root, approximately 0.4.

After this, a computer program may be used to find a more accurate value; however, the most crucial part of the solution has been accomplished by the graphic method. Knowing the behavior of the function, the number of roots, and its approximate value, the rest can be easily done by a computer program, or even with a hand-held calculator.

The approach of the mathematician is exactly what we will do with the graphics of MATLAB. Indeed, we can easily plot $y = x\sin(1/x)$ and $y = 0.2\exp(-x)$, as illustrated in Figure 7.1. Alternatively, $f(x) = x\sin(1/x) - 0.2\exp(-x)$ may be directly plotted, as shown in Figure 7.2. The figures show that the root is approximately 0.38. The graphic method can still be used to find a more accurate value by zooming up the plot. It would be more efficient, however, if one of the methods discussed in the following sections is applied in order to calculate much more accurately.

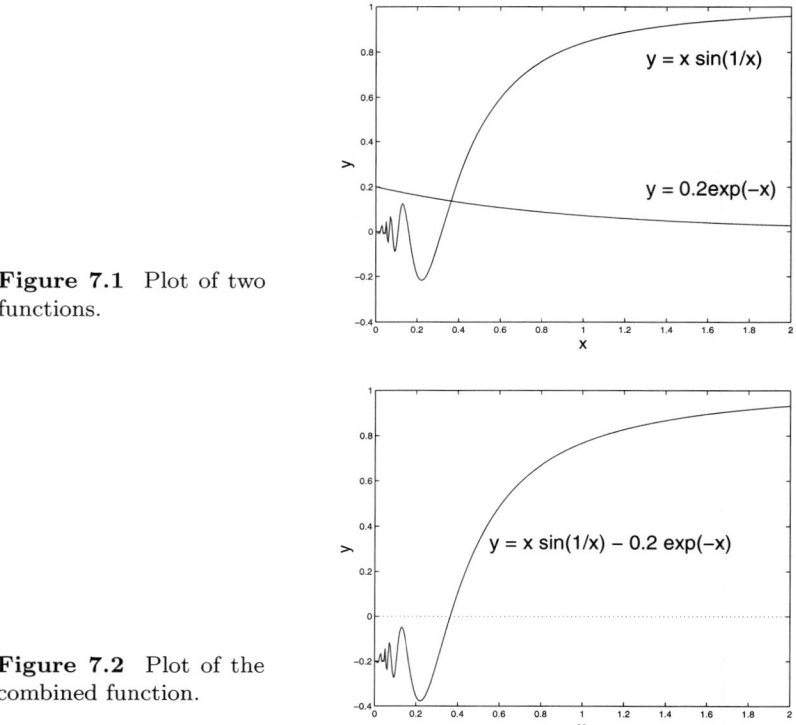

Figure 7.1 Plot of two functions.

Figure 7.2 Plot of the combined function.

Example 7.1

The natural frequencies of vibration of a uniform beam clamped at one end is the solution of the following equation:

$$\cos(x)\cosh(x) + 1 = 0 \tag{A}$$

where
$$\begin{aligned} x &= \rho\omega^2 L/EI \\ L &= \text{length of the beam}(\text{m}) \\ w &= \text{frequency}(\text{s}^{-1}) \\ EI &= \text{flexural rigidity}(\text{Nm}^2) \\ \rho &= \text{density of the beam material}(\text{kg/m}^3) \end{aligned}$$

Determine approximate values of the lowest three positive roots by the graphic method.

Solution

We first set
$$f(x) = \cos(x)\cosh(x) + 1 \tag{B}$$

Because we know little of the function, a graphical analysis at this point is helpful. We first plot without limits of y in $0 \leq x \leq 20$. The plotted graph is shown in Figure 7.3 (see List 7.1 for the script to plot). From this figure, we learn that one root is approximately $x = 17.5$, but other roots may also exist in $0 \leq x < 15$.

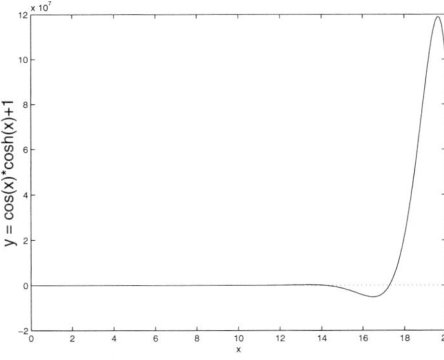

Figure 7.3 Plot of $y = \cos(x)\cosh(x) + 1$.

List 7.1

```
clf;clear
x = 0:0.1:20;
```

```
y = cos(x).*cosh(x) + 1;
plot(x,y, x, zeros(x));
xlabel('x'); ylabel('y = cos(x)*cosh(x)+1')
```

While the figure plotted by the foregoing script is still on the screen, the limits of the graph may be changed by the `axis` command or manually by zooming. For example, `axis([0 20 -10 20])` changes the graph to that shown in Figure 7.4.

By reading from Figure 7.4, the three smallest positive roots are found to be $x = 1.8$, 4.6, and 7.8, approximately.

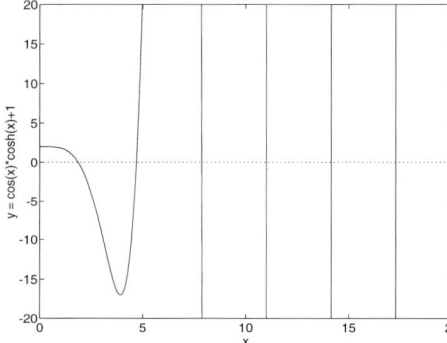

Figure 7.4 Zoomed plot of $y = \cos(x)\cosh(x) + 1$.

As is obvious from the example just described, the graphic method is not without difficulties and pitfalls. One problem is that a graph may be very poorly depicted in some cases. For example, the quality of plot becomes poor in the vicinity of a singularity. If a graph is carelessly plotted, singular points may look like roots. When a singularity is suspected, zoom up the graph and then determine if the function is really singular. Another example is that if a function is plotted with equispaced intervals, fast oscillation may not be captured, so the plotted curve may significantly misrepresent the true function. It is advisable, therefore, to plot the function several times with a finer grid, different zooming, and focus until the function is well understood.

7.2 BISECTION METHOD

The bisection method is a simple but robust numerical method for finding one real root in a given interval where the root is known to exist. Its unique advantage is that it works even for nonanalytic functions; however, the method should be used only after a graphic analysis.

Suppose that a root of $f(x) = 0$ is located in an interval between $x = a$ and $x = c$ denoted by $[a, c]$, or equivalently, $a \leq x \leq c$. The bisection method is based on the fact that the sign of $y(x)$ at $x = a$ and $x = b$ are opposite, namely, $f(a)f(c) < 0$ (see Figure 7.5). We now bisect the interval $[a, c]$ into two halves, namely, $[a, b]$ and $[b, c]$, where $b = (a + c)/2$ (see circle 1 in Figure 7.5). By checking the signs of $f(a)f(b)$ and $f(b)f(c)$, the half interval that contains the root is found. Indeed, since $f(b)f(c) \leq 0$, the interval $[b, c]$ including $x = b$ and $x = c$ has the root, otherwise, the root would be in the other interval $[a, b]$. The new interval containing the root is bisected again. As this procedure is repeated, the size of the interval containing the root becomes smaller and smaller. In each step, the midpoint of the interval is taken as the most updated approximation for the root. The iteration is stopped when the half interval size is less than a given tolerance.

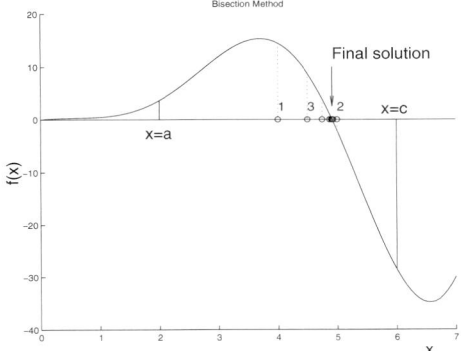

Figure 7.5 Bisection method (plotted by bisec_g).

The interval size after n iteration steps becomes

$$\frac{c_0 - a_0}{2^n} \qquad (7.2.1)$$

where a_0 and c_0 are initial values of a and c, so the numerator is the initial interval size. Equation (7.2.1) equals the maximum possible error when the root is approximated by the nth midpoint. Therefore, the number of iteration steps required is the smallest integer n satisfying

$$\tau \geq \frac{c_0 - a_0}{2^n} \qquad (7.2.2)$$

or equivalently

$$n \geq \frac{\log\left(\frac{c_0 - a_0}{\tau}\right)}{\log(2)} \qquad (7.2.3)$$

where τ is the tolerance. For example, if $c_0 - a_0 = 1$ and $\tau = 0.0001$, then $n = 14$.

Two functions, bisec_g, and bisec_n, listed in Section 7.7, may be used for bisection computations. The former graphically displays the progress of bisection iteration, as illustrated in Figure 7.5. The latter does not plot a graph, but is faster.

The synopsis for bisec_g is as follows:

    bisec_g('f_name', a, c, xmin, xmax, n_points)

where f_name is the name of the function that defines the equation to be solved, a and c are endpoints of the initial interval, xmin and xmax are minimum and maximum x values of the graph, and n_points is the number of points to plot the function. The tolerance is set to $\tau = 10^{-6}$ by default.

The synopsis of bisec_n is

    bisec_n('f_name', a, c)

Example 7.2

Find the intersection of the following two functions:

$y = \sqrt{x^2 + 1}$
$y = \tan(x), \quad 0 < x < \pi/2$

Solution

The problem is equivalent to finding a zero of

$$f = \sqrt{x^2 + 1} - \tan(x), \quad 0 < x < \pi/2 \qquad (A)$$

By plotting the function, we find the root is approximately $x = 0.9$. To use bisec_n (or bisec_g), we write a function m-file to define Eq.(A):

```
        function f = fun_ex2(x)
        f = sqrt(1+x.^2) - tan(x);
```

Then, bisec_n is used as

```
        bisec_n('fun_ex2', 0.8, 1.0)
```

The output is:

```
Bisection Scheme:
It.  a         b        c         f(a)      f(b)       f(c)
 1  0.800000  0.900000  1.000000   0.250986  0.085204  -0.143194
 2  0.900000  0.950000  1.000000   0.085204 -0.019071  -0.143194
 3  0.900000  0.925000  0.950000   0.085204  0.035236  -0.019071
 4  0.925000  0.937500  0.950000   0.035236  0.008660  -0.019071
 5  0.937500  0.943750  0.950000   0.008660 -0.005056  -0.019071
 6  0.937500  0.940625  0.943750   0.008660  0.001838  -0.005056
 7  0.940625  0.942187  0.943750   0.001838 -0.001600  -0.005056
 8  0.940625  0.941406  0.942187   0.001838  0.000122  -0.001600
 9  0.941406  0.941797  0.942187   0.000122 -0.000738  -0.001600
10  0.941406  0.941602  0.941797   0.000122 -0.000308  -0.000738
11  0.941406  0.941504  0.941602   0.000122 -0.000093  -0.000308
12  0.941406  0.941455  0.941504   0.000122  0.000014  -0.000093
13  0.941455  0.941479  0.941504   0.000014 -0.000040  -0.000093
14  0.941455  0.941467  0.941479   0.000014 -0.000013  -0.000040
15  0.941455  0.941461  0.941467   0.000014  0.000001  -0.000013
16  0.941461  0.941464  0.941467   0.000001 -0.000006  -0.000013
17  0.941461  0.941463  0.941464   0.000001 -0.000003  -0.000006
18  0.941461  0.941462  0.941463   0.000001 -0.000001  -0.000003
19  0.941461  0.941462  0.941462   0.000001  0.000000  -0.000001
Tolerance is satisfied.
Final result: Root =  0.941462
```

If the bisection method is applied with a hand-held computer, follow the format of the table in the foregoing example.

7.3 NEWTON ITERATION

Newton iteration is an iterative scheme to find a root of a nonlinear equation. It is applicable also on the complex domain to find a complex root, as well as extendable to simultaneous nonlinear equations, as described in more detail in Section 7.6.

Newton iteration is derived by Taylor expansion. Suppose the problem is to find a root of $f(x) = 0$. The first order truncated Taylor expansion of $f(x)$ about an initial estimate, x_0, is written by

$$f(x) \approx f(x_0) + f'(x_0)(x - x_0) \tag{7.3.1}$$

which is regarded as an approximation for $f(x)$. By setting Eq.(7.3.1) to zero, an approximation for the root is obtained as

$$x_1 = x_0 - \frac{f(x_0)}{f'(x_0)}$$

The same process is repeated by

$$x_n = x_{n-1} - \frac{f(x_{n-1})}{f'(x_{n-1})} \tag{7.3.2}$$

The algorithm is also graphically illustrated in Figure 7.6. For the initial value x_0, the line passing tangentially through (x_0, f_0) is drawn. The intersection of the tangential line with the x-axis is x_1. Then, the line passing tangentially through (x_1, f_1) is drawn. The same procedure is repeated, using the most updated value as a guess for the next iteration cycle.

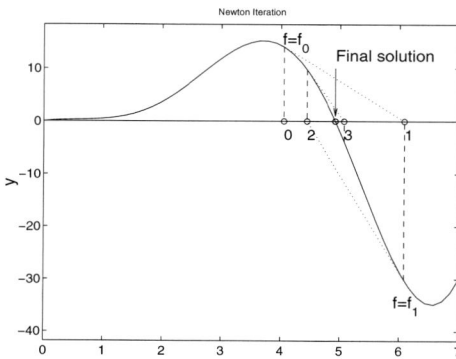

Figure 7.6 Newton iteration.

Deriving the first derivative of a given function could be cumbersome. In such a case, $f'(x)$ in Eq.(7.3.2) may be evaluated by a difference approximation rather than analytically. For example, $f'(x_{n-1})$ may be approximated by

$$f'_{n-1} = \frac{f(x_{n-1} + h) - f(x_{n-1})}{h} \tag{7.3.3}$$

or

$$f'_{n-1} = \frac{f(x_{n-1}) - f(x_{n-1} - h)}{h} \qquad (7.3.4)$$

where h is a small value (such as $h = 0.001$ for most exercise problems). Equations (7.3.3) and (7.3.4) are the forward and backward difference approximations, respectively. Small errors in the difference approximation have no noticeable effect on the convergence rate of Newton iteration. The accuracy of the final result is not affected by the error of a difference approximation; however, when a singularity is near the root, difference approximation needs to be used with much caution.

Example 7.3

Derive an iterative scheme to find the cubic root of a number using Newton iteration. Find the cubic root of $a = 155$ by the scheme derived.

Solution

The problem is to find the zero of

$$f(x) = x^3 - a$$

Newton iteration is reduced to

$$\begin{aligned} x_{n+1} &= x_n - \frac{f(x_n)}{f'(x_n)} \\ &= x_n - \frac{x_n^3 - a}{3x_n^2} \\ &= \frac{2}{3} x_n + \frac{a}{3x_n^2} \end{aligned}$$

We set $a = 155$ and an initial guess to $x_0 = 5$. The iteration proceeds as

```
List 7.1a
    n       x
    0       5
    1       5.4
    2       5.371834
    3       5.371686 (exact)
```

The exact solution is obtained after only three iteration steps. We try again with a much poorer initial guess of $x_0 = 10$:

List 7.1b

n	x
0	10
1	7.183334
2	5.790176
3	5.401203
4	5.371847
5	5.371686 (exact)

The exact value of the cubic root is obtained with five iteration steps.

Two functions, Newt_g, and Newt_n (listed in Section 7.7), solve nonlinear equations by Newton iteration. The former displays the procedure of Newton iteration graphically, while the latter performs only computations. The synopses are

```
Newt_g('f_name', x0, xmin, xmax, n_points)
Newt_n('f_name', x0)
```

where f_name is the name of the function m-file that defines the equation to be solved, and x0 is an initial guess for the root. The meanings of xmin, xmax, and n_points are the same as for bisec_g.

For illustration purposes, we define the equation to be solved by

$$y = (0.01x + 1)\sin(x) - (x - 0.01)/(x^2 + 1) - 0.0096$$

The foregoing equation is written in an m-file named eqn_1.m listed in FM 7-3. Then, we execute Newt_n('eqn_1', 4). The output becomes

```
Newton Iteration
  Type name of the function (enclosed with single quote):
          'eqn_1'
  f_name =
          eqn_1
  Type initial guess of the root: 4
  n=  1, x= 2.36795e+00, y = -1.031e+00,  yd = -6.319e-01
  n=  2, x= 2.92631e+00, y =  3.488e-01,  yd = -6.247e-01
  n=  3, x= 2.82370e+00, y = -9.467e-02,  yd = -9.226e-01
  n=  4, x= 2.82171e+00, y = -1.774e-03,  yd = -8.895e-01
  n=  5, x= 2.82170e+00, y = -4.498e-06,  yd = -8.888e-01
  n=  6, x= 2.82170e+00, y = -9.553e-09,  yd = -8.888e-01
          Final answer = 2.82170e+00
```

The output of Newt_g is identical to that of Newt_n except the former plots a graph of progress. Indeed, Figure 7.6 was plotted by Newt_g('eqn_1', 4, 0, 7, 50) for this example.

Example 7.4

Imagine a furnace made of a single layer of bricks of 0.05 m thick. The temperature of the inner wall surface, T_0, is 625K, but the outer surface temperature, T_1, is unknown. The heat loss from the outer surface is due to convection as well as radiation. The temperature T_1 is determined by the equation

$$f(T_1) \equiv \frac{k}{\Delta x}(T_1 - T_0) + \varepsilon\sigma(T_1^4 - T_\infty^4) + h(T_1 - T_f) = 0 \quad \text{(A)}$$

where

k: thermal conductivity of the wall, 1.2W/mK

ε: emissivity, 0.8

T_0: inner wall temperature, 625K

T_1: outer wall temperature (unknown), K

T_∞: temperature of the surrounding environment, 298K

T_f: temperature of the air, 298K

h: heat transfer coefficient, 20W/m^{2}K

σ: Stefan-Boltzmann constant, 5.67×10^{-8} W/m^{2}K^4

Δx: thickness of the wall, 0.05m

Determine T_1 by Newton iteration.

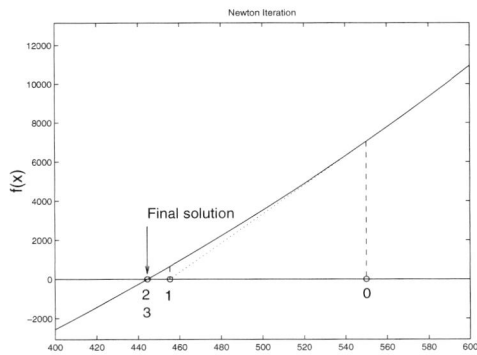

Figure 7.7 $f(T_1)$ versus T_1. TT is represented by x.

Solution

We solve the problem by `Newt_g`. The equation to be solved is written in a function m-file as shown:

```
List 7.2
function  f = wall_ht(T1)
k =1.2; e = 0.8; Tinf = 298;
Tf=298; h = 20; T0=625;
sig = 5.67E-8 ; wall_thick = 0.05;
f = k/wall_thick*(T1-T0) +e*sig*(T1.^4-Tinf^4)  ...
                        + h*(T1 - Tf);
```

After saving the foregoing function m-file as `wall_ht.m`, we execute the following command:

```
Newt_g('wall_ht', 550,400,600, 50)
```

The result is:

```
Newton Iteration
  n=   0,   x= 5.50000e+02,   y= 7.03301e+03
  n=   1,   x= 4.55199e+02,   y= 6.58551e+02
  n=   2,   x= 4.44423e+02,   y= 6.44623e+00
  n=   3,   x= 4.44316e+02,   y= 6.27680e-04
  n=   4,   x= 4.44316e+02,   y= 5.70253e-10
ans =
   444.3157
```

The final answer is $T_1 = 444.3$K. The graphic output is shown in Figure 7.7, where x and y denote T_1 and $f(T_1)$, respectively.

7.4 SECANT METHOD

The secant method is a variant of Newton iteration. We have used a difference approximation to evaluate f' in Newton iteration; however, f' can also be evaluated approximately using the past two consecutive values of f. The iterative scheme based on this concept is written as

$$x_n = x_{n-1} - f_{n-1} \frac{x_{n-1} - x_{n-2}}{f_{n-1} - f_{n-2}}, \quad n = 2, 3, ...$$

To start the iteration, x_0 has to be specified. The value of x_1 may be set to $x_1 = x_0 + \Delta x$, where Δx is an arbitrarily small number such as 0.01, for example. Then, the iteration can be continued until a tolerance is satisfied.

Example 7.5

A bullet of $M = 0.002$kg has been shot vertically into the air and is descending at its terminal speed.[1] The terminal speed is determined

---

[1] Never shoot bullets into the air. Many people are wounded every year by randomly shot bullets.

by $gM = F_{\text{drag}}$, where g is gravity M is the mass, and F_{drag} is the drag force that depends on the bullet velocity. The whole equation may be written, after evaluating the constants, as

$$(0.002)(9.81) = 1.4 \times 10^{-5} v^{1.5} + 1.15 \times 10^{-5} v^2 \qquad \text{(A)}$$

where v is the terminal velocity, m/s. The first term on the right side represents the friction drag and the second term represents the pressure drag. Determine the terminal velocity by the secant method. A crude guess is given by $v \approx 30$m/s.

Solution

The task is to find the root of

$$f(v) = (0.002)(9.81) - 1.4 \times 10^{-5} v^{1.5} - 1.15 \times 10^{-5} v^2 \qquad \text{(B)}$$

We set $v_0 = 30$ and $v_1 = 30.1$ based on the crude guess given, and compute f_0 and f_1 by Eq.(B). The iterative solution is shown below:

```
n        v              f(v)
0        30.00000       1.9620001E-02
1        30.10000       6.8889391E-03
2        30.15411       6.8452079E-03
3        38.62414      -8.9657493E-04
4        37.64323       9.0962276E-05
5        37.73358       9.9465251E-07
6        37.73458      -1.8626451E-09
```

Thus, the terminal velocity is $v = 37.7$m/s.

7.5 SUCCESSIVE SUBSTITUTION METHOD

The term *successive substitution* method refers to a large class of iterative solution schemes for nonlinear equations. Newton iteration and the secant method may be viewed as applications of successive substitution. Since successive substitution is employed in many numerical algorithms to solve nonlinear equations including differential equations and simultaneous nonlinear equations, we introduce some fundamental aspects of it in this section.

If the equation to be solved, $f(x) = 0$, is rearranged to the form

$$x = g(x) \qquad (7.5.1)$$

then an iterative scheme may be written as

$$x_n = g(x_{n-1}) \tag{7.5.2}$$

where n is the number of iteration steps and x_0 is an initial guess. This method is called the successive substitution method, or *fixed-point iteration*.

The advantage of this method is in its simplicity and flexibility to choose the form of $g(x)$. The disadvantage, however, is that the iteration does not always converge for an arbitrarily chosen form of $g(x)$. To ensure convergence of the iteration, the following condition must be satisfied:

$$|g'(x)| < 1 \tag{7.5.3}$$

Figure 7.8 illustrates how $g'(x)$ affects the convergence of the iterative method. It can be observed that the convergence is asymptotic if $0 < g' < 1$, and oscillatory if $-1 < g' < 0$. Otherwise, the iteration diverges. Further-

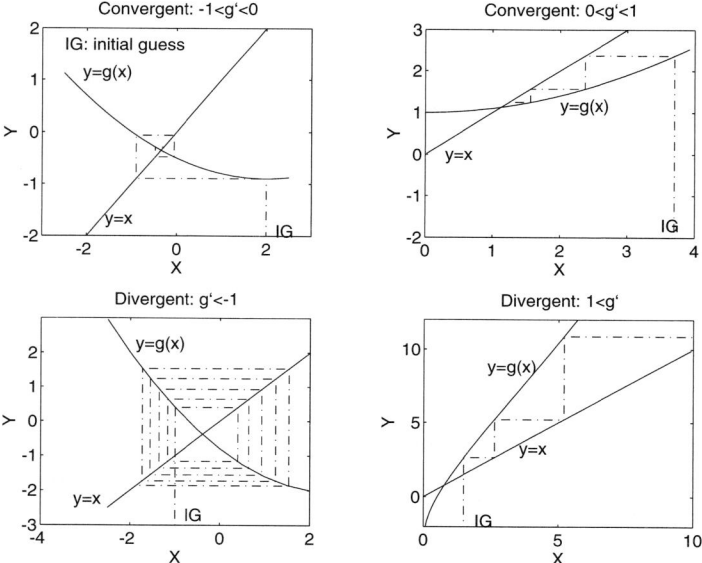

Figure 7.8 Convergence of the successive substitution method (IG denotes an initial guess).

more, it can be shown easily that the convergence rate becomes fastest as g' approaches 0.

Example 7.6

The function
$$y = x^2 - 3x + e^x - 2 \qquad (A)$$

is known to have two roots: one negative and one positive. Find the smaller root by successive substitution.

Solution

By checking the sign of y at $x = -1$ and $x = 0$ (namely, $y(-1) = 2.367$ and $y(0) = -1$), we locate the smaller root in $-1 < x < 0$. We rewrite the given equation to

$$x = g(x) = \frac{x^2 + e^x - 2}{3} \qquad (B)$$

Then, an iterative scheme is written as

$$x_n = g(x_{n-1}) \qquad (C)$$

The first derivative of $g(x)$ satisfies Eq.(7.5.3) in the range of $-1 < x < 0$, so the scheme is convergent. The results of iteration are shown next.

```
Iteration Count    Successive Approx.
n                  x(n)
0                  0 (initial guess)
1                  -0.333333
2                  -0.390786
3                  -0.390254
4                  -0.390272
5                  -0.390272
```

Alternative equations are

$$x = -\sqrt{3x - e^x + 2} \qquad (D)$$

and

$$x = \sqrt{3x - e^x + 2} \qquad (E)$$

Equations (D) and (E), however, have discontinuities in the vicinity of the smaller root. Furthermore, the first derivatives of both equations violate the condition of Eq. (7.5.3). Therefore, neither equation works.

One systematic way of finding a form of $g(x)$ is to set

$$g(x) = x - \alpha f(x) \tag{7.5.4}$$

so the iterative scheme becomes

$$x_n = x_{n-1} - \alpha f(x_{n-1}) \tag{7.5.5}$$

where α is a constant. The constant α may be determined as follows: By substituting Eq.(7.5.5) into Eq.(7.5.3), it is seen that iteration converges when

$$-1 < 1 - \alpha f'(x) < 1 \tag{7.5.6}$$

or equivalently

$$0 < \alpha f'(x) < 2 \tag{7.5.7}$$

The foregoing equation indicates that first, α must have the same sign as f', and second, the convergence rate is optimal when $\alpha \approx 1/f'$.

The present scheme reduces to Newton iteration if α is set to $1/f'(x_n)$ for each iteration.

Example 7.7

The critical size of a nuclear reactor is determined by a criticality equation. A simple form of the criticality equation is given by

$$\tan(0.1x) = 9.2e^{-x} \tag{A}$$

The solution that is physically meaningful is the smallest positive root satisfying $3 < x < 4$. Determine the smallest positive root.

Solution

We apply the iterative scheme of Eq.(7.5.5) to

$$f(x) = \tan(0.1x) - 9.2e^{-x} \tag{B}$$

An approximate value of f' in $3 < x < 4$ is estimated by

$$f' \approx \frac{f(4) - f(3)}{4 - 3} = 0.40299 \qquad \text{(C)}$$

Then, the parameter α is set to

$$\alpha = \frac{1}{0.40299} \qquad \text{(D)}$$

The iteration of Eq.(7.5.5) converges as follows:

```
Iteration     Iterative
number        solution
n             x
0             4.00000
1             3.36899
2             3.28574
3             3.29384
4             3.28280
5             3.29293
6             3.29292
7             3.29292
```

7.6 SIMULTANEOUS NONLINEAR EQUATIONS

The necessity to solve simultaneous nonlinear equations occurs rather frequently. We introduce two methods of solving simultaneous nonlinear equations.

successive substitution iteration: A nonlinear system of equations may often be written in the same form as the linear system, $Ax = y$, except that the coefficient matrix A, and even the inhomogeneous term y, may be dependent on the solution. An iterative solution for a nonlinear system based on successive substitution may be written as

$$\mathbf{A}_{n-1}\mathbf{x}_n = \mathbf{y}_{n-1} \qquad (7.6.1)$$

where $\mathbf{A}_{n-1}$ is computed by the most updated iterative solution, $\mathbf{x}_n$ is the nth iterative solution, and $\mathbf{y}_{n-1}$ is an inhomogeneous term that is assumed to also be a function of the solution.

Initially, the coefficient matrix is computed using an initial guess for the solution. Once the coefficient matrix is determined, the equation is solved as a linear system. After the solution is obtained, the coefficient matrix is revised and the equation is solved again. If instability occurs during iteration, use under-relaxation:

$$\mathbf{x_n} = \omega \mathbf{A}_{n-1}^{-1} \mathbf{y_{n-1}} + (1-\omega)\mathbf{x_{n-1}} \qquad (7.6.2)$$

where ω is an under-relaxation parameter satisfying $0 < \omega < 1$.

Example 7.8

Electric heating elements are connected as shown in Figure 7.9. The resistance of the jth heating element is a function of temperature and is given by

$$R_j = a_j + b_j T_j + c_j T_j^2 \qquad (A)$$

where a_j, b_j, and c_j are constants, and T_j is the temperature of the jth element, in Kelvin. The temperature of each heating element is determined by

$$I_j^2 R_j = A_j \sigma \left(T_j^4 - T_\infty^4\right) + A_j h (T_j - T_\infty) \qquad (B)$$

where T_∞ is the temperature of the surrounding environment and A_j is the surface area of the jth element. See Example 7.4 for other notations and constants. Equation (B) is an energy equation that includes the effects of the heat generated, and convection and radiation heat transfer. Discuss how the present problem may be solved.

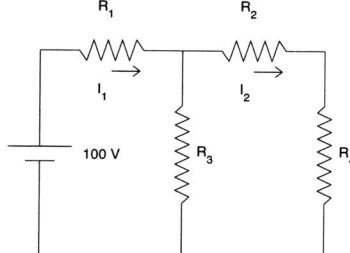

Figure 7.9 Circuit of heating elements.

Solution
The electric currents I_1 and I_2 satisfy

Section 7.6 Simultaneous Nonlinear Equations

$$\begin{aligned}(R_1 + R_3)I_1 - R_3 I_2 &= 100 \\ -R_3 I_1 + (R_2 + R_4 + R_3)I_2 &= 0\end{aligned} \quad \text{(C)}$$

The foregoing equations are nonlinear because each resistance is a function of temperature, while temperature is, in turn, a function of current and resistance. If the temperature is low, the nonlinear effects vanish and the equations become linear. The solution algorithm may be developed as follows: Solve Eq.(C) as simultaneous linear equations, first with cold values of resistances. Solve Eq.(B) for the temperature. Calculate the resistance of each resistor as a function of temperature by Eq.(A). Repeat solution of Eq.(C) using the updated values of the resistances. The whole procedure is repeated until the solution for every quantity converges.

Newton Iteration: Nonlinear equations may be linearized by Taylor expansion. Suppose the system of equations is in the form

$$f_i(x_1, x_2, .., x_n) = 0, \ i = 1, 2, ...n \quad (7.6.3)$$

where f_i is a nonlinear function of x_js. If we know an initial guess for the solution, the solution may be written as

$$x_j = \hat{x}_j + \Delta x_j \quad (7.6.4)$$

where $\hat{x}_j$ is the initial guess and Δx_j is an unknown correction. If we expand Eq.(7.6.3) into a first-order truncated Taylor expansion about $\hat{x}_j$, we get

$$\sum_j \frac{\partial f_i}{\partial x_j} \Delta x_j = -f_i(\hat{x}_1, \hat{x}_2, ...\hat{x}_n) \quad (7.6.5)$$

where the partial derivatives are evaluated with the initial guesses. Equation (7.6.5) may be written in a matrix form as

$$\mathbf{J}\Delta\mathbf{x} = -\mathbf{f} \quad (7.6.6)$$

where $\mathbf{J}$ is the Jacobian matrix given by

$$\mathbf{J} = \left[\frac{\partial f_i}{\partial x_j}\right] \quad (7.6.7)$$

and

$$\Delta \mathbf{x} = \begin{bmatrix} \Delta x_1 \\ \Delta x_2 \\ ... \\ \Delta x_n \end{bmatrix}, \quad \mathbf{f} = \begin{bmatrix} f_1(\hat{x}_1, \hat{x}_2, ...\hat{x}_n) \\ f_2(\hat{x}_1, \hat{x}_2, ...\hat{x}_n) \\ ... \\ f_n(\hat{x}_1, \hat{x}_2, ...\hat{x}_n) \end{bmatrix} \quad (7.6.8)$$

The partial derivatives may be evaluated by a difference approximation, for example,

$$\frac{\partial f_i}{\partial x_j} \approx \frac{f_i(\hat{x}_1, ..., \hat{x}_j + \delta x_j, ...\hat{x}_n) - f_i(\hat{x}_1, ..., \hat{x}_j, ... \hat{x}_n)}{\delta x_j} \quad (7.6.9)$$

where δx_j is an arbitrarily chosen small value.

Example 7.9

Using the method described in this section, find the solutions of

$$f_1(x, y) = f_2(x, y) = 0$$

where

$$\begin{aligned} f_1(x, y) &= x\exp(xy + 0.8) + \exp(y^2) - 3 \\ f_2(x, y) &= x^2 - y^2 - 0.5\exp(xy) \end{aligned}$$

satisfying $x > 0$.

Solution

We first plot $f_1(x, y) = 0$ and $f_2(x, y) = 0$ in Figure 7.10 by the following script based on the plotting technique mentioned in Section 2.3.

```
List 7.3
clear, clf, hold off
x1 = 0:0.1:2;
y1 = -2:0.1:2;
[x,y] = meshgrid(x1,y1);
f1 = f_f1(x,y) ;
f2 = f_f2(x,y) ;
contour(f1, [0.00, 0.00], x1,y1)
hold on
contour(f2, [0.00, 0.00], x1,y1)
xlabel(x); ylabel(y)
```

f_f1.m

Section 7.6 Simultaneous Nonlinear Equations

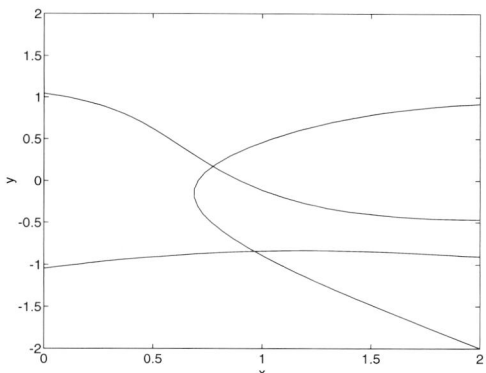

Figure 7.10 Graphic solution for Example 7.9.

```
function f = f_f1(x,y)
f = x.*exp(x.*y+0.8)  + exp(y.^2) - 3;
```
f_f2.m
```
function f = f_f2(x,y)
f = x.^2 - y.^2 - 0.5*exp(x.*y);
```

The curves in Figure 7.10 indicate that there are two roots in the positive domain of x; one is approximately $(x = 0.8, y = 0.2)$ and the other is $(x = 1, y = -0.8)$. We find more accurate solutions by Newton iteration. A script is in List 7.4.

List 7.4
```
% Newton Iteration 2D
clear,clf, fprintf('\n')
dx = 0.01; dy = 0.01;
x = input('Initial guess for x? ');
y = input('Initial guess for y? ');
for n=1:50
  s = [x,y];
  xp = x + dx;
  yp = y + dy;
  J(1,1) = (f_f1(xp, y) - f_f1(x,y))/dx;
  J(1,2) = (f_f1(x, yp) - f_f1(x,y))/dy;
  J(2,1) = (f_f2(xp, y) - f_f2(x,y))/dx;
  J(2,2) = (f_f2(x, yp) - f_f2(x,y))/dy;
  f(1) = f_f1(x,y);
  f(2) = f_f2(x,y);
  ds = - J\f';
  x = x + ds(1);
  y = y + ds(2);
fprintf('n=%2.0f,   x=%12.5e,   y=%12.5e', n,x,y)
fprintf('f(1)=%10.2e, f(2)=%10.2e\n', f(1), f(2))
   if (abs(f(1))<1.0e-9 & abs(f(2))<1.0e-9), break; end
```

end

The output of Newton iteration is:

```
Initial guess for x? 1
Initial guess for y? 1
n=1, x= 9.237e-01, y= 5.828e-01  f(1)= 5.77e+00, f(2)=-1.36e+00
n=2, x= 8.086e-01, y= 3.295e-01  f(1)= 1.93e+00, f(2)=-3.43e-01
n=3, x= 7.754e-01, y= 2.009e-01  f(1)= 4.64e-01, f(2)=-1.07e-01
n=4, x= 7.748e-01, y= 1.729e-01  f(1)= 5.81e-02, f(2)=-2.33e-02
n=5, x= 7.749e-01, y= 1.716e-01  f(1)= 1.92e-03, f(2)=-1.26e-03
n=6, x= 7.749e-01, y= 1.716e-01  f(1)= 2.24e-05, f(2)=-1.82e-05
n=7, x= 7.749e-01, y= 1.716e-01  f(1)= 2.69e-07, f(2)=-2.30e-07
n=8, x= 7.749e-01, y= 1.716e-01  f(1)= 3.31e-09, f(2)=-2.87e-09
n=9, x= 7.749e-01, y= 1.716e-01  f(1)= 4.10e-11, f(2)=-3.58e-11

Initial guess for x? 1
Initial guess for y? -1
n=1, x= 9.863e-01, y=-8.815e-01  f(1)= 5.37e-01, f(2)=-1.84e-01
n=2, x= 9.695e-01, y=-8.489e-01  f(1)= 9.53e-02, f(2)=-1.38e-02
n=3, x= 9.687e-01, y=-8.476e-01  f(1)= 3.43e-03, f(2)=-3.75e-04
n=4, x= 9.687e-01, y=-8.477e-01  f(1)=-6.65e-05, f(2)= 1.98e-05
n=5, x= 9.687e-01, y=-8.477e-01  f(1)= 1.45e-06, f(2)=-3.67e-07
n=6, x= 9.687e-01, y=-8.477e-01  f(1)=-3.14e-08, f(2)= 8.20e-09
n=7, x= 9.687e-01, y=-8.477e-01  f(1)= 6.82e-10, f(2)=-1.77e-10
```

A summary of the solutions is:

```
x = 0.7749, y = 0.1716
x = 0.9687, y =-0.8477
```

7.7 M-FILES

FM 7-1. Bisection
Purpose: To find a root of a function.
Synopsis: bisec_n('f_name', a, b)
      f_name: the name of the function
      a and b: endpoints of the initial interval
Example: bisec_n('eqn_w3', 0, 1.3)

bisec_n.m
```
function bisec_n(f_name, a,c)
f_name
%        a, c : endpoints of initial interval
%        tolerance : tolerance
%        it_limit : limit of iteration number
```

Section 7.7 M-Files

```
%          Y_a, Y_c : y values of the current end points
%          fun_f(x) : functional value at x
fprintf( 'Bisection Scheme\n\n' );
tolerance = 0.000001;  it_limit = 30;
fprintf( ' It.     a            b            c          fa=f(a)    ');
fprintf( '     fc=f(c)     abs(fc-fa) \n' );
it = 0;
Y_a = feval(f_name, a ); Y_c = feval(f_name, c );
if ( Y_a*Y_c > 0 )
    fprintf( '\n \n Stopped because   f(a)f(c) > 0 \n' );
else
    while 1
       it = it + 1;
       b = (a + c)/2;  Y_b = feval(f_name, b );
       fprintf('%3.0f %10.6f, %10.6f', it, a, b );
       fprintf('%10.6f, %10.6f, %10.6f', c, Y_a, Y_c );
       fprintf( ' %12.3e\n', abs((Y_c - Y_a)));
       if ( abs(c-a)/2<=tolerance )
          fprintf( '    Tolerance is satisfied. \n' );break
          fprintf( '\n Change a or b and run again.\n' );
       end
       if ( it>it_limit )
          fprintf( 'Iteration limit exceeded.\n' ); break
       end
       if( Y_a*Y_b <= 0 )     c = b;    Y_c = Y_b;
       else                   a = b;    Y_a = Y_b;
       end
    end
    fprintf('Final result: Root = %12.6f \n', b );
end
```

eqn_w3.m

```
function y = eqn_w3(x)
   y = sqrt(x^2 + 1) - tan(x);
```

FM 7-2. Bisection method with graphics

Purpose: To find a root of a function and display the iterative process.
Synopsis: bisec_g('f_name', a, b, xmin, xmax,n_points)

      f_name: the name of the function.

      a and b: endpoints of the initial interval

      xmin, xmax: minimum and maximum x coordinates of the graph

      b_points: number of points used to plot the curve

Example: bisec_g('dem_bs', 2, 6, 0, 7, 100) (see Figure 7.5).

bisec_g.m

```
function bisec_g(f_name, a,c, xmin, xmax, n_points)
```

```
f_name
%       a, c : end points of initial interval
%       tolerance : tolerance
%       it_limit : limit of iteration number
%       Y_a, Y_c : y values of the current end points
%       fun_f(x) : functional value at x
clf, hold off
clear Y_a, clear Y_c
wid_x = xmax - xmin;   dx = (xmax- xmin)/n_points;
xp=xmin:dx:xmax;    yp=feval(f_name, xp);
plot(xp,yp); xlabel('x');ylabel('f(x)');
title('Bisection Method'),hold on
ymin=min(yp); ymax=max(yp);wid_y = ymax-ymin;
yp=0.*xp;  plot(xp,yp)
fprintf( 'Bisection Scheme\n\n' );
tolerance = 0.000001;   it_limit = 30;
fprintf( ' It.    a           b           c           fa=f(a)      ');
fprintf( '   fc=f(c)    abs(fc-fa) \n' );
it = 0;
Y_a = feval(f_name, a ); Y_c = feval(f_name, c );
plot([a,a],[Y_a,0]); text(a,-0.1*wid_y,'x=a')
plot([c,c],[Y_c,0]); text(c,-0.1*wid_y,'x=c')
if ( Y_a*Y_c > 0 )  fprintf( '    f(a)f(c) > 0 \n' );
else
   while 1
      it = it + 1;
      b = (a + c)/2;   Y_b = feval(f_name, b );
      plot([b,b],[Y_b,0],':'); plot(b,0,'o')
      if it<4, text(b, wid_y/20, [num2str(it)]), end
       fprintf('%3.0f %10.6f, %10.6f', it, a, b );
       fprintf('%10.6f,  %10.6f, %10.6f', c, Y_a, Y_c );
       fprintf( ' %12.3e\n', abs((Y_c - Y_a) ));
      if ( abs(c-a)<=tolerance )
         fprintf( '    Tolerance is satisfied. \n' );break
      end
      if ( it>it_limit )
        fprintf( 'Iteration limit exceeded.\n' ); break
      end
      if( Y_a*Y_b <= 0 )    c = b;     Y_c = Y_b;
      else                  a = b;     Y_a = Y_b;
      end
   end
   fprintf('Final result: Root = %12.6f \n', b );
end
x=b;
plot([x x],[0.05*wid_y 0.2*wid_y])
text( x, 0.25*wid_y, 'Final solution')
```

Section 7.7 M-Files

```
plot([x (x-wid_x*0.004)],[0.05*wid_y  0.09*wid_y])
plot([x (x+wid_x*0.004)],[0.05*wid_y  0.09*wid_y])
```

dem_bs.m
```
function y = dem_bs(x)
y = (1 - x.*cos(x)).*x;
```

FM 7-3. Newton iteration with no graphics
Purpose: Solve a nonlinear equation by Newton iteration.
Synopsis: Newt_n('f_name', x0)
      f_name: name of the function that defines the nonlinear equation
      x0: initial guess
Example: Newt_n('eqn_1', 2)

Newt_n.m
```
function x = Newt_n(f_name, x0)
% Newton iteration with no graphics
x = x0; xb=x-999;
n=0;  del_x = 0.01;
while abs(x-xb)>0.000001
    n=n+1;   xb=x;
    if n>300 break; end
    y=feval(f_name, x);
    y_driv=(feval(f_name, x+del_x) - y)/del_x;
    x = xb - y/y_driv;
    fprintf(' n=%3.0f, x=%12.5e, y = %12.5e, ', n,x,y)
    fprintf(' yd = %12.5e \n', y_driv)
end
fprintf('\n    Final answer = %12.6e\n', x);
```

eqn_1.m
```
function y = eqn_1(x)
y = (0.01*x + 1).*sin(x) ...
    - (x - 0.01).*(x.^2 +1).^(-1) - 0.0096;
```

FM 7-4. Newton iteration with graphics
Purpose: To solve a nonlinear equation by Newton iteration.
Synopsis: Newt_g(f_name, x0, xmin, xmax, n_points)
      f_name: name of the function that defines the nonlinear equation
      x0: initial guess
      xmin, xmax: minimum and maximum x coordinates of the graph
      b_points: number of points used to plot the curve
Example: Newt_g('eqn_1', 2, 0, 5, 50)

Newt_g.m

```
function x = Newt_g(f_name, x0, xmin, xmax, n_points)
clf, hold off
% Newton_Method with graphic illustration
del_x=0.001;
wid_x = xmax - xmin;   dx = (xmax- xmin)/n_points;
xp=xmin:dx:xmax;   yp=feval(f_name, xp);
plot(xp,yp); xlabel('x');ylabel('f(x)');
title('Newton Iteration'),hold on
ymin=min(yp); ymax=max(yp);wid_y = ymax-ymin;
yp=0.*xp;   plot(xp,yp)
x = x0;    xb=x+999; n=0;
while abs(x-xb)>0.000001
   if n>300 break; end
   y=feval(f_name, x);    plot([x,x],[y,0]); plot(x,0,'o')
   fprintf(' n=%3.0f,   x=%12.5e,   y=%12.5e\n', n,x,y);
   xsc=(x-xmin)/wid_x;
   if n<4, text(x, wid_y/20, [ num2str(n)]), end
   y_driv=(feval(f_name, x+del_x) - y)/del_x;
   xb=x;
   x = xb - y/y_driv; n=n+1;
   plot([xb,x],[y,0])
end
plot([x x],[0.05*wid_y 0.2*wid_y])
text( x, 0.2*wid_y, 'Final solution')
plot([x (x-wid_x*0.004)],[0.01*wid_y  0.09*wid_y])
plot([x (x+wid_x*0.004)],[0.01*wid_y  0.09*wid_y])
```

PROBLEMS

(7.1) Find approximate values of the solutions for the following equations by the graphic method:

(a) $0.5 \exp(x/3) - \sin(x) = 0, \ x > 0$
(b) $\log(1 + x) - x^2 = 0$

(7.2) Find all the positive solutions of the following equations approximately by the graphic method:

(a) $\tan(x) - x + 1 = 0, \quad 0 < x < 3\pi$
(b) $\sin(x) - 0.3 e^x = 0, \quad x > 0$
(c) $0.1x^3 - 5x^2 - x + 4 + e^{-x} = 0$

(d) $\log(x) - 0.2x^2 + 1 = 0$

(7.3) Calculate $\tan^{-1}(3.5)$ in the interval $[0,\pi]$ by the bisection method. (*Hint*: Solve $\tan(x) = 3.5$ satisfying $0 \le x \le \pi$.)

(7.4) Repeat Problem 7.1 by the bisection method.

(7.5) The surface configuration of the NACA0012 airfoil of chord length 1 m and maximum thickness of 0.2 m is given by

$$y(x) = \pm[0.2969\sqrt{x} - 0.126x - 0.3516x^2 + 0.2843x^3 - 0.1015x^4]$$

where + and − signs refer to upper and lower surfaces, respectively. The design engineer has to find the following information:

(a) The x coordinate where the airfoil thickness becomes the maximum.
(b) The x and y coordinates of the airfoil where thickness becomes half of the maximum.

Find the answers by the bisection method. (Hint: Consider solving $y'(x) = 0$ for the first question.)

(7.6) A design engineer has to find the coordinates of the intersections of the NACA 0012 airfoil surface (given in the previous problem) and the curve given by

$$y(x) = 0.2x(x - 0.6)$$

Compute the value by a method of your choice.

(7.7) The CO gas is contained in a vessel at $T = 215$ K and $P = 70$ bars. The van der Waals equation of state for a non-ideal gas is given by

$$\left(P + \frac{a}{v^2}\right)(v - b) = RT$$

where $R = 0.08314$ bar m^3/(kg mol K), $a = 1.463$ bar m^6/(kg mol)^2, and $b = 0.0394$ m^3/kg mol. Determine the specific volume v (m^3/kg mol) and compare the result to the specific volume calculated by the ideal gas equation, $Pv = RT$. You can choose any solution method.

(7.8) Find the positive roots of the following functions by Newton iteration:

(a) $f(x) = 0.5\exp(x/3) - \sin(x)$, $x > 0$
(b) $f(x) = \log(1 + x) - x^2$
(c) $f(x) = \exp(x) - 5x^2$
(d) $f(x) = x^3 + 2x - 1$

(e) $f(x) = \sqrt{x+2} - x$

(7.9) The following equation has two positive roots, one of which is very close to a singular point:
$$y = \exp(x) - 1/\sin(x)$$

(a) Find both positive roots by Newton iteration using an analytically differentiated derivative.
(b) Repeat (a) using difference approximation given by Eq.(7.3.3) or Eq.(7.3.4).
(c) State what efforts are necessary for both approaches in order to find the two roots successfully.

(7.10) Two ellipses have to four intersections at most as illustrated in Figure 7.11. The following equations represent two ellipses. Find the coordinates of the intersections by a graphic method first and then by Newton iteration.[2] (*Hint:* Eliminate x or y and work with a single unknown.)

$$(x-2)^2 + (y-3+2x)^2 = 5$$
$$2(x-3)^2 + (y/3)^2 = 4$$

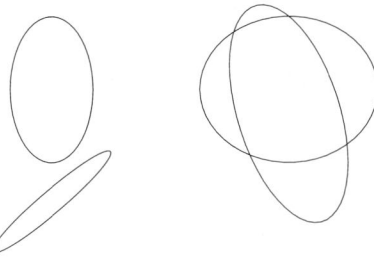

Figure 7.11
Two ellipses.   Pair A   Pair B

(7.11) The natural frequencies of vibration of a uniform beam clamped at one end and free at the other end are solutions of

$$\tan(\beta)\tanh(\beta) + 1 = 0 \qquad (A)$$

where

---
[2]This problem was provided by Professor S.V. Sreenivasan of University of Texas, Austin, TX.

$\beta = \rho \omega^2 L / EI$
L = length of the beam, m
ω = frequency, s^{-1}
EI = flexural rigidity, Nm^2
ρ = density of the beam material, kg/m^3

Investigate the β values that satisfy Eq.(A) first by the graphic method and then determine the lowest three values of β satisfying Eq.(A) by Newton iteration.

(7.12) An equimolar mixture of carbon monoxide and oxygen is to attain equilibrium at 3000K and 5bar pressure. The theoretical reaction is

$$CO + (1/2)O_2 \leftrightarrow CO_2$$

The actual chemical reaction is written as

$$CO + O_2 \rightarrow xCO + (1/2)(1+x)O_2 + (1-x)CO_2$$

The chemical equilibrium equation to determine the fraction of remaining CO, namely, x, is given by

$$K_p = \frac{(1-x)\sqrt{3+x}}{x\sqrt{1+x}\sqrt{P/P_o}}, \quad 0 < x < 1$$

where $K_p = 3.06$ is the equilibrium constant for $CO + (1/2)O_2 = CO_2$ at 3000K, P = 5bar, and P_o = 1bar. Determine the value of x by the secant method.

(7.13) Consider the same chemical reaction as in the previous problem, except that it occurs with the existence of N_2 at atmospheric pressure. The reaction is

$$CO + O_2 + 3.76N_2 \rightarrow xCO + \frac{1}{2}(1+x)O_2 + (1-x)CO_2 + 3.76N_2$$

The equation of equilibrium is

$$3.06 = \frac{(1-x)\sqrt{10.52+x}}{x\sqrt{1+x}}$$

Determine the value of x by Newton iteration.

(7.14) The equation $x^2 - 2x - 3 = 0$ may be reformulated for the successive substitution method as follows:

(a) $x = (x^2 - 3)/2$
(b) $x = \sqrt{2x + 3}$

(c) $x = (2x+3)/\sqrt{x}$
(d) $x = x - 0.2(x^2 - 2x - 3)$

The solutions of the equation are $x = 3$ and $x = -1$. Determine graphically which formulas above converge when used for successive substitution to find the root, $x = -1$. Verify the conclusions of the graphic analysis by the criterion of Eq.(7.5.3). Repeat the same analysis for $x = 3$.

(7.15) Find all the solutions of the equations in Problem 7.2 using successive substitution in the form

$$x = x - \alpha f(x)$$

(*Hint*: Determine α using the gradient of the linear interpolation fitted to the two endpoints of the interval found in problem 7.4.)

(7.16) The friction factor f for the turbulent flows in a pipe is given by

$$\frac{1}{\sqrt{f}} = 1.14 - 2\log_{10}\left(\frac{e}{D} + \frac{9.35}{Re\sqrt{f}}\right)$$

named Colebrook correlation, where Re is the Reynolds number, e is the roughness of the pipe surface, and D is the pipe diameter.[3] Write a computer program to solve the equation for f using the successive substitution method. Then evaluate f by running the program for the following cases:

(a) $D = 0.1$m, $e = 0.0025$m, $Re = 3 \times 10^4$
(b) $D = 0.1$m, $e = 0.0001$m, $Re = 5 \times 10^6$

Hint: Rewrite the equation to the following form first:

$$f = \left[1.14 - 2\log_{10}\left(\frac{e}{D} + \frac{9.35}{Re\sqrt{f}}\right)\right]^{-2}$$

Introduce an initial guess to f on the right side, and then calculate the right side. Reintroduce f calculated to the right side again, and repeat this calculation until f converges. The initial guess may be set to zero. The results of the calculations can be checked with a Moody's chart in a fluid mechanics text.

---

[3] See Fox and McDonald, *Introduction to Fluid Mechanics*, 4th ed., John Wiley, 1992.

Chapter 8

CURVE FITTING TO MEASURED DATA

Curve fitting helps to fit a function $g(x)$ to a set of given data, (x_i, y_i), $i = 1, 2, ..., L$. The function $g(x)$ can be a polynomial, a nonlinear function, or a linear combination of known functions. The function $g(x)$ selected for curve fitting must have a certain number of undetermined coefficients. In general, the number of data points to be fitted, L, is much greater than the number of undetermined coefficients, k. Therefore, the principle of determining the coefficients is based on the minimization of the discrepancies between the determined function and the data points and is named the *least square method*. In the special case of $L = k$, the curve fitting reduces to an interpolation problem because the fitted curve passes through the data points.

8.1 LINE FITTING

Suppose we want to fit a linear function to the data set, as illustrated in Table 8.1. The line fitted to a data set is called a *regression line*.

Table 8.1 Sample Data Set

i	$x(i)$	$y(i)$
1	0.1	0.61
2	0.4	0.92
3	0.5	0.99
4	0.7	1.52
5	0.7	1.47
6	0.9	2.03

The linear function is expressed by

$$g(x) = c_1 x + c_2 \qquad (8.1.1)$$

where c_1 and c_2 are undetermined constants. Since the number of data points is greater than two, the line cannot be fitted to every point, but is determined by minimizing the discrepancies between the line and data. The deviation of the line from data points, namely *residual*, is defined by

$$r_i = y_i - g(x_i) = y_i - (c_1 x_i + c_2), \quad i = 1, 2, \ldots L \qquad (8.1.2)$$

where L is the total number of data points (six in this example), and c_1 and c_2 are the constants to be determined.

The sum of the squared residuals is

$$R = \sum_{i=1}^{L} r_i^2 = \sum_{i=1}^{L} (y_i - c_1 x_i - c_2)^2 \qquad (8.1.3)$$

The minimum of R occurs when partial derivatives of R with respect to c_1 and c_2 both become zero:

$$\begin{aligned}
\frac{\partial R}{\partial c_1} &= -2 \sum_{i=1}^{L} x_i (y_i - c_1 x_i - c_2) = 0 \\
\frac{\partial R}{\partial c_2} &= -2 \sum_{n=1}^{L} (y_i - c_1 x_i - c_2) = 0
\end{aligned} \qquad (8.1.4)$$

Equation (8.1.4) may be rewritten as

$$\begin{bmatrix} a_{1,1} & a_{1,2} \\ a_{2,1} & a_{2,2} \end{bmatrix} \begin{bmatrix} c_1 \\ c_2 \end{bmatrix} = \begin{bmatrix} z_1 \\ z_2 \end{bmatrix} \qquad (8.1.5)$$

where

$$a_{1,1} = \sum_{i=1}^{L} x_i^2$$

$$a_{1,2} = a_{2,1} = \sum_{i=1}^{L} x_i$$

$$a_{2,2} = \sum_{i=1}^{L} 1 = L$$

Section 8.1 Line Fitting

$$z_1 = \sum_{i=1}^{L} x_i y_i$$

$$z_2 = \sum_{i=1}^{L} y_i$$

The solution of Eq.(8.1.5) is

$$\begin{aligned} c_1 &= (a_{2,2}z_1 - a_{1,2}z_2)/(a_{1,1}a_{2,2} - a_{1,2}a_{2,1}) \\ c_2 &= (a_{1,1}z_2 - a_{2,1}z_1)/(a_{1,1}a_{2,2} - a_{1,2}a_{2,1}) \end{aligned} \tag{8.1.6}$$

An equivalent way of determining the coefficients is to consider the problem as an *over-determined* linear equation, as explained in Section 3.4. Consider the data in Table 8.1 as an example. As if every data point satisfies Eq.(8.1.1), we write

$$c_1 x_i + c_2 = y_i, \quad i = 1, 2, \ldots L$$

or

$$Ac = y \tag{8.1.7}$$

where

$$A = \begin{bmatrix} 0.1 & 1 \\ 0.4 & 1 \\ 0.5 & 1 \\ 0.7 & 1 \\ 0.7 & 1 \\ 0.9 & 1 \end{bmatrix}, \quad c = \begin{bmatrix} c_1 \\ c_2 \end{bmatrix}, \quad y = \begin{bmatrix} 0.61 \\ 0.92 \\ 0.99 \\ 1.52 \\ 1.47 \\ 2.03 \end{bmatrix}$$

Equation (8.1.7) is an over-determined linear equation that is not solvable because the number of equations, L, is greater than the number of unknowns. To make the equation solvable, Eq. (8.1.7) is premultiplied by the transpose of A:

$$A^t A c = A^t y \tag{8.1.8}$$

Since $A^t A$ becomes a 2-by-2 square matrix, and $A^t y$ becomes a vector of length 2, Eq.(8.1.8) is a regular 2-by-2 problem. The solution is obtained by

```
c = (A'*A)\(A'*y)
```

The foregoing solution becomes identical with that of Eq.(8.1.5). Indeed, Eq.(8.1.8) can be easily shown to be identical to Eq.(8.1.5).

An over-determined equation can also be solved in MATLAB simply by

```
c = A\y
```

The same can be achieved by `polyfit`, too. Suppose x and y are the data sets to be fitted, then

```
c = polyfit(x,y,1)
```

will return the coefficients c_1 and c_2 in the vector c, where "1" in the third place of the argument is the order of polynomial fitted, which is unity for line fitting.

Example 8.1

Determine the regression line for the data in Table 8.1 by (a) solving Eq.(8.1.5), and (b) using the `polyfit` command. After the regression line is obtained, examine the deviation of the line from the data.

Solution

We calculate the coefficients of Eq.(8.1.5) as follows:

	a_{21}	z_2	a_{11}	z_1
i	x_i	y_i	x_i^2	$x_i y_i$
1	0.1	0.61	0.01	0.061
2	0.4	0.92	0.16	0.368
3	0.5	0.99	0.25	0.495
4	0.7	1.52	0.49	1.064
5	0.7	1.47	0.49	1.029
6	0.9	2.03	0.81	1.827
Total	3.3	7.54	2.21	4.844

From the foregoing table, we get

$$a_{1,1} = 2.21, a_{1,2} = 3.3, z_1 = 4.844$$
$$a_{2,1} = 3.3, a_{2,2} = 6, z_2 = 7.54$$

Thus, Eq.(8.1.5) becomes

$$\begin{bmatrix} 2.21 & 3.3 \\ 3.3 & 6 \end{bmatrix} \begin{bmatrix} c_1 \\ c_2 \end{bmatrix} = \begin{bmatrix} 4.844 \\ 7.54 \end{bmatrix} \quad (A)$$

The solution is

$$c_1 = 1.7645, c_2 = 0.2862$$

The line therefore becomes

$$g(x) = 1.7645x + 0.2862 \qquad (B)$$

Figure 8.1 plots Eq.(B) with the data points.

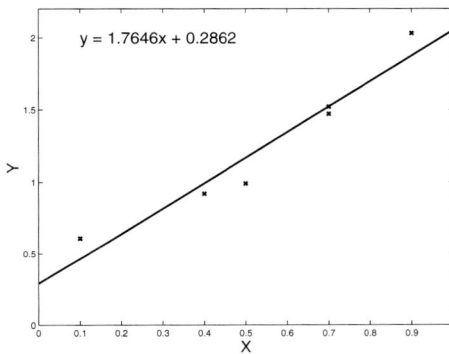

Figure 8.1 The line fitted to the data.

We now solve the same problem again using the `polyfit` command. The script has only three lines, as follows:

```
x = [0.1,  0.4,  0.5,  0.7   0.7    0.9]
y = [0.61, 0.92, 0.99, 1.52, 1.47, 2.03]
c = polyfit(x,y,1)
```

The result is:

```
c =
      1.7646     0.2862
```

which is identical to the coefficients of Eq.(B).

Deviation of the fitted line is analyzed as follows:

i	$x(i)$	$y(i)$	$g = c_1 x + c_2$	Deviation
1	.1	.61	0.4626	0.14738
2	.4	.92	0.9919	-0.07198
3	.5	.99	1.1684	-0.17844
4	.7	1.52	1.5213	-0.00135
5	.7	1.47	1.5213	-0.05135
6	.9	2.03	1.8742	0.15574

8.2 NONLINEAR CURVE FITTING WITH A POWER FUNCTION

For some types of data, fitting the power function given by

$$g(x) = \beta x^\alpha \qquad (8.2.1)$$

may be suitable where α and β are undetermined coefficients. To determine the coefficients, we first take the logarithm of Eq.(8.2.1):

$$\log(g) = \alpha \log(x) + \log(\beta) \qquad (8.2.2)$$

With the definitions

$$G = \log(g) \qquad (8.2.3)$$
$$c_1 = \alpha \qquad (8.2.4)$$
$$c_2 = \log(\beta) \qquad (8.2.5)$$
$$X = \log(x) \qquad (8.2.6)$$

Eq.(8.2.2) becomes

$$G = c_1 X + c_2 \qquad (8.2.7)$$

Then, the problem is reduced to line regression, as described in Section 8.1. Equation (8.2.7) is fitted to the data set, $(\log(y_i), \log(x_i))$.

Example 8.2[1]

A data set plotted in Figure 8.2 is given by

x = [0.15, 0.4,   0.6,   1.01, 1.5,   2.2,   2.4,   2.7,
     2.9,   3.5,   3.8,   4.4,   4.6,   5.1,   6.6,   7.6]
y = [4.4964,5.1284,5.6931,6.2884,7.0989,7.5507,7.5106,8.0756,
     7.8708,8.2403,8.5303,8.7394,8.9981,9.1450,9.5070,9.9115]

Fit the data by the power function.

Solution

The MATLAB script may be developed as follows:

---
[1] This example was provided by Professor Y. Guezennec of The Ohio State University.

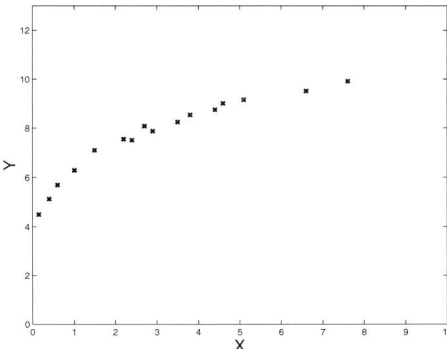

Figure 8.2 Plot of data points.

List 8.1
```
x = [0.15,  0.4,    0.6,    1.01,   1.5,    2.2,    2.4,    ...
     2.7,   2.9,    3.5,    3.8,    4.4,    4.6,    5.1,    ...
     6.6,   7.6]
y = [4.4964,5.1284,5.6931,6.2884,7.0989,7.5507,7.5106, ...
     8.0756,7.8708,8.2403,8.5303,8.7394,8.9981,9.1450, ...
     9.5070,9.9115]
c = polyfit(log(x), log(y),1)
```

The script yields

```
c =
        0.2093    1.8588
```

The constants of the power function become

$$\begin{aligned} \alpha &= c_1 = 0.2093 \\ \beta &= \exp(c_2) = \exp(1.8588) = 6.4160 \end{aligned} \qquad (8.2.8)$$

Finally, the power function becomes

$$g(x) = \beta x^\alpha = 6.4160 x^{0.2093}$$

The data set and the fitted curve are plotted in three different ways in Figure 8.3.

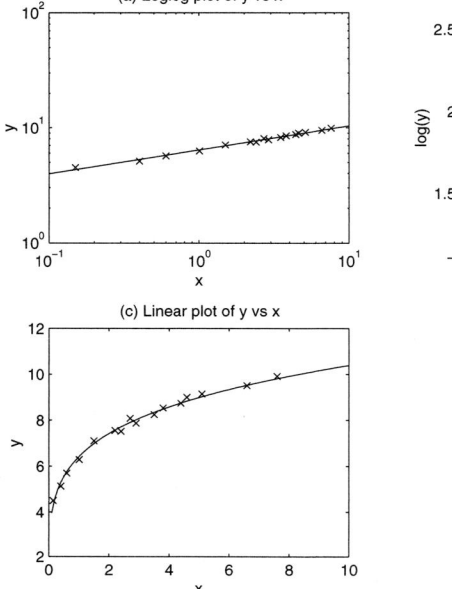
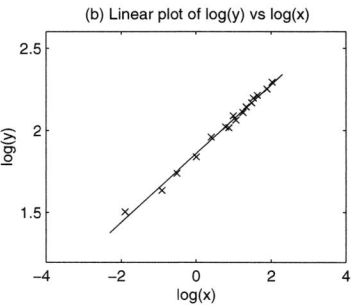

Figure 8.3 Fitted function and data points (plotted in three different ways).

8.3 CURVE FITTING WITH A HIGHER-ORDER POLYNOMIAL

The principle of least square can be extended to fitting a higher-order polynomial to measured data. An nth-order polynomial is written as

$$g(x) = c_1 x^n + c_2 x^{n-1} + ... + c_{n+1} \tag{8.3.1}$$

Residual of the curve from each data point is

$$r_i = y_i - g(x_i), \quad i = 1, 2, ... L \tag{8.3.2}$$

where L is the number of data points. The sum of the squared residuals is

$$R = \sum_{i=1}^{L} r_i^2 \tag{8.3.3}$$

In order to minimize R, we set the partial derivatives of R, with respect to c_j, to zero:

$$\frac{\partial R}{\partial c_j} = 0, \quad j = 1, 2, ..., n+1 \tag{8.3.4}$$

Section 8.3 Curve Fitting with a Higher-Order Polynomial

or equivalently

$$\sum_{j=1}^{n+1}\left(\sum_{i=1}^{L} x_i^{2n+2-j-k}\right) c_j = \sum_{i=1}^{L} x_i^{n+1-k} y_i, \quad k = 1, 2, \ldots n+1 \qquad (8.3.5)$$

or in matrix form as

$$\begin{bmatrix} \sum_{i=1}^{L} x_i^{2n} & \sum_{i=1}^{L} x_i^{2n-1} & \cdot & \sum_{i=1}^{L} x_i^{n} \\ \sum_{i=1}^{L} x_i^{2n-1} & \cdot & \cdot & \sum_{i=1}^{L} x_i^{n-1} \\ \cdot & \cdot & \cdot & \cdot \\ \sum_{i=1}^{L} x_i^{n} & \cdot & \cdot & \sum_{i=1}^{L} x_i^{0} \end{bmatrix} \begin{bmatrix} c_1 \\ c_2 \\ \cdot \\ c_{n+1} \end{bmatrix} = \begin{bmatrix} \sum_{i=1}^{L} x_i^{n} y_i \\ \sum_{i=1}^{L} x_i^{n-1} y_i \\ \cdot \\ \sum_{i=1}^{L} y_i \end{bmatrix} \qquad (8.3.6)$$

An equivalent way of deriving Eq.(8.3.6) is to write an over-determined equation. The matrix form of the equation is

$$Ac = y \qquad (8.3.7)$$

where

$$A = \begin{bmatrix} x_1^n & x_1^{n-1} & \cdot & 1 \\ x_2^n & \cdot & \cdot & 1 \\ \cdot & \cdot & \cdot & \cdot \\ x_L^n & \cdot & \cdot & 1 \end{bmatrix}, \quad c = \begin{bmatrix} c_1 \\ c_2 \\ \cdot \\ c_{n+1} \end{bmatrix}, \quad y = \begin{bmatrix} y_1 \\ y_2 \\ \cdot \\ y_L \end{bmatrix}$$

When $L > n+1$, the equation is over-determined, that is, unsolvable by itself because the number of equations is greater than the number of undetermined coefficients. To make it solvable, both sides are premultiplied by A^t to yield

$$A^t A c = A^t y \qquad (8.3.8)$$

which becomes identical with Eq.(8.3.6) and solvable as a regular problem by

```
c = (A'*A)\(A'*y)
```

In MATLAB, the solution of Eq.(8.3.7) can be obtained simply by

```
c = A\y
```

As already mentioned in Section 8.1, another equivalent but simpler way of finding coefficents of a polynomial fitted to a data set is by means of `polyfit`:

```
c = polyfit(x,y,n)
```

This format is identical to that used for interpolation discussed in Chapter 4, "Polynomials and Interpolation," except that for interpolation n is replaced by `length(x)-1`, but for curve fitting, `n < length(x)-1`.

Example 8.3

Fit the following data set by a quadratic polynomial:

```
x = [0.1, 0.4, 0.5, 0.7, 0.7, 0.9];
y = [0.61, 0.92, 0.99, 1.52, 1.47, 2.03];
```

and plot both data set and the fitted curve.

Solution

We find the coefficients of the quadratic polynomial by the `polyfit` command, and then plot the curve. A script to complete the answer is as follows:

List 8.2
```
clear, clf
x = [0.1, 0.4, 0.5, 0.7, 0.7, 0.9];
y = [0.61, 0.92, 0.99, 1.52, 1.47, 2.03];
cc = polyfit(x,y,2)
xx = x(1):0.1:x(length(x))
yy = polyval(cc,xx)
plot(xx,yy); hold on
plot(x,y,'x')
axis([0, 1, 0, 3])
xlabel('X')
ylabel('Y')
```

The plot of the result is shown in Figure 8.4.

The linear equations in curve fitting can become ill-conditioned. This occurs if (1) the abscissas of the data points include both very small and very large numbers, or (2) when the order of the polynomial is high. A high-order polynomial is not desirable because the polynomial may oscillate just as a high-order polynomial is not desirable for interpolation.

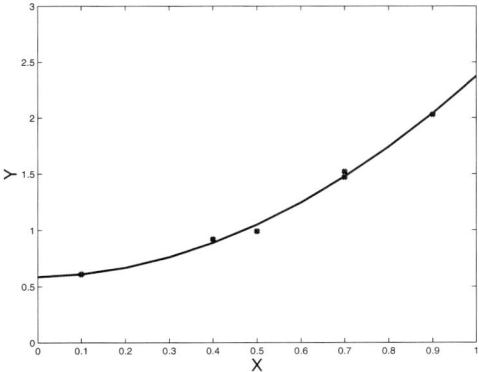

Figure 8.4 Plot of the fitted quadratic polynomial.

8.4 CURVE FITTING BY A LINEAR COMBINATION OF KNOWN FUNCTIONS

In fitting a function to data points, a linear combination of any known functions, including polynomials, may be used:

$$g(x) = c_1 f_1(x) + c_2 f_2(x) + c_3 f_3(x) + \ldots + c_n f_n(x) \qquad (8.4.1)$$

where f_1, f_2, ... are prescribed functions, c_1, c_2, ... are undetermined coefficients, and n is the total number of prescribed functions. By fitting Eq.(8.4.1) to each data point, an over-determined equation is written as

$$Ac = y \qquad (8.4.2)$$

with

$$A = \begin{bmatrix} f_1(x_1) & f_2(x_1) & . & f_n(x_1) \\ f_1(x_2) & f_2(x_2) & . & f_n(x_2) \\ . & . & . & . \\ f_1(x_L) & f_2(x_L) & . & f_n(x_L) \end{bmatrix}, \quad c = \begin{bmatrix} c_1 \\ c_2 \\ . \\ c_n \end{bmatrix}, \quad y = \begin{bmatrix} y_1 \\ y_2 \\ . \\ y_L \end{bmatrix}$$

where $L > n$. The coefficients are determined by

```
c = A\y
```

Any function may be used for f in Eq.(8.4.1). Knowledge, experience, and trials help select appropriate functions for linear combinations.

Example 8.4

Determine the coefficients of the function

$$g(x) = c_1 + c_2 x + c_3 \sin(x) + c_4 \exp(x)$$

fitted to the data in the following table:

x	y
0.1	0.61
0.4	0.92
0.5	0.99
0.7	1.52
0.7	1.47
0.9	2.03

Solution

The solution algorithm is implemented in List 8.3. The curve determined is plotted in Figure 8.5.

List 8.3
```
clc; clear; clf
data=[   0.1    0.61;
         0.4    0.92;
         0.5    0.99;
         0.7    1.52;
         0.7    1.47;
         0.9    2.03]
x = data(:,1);     y = data(:,2);
A(:,1)=ones(x);    A(:,2)=x;    A(:,3)=sin(x);    A(:,4)=exp(x);
```

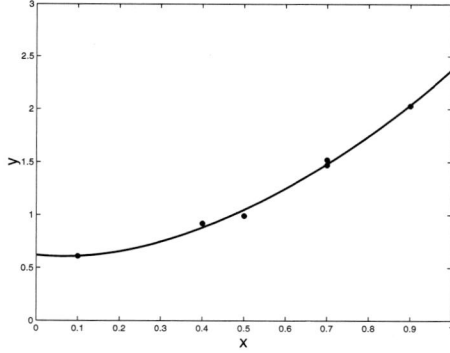

Figure 8.5 Plot of the linearly combined functions.

```
c = A\y
xx = 0:0.01:1;
g= c(1)*ones(xx) + c(2)*xx + c(3)*sin(xx) + c(4)*exp(xx);
axis('square');
plot(x, y,'*', xx, g);   xlabel('x'); ylabel('y')
```

PROBLEMS

(8.1) Determine a line fitted to the following data set by the least square method. (Work by hand calculation first and then verify the answer with `polyfit`.)

i	x_i	y_i
1	1.0	2.0
2	1.5	3.2
3	2.0	4.1
4	2.5	4.9
5	3.0	5.9

(8.2) Using MATLAB, determine a linear function fitted to the following data set by solving an over-determined linear equation. Verify the result by `polyfit`.

i	x_i	y_i
1	0.1	9.9
2	0.2	9.2
3	0.3	8.4
4	0.4	6.6
5	0.5	5.9
6	0.6	5.0
7	0.7	4.1
8	0.8	3.1
9	0.9	1.9
10	1.0	1.1

(8.3) The data set below is to be fitted by

$$y = \alpha \exp(\beta x)$$

Determine the constants. Plot the curve with the data on a linear scale as well as on a log scale.

x	y
0.0129	9.5600
0.0247	8.1845
0.0530	5.2616
0.1550	2.7917
0.3010	2.2611
0.4710	1.7340
0.8020	1.2370
1.2700	1.0674
1.4300	1.1171
2.4600	0.7620

(8.4) Prove that Eq.(8.1.8) is equivalent to Eq.(8.1.5).

(8.5) (a) Fit a quadratic polynomial to the following data set using `polyfit` command. (b) Plot the determined polynomial with the data.

i	x_i	y_i
1	0	0
2	1	2.3
3	2	4.2
4	3	5.7
5	4	6.5
6	5	6.9
7	6	6.8

(8.6) Repeat the previous problem with 1st-order and 3rd-order polynomials.

(8.7) Prove that Eq.(8.3.8) is equivalent to Eq.(8.3.6).

(8.8) Fit polynomials of order 1, 2, and 3 to the following data set and compare deviations of the three polynomials. Plot the polynomial with the data.

x_i	y_i
0	0
.002	0.618
.004	1.1756
.006	1.6180
.008	1.9021

(8.9) Fit a cubic polynomial to the following data. Plot the polynomial with the data.

i	x_i	y_i
1	0	0
2	0.2	7.78
3	0.4	10.68
4	0.6	8.37
5	0.8	3.97
6	1	0

(8.10) Fit the function given by

$$g(x) = c_1 + c_2 x + c_3 \sin(\pi x) + c_4 \sin(2\pi x)$$

to the following data. Plot $g(x)$ with the data.

i	$x(i)$	$y(i)$
1	.1	0.0000
2	.2	2.1220
3	.3	3.0244
4	.4	3.2568
5	.5	3.1399
6	.6	2.8579
7	.7	2.5140
8	.8	2.1639
9	.9	1.8358

Chapter 9

SPLINE FUNCTIONS AND NONLINEAR INTERPOLATION

This chapter presents three subjects namely, *b-spline*, *c-spline*, and nonlinear interpolation. The c-spline function consists of piecewise cubic polynomials that fit to given data points. It is suitable to fit a smooth curve to a large data set. The cubic b-spline function consists of piecewise cubic polynomials that do not fit to the data points exactly, but its purpose is to generate smooth curves that are pleasing to the eyes. The nonlinear interpolation methods are useful when an exponential behavior of the fitted function is desired.

9.1 C-SPLINE INTERPOLATION

An incentive for the c-spline (cubic spline) function is illustrated by the question: How can a large number of points on the x-y plane, such as those shown in Figure 9.1, be fitted by a smooth curve?

Attempts to fit a single polynomial to a large data set will fail. The reason is that, as the number of points increases, errors of the Lagrange interpolation increase rapidly.

The essence of the c-spline interpolation is to apply a cubic polynomial to each interval between two consecutive data points. The first and second derivatives of the cubic polynomials, however, are also required to be continuous across each data point. Therefore, the functional value, first derivative, and second derivative all become continuous in the entire domain. To determine the coefficients of the c-spline function, however, the coefficients for all the intervals must be determined simultaneously.

In order to fit a c-spline function $f(s)$ to data points (s_i, f_i), the following

Section 9.1 C-Spline Interpolation

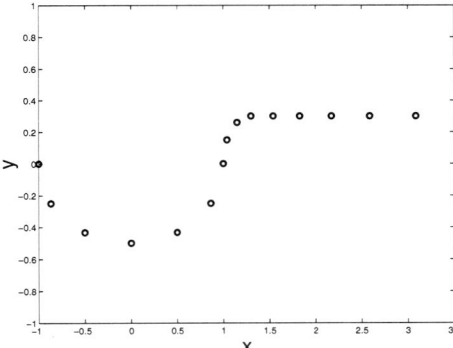

Figure 9.1 Points to be connected by a smooth curve.

quantities are involved:

$$s_i, \quad i = 1, 2, ..., n : \quad \text{known}$$
$$f_i, \quad i = 1, 2, ..., n : \quad \text{known}$$
$$f'_i, \quad i = 1, 2, ..., n : \quad \text{to be determined}$$
$$f''_i, \quad i = 1, 2, ..., n : \quad \text{to be determined}$$

where s has the following meaning. We use s as the independent variable rather than x or y. The s measures the location on a given curve, and increases with the distance on the curve measured from the end of the point. We also use t as a local coordinate in place of s, that is, $dt = ds$ but $t = 0$ can be set at any point along the curve whenever convenient.

Consider one interval, $s_i < s < s_{i+1}$ with $h_i = s_{i+1} - s_i$, as shown in Figure 9.2. Using the local coordinate $t = s - s_i$, a cubic polynomial for one interval may be written as

$$f(t) = a + bt + ct^2 + et^3 \qquad (9.1.1)$$

where $0 \leq t \leq h_i$.

We first require $f(t)$ to equal the known values of the function $f(t)$ at $t = 0$ and $t = h_i$:

$$f_i = a \qquad (9.1.2)$$
$$f_{i+1} = a + bh_i + ch_i^2 + eh_i^3 \qquad (9.1.3)$$

The foregoing two equations are insufficient to determine the four constants, a, b, c, and e. If two more conditions are specified, however, the equations to determine the constants will be closed. These conditions are provided by

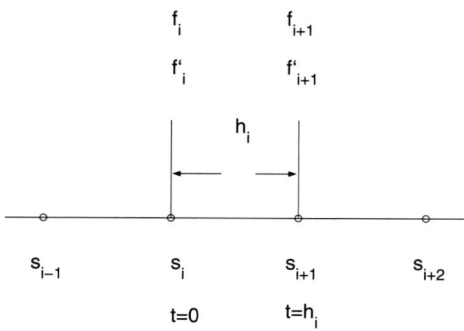

Figure 9.2 An interval between two data points for c-spline.

the requirements that f'' and f' become continuous across each data point. If this is achieved, the entire curve will become continuous in the function fitted, the first derivative, and the second derivative.

The second derivative of Eq.(9.1.1) is

$$f''(t) = 2c + 6et \qquad (9.1.4)$$

which becomes, at points i and $i+1$, respectively,

$$f''_i = 2c \qquad (9.1.5)$$
$$f''_{i+1} = 2c + 6eh_i \qquad (9.1.6)$$

where f''_i and f''_{i+1} are values of f'' at i and $i+1$, respectively, which are yet to be determined. The foregoing two equations can be written as

$$c = f''_i/2 \qquad (9.1.7)$$
$$e = \frac{f''_{i+1} - f''_i}{6h_i} \qquad (9.1.8)$$

The coefficient a is already given by Eq.(9.1.2). The coefficient b is determined by eliminating a, c, and e in Eq.(9.1.3) by Eqs.(9.1.2), (9.1.7), and (9.1.8),

$$b = \frac{f_{i+1} - f_i}{h_i} - \frac{f''_{i+1} + 2f''_i}{6}h_i \qquad (9.1.9)$$

Thus, the cubic polynomial in Eq.(9.1.1) is expressed by

$$f(t) = f_i + \left(\frac{f_{i+1} - f_i}{h_i} - \frac{f''_{i+1} + 2f''_i}{6}h_i\right)t + \frac{f''_i}{2}t^2 + \frac{f''_{i+1} - f''_i}{6h_i}t^3 \qquad (9.1.10)$$

We differentiate Eq.(9.1.10), and set the first derivative of f at $t = 0$ and $t = h_i$ to f_i' and f_{i+1}', respectively,

$$f_i' = -\frac{h_i}{6}\left(f_{i+1}'' + 2f_i''\right) + \frac{1}{h_i}(f_{i+1} - f_i) \qquad (9.1.11)$$

$$f_{i+1}' = \frac{h_i}{6}\left(2f_{i+1}'' + f_i''\right) + \frac{1}{h_i}(f_{i+1} - f_i) \qquad (9.1.12)$$

For the adjacent interval of $s_{i-1} < s < s_i$, Eq.(9.1.12) becomes

$$f_i' = \frac{h_{i-1}}{6}\left(2f_i'' + f_{i-1}''\right) + \frac{1}{h_{i-1}}(f_i - f_{i-1}) \qquad (9.1.13)$$

where $h_{i-1} = s_i - s_{i-1}$. The f_i' of Eq.(9.1.13) must equal that of f_i' in Eq.(9.1.11) for continuity. Eliminating f_i' between the two equations yields

$$h_{i-1}f_{i-1}'' + (2h_{i-1} + 2h_i)f_i'' + h_i f_{i+1}''$$
$$= 6\left(\frac{1}{h_{i-1}}f_{i-1} - (\frac{1}{h_{i-1}} + \frac{1}{h_i})f_i + \frac{1}{h_i}f_{i+1}\right) \qquad (9.1.14)$$

where the equation has been multiplied through by 6.

The foregoing equation can be written for all the points except for the two endpoints. That is, there are $n - 2$ equations, while the number of undetermined f_i'' is n. Therefore, two additional equations are necessary to determine all the undetermined f_i''s, which may be provided by the boundary conditions. Three ways of specifying boundary conditions at the endpoints are explained in the following:

(a) Specifying f_i'' at the endpoints: If we prescribe f_1'' and f_n'', the set of equations becomes

$$(2h_1 + 2h_2)f_2'' + h_2 f_3''$$
$$= 6\left(\frac{1}{h_1}f_1 - (\frac{1}{h_1} + \frac{1}{h_2})f_2 + \frac{1}{h_2}f_3\right) - h_1 f_1''$$
$$h_{i-1}f_{i-1}'' + (2h_{i-1} + 2h_i)f_i'' + h_i f_{i+1}''$$
$$= 6\left(\frac{1}{h_{i-1}}f_{i-1} - (\frac{1}{h_{i-1}} + \frac{1}{h_i})f_i + \frac{1}{h_i}f_{i+1}\right) \qquad (9.1.15)$$
$$h_{n-2}f_{n-2}'' + (2h_{n-2} + 2h_{n-1})f_{n-1}''$$
$$= 6\left(\frac{1}{h_{n-2}}f_{n-2} - (\frac{1}{h_{n-2}} + \frac{1}{h_{n-1}})f_{n-1} + \frac{1}{h_{n-1}}f_n\right) - h_{n-1}f_n''$$

The foregoing equations constitute $n-2$ equations for $n-2$ unknowns, f_i''. When the equations are written in matrix form, the coefficient matrix becomes a special form, called the *tridiagonal matrix*, in which all the elements are zero except the three diagonal lines. Although the equation may be solved by the standard solution for the linear equations, the tridiagonal solution scheme explained in Section 11.3 is significantly more efficient. Although f'' at the endpoints is not known in most situations, one approach is to assume $f'' = 0$ at the endpoints. Geometrically, this is equivalent to assuming that the curve becomes a straight line toward the endpoints.

(b) Extrapolating f'' from inside: Extrapolation of f_1'' from f_2'' and f_3'' is written as

$$f_1'' = (1 + \frac{h_1}{h_2})f_2'' - \frac{h_1}{h_2}f_3'' \qquad (9.1.16)$$

By setting $i=2$ in Eq.(9.1.14) and eliminating f_1'' by using Eq.(9.1.16), we get

$$\left(3h_1 + 2h_2 + \frac{(h_1)^2}{h_2}\right)f_2'' + \left(h_2 - \frac{(h_1)^2}{h_2}\right)f_3''$$
$$= 6\left(\frac{1}{h_1}f_1 - (\frac{1}{h_1} + \frac{1}{h_2})f_2 + \frac{1}{h_2}f_3\right) \qquad (9.1.17)$$

The foregoing equation replaces the first equation of Eq.(9.1.15). A similar equation may be written for point $n-1$, which replaces the last equation in Eq.(9.1.15). The system of the equation has the same form as Eq.(9.1.15) except for a few coefficients. Therefore, the set of equations may be solved by the same scheme as for **(a)**.

(c) Cyclic boundary condition: The cyclic boundary condition is applied if the first and last data are identical, and the derivatives at these data points are identical also. This occurs if the whole data set represents one cycle of a curve that repeats. A closed curve on a plane may be fitted by the cyclic boundary conditions, for example.

The MATLAB command `interp1` performs a c-spline interpolation (see Section 4.1). Its synopsis is

`yi=interp1(x,y,xi,'spline')`

where `x` and `y` are data points in the vector form, and `xi` is a vector of the abscissa for which the interpolation is performed. Therefore, the command returns the interpolated y values for `xi` in vector `yi`.

Section 9.1 C-Spline Interpolation

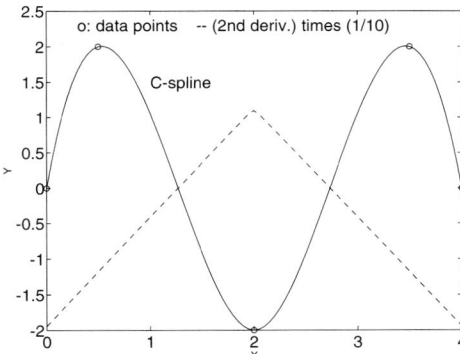

Figure 9.3 Investigation of BC (the spline BC in MATLAB is extrapolation).

No boundary conditions are necessary in the argument, but the boundary condition of type (b) explained earlier is assumed. Although the MATLAB Reference Manual does not explain this, we can verify it by examining the result of `spline` applied with a test data set. We set test data as:

```
x = [0, 0.5, 2, 3.5, 4]
y = [0, 2,  -2, 2,   0]
```

In order to find the spline function for $0 \leq x \leq 4$, we also set

```
xi = 1:0.05:4
```

which is significantly finer than the test data. We get the c-spline function for `xi` by `yi=interp1(x,y,xi,'spline')`. The second derivative of the spline function can be computed from `yi` by the second-order difference approximation. In Figure 9.3, the spline function (solid curve) and its second derivative (dotted curve), computed from the spline function, are plotted. Notice that the second derivative is linear from $x = 0$ to $x = 2$, spanning two data intervals. The same is true for the last two intervals. The script used to plot Figure 9.3 is listed in List 9.1.

List 9.1
```
clear, clf, hold off
x=0:4;
x(2) = 0.5; x(4)=3.5;x
y = [0 2 -2 2 0]
xp=0:0.05:4; % fine points for which spline
             % function is to be computed
h = xp(2)-xp(1)
yp = spline(x,y,xp);
n=length(xp)
for i=2:n-1
```

```
          ypd(i) = (yp(i-1) - 2*yp(i) + yp(i+1))/h^2;
    end
    ypd(1)=ypd(2)*2 - ypd(3);     %for graphics only
    ypd(n)=ypd(n-1)*2 - ypd(n-2); %for graphics only
    plot(xp,yp,  xp,ypd/10, '--')
    hold on
    plot(x,y,'o')
    xlabel('X')
    ylabel('Y')
    set(gca, 'FontSize',[18])
    text(1,1.5,'C-spline','FontSize',[18])
    text(0.3,2.3,'o: data points   -- (2nd deriv.) times (1/10)', ...
    'FontSize',[18])
```

Like the Lagrange interpolation, the c-spline interpolation may develop an oscillatory behavior of errors. If abscissas of the data points can be chosen freely, use smaller intervals near the endpoints as well as where the curvature is high.

Example 9.1

The data points in Figure 9.1 are given by

```
xx =
[-1.0000 -0.8660 -0.5000 -0.0000  0.5000  0.8660 ...
  1.0000  1.0000  1.0402  1.1500  1.3000  1.5400 ...
  1.8280  2.1736  2.5883  3.0860]

yy =
[ 0.0000 -0.2500 -0.4330 -0.5000 -0.4330 -0.2500 ...
 -0.0000  0.0000  0.1500  0.2598  0.3000  0.3000 ...
  0.3000  0.3000  0.3000  0.3000]
```

Determine the spline function that fits the data.

Solution

We use s as a parameter and fit spline functions to x and y separately as functions of s. A script is given in List 9.2. The result is shown in Figure 9.4.

List 9.2
```
clear, clf, hold off
xx = ...
[-1.0000 -0.866 -0.5000 -0.0000  0.5000 0.8660  1.0000 ...
 1.0000  1.0402  1.1500  1.3000  1.5400  1.8280  2.1736 ...
 2.5883 3.0860]
yy = ...
```

Section 9.2 Cubic B-Spline

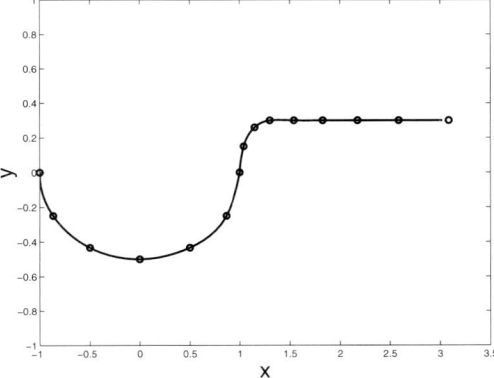

Figure 9.4 C-spline curve on the x-y plane.

```
[0.0000 -0.2500 -0.4330 -0.5000 -0.4330 -0.2500 -0.0000 ...
 0.0000  0.1500  0.2598  0.3000  0.3000  0.3000  0.3000 ...
 0.3000  0.3000]
s=1:length(xx);sp=1:(length(xx)/100):length(xx);
xp=spline(s,xx,sp);
yp=spline(s,yy,sp);
clf
plot(xp,yp); hold on
plot(xx,yy, 'o');xlabel('x'); ylabel('y');
hold off; axis ([-1 3 -1 1])
```

9.2 CUBIC B-SPLINE

The b-spline function consists of piecewise polynomials determined by a series of control points: (s_i, p_i), $i = 1, 2, ..., n$. The b-spline function based on cubic polynomials is named cubic b-spline, a sibling of the c-spline studied in the preceding section but with different characters. We call (s_i, p_i) control points, because b-spline does not pass through the points except under special conditions. The b-spline function is useful to generate a smooth curve in design and graphics when artistic impression or a visually comfortable curve is more important than strict fitting. In the remainder of this section, we will discuss mathematical expression and behaviors of the cubic b-spline.

A segment of the cubic b-spline is determined with four consecutive control points, (s_{i-1}, p_{i-1}), (s_i, p_i), (s_{i+1}, p_{i+1}), and (s_{i+2}, p_{i+2}), by

$$f(s) = \frac{1}{6}[(1-t)^3 p_{i-1} + (3t^3 - 6t^2 + 4)p_i$$
$$+ (-3t^3 + 3t^2 + 3t + 1)p_{i+1} + t^3 p_{i+2}], \quad 0 \leq t \leq 1 \quad (9.2.1)$$

where $t = s - s_i$ is a local coordinate, and $s_i = i$. For $s = s_i$ and $s = s_{i+1}$ (or equivalently $t = 0$ and $t = 1$, respectively), f, f', and f'' have the following values:

$$f(s_i) = \frac{p_{i-1} + 4p_i + p_{i+1}}{6}, \quad f'(s_i) = \frac{p_{i+1} - p_{i-1}}{2}, \quad f''(s_i) = \frac{p_{i+1} - 2p_i + p_{i-1}}{2}$$
$$f(s_{i+1}) = \frac{p_i + 4p_{i+1} + p_{i+2}}{6}, \quad f'(s_{i+1}) = \frac{p_{i+2} - p_i}{2}, \quad f''(s_{i+1}) = \frac{p_{i+2} - 2p_{i+1} + p_i}{2}$$
(9.2.2)

The cubic b-spline curves determined by four control points are illustrated in Figure 9.5, where s values are set to 1, 2, 3, and 4, while p values are varied from case to case. It is seen that $f(s)$ does not pass through control points in Cases A and B. If three consecutive ordinates are identical, however, as in Case C, or if the three consecutive ordinates change linearly, as in Case D, the curve passes through the middle of the three.

If the number of control points is greater than 4, a series of cubic b-spline curves becomes a single curve, as illustrated in Figure 9.6. The b-spline function and its first and second derivatives all become continuous.

The curve in Figure 9.6 does not pass through any boundary points. By repeating $f = 1$ three times in the beginning of the control points, and repeating $f = 2$ three times at the end of the control points, however, the

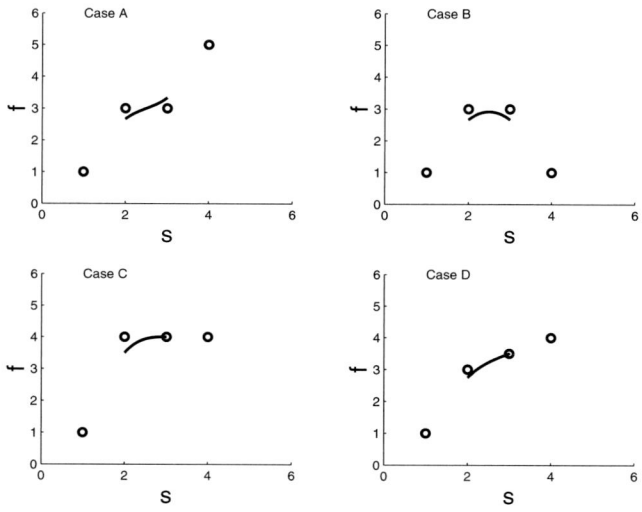

Figure 9.5 Pieces of b-spline determined by four control points.

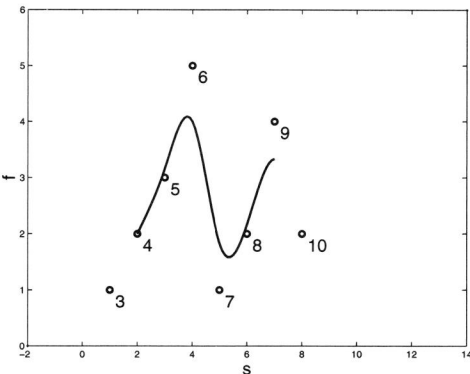

Figure 9.6 A b-spline function determined by 10 control points.

curve satisfies these boundary conditions, as illustrated in Figure 9.7. The script used to plot Figure 9.7 is given in List 9.3.

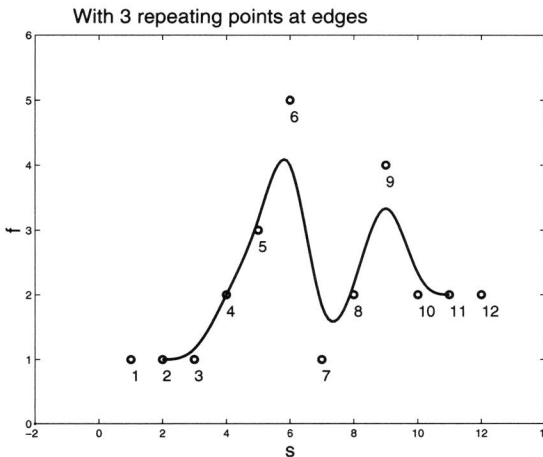

Figure 9.7 The b-spline function satisfying the boundary conditions.

List 9.3
```
clear; clf; hold off
f = [ 1 1 1 2 3 5 1 2 4 2 2 2 ];   m = length(f)
s=1:m;
plot([-2 14], [0 6], '.');  hold on
xlabel('s'); ylabel('f');   plot(s,f,'o')
for k=1:m
  z=int2str(k);  sk = s(k);  fk=f(k);  text(sk+0.2,fk-0.2,z)
end
```

```
t = 0:0.1:1; t2=t.^2; t3=t.^3;
for i=2:m-2
    fb = 1/6*((1-t).^3*f(i-1)+(3*t3-6*t2+ 4)*f(i) + ...
        (-3*t3+3*t2 + 3*t + 1)*f(i+1) + t3*f(i+2) );
    plot(s(i)+t,fb)
end
title (' With 3 repeating points at edges')
```

The rule of repeating the same ordinates three times also applies to a control point in the middle. That is, if the curve is required to pass through a point in the middle, repeat that point three times in the control point vector.

We now apply the cubic b-spline on the x-y plane. The control points are given by

(x,y): (0,0), (0.2,1), (1,1), (2,0), (2.8,0), (3,1)

Assume that the curve is required to pass through the first point (0,0) and the last point (3,1). Each of x and y must be determined as a function of parameter s. Therefore, the control points of the s-x space as well as the s-y space are set to

```
s = (1, 2, 3, 4,  5, 6, 7,   8, 9, 10)
x = (0, 0, 0, 0.2,1, 2, 2.8, 3, 3, 3)

s = (1, 2, 3, 4, 5, 6, 7, 8, 9, 10)
y = (0, 0, 0, 1, 1, 0, 0, 1, 1, 1)
```

Here, the value x=0 and y=0 are repeated three times in the beginning of the control point vectors, while x=3 and y=1 are repeated three times at the end of the control point vectors. The plot of the curve on the x-y plane is shown in Figure 9.8. Notice that the curve passes through x=y=0 at the left end, while the curve passes through x=3 and y=1 at the right end. The script to plot Figure 9.8 is listed in List 9.4.

List 9.4
```
clear; clf; hold off
y = [0 0 0 1    1 0 0    1 1 1];
x = [0 0 0 0.2  1 2 2.8 3 3 3];
m = length(y); plot([-1 4], [-1 2], '.'); hold on
xlabel('x'); ylabel('y');  plot(x,y,'o')
for k=1:m
    z=int2str(k); xk = x(k); yk=y(k); text(xk+0.1,yk,z)
end
t = 0:0.2:1; t2=t.^2; t3=t.^3;
```

Section 9.2 Cubic B-Spline

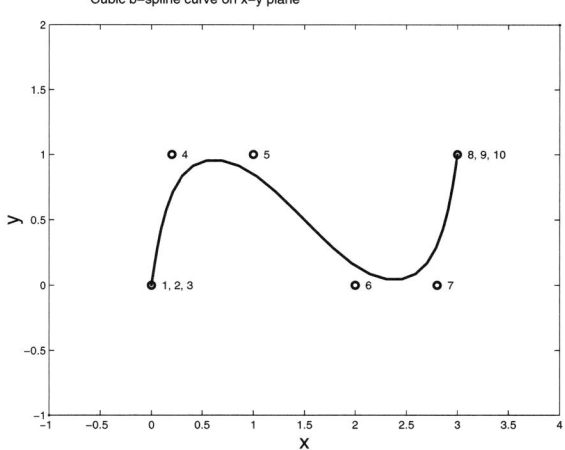

Figure 9.8 The b-spline curve passing through two endpoints.

```
for i=2:m-2
    yb = 1/6*((1-t).^3*y(i-1) + (3*t3-6*t2+4)*y(i) + ...
         (-3*t3 + 3*t2 + 3*t + 1)*y(i+1) + t3*y(i+2) );
    xb = 1/6*((1-t).^3*x(i-1) + (3*t3-6*t2+4)*x(i) +  ...
         (-3*t3 + 3*t2 + 3*t + 1)*x(i+1) + t3*x(i+2) );
    plot(xb,yb)
end
title(' Cubic b-spline curve on x-y plane ')
```

Example 9.2

The data file car.dat specifies a side-view profile of an automobile. Plot the data without any modification. Then, smooth out the profile by b-spline.

Solution

Two profiles plotted by List 9.5 are shown in Figure 9.9.

```
List 9.5
clear, clf, hold off
load car.dat
x=car(:,1)'; y=car(:,2)';
subplot(2,1,1)
hold on
plot(x,y) % plot of car profile
dth=pi/10;
th=0:dth:2*pi; xt=1.2*cos(th); yt=1.2*sin(th);
```

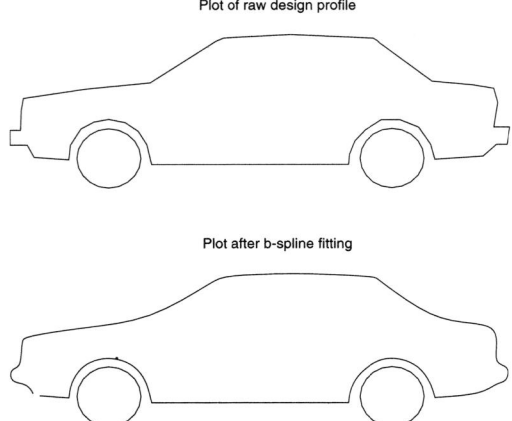

Figure 9.9 Car profiles before and after b-spline fitting.

```
plot(xt+3.7, yt+0.45)     %front tire
plot(xt+14.3, yt+0.45)    %front tire
title('Plot of raw design profile')
axis([-0,20,-0.9,6.0]); axis('off')
disp 'Hit return to plot the profile after smoothing'
pause
subplot(2,1,2)
hold on
m = length(y); plot([-1 4], [-1 2], '.');
x=[x(1),x,x(m)]; y=[y(1),y,y(m)];
m=length(x);
t = 0:0.25:1; t2=t.^2; t3=t.^3;
for i=2:m-2
   yb = 1/6*((1-t).^3*y(i-1) + (3*t3-6*t2+4)*y(i) + ...
        (-3*t3 + 3*t2 + 3*t + 1)*y(i+1) + t3*y(i+2) );
   xb = 1/6*((1-t).^3*x(i-1) + (3*t3-6*t2+4)*x(i) + ...
        (-3*t3 + 3*t2 + 3*t + 1)*x(i+1) + t3*x(i+2) );
   plot(xb,yb)
end
plot(xt+3.7, yt+0.45), plot(xt+14.3, yt+0.45) % tires
title('Plot after b-spline fitting'); hold off
```

Example 9.3

A ceramic pot image may be created on the screen by k_wheel. The script collects data points clicked on the screen by the mouse. The

Section 9.2 Cubic B-Spline   **337**

points are used as control points for b-spline, and a pot is created by rotating the shape determined by b-spline (see Figure 9.10). Run `k_wheel` and create a pot. (Script of `k_wheel` is listed in Section 9.4)

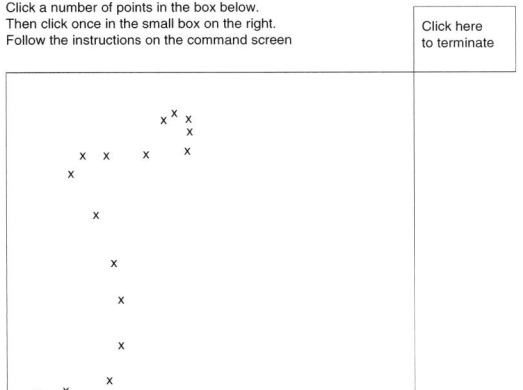

Figure 9.10 Input for pot making.

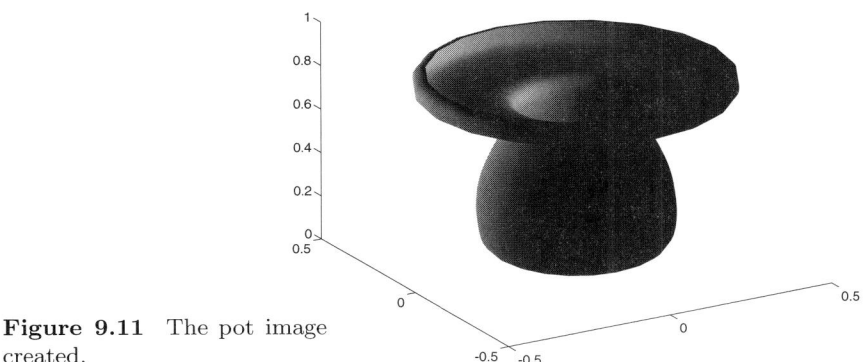

Figure 9.11 The pot image created.

Solution

To run the script, we type `k_wheel`. Now input the coordinate values by clicking points on the graphic window from the bottom to the top of the pot. When input is completed, click inside the box to terminate input. Figure 9.10 illustrates the points clicked for input. Figure 9.11 shows the pot image created.

9.3 INTERPOLATION WITH A NONLINEAR FUNCTION

Interpolation by a nonpolynomial function can produce effects different from interpolation by a polynomial. In this section, we present a few applications of exponential functions fitted to a given data set.

In the first approach we use

$$f(x) = a\exp(bx) + c \qquad (9.3.1)$$

where a, b, and c are undetermined coefficients. With the three free parameters, a, b, and c, Eq.(9.3.1) may be fitted to three data points, (x_i, f_i), $i = 1, 2$, and 3. Setting Eq.(9.3.1) to each data point, we get

$$\begin{aligned} f(x_1) &= a\exp(bx_1) + c = f_1 \\ f(x_2) &= a\exp(bx_2) + c = f_2 \\ f(x_3) &= a\exp(bx_3) + c = f_3 \end{aligned} \qquad (9.3.2)$$

By eliminating c between the first and second equations, we get

$$a = \frac{f_1 - f_2}{\exp(bx_1) - \exp(bx_2)} \qquad (9.3.3)$$

Also, by eliminating c between first and third equations, we get

$$a = \frac{f_1 - f_3}{\exp(bx_1) - \exp(bx_3)} \qquad (9.3.4)$$

Equating the two foregoing equations yields

$$\frac{\exp(bx_2) - \exp(bx_1)}{f_2 - f_1} = \frac{\exp(bx_3) - \exp(bx_1)}{f_3 - f_1} \qquad (9.3.5)$$

or by dividing through by $\exp(bx_1)$,

$$\frac{\exp\{b(x_2 - x_1)\} - 1}{f_2 - f_1} = \frac{\exp\{b(x_3 - x_1)\} - 1}{f_3 - f_1} \qquad (9.3.6)$$

The constant b is determined by solving the foregoing nonlinear equation by one of the schemes described in Chapter 7, "Roots of Nonlnear Equations." Once b is known, a is evaluated by Eq.(9.3.3), and c by one of the equations in Eq.(9.3.2); for example

$$c = f_1 - a \exp(bx_1) \tag{9.3.7}$$

Example 9.4

A bar of length L is to be cut into seven sections such that the lengths change monotonically and smoothly from one section to the next. The first section should be $1/12$ of the total length L. Determine the length of each section.

Solution

The problem can be restated as follows: Determine a smooth and monotonic function

$$f(s)/L = a \exp(bs) + c \tag{A}$$

where s is a parameter satisfying $0 \leq s \leq 7$; f is the length of the bar measured from the left end while at $s = 7$, f equals L; a, b, and c are undetermined constants. We summarize the conditions for f as

$$s = 0 : f(0) = 0$$
$$s = 1 : f(1) = L/12$$
$$s = 7 : f(7) = L$$

Introducing these three conditions to Eq.(9.3.1) yields

$$\begin{aligned} a + c &= 0 \\ a \exp(b) + c &= 1/12 \\ a \exp(7b) + c &= 1 \end{aligned} \tag{9.3.8}$$

Eliminating a and c yields

$$\frac{\exp(b) - 1}{1/12} = \exp(7b) - 1 \tag{D}$$

Applying Newton iteration, b is found to be 0.16229 so

$$a = 0.472931, \quad b = 0.16229, \quad c = -0.472931 \qquad \text{(E)}$$

The exponential function determined is plotted in Figure 9.12. Length of each segment becomes as follows:

Section #	Relative length
1	0.083333
2	0.098017
3	0.115288
4	0.135602
5	0.159496
6	0.187601
7	0.220657

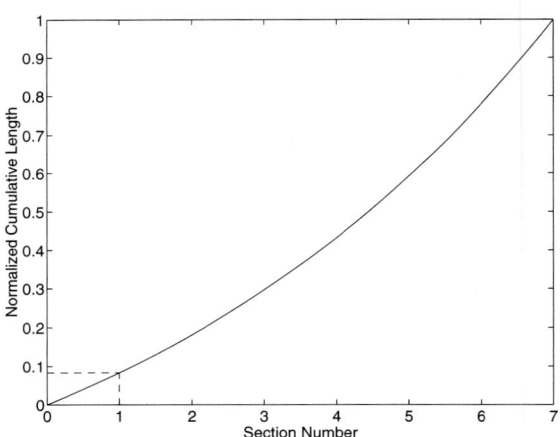

Figure 9.12 Plot of f.

List 9.6
```
% A script to plot Figure 9.12
clear, hold off, clf
b = 0.162294
c = 1/12/(1- exp(b))
a = -c
x = 0:0.1:7;
y =  a*exp(b*x) + c;
plot(x,y)
xlabel('s')
ylabel('f(s)/L')
y1 =  a*exp(b) + c
```

```
hold on
plot([1,1], [0,y1], '--')
plot([0,1], [y1,y1], '--')
```

Example 9.5

Fit the function
$$y = ae^{-\gamma x} + be^{\gamma x} + c$$
to the following data:

x1 = 0,	x2 = 0.01,	x3 = 0.95,	x4 = 1
y1 = 0,	y2 = 0.01,	y3 = 0.8,	y4 = 1

where a, b, c, and γ are undetermined constants.

Solution

We first define
$$f(x,y) = ae^{-\gamma x} + be^{\gamma x} + c - y \qquad (A)$$

By setting Eq. (A) to each data point, we get four equations:

$$\begin{aligned}
f_1 &\equiv f(x_1, y_1) = a \quad\;\; + \quad b \quad\;\; + \quad c = 0 \\
f_2 &\equiv f(x_2, y_2) = ae^{-0.01\gamma} + be^{0.01\gamma} + c - 0.01 = 0 \\
f_3 &\equiv f(x_3, y_3) = ae^{-0.95\gamma} + be^{0.95\gamma} + c - 0.8 = 0 \\
f_4 &\equiv f(x_4, y_4) = ae^{-\gamma} \;\;+ \;\; be^{\gamma} \;\;+ \;\; c - 1 = 0
\end{aligned}$$

In the foregoing equations, each f may now be regarded as a function of a, b, c, and γ, and written as

$$f_k(\hat{a} + \delta a,\; \hat{b} + \delta b,\; \hat{c} + \delta c,\; \hat{\gamma} + \delta\gamma) = 0, \quad k = 1 \sim 4 \qquad (B)$$

where $\hat{a}$, $\hat{b}$, $\hat{c}$, and $\hat{\gamma}$ are guesses, while δa, δb, δc, and $\delta\gamma$ are unknown corrections, and $a = \hat{a} + \delta a$, $b = \hat{b} + \delta b$, $c = \hat{c} + \delta c$, and $\gamma = \hat{\gamma} + \delta\gamma$. Assuming that the corrections are small, the first-order approximation (using the Taylor expansion) may be written as

$$\frac{\partial f_k}{\partial a}\delta a + \frac{\partial f_k}{\partial b}\delta b + \frac{\partial f_k}{\partial c}\delta c + \frac{\partial f_k}{\partial \gamma}\delta\gamma = -f_k(\hat{a}, \hat{b}, \hat{c}, \hat{\gamma}), \quad k = 1 \sim 4$$
$$(C)$$

Equation (C) may be solved as a linear system. The solution is then updated by $a = \hat{a} + \delta a$, $b = \hat{b} + \delta b$, $c = \hat{c} + \delta c$, and $\gamma = \hat{\gamma} + \delta\gamma$. The procedure is iterated using the most updated values of a, b, c, and γ as new guesses until δa, δb, δc, and $\delta\gamma$ all approach zero. This scheme is indeed the Newton iteration. The problem is solved by the script in List 9.70. The function determined is plotted in Figure 9.13.

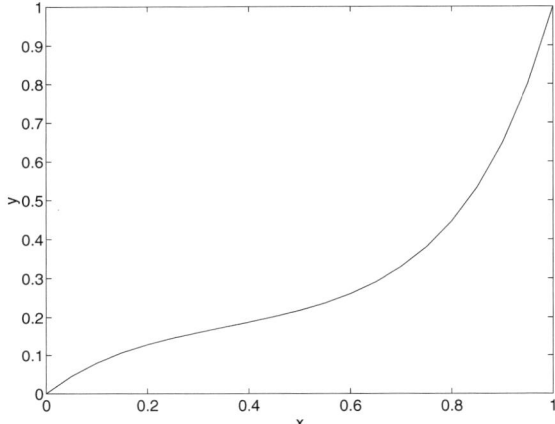

Figure 9.13 Nonlinear function fitted to four data points.

List 9.7
```
clear, clf, hold off
a=1;
b=1;
c=1; g = 1;
x1 = 0.01; y1 = 0.01; x2 = 0.95; y2 = 0.8;
for it = 1:20
  A=zeros(4);
  A(1,1)=1; A(1,2)=1; A(1,3)=1; A(1,4) = 0;
  y(1) = -(a + b + c);
  A(2,1) = exp(-g*x1); A(2,2) = exp(g*x1); A(2,3)=1;
  A(2,4) = a*(-x1)*A(2,1) + b*(x1)*A(2,2);
  y(2) = -(a*A(2,1) + b*A(2,2) + c - y1);
  A(3,1) = exp(-g*x2); A(3,2) = exp(g*x2); A(3,3)=1;
  A(3,4) = a*(-x2)*A(3,1) + b*(x2)*A(3,2);
  y(3) = -(a*A(3,1) + b*A(3,2) + c - y2);
  A(4,1) = exp(-g); A(4,2) = exp(g); A(4,3)=1;
  A(4,4) = a*(-1)*A(4,1) + b*(1)*A(4,2);
  y(4) = -(a*A(4,1) + b*A(4,2) + c - 1);
  da=A\y'
```

```
    a = a+da(1); b = b+da(2); c=c+da(3); g=g+da(4);
    if sum(abs(da)) < 0.00001, break;end
end
x =0:0.05:1;
yy = a*exp(-g*x) + b*exp(g*x) + c;
clf
plot(x,yy)
ylabel('y'), xlabel('x')
```

The need of dividing a length to a specified number of segments such that the length of the first and last segments are both prescribed and yet the segment lengths change from one to the next as gradually as possible is fulfilled by the Vinokur's stretching function.[1] Its algorithm is as follows:

Consider an arc of length L. A point on the arc is measured by the arc length s from one end. Assume also a total of n points is to be distributed along the arc including the two endpoints, one at $s = 0$, and another at $s = L$. We assume that the points are numbered by index i and the s value at the points are denoted by s_i, with $i = 1, 2, ...n$. If the desired increment of s between $i = 1$ and $i = 2$ equals Δs_a, while the desired length between $i = n - 1$ and $i = n$ equals Δs_b, then s_i values are determined by

$$s_i = \frac{L u_i}{A + (1 - A) u_i}$$

where

$$u_i = 0.5 \left[1 + \frac{\tanh\left(\delta(\frac{i-1}{n-1} - 0.5)\right)}{\tanh(\delta/2)} \right]$$

$$A = \sqrt{\Delta s_b / \Delta s_a}$$

In the foregoing equations, δ satisfies

$$\sinh(\delta) = B\delta$$

with

$$B = \frac{L}{(n-1)\sqrt{\Delta s_a \Delta s_b}}$$

The foregoing equations are computed by stret_, listed as FM 9-2. Suppose a line of unit length is desired to be divided into 19 intervals, with the first interval to be approximately 0.01, and the last interval to be approximately 0.02. Then,

---

[1] M. Vinokur, "On the Stretching Functions for Finite-Difference Calculations," J. Comput. Phys., Vol. 50, p. 215 (1983).

```
x = stret_(20, 1, 0.01, 0.02)
```

yields

```
x =
         0    0.0117   0.0277   0.0491   0.0776   0.1147   0.1620
    0.2206   0.2907   0.3711   0.4587   0.5495   0.6385   0.7212
    0.7942   0.8560   0.9064   0.9462   0.9768   1.0000
```

The lengths of the segments are plotted in Figure 9.14.

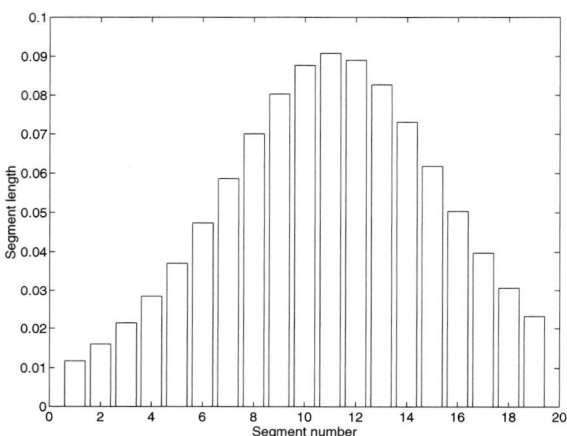

Figure 9.14 Lengths of segments determined by the stretching function.

Example 9.6

Data points along the upper surface of a prototype airfoil are given by

```
x_af=[1.0000   0.6638   0.4397   0.2900   0.1896   0.1221   ...
      0.0765   0.0455   0.0243   0.0099        0 ]
y_af=[0.0021   0.0668   0.0939   0.1000   0.0946   0.0836   ...
      0.0705   0.0569   0.0431   0.0282        0 ]
```

where the data points start at the trailing edge and are in counterclockwise order. The chord length of the airfoil is set to unity (nondimensional). The manufacturer desires to partition the upper airfoil surface into 15 intervals so the arc length of the interval at the leading edge is approximately 0.05, and the length of the interval at the trailing edge is approximately 0.1, while the arc length of the segments should change as gradually as possible. Determine the

Section 9.3 Interpolation with a Nonlinear Function   **345**

points where the airfoil is cut to pieces, and show the location of the cuts in a plot of the airfoil profile. Assume the airfoil is symmetric about the chord.

Solution

Although data points of the only upper half of the surface are given, we can plot the whole profile because the airfoil is symmetric. The top plot in Figure 9.15 illustrates the airfoil with data points along the upper surface. The arc lengths at the points measured from the trailing edge are then calculated. The coordinates x and y will be expressed as functions of arc length s. The total arc length from the trailing edge to the leading edge will be denoted by L. The lengths of arcs to satisfy the manufacturer's need are determined by `stret_` that partitions the length L into 15 segments. The coordinates, x and y, at the points are determined by c-spline. A script to perform the computations is shown in List 9.8. The result of the points cutting the airfoil surface are shown in the second plot in Figure 9.15.

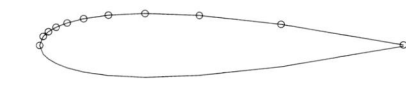

o: the given data points

Figure 9.15 Airfoil profile.   x: the points determined

List 9.8
```
clear,clf
x_af=[1.0000   0.6638   0.4397   0.2900   0.1896   0.1221   ...
      0.0765   0.0455   0.0243   0.0099        0 ];
y_af=[0.0021   0.0668   0.0939   0.1000   0.0946   0.0836   ...
      0.0705   0.0569   0.0431   0.0282        0 ];
m=length(x_af);
x = [x_af, x_af(m-1:-1:1)];   % Whole airfoil profile
y = [y_af, -y_af(m-1:-1:1)];
plot(x,y+0.3)
```

```
hold on
plot(x_af,y_af+0.3,'or')
axis([-0.1, 1.1 ,-0.6, 0.6])
n=length(x);
arc(1)=0;   % Arc length measured from trailing edge
for i=2:n
    arc(i)=arc(i-1)+sqrt((x(i)-x(i-1))^2+(y(i)-y(i-1))^2);
end
L = arc(m);
s = stret_(15+1, L,  0.02, 0.02);
xcut=interp1(arc, x, s, 'spline');   % c-spline
ycut=interp1(arc, y, s, 'spline');   % c-spline
plot(x,y-0.3)
plot(xcut,ycut-0.3,'x')
axis([-0.2, 1.1 ,-0.6, 0.6])
text(0, 0.1, 'o: given data points','Fontsize',[18])
text(0,-0.5, 'x: points to cut the surface','Fontsize',[18])
axis('off')
```

9.4 M-FILES

FM 9-1. Kickwheel ceramic game

Purpose: To collect data of points, fit them by b-spline, and draw a ceramic image.

Synopsis: k_wheel. Follow instructions on the screen.

k_wheel.m

```
% Simulation of kickwheel
clear; clf; hold off
axis([0, 1.25, 0,1.2 ])
text(1.02,1.14,'Click here','Color', 'r')
text(1.02,1.09,'to terminate','Color', 'r')
hold on
axis('off')
plot([1,1.25,1.25,1,1],[1,1,1.2,1.2,1])
plot([0,1,1,0,0],[0,0,1,1,0])
text(0,1.2,'Click a number of points in the box below.', ...
                                         'Color', 'g')
text(0,1.15,'Then click once in the small box on the right.', ...
                                         'Color', 'g')
text(0,1.10,'Follow the instructions on the command screen', ...
                                         'Color', 'g')
for n=1:100
```

Section 9.4 M-Files

```
[xg,yg]=ginput(1);
if xg>0.99 & yg>0.99, break; end
x(n)=xg; y(n)=yg;
text(x(n),y(n),'x')
end
m = length(y);
xlabel('x'); ylabel('y');  plot(x,y,'o')
for k=1:m
  z=int2str(k); xk = x(k); yk=y(k); text(xk+0.1,yk,z)
end
t = 0:0.25:1; t2=t.^2; t3=t.^3;
lt = length(t); ltm=lt-1;
rs=[]; zs=[];
for i=2:m-2
   yb = 1/6*((1-t).^3*y(i-1) + (3*t3-6*t2+4)*y(i) + ...
        (-3*t3 + 3*t2 + 3*t + 1)*y(i+1) + t3*y(i+2) );
   xb = 1/6*((1-t).^3*x(i-1) + (3*t3-6*t2+4)*x(i) + ...
        (-3*t3 + 3*t2 + 3*t + 1)*x(i+1) + t3*x(i+2) );
   plot(xb,yb)
   rs=[rs,xb(1:ltm)];
   zs=[zs,yb(1:ltm)];
end
   rs=[rs,xb(lt)];
   zs=[zs,yb(lt)];
title(' Cubic b-spline curve on x-y plane ')
fprintf('Hit RETURN to proceed')
pause
clf
dth=pi/10;
th=0:dth:2*pi;
for i=1:length(th)
zz(i,:)=zs;
xx(i,:)=rs.*(cos(th(i)) + 0*0.2*cos(5*th(i)));
yy(i,:)=rs.*(sin(th(i))+ 0*0.2*sin(5*th(i)));
end
mesh(xx,yy,zz,zz)
colormap default
caxis([-0.5, 1.5])
shading interp
fprintf('Hit RETURN to proceed')
pause
surfl(xx,yy,zz,[30,30])
fprintf('Hit RETURN to proceed')
pause
caxis([-1,3])
fprintf('Hit RETURN to proceed')
pause
```

```
clf
colormap default
[nx,ny,nz]=surfnorm(xx,yy,zz);
r=specular(nx,ny,nz,[30,30], [50,10]);
r=diffuse(nx,ny,nz, [-50,10]);
surface(xx,yy,zz,r*0.3+ 0.1*zz)
view([-30,30])
shading interp
colormap jet
caxis([-0,1])
pause
clf
```

FM 9-2. Stretching and clustering

Purpose: To distribute points with stretching and clustering.
Synopsis: stret_(n,L,ds0,ds1)
       n: total number of points including endpoints
       L: total length
       ds0: desired size of first interval
       ds1: desired size of last interval
Example: stret_(20,1,0.01, 0.1)

stret_.m
```
% Distribution of points with stretching function
function s=stret_(n,L,ds0,ds1)
A=sqrt(ds1/ds0);
B=L/(n-1)/sqrt(ds0*ds1);
if (B<1.0), fprintf('B is less than 1'),pause; end
DL= delta_(B) ;
if DL==0, retern, end
for I=1:n
        X=DL*(I-1)/(n-1) - .5*DL;
        U=.5*(1+tanh(X)/tanh(DL/2.));
        s(I)=U*L/( A + (1.-A)*U);
end
```

delta_.m
```
% Solves sinh(delta)=B*delta by Newton iteration
function DELTA = delta_(B)
if (B<1.0 ),
   fprintf('B IS LESS THAN 1. CODE IS STOPPED IN SUB. DELTA' )
   B=0.0;
return
end
```

```
DELTA=0;
K=0;
X=sqrt(6*B-6.);
XB = 0;
x=6.0;
     if (B< 3) x=B;   end
     if (B>=3 & B< 80) x=7. ;end
     if (B>=80 & B<100) x=7.3;end
     if (B>=100 & B<200) x=8.  ;end
     if (B>=200 & B<300) x=8.65;end
     if (B>=300 ) x=8.86;end
X = x;
flag = 0;
while abs(X-XB)>0.000001*abs(X) ,
     XB=X;
     XP = exp(X);
     XM=1./XP;
     F=XP-XM -B*2.0*X;
     FD=XP+XM -B*2.0 ;
     X= XB-F/FD ;
     K=K+1
       if  (K>40)
          fprintf(' ITERATION LIMIT EXCEEDED.   STOPPED IN SUB. DELTA')
          flag = 1;return
       end
     if flag==1; return ,end
end
DELTA=X;
```

PROBLEMS

(9.1) Determine the c-spline curve that passes through the following points using the extrapolation boundary conditions. Plot the curve with the data points:

	s:	0	-0.5	0	1	2	3	3.5	3
	f:	0	1	2	2	2	2	1	0

(9.2) Determine a closed c-spline curve that passes through the following points. The curve is required to be smooth across the endpoints. Plot the curve with the data points:

s:	0	1	2	3	3.5	3.7	3.5	3	2	1	0
f:	0	1	1.5	1.5	1	0	-1	-1.5	-1.5	-1	0

(9.3) Determine a b-spline curve using the following control points. Plot the curve with the data points:

```
s: 0    0    1    1    2    2    4    4
f: 0    1    1    0.5  0.5  2    2    0
```

The curve is required to pass through the endpoints of the data above.

(9.4) Determine the function

$$f(x) = a \exp(bx) + c$$

that passes through

```
x: 0    1    5
y: 0    2    4
```

(9.5) Determine the function

$$y = ae^{-\gamma x} + be^{\gamma x} + c$$

that passes through

```
x: 0    1    4    5
y: 0    0.5  3.5  4
```

(9.6) Divide a bar of one unit length into 11 segments such that the first segment length will be $1/20$ and the last segment length will be $1/15$. The lengths of the segments must change as gradually as possible. Determine the length of all the 11 segments by stret_.

Chapter 10

INITIAL-VALUE PROBLEMS OF ORDINARY DIFFERENTIAL EQUATIONS

The dynamic behavior of systems is an important subject. A mechanical system involves displacements, velocities, and accelerations. An electric or electronic system involves voltages, currents, and time derivatives of these quantities. In general, the equations to describe dynamics include time-dependent unknowns such as displacement or electric current and its derivatives.

An equation that involves one or more ordinary derivatives of the unknown function is called an ordinary differential equation, abbreviated as *ODE*. The order of the equation is determined by the order of the highest derivative. For example, if the first derivative is the only derivative, the equation is called a first-order ODE. Likewise, if the highest derivative is second order, the equation is called a second-order ODE.

The problems of solving an ODE are classified into initial-value problems and boundary-value problems, depending on how the conditions at the endpoints of the domain are specified. All the conditions of an initial-value problem are specified at the initial point. On the other hand, the problem becomes a boundary-value problem if conditions are spread between both initial and final points. The ODEs in the time domain are initial-value problems, so all the conditions are specified at the initial time, such as $t = 0$. The subject of this chapter is the solution of initial-value problems; boundary-value problems are discussed in the next chapter.

10.1 FIRST-ORDER ODEs

The initial-value problem of a first-order ODE may be written in the form

$$y'(t) = f(y,t), \quad y(0) = y_0 \qquad (10.1.1)$$

where $f(y,t)$ is a function of y and t, and the second equation is an initial condition without which the solution cannot be evaluated. In the foregoing equation, the first derivative of y is given as a function of y and t, and we desire to compute the unknown function y by numerically integrating $f(y,t)$. If f were independent of y, the computation would be one of the straightforward integrations discussed in Chapter 5, "Numerical Integration." The fact that f is a function of y, however, makes the integration procedure different. If f is a linear function of y, for example

$$f = ay + b$$

with a and b being constant or functions of t, Eq.(10.1.1) is a *linear ODE*. If f is not a linear function of y, the equation is called a *nonlinear ODE*. An analytical solution of some ODEs can be found, but the majority of nonlinear ODEs have no analytical solution. This is one of the reasons why numerical methods become important. We solve even linear ODEs by numerical methods, particularly when the ODEs are coupled.

For those who have not yet been exposed to differential equations, derivations of ODEs are illustrated next.

Example 10.1

Carbon-11 is a radioisotope that disintegrates at the rate of 3.46 %/min, which is equivalent to a half life of 20 minutes. The rate of decay is expressed by $\lambda = 0.0346$ min^{-1} or $\lambda = 2.076$ s^{-1} called decay constant. The initial atomic number density at $t = 0$ is denoted by N_0 atoms/cm^3. Derive a differential equation for the atomic number density.

Solution

Denoting the number density at t by $N(t)$, $N(t + dt)$ becomes

$$N(t + dt) = N(t) - \lambda N(t) dt \qquad (A)$$

where dt is an infinitesimally small time interval. The foregoing equation can be written as

$$\frac{dN}{dt} = -\lambda N(t) \tag{B}$$

with the initial condition,

$$N(0) = N_0$$

where N_0 is the number density at $t = 0$.

Comment: Equation (B) is one of the simplest ODEs. Its analytical solution is given by $N(t) = exp(-\lambda t)N_0$. From a practical point of view, there is no need to solve Eq.(B) numerically. We will often use an equation of this type, however, to investigate the accuracy of the numerical methods.

Example 10.2

A skydiver of mass M kg jumps into the air from an airplane at $t = 0$. We assume the initial vertical velocity of the skydiver is zero at $t = 0$ and that the skydiver falls vertically for the sake of simplicity. If the aerodynamic drag is given by $F_{air} = Cv^2$, where C is a constant and v is the vertical velocity which is positive downward, derive an ODE to determine the vertical velocity of the diver.

Solution

Applying Newton's second law, the balance of forces satisfies

$$M\frac{dv(t)}{dt} = -F_{air} + gM \tag{A}$$

where v is the diver's velocity (m/s) positive downward and g is the gravity acceleration, 9.8 m/s^2. Equation (A) can be written as

$$\frac{dv(t)}{dt} = -\frac{C}{M}v^2 + g, \qquad v(0) = 0 \tag{B}$$

or equivalently

$$v' = f(v, t), \qquad v(0) = 0 \tag{C}$$

with

$$f(v,t) = -\frac{C}{M}v^2 + g$$

Comment: The equation may be rewritten in terms of $y(t)$, which is the distance the skydiver fell. The relation between the velocity and height is $v = y'$. Introducing this into Eq.(B) yields

$$\frac{d^2 y(t)}{dt^2} = -\frac{C}{M}{y'}^2 + g$$

which is a second-order ODE with initial conditions, $y(0) = 0$ and $y'(0) = 0$.

Example 10.3

Consider the electrical circuit shown in Figure 10.1. The switch is closed at $t = 0$. Write an equation for current $I(t)$.

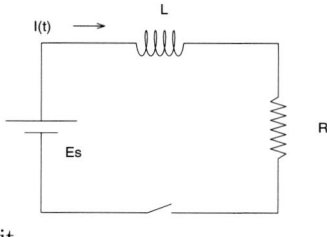

Figure 10.1 Electrical circuit.

Solution

Kirchhoff's first law states that the total of the voltages through a loop is zero; that is

$$E_L + E_R + E_S = 0 \qquad \text{(A)}$$

where E_S is the voltage of the source that may be time-dependent, E_L is the voltage across the inductor, and E_R is the voltage across the resistor. Voltages E_L and E_R are related to the electric current, respectively, by

$$E_L = -L\frac{dI(t)}{dt}$$
$$E_R = -RI(t)$$

where L is self-inductance, R resistance, and $I(t)$ the electric current. Therefore, Eq.(A) becomes

$$\frac{dI(t)}{dt} = -\frac{R}{L}I(t) + \frac{E_s}{L} \tag{B}$$

The foregoing equation is a first-order ODE and its initial condition is $I(0) = 0$.

10.2 EULER METHODS

The Euler methods are simple methods of solving first-order ODEs, particularly suitable for quick programming because of their great simplicity, although their accuracy is not high. Euler methods include three versions, namely, (a) forward Euler, (b) modified Euler, and (c) backward Euler methods. We study these methods primarily for the sake of understanding the basic concepts of numerical solution for initial-value problems.

10.2.1 Forward Euler Method

The forward Euler method for $y' = f(y, t)$ is derived by rewriting the forward difference approximation,

$$(y_{n+1} - y_n)/h \approx y'_n \tag{10.2.1}$$

to

$$y_{n+1} = y_n + hf(y_n, t_n) \tag{10.2.2}$$

where $y'_n = f(y_n, t_n)$ is used. In order to advance time steps, Eq.(10.2.2) is recursively applied as

$$\begin{aligned}
y_1 &= y_0 + hy'_0 = y_0 + hf(y_0, t_0) \\
y_2 &= y_1 + hf(y_1, t_1) \\
y_3 &= y_2 + hf(y_2, t_2) \\
&\cdots \\
y_n &= y_{n-1} + hf(y_{n-1}, t_{n-1})
\end{aligned} \tag{10.2.3}$$

Example 10.4

Find the velocity of the skydiver in Example 10.2, and plot the solution for $t \leq 20$s after the skydiver jumps from the airplane. Assume $M = 70$kg and $C = 0.27$kg/m. Use $h = 0.1$s.

Solution

The script in List 10.1 solves Eq.(C) of Example 10.2 by the forward Euler method:

```
List 10.1
clear, clf, hold off
t = 0; n=0; v=0;
C = 0.27; M = 70; cm=C/M; g = 9.8; h = 0.1;
t_rec(1)=t; v_rec(1) = v;
while t<=20
    n=n+1;
    v = v + h*( -cm*v^2 + g);
    t = t+h;
    v_rec(n+1) = v;
    t_rec(n+1) = t;
end
plot(t_rec,v_rec)
xlabel('time (s)')
ylabel('velocity (m/s)')
```

The results are shown in Figure 10.2.

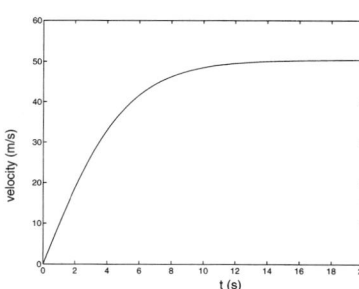

Figure 10.2 Skydiver's velocity.

Example 10.5

(a) Solve
$$y' = f(y,t), \quad y(0) = 5 \tag{A}$$

where
$$f(y,t) = -20y + 7\exp(-0.5t) \tag{B}$$

using the forward Euler method with $h = 0.01$ for $0 < t \leq 0.02$. Do this part by hand calculation.

(b) Repeat the same for $0 < t \leq 0.1$ with $h = 0.01$, 0.001, and 0.0001 for $0 \leq t \leq 0.1$ by MATLAB. Evaluate errors of the three calculations by comparison to the analytical solution given by

$$y = 5e^{-20t} + (7 - 19.5)(e^{-0.5t} - e^{-20t}) \tag{C}$$

Solution

(a) The first two time steps of calculations with $h = 0.01$ are

$t_0 = 0$, $\quad y_0 = y(0) = 0$
$t_1 = 0.01$, $\quad y_1 = y_0 + hy_0' = 5 + (0.01)(-20(5) + 7\exp(0)) = 4.07$
$t_2 = 0.02$, $\quad y_2 = y_1 + hy_1' = 4.07 + (0.01)(-20(4.07) + \exp(-0.01))$
$\quad = 3.326$

(b) The computational results for selected values of t with three different values of h are shown in Table 10.1.

Table 10.1 Solution of the Forward Euler Method

	$y(t)$ and percent errors in parentheses		
t	$h=0.01$	$h=0.001$	$h=0.0001$
0.01	4.07000 (8.710)	4.14939 (0.771)	4.15634 (0.076)
0.02	3.32600 (14.099)	3.45438 (1.261)	3.46574 (0.125)
0.03	2.73080 (17.117)	2.88650 (1.547)	2.90044 (0.153)
0.04	2.25464 (18.474)	2.42251 (1.687)	2.43771 (0.167)
0.05	1.87371 (18.693)	2.04339 (1.725)	2.05893 (0.171)
0.06	1.56897 (18.158)	1.73362 (1.693)	1.74887 (0.168)
0.07	1.32518 (17.150)	1.48052 (1.616)	1.49507 (0.161)
0.08	1.13014 (15.868)	1.27372 (1.510)	1.28732 (0.150)
0.09	0.97411 (14.453)	1.10474 (1.390)	1.11726 (0.138)
0.10	0.84929 (13.002)	0.96668 (1.263)	0.97805 (0.126)

Comment: Accuracy of the forward Euler method increases with the decrease in step size h. It is observed that magnitudes of errors are approximately proportional to h. The errors (in percentage) are due to truncation associated with the forward Euler method. Further reduction of h is not advantageous, however, because computational time becomes longer and rounding errors may increase.

Although the forward Euler method is simple, it has to be used carefully because two kinds of errors may emerge. The first is the truncation error which is mentioned in Example 10.5, and the second is *instability*. The latter occurs when the time constant of the equation is negative (solution approaches zero if source is removed), but time step h is not sufficiently small. A typical equation with a negative time constant is $y' = \alpha y$, with $y(0) = y_0 > 0$ and $\alpha < 0$ (see Example 10.1). The exact solution is $y = y_0 e^{\alpha t}$. The forward Euler scheme for this problem becomes

$$y_{n+1} = (1 + \alpha h) y_n$$

If $0 > \alpha h > -1$, the numerical solution is positive and approaching zero, but if $\alpha h < -1$, the sign of the solution alternates as n is advanced. Furthermore, if $\alpha h > 2$, the magnitude of the solution increases after each step while the sign alternates, and eventually the solution diverges. This erratic behavior of the solution is referred to as instability of the scheme.

10.2.2 Modified Euler Method

The motivation for the modified Euler method is twofold. First, the modified Euler method is more accurate than the forward Euler method. Second, it is more stable than the forward Euler method.

The modified Euler method is derived by applying the trapezoidal rule to the solution of $y' = f(y, x)$:

$$y_{n+1} = y_n + \frac{h}{2}[f(y_{n+1}, t_{n+1}) + f(y_n, t_n)] \qquad (10.2.4)$$

If f is a linear function of y, Eq.(10.2.4) may be easily solved for y_{n+1} in a closed form. As an example, let

$$f(y, t) = ay + \cos(t)$$

then, Eq.(10.2.4) becomes

$$y_{n+1} = y_n + \frac{h}{2}[ay_{n+1} + \cos(t_{n+1}) + ay_n + \cos(t_n)]$$

Therefore, solving for y_{n+1} yields

$$y_{n+1} = \frac{1+ah/2}{1-ah/2}y_n + \frac{h}{1-ah/2}\frac{\cos(t_{n+1}) + \cos(t_n)}{2} \qquad (10.2.5)$$

If f is a nonlinear function of y, Eq.(10.2.4) becomes a nonlinear function of y_{n+1}, so an algorithm to solve the nonlinear equation should be applied. A widely used method is the *successive substitution method*,[1] which is written as

$$y_{n+1}^{(k)} = y_n + \frac{h}{2}[f(y_{n+1}^{(k-1)}, t_{n+1}) + f(y_n, t_n)] \qquad (10.2.6)$$

where $y_{n+1}^{(k)}$ is the kth iterative approximation for y_{n+1}, and $y_{n+1}^{(0)}$ is an initial guess for y_{n+1}. The iteration is terminated when $|y_{n+1}^{(k)} - y_{n+1}^{(k-1)}|$ becomes less than a prescribed tolerance. If the initial guess is set to y_n, the first iteration step becomes identical with the forward Euler method. If only two iteration steps are used, the scheme becomes the second-order Runge-Kutta method.

The next example shows an application of the modified Euler method to a nonlinear first-order ODE.

Example 10.6

(a) Determine $y(0.1)$ for the following initial-value problem

$$y' = -y^{1.5} + 1, \quad y(0) = 10 \qquad (A)$$

by the modified Euler method with $h = 0.1$. Set the tolerance of convergence to 0.00001.

(b) Continue computation by advancing time steps until $t = 0.5$ is reached.

(c) Develop a MATLAB script to compute the solution for $0 < t \leq 1$ by both forward Euler and modified Euler methods and plot the results.

Solution

(a) The modified Euler scheme is written

$$y_{n+1} = y_n + (h/2)[-(y_{n+1})^{1.5} - (y_n)^{1.5} + 2] \qquad (B)$$

---

[1] See also Section 7.5.

Its iterative solution based on successive substitution is

$$y_{n+1}^{(k)} = y_n + (h/2)[-(y_{n+1}^{(k-1)})^{1.5} - (y_n)^{1.5} + 2] \quad (C)$$

where k is the iteration number. The iteration for y_1 starts with the initial guess $y_1^{(0)} = y(0) = 10$, and is continued as follows:

$$y_1^{(1)} = 10 + (0.1/2)[-(10)^{1.5} - (10)^{1.5} + 2] = 6.93772$$
$$y_1^{(2)} = 10 + (0.1/2)[-(6.93772)^{1.5} - (10)^{1.5} + 2] = 7.60517$$
$$y_1^{(3)} = 10 + (0.1/2)[-(7.60517)^{1.5} - (10)^{1.5} + 2] = 7.47020$$
$$y_1^{(4)} = 10 + (0.1/2)[-(7.47020)^{1.5} - (10)^{1.5} + 2] = 7.49799$$
$$y_1^{(5)} = 10 + (0.1/2)[-(7.49799)^{1.5} - (10)^{1.5} + 2] = 7.49229$$
$$\cdots$$
$$y_1 = 10 + (0.1/2)[-(7.49326)^{1.5} - (10)^{1.5} + 2] = 7.49326$$

(b) The computed results for five time steps are:

t	y
0.0	10.0000
0.1	7.4932
0.2	5.8586
0.3	4.7345
0.4	3.9298
0.5	3.3357

(c) A MATLAB script to obtain the solutions is in List 10.2. In the script, the solution of the forward Euler scheme is denoted by yf, while that of the modified Euler scheme is ym. The modified Euler scheme is computed iteratively by the successive substitution method. The number of iterations is limited to 10 times at most. If the iteration count exceeds nine, a message is printed out.

List 10.2
```
clear, clf
%===== Forward Euler
yf(1) = 10;   t(1) = 0;   h = 0.1; n=1;
while t(n)<1
    n = n+1; t(n) = t(n-1) + h;
    yf(n) = yf(n-1) +  h*( -yf(n-1)^1.5 + 1);
end
%==== Modifed Euler
ym(1) = 10;   t(1) = 0;   h = 0.1; n=1;
while t(n)<1
    n = n+1;  t(n) = t(n-1) + h;
```

```
            ym(n) = ym(n-1) +  h*( - ym(n-1)^1.5 + 1);
            ymb = 1e10;
            while abs(ym(n) - ymb) > 0.00001
               ymb = ym(n);
               ym(n) = ym(n-1) ...
                   + 0.5*h*( -ym(n)^1.5 - ym(n-1)^1.5 + 2);
            end
        end
        plot(t,yf,'--', t,ym, '-')
        legend( 'Forward Euler ','Modified Euler')
        text(0.7, -1.0, 't', 'FontSize',[18])
        text(-0.15, 5, 'y', 'FontSize',[18])
        axis([0,1.2, 0,10])
        set(gca, 'FontSize',[18])
```

The results are shown in Figure 10.3.

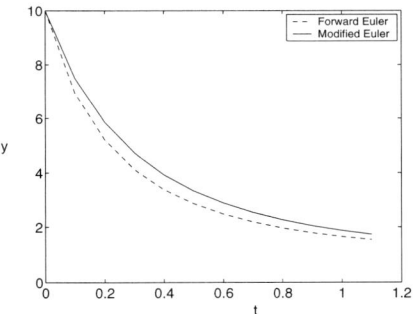

Figure 10.3 Comparison of Euler and modified Euler results.

10.2.3 Backward Euler Method

The backward Euler method is based on the backward difference approximation and written as

$$y_{n+1} = y_n + hf(y_{n+1}, t_{n+1}) \qquad (10.2.7)$$

The order of accuracy of this method is the same as that of the forward Euler method. Besides, if f is a nonlinear function of y, an iterative scheme (successive substitution) has to be used in each step just as in the modified Euler method. The advantages, however, are (a) the method is unconditionally stable, and (b) positivity of solution is guaranteed when the solution is supposed to be positive.

10.2.4 Accuracy of Euler Methods

Why is the accuracy of the modified Euler method higher than that of the forward or backward Euler methods? To find out the reason analytically, let us consider the test equation $y' = \alpha y$. Equation (10.2.4) may then be written for this problem as

$$y_{n+1} = y_n + \frac{1}{2}\alpha h(y_{n+1} + y_n) \qquad (10.2.8)$$

or equivalently,

$$y_{n+1} = \frac{1 + \frac{1}{2}\alpha h}{1 - \frac{1}{2}\alpha h} y_n$$

Expanding the foregoing equation yields

$$y_{n+1} = (1 + \alpha h + \frac{1}{2}(\alpha h)^2 + \frac{1}{4}(\alpha h)^3 + \cdots)y_n \qquad (10.2.9)$$

Here we assume that y_n is given. On the other hand, Taylor expansion of the exact solution $(y_{n+1})_{\text{exact}} = \exp(\alpha h)y_n$ is

$$(y_{n+1})_{\text{exact}} = (1 + \alpha h + \frac{1}{2}(\alpha h)^2 + \frac{1}{6}(\alpha h)^3 + \cdots)y_n \qquad (10.2.10)$$

The discrepancy between Eqs.(10.2.9) and (10.2.10) is due to the error generated in $t_n < t < t_{n+1}$, named *local error*. The two equations agree to the second-order term, and the discrepancy is in the order h^3. Thus, the modified Euler method is second-order accurate. Errors are accumulated as time steps proceed. Assuming that a fixed interval of time, h, is used repeatedly, the order of the total errors accumulated during a given period of time, say t, equals the number of time intervals times h^3, that is, $(t/h)h^3 = h^2 t$. The total of the accumulated errors is named *global error*. Therefore, the order of global error is one order lower than that of the local error.

A similar analysis may be applied to the forward and backward Euler methods, which will show that both are first-order accurate. The proof is left for the reader. Table 10.2 summarizes the local and global errors of the three Euler methods.

Table 10.2 Order of Errors of Euler Methods

	Forward Euler	Modified Euler	Backward Euler
Order of local error	h^2	h^3	h^2
Order of global error	h	h^2	h

10.2.5 Second-Order ODEs

When the highest derivative in an ODE is in the second order, the equation is called a *second-order ODE*. The second-order ODEs may be written as

$$u''(t) + au'(t) + bu(t) = s(t), \quad u(0) = u_0, \quad u'(0) = u'_0 \qquad (10.2.11)$$

where a, b, and s are constants or functions of t, u, and u', and the second and third equations are initial conditions. Notice that a second-order ODE uses two initial conditions, which are given for $u(0)$ and $u'(0)$. If a, b, and s are independent of u, the foregoing equation is a linear ODE. On the other hand, if any of a, b, and s are a function of u or u', or both, the equation is a nonlinear equation. In this subsection, we study how to solve second-order ODEs by the forward Euler method. We will also learn how to write MATLAB scripts, which can be easily extended to a more accurate method such as the fourth-order Runge-Kutta method.

An important step before applying an Euler scheme is to break up the second-order ODE to a pair of first-order ODEs. Define

$$v = u'$$

then Eq.(10.2.11) may be written as

$$v'(t) + av(t) + bu(t) = s(t), \quad v(0) = u'_0$$

Here, the initial condition in terms of the new variable v comes from the second initial condition in Eq.(10.2.11). Equation (10.2.11) is now equivalently expressed by a set of first-order ODEs as follows:

$$\begin{array}{rl} u' = & f_1(u,v,t), \quad u(0) = u_0 \\ v' = & f_2(u,v,t), \quad v(0) = v_0 = u'_0 \end{array} \qquad (10.2.12)$$

where

$$f_1(u,v,t) = v$$
$$f_2(u,v,t) = -av - bu + s$$

A step-by-step computation for the first few time steps are as follows:

$t = h$,
$$u_1 = u_0 + hf_1(u_0, v_0, 0) = u_0 + hv_0$$
$$v_1 = v_0 + hf_2(u_0, v_0, 0) = v_0 + h(-av_0 - bu_0 + s_0)$$
$t = 2h$,
$$u_2 = u_1 + hf_1(u_1, v_1, h) = u_1 + hv_1$$
$$v_2 = v_1 + hf_2(u_1, v_1, h) = v_1 + h(-av_1 - bu_1 + s_1)$$
where $s_n = s(nh)$.

For MATLAB, the computation for each time step may be written in a vector form. We first define $\mathbf{y}$ and $\mathbf{f}$, respectively, by

$$\mathbf{y} = \begin{bmatrix} u \\ v \end{bmatrix} \qquad (10.2.13)$$

$$\mathbf{f} = \begin{bmatrix} f_1 \\ f_2 \end{bmatrix} = \begin{bmatrix} v \\ -av - bu + s \end{bmatrix} \qquad (10.2.14)$$

Then, the set of equations in Eq.(10.2.12) is written in a single equation as

$$\mathbf{y}' = \mathbf{f}(\mathbf{y}, t)$$

The forward Euler scheme for the foregoing equation is written as

$$\mathbf{y}_{n+1} = \mathbf{y}_n + h\mathbf{f}(\mathbf{y}_n, t_n) \qquad (10.2.15)$$

which is the same as Eq.(10.2.2) except that $\mathbf{y}$ and $\mathbf{f}$ are vectors.

Example 10.7

A cubic object of mass $M = 10$kg is fixed to the lower end of a spring-damper system (see Figure 10.4). The upper end of the spring is fixed to a structure at rest. The force of damper is $R = -B|u'|u'$, where B is a constant and u is the displacement distance from the initial position in meters. The equation of motion is

$$Mu'' + B|u'|u' + ku = 0, \quad u(0) = 0, \quad u'(0) = 1 \qquad (A)$$

where k is the spring constant of 200N/m, and $B = 50\text{Ns}^2/\text{m}^2$.

(a) Calculate $u(t)$ for $0 < t \le 0.1$ using the forward Euler method with $h = 0.05$ by hand calculations.

(b) Calculate $u(t)$ for $0 < t \le 5$ s by MATLAB using the forward Euler method with $h = 0.05$. Plot the results.

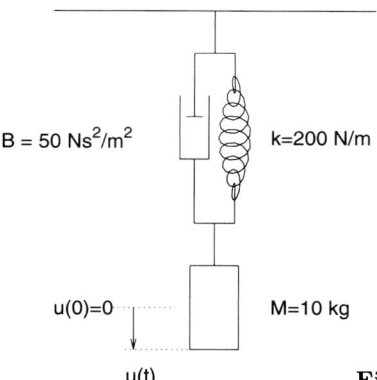

Figure 10.4 A spring-mass system.

Solution

Equation (A) may be written as

$$\begin{aligned} u' &= v, & u(0) &= 0 \\ v' &= -a|v|v - cu, & v(0) &= 1 \end{aligned} \quad (B)$$

where $a = B/M = 5$ and $c = k/M = 20$.

(a):
$t = 0$,

$$u_0 = u(0) = 0$$
$$v_0 = u'(0) = 1$$

$t = 0.05$,

$$\begin{aligned} u_1 &= u_0 + hv_0 \\ &= 0 + (0.05)(1) = 0.05 \\ v_1 &= v_0 + h(-a|v_0|v_0 - cu_0) \\ &= 1 + (0.05)[-5|1|(1) - (20)(0)] = 0.75 \end{aligned}$$

$t = 0.1$,

$$\begin{aligned} u_2 &= u_1 + hv_1 \\ &= 0.05 + (0.05)(0.75) = 0.0875 \end{aligned}$$

$$z_2 = v_1 + h(-a|v_1|v_1 - cu_1)$$
$$= 0.75 + (0.05)\left[-5|0.75|(0.75) - (20)(0.05)\right] = 0.5594$$

(b): A script for MATLAB is most easily developed by writing the equations in vector form:

$$\mathbf{y}' = \mathbf{f}(\mathbf{y}, t) \tag{C}$$

where

$$\mathbf{y} = \begin{bmatrix} u \\ v \end{bmatrix}$$

$$\mathbf{f} = \begin{bmatrix} v \\ -a|v|v - cu \end{bmatrix}$$

The forward Euler scheme for the foregoing equation is written as

$$\mathbf{y}_{n+1} = \mathbf{y}_n + h\mathbf{f}(\mathbf{y}_n, t_n) \tag{D}$$

A script to complete the solution is given in List 10.3. The results are shown in Figure 10.5.

List 10.3
```
clear,clf,hold off
h = 0.05; t_max=5; n=1;
y(:,1) = [0; 1];
t(1) = 0;
while t(n)< t_max
    y(:,n+1) = y(:,n) + h*f_def(y(:,n),t); yb=y;
    t(n+1) = t(n)+h ;
    n=n+1;
end
axis([0 5 -1 1])
```

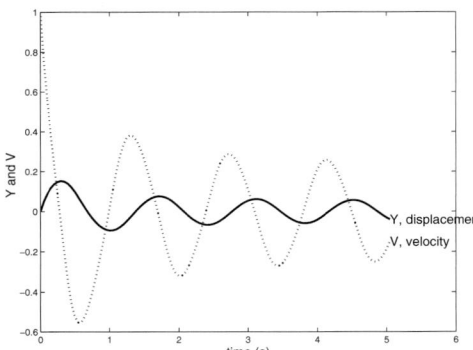

Figure 10.5 Forward Euler solution of mass-spring problem.

```
plot(t, y(1,:), t, y(2,:),':')
xlabel('time (s)'); ylabel('Y and V  ')
L=length(t);
text(t(L), y(1,L), 'Y, displacement')
text(t(L), y(2,L), 'V, velocity')
```

f_def.m
```
function f = f_def(y, t)
a = 5; c=20;
f = [y(2);  (-a*abs(y(2))*y(2) - c*y(1))];
```

Comment: Since the computation is very easy, we may be tempted to apply the foregoing script for the case with $B = 0$. If you do this, somewhat puzzling results will occur. For $B = 0$, the solution must be purely harmonic; in other words, the oscillation should be a sustaining sinusoidal motion. The computational result of the forward Euler method with $h = 0.05$, however, will show a slowly diverging oscillation because of numerical errors. In order to decrease the error, a substantially smaller h is necessary. This not only increases computing time significantly, but also risks the danger of introducing a significant amount of rounding errors. This is one of the reasons why we should use more accurate methods such as the fourth-order Runge-Kutta method described in Section 10.3.

10.2.6 Higher-Order ODEs

The methods described in the preceding subsections may be extended further to higher-order ODEs. For example, consider

$$y''''(t) + ay'''(t) + by''(t) + cy'(t) + ey(t) = g(t) \qquad (10.2.16)$$

where a, b, c, e, and g are constants or known functions of t if the equation is a linear ODE. If the equation is nonlinear, at least one of a, b, c, e, and g is a function of one or more of y, y', y'', and y'''. The initial conditions are given as

$$\begin{aligned} y(0) &= y_0, & y'(0) &= y_0', \\ y''(0) &= y_0'', & y'''(0) &= y_0''' \end{aligned}$$

where y_0, y_0', y_0'' and y_0''' are prescribed values.

If we consider each of y, y', y'' and y''' as an unknown variable, Eq.(10.2.16) can be equivalently written as a set of four first-order ODEs:

$$\begin{aligned} y' &= u, & y(0) &= y_0 \\ u' &= v, & u(0) &= y_0' \\ v' &= w, & v(0) &= y_0'' \\ w' &= g - aw - bv - cu - ey, & w(0) &= y_0''' \end{aligned} \qquad (10.2.17)$$

Equation (10.2.17) may be equivalently written in a vector form as

$$\mathbf{y}' = \mathbf{f}(\mathbf{y}, t) \qquad (10.2.18)$$

with

$$\mathbf{y} = \begin{bmatrix} y \\ u \\ v \\ w \end{bmatrix}$$

$$\mathbf{f} = \begin{bmatrix} u \\ v \\ w \\ g - aw - bv - cu - ey \end{bmatrix}$$

The expression of the forward Euler scheme for Eq.(10.2.18) is the same as Eq.(10.2.15).

Numerical methods also be applied to integro-differential equations. For example, consider

$$y'' + ay + \int_0^t y(s)ds = c, \quad y(0) = y_0, \quad y'(0) = y_0' \qquad (10.2.19)$$

We define u and v as

$$u = y', \quad v = \int_0^t y(s)ds$$

the latter of which may be equivalently written, after differentiation, as

$$v' = y, \quad v(0) = 0$$

Then, Eq.(10.2.19) becomes

$$\begin{aligned} y' &= u, & y(0) &= y_0 \\ u' &= -ay - v + c, & u(0) &= y_0' \\ v' &= y, & v(0) &= 0 \end{aligned} \qquad (10.2.20)$$

Section 10.2 Euler Methods

The foregoing equation can be written in the vector form as

$$\mathbf{y}' = \mathbf{f}(\mathbf{y}, t) \tag{10.2.21}$$

with

$$\mathbf{y} = \begin{bmatrix} y \\ u \\ v \end{bmatrix}$$

$$\mathbf{f} = \begin{bmatrix} u \\ -ay - v + c \\ y \end{bmatrix}$$

For Eq.(10.2.21), the forward Euler scheme is again the same as Eq.(10.2.15).

Example 10.8

The electric current of the circuit shown in Figure 10.6 satisfies the integro-differential equation

$$L\frac{di(t)}{dt} + Ri(t) + \frac{q(t)}{C} = E(t), \quad t > 0 \tag{A}$$

$$q(t) = \int_0^t i(t')dt' + q(0) \tag{B}$$

where $q(t)$ is the capacitor charge (coulombs), the switch is closed at $t = 0$, $i = i(t)$ is the current (amperes), and the constants are given by

$R = 100\Omega$
$L = 200\text{mH}$

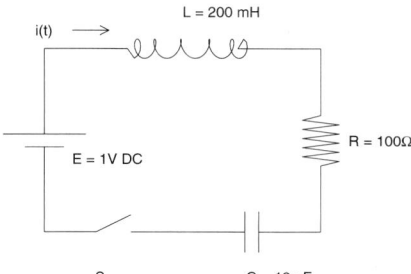

Figure 10.6 Electrical circuit.

$$C = 10\mu F$$
$$E = 1V$$

Initial conditions are $q(0) = 0$ (capacitor's initial charge) and $i(0) = 0$. Calculate the current for $0 < t \leq 0.025$s with $h = 0.00025$s.

Solution

Differentiating Eq.(B) yields

$$\frac{dq(t)}{dt} = i(t), \quad q(0) = 0 \tag{C}$$

We rewrite Eq.(A) to

$$\frac{di(t)}{dt} = -\frac{R}{L}i(t) - \frac{1}{LC}q(t) + \frac{E(t)}{L}, \quad i(0) = 0 \tag{D}$$

Then, the vector form of the equations is

$$\mathbf{y}' = \mathbf{f}(\mathbf{y}, t) = \mathbf{My} + \mathbf{S} \tag{E}$$

with

$$\mathbf{y} = \begin{bmatrix} q \\ i \end{bmatrix}, \quad \mathbf{M} = \begin{bmatrix} 0, & 1 \\ -1/LC, & -R/L \end{bmatrix}, \quad \mathbf{S} = \begin{bmatrix} 0 \\ E(t)/L \end{bmatrix}$$

Computation is performed in the script shown in List 10.4, and the results are plotted in Figure 10.7.

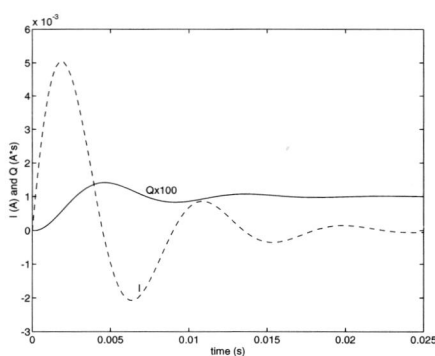

Figure 10.7 Graph of computed results.

List 10.4
```
clear, clf, hold off
R = 100;       %ohm
L = 200e-3;    %H
C = 10e-6;     %F
E = 1;
h = 0.25e-3;
n=1;
t(1)=0; y(:,1)=[0;0];
M=[0,1;-1/(L*C), -R/L]; S = [0;E/L];
while n<101
    y(:,n+1) = y(:,n) + h*(M*y(:,n)+S);
    t(n+1) = n*h;
    n=n+1;
end
plot(t,100*y(1,:),t,y(2,:),'--' )
text(t(30), 119*(y(1,30)), 'Qx100')
text(t(28), y(2,30), 'I')
xlabel('time (s)')
ylabel('I (A) and Q (A*s)')
```

10.3 RUNGE-KUTTA METHODS

A major drawback of the Euler methods is that the order of accuracy is low. To maintain a high accuracy requires a very small h, which not only increases computational time but also causes rounding errors.

In Runge-Kutta methods, the order of accuracy is increased using a more accurate numerical integration method. A higher accuracy implies that the computed result is more accurate and that errors decrease more rapidly when h is decreased.

Consider an ordinary differential equation

$$y' = f(y,t), \quad y(0) = y_0 \tag{10.3.1}$$

In order to calculate y_{n+1} with a known value of y_n, we integrate Eq.(10.3.1) in the interval $t_n \geq t \geq t_{n+1}$ to yield

$$y_{n+1} = y_n + \int_{t_n}^{t_{n+1}} f(y,t)dt \tag{10.3.2}$$

Then, Runge-Kutta methods are derived by applying a numerical integration method to the right side of the foregoing equation. In the remainder of this section, the second-, third-, and fourth-order Runge-Kutta methods are explained.

10.3.1 Second-Order Runge-Kutta Method

Here we examine the application of the trapezoidal rule to the right side of Eq.(10.3.2):

$$\int_{t_n}^{t_{n+1}} f(y,t)dt \approx \frac{h}{2}[f(y_n,t_n) + f(y_{n+1},t_{n+1})] \qquad (10.3.3)$$

where $h = t_{n+1} - t_n$. In the foregoing equation, y_{n+1} is not known, so that the second term is approximated by $f(\bar{y}_{n+1}, t_{n+1})$, where $\bar{y}_{n+1}$ is an estimate calculated by the forward Euler method. The scheme derived in this way is called the second-order Runge-Kutta method, and is written as

$$\bar{y}_{n+1} = y_n + hf(y_n, t_n)$$
$$y_{n+1} = y_n + \frac{h}{2}[f(y_n, t_n) + f(\bar{y}_{n+1}, t_{n+1})]$$

or, equivalently,

$$k_1 = hf(y_n, t_n)$$
$$k_2 = hf(y_n + k_1, t_{n+1}) \qquad (10.3.4)$$
$$y_{n+1} = y_n + \frac{1}{2}(k_1 + k_2)$$

The second-order Runge-Kutta method is equivalent to the modified Euler method with only two iteration steps.

Example 10.9

The circuit shown in Figure 10.8 has a self-inductance of $L = 50\text{mH}$, a resistance of $R = 20\Omega$, and a voltage source of $E = 10\text{V}$. If the switch is closed at $t = 0$, the current $I(t)$ satisfies

$$L\frac{dI(t)}{dt} + RI(t) = E, \quad I(0) = 0 \qquad (A)$$

Find the value of the current for $0 < t < 0.02\text{s}$ by the second-order Runge-Kutta method with $h = 0.0001$.

Section 10.3 Runge-Kutta Methods

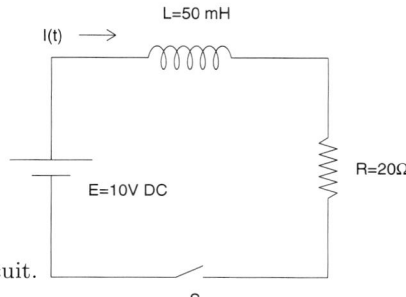

Figure 10.8 An electrical circuit.

Solution

We rewrite Eq.(A) as

$$\frac{dI}{dt} = f(I,t) \tag{B}$$

where

$$f(I,t) = -\frac{R}{L}I + \frac{E}{L}$$

Then, the second-order Runge-Kutta method becomes

$$k_1 = h\left(\frac{-R}{L}I_n + \frac{E}{L}\right)$$

$$k_2 = h\left(\frac{-R}{L}(I_n + k_1) + \frac{E}{L}\right)$$

$$I_{n+1} = I_n + \frac{1}{2}(k_1 + k_2)$$

Calculations for the first two steps are shown:

$t = 0$,
$\quad I_0 = 0$

$t = 0.0001$,
$\quad k_1 = 0.0001[(-400)(0) + 200] = 0.02$
$\quad k_2 = 0.0001[(-400)(0 + 0.02) + 200] = 0.0192$
$\quad I_1 = I_0 + (1/2)(k_1 + k_2) = 0 + (1/2)(0.02 + 0.0192) = 0.0196$

$t = 0.0002$,
$\quad k_1 = 0.0001[(-400)(0.0196) + 200] = 0.019216$
$\quad k_2 = 0.0001[(-400)(0.0196 + 0.019216) + 200] = 0.018447$
$\quad I_2 = I_1 + (1/2)(k_1 + k_2) = 0.0196 + (1/2)(0.019216 + 0.018447)$
$\quad\quad = 0.038431$

The remainder of computation is performed by MATLAB (see List 10.5) and the final result of the computation is plotted in Figure 10.9.

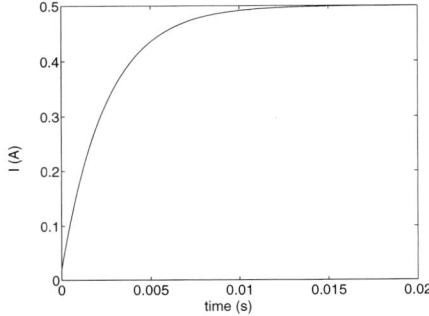

Figure 10.9 Electric current.

List 10.5
```
clear,clf    %x10_8mains.m
R = 20;      %ohm
L = 50e-3;   %H
E = 10;      %V
y=0;
h = 0.1e-3;
n=0;
y_rec(1)=y;  t_rec(1)=0;t=0;
RL = R/L;   EL=E/L;
while t<0.02
   n=n+1; RL;EL;
   k1 = h*f_x10_9(y, RL, EL);
   k2 = h*f_x10_9(y+k1, RL, EL);
   y = y + 0.5*(k1+k2);
   t = (n-1)*h;
   y_rec(n+1)=y; t_rec(n+1)=t;
end
plot(t_rec,y_rec )
text(0.008, -0.047, 'time (s)','FontSize',[18])
text(-0.0027, 0.2,'I (A) ','FontSize',[18],'Rotation',[90])
set(gca,'FontSize',[18])
```

f_x10_9
```
function f = f_x10_9(y, RL, EL)
f = -RL*y + EL;
```

Example 10.10

A thin plate at 200C (or 473K) is suddenly placed in a room of 24C (or 297K), where the plate is cooled by both natural convection and radiation heat transfer. The following physical constants are given:

$\rho = 300 \text{kg/m}^3$ (density)
$V = 0.001 \text{m}^3$ (volume)
$A = 0.25 \text{m}^2$ (surface area)
$C = 900 \text{J/kgK}$ (specific heat)
$h_c = 30 \text{J/m}^2\text{K}$ (heat transfer coefficient)
$\epsilon = 0.8$ (emissivity)
$\sigma = 5.67 \times 10^{-8} \text{W/m}^2\text{K}^4$ (Stefan-Boltzmann constant)

Assuming the temperature distribution in the metal is uniform, the equation for the temperature is

$$\frac{dT}{dt} = \frac{A}{\rho CV}\left[\epsilon\sigma(297^4 - T^4) + h_c(297 - T)\right], \quad T(0) = 473 \quad \text{(A)}$$

where T is the temperature in Kelvin. Find the temperature for $0 < t < 180\text{s}$, using the second-order Runge-Kutta scheme with $h = 1\text{s}$.

Solution

The second-order Runge-Kutta scheme is implemented in List 10.6. When the right side of the ODE is a nonlinear function like the present problem, it is convenient to write a function m-file to compute the right side of the ODE. The results are plotted in Figure 10.10.

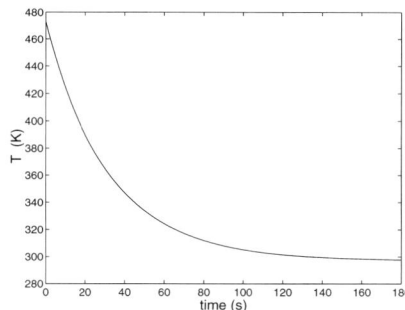

Figure 10.10 Temperature of the metal piece.

List 10.6

```
clear, clf, hold off
ro=300; V=0.001; A = 0.25; C = 900;
hc=30;
epsi=0.8; sig=5.67e-8; n=1;
h = 1; T(1)=473; t(1)=0;
Arcv = A/(ro*C*V);   Epsg = epsi*sig;
while t(n)<180
  k1 = h*fn10_10(T(n),Arcv,Epsg,hc);
```

```
k2 = h*fn10_10(T(n)+k1,Arcv,Epsg,hc);
T(n+1) = T(n) + 0.5*(k1 + k2);
t(n+1)=t(n) + h;
n=n+1;
end
plot(t,T); xlabel('time, sec'), ylabel(' T  (Kelvin)')
```

fn10_10

```
function f = fn10_10(TB,Arcv,Epsg,hc)
y=Arcv*( Epsg*(297^4 - TB^4) + hc*(297-TB));
```

10.3.2 Accuracy of the Second-Order Runge-Kutta Method

Accuracy of the second-order Runge-Kutta method may be analyzed by the test equation

$$y' = f(y,t) = \alpha y \qquad (10.3.5)$$

Provided that y_n is given, the exact solution for y_{n+1} is obviously

$$(y_{n+1})_{\text{exact}} = e^{\alpha h} y_n \qquad (10.3.6)$$

Its Taylor expansion is

$$(y_{n+1})_{\text{exact}} = [1 + \alpha h + \frac{1}{2}(\alpha h)^2 + \frac{1}{6}(\alpha h)^3 ...] y_n \qquad (10.3.7)$$

On the other hand, applying Eq.(10.3.4) to Eq.(10.3.5) yields

$$y_{n+1} = [1 + \alpha h + \frac{1}{2}(\alpha h)^2] y_n \qquad (10.3.8)$$

By comparing Eq.(10.3.8) with Eq.(10.3.7), the former is found to be accurate to order h^2 and the discrepancy (error generated in one step) is proportional to h^3. Notice that the second-order Runge-Kutta method is identical to the modified Euler method given by Eq.(10.2.6) with two iteration steps. The order of accuracy of the second-order Runge-Kutta scheme, however, is found to be identical to that of the modified Euler method which requires iterative convergence. This indicates that the iteration beyond the second step in the modified Euler method does not increase the order of accuracy. (Indeed, using the second-order Runge-Kutta method with a smaller h is far more effective in improving accuracy than strict iterative convergence only.) The accuracy may be analyzed more formally without using a test equation.[2]

---

[2]Given the value of y_n, the solution of $y' = f(y,t)$ may be expressed by the Taylor

10.3.3 Higher-Order ODEs

The application of the second-order Runge-Kutta method to a higher-order ordinary differential equation is similar to that of the forward Euler method. For illustration, we consider the second-order differential equation:

$$u'' + au' + bu = q(t), \quad u(0) = 1, \quad u'(0) = 0 \qquad (10.3.9)$$

where a, b, and q are constants or functions of t, u, and u'. By defining

$$v(t) = u'(t) \qquad (10.3.10)$$

Eq.(10.3.9) can be reduced to a set of coupled first-order differential equations:

$$\begin{aligned} u' &= f(u, v, t) = v, \quad u(0) = 1 \\ v' &= g(u, v, t) = -av - bu + q, \quad v(0) = 0 \end{aligned} \qquad (10.3.11)$$

The second-order Runge-Kutta method for the foregoing equations is written as

$$\begin{aligned} k_1 &= hf(u_n, v_n, t_n) = hv_n \\ m_1 &= hg(u_n, v_n, t_n) = h(-av_n - bu_n + q_n) \\ k_2 &= hf(u_n + k_1, v_n + m_1, t_{n+1}) = h(v_n + m_1) \\ m_2 &= hg(u_n + k_1, v_n + m_1, t_{n+1}) \\ &= h(-a(v_n + m_1) - b(u_n + k_1) + q_{n+1}) \\ u_{n+1} &= u_n + \tfrac{1}{2}(k_1 + k_2) \\ v_{n+1} &= v_n + \tfrac{1}{2}(m_1 + m_2) \end{aligned} \qquad (10.3.12)$$

For MATLAB implementation, we write the ODEs in the vector form as

$$\mathbf{y}' = \mathbf{f} \qquad (10.3.13)$$

---

expansion of y_{n+1} about t_n as

$$\begin{aligned} (y_{n+1})_{\text{exact}} &= y_n + hf + (h^2/2)[f_t + f_y f] \\ &+ (h^3/6)[f_{tt} + 2f_{ty}f + f_{yy}f^2 + f_t f_y + f_y^2 f] + O(h^4) \end{aligned} \qquad (\text{F1})$$

where all the derivatives of y are expressed in terms of f and the partial derivatives of f at t_n.

Next, we expand the third equation in Eq.(10.3.4) in a Taylor series:

$$\begin{aligned} y_{n+1} &= y_n + hf + (h^2/2)[f_t + f_y f] \\ &+ (h^3/4)[f_{tt} + 2f_{ty}f + f_{yy}f^2] + O(h^4) \end{aligned} \qquad (\text{F2})$$

Comparison of Eq.(F2) with Eq.(F1) reveals that Eq.(10.3.4) is accurate up to order h^2; in other words, the order of its local error is h^3.

with
$$\mathbf{y} = \begin{bmatrix} u \\ v \end{bmatrix}$$
$$\mathbf{f} = \begin{bmatrix} f \\ g \end{bmatrix} = \begin{bmatrix} v \\ -av - bu + q \end{bmatrix}$$

Then, the second-order Runge-Kutta scheme becomes

$$\begin{aligned} \mathbf{k}_1 &= h\mathbf{f}(\mathbf{y}_n, t_n) \\ \mathbf{k}_2 &= h\mathbf{f}(\mathbf{y}_n + \mathbf{k}_1, t_{n+1}) \\ \mathbf{y}_{n+1} &= \mathbf{y}_n + \frac{1}{2}(\mathbf{k}_1 + \mathbf{k}_2) \end{aligned} \qquad (10.3.14)$$

In case a, b, and q are constants or functions of only t, Eq.(10.3.13) may be written as

$$\mathbf{y}' = \mathbf{M}\mathbf{y} + \mathbf{S}$$

where

$$\mathbf{M} = \begin{bmatrix} 0 & 1 \\ -b & -a \end{bmatrix}, \qquad \mathbf{S} = \begin{bmatrix} 0 \\ q \end{bmatrix}$$

Then, Eq.(10.3.14) is written equivalently

$$\begin{aligned} \mathbf{k}_1 &= h\left[\mathbf{M}\mathbf{y_n} + \mathbf{S}\right] \\ \mathbf{k}_2 &= h\left[\mathbf{M}(\mathbf{y_n} + \mathbf{k}_1) + \mathbf{S}\right] \\ \mathbf{y}_{n+1} &= \mathbf{y}_n + \frac{1}{2}(\mathbf{k}_1 + \mathbf{k}_2) \end{aligned} \qquad (10.3.15)$$

Example 10.11

A rectangular box of mass $M = 0.5$kg is fixed to the lower end of a massless spring-damper system, as illustrated in Figure 10.11. The upper end of the spring is fixed to a structure at rest. The box receives a force of $R = -B du/dt$ from the damper, where B is a damping constant. The equation of motion is

$$Mu'' + Bu' + ku = 0, \quad u(0) = 1, \quad u'(0) = 0 \qquad (A)$$

where u is the displacement from the static position, k is the spring constant equal to 100N/m, and $B = 10$Ns/m.

(a) Calculate $u(t)$ for $0 < t \leq 0.05$s, using the second-order Runge-Kutta method with $h = 0.025$s, by hand calculations.

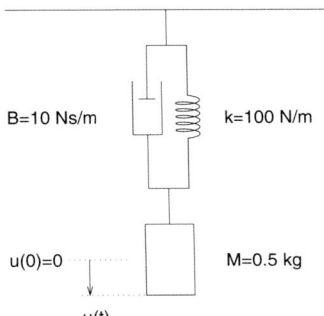

Figure 10.11 A spring-damper system.

(b) Calculate $u(t)$ for $0 < t \leq 1$s, using the second-order Runge-Kutta method with $h = 0.025$s.

Solution

Equation (A) may be written as

$$u' = f \equiv v, \quad u(0) = 1$$
$$v' = g \equiv -(B/M)v - (k/M)u, \quad v(0) = 0$$

By setting $a = B/M = 20$ and $b = k/M = 200$, the second-order Runge-Kutta method for Eq.(A) becomes the form of Eq.(10.3.14);
(a):
$t = 0$,
$\quad u_0 = u(0) = 1$
$\quad v_0 = u'(0) = 0$
$t = 0.025$,
$\quad k_1 = hf(u_0, v_0, t_0) = hv_0 = 0.025(0) = 0$
$\quad m_1 = hg(u_0, v_0, t_0) = h(-20v_0 - 200u_0)$
$\quad \quad = 0.025(-20(0) - 200(1)) = -5$
$\quad k_2 = hf(u_0 + k_1, v_0 + m_1, t_1) = h(v_0 + m_1)$
$\quad \quad = 0.025(0 - 5) = -0.125$
$\quad m_2 = hg(u_0 + k_1, v_0 + m_1, t_1)$
$\quad \quad = h[-20(v_0 + m_1) - 200(u_0 + k_1)]$
$\quad \quad = 0.025[-20(0 - 5) - 200(1 + 0)] = -2.5$
$\quad u_1 = u_0 + (1/2)(0 - 0.125) = 0.9375$
$\quad v_1 = v_0 + (1/2)(-5 - 2.5) = -3.75$
$t = 0.05$,
$\quad k_1 = hf(u_1, v_1, t_1) = hv_1 = 0.025(-3.75) = -0.09375$
$\quad m_1 = hg(u_1, v_1, t_1) = h(-20v_1 - 200u_1)$
$\quad \quad = 0.025[-20(-3.75) - 200(0.9375)] = -2.8125$

$$k_2 = hf(u_1 + k_1, v_1 + m_1, t_2) = h(v_1 + m_1)$$
$$= 0.025(-3.75 - 2.8125) = -0.16406$$
$$m_2 = hg(u_1 + k_1, v_1 + m_1, t_2)$$
$$= h[-20(v_1 + m_1) - 200(u_1 + k_1)]$$
$$= 0.025[-20(-3.75 - 2.8125) - 200(0.9375 - 0.09375)]$$
$$= -0.9375$$
$$u_2 = u_1 + (1/2)(-0.09375 - 0.16406) = 0.80859$$
$$v_2 = v_1 + (1/2)(-2.8125 - 0.9375) = -5.625$$

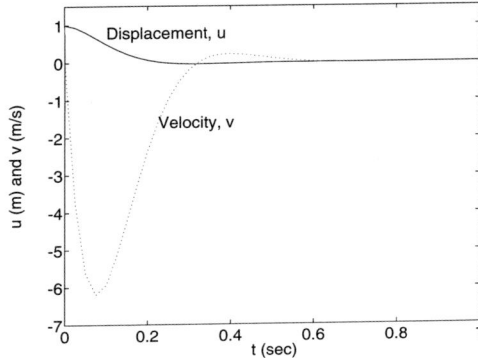

Figure 10.12 Dynamic responses of spring-mass system.

(b): For MATLAB computations, we may rewrite the equations as

$$\mathbf{y}' = \mathbf{M}\mathbf{y} + \mathbf{S}$$

where

$$\mathbf{M} = \begin{bmatrix} 0 & 1 \\ -b & -a \end{bmatrix}, \quad \mathbf{y} = \begin{bmatrix} u \\ v \end{bmatrix}, \quad \mathbf{S} = \begin{bmatrix} 0 \\ 0 \end{bmatrix}$$

The script in List 10.7 is developed based on Eq.(10.3.14) applied to the foregoing equation. Since $\mathbf{S}$ is a null vector, it is not considered. The results are plotted in Figure 10.12.

List 10.7
```
clear;     %x10_8mains.m
clear, clf
y= [1,0]'; % initial condition
M=0.5; k = 100; B=10; a = B/M;
b = k/M; n=0; t=0; h = 0.025;
y_rec(:,1) = y; t_rec(1)=0;
while t<=1
  n=n+1;
  k1 = h*f_sm(y,t,a,b);
  k2 = h*f_sm(y+k1,t+h,a,b);
```

```
            y = y + 0.5*(k1 + k2);
            t_rec(n+1) = n*h;
            y_rec(:,n+1) = y;
            t = t+h;
        end
        clear y    t
        y=y_rec; t=t_rec;
        plot(t,y(1,:), '-', t,y(2,:),':');
        text(0.45, -7.7, 't (s)','FontSize',[18])
        text(-0.12, -4.5, ' u (m) and v (m/s)','FontSize',[18],'Rotation',[90])
        text(t(5),y(1,5)+0.3,'Displacement, u','FontSize',[18])
        text(t(10),y(2,10),'Velocity, v','FontSize',[18])
        axis([0,1,-7,1.5])
```

Comment: The present problem is repeated in Example 10.14 by the fourth-order Runge-Kutta method with application to the case of $B = 0$.

Example 10.12

Motion of an electron in a uniform electromagnetic field is given by[3]

$$m\frac{d\mathbf{V}}{dt} = e\mathbf{V} \times \mathbf{B} + e\mathbf{E} \qquad (A)$$

where $\mathbf{V}$ is the velocity vector, $\mathbf{B}$ the magnetic field vector, $\mathbf{E}$ the electric field vector, m the mass of electron, and e the charge of electron:

Initial condition: $\mathbf{V} = (-10, 2, 0.1) \times 10^5 \text{m/s}$
Initial position of electron: $\mathbf{R} = (0, 0, 0)\text{m}$
Magnetic field vector: $\mathbf{B} = (0, 0, 0.1)\text{T}$
Electric field vector: $\mathbf{E} = (0, 2, 0) \times 10^4 \text{V/m}$
Mass of electron: $m = 9.1 \times 10^{-31}\text{kg}$
Charge of electron, $e = 1.6 \times 10^{-19}\text{c}$

Solve Eq.(A) by the second-order Runge-Kutta method with $h = 0.5 \times 10^{-11}\text{s}$, for $0 < t \leq 2 \times 10^{-9}\text{s}$, and determine the locus of the electron. Plot the trajectory of the electron in a three-dimensional view, and the velocity components as functions of time as well as in the three-dimensional phase space.

---

[3]This example was provided by Professor Y. Funato of Suzuka College of Technology, Japan.

Solution

A script may be developed in a straightforward manner using vxv_, which is a function to compute a vector product. The solutions computed by the following script are shown in Figure 10.13.

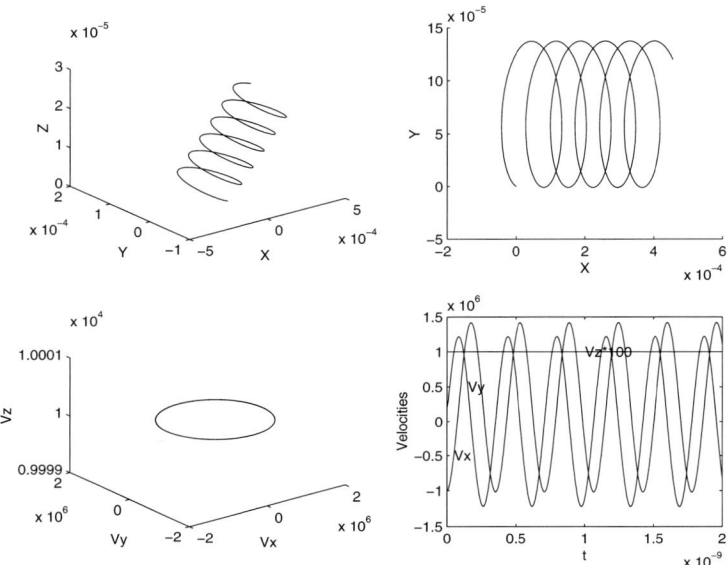

Figure 10.13 Trajectory and velocity of electron.

List 10.8

```
clear,clf,hold off
e=1.6e-19;          % Charge of electron, coulomb
m=9.1e-31;          % Electron mass, kg
B=[0;0;0.1]*e/m;    % Magnetic field strength, tesla
E=[0;2e4;0]*e/m;    % Electric field strength, volt/meter
h=0.5e-11;          % Time step, second
v(:,1)=1e5*[-10;2;0.1];
                    % Initial velocity of electron, meter/sec
t(1)=0;             % Time initialization, sec
xyz(:,1)=[0;0;0];
epm=e/m;
for i=2:400
  t(i)=h*i;
  k1=h*(vxv_(v(:,i-1),B) + E) ;
  k2=h*(vxv_(v(:,i-1)+k1,B) + E) ;
  v(:,i)=v(:,i-1) + 0.5*(k1+k2);
  xyz(:,i)=xyz(:,i-1)+0.5*(v(:,i-1)+v(:,i))*h;
```

```
end
figure(1)
plot3(xyz(1,:), xyz(2,:),xyz(3,:))
axis([-5,5,-1,2,0,0.3]*1e-4)
xlabel('X'); ylabel('Y'); zlabel('Z');
figure(2)
plot3(xyz(1,:), xyz(2,:),xyz(3,:))
xlabel('X'); ylabel('Y'); zlabel('Z');
view([0,0,1])
figure(3)
plot3(v(1,:), v(2,:),v(3,:))
xlabel('Vx'); ylabel('Vy'); zlabel('Vz');
figure(4)
plot(t,v(1,:),t, v(2,:),t,v(3,:)*100)
xlabel('t'); ylabel('Velocities');
text(t(10),v(1,10), 'Vx')
text(t(30),v(2,30), 'Vy')
text(t(200),v(3,200)*100, 'Vz*100')

function c=vxv_(a,b)
% [c] = [a]  x [b]
% a, b, c:  vectors
c=[a(2)*b(3)-a(3)*b(2);
  -a(1)*b(3)+a(3)*b(1);
   a(1)*b(2)-a(2)*b(1)];
```

10.3.4 Third-Order Runge-Kutta Method

The third-order Runge-Kutta method is derived by a higher-order numerical integration scheme for the second term of Eq.(10.3.2). Using Simpson's 1/3 rule, Eq.(10.3.2) may be written as

$$y_{n+1} = y_n + \frac{h}{6}[f(y_n,t_n) + 4f(\overline{y}_{n+1/2},t_{n+1/2}) + f(\overline{y}_{n+1},t_{n+1})] \quad (10.3.16)$$

where $\overline{y}_{n+1/2}$ and $\overline{y}_{n+1}$ are estimates because $y_{n+1/2}$ and y_{n+1} are not known.

The estimate $\overline{y}_{n+1/2}$ is obtained by the forward Euler method as

$$\overline{y}_{n+1/2} = y_n + \frac{h}{2}f(y_n,t_n) \quad (10.3.17)$$

The estimate $\overline{y}_{n+1}$ may be obtained by

$$\overline{y}_{n+1} = y_n + hf(y_n,t_n)$$

or
$$\overline{y}_{n+1} = y_n + hf(\overline{y}_{n+1/2}, t_{n+1/2})$$
or a linear combination of both
$$\overline{y}_{n+1} = y_n + h[\theta f(y_n, t_n) + (1-\theta)f(\overline{y}_{n+1/2}, t_{n+1/2})] \quad (10.3.18)$$

Here, θ is an undetermined parameter, which will be determined to maximize the accuracy of the numerical method. With Eq.(10.3.18), the whole scheme is written in the following form:

$$\begin{aligned} k_1 &= hf(y_n, t_n) \\ k_2 &= hf(y_n + \frac{1}{2}k_1, t_{n+1/2}) \\ k_3 &= hf(y_n + \theta k_1 + (1-\theta)k_2, t_{n+1}) \\ y_{n+1} &= y_n + \frac{1}{6}(k_1 + 4k_2 + k_3) \end{aligned} \quad (10.3.19)$$

To analyze the accuracy and optimize θ, we apply the foregoing equations to our test equation, Eq.(10.3.5). If applied to Eq.(10.3.5), Eq.(10.3.19) becomes

$$\begin{aligned} k_1 &= h\alpha y_n \\ k_2 &= h\alpha(1 + \tfrac{1}{2}h\alpha)y_n \\ k_3 &= h\alpha\left[1 + \theta h\alpha + (1-\theta)h\alpha(1 + \tfrac{1}{2}h\alpha)\right] y_n \\ y_{n+1} &= \left[1 + h\alpha + \tfrac{1}{2}(h\alpha)^2 + \tfrac{1-\theta}{12}(h\alpha)^3\right] y_n \end{aligned} \quad (10.3.20)$$

Comparing with the expansion of $(y_{n+1})_{\text{exact}}$ given by Eq.(10.3.7), we find that the optimum is $\theta = -1$.

Therefore, the third-order Runge-Kutta method is written as

$$\begin{aligned} k_1 &= hf(y_n, t_n) \\ k_2 &= hf(y_n + k_1/2, t_{n+1/2}) \\ k_3 &= hf(y_n - k_1 + 2k_2, t_{n+1}) \\ y_{n+1} &= y_n + \frac{1}{6}(k_1 + 4k_2 + k_3) \end{aligned} \quad (10.3.21)$$

The foregoing equations may also be derived without assuming any particular model equation.[4]

---

[4] Taylor expansions of k_1, k_2 and k_3 in Eq.(10.3.18) are

$$k_1 = hf \quad (\text{F3a})$$

10.3.5 Fourth-Order Runge-Kutta Method

Derivation of the fourth-order Runge-Kutta method is similar to that of the third-order method, except that one more intermediate step of evaluating the derivative is used. There are several alternative choices for the numerical integration scheme to be used in Eq.(10.3.2). The fourth-order Runge-Kutta method is accurate to the fourth-order term of the Taylor expansion, so the local error is proportional to h^5.

The following two versions of the fourth-order Runge-Kutta method are most popularly used. The first version is based on Simpson's 1/3 rule and is written as

$$k_1 = hf(y_n, t_n)$$
$$k_2 = hf(y_n + k_1/2, t_{n+1/2})$$
$$k_3 = hf(y_n + k_2/2, t_{n+1/2})$$
$$k_4 = hf(y_n + k_3, t_{n+1})$$
$$y_{n+1} = y_n + \frac{1}{6}(k_1 + 2k_2 + 2k_3 + k_4) \qquad (10.3.22)$$

The second version is based on Simpson's 3/8 rule and is written as

$$k_1 = hf(y_n, t_n)$$
$$k_2 = hf(y_n + k_1/3, t_{n+1/3})$$
$$k_3 = hf(y_n + k_1/3 + k_2/3, t_{n+2/3})$$
$$k_4 = hf(y_n + k_1 - k_2 + k_3, t_{n+1})$$
$$y_{n+1} = y_n + \frac{1}{8}(k_1 + 3k_2 + 3k_3 + k_4) \qquad (10.3.23)$$

Example 10.13

Calculate $y(1)$ for

$$y' = -1/(1 + y^2), \qquad y(0) = 1$$

$$k_2 = hf + (1/2)h^2(f_t + f_y f) + \tfrac{1}{8}h^3(f_{tt} + 2f_{ty}f + f_y f^2) \qquad \text{(F3b)}$$

$$k_3 = hf + h^2(f_t + f_y f) + \tfrac{1}{2}h^3[f_{tt} + 2f_{ty}f + f_{yy}f^2 + (1-\theta)(f_t + f_y f)f_y] \qquad \text{(F3c)}$$

where f and its derivatives are evaluated at t_n. We introduce Eq.(F3) into Eq.(10.3.20) and compare it with the exact value of y_{n+1} in the Taylor series written in Footnote 2. We then find that Eq.(10.3.20) agrees with the Taylor expansion of the exact solution to the third-order term if $\theta = -1$.

using the fourth-order Runge-Kutta method with $h = 1$.

Solution

We set
$$f(y, t) = -1/(1 + y^2)$$
with $y_0 = 1$ and $t_0 = 0$. Since we have only one interval, the answer is obtained by

$$k_1 = hf(y_0, t_0) = -1/(1 + 1) = -0.5$$
$$k_2 = hf(y_0 + k_1/2, t_{1/2}) = -1/(1 + (0.75)^2) = -0.64$$
$$k_3 = hf(y_0 + k_2/2, t_{1/2}) = -1/(1 + (0.68)^2) = -0.6838$$
$$k_4 = hf(y_0 + k_3, t_1) = -1/(1 + (0.3161)^2) = -0.9091$$

$$y_1 = y_0 + \frac{1}{6}[k_1 + 2k_2 + 2k_3 + k_4]$$
$$= 1 + \frac{1}{6}[-0.5 - 2(0.64) - 2(0.6838) - 0.9091] = 0.3238$$

Application of the fourth-order Runge-Kutta method to a set of ordinary differential equations is very similar to that of the second-order Runge-Kutta method. For the simplicity of explanation, we consider a set of two equations:

$$\begin{aligned} u' &= f(u, v, t) \\ v' &= g(u, v, t) \end{aligned} \qquad (10.3.24)$$

The fourth-order Runge-Kutta method for the set of two equations becomes

$$k_1 = hf(u_n, v_n, t_n)$$
$$m_1 = hg(u_n, v_n, t_n)$$
$$k_2 = hf(u_n + k_1/2, v_n + m_1/2, t_{n+1/2})$$
$$m_2 = hg(u_n + k_1/2, v_n + m_1/2, t_{n+1/2})$$
$$k_3 = hf(u_n + k_2/2, v_n + m_2/2, t_{n+1/2})$$
$$m_3 = hg(u_n + k_2/2, v_n + m_2/2, t_{n+1/2})$$
$$k_4 = hf(u_n + k_3, v_n + m_3, t_{n+1})$$
$$m_4 = hg(u_n + k_3, v_n + m_3, t_{n+1})$$
$$u_{n+1} = u_n + \frac{1}{6}(k_1 + 2k_2 + 2k_3 + k_4) \qquad (10.3.25)$$

Section 10.3 Runge-Kutta Methods

$$v_{n+1} = v_n + \frac{1}{6}(m_1 + 2m_2 + 2m_3 + m_4)$$

If Eq.(10.3.24) is written in the vector form,

$$\mathbf{y}' = \mathbf{f}(\mathbf{y}, t) \tag{10.3.26}$$

where

$$\mathbf{y} = \begin{bmatrix} u \\ v \end{bmatrix}$$
$$\mathbf{f} = \begin{bmatrix} f \\ g \end{bmatrix} \tag{10.3.27}$$

then the fourth-order Runge-Kutta scheme is written as

$$\begin{aligned}
\mathbf{k}_1 &= hf(\mathbf{y}_n, t_n) \\
\mathbf{k}_2 &= hf(\mathbf{y}_n + \mathbf{k}_1/2, t_{n+1/2}) \\
\mathbf{k}_3 &= hf(\mathbf{y}_n + \mathbf{k}_2/2, t_{n+1/2}) \\
\mathbf{k}_4 &= hf(\mathbf{y}_n + \mathbf{k}_3, t_{n+1}) \\
\mathbf{y}_{n+1} &= \mathbf{y}_n + \frac{1}{6}(\mathbf{k}_1 + 2\mathbf{k}_2 + 2\mathbf{k}_3 + \mathbf{k}_4)
\end{aligned} \tag{10.3.28}$$

MATLAB scripts implementing the fourth-order Runge-Kutta method can be developed using the form of Eq.(10.3.28); however, if Eq.(10.3.26) can be written in a linear form as

$$\mathbf{y}' = \mathbf{M}\mathbf{y} + \mathbf{S}$$

then Eq.(10.3.28) is written as

$$\begin{aligned}
\mathbf{k}_1 &= h[\mathbf{M}\mathbf{y_n} + \mathbf{S}] \\
\mathbf{k}_2 &= h[\mathbf{M}(\mathbf{y_n} + \mathbf{k}_1/2) + \mathbf{S}] \\
\mathbf{k}_3 &= h[\mathbf{M}(\mathbf{y_n} + \mathbf{k}_2/2) + \mathbf{S}] \\
\mathbf{k}_4 &= h[\mathbf{M}(\mathbf{y_n} + \mathbf{k}_3) + \mathbf{S}] \\
\mathbf{y}_{n+1} &= \mathbf{y}_n + \frac{1}{6}[\mathbf{k}_1 + 2\mathbf{k}_2 + 2\mathbf{k}_3 + \mathbf{k}_3]
\end{aligned} \tag{10.3.29}$$

Example 10.14

(a) Repeat part (a) of the problem in Example 10.11 by the fourth-order Runge-Kutta method. (b) Repeat part (b) of Example 10.11 for $B = 0$, using MATLAB.

Solution

(a): Referring to Example 10.11, the equations to be solved are

$$u' = f \equiv v, \quad u(0) = 1$$
$$v' = g \equiv -(B/M)v - (k/M)u, \quad v(0) = 0$$

By setting $a = B/M = 20$ and $b = k/M = 200$, the fourth-order Runge-Kutta method for Eq.(A) in Example 10.11 becomes the form of Eq.(10.3.25).

$t = 0$,
  $u_0 = u(0) = 1$
  $v_0 = u'(0) = 0$
$t = 0.025$,
  $k_1 = hf(u_0, v_0, t_0) = hv_0 = 0.025(0) = 0$
  $m_1 = hg(u_0, v_0, t_0) = h(-20v_0 - 200u_0)$
    $= 0.025(-20(0) - 200(1)) = -5$
  $k_2 = hf(u_0 + k_1/2, v_0 + m_1/2, t_0 + h/2) = h(v_0 + m_1/2)$
    $= 0.025(0 - 5/2) = -0.0625$
  $m_2 = hg(u_0 + k_1/2, v_0 + m_1/2, t_0 + h/2)$
    $= h[-20(v_0 + m_1/2) - 200(u_0 + k_1/2)]$
    $= 0.025[-20(0 - 5/2) - 200(1 + 0/2)] = -3.75$
  $k_3 = hf(u_0 + k_2/2, v_0 + m_2/2, t_0 + h/2) = h(v_0 + m_1/2)$
    $= 0.025(0 - 3.75/2) = -0.046875$
  $m_3 = hg(u_0 + k_2/2, v_0 + m_2/2, t_0 + h/2)$
    $= h[-20(v_0 + m_2/2) - 200(u_0 + k_2/2)]$
    $= 0.025[-20(0 - 3.75/2) - 200(1 - 0.0625/2)] = -3.9062$
  $k_4 = hf(u_0 + k_3, v_0 + m_3, t_0 + h) = h(v_0 + m_3)$
    $= 0.025(0 - 5/2) = -0.09765$
  $m_4 = hg(u_0 + k_3, v_0 + m_3, t_0 + h)$
    $= h[-20(v_0 + m_3/2) - 200(u_0 + k_3/2)]$
    $= 0.025[-20(0 - 3.90625) - 200(1 - 0.046875)] = -2.8125$
  $u_1 = u_0 + (1/6)(0 + 2(-0.0625) + 2(-0.046875) - 0.097656)$
    $= 0.947266$
  $v_1 = v_0 + (1/6)(-5 + 2(-3.75) + 2(-3.9062) - 2.8125)$
    $= -3.8541$
$t = 0.05$,
  $k_1 = hf(u_1, v_1, t_1) = hv_1 = 0.025(-3.85416) = -0.096354$
  $m_1 = hg(u_1, v_1, t_1) = h(-20v_1 - 200u_1)$
    $= 0.025(-20(-3.8541) - 200(0.947265)) = -2.8092$
  $k_2 = hf(u_1 + k_1/2, v_1 + m_1/2, t_1 + h/2) = h(v_1 + m_1/2)$
    $= 0.025(-3.8541666 - 2.809244/2) = -0.1314697$

Section 10.3 Runge-Kutta Methods

$$m_2 = hg(u_1 + k_1/2, v_1 + m_1/2, t_1 + h/2)$$
$$= h[-20(v_1 + m_1/2) - 200(u_1 + k_1/2)]$$
$$= 0.025[-20(-3.85416 - 2.809244/2) - 200(0.947266 - 0.096354/2)]$$
$$= -1.866054$$
$$k_3 = hf(u_1 + k_2/2, v_1 + m_2/2, t_1 + h/2) = h(v_1 + m_2/2)$$
$$= 0.025(-3.85416 - 1.866054/2) = -0.1196797$$
$$m_3 = hg(u_1 + k_2/2, v_0 + m_2/2, t_1 + h/2)$$
$$= h[-20(v_1 + m_2/2) - 200(u_1 + k_2/2)]$$
$$= 0.025[-20(-3.85416 - 1.866054/2) - 200(0.947266 - 0.1314697/2)]$$
$$= -2.014058$$
$$k_4 = hf(u_1 + k_3, v_1 + m_3, t_1 + h) = h(v_1 + m_3)$$
$$= 0.025(-3.85416 - 2.014058) = -0.146706$$
$$m_4 = hg(u_1 + k_3, v_1 + m_3, t_1 + h)$$
$$= h[-20(v_1 + m_3) - 200(u_1 + k_3)]$$
$$= 0.025[-20(-3.85416 - 2.014058) - 200(0.947266 - 0.1196797)]$$
$$= -1.203821$$
$$u_2 = u_1 + (1/6)(-0.0963541 + 2(-0.131469) + 2(-0.119679)$$
$$-0.146705) = 0.823039$$
$$v_2 = v_1 + (1/6)(-2.809244 + 2(-1.866048) + 2(-2.014058)$$
$$-1.203816) = -5.816375$$

(b): For MATLAB computations, we rewrite the equations to the following form:
$$\mathbf{y}' = \mathbf{M}\mathbf{y} + \mathbf{S}$$
where
$$\mathbf{y} = \begin{bmatrix} u \\ v \end{bmatrix}, \quad \mathbf{M} = \begin{bmatrix} 0, & 1 \\ -b, & -a \end{bmatrix}, \quad \mathbf{S} = \begin{bmatrix} 0 \\ 0 \end{bmatrix}$$

List 10.9 is developed based on Eq.(10.3.29) applied to the foregoing equations. The result is shown in Figure 10.14.

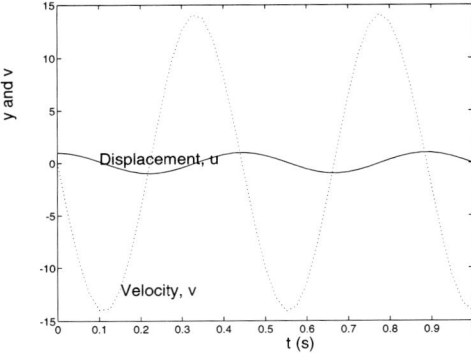

Figure 10.14 Dynamic responses of spring-mass system.

List 10.9
```
clear,clf
M=0.5; k = 100; B=0; a = B/M;
b = k/M; n=0; t=0; h = 0.025;
y(:,1) = [1;0]; t(1)=0; % initial condition
M=[0,1; -b,-a];
while t<=1
  n=n+1;
  k1 = h*M*y(:,n);
  k2 = h*M*(y(:,n)+k1/2);
  k3 = h*M*(y(:,n)+k2/2);
  k4 = h*M*(y(:,n)+k3);
  y(:,n+1) = y(:,n) + (k1 + 2*k2 + 2*k3 + k4)/6;
  t(n+1) = n*h;
end
plot(t,y(1,:), '-', t,y(2,:),':');
xlabel('t (s)'), ylabel(' y and v')
text(t(5),y(1,5)+0.3,'Displacement, u','FontSize',[18])
text(t(7),y(2,7),'Velocity, v','FontSize',[18])
axis([0,1,-15,15])
```

Comment: Part B is a simple problem but not necessarily trivial (see comments in Example 10.7). Since the solution is analytically known, however, it is a good benchmark problem to examine a solution method.

Example 10.15

The three-mass system is shown in Figure 10.15.[5] The displacements of the three masses satisfy the equations given by

$$M_1 y_1'' + B_1 y_1' + K_1 y_1 - B_1 y_2' - K_1 y_2 = F_1(t)$$
$$-B_1 y_1' - K_1 y_1 + M_2 y_2'' + B_1 y_2' + (K_1 + K_2) y_2 - K_2 y_3 = 0 \quad \text{(A)}$$
$$-K_2 y_2 + M_3 y_3'' + B_3 y_3' + (K_2 + K_3) y_3 = F_3(t)$$

where y_1, y_2, and y_3 are displacements. Constants and initial conditions are

$K_1 = K_2 = K_3 = 1$ (spring constants, N/m)
$M_1 = M_2 = M_3 = 1$ (mass, kg)
$F_1(t) = 0.01$, $F_3(t) = 0$ (force, N)
$B_1 = B_3 = 0.1$ (damping coefficients, Ns/m)

---

[5]This example was provided by Professor Doebelin of The Ohio State University.

$$y_1(0) = y_1'(0) = y_2(0) = 0 \quad \text{(initial displacement, m)}$$
$$y_2'(0) = y_3(0) = y_3'(0) = 0 \quad \text{(initial velocity, m/s)}$$

Solve the foregoing equations by the fourth-order Runge-Kutta method for $0 \leq t \leq 30$s with $h = 0.1$s.

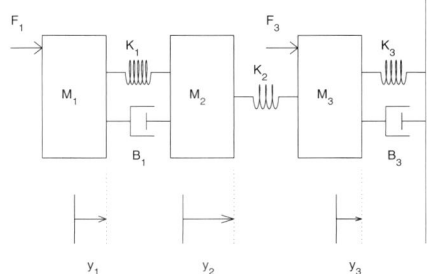

Figure 10.15 Mass-spring system.

Solution

We define
$$y_4 = y_1', \quad y_5 = y_2', \quad \text{and} \quad y_6 = y_3' \tag{B}$$

Then, Eq.(A) is written as a set of six first-order ODEs:

$$\begin{aligned}
y_1' &= y_4 \\
y_2' &= y_5 \\
y_3' &= y_6 \\
y_4' &= [-B_1 y_4 - K_1 y_1 + B_1 y_5 + K_2 y_2 + F_1]/M_1 \\
y_5' &= [B_1 y_4 + K_1 y_1 - B_1 y_5 - (K_1 + K_2) y_2 + K_2 y_3]/M_2 \\
y_6' &= [K_2 y_2 - B_3 y_6 - (K_2 + K_3) y_3 + F_3]/M_3
\end{aligned}$$

Equation (C) can be written in matrix form as

$$\mathbf{y}' = \mathbf{f}(\mathbf{y}, t) \tag{D}$$

with

$$\mathbf{y} = \begin{bmatrix} y_1 \\ y_2 \\ y_3 \\ y_4 \\ y_5 \\ y_6 \end{bmatrix}$$

$$\mathbf{f} = \begin{bmatrix} 0 & 0 & 0 & 1 & 0 & 0 \\ 0 & 0 & 0 & 0 & 1 & 0 \\ 0 & 0 & 0 & 0 & 0 & 1 \\ \frac{-K_1}{M_1} & \frac{K_2}{M_1} & 0 & \frac{-B_1}{M_1} & +\frac{B_1}{M_1} & 0 \\ \frac{K_1}{M_2} & -\frac{K_1+K_2}{M_2} & \frac{K_3}{M_2} & \frac{B_1}{M_2} & \frac{-B_1}{M_2} & 0 \\ 0 & \frac{K_2}{M_3} & -\frac{K_2+K_3}{M_3} & 0 & 0 & \frac{-B_3}{M_3} \end{bmatrix} \mathbf{y} + \begin{bmatrix} 0 \\ 0 \\ 0 \\ F_1/M_1 \\ 0 \\ F_3/M_3 \end{bmatrix}$$

The computational results are shown in Figure 10.16.

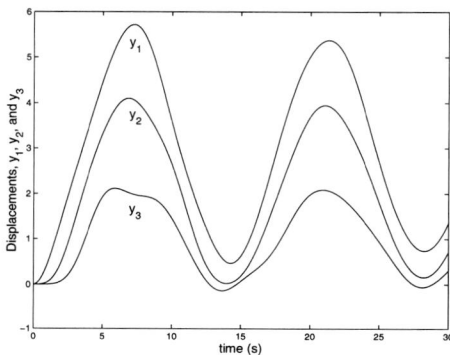

Figure 10.16 Results of computations.

List 10.10
```
clear, clf
M1 = 1; M2 = 1; M3 = 1;
K1 = 1; K2 = 1; K3 = 1;
F1 = 0.01; F3 = 0; F = [0, 0, 0, F1/M1, 0, F3/M3]';
B1 = 0.1; B3 = 0.1;
y(:,1)=[0; 0; 0; 0; 0; 0]; t(1) = 0; n=1;
h = 0.1;
C = [0,      0,           0,      1,      0,      0; ...
     0,      0,           0,      0,      1,      0; ...
     0,      0,           0,      0,      0,      1; ...
    -K1/M1,  K2/M1,       0,     -B1/M1,  B1/M1,  0; ...
     K1/M2,-(K1+K2)/M2,   K2/M2,  B1/M2, -B1/M2,  0; ...
     0,      K2/M3,  -(K2+K3)/M3, 0,      0,     -B3/M3]
while t<=30
    k1 = h*F3m(y(:,n),      C, F);
    k2 = h*F3m(y(:,n)+k1/2, C, F);
    k3 = h*F3m(y(:,n)+k2/2, C, F);
    k4 = h*F3m(y(:,n)+k3,   C, F);
    y(:,n+1) = y(:,n) + (1/6)*(k1 + 2*k2 + 2*k3 + k4);
    t(n+1) = n*h;
    n=n+1;
end
plot(t,y(1:3,:))
```

```
text( t(70), y(1,70), 'y1')
text( t(70), y(2,70), 'y2')
text( t(70), y(3,70), 'y3')
xlabel('time (s)')
ylabel('Displacements, y1, y2, and y3')
```
F3m.m
```
function f = F3m(y,C,F)
f = C*y + F;
```

Example 10.16

The behavior of an electric circuit changes significantly depending upon the values of the parts used. Consider the circuit shown in Figure 10.17, for which differential equations are written as

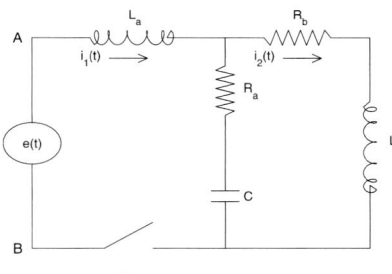

Figure 10.17 Electrical circuit.

$$L_a \frac{di_1}{dt} + R_a(i_1 - i_2) + \frac{q(t)}{C} = e(t)$$

$$-\frac{q(t)}{C} - R_a(i_1 - i_2) + R_b i_2 + L_b \frac{di_2}{dt} = 0$$

with

$$q(t) = \int_0^t (i_1(t') - i_2(t'))dt' + q(0)$$

where $e(t) = 0$ except $e(t)=1$ when $0 < t < 0.01$s, $q(t)$ is the capacitor charge, and $i_1(t)$ and $i_2(t)$ are currents; meanings of other notations and units are shown in Figure 10.17. Initial conditions are $i_1(0) = i_2(0) = q(0) = 0$ for all cases. In order to investigate the effects of the parts, solve the equations for the following four sets of constants:
(a) $L_a = 0.01$; $L_b = 0.5$; $R_a = 200$; $R_b = 20$; $C = 0.002$
(b) Same as (a) except $L_a = 0.1$
(c) Same as (a) except $L_b = 0.25$

(d) Same as (a) except $R_a = 20$

Solution

The solutions are obtained by List 10.11. The results are shown in Figure 10.18.

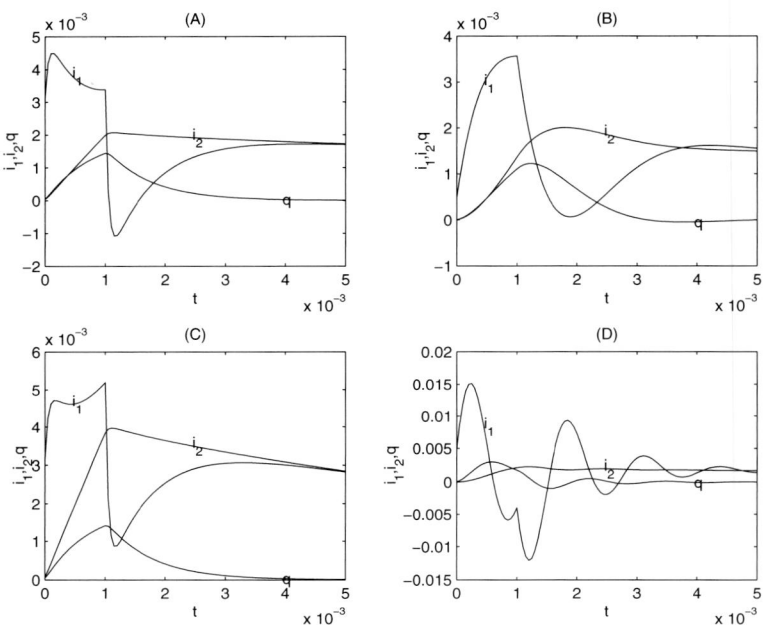

Figure 10.18 Behavior of the circuit.

List 10.11[6]
```
clear;clf
subplot(221)
for k=1:4
  e=1;
  if k==1; subplot(221);
     La=0.01; Lb=0.5;   Ra=200; Rb=20;C=0.002; end
  if k==2, subplot(222);
     La=0.1;  Lb= 0.5;  Ra=200 ; Rb=20; C=0.002; end
  if k==3; subplot(223);
     La=0.01; Lb= 0.25; Ra=200 ; Rb=20   ;C=0.002; end
```

---

[6]If no vector form of the equation is used, the programming would be much longer and messier.

```
        if k==4; subplot(224)
          La=  0.01; Lb= 0.5; Ra=20 ; Rb=20  ;C=0.002; end
        M=[ -Ra/La,    Ra/La,         -1/(La*C) ; ...
            Ra/Lb,  -(Ra+Rb)/Lb,    1/(Lb*C) ;    ...
                 1/C,       -1/C,              0           ]
        S=[0;0;0]; x=[0; 0; 0];
        h=0.00005;
        for n=1:101
          t=(n-1)*h;
          %S=[ sin(t*600)*exp(-t*600)/La; 0; 0];
          %S=[ cos(t*600)/La; 0; 0];
          S=[ 1/La; 0; 0];
          if t>0.001, S=[0;0;0];end
          k1=h*(M*x+S);
          k2=h*(M*(x+k1/2)+S);
          k3=h*(M*(x+k2/2)+S);
          k4=h*(M*(x+k3)+S);
          x=x+(k1+k2*2+k3*2+k4)/6;
          x_r(:,n)=x;
          t_r(n)=t;
        end
        plot(t_r, x_r(1:2,:), t_r, x_r(3,:))
        xlabel('t'),ylabel('i1,i2,q')
        L= length(t_r)
        text(t_r(L/10),x_r(1,L/10),'i1')
        text(t_r(L/2),x_r(2,L/2),'i2')
        text(t_r(L*0.8),x_r(3,L*0.8),'q')
        if k==1;title('(A)');end
        if k==2;title('(B)');end
        if k==3;title('(C)');end
        if k==4;title('(D)');end
    end
```

10.3.6 Error, Stability, and Time-interval Optimization

The Runge-Kutta methods are subject to two kinds of errors; namely, truncation error and instability. As discussed earlier, the truncation error can be found as the discrepancy between the Taylor expansion of the numerical method and that of the exact solution. The amount of error decreases faster with a decrease in h as the order of the method becomes higher. On the other hand, instability is an accumulated effect of the local errors.

To analyze the instability of a Runge-Kutta method, let us consider our model equation

$$y' = \alpha y \qquad (10.3.30)$$

where $\alpha < 0$. For a given value of y_n, the exact value for y_{n+1} is analytically given as

$$(y_{n+1})_{\text{exact}} = e^{\alpha h} y_n = e^{n\alpha h} y_0 \qquad (10.3.31)$$

Notice that, since $\alpha < 0$, $|(y_{n+1})_{\text{exact}}|$ decreases as n (or time) increases.

Although the methodology of analysis described in this section is applicable to the Runge-Kutta method of any order, we will first illustrate an application to the fourth-order Runge-Kutta method. The numerical solution of Eq.(10.3.30) by the fourth-order Runge-Kutta method, Eq.(10.3.22), becomes

$$k_1 = \alpha h y_n$$
$$k_2 = \alpha h(y_n + k_1/2) = \alpha h(1 + \frac{1}{2}\alpha h)y_n$$
$$k_3 = \alpha h(y_n + k_2/2) = \alpha h(1 + \frac{1}{2}\alpha h(1 + \frac{1}{2}\alpha h))y_n$$
$$k_4 = \alpha h(y_n + k_3) = \alpha h(1 + \alpha h(1 + \frac{1}{2}\alpha h(1 + \frac{1}{2}\alpha h)))y_n$$
$$y_{n+1} = \left(1 + \alpha h + \frac{1}{2}(\alpha h)^2 + \frac{1}{6}(\alpha h)^3 + \frac{1}{24}(\alpha h)^4\right) y_n \qquad (10.3.32)$$

Equation (10.3.32) equals the first five terms of the Taylor expansion for the right side of Eq.(10.3.31) about t_n. The amplification factor

$$\gamma = 1 + \alpha h + \frac{1}{2}(\alpha h)^2 + \frac{1}{6}(\alpha h)^3 + \frac{1}{24}(\alpha h)^4 \qquad (10.3.33)$$

in Eq.(10.3.32) is an approximation for $\exp(\alpha h)$ of Eq.(10.3.31), so the truncation error and instability of Eq.(10.3.23) both originate from this approximation.

Equation (10.3.33) and $\exp(\alpha h)$ are plotted together in Figure 10.19 for comparison. The figure indicates that if $\alpha < 0$ and the modulus (absolute value) of αh increases, the deviation of γ from $\exp(\alpha h)$ increases; that is, the error of the Runge-Kutta method increases. Particularly, if $\alpha h \leq -2.785$, the method becomes unstable because the modulus of the numerical solution grows while the modulus of the true solution decreases by a factor, $\exp(\alpha h)$, in each step.

In practical applications of the Runge-Kutta method, an optimal time interval can be determined in the following way: For illustration purposes, suppose we desire to keep the local error of the third-order Runge-Kutta

Section 10.3 Runge-Kutta Methods

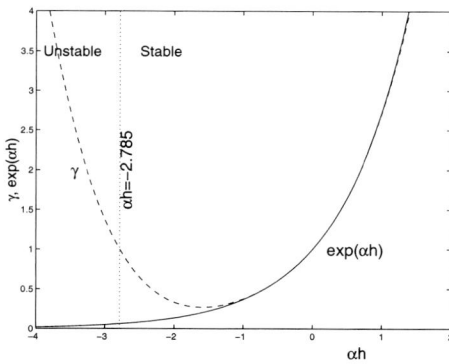

Figure 10.19 Domain of stability.

method less than ξ. The local error of the third-order Runge-Kutta method is proportional to h^4, so we express the local error in the form

$$E_h = Bh^4 \qquad (10.3.34)$$

where B is a constant that depends on the given problem. If we apply the same Runge-Kutta method in two steps with time interval $h/2$, the error becomes proportional to $2(h/2)^4$, where the factor 2 is due to the accumulation of errors in two steps. The error accumulated in two steps is written as

$$2E_{h/2} = 2B(h/2)^4 = (1/8)Bh^4 \qquad (10.3.35)$$

By subtracting Eq.(10.3.35) from Eq.(10.3.34), we get

$$E_h - 2E_{h/2} = Bh^4 - (1/8)Bh^4 = (7/8)Bh^4 \qquad (10.3.36)$$

The left side of Eq.(10.3.36) may be evaluated by a numerical experiment; that is, to run the scheme twice starting from the same initial value. In the first run, only one time step is advanced using a trial value of h. We denote the result of this calculation as $[y_1]_h$. In the second run, $[y_2]_{h/2}$ is calculated in two time steps using time interval $h/2$. Using the results of those two calculations, the left side of Eq.(10.3.36) becomes

$$E_h - 2E_{h/2} = [y_1]_h - [y_2]_{h/2} \qquad (10.3.37)$$

Eliminating the left side of Eq.(10.3.36) by Eq.(10.3.37) and solving for B yields

$$B = (8/7)([y_1]_h - [y_2]_{h/2})/h^4 \qquad (10.3.38)$$

Once B is determined, the maximum (or optimum) h that satisfies the criterion $|E_h| \le \xi$ is found by taking the absolute of Eq.(10.3.35) and setting $|E_h| = \xi$:

$$h = (\xi/|B|)^{0.25} \qquad (10.3.39)$$

The present approach is reminiscent of the Romberg integration explained in Section 5.1.

Example 10.17

Assuming a fourth-order Runge-Kutta method is applied to

$$y' = -y/(1+t^2), \; y(0) = 1$$

find an optimal step interval satisfying $|E_h| \le 0.00001$.

Solution

For the fourth-order Runge-Kutta method, the local error is expressed by

$$E_h = Bh^5 \qquad (A)$$

The approach is very similar to Eqs.(10.3.34) through (10.3.39) except that the order of error is five. The error accumulated in two steps using $h/2$ is $2E_{h/2} = 2B(h/2)^5$. The difference between the errors of one-step and two-step calculations, namely $E_h - 2E_{h/2}$, is numerically evaluated by

$$E_h - 2E_{h/2} = [y_1]_h - [y_2]_{h/2} \qquad (B)$$

In the above equation, $[y_1]_h$ is the result of the fourth-order Runge-Kutta method for only one step with h, and $[y_2]_{h/2}$ is the result of the same for two steps with $h/2$. Introducing Eq.(A) into Eq.(B) and solving for B, we have

$$B = (16/15)([y_1]_h - [y_1]_{h/2})/h^5 \qquad (C)$$

Now, we actually run the fourth-order Runge-Kutta method for only one step with $h = 1$ starting with the given initial condition, then for two steps with $h/2 = 1/2$. The results are

$$[y_1]_1 = 0.4566667 \quad \text{(one interval only)}$$
$$[y_2]_{1/2} = 0.4559973 \quad \text{(two intervals)}$$

From Eq.(C) we obtain B as

$$B = (16/15)(0.4566667 - 0.4559973)/(1)^5 = 6.3 \times 10^{-4} \quad \text{(D)}$$

By introducing this into Eq.(A), the local error for any h is expressed by

$$E_h = 6.3 \times 10^{-4} h^5$$

The maximum h that satisfies the given criterion, $|E_h| < 0.00001$, is

$$h = \left(\frac{0.00001}{6.3 \times 10^{-4}}\right)^{1/5} = 0.44 \quad \text{(E)}$$

10.4 SHOOTING METHOD

The numerical methods for initial-value problems may be used to solve boundary-value problems. This approach is named the *shooting method*.

We consider a second-order ODE

$$\frac{d^2 y(x)}{dx^2} + a \frac{dy(x)}{dx} + by(x) = 0 \quad (10.4.1)$$

with

$$y(0) = 0, \quad y(1) = 1$$

The foregoing equation has nothing new as a second-order ODE, except that the second condition is not an initial condition. Since the end conditions are spread between the initial and final points, the equation is called a boundary-value problem.

In order to apply any numerical method for initial-value problems to Eq.(10.4.1), we have to consider Eq.(10.4.1) as if it were an initial-value problem. We will estimate the second initial condition on a trial basis and see if the second boundary condition in Eq.(10.4.1) is satisfied. If not, we will make another guess and try again. This process will be repeated until the end condition is satisfied. Of course, after a few trials, we learn how to estimate the initial condition more skillfully just like in shooting a gun at a target.

Example 10.18

A rod 0.2m long is placed in a stream of air at 293K. The temperature at the left end at $x = 0$ is fixed at 493K, but the right end is insulated. The heat is removed from the surface by convection heat transfer. Using the following constants, determine the temperature distribution in the axial direction:

$$k = 60 \text{W/mK} \text{ (thermal conductivity)}$$
$$h_c = 20 \text{W/m}^2\text{K} \text{ (heat transfer coefficient)}$$
$$A = 0.0001 \text{m}^2 \text{ (cross sectional area)}$$
$$P = 0.01 \text{m} \text{ (perimeter of the rod)}$$

Solution

The heat conduction equation in the axial direction x is written as

$$-Ak\frac{d^2T}{dx^2} + Ph_c(T - 293) = 0, \quad 0 < x < 0.2 \text{ m} \quad \text{(A)}$$

with the boundary conditions

$$T(0) = 493\text{K}, \quad T'(0.2) = 0$$

The present problem is a boundary-value problem (boundary conditions are specified at $x = 0$ and $x = 0.2$m), but can be solved as an initial-value problem on the trial-and-error basis. By defining

$$y_1(x) = T(x)$$
$$y_2(x) = T'(x)$$

Eq.(A) may be rewritten as a set of two first-order ODEs:

$$\begin{array}{rcl} y_1' & = & y_2(x) \\ y_2' & = & (Ph_c/Ak)(y_1(x) - 293) \end{array} \quad \text{(B)}$$

Only one initial condition, $y_1(0) = 493$, is known from the boundary conditions (but $y_2(0)$ is not known). So, we solve Eq.(A) with trial values for $y_2(0)$ until the boundary condition for the right end, namely, $y_2(0.2) = T'(0.2) = 0$, is satisfied. A MATLAB script to perform the computation is developed as List 10.12. When executed, the program asks for the value of $y_2(0)$, then the computed temperature distribution is plotted. By looking at the plot of $y_2(x)$, the next guess may be determined.

We use the fourth-order Runge-Kutta method. After a number of trial and errors, we find that $y_2(0) = -2813.57$ satisfies the second boundary condition accurately, as shown in Figure 10.20.

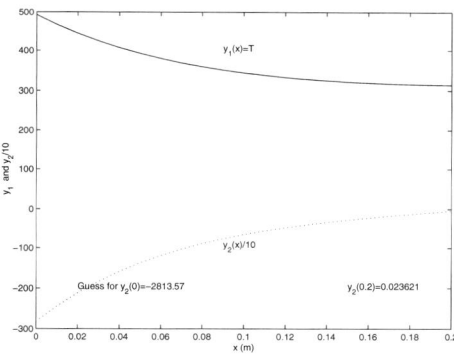

Figure 10.20 Computed results of the shooting method.

List 10.12
```
clear, clf
while 1
  y2 = input('Type gradient, y2(0); or -99999 to quit:  ')
  if y2 < -88888, break, end
  A = 0.0001; P=0.01; hc = 120; k = 60; b=293;
  a=P*hc/A/k;
  n=1; x(1)=0; h = 0.01;
  y(:,1) = [493;y2];
    while x<=0.3
      k1 = h*f_shoot(y(:,n),     x(n),     a,b);
      k2 = h*f_shoot(y(:,n)+k1/2, x(n)+h/2, a,b);
      k3 = h*f_shoot(y(:,n)+k2/2, x(n)+h/2, a,b);
      k4 = h*f_shoot(y(:,n)+k3,   x(n)+h,   a,b);
      y(:,n+1) = y(:,n) + (1/6)*(k1 + 2*k2 + 2*k3 + k4);
      x(n+1) = n*h;
      if (x(n)-0.2001)*(x(n)-0.1999)<0
```

```
            y2_end = y(2,n+1), break,
         end
         n=n+1;
      end
%   y2_end=(y(1,n+1)-y(1,n))/h;
     plot(x,y(1,:), '-', x,y(2,:)/10,':');
     xlabel('x (s)'), ylabel(' y:-    and v/10:...')
     text(0.15, -200, ['y2(0.2)=', num2str(y2_end)] )
     text(0.02, -200, ['Guess for y2(0)=', num2str(y2)] )
     text(x(10),   y(1,10)-20, 'y1(x)' )
     text(x(10),   y(2,10)/10-20  , 'y2(x)/10' )
     axis([0,0.2,-300,500])
end

f_sm
function  f = f_shoot(y,x,a,b)
f = [y(2); a*(y(1)-b)];
```

Comment: Although writing a program using the shooting method is easy, much patience is necessary in the trial-and-error effort to determine the initial condition that satisfies the boundary condition at the endpoint. The boundary-value problem as in this example can be solved much more easily and efficiently by the method described in Chapter 11, "Boundary-Value Problems of Ordinary Differential Equations."

10.5 METHOD OF LINES

Method of lines is another application of numerical methods of initial-value problems to boundary-value problems. The method of lines is suitable particularly for parabolic PDEs.

We consider an unsteady heat conduction equation:

$$\frac{\partial T(x,t)}{\partial t} = \alpha \frac{\partial^2 T(x,t)}{\partial x^2}, \quad 0 < x < H \tag{10.5.1}$$

with the initial condition

$$T(x,0) = T_0$$

and boundary conditions

$$T(0,t) = T_L, \quad T(H,t) = T_R$$

where α is a constant (thermal diffusivity).

In order to derive a solution algorithm, we divide the domain of $0 \leq x \leq H$ into $K+1$ equispaced intervals, so the mesh size is $\Delta x = H/(K+1)$. The points are indexed by i and the temperature value at point i is denoted by

$$T_i(t) = T(x_i, t)$$

A semidifference approximation for Eq.(10.5.1) is written as

$$\frac{dT_i(t)}{dt} = \frac{\alpha}{\Delta x^2}\left(T_{i-1}(t) - 2T_i(t) + T_{i+1}(t)\right), \quad 1 \leq i \leq K \quad (10.5.2)$$

with boundary conditions

$$T_0(t) = T_L, \quad T_{K+1}(t) = T_R$$

We can now express Eq.(10.5.2) in vector form by

$$\frac{d}{dt}\mathbf{T} = \mathbf{MT} + \mathbf{S} \quad (10.5.3)$$

where

$$\mathbf{T} = \begin{bmatrix} T_1 \\ T_2 \\ T_3 \\ \cdot \\ T_K \end{bmatrix}$$

$$\mathbf{M} = \frac{\alpha}{\Delta x^2}\begin{bmatrix} -2 & 1 & 0 & \cdots & 0 \\ 1 & -2 & 1 & \cdots & 0 \\ 0 & 1 & -2 & \cdots & 0 \\ \cdot & \cdot & \cdot & \cdots & 0 \\ 0 & 0 & 0 & \cdots & -2 \end{bmatrix}, \quad \mathbf{S} = \frac{\alpha}{\Delta x^2}\begin{bmatrix} T_L \\ 0 \\ 0 \\ \cdot \\ T_R \end{bmatrix} \quad (10.5.4)$$

The foregoing equation can be solved by one of the Runge-Kutta methods.

Example 10.19

The temperature of a perfectly insulated iron bar 50cm long is initially at $200°C$. The temperature of the left edge is suddenly reduced and fixed to $0°C$ at $t = 0$s, but the temperature of the right end is maintained at $200°C$. Plot the temperature distribution at every increment of 200s until 1000s is reached. The material properties are

$k = 80.2\text{W/mK}$ (thermal conductivity)

$\rho = 7870\text{kg/m}^3$ (density)

$c = 447\text{kJ/kgK}$ (specific heat)

Solution

We first divide the rod into ten intervals (see Figure 10.21). The thermal diffusivity is calculated by

$$\alpha = \frac{k}{\rho C} = \frac{80.2}{(7870)(447)} = 2.28 \times 10^{-5}$$

The equation to be solved is given by Eq.(10.5.3) with $K = 9$. The values of T_L and T_R in Eq.(10.5.4) are set to $T_L = 0$ and $T_R = 200$, respectively. A MATLAB script using the fourth-order Runge-Kutta scheme in the vector form given by Eq.(10.3.29) is shown in List 10.13. The results are plotted in Figure 10.22.

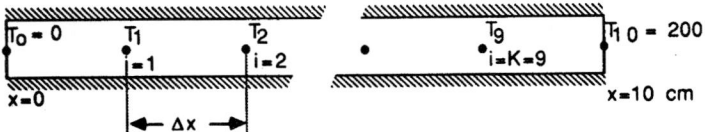

Figure 10.21 An insulated bar.

List 10.13
```
clear, clf, hold off
k=80.2; ro=7870;c=447;TL=0;TR=200;
alpha = k/ro/c; Dx=.05;
M = [-2  1  0  0  0  0  0  0  0; ...
      1 -2  1  0  0  0  0  0  0; ...
      0  1 -2  1  0  0  0  0  0; ...
      0  0  1 -2  1  0  0  0  0; ...
      0  0  0  1 -2  1  0  0  0; ...
      0  0  0  0  1 -2  1  0  0; ...
      0  0  0  0  0  1 -2  1  0; ...
      0  0  0  0  0  0  1 -2  1; ...
      0  0  0  0  0  0  0  1 -2]*alpha/Dx^2;
S=[TL; 0; 0; 0; 0; 0; 0; 0;TR]*alpha/Dx^2;
T=[40;40;40;40;40;40;40;40;40]  ;
T=200*ones(T);
```

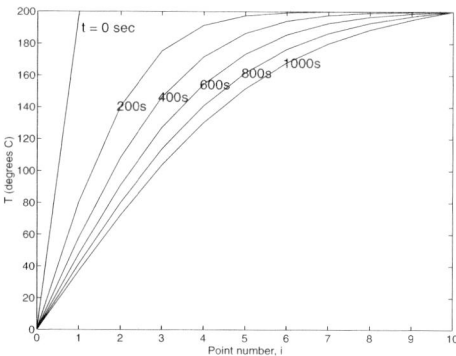

Figure 10.22 Results of method of lines.

```
n=0; t=0; h=20; m=0;
%
  axis([0,10,0,220])
  j=[0,1:length(T),length(T)+1];
  T_plot=[TL, T',TR];
  plot(j,T_plot)
  text( j(2), T_plot(2),['t=',int2str(t),'s'])
  xlabel('Point number, i')
  ylabel('T (degrees C)')
%
for k=1:5
  for m=1:10
    n=n+1;
    k1 = h*(M*T + S);
    k2 = h*(M*(T+k1/2) + S);
    k3 = h*(M*(T+k2/2) + S);
    k4 = h*(M*(T+k3) + S);
    T = T+(k1 + 2*k2 + 2*k3 + k4)/6;
    t=h*n;
  end
  hold on
  j=[0,1:length(T),length(T)+1];
  T_plot=[TL, T',TR];
  plot(j,T_plot)
  text( j(k+1), T_plot(k+1),int2str(t))
end
```

PROBLEMS

(10.1) (a) Solve the following problems in $0 \leq t \leq 0.5$ using the forward Euler method with $h = 0.1$ by hand calculation. (b) Repeat the same with $h = 0.01$

by MATLAB in $0 \leq t \leq 5$. (c) Evaluate the errors by comparing to the exact solutions shown here. (d) Plot the solution of each equation.

(1) $y' + ty = 1$, $y(0) = 1$
(2) $y' + 3y = e^{-t}$, $y(0) = 1$
(3) $y' = (t^2 - y)$, $y(0) = 0.5$
(4) $y' + y|y| = 0$, $y(0) = 1$
(5) $y' + |y|^{1/2} = \sin(t)$, $y(0) = 1$

Exact Solution:

Case t	(1) y	(2) y	(3) y	(4) y	(5) y
0	1.0000	1.0000	0.5000	1.0000	1.0000
0.1	1.0947	0.8228	0.4527	0.9091	0.9074
0.2	1.1775	0.6837	0.4119	0.8333	0.8292
0.3	1.2471	0.5736	0.3788	0.7692	0.7648
0.4	1.3024	0.4857	0.3545	0.7143	0.7131
0.5	1.3428	0.4148	0.3402	0.6666	0.6734
1	1.3313	0.2088	0.4482	0.5000	0.6147
2	0.7753	0.06890	1.7969	0.3333	0.7458
3	0.4043	2.4955E-2	4.9253	0.2500	0.4993
4	0.2707	9.1610E-3	9.9725	0.2000	−0.2714
5	0.2092	3.3692E-3	16.980	0.1666	−2.2495

(10.2) Solve the initial-value problem given by

$$y''(t) - 0.05y'(t) + 0.15y(t) = 0, \quad y'(0) = 0, \quad y(0) = 1$$

and find the values of $y(1)$ and $y(2)$ using the forward Euler method with $h = 0.5$.

(10.3) (a) Solve the following problems in $0 \leq t \leq 5$ using the forward Euler method with $h = 0.1$ and $h = 0.01$ (write your own program in MATLAB). (b) Evaluate the errors with the exact solutions shown below. (c) Plot the solution for each equation:

(1) $y'' + 8y = 0$, $y(0) = 1$, $y'(0) = 0$
(2) $y'' - 0.01(y')^2 + 2y = \sin(t)$, $y(0) = 0$, $y'(0) = 1$
(3) $y'' + 2ty' + ty = 0$, $y(0) = 1$, $y'(0) = 0$
(4) $(e^t + y)y'' = t$, $y(0) = 1$, $y'(0) = 0$

Exact Solution

Case	(a)	(b)	(c)	(d)
t	y	y	y	y
0	1.0	0.0000	1.0000	1.0000
1	−0.9514	0.8450	0.8773	1.0629
2	0.8102	0.9135	0.5372	1.3653
3	−0.5902	0.1412	0.3042	1.8926
4	0.3128	−0.7540	0.1763	2.5589
5	−0.0050	−0.9589	0.1035	3.2978

(10.4) Solve the following set of equations for $0 < t < 5$ by the modified Euler method:

$$4y' = -3y + 7z, \quad y(0) = 1$$
$$7z' = 2y - 8z, \quad z(0) = 0$$

Use both $h = 0.01$ and 0.001. Plot the solution separately for each h, but compare the solutions with two values of h for each equation in the same figure.

(10.5) A conical tank contains water up to 0.5m high from the bottom. The tank has a hole of 0.02m radius at the bottom. The radius of the tank at y is given by $r = 0.25y$, where r is the radius and y is the height measured from the bottom. The velocity of the water that drains through the hole is given by $v^2 = 2gy$, where $g = 9.8 \text{m/s}^2$. Using the forward Euler method (use $h = 0.001\text{s}$), find out how many minutes it will take until the tank becomes empty. Plot y and v computed.

(10.6) A circuit, shown in Figure 10.23, has a self-inductance of $L = 100\text{H}$, a resistance of $R = 200\Omega$, and a DC voltage source of 10V. If the switch is closed at $t = 0\text{s}$, the current, $I(t)$, changes in accordance with

$$L\frac{dI(t)}{dt} + I(t)R = E, \quad I(0) = 0$$

(a) Find the current I at $t = 1, 2, 3, 4,$ and 5s by the forward Euler method with $h = 0.01\text{s}$. Plot solutions in one figure.

(b) Evaluate the error by comparing the numerical solution to the analytical solution given by $I(t) = (E/R)(1 - \exp(-Rt/L))$.

(c) Investigate the effect of h by repeating the above calculations with $h = 0.1\text{s}$.

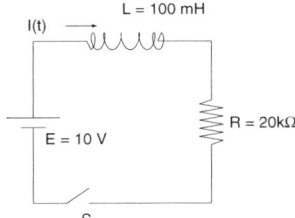

Figure 10.23 Electrical circuit.

(10.7) A U-tube of 0.05m radius is initially filled with water, but separated by a partition so that the water level of the left vertical part is 0.1m higher than the water level of the right vertical part. At $t = 0$, the partition is suddenly removed. The water level of the left vertical portion, y_A, measured from the midplane between two surfaces, satisfies

$$Ly_A'' = -2gy_A$$

where L is the total length of water in the U-tube, which is assumed to be 1m, and $g = 9.81\text{m/s}^2$. Ignoring the friction on the wall of the tube, calculate the water level by the forward Euler method for $0 < t < 10\text{s}$, and find when y_A reaches minimums and maximums. Use $h = 0.001\text{s}$. Plot displacement and velocity in one figure with proper scaling.

(10.8) Repeat the previous problem assuming that there is friction between the fluid and the wall of the pipe, so that the equation of motion is given by

$$Ly_A'' = -2gy_A - \beta y_A'$$

where $\beta = 0.8\text{m/s}$. Use $h = 0.001\text{s}$.

(10.9) The number density (number of atoms per cm^3) of iodine-135 (radioisotope) satisfies

$$\frac{dN_i(t)}{dt} = -\lambda_i N_i(t)$$

where $N(t)$ is the number density of iodine-135; λ_i is its decay constant equal to 0.1044hr^{-1}. If $N_i(0) = 10^5 \text{atoms/cm}^3$ at $t = 0$, compute $N_i(t)$ at $t = 1\text{h}$ by the modified Euler method. Set $h = 0.5\text{hr}$.

(10.10) The decay product of iodine-135 (considered in the previous problem) is xenon-135, and is also radioactive. Its decay constant is $\lambda_x = 0.0753\text{h}^{-1}$. The number density of xenon satisfies

$$\frac{dN_x(t)}{dt} = -\lambda_x N_x(t) + \lambda_i N_i(t)$$

where N_x is the number density of xenon and N_i is the number density of iodine defined in the previous problem. Assuming that $N_x(0) = 0$, develop a program to compute N_i and N_x based on the modified Euler method. (Since the differential equations are linear, use closed form solutions for each time step.) Find the solution for $0 < t \leq 50$h and plot. Use $h = 0.1$hr. Plot both N_i and N_x.

(10.11) Find $y(1)$ for the following equation using the second-order Runge-Kutta method with $h = 0.5$:

$$y' = -\frac{y}{t+y^2}, \quad y(0) = 1$$

(10.12) Calculate $y(2)$ for the following equation using the second-order Runge-Kutta method with $h = 1$:

$$y'' + 0.2y' + 0.003y\sin(t) = 0, \quad y(0) = 0, \quad y'(0) = 1$$

(10.13) Find the value of $y(1)$ by solving

$$y'' - 0.05y' + 0.15y = 0, \quad y(0) = 1, \quad y'(0) = 0$$

Use the second-order Runge-Kutta method with $h = 0.5$.

(10.14) Solve the following differential equation

$$2y'' + (y')^2 + y = 0, \quad y(0) = 0, \quad y'(0) = 1$$

by the second-order Runge-Kutta method with $h = 0.5$ and evaluate $y(1)$ and $y'(1)$.

(10.15) An initial-value problem of an ordinary differential equation is given by

$$y''' = -y, \quad y(0) = 1, \quad y'(0) = y''(0) = 0$$

Using the second-order Runge-Kutta method with $h = 0.2$, calculate $y(0.4)$ and $y(1)$.

(10.16) (a) A 50L tank full of water contains salt at a concentration of 10g/L. In order to dilute the salt content, fresh water is supplied at the rate of 2L/min. If the tank is well mixed, and the water leaves the tank with the same flow rate, the salt content satisfies

$$y_1'(t) = -(2/50)y_1$$

where $y_1(t)$ is the salt concentration in g/L, and t is time in minutes. By the second-order Runge-Kutta method with $h = 1$min, find out how long it takes until the salt concentration reaches 1/10 of its initial value.

(b) The water that leaves the tank enters another tank of 20L capacity, into which fresh water is also poured at the rate of 3L/min and well mixed. The salt concentration in this tank satisfies

$$y_2'(t) = -(5/20)y_2(t) + (2/20)y_1(t), \quad y_2(0) = 0$$

where $y_1(t)$ is the salt concentration of the 50L tank mentioned in (a). By the second-order Runge-Kutta method, find when the salt concentration of the 20L tank reaches its maximum. Assume that the water in the second tank is fresh at $t = 0$.

(10.17) Calculate $y(1)$ by solving the following equation using the fourth-order Runge-Kutta method with $h = 1$:

$$y' = -y/(t + y^2), \quad y(0) = 1$$

(10.18) Find the solution of

$$y'(t) = -1/(1 + y^2), \quad y(0) = 1$$

for $t = 1$ and $t = 2$ using the fourth-order Runge-Kutta method with $h = 0.5$ and $h = 1$.

(10.19) A bullet is shot into the air at a 45 degree angle from the ground at $u = v = 150$m/s, where u and v are horizontal and vertical velocities, respectively. The equations of motion are given by

$$\begin{aligned} u' &= -cVu, \quad u(0) = 150\text{m/s} \\ v' &= -g - cVv, \quad v(0) = 150\text{m/s} \end{aligned} \quad (A)$$

where u and v are functions of time, $u = u(t)$, $v = v(t)$, and

$$\begin{aligned} V^2 &= u^2 + v^2 \\ c &= 0.005\text{m}^{-1} \text{ (coefficient of drag)} \\ g &= 9.8\text{m/s}^2 \text{ (gravity)} \end{aligned}$$

The equations of motion may be solved by one of the Runge-Kutta methods. The trajectory of the bullet may be calculated by integrating

$$x' = u, \quad \text{and} \quad y' = v$$

or

$$x = \int_0^t u(t')dt'$$
$$y = \int_0^t v(t')dt'$$
(B)

A script based on the forward Euler method to solve Eq.(A) and evaluate Eq.(B) is in List 10.14.

List 10.14
```
clear; close all
u = 150; v=150;  h=.1; c=0.005; t=0;
ub=u; vb=v;
y=0; x=0; n=1;
u_rec(1)=u;  v_rec(1)=v; t_rec(1)=t;
x_rec(1)=x; y_rec(1)=y;
while y>=0
   vel1= sqrt( ub*ub + vb*vb);
   k1 = h*(-c*vel1*ub);
   l1 = h*(-9.8-c*vel1*vb);
   u=ub+ k1;   v=vb+l1;
   x=x+h*(ub+u)/2;  y=y+h*(vb+v)/2;
   ub=u;   vb=v;
   n=n+1; t=t+1;
   u_rec(n)=u;  v_rec(n)=v; t_rec(n)=t;
   x_rec(n)=x; y_rec(n)=y;
end
plot(x_rec,y_rec)
xlabel('x(m)'); ylabel('y(m)')
title('Proble 10.19, Trajectory')
```

(a) Run the script and plot the trajectory of the bullet. (b) Plot x and y as a function of time in the same graph. (c) Plot u and v as a function of time in the same graph. (d) Rewrite the script using the fourth-order Runge-Kutta method in a vector form. Find the horizontal distance that the bullet reaches with an error of less than 0.1 percent.

(10.20) The solution of $y' = -1/(1+y^2)$ by the second-order Runge-Kutta method is shown for two different h values.

t	$h = 0.1$ y	$h = 0.2$ y
0.0	1.0000000	1.0000000
0.1	0.9487188	
0.2	0.8946720	0.8947514

(a) Estimate the local error of $y(0.2)$ with $h = 0.1$.

(b) Estimate a more accurate value of $y(0.2)$.

(c) If the local error is required to satisfy $|E_h| < 0.00001$, estimate h.

(10.21) For the equation given by

$$y' = 3y + \exp(1-t), \ y(0) = 1$$

find an optimal time step for the second-order Runge-Kutta method that satisfies $|E_h| < 0.0001$. (Run the second-order Runge-Kutta method for one interval with a value of h, and rerun for two intervals with $h/2$.)

(10.22) Repeat Problem 10.21 for the fourth-order Runge-Kutta method.

(10.23) By repeating the analysis of Eqs.(10.3.33) through (10.3.39), derive the equation corresponding to Eq.(10.3.38) for the third-order Runge-Kutta method.

(10.24) If the third-order Runge-Kutta method is applied to $y' = -\alpha y$, find in what range of h the method is unstable.

(10.25) The initial temperature of a metal piece is 25°C. The metal piece is internally heated electrically at the rate of $Q = 3000$W. The equation for the temperature is written as

$$\frac{dT}{dt} = \frac{1}{V\rho c}\left[Q - \epsilon\sigma A\left(T^4 - 298^4\right) - h_c A(T - 298)\right], \ T(0) = 298 \text{ K}$$

where T is in Kelvin, and

$k = 60$W/mK (thermal conductivity)

$\sigma = 5.67 \times 10^{-8}$ W/m²K⁴ (Stefan-Boltzmann constant)

$A = 0.25$m² (surface area)

$V = 0.001$m (volume)

$c = 900$J/kgK (specific heat)

$\rho = 3000$kg/m³ (density)

$h_c = 30$J/m²K (heat transfer coefficient)

$\epsilon = 0.8$ (emissivity)

Calculate the temperature for $0 < t < 10$ min, by the fourth-order Runge-Kutta method with $h = 0.1$ min. Plot the solution.

(10.26) The motion of the mass system illustrated in Figure 10.24 is given by

$$y'' + 2\zeta\omega y' + \omega^2 y = F(t)/M, \ y(0) = y'(0) = 0$$

where

Problems

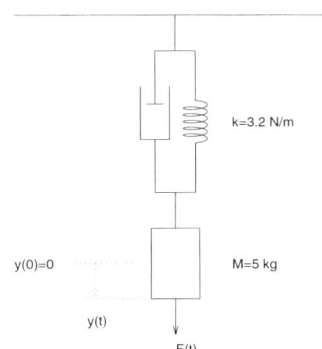

Figure 10.24 Spring-mass system.

$$\omega = (k/M)^{1/2} \text{ (undamped natural frequency, s}^{-1})$$
$$\zeta = 0.5 \text{ (damping factor)}$$
$$k = 3.2 \text{ (spring constant, N/m)}$$
$$M = 5 \text{ (mass, kg)}$$
$$F(t) = 0 \text{ (force, N)}$$

If $F(t) = 1$ for $0 \leq t \leq 1$ s, and $F(t) = 0$ for $t > 1$s, determine the motion of the mass for $0 < t < 10$s, using the fourth-order Runge-Kutta method.

(10.27) Determine the response of the spring-mass system of the previous problem subject to a triangular force pulse

$$F(t) = 2F_0 t, \ 0 \leq t \leq 1 \text{ s}$$
$$= 2F_0(1-t), \ 1 \leq t \leq 2 \text{ s}$$
$$= 0, \ t > 2 \text{ s}$$

where $F_0 = 1$N. Use the fourth-order Runge-Kutta method and plot the result.

(10.28) Repeat the problem in Example 10.16, except change $e(t)$ to

$$e(t) = \sin(1200t)\exp(-1200t)$$

and for $0 < t < 0.01$s.

(10.29) Solve the following problem by the shooting method based on the fourth-order Runge-Kutta method:

$$Ak\frac{dT^2}{dx^2} + P\sigma(T^4 - 273^4) = AQ, \quad 0 < x < 0.5$$
$$T(0) = 0$$
$$T'(0.5) = 0$$

where A and P are given in Example 10.17, and $\sigma = 5.67 \times 10^{-8}$w/m^{2}K^4. (*Hint*: Change $T'(0.5)$ by trial and error until $T'(0.5) = 0$ is satisfied.)

Chapter 11

BOUNDARY-VALUE PROBLEMS OF ORDINARY DIFFERENTIAL EQUATIONS

One-dimensional boundary-value problems appear in almost every branch of science and engineering. The numerical solution of these equations is not only important to investigate the physical nature of the problems, but it also is an introduction to the numerical solution of two- and three-dimensional boundary-value problems. In this chapter we study numerical methods for the one-dimensional boundary-value problems, considering heat conduction equations and particle diffusion equations as examples. After that, the numerical solution of boundary-value problems of nonlinear and higher-order ODEs will be discussed.

11.1 INTRODUCTION

For the one-dimensional boundary-value problem of ordinary differential equations, the solution is required to satisfy boundary conditions at both ends of the domain. The definition of boundary conditions is an important part of each boundary-value problem. For example, consider a thin metal rod of length H with each end connected to a different heat source (see Figure 11.1). If heat escapes from the surface of the rod to the air only by convection heat transfer, the equation for the temperature is

$$-A\frac{d}{dx}k(x)\frac{dT(x)}{dx} + h_c PT(x) = h_c PT_\infty + AS(x) \qquad (11.1.1)$$

where $T(x)$ is the temperature at distance x from the left end, A the constant cross-sectional area of the rod, k the thermal conductivity, P the perimeter of

Section 11.1 Introduction

the rod, h_c the convection heat-transfer coefficient, T_∞ the bulk temperature of the air, and S the heat source. The boundary conditions are

$$\begin{aligned} T(0) &= T_L \\ T(H) &= T_R \end{aligned} \qquad (11.1.2)$$

where T_L and T_R are known temperatures at the left and right ends, respectively.

If θ is defined as

$$\theta = T - T_\infty$$

Eq.(11.1.1) may be written as

$$-\frac{d}{dx}k(x)\frac{d\theta(x)}{dx} + \sigma\theta(x) = S(x) \qquad (11.1.3)$$

where $\sigma = h_c P/A$ and the equation has been divided by A. The first term represents the conduction of heat, the second term is the removal of heat by convection to the air, and the right side is the heat source.

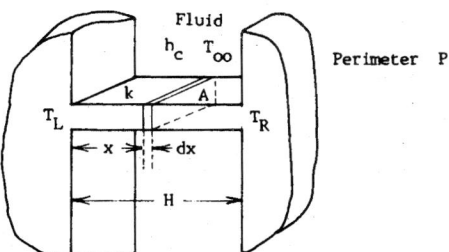

Figure 11.1 A fin connected to two heat sources.

Another example of ODE in a similar form is the neutron diffusion equation given by

$$-\frac{d}{dx}D(x)\frac{d\psi(x)}{dx} + \Sigma_a\psi(x) = S(x) \qquad (11.1.4)$$

where ψ is the neutron flux, D is the diffusion coefficient, and S is the neutron source. The meaning of the first term is the diffusion of neutrons, while the second term is the removal by absorption.

In the remainder of this chapter, we consider the equation

$$-\frac{d}{dx}p(x)\frac{d\phi(x)}{dx} + q(x)\phi(x) = S(x) \qquad (11.1.5)$$

or similar equations on cylindrical or spherical coordinates. The first term is the diffusion term, the second is the removal term, and the right side is the source term.

It should be emphasized that Eq.(1.1.5) is a conservation law of diffusion. Indeed, integrating Eq.(1.1.5) in $[a, b]$ yields

$$Z(b) - Z(a) + \int_a^b q(x)\phi(x)dx = \int_a^b S(x)dx \qquad (11.1.6)$$

where

$$Z(x) = -p(x)\frac{d\phi(x)}{dx}$$

is heat flux at x if heat conduction is considered, or neutron current if neutron diffusion is considered. In any case, the first and second terms in the equation above are, respectively, inflow and outflow of the physical quantity associated with ϕ, the third term is the total removal in $[a, b]$, and the right side is the total source in $[a, b]$. Thus, Eq.(11.1.6) represents conservation of the physical quantity in $[a, b]$.

If Eq.(11.1.1) were an initial-value problem, two boundary conditions would be specified at only one boundary, so the numerical solution could proceed from that end to the other by a numerical method such as the fourth-order Runge-Kutta method. Although the solution methods for initial-value problems can be used for boundary-value problems, as illustrated in Chapter 10, "Initial Value Problems of Ordinary Differential Equations," they work only on a trial-and-error basis (known as the shooting method; see Example 10.17). An advantage of the shooting method is that an existing program for initial-value problems may be utilized. The shooting method, however, often becomes unsuccessful because it may face numerical instability. Furthermore, its application becomes very difficult if the order of the ODE exceeds two.

A more general way of solving boundary-value problems consists of (a) deriving difference equations and (b) solving all the difference equations simultaneously. In this chapter, we first study the derivation of difference approximations for boundary-value problems and their simultaneous solution.

11.2 BOUNDARY-VALUE PROBLEMS FOR RODS AND SLABS

In this section, we derive finite difference equations for second-order ordinary differential equations with boundary conditions.

In order to explain the principle of the method, we consider the equation

$$-\phi''(x) + q\phi(x) = S(x), \quad 0 < x < H \qquad (11.2.1)$$

with the boundary conditions

$$\begin{aligned} \phi'(0) &= 0 & \text{(left B.C.)} \\ \phi(H) &= \phi_R & \text{(right B.C.)} \end{aligned} \qquad (11.2.2)$$

where q is a constant coefficient. By dividing the domain into N equispaced intervals, we obtain a grid, as shown in Figure 11.2, where the grid intervals are $h = H/N$. Applying the central difference approximation (see (f) of Table 6.1) to the first term of Eq.(11.2.1), the difference equation for point i is derived as

$$\frac{-\phi_{i-1} + 2\phi_i - \phi_{i+1}}{h^2} + q\phi_i = S_i \qquad (11.2.3)$$

where $\phi_i = \phi(x_i)$, $S_i = S(x_i)$, and q is assumed to be constant. Multiplying Eq.(11.2.3) by h^2 yields

$$-\phi_{i-1} + (2+w)\phi_i - \phi_{i+1} = h^2 S_i \qquad (11.2.4)$$

where $w = h^2 q$. The foregoing equation applies to all the grid points except for $i = 1$ and $i = N + 1$.

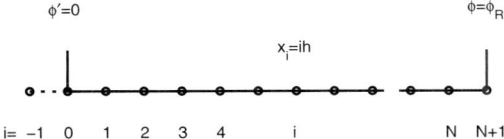

Figure 11.2 One-dimensional grid for a slab

The left boundary condition given by Eq.(11.2.2) is equivalent to a symmetry boundary condition called an *adiabatic* boundary condition in heat transfer. If a hypothetical grid point $i = 0$, located at $x = -h$, is considered, Eq.(11.2.4) for $i = 1$ becomes

$$-\phi_0 + (2+w)\phi_1 - \phi_2 = h^2 S_1 \qquad (11.2.5)$$

In the foregoing equation, ϕ_0 can be set to $\phi_0 = \phi_2$ because the left boundary condition can be interpreted as

$$\phi_1' \approx \frac{\phi_2 - \phi_0}{2h} = 0$$

Then, dividing the resulting equation by 2 yields

$$(1 + w/2)\phi_1 - \phi_2 = h^2 S_1/2 \qquad (11.2.6)$$

Since $\phi_{N+1} = \phi(H) = \phi_R$ at the right boundary, Eq.(11.2.4) for $i = N$ is written as

$$-\phi_{N-1} + (2+w)\phi_N = h^2 S_N + \phi_R \qquad (11.2.7)$$

where all the known terms are brought to the right side.

The set of Eqs.(11.2.5), (11.2.4), and (11.2.7) is written together as

$$\begin{aligned}
(1+w/2)\phi_1 - \phi_2 &= h^2 S_1/2 \\
-\phi_1 + (2+w)\phi_2 - \phi_3 &= h^2 S_2 \\
-\phi_2 + (2+w)\phi_3 - \phi_4 &= h^2 S_3 \\
&\cdots \\
-\phi_{N-1} + (2+w)\phi_N &= h^2 S_N + \phi_R
\end{aligned} \qquad (11.2.8)$$

or equivalently in matrix form,

$$\begin{bmatrix} 1+w/2 & -1 & & & \\ -1 & 2+w & -1 & & \\ & -1 & 2+w & -1 & \\ & & \ddots & \ddots & \ddots \\ & & & -1 & 2+w \end{bmatrix} \begin{bmatrix} \phi_1 \\ \phi_2 \\ \phi_3 \\ \cdots \\ \phi_N \end{bmatrix} = \begin{bmatrix} h^2 S_1/2 \\ h^2 S_2 \\ h^2 S_3 \\ \cdots \\ h^2 S_N + \phi_R \end{bmatrix}$$

$$(11.2.9)$$

The coefficient matrix of Eq.(11.2.9) are all zero except along the three diagonal lines. This special form of the matrix is called a *tridiagonal matrix*,

Section 11.2 Boundary-Value Problems for Rods and Slabs

which appears very often in the numerical method for boundary-value problems. Equation (11.2.9) is solved by the tridiagonal solution described in Section 11.3.

Boundary conditions are classified into the three types as shown in Table 11.1. To discuss the implementation of a mixed-type boundary condition, suppose both boundary conditions for Eq.(11.2.1) are given by the mixed type, namely

$$-\phi'(0) + f_L \phi(0) = g_L \tag{11.2.10}$$
$$\phi'(H) + f_R \phi(H) = g_R \tag{11.2.11}$$

where f_L, f_R, g_L, and g_R are constants. We will consider the grid shown in Figure 11.3 (which is the same as Figure 11.2, except that the last grid point is numbered N rather than $N+1$).

Table 11.1 Three Types of Boundary Conditions

Type	Explanation	Examples
Fixed value boundary condition (Dirichlet type)	Functional value of the solution is given.	$\phi(0) = 0$, or $\phi(0) = 1$
Derivative boundary condition (Neumann type)	Derivative of the solution is given.	$\phi'(0) = 0$, or $\phi'(0) = 1$
Mixed boundary condition (Mixed type)	Functional value is related to the derivative.	$\phi'(0) + \alpha \phi(0) = \beta$

The difference equation, Eq.(11.2.4), is unchanged for $i = 2$ through $N - 1$, but the ones for $i = 1$ and N need to be revised because of the new boundary conditions. We consider the left boundary first. Using the forward difference approximation based on an interval of $h/2$ for Eq.(11.2.1) at $x = 0$ yields

$$-\frac{\phi'(h/2) - \phi'(0)}{h/2} + q\phi_1 = S_1 \tag{11.2.12}$$

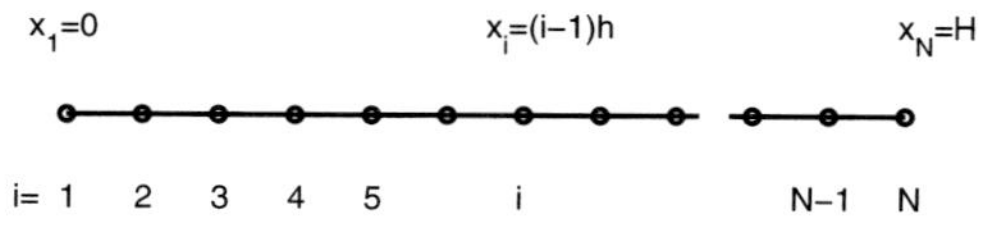

Figure 11.3 One-dimensional grid.

Here, $\phi'(h/2)$ is substituted by the central difference approximation,
$$\phi'(h/2) = (\phi_2 - \phi_1)/h$$
and $\phi'(0)$ may be eliminated by using Eq.(11.2.10). Thus, we obtain
$$-\frac{(\phi_2 - \phi_1)/h + g_L - f_L\phi_1}{h/2} + q\phi_1 = S_1$$
or equivalently
$$(1 + \frac{w}{2} + hf_L)\phi_1 - \phi_2 = \frac{h^2 S_1}{2} + hg_L \qquad (11.2.13)$$
where $w = qh^2$, and all known terms are on the right side.

The difference equation for the right boundary is derived by a similar procedure:
$$-\phi_{N-1} + (1 + \frac{w}{2} + hf_R)\phi_N = \frac{h^2 S_N}{2} + hg_R \qquad (11.2.14)$$

The set of Eqs.(11.2.13), (11.2.4), and (11.2.14) forms a tridiagonal equation set.

Example 11.1

Derive difference equations for the following boundary-value problem:
$$-2y''(x) + y(x) = \exp(-0.2x) \qquad (A)$$
with the boundary conditions
$$y(0) = 0.1$$
$$y'(10) = -y(10)$$

Section 11.2 Boundary-Value Problems for Rods and Slabs

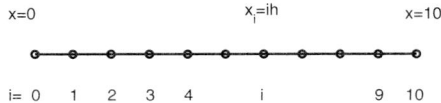

Figure 11.4 Grid for Example 11.1.

Assume the grid spacing is unity.

Solution

We consider the grid shown in Figure 11.4. The difference equations for $i = 2$ through 9 are

$$2(-y_{i-1} + 2y_i - y_{i+1}) + y_i = \exp(-0.2i) \tag{B}$$

where $x_i = ih$, with $h = 1$, is used.

For $i = 1$, the boundary condition $y_0 = y(0) = 1$ is introduced into Eq.(B) to yield

$$5y_1 - 2y_2 = \exp(-0.2) + 0.2 \tag{C}$$

For $i = 10$, we approximate Eq.(A) first by

$$-\frac{2[y'(10) - y'(9.5)]}{1/2} + y(10) = \exp(-2) \tag{D}$$

Using the central difference approximation, the term $y'(9.5)$ becomes

$$y'(9.5) = [y(10) - y(9)]/1 \tag{E}$$

Introducing Eq.(E) and the right boundary condition $y'(10) = -y(10)$ into Eq.(D) yields

$$-2y_9 + 4.5y_{10} = 0.5\exp(-2) \tag{F}$$

Summarizing the difference equations obtained, we write

$$\begin{aligned} 5y_1 - 2y_2 &= \exp(-0.2) + 0.2 \\ -2y_{i-1} + 5y_i - 2y_{i+1} &= \exp(-0.2x_i), \text{ for } i = 2 \text{ to } 9 \\ -2y_9 + 4.5y_{10} &= 0.5\exp(-2) \end{aligned} \tag{G}$$

where $x_i = i$ is used. The numerical results are shown in Example 11.2.

11.3 SOLUTION OF TRIDIAGONAL EQUATIONS

We write the tridiagonal equation derived in Section 11.2 in the form

$$\begin{bmatrix} B_1 & C_1 & & & & & \\ A_2 & B_2 & C_2 & & & & \\ & A_3 & B_3 & C_3 & & & \\ & & \ddots & \ddots & & & \\ & & & A_i & B_i & C_i & \\ & & & & \ddots & \ddots & \\ & & & & & A_N & B_N \end{bmatrix} \begin{bmatrix} \phi_1 \\ \phi_2 \\ \phi_3 \\ \cdots \\ \phi_i \\ \cdots \\ \phi_N \end{bmatrix} = \begin{bmatrix} D_1 \\ D_2 \\ D_3 \\ \cdots \\ D_i \\ \cdots \\ D_N \end{bmatrix} \qquad (11.3.1)$$

The solution algorithm, called the tridiagonal solution, is a variant of Gauss elimination and given next.

(a) Initialize the two new variables: $B'_1 = B_1$ and $D'_1 = D_1$

(b) Calculate recurrently the following equations in increasing order of i, until $i = N$ is reached:

$$\begin{aligned} R &= A_i/B'_{i-1} \\ B'_i &= B_i - RC_{i-1} \\ D'_i &= D_i - RD'_{i-1} \end{aligned} \qquad (11.3.2)$$

for $i = 2, 3, ..., N$.

(c) Calculate the solution for the last unknown by

$$\phi_N = D'_N / B'_N \qquad (11.3.3)$$

(d) Calculate the following equation in decreasing order of i:

$$\phi_i = (D'_i - C_i \phi_{i+1})/B'_i, \quad i = N-1, ..., 2, 1 \qquad (11.3.4)$$

In a computer program, the primed variables B'_i and D'_i need not be distinguished from B_i and D_i, respectively, because B'_i and D'_i are stored in the same memory as for B_i and D_i. Therefore, step (a) is not necessary in real programming.

A function M-file, tri_diag.m, to solve the tridiagonal equation appears in List 11.1.

List 11.1
tri_diag.m

```
function f = tri_diag(a,b,c,d,n)
for i=2:n
   r=a(i)/b(i-1)
   b(i)=b(i)-r*c(i-1)
   d(i)=d(i)-r*d(i-1)
end
d(n)=d(n)/b(n)
for i=n-1:-1:1
   d(i)=(d(i)-c(i)*d(i+1))/b(i)
end
f=d;
```

When the computation in the function is completed, the solution is returned in array f.

Example 11.2
Solve Eq.(D) in Example 11.1 and plot the results.

Solution
The answer is computed by the following script. The solution is plotted in Figure 11.5.

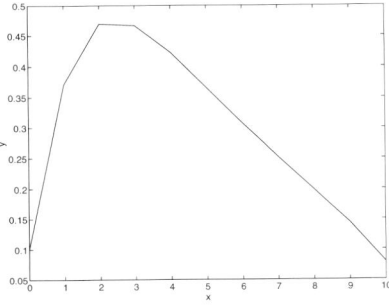

Figure 11.5 Plot of the solution.

List 11.2
```
clear,clf, y0=0.1;
b(1)=5; c(1)=-2; s(1)=exp(-0.2) + y0;
for i=2:9
a(i)=-2; b(i)=5; c(i)=-2; s(i)=exp(-0.2*i);
end
a(10)=-2; b(10)=4.5; s(10)=0.5*exp(-2);
y=tri_diag(a,b,c,s,10)
plot(0:10,[y0,y])
xlabel('x');ylabel('y')
```

11.4 VARIABLE COEFFICIENTS AND NONUNIFORM GRIDS

In many problems, the coefficients of the differential equation are space-dependent. A nonequispaced grid is used when the geometry consists of layers of different properties, for example.

The second-order ordinary differential equation for the slab geometry with variable coefficients is written here as

$$-(p(x)\phi'(x))' + q(x)\phi(x) = S(x) \qquad (11.4.1)$$

with the boundary conditions given by Eqs.(11.2.10) and (11.2.11). The grid spacing between x_i to x_{i+1} will be denoted by h_i. We assume that p, q, and S in each grid interval are constant and denoted by p_i, q_i, and S_i, respectively, as shown in Figure 11.6.

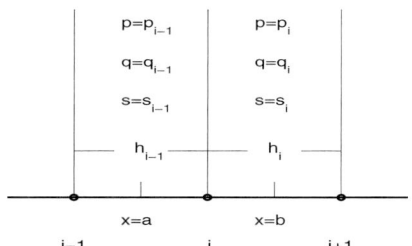

Figure 11.6 Constants in grid intervals.

One natural way of deriving difference equations with piecewise-constant coefficients is the method of integration. In this method, Eq.(11.4.1) is integrated from a to b (see Figure 11.6):

$$-\int_a^b (p(x)\phi'(x))' dx + \int_a^b q(x)\phi(x) dx = \int_a^b S(x) dx \qquad (11.4.2)$$

where $a = x_i - h_{i-1}/2$, and $b = x_i + h_i/2$ (which are midpoints between i-1 and i, and i and $i+1$, respectively).

The first term of Eq.(11.4.2) becomes

$$-\int_a^b (p\phi')' dx = -(p\phi')_{i+1/2} + (p\phi')_{i-1/2} \qquad (11.4.3)$$

The derivatives on the right side are approximated by the central difference approximation:

Section 11.4 Variable Coefficients and Nonuniform Grids

$$(p\phi')_{i-1/2} \approx p_{i-1}(\phi_i - \phi_{i-1})/h_{i-1}$$
$$(p\phi')_{i+1/2} \approx p_i(\phi_{i+1} - \phi_i)/h_i \tag{11.4.4}$$

where $p(x) = p_i$ for $x_i < x < x_{i+1}$. Thus, the first term of Eq.(11.4.2) becomes

$$-\int_a^b (p\phi')' dx \approx -\frac{p_{i-1}}{h_{i-1}}\phi_{i-1} + \left(\frac{p_{i-1}}{h_{i-1}} + \frac{p_i}{h_i}\right)\phi_i - \frac{p_i}{h_i}\phi_{i+1}h_i \tag{11.4.5}$$

The second term of Eq.(11.4.2) becomes

$$\int_a^b q(x)\phi(x)dx \approx (q_{i-1}h_{i-1} + q_i h_i)\phi_i/2 \tag{11.4.6}$$

where $\phi(x)$ is approximated by ϕ_i. The right side of Eq.(11.4.2) becomes

$$\int_a^b S(x)dx \approx (S_{i-1}h_{i-1} + S_i h_i)/2 \tag{11.4.7}$$

Introducing Eqs.(11.4.5), (11.4.6), and (11.4.7) into Eq.(11.4.2) yields

$$-\frac{p_{i-1}}{h_{i-1}}\phi_{i-1} + \left(\frac{p_{i-1}}{h_{i-1}} + \frac{p_i}{h_i}\right)\phi_i - \frac{p_i}{h_i}\phi_{i+1} + \frac{(q_{i-1}h_{i-1} + q_i h_i)}{2}\phi_i = \frac{S_{i-1}h_{i-1} + S_i h_i}{2} \tag{11.4.8}$$

Equation (11.4.8) can now be written in the form

$$A_i\phi_{i-1} + B_i\phi_i + C_i\phi_{i+1} = D_i \tag{11.4.9}$$

where
$$\begin{aligned} A_i &= -\frac{p_{i-1}}{h_{i-1}} \\ B_i &= \frac{p_{i-1}}{h_{i-1}} + \frac{p_i}{h_i} + \frac{(q_{i-1}h_{i-1} + q_i h_i)}{2} \\ C_i &= -\frac{p_i}{h_i} \\ D_i &= \frac{S_{i-1}h_{i-1} + S_i h_i}{2} \end{aligned} \tag{11.4.10}$$

With the boundary conditions given by Eqs.(11.2.10) and (11.2.11), difference equations for the left and right boundary points are also derived by integrating Eq.(11.4.1). Considering the left boundary point, a and b in

Eq.(11.4.2) are set to:

$a = x_1$ (the left boundary point)
$b = x_1 + h_1/2$ (the midpoint between x_1 and x_2)

Then, the first term of Eq.(11.4.2) becomes

$$-\int_a^b (p\phi')' dx = -(p\phi')_b + (p\phi')_a \qquad (11.4.11)$$

The first term on the right side is approximated by the central difference approximation,

$$-(p\phi')_b \approx -p_1 \frac{\phi_2 - \phi_1}{h_1} \qquad (11.4.12)$$

The ϕ' in the second term on the right side of Eq.(11.4.11) is eliminated by Eq.(11.2.10). Therefore, Eq.(11.4.11) becomes

$$-\int_a^b (p\phi')' dx \approx -p_1 \frac{\phi_2 - \phi_1}{h_1} + p_1(-g_L + f_L \phi_1) \qquad (11.4.13)$$

The second term and right side of Eq.(11.4.2) become, respectively,

$$\int_a^b q(x)\phi(x) dx \approx \frac{q_1 h_1}{2} \phi_1 \qquad (11.4.14)$$

$$\int_a^b S(x) dx \approx \frac{S_1 h_1}{2} \qquad (11.4.15)$$

Introducing Eqs.(11.4.12) through (11.4.15) in Eq.(11.4.2) yields

$$(\frac{p_1}{h_1} + p_1 f_L + \frac{q_1 h_1}{2})\phi_1 - \frac{p_1}{h_1}\phi_2 = \frac{S_1 h_1}{2} + p_1 g_L \qquad (11.4.16)$$

which may be rewritten more compactly as

$$B_1 \phi_1 + C_1 \phi_2 = D_1 \qquad (11.4.17)$$

The difference equation for the right boundary point can also be derived similarly and written as

$$A_N \phi_{N-1} + B_N \phi_N = D_N \qquad (11.4.18)$$

The set of difference equations thus derived, namely, Eqs.(11.4.17), (11.4.9), and (11.4.18), fits exactly in the form of Eq.(11.3.1).

Provided that physically correct boundary conditions are imposed and that the coefficient of the removal term is non-negative, the coefficient matrix of the difference equations in the conservation form has the following five properties:

(1) the coefficient matrix in Eq.(11.3.1) is symmetric

(2) the diagonal coefficients are all positive

(3) A_i and C_i are all negative

(4) the coefficients in each row satisfy

$$B_i \geq -A_i - C_i$$

with strict inequality for at least one row, and

(5) no part of the equation can be solved independently of other parts.

The inverse of the matrix satisfying all the foregoing conditions is shown to be a positive matrix; that is, all the elements of the inverse matrix are positive. This implies that, if $S_i \geq 0$ with strict inequality for at least one i, the solution is positive everywhere.

11.5 CYLINDERS AND SPHERES

The derivation of difference equations for second-order ordinary differential equations for cylindrical and spherical geometries is very similar to that discussed in Section 11.4. The difference equations for these two geometries will have the form of Eq.(11.3.1).

The second-order ordinary differential equation for cylindrical and spherical geometries may be written as

$$-\frac{1}{r^m}\frac{d}{dr}p(r)r^m\frac{d}{dr}\phi(r) + q(r)\phi(r) = S(r) \qquad (11.5.1)$$

where
$\quad m = 1$ for cylinder
$\quad m = 2$ for sphere

Notice also that the equation reduces to Eq.(11.4.1) for a slab if $m = 0$.

Considering space-dependent coefficients and a nonequispaced grid, as discussed in the preceding section, we derive difference approximations by the method of integration. That is, to integrate the equation over a cylindrical or spherical control volume, depending on the geometry.

The derivation of difference equations is now shown using the notations for h, p, q, and S defined in Figure 11.6, where p, q, and S are assumed to be constant between two consecutive points. We multiply Eq.(11.5.1) by r^m and integrate from $a = r_{i-1/2}$ to $b = r_{i+1/2}$, which are midpoints of $[r_{i-1}, r_i]$ and $[r_i, r_{i+1}]$, respectively:

$$-\int_a^b \frac{d}{dr} r^m p(r) \frac{d}{dr} \phi(r) dr + \int_a^b q(r)\phi(r) r^m dr = \int_a^b S(r) r^m dr \qquad (11.5.2)$$

Here, for a cylindrical geometry ($m = 1$), $r^m dr$ represents an infinitesimal volume element divided by $2\pi L$, where L is the height of the circular cylinder. For a spherical geometry, $r^m dr$ represents an infinitesimal volume element divided by 4π. The first term of Eq.(11.5.2) becomes

$$p_{i-1} r_{i-1/2}^m \left[\frac{d}{dr}\phi(r)\right]_a - p_i r_{i+1/2}^m \left[\frac{d}{dr}\phi(r)\right]_b \qquad (11.5.3)$$

Using the difference approximation for the derivatives then yields

$$p_{i-1} r_{i-1/2}^m \frac{\phi_i - \phi_{i-1}}{h_{i-1}} - p_i r_{i+1/2}^m \frac{\phi_{i+1} - \phi_i}{h_i} \qquad (11.5.4)$$

For the cylindrical geometry, the first term times $2\pi L$ is the total flow of the physical quantity through the cylindrical surface at $a = r_{i-1/2}$, and the second is the same for $b = r_{i+1/2}$. For the spherical geometry, the first term times 4π is the total flow.

The second term of Eq.(11.5.2) may be approximated by

$$\int_a^b q(r)\phi(r) r^m dr \approx (v_L q_{i-1} + v_R q_i)\phi_i \qquad (11.5.5)$$

and represents the total removal of the physical property in $[r_{i-1/2}, r_{i+1/2}]$, where for $m = 1$,

$$v_L = \frac{1}{2}[r_i^2 - (r_i - \frac{h_{i-1}}{2})^2] = \frac{h_{i-1}}{2}(r_i - \frac{h_{i-1}}{4}) \qquad (11.5.6)$$

$$v_R = \frac{1}{2}[(r_i + \frac{h_i}{2})^2 - r_i^2] = \frac{h_i}{2}(r_i + \frac{h_i}{4}) \qquad (11.5.7)$$

and for $m = 2$,
$$v_L = \frac{1}{3}[r_i^3 - (r_i - \frac{h_{i-1}}{2})^3] \tag{11.5.8}$$
$$v_R = \frac{1}{3}[(r_i + \frac{h_i}{2})^3 - r_i^3] \tag{11.5.9}$$

Note here for $m = 1$ that, v_L times $2\pi L$ becomes the volume of a cylindrical cell between $r = r_{i-1/2}$ and $r = r_i$, while v_R becomes the same between r_i and $r_{i+1/2}$. The third term of Eq.(11.5.2) may be approximated similarly by

$$\int S(r) r\, dr \approx v_L S_{i-1} + v_R S_i \tag{11.5.10}$$

Collecting all the terms, the difference approximation for Eq.(11.5.1) becomes the tridiagonal form.

The difference equations derived in this section are in the conservation form. The coefficient matrix for a cylinder has exactly the same mathematical properties as for the slab geometry (see Section 11.4), so it has a positive inverse matrix.

11.6 NONLINEAR ORDINARY DIFFERENTIAL EQUATIONS

An ordinary differential equation is nonlinear if the unknown appears in a nonlinear form, or if its coefficients depend on the solution. For example, the heat-conduction equation for a cooling fin becomes nonlinear if radiation heat transfer from the surface is involved. The diffusion equation for a chemical species is nonlinear if it has a removal term that is dependent on the density of the species. In a nuclear reactor, properties of the materials are significantly affected by the neutron population when the power level is high, so the governing equation for the neutron flux becomes nonlinear.

The solution of nonlinear boundary-value problems requires iterative applications of a solution method for linear boundary-value problems. Two general methods will be discussed, considering a nonlinear diffusion equation given by

$$-\phi'' + 0.01\phi^2 = \exp(-x), \quad 0 < x < H \tag{11.6.1}$$

where
$$\phi(0) = \phi(H) = 0$$

We note here some peculiar aspects of nonlinear boundary-value problems. First, unlike a linear boundary-value problem, existence of the solution may be hard to prove. Second, a nonlinear boundary-value problem can have more than one solution. Indeed, different solutions may be obtained for different initial guesses for an iterative algorithm. Therefore, when a numerical solution is obtained, one must examine whether that solution is physically meaningful.

11.6.1 Successive Substitution

Equation (11.6.1) is now rewritten as

$$-\phi'' + \alpha(x)\phi(x) = \exp(-x) \qquad (11.6.2)$$

where

$$\alpha(x) = 0.01\phi(x)$$

The method explained here is an extension of the successive substitution method described in Chapter 3, "Linear Algebra," and proceeds as follows:

(a) Set $\alpha(x)$ to an estimate, for example $\alpha(x) = 0.01$.

(b) Solve Eq.(11.6.2) numerically as a linear boundary-value problem (since α is fixed, the equation is linear).

(c) Revise $\alpha(x) = 0.01\phi(x)$ with the updated value of $\phi(x)$ from (b).

(d) Repeat (b) and (c) until $\phi(x)$ in two consecutive solutions agree within a prescribed tolerance.[1]

11.6.2 Newton Iteration

If we denote an estimate for $\phi(x)$ by $\psi(x)$, the exact solution may be expressed as

$$\phi(x) = \psi(x) + \delta\psi(x) \qquad (11.6.3)$$

where $\delta\psi(x)$ is a correction for the estimate. Introducing Eq.(11.6.3) into Eq.(11.6.1) gives

$$-\delta\psi'' + (0.01)[2\psi\delta\psi + (\delta\psi)^2] = \psi'' - 0.01\psi^2 + \exp(-x) \qquad (11.6.4)$$

---

[1] The iterative solution of the nonlinear equation may be slow due to oscillation of the solution from one pattern to another in two consecutive iteration cycles. Such oscillation can be suppressed by under-relaxation, $\alpha(x) = 0.01(\theta\phi^{(t-1)}(x) + (1-\theta)\phi^{(t-2)}(x))$ for the present case as an example, where θ is an under-relaxation parameter satisfying $0 < \theta < 1$, and t is the iteration number.

Section 11.6 Nonlinear Ordinary Differential Equations

Ignoring the second-order term $(\delta\psi)^2$ yields

$$-\delta\psi'' + 0.02\psi\delta\psi = \psi'' - 0.01\psi^2 + \exp(-x) \qquad (11.6.5)$$

which may be solved as a linear boundary-value problem. An approximate solution for Eq.(11.6.1) is then obtained by $\psi(x) + \delta\psi(x)$. The solution may be further improved by repeating the procedure, using the most updated result as a new estimate. This procedure is an extension of the Newton iteration described in Chapter 6, "Numerical Differentiation."

Example 11.3

Derive linearized difference equations based on the Newton iteration for Eq.(11.6.1) in the domain $0 < x < 2$ with the boundary conditions $\phi(0) = \phi(10) = 0$ using 10 grid intervals. Solve the equations.

Solution

The linearized form of Eq.(11.1.1) is given by Eq.(11.6.5). With the grid spacing $h = 2/10 = 0.2$, the difference equation for Eq.(11.5.5) is written as

$$\delta\psi_{i-1} + 2\delta\psi_i - \delta\psi_{i+1} + 0.02h^2\psi_i\delta\psi_i$$
$$= \psi_{i-1} - 2\psi_i + \psi_{i+1} - 0.01h^2\psi_i^2 + h^2\exp(-ih) \qquad (11.6.6)$$
$$i = 1, 2, ...9$$

where $i = 0$ for $x = 0$, and the equation has been multiplied by h^2. The foregoing equation may be written in the form of Eq.(11.3.1) if we define

$$A_i = -1$$
$$B_i = 2 + 0.02h^2\psi_i$$
$$C_i = -1$$
$$D_i = \psi_{i-1} - 2\psi_i + \psi_{i+1} - 0.01h^2\psi_i^2 + h^2\exp(-ih)$$

We start the Newton iteration by setting an estimate as $\psi_i = 0$ for all the grid points. Then, the difference equations for $i=1, 2, 3, ..9$ are solved by the tridiagonal solution. The iterative solution for the first five grid points is listed next.

Iteration number	Grid Points				
	i=1	i=2	i=3	i=4	i=5
1	0.0850	0.1406	0.1720	0.1837	0.1792
2	0.0935	0.1546	0.1891	0.2019	0.1970
3	0.0943	0.1560	0.1908	0.2038	0.1988
4	0.0944	0.1561	0.1910	0.2040	0.1990

Example 11.4

The Blasius boundary layer equation is given by

$$f''' + 0.5 f f'' = 0 \tag{A}$$

with boundary condtions,

$$f(0) = 0, \quad f'(0) = 0, \quad f'(\infty) = 1$$

The third boundary condition may be replaced by $f'(10) = 1$. Derive the finite difference approximation and solve as a boundary value problem.

Solution

Equation (A) may be reduced to a second-order boundary-value problem by defining

$$g(\eta) = f'(\eta) \tag{B}$$

or equivalently

$$f(\eta) = \int_0^\eta g(\tau) d\tau \tag{C}$$

which satisfies the boundary condition, $f(0) = 0$. By introducing Eq.(B) into Eq.(A), we obtain

$$g'' + 0.5 f g' = 0 \tag{D}$$

with boundary condtions,

$$g(0) = 0, \quad g(10) = 1$$

Equation (D) is a nonlinear second-order boundary-value problem, and can be solved by successive substitution as follows. The difference approximation for Eq.(D) may be written as

$$\frac{g_{i-1} - 2g_i + g_{i+1}}{(\Delta\eta)^2} + 0.5 f_i \frac{g_{i+1} - g_{i-1}}{2\Delta\eta} = 0 \qquad (E)$$

where

$$f_i = \Delta\eta \sum_{i=1}^{i} \frac{g_{k-1} + g_k}{2} \qquad (F)$$

In Eq.(F) the trapezoidal rule is applied with $g_0 = 0$. Equation (E) is solved iteratively as follows:

(a) Assume an initial distribution of g_i, and calculate f_i by Eq.(F).

(b) Solve Eq.(E) by the tridiagonal scheme.

(c) Update f_i by introducing g_i just calculated into Eq.(F).

(d) Repeat (b) and (c) until the solution converges.

The results computed by List 11.2 are shown in Figure 11.7.

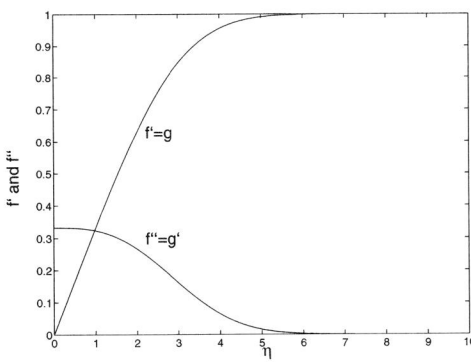

Figure 11.7 Solution of Blasius boundary layer equation.

List 11.2
```
blasius.m
clear,clf
ni=200;
h=10/ni; h2inv = 1/h^2; hinv=1/h;
eta=h*(1:ni); f=ones(1,ni);
for k=1:9
  for i=1:ni
    a(i) = h2inv - 0.25*f(i)*hinv;
    b(i) = -2*h2inv;
    c(i) = h2inv + 0.25*f(i)*hinv;
    s(i)=0;
```

```
        end
        s(ni)=-c(ni);
        g=tri_diag(a,b,c,s,ni);
        f(1)=0.5*g(1)*h;
        for i=2:ni
          f(i)=0.5*(g(i) + g(i-1))*h+f(i-1);
        end
    end
    if k==1 hold on, end
    axis([0,10,0,2])
    fdd0 = (-g(2) + 4*g(1))/2/h
    fdd(1)= (g(2)-0)/h/2;
    for i=2:ni-1
    fdd(i)=(g(i+1)-g(i-1))/h/2;
    end
    fdd(ni) = (3*g(ni) - 4*g(ni-1) + g(ni-2))/h/2;
    plot([0,eta],[0,g],[0,eta],[fdd0,fdd])
    [[0,eta(20:20:ni)]', [0,g(20:20:ni)]', [fdd0,fdd(20:20:ni)]']
    text(2.2, 0.63, 'f'=g', 'Fontsize', [18])
    h=text(2.2, 0.3, 'f''=g'', 'Fontsize', [18])
    text(5, -0.05, 'h', 'FontName', 'Symbol','Fontsize',[18])
    text(-1.0,0.4, 'f' and f''', 'Fontsize',[18],'Rotation',[90])
```

PROBLEMS

(11.1) Derive difference equations for $i=1$ and $i=10$ in Example 11.1 assuming that the boundary conditions are changed to $y'(1) = y(1)$ and $y'(10) = 0$.

(11.2) Derive difference equations for

$$-(p(x)\phi'(x))' + q(x)\phi(x) = S(x), \quad 0 < x < H$$

$$\phi'(0) = \phi(H) = 0$$

The geometry, grid, and constants are shown in Figure 11.8. Grid spacings are $h = H/4$ for all the intervals.

(11.3) Repeat the previous problem assuming that the grid spacing for the first two intervals is h_1 and for the last two intervals is h_2.

(11.4) The differential equation for a flexible cable, 50m long, fixed at two ends, is given by

$$y''(x) = -w(x)/T, \quad y(0) = y(50) = 0$$

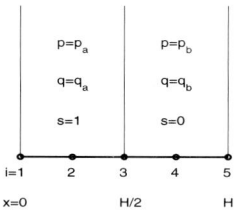

Figure 11.8 Grid and constants.

where x is in meters, $y(x)$ is the displacement of the wire measured from the level of the endpoints of the wire (positive downward), T is the horizontal component of tension (5000kg), and $w(x)$ is the load distribution given by

$$w(x) = 20(1 + \exp(x/25)) \text{ kg/m}$$

Determine the shape of the cable. (Use 10 grid intervals.)

(11.5) Consider a cooling fin with a variable cross-sectional area and a variable perimeter. Assuming that the temperature across any cross-section, perpendicular to the axis is uniform, the temperature in the axial direction is the solution of the equation

$$-(kA(x)T'(x))' + P(x)h_cT(x) = P(x)h_cT_\infty$$

where k is the thermal conductivity, $P(x)$ is the perimeter, $A(x)$ is the cross-sectional area, and T_∞ is the temperature of the surroundings. The boundary conditions are given by

$$T(0) = 100°C$$

$$-kT'(H) = h_c(T(H) - T_\infty)$$

where H is the length of the fin, and h_c is the convection heat-transfer coefficient. Solve the problem with the following constants:

$$h_c = 30 \text{w/m}^2\text{K}, \quad H = 0.1 \text{ m}, \quad k = 100 \text{ w/mK}, \quad T_\infty = 20°C$$
$$A(x) = (0.005)(0.05 - 0.25x) \text{ m}^2$$
$$P(x) = A(x)/0.005 + 0.01 \text{ m}$$

(Use 10 grid intervals.)

(11.6) The boundary condition in the form of Eq.(11.2.10) becomes numerically equivalent to $\phi(0) = 0$ if g_L is set to 0 and f_L is set to a very large value such as 10^{10}. What values for g_L and f_L make Eq.(11.2.10) equivalent to $\phi(0) = 2$?

(11.7) Consider a cylindrical unit cell in a light water nuclear reactor consisting of a fuel pin and moderator, as shown in Figure 11.9.

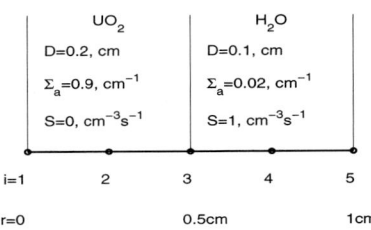

Figure 11.9 Unit cell.

The thermal neutron flux in the cell satisfies the neutron diffusion equation given by

$$-\frac{1}{r}\frac{d}{dr}Dr\frac{d}{dr}\phi(r) + \Sigma_a\phi(r) = S(r)$$

where D is the diffusion coefficient, Σ_a is the absorption cross-section and S is the neutron source. The constants for UO_2 and H_2O are shown in the figure. The boundary conditions are

$$\phi'(0) = \phi'(1) = 0$$

(a) Using five grid points for the whole domain with a constant interval of 0.25 cm, derive difference equations for each grid point.

(b) Solve the difference equations derived in (a) by the tridiagonal solution.

(11.8) For a slab material of thickness 0.2 cm, the left side is perfectly insulated, but the right surface temperature is fixed at 0°C. The slab has a distributed heat source. The temperature equation is given by $-T''(x) = q(x)/k$. Develop a program to compute the temperature distribution using 10 grid intervals. Assuming the thermal conductivity is $k = 30$ W/m²K, run the program for the following two heat source distributions:

(a) $q(x) = 200$ kW/m³

(b) $q(x) = 100\exp(-10x)$ kW/m³

Compare the results with the following analytical solutions:

(a) $T(x) = (10/3)(0.04 - x^2)$

(b) $T(x) = 0.033(e^{-2} + 2 - 10x - e^{-10x})$

(11.9) The diffusion equation for a cylindrical geometry is given by

$$-\frac{1}{r}(p(r)r\phi'(r))' + q(r)\phi(r) = S(r)$$

Considering the three grid points as shown in Figure 11.10, difference equations may be derived by integrating the equation from the midpoint between $i-1$ and i to the midpoint between i and $i+1$. Assuming the coefficients are constants as illustrated in the figure and grid spacings are not uniform, derive the difference equations by integrating in the volume between a and b.

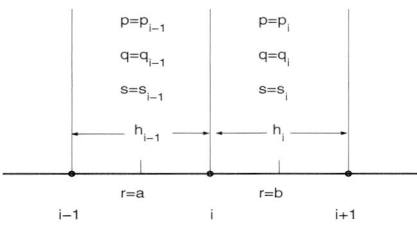

Figure 11.10 Cylindrical geometry.

(11.10) The equation for the displacement of a concentric circular membrane loaded with a constant pressure P (see Figure 11.11) is given by

$$y''(r) + \frac{1}{r}y'(r) = -P/T, \quad 0.2\text{m} \le r \le 0.5\text{m}$$

where r is the radial coordinate, y is the displacement of the membrane (positive downward), T is the tension (400kg/m), and the pressure is given as $P = 800$ kg/m^2. The boundary conditions are $y(0.2) = y(0.5) = 0$. Determine the displacement of the membrane, $y(r)$.

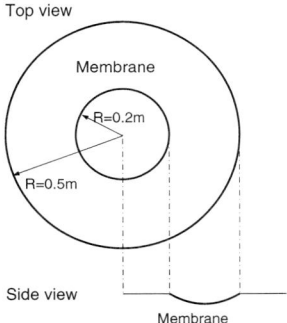

Figure 11.11 A membrane under pressure.

(11.11) The spherical body of a material of radius 0.05m is heated with a heat source distributed by

$$S(r) = 300 \exp[20(r - 0.05)]$$

where r is the radius in meters, and the unit of S is W/m^3. The surface of the sphere is exposed to air. Heat escapes to the surrounding air by convection with the heat-transfer coefficient, $h_c = 20$W/m^{2}K. At steady state, the temperature distribution is the solution of the equation,

$$-\frac{1}{r^2}\frac{d}{dr}r^2 k\frac{d}{dr}T(r) = S(r)$$

The boundary conditions are

$$T'(0) = 0$$
$$kT' = h_c(T_\infty - T(R)), \quad T_\infty = 20°\text{C}$$

(a) Write the difference equations for the temperature using four equally spaced grid intervals. (b) Solve the difference equations by the tridiagonal solution.

(11.12) One end of a rectangular cooling fin of length $H = 0.1$ m is attached to a heat source of 200°C. The fin transfers heat by both radiation and convection to the environment of 20°C. Assuming the fin and environment are both black bodies, the temperature of the fin satisfies the nonlinear diffusion equation

$$-AkT''(x) + Ph_c(T(x) - T_\infty) + P\sigma(T^4(x) - T_\infty^4) = 0$$

where

$k = 120$ W/mK (thermal conductivity)

$A = 1.5x10^{-4}$ m^2 (cross-sectional area of the fin)

$P = 0.106$ m (perimeter of the fin)

$h_c = 100$ W/m^{2}K (convection heat-transfer coefficient)

$\sigma = 5.67x10^{-8}$ W/m^{2}K^4 (Stefan-Boltzmann constant)

$T_\infty = 293$ K (temperature of the environment)

The boundary conditions are given by

$$T(0) = 500 + 273 \text{ K}$$
$$T'(H) = 0$$

where the right end of the fin is assumed to be perfectly insulated.

(a) Derive the difference equation for the above differential equation using 10 equally spaced grid intervals.

(b) Solve the difference equation by means of successive substitution.

(c) Repeat (b) using Newton iteration.

(11.13) Solve the following equation by Newton iteration:

$$-\phi''(x) + [2 + \sin(\phi(x))]\phi(x) = 2, \quad \phi(0) = \phi(2) = 0$$

Use 20 mesh intervals.

(11.14) In a chemical reactor, the density of a material is governed by

$$-\phi''(x) + 0.1\phi'(x) = \exp(1 + 0.05\phi), \quad 0 < x < 2$$

Boundary conditions are $\phi(0) = 0$ and $\phi'(2) = 0$. With 10 equally spaced grid intervals, solve the equation by (a) successive substitution, and (b) Newton iteration.

Appendix A

COLORS

A color may be defined by mixing three basic colors, namely, red, green, and blue, and is expressed by a triplet (r, g, b), where r, g, and b represent the relative intensities of the basic colors, which are red, green, and blue, respectively. The highest value is 1 and the lowest is 0 for each basic color. Ten examples of color definitions by triplets are given here.

	r	g	b
white	1	1	1
red	1	0	0
yellow	1	1	0
green	0	1	0
cyan	0	1	1
gray	0.5	0.5	0.5
dark red	0.5	0	0
blue	0	0	1
aquamarine	0.5	1	0.83
black	0	0	0

color map: The color map is an $n \times 3$ matrix. Each row is a triplet of the three colors. The default value of n in MATLAB is 64. The first row corresponds to the minimum value of the color axis and the last row to the maximum. By defining a different intensity distribution of the three basic colors, different color maps are developed. Some predetermined color maps in MATLAB are

   `hsv, cool, hot, jet, gray, flag`

where `hsv` stands for the *hue saturation value* color set.

The color map for the `hsv` color is illustrated in Table A.1. A color map may be displayed in graphic form by `rgbplot`. The intensities of the three colors in the `hsv` color map are plotted in Figure A.1. The actual colors of several color maps are illustrated in color plates similar to Figure A.2. To

439

assign a color map to a figure, use `colormap`; for example, `colormap jet` or `colormap(jet)` sets the current color map to jet.

color axis: Color axis is a one-dimensional coordinate with its minimum and maximum. The minimum and maximum can be prescribed by `caxis([cmin, cmax])`. The minimum value of the color axis points to the first row (or the first index) in the color map and the maximum value of the color axis points to the last row (or the last index). Unless `cmin` and `cmax` are specified by `caxis`, the lowest color index is automatically set to the minimum value of the color data in `mesh`, `surface`, and similar commands.

Table A.1 The RGB Color Map

Color Index	Intensities		
	Red	Green	Blue
1	1.0000	0	0
2	1.0000	0.0938	0
3	1.0000	0.1875	0
4	1.0000	0.2812	0
5	1.0000	0.3750	0
6	1.0000	0.4688	0
7	1.0000	0.5625	0
8	1.0000	0.6562	0
9	1.0000	0.7500	0
10	1.0000	0.8438	0
11	1.0000	0.9375	0
12	0.9688	1.0000	0
13	0.8750	1.0000	0
14	0.7812	1.0000	0
15	0.6875	1.0000	0
16	0.5938	1.0000	0
17	0.5000	1.0000	0
18	0.4062	1.0000	0
19	0.3125	1.0000	0
20	0.2188	1.0000	0
21	0.1250	1.0000	0
22	0.0312	1.0000	0
23	0	1.0000	0.0625
24	0	1.0000	0.1562
25	0	1.0000	0.2500
26	0	1.0000	0.3438
27	0	1.0000	0.4375
.	.	.	.

```
     .          .             .        .
     .          .             .        .
    59        1.0000          0      0.5625
    60        1.0000          0      0.4688
    61        1.0000          0      0.3750
    62        1.0000          0      0.2812
    63        1.0000          0      0.1875
    64        1.0000          0      0.0938
    ----------------------------------------
```

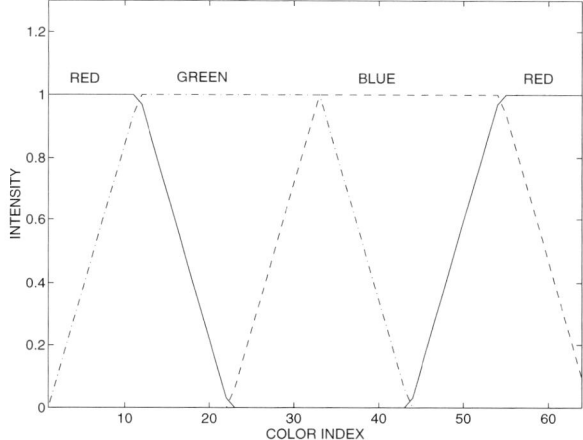

Figure A.1 RGB plot of an hsv color map.

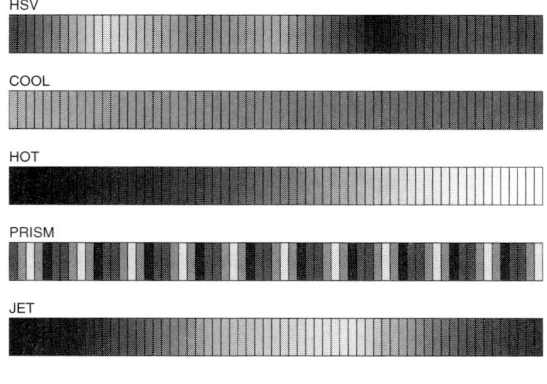

Figure A.2 Color bars.

multiple color maps: Only one color map can be assigned to a figure. Often, however, it becomes desirable to use multiple color maps to finish a figure. This conflicting situation can be resolved by developing a composite color map. For example, if cool, hot, and jet are all necessary in a single figure, make the composite color map by combining them into a single color map, such as

```
ccm=[ cool(64); hot(64); jet(64)]
```

The color map ccm becomes a matrix of 192×3, and the top 64 rows correspond to cool, the next 64 rows to hot, and the last 64 to jet.

One word of caution is *not* to omit 64 in the definition of ccm for the following reason: once the length of the color map other than 64 is used, the default length of the color map is also changed to that value. In the present case, the default length of color maps becomes $64 \times 3 = 192$ in the next call, so that even the length of hsv or jet becomes 192, unless their lengths are specified. If ccm is computed without 64 for the second time, its length becomes 192×3. In a few times of repeat, the computer memory and disk space are exhausted.

List A.1 plots the color bars in Figure A.1 and is an example of using a composite color map.

List A.1
```
% col_bar.m
clear,clf
C=[hsv(64);cool(64);hot(64);prism(64);jet(64)];
colormap(C);   hold on
for M=1:5
  for i=1:64;
    for j=1:2
      x(i,j)=(i-1)/63;
      y(i,j)=(j+8)*1.1 - (M-1)*2.2;
      z(i,j)=i+64*(M-1);
      if i==1 z(i,j)=z(i,j)+0.0001;end
      if i==64 z(i,j)=z(i,j)-0.0001;end
    end
  end
  surface(x,y,z, z)
end
text(0, 2.4+0.1,'JET')
text(0, 4.6+0.1,'PRISM')
text(0, 6.8+0.1,'HOT')
text(0, 9.0+0.1,'COOL')
text(0,11.2+0.1,'HSV')
axis([0,1,0,12]) ; axis('off')
text(0.3,0,' <-----   Color Index   -----> ')
text(1,0,'64')
text(0,0,'1')
```

Appendix B

DRAWING THREE-DIMENSIONAL OBJECTS

Developing a complicated three-dimensional object as a single surface or mesh is usually very difficult or inefficient. Instead, the object may be assembled using parts that can easily be developed as a single surface or mesh. The coordinate set of x, y, and z for a part may be developed using a local coordinate system. In order to locate the parts at appropriate positions, rotation, translation, and scaling of the coordinates of each part are necessary. The objectives of this appendix are first, to introduce basic methods for moving objects and second, to illustrate a few objects developed.

MOVING OBJECTS IN 3-D SPACE

Transformation of origin: Suppose a part of the whole object is defined in a local coordinate system (x, y, z). If the origin of the local system is translated by (x_a, y_a, z_a), the new coordinates $(\overline{x}, \overline{y}, \overline{z})$ become

$$\begin{aligned} \overline{x} &= x + x_a \\ \overline{y} &= y + y_a \\ \overline{z} &= z + z_a \end{aligned} \tag{B.1}$$

Change of scale: If the scale in the local system is changed by a scale factor α, the new coordinates in the local system become

$$\begin{aligned} \overline{x} &= \alpha x \\ \overline{y} &= \alpha y \\ \overline{z} &= \alpha z \end{aligned} \tag{B.2}$$

Rotation about the x-axis: If the local system is rotated counterclockwise θ degrees about the x-axis, the new coordinates become

$$\begin{aligned} \overline{x} &= x \\ \overline{y} &= \cos(\theta)y - \sin(\theta)z \\ \overline{z} &= \sin(\theta)y + \cos(\theta)z \end{aligned} \tag{B.3}$$

Rotation about the y-axis: If the local system is rotated counterclockwise θ degrees about the y-axis, the new coordinates become

$$\begin{aligned} \overline{x} &= \sin(\theta)z + \cos(\theta)x \\ \overline{y} &= y \\ \overline{z} &= \cos(\theta)z - \sin(\theta)x \end{aligned} \tag{B.4}$$

Rotation about the z-axis: If the local system is rotated counterclockwise θ degrees about the z-axis, the new coordinates become

$$\begin{aligned} \overline{x} &= \cos(\theta)x - \sin(\theta)y \\ \overline{y} &= \sin(\theta)x + \cos(\theta)y \\ \overline{z} &= z \end{aligned} \tag{B.5}$$

Three functions to rotate a system are

List B.1
rotx_.m
```
function [xd,yd,zd]=rotx_(x,y,z,th)
cosf=cos(th*pi/180);sinf=sin(th*pi/180);
xd =x;
yd =   cosf.*y - sinf.*z;
zd =   sinf.*y + cosf.*z;
```

roty_.m
```
function [xd,yd,zd]=roty_(x,y,z,th)
cosf=cos(th*pi/180);sinf=sin(th*pi/180);
yd =y;
xd =   cosf.*x + sinf.*z;
zd = - sinf.*x + cosf.*z;
```

rotz_.m
```
function [xd,yd,zd]=rotz_(x,y,z,th)
cosf=cos(th*pi/180);sinf=sin(th*pi/180);
xd =   cosf *x - sinf *y;
yd =   sinf *x + cosf *y;
zd =z;
```

Example B.1 Fan Rotor

Figure B.1 illustrates a fan rotor that consists of one cylindrical shaft and six blades. In List B.2, a mesh for a blade is developed by an array of section profiles. The cross-sectional profile of the blades is first developed in b_design.m. The mesh for a blade is expressed by a triplet of x, y, and z.

The rotor can then be constructed by copying the blade to five other locations after rotations. The shaft is developed as a hollow cylinder.

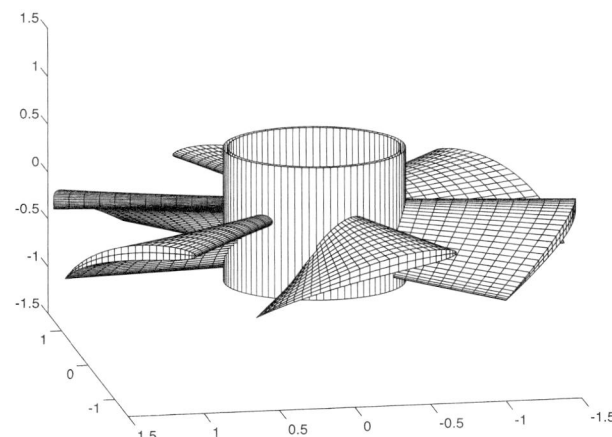

Figure B.1 Fan rotor.

List B.2
fan_rot.m

```
% Plots a fan rotor (Fig.B.1)
clear,clf    %ref: t_blade.m
colormap jet
r=0.601:0.1:2;
imax=length(r);
dth=pi/16;
th=-2*dth:dth:2*dth;
[th,zb]=b_design;
jmax=length(th);
%          minz=-0.5, maxz=0.1
%          minth=-0.4, maxth=0.4
for i=1:imax
for j=1:jmax
x(i,j)=r(i)*cos(th(j));
y(i,j)=r(i)*sin(th(j));
z(i,j)=zb(j);
end
end
zc=z;
```

```
        for i=imax-1:imax
        for j=1:jmax
        x(i,j)=r(imax-2)*cos(th(j));
        y(i,j)=r(imax-2)*sin(th(j));
        if i== imax, z(i,j)=(zb(j)+zb(jmax+1-j))*0.5;, end
        zc(i,j)=1;
        end
        end
        hold on
        for k=1:6
        angl=60*k
        [xb,yb,zb] = rotz_(x,y,z,angl);
        mesh(xb,yb,zb, zc)
        end
        axis([-1.5,1.5,-1.5,1.5,-1.5,1.5])
        [xc,yc,zc]=cylinder(0.595,80);
        xc(2,:)=xc(1,:);
        yc(2,:)=yc(1,:);
        zc(1,:)=-ones(size(xc(1,:)))*0.7;
        zc(2,:)=ones(size(xc(1,:)))*0.7;
        colr=0.7*ones(size(zc));
        mesh(xc,yc,zc, colr*0.6)
        mesh(xc*0.95,yc*0.95,zc, colr*0.99)
        view([-100,20])
```

b_design.m

```
        function [thb,zb]=b_design
        % Analytical airfoil section design
        minz=-0.5;
        maxz=0.1;
        minth=-0.4;
        maxth=0.4;
        r=0.4;
        dth=pi/32;
        th=0:dth:2*pi;
        x=r*cos(th);
        y=r*sin(th).* (x+0.5).*(5-x)/15  ...
               - (x+0.4).*(x-0.4)+ (0.6/0.8)*(x)-0.2 ;
        thb=x;
        zb=y;
```

Example B.2   Spiral Pipe

A pipe is constructed by connecting an array of circles (see Figure B.2). Because all circles are identical except for locations and orientations, they can be drawn by translating and rotating one reference circle drawn at the origin on the x-y plain. The reference unit circle on the x-y plane is expressed by points on the circle. The circle is rotated first about the x-axis and then about the z-axis. The pipe is drawn by List B.3.

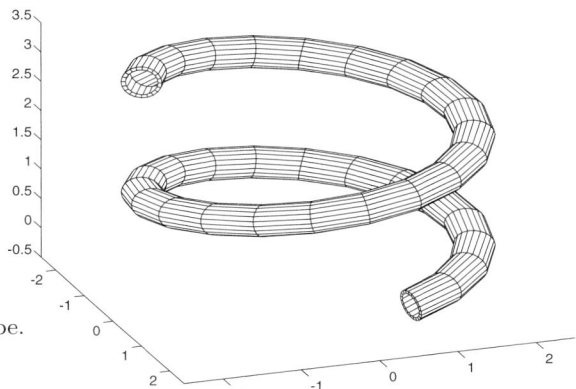

Figure B.2 Spiral pipe.

List B.3
pipe_.m

```
clear,clf,hold off
%-------Construction of basic pipe cross-section (circle)
dth=pi/10;
th=0:dth:2*pi;
x=0.25*cos(th);y=0.25*sin(th);z=0.25*zeros(size(x));
%-------Spiral shape of axis of pipe
ths=0:dth:pi*3.5;
xs=2*cos(ths);ys=2*sin(ths);zs=zeros(size(xs))+ 0.3*ths ;
m=length(xs) ;
%-------Construction of pipe section to axial direction
for i=2:m
  xn=xs(i)-xs(i-1) ;
  yn=ys(i)-ys(i-1) ;
  zn=zs(i)-zs(i-1) ;
  rn=sqrt(xn^2+yn^2+zn^2);
  el=acos(zn/rn)*180/pi;
  az=0;
  rxy=sqrt(xn^2+yn^2);
  if xn==0, xn=1e-10;end
  az=atan2(yn,xn)*180/pi;
  [xd,yd,zd]=rotx_(x ,y ,z ,-el);
  b=-(az+90);
  [xp(i,:),yp(i,:),zp(i,:)]=rotz_(xd,yd,zd,b);
  xp(i,:)=xp(i,:)+xs(i);
  yp(i,:)=yp(i,:)+ys(i);
  zp(i,:)=zp(i,:)+zs(i);
```

```
end
%------------- Pipe structure is now in xpp,ypp,zpp
xav=sum(xp(2,:))/length(xp(2,:));
yav=sum(yp(2,:))/length(yp(2,:));
zav=sum(zp(2,:))/length(zp(2,:));
xp(1,:)=xav*0.2+ xp(2,:)*0.8;
yp(1,:)=yav*0.2+ yp(2,:)*0.8;
zp(1,:)=zav*0.2+ zp(2,:)*0.8;
j=m-1;
xav=sum(xp(j,:))/length(xp(j,:));
yav=sum(yp(j,:))/length(yp(j,:));
zav=sum(zp(j,:))/length(zp(j,:));
xp(m,:)=xav*0.2+ xp(j,:)*0.8;
yp(m,:)=yav*0.2+ yp(j,:)*0.8;
zp(m,:)=zav*0.2+ zp(j,:)*0.8;

xpp=xp;
ypp=yp;
zpp=zp;
%------------------------------------
colormap hsv
mesh(xpp,ypp,zpp)
view([70,30])
axis([-2.5 ,2.5 ,-2.5 ,2.5 ,-.5,3.5])
title('Plot by "mesh" with "colormap hsv" ')
```

Example B.3 Airplane

An airplane frame (see Figure B.3) is developed by putting five parts together. The fuselage is first developed by an array of circles. One side of the main wing is developed by function wing_2d, which uses NACA0012 airfoil (see Problem 7.5). The ladder and stabilizer are essentially copies of the main wing after scaling, rotation, and translation. See List B.4.

List B.4
plane_.m
```
clear, clf    % Next part develops fuselage
dth=pi/16; fuselen=6;  thf=pi:-dth:pi/2;
xa = 0:0.5:fuselen
xt=fuselen+0.25:0.25:fuselen+2;
dxt = 1.4/(length(xt)-0) ;
yt = -1+dxt:dxt:0.4;
length(yt)
xft=[cos(thf),xa, xt]
yft=[sin(thf)- 0.3*sin(2*thf).^4, ones(size(xa)),...
                              ones(size(yt))];
xfb=[cos(thf),xa,xt]
```

Commuter Airplane

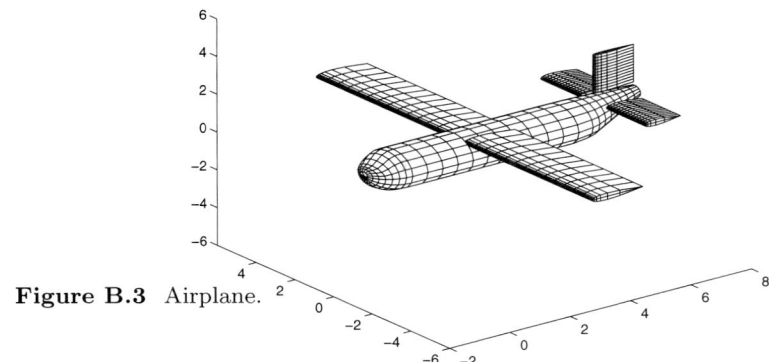

Figure B.3 Airplane.

```
yfb=[-sin(thf),-ones(size(xa)),yt ];
k=length([thf, xa])
yfb(k)=( yfb(k-1)+yfb(k+1))/2
xc =(xfb+xft)/2;
yc = (yfb+yft)/2;
L=length(xc);
for i=1:L
   if xc(i)<0   yc(i)=0; end
end

a=0.5; b=0.5;
dth=pi/8;  th=0:dth:2*pi; jmax=length(th);
xr=cos(th); yr=sin(th);
L=length(xc);
for i=1:L
  xr=cos(th);
  yr=sin(th);
  a = (yft(i)-yc(i))/(-yfb(i) + yc(i));
  b = (-yfb(i)     +yc(i));
  for j=1:jmax
      y(i,j)=yr(j)*b+yc(i);
      if th(j)<pi    y(i,j)=yr(j)*b*a + yc(i); end
    x(i,j)=xr(j)*b;
    z(i,j)=xc(i);
  end
end
mesh(z, x,y)
axis([-2 8 -6 6 -6 6])
hold on
[xw,yw,zw] = wing_2d         % Airfoil section profile
F = 1.7;
```

```
xw=F*xw; yw=F*yw; zw=F*zw;
[x1,y1,z1] = rotz_(xw,yw,zw,90);
[x2,y2,z2] = rotx_(xw,yw,zw,180);
[x2,y2,z2] = rotz_(x2,y2,z2,270);
mesh(x1+2,y1-0.5,z1+ 0.7);
mesh(x2+2,y2+0.5,z2+ 0.7);
mesh(0.8*x1+6.6,0.5*z1-0,-0.3*y1+1.2)
pause
mesh(0.7*x1+6.6,0.3*y1-0.7,0.9*z1+ 0.7);
mesh(0.7*x2+6.6,0.3*y2+0.7,0.9*z2+ 0.7);
caxis([-3,1])
axis([-2 8 -6 6 -6 6])
title('Commuter Airplane')
caxis([-2, 2])
colormap(hsv)
```

wing_2d.m
```
function [zw,xw,yw] = naca0012
x=0:0.1:1;
n=length(x);
for k=1:30
  for i=2:n-1
    x(i)=0.5*x(i-1)+0.4*x(i+1);
  end
end
for i=2:n
  x(n+i-1)=x(n-i+1);
end
y=0.2969*sqrt(x) - 0.126*x - 0.3516*x.^2 + ...
    0.2843 * x.^3 - 0.1015*x.^4;
for i=n+1:length(y)
  y(i)=-y(i);
end
jmax=15
for j=1:jmax
  for i=1:2*n-1
    xw(i,j)=x(i);
    yw(i,j)=y(i);
    zw(i,j)=0.3*(j-1);
  end
end
yw(:,jmax)=zeros(size(yw(:,jmax)));
zw(:,jmax)=zw(:,jmax-1);
```

Example B.4 A Lobe of Oscillating Liquid Jet

A three-dimensional view of an oscillating liquid jet lobe is developed and displayed using the surfl command. The script is shown in List B.5 and the view is plotted in Figure B.4.

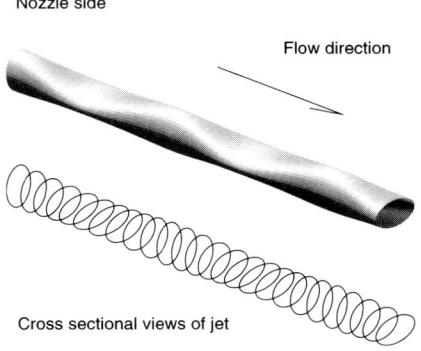

Figure B.4 A lobe of oscillating liquid jet.

List B.5
lobe_.m

```
% Plots a lobe of liquid jet.
clear, clf
hold on
dth=2*pi/40;
th=0:dth:2*pi;
r = ones(size(th));
colormap gray
for n=1:51
   b=n-1;
   x(n,:)=cos(th)*(1-0.25*cos(b*0.3));
   y(n,:)=sin(th)*(1+0.25*cos(b*0.3));
   z(n,:)=n*0.3*ones(size(th));
   m=n+9;
   if floor(m/2)*2 == m
      plot3(z(n,:), x(n,:), y(n, :)-5)
   end
end
surfl(z,x,y+2, [-10, 60])
axis([0 13 -5 15 -10 5])
shading flat
view([10 -10 10])
text(5.2, 8.4,3, ' Flow direction')
text(-5, 8, 'Nozzle side')
xd= [5, 10, 9];
yd=[5,5, 4.5];
zd=[ 3,3,3];
plot3(xd, yd, zd)
```

```
axis('off')
text(10,-15, -2,'Cross-sectional views of jet')
hold off
```

Appendix C

MOVIES

Showing time-dependent phenomena is a natural application of a movie. Movies can also be used to show complicated objects from different angles and with different zooming rates. The principle of a movie is simple; that is, to show a series of figures or images. This appendix shows how to make and play movies, with an illustration.

Making movies using MATLAB is simple and great fun. In essence, it consists of only three commands, getframe, moviein, and movie. Since a movie is a sequence of figures or images, you must think about how to prepare them.

MATLAB COMMANDS TO MAKE MOVIES

getframe: getframe captures a movie frame from the current axis of a figure. A frame is written in a column vector. It uses one of the following formats:

```
geframe
getframe(h)
```

With the first format, the entire current axis is captured. In the second format, h is the handle to the root, a figure, or axes. Therefore, getframe(h) gets a frame from object (or the window of the handle h).

moviein: M = moviein(n) initializes a matrix M to hold n frames ftom the current figure window. M = moviein(n, h) initializes matrix M to hold n frames from the window of the handle h.

movie: movie(M) plays the movie in matrix M once. It can also take one of the following formats:

```
movie(M,n)
movie(M,n,fps)
movie(h,M,n,fps)
movie(h,M,n,fps,loc)
```

Command `movie(M,n)` plays a movie n times. If n is negative, the movie is played n times, but the plays in the even times are backward. Parameter `fps` in the third format specifies the number of frames per second. Without `fps`, the default is 1 frame per second. Parameter `h` is the handle of the figure or axis where the movie is to be played. The parameter `loc` in the fourth format is a vector of length 4 that specifies the location of the movie relative to the left bottom corner of the current window. Only the first two elements are used; the first is the pixel number counted from the left and the second is the pixel number counted from the bottom.

Example C.1   Rotating Ball

The colored surface of a ball is rotated around its x-axis. List C.1 illustrates the script.

List C.1
movie_1.m

```
clear clf
h=figure(8)
fprintf('ADJUST SCREEN SIZE MANUALLY')
fprintf('(A 3 inch square is suggested.)\n')
fprintf('Hit RETURN after ajustment\n')
pause
M=moviein(10,gcf);
dth=pi/10; th=0:dth:pi; fi=0:dth:2*pi;
nk=length(th); nj = length(fi);
for j=1:nj
  for k=1:nk
    x(k,j) = sin(th(k)) *cos(fi(j));
    y(k,j) = sin(th(k))* sin(fi(j));
    z(k,j) =cos(th(k));
  end
end
[xd,yd,zd] = rotx_(x,y,z, 30);
axis([-1.5 1.5 -1.5 1.5 -1 1])
c=zd;
for k=1:11
  kk=36*k;
  [xd,yd,zd] = rotx_(x,y,z, kk);
```

```
        surf(xd,yd,zd,c)
        M(:,k) = getframe(gcf);
    end
    n=10; fps=10; save m_ball M n fps
```

In order to play the movie:

```
    gcf;cla;clf
    load m_ball
    loc=[30,30,0,0];
    movie(gcf,M,n,fps,loc)
```

MAKING MOVIES USING PICTURES IN GIF FORMAT

A more convenient way of making movie footage is to use a commercially available software[1] that takes figures in the GIF format. To make movie footage for a technical presentation, 50 to 200 frames of figures must be prepared in the GIF format. These figure files can then be moved to the animation software using a mouse. Whether the animation software automatically sets the figures sequentially in order of the alphabet or numbers in the file names depends on the design of the software. In the case of Gifanime, the pictures have to be transferred one by one sequentially, otherwise the order of the pictures is altered. In Lview, however, the pictures are automatically set in order of increasing numbers and the alphabet in the picture file names.

The following two recommendations should be considered when making a movie in this way. First, MATLAB cannot create picture files in the GIF format. So, a recommended approach is to use the JPEG format with the command `print -djpeg filename`, which generates the files as `filename.jpg`. The JPEG files can then be converted to GIF files by the Image Alchemy software described in the first footnote of Appendix D.

The second consideration is to use the same alphabetic characters in the file name for all the figures in a movie, which is followed by three-digit numbers including 0. For example, the figure number 1 should be numbered as 001. See Section 1.12 on how to automatically create file names with three-digit numbers.

---

[1] For example Microsoft Gifanime or LView Pro. For more information, see:
http://www.microsoft.com/frontpage/imagecomposer/imagecomposer5.htm
http://www.wugnet.com/shareware/98/week103/
http://www.mindworkshop.com/alchemy/gifcon.html
http://members.aol.com/royalef/toolbox.htm
http://www.webreference.com/dev/gifanim/

Appendix D

IMAGE PROCESSING

IMAGES IN MATLAB

Graphics created in MATLAB can be saved as an image file using the `print` command or the `export` menu on the figure window. Graphic files in a certain format can also be imported in MATLAB.

Graphic images in MATLAB are classified into three types: (a) RGB (truecolor), (b) indexed, and (c) intensity.

An RGB image file includes three sets of m-by-n arrays, or equivalently, an m-by-n-by-3 array, where m and n are the number of pixels in the horizontal and vertical directions, respectively. The first array is for the red color, the second the green, and the third the blue. A set of red, green, and blue comprise the color of a pixel. The variable to represent an image will be denoted by w in this appendix. Values in the arrays are 8-bit or 16-bit integers.[1] If the 8-bit integers are used, the numbers in the RGB array are integers ranging from 0 to 255. Similarly, if the 16-bit integers are used, the numbers are from 0 to 65535. The structure of RGB images in MATLAB closely matches to those of well known formats of images outside MATLAB. For example, 'jpeg' or 'jpg', 'tiff' or 'tif', and 'png' belongs to the RGB type.

An indexed image file is an m-by-n array of indices, and a colormap. An index k refers to the $k+1$th color in the colormap. The values in the array are 8-bit integers or 16-bit integers: 0 refers to the first color set of the colormap, 1 refers to the second, and so on. With the 8-bit integers, the length of the colormap is 256. Among the image formats used outside MATLAB, 'bmp'

---

[1] This is an exceptional feature, because in MATLAB all integers for computations are expressed in double precision (64 bits) without any distinction from the floating values. For graphics, however, MATLAB uses 8-bit and 16-bit integers to save the memory space.

is an example of the indexed type.

An intensity image file consists of an intensity matrix and a colormap. Usually a grayscale colormap is used. The intensity matrix is written in the 8-bit integers, 16-bits, or floating values.

imread:[2] The `imread` command reads an image file into MATLAB. Its synopsis is:

`[w,map,alpha]=imread('filename.fmt')`

where `w` is the array, `map` is the colormap if any, and `alpha` is the properties of the graphic object if any; `filename` is the name of the file, `fmt` is the format. The supported formats include: 'jpg' or 'jpeg', Joint Photographic Experts Group (JPEG); 'tif' or 'tiff', Tagged Image File Format (TIFF); 'gif', Graphics Interchange Format (GIF); 'bmp', Windows Bitmap (BMP); 'png', Portable Network Graphics; 'hdf', Hierarchical Data Format (HDF); 'pcx', Windows Paintbrush (PCX); 'xwd', X Window Dump (XWD); 'cur', Windows Cursor resources (CUR); 'ico', Windows Icon resources (ICO).
If there are no colormap and alpha associated, the foregoing command simply returns empty `map` and `alpha`. For the RGB type image files such as 'jpg', `map` and `alpha` on the left side of the command can be omitted.

imwrite: The `imwrite` command write an image file. For an indexed image, the synopsis is `imwrite(w, map, 'filename', 'fmt')`, while for a RGB image the synopsis is `imwrite(w, 'filename', 'fmt')`. This command supports 'tif', 'jpg', 'bmp', 'png', 'hdf', 'pxc', and 'xwd'.

image: `image` displays an image in the figure window. Its use for RGB images includes:

`image(w)`

---

[2] If you have an earlier versions of MATLAB, the only format to import and export image files from and to other software may be in the raw image format, unless Image Processing Toolbox is used.

The raw image files are produced by the Image Alchemy program developed by Handmade Software, Inc. This program allows one to convert to and from many different formats, including TARGA, ADEX, FOP, EPS, GIF, Gem VDI, ILBM, Vivid IMG, JPEG, HP RTL, PBM, Stork, PALette, AutoLogic, Macintosh PICT, MTV, SGI, QDV, PCX, PCL, HSI Raw, Erdas Image, Sun RASter, Grasp, TIFF, QRT Raw, Utah RLE, Windows BMP, and WPG.

Contact Handmade Software, Inc., 15951 Los Gatos Blvd., Suite 7, Los Gatos, CA 95032, Phone: (408) 358-1292, Fax: (408) 358-2694, Internet: hsi@netcom.COM.

```
image(x,y,w)
h=image(w)
```

The first format `image(w)` displays matrix `w` as an image. Each element of `w` specifies the color of a rectangular tile in the image. In order to display the image of a file, the file must be read in first by the `imread`, and then displayed. In order to read and display `'filename.jpg'` as an example, use `w=imread('filename.jpg')` and, then, `image(w)`.

The command `image(x,y,w)` is useful only if you wish to print out the tic marks of the coordinate values, where `x` and `y` are vectors and specify the labeling of x and y axes. However, only the first and last elements of `x` and `y` are used for the axis limits. Commands `image(w)` and `image(x,y,w)` produce exactly the same image except that the tic marks are altered by the latter.

The third format `h=image(w)` returns a handle of objects associated with `image`. In order to see a list of image object properties and their current values, execute `set(h)`.

For an indexed images, a colormap must be specified. For example

```
image(w); colormap(map)
```

To read and display a 'filename.bmp' that is an indexed type, use `[w, map]=imread('filename.bmp')` and, then, `image(w); colormap(map)`. Some parameters to specify additional properties of the image can be added after `w` in the arguments of the `image` command.

imfinfo: The `imfinfo` command collects information of an image file. Its synopsis is `imfinfo('filename.fmt')`.

pcolor: Stands for pseudocolor (checkerboard) plot. The formats are

```
pcolor(w)
pcolor(x,y,w)
h=pcolor(w)
```

Command `pcolor(w)` displays a pseudocolor or "checkerboard" plot of matrix `w`. The first row of `w` becomes the bottom of the figure (reverse of `image(w)` unless `hold on` is used). If `view(0,-90)` is applied, its vertical order becomes identical with that of `image`. The values of the elements of `w` specify the color in each cell of the plot. The `shading` and `caxis` commands are both applicable to `pcolor`. Indeed, `shading faceted` is its default mode, in which each cell has a constant color and the last row and column of `w` are not used. Furthermore, the tiles are separated by black lines. When the size of tiles becomes small, the black lines may dominate the color tiles and tend to darken the image. The black lines may be removed by using `shading flat`. If `shading interp` is used as another option, colors in a tile are changed continuously by bilinear interpolation, so the whole image becomes smooth. With the default mode of `caxis`, the smallest and largest elements of `w` are assigned the first and last colors given in the color table; the colors for all the remaining elements in `w` are determined by table-lookup within the remainder of the colormap. By the `caxis` command, however, the color range may be changed.

Here is an easy way for the reader to experiment with `image` and `pcolor`; that is, to plot an image of a random matrix by running the following script:

List D.1
rand_im.m

```
% Plots image of random matrix
m=input('m= ');
n=input('n= ');
W = ceil(64*rand(m,n));
    % Generates a m-by-n random matrix.
colormap(hot)
image(W);
```

Multiplication of the random matrix by 64 is necessary because the random numbers from `rand` are between 0 and 1. On the other hand, the color indices are between 1 and 64. Therefore, `ceil(64*ran(m,n))` is used to produce a matrix of random numbers from 1 to 64. Try a small number of tiles, such as 5-by-5 (m = n = 5) or 20-by-30 (m = 20, n = 30) first, then a larger one such as 200-by-300. After the display with the `hot` colormap is completed, the colormap can be changed to any other colormap as often as desired. Try `colormap jet`, `colormap cool`, `colormap hsv`, and `colormap flag` from the command window. Unlike `pcolor`, the commands `caxis`, `shading flat`, and `shading interp` are not applicable to `image`.

Once you understand what works and what doesn't with `image`, replace `image` by `pcolor` in List D.1 and run the program. With `pcolor`, the `caxis`, `shading`, and `view` commands work. For example, with `view(0,-90)`, the top and bottom of the `pcolor` image are flipped. Also, with `caxis([-100, 100])`, the color range in the image is narrowed. Apply `shading interp` as well as `shading flat`. You should notice that with `shading flat`, the black lines that separate tiles are removed, so the image becomes much brighter than with the default option `shading faceted`. With `shading interp`, the image becomes smooth.

IMAGES FROM DIGITAL CAMERAS

Example D.1 Pictures from Qtake

The photographs in Figure D.1 show the sculptures titled *Mobius Trilogy* (left)[3] and *Closed Loop Drifter* (right) by Ralph Williams, which were taken by Quick100[4] and downloaded to a PC. The format of the images from the digital camera was QTK, which was first converted to the TIF format by the Quick100 software.

Figure D.1 Mobius Trilogy (left) and Closed Loop Drifter (right) by Ralph Williams.

Example D.2 Pictures from Digital Mavica

The pictures in Figure D.2 were taken using the Digital Mavica camera by Sony. This camera creates JPG image files that can be immediately taken into MATLAB.

---

[3] German mathematician A.G.R. Mobius first described a surface that twists in such a way that its top side is continuous with its underside and so, in effect, it has only one side.

[4] A digital camera manufactured by Apple that takes photographs in an electronic form.

Figure D.2 Digital photos: numbers on the campus (left) and raccoon (right).

SAVING AND LOADING IMAGES IN STANDARD FORMAT

The standard image data in MATLAB consists of an image matrix `w` and an associated colormap `map`. To save an image in the standard format,

    save filename w map

In order to load the file,

    [w, map] = load filename

ELEMENTS OF IMAGE PROCESSING

Because an image consists of a matrix of color indices and an associated colormap, the image can be altered in many different ways by modifying the matrix and the colormap. Changing color and contrast is the most elementary use of image processing. Changing a color scheme can often provide different information from the same image file. Image Processing Toolbox has numerous tools for image processing. In the remainder of this section, we describe the fundamental aspects of a few elementary image-processing techniques.

Example D.3   Edge Extraction and Diffusion

Figure D.3 displays an image of overlapping circular disks plotted by List D.2.

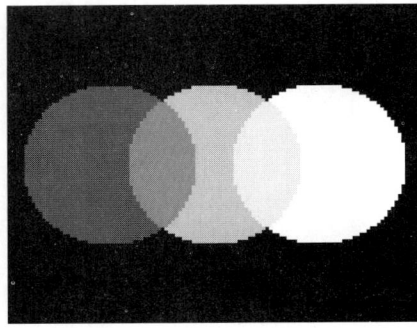

Figure D.3 Three disks.

List D.2
disk_ptn.m

```
% disk_ptn.m   Plots three disks by pcolor.
clear;clf
map=jet;
colormap(map)
disp 'For Student Edition users, ni < 25'
%ni=input('ni = ')
ni=100;
nj= ni*1.20;
ic1=ni/2;  ic2=ni/2;  ic3=ni/2;
jc1=nj/4;  jc2=nj/2;  jc3=nj/4*3;
w=ones(ni,nj);
ni20=ni/4;
for i=1:ni
   for j=1:nj
     r1 = sqrt((i-ic1)^2 + (j-jc1)^2);
     r2 = sqrt((i-ic2)^2 + (j-jc2)^2) ;
     r3 =  sqrt((i-ic3)^2 + (j-jc3)^2);
     if r1  <  ni20   w(i,j)=20; end
     if r2  < ni20 ,  w(i,j)=40; end
     if r3  < ni20 ,  w(i,j)=60; end
     if r1< ni20 & r2 < ni20,   W(i,j)=30; end
     if r2< ni20 & r3 < ni20,   W(i,j)=50; end
   end
end
pcolor(w);
shading flat;
save disksda w map  ; axis('off')
text(ni/10,ni/10,'Disk pattern','FontSize',[18])
```

Edges of disks may be identified by sudden changes of the color index in the image matrix w. For example,

$$c(i,j) = [w(j,i) - w(j-1,i)]^2 + [w(j,i) - w(j+1,i)]^2$$
$$+ [w(j,i) - w(j,i-1)]^2 + [w(j,i) - w(j,i+1)]^2$$

will become zero unless the tile (i,j) is not adjacent to an edge, but becomes nonzero if it is. The edge pattern image illustrated in Figure D.4 is drawn by List D.3.

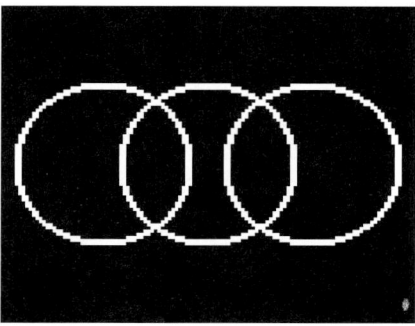

Figure D.4 Edges of three disks.

List D.3
disk_edg.m

```
% disk_edg.m    Plots edges extracted from three disks.
clear,clf
load   disksda    %reads W and map
[ni,nj]=size(W);
colormap(map)
c = zeros(size(W));
for i=2:ni-1
for j=2:nj-1
 c(i,j)= (W(i-1,j)-W(i,j))^2 + (W(i+1,j)-W(i,j))^2 ...
     + (W(i,j-1)-W(i,j))^2 + (W(i,j+1)-W(i,j))^2;
  if c(i,j) > 0, c(i,j) = 55; end
end
end
image(c);axis('off')
text(ni/10,ni/10,'Extracted edge pattern','FontSize',[18])
save edgeda c map
```

The edge pattern may be diffused by applying a diffusion operator, or equivalently, by solving the following equation:

$$(4 + \alpha)d_{j,i} = d_{j-1,i} + d_{j+1,i} + d_{j,i-1} + d_{j,i+1} + c(j,i) \qquad \text{(D.1)}$$

where α is a parameter to control how far the diffusion effect reaches. The higher α is, the shorter the distance of diffusion. An iterative solution scheme based on the Gauss-Seidel method is written as

$$(4+\alpha)d_{j,i}^{(t)} = d_{j-1,i}^{(t)} + d_{j+1,i}^{(t-1)} + d_{j,i-1}^{(t)} + d_{j,i+1}^{(t-1)} + c(j,i) \qquad \text{(D.2)}$$

where t is the iteration number. For image processing, a strict convergence is not necessary. In fact, a small number of iteration steps will achieve the diffusion effect.

A variant of the foregoing processing is the *convective-diffusion* effect produced by

$$(2+a)d_{j,i}^{(t)} = d_{j+1,i}^{(t-1)} + d_{j,i+1}^{(t-1)} + c(j,i) \qquad \text{(D.3)}$$

The foregoing scheme diffuses the image only in one direction from the edges. List D.4 displays the diffused pattern in Figure D.5.

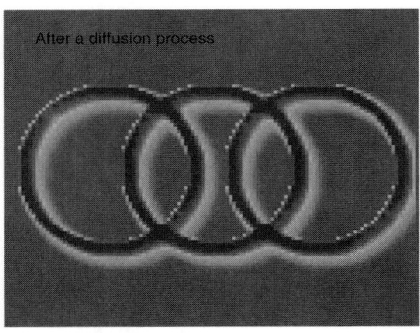

Figure D.5 Three disks after diffusion.

List D.4
edge_dif.m

```
% edge_dif.m  Edges of three disks after diffusion.
clear,clf
load   edgeda
[ni,nj]=size(c);
d=c;
colormap(map)
for iter=1:7
for i=2:ni-1
for j=2:nj-1
 d(i,j)= (d(i-1,j)+d(i,j) + d(i,j-1)+d(i,j) + c(i,j))/(4+0.1);
 end
end
```

```
end
end
image(d)

text(ni/10,ni/10,'After a diffusion process','FontSize',[18])
axis('off')
```

Example D.4   Fractal

Figure D.6 displays a fractal image plotted by List D.4 based on the Henon's model[5]:
$$x_{n+1} = ax_n - b(y_n - x_n^2)$$
$$y_{n+1} = bx_n + a(y_n - x_n^2)$$
where $a = 0.24$ and $b = 0.9708$.

The same fractal image becomes significantly different if the color scheme is altered.

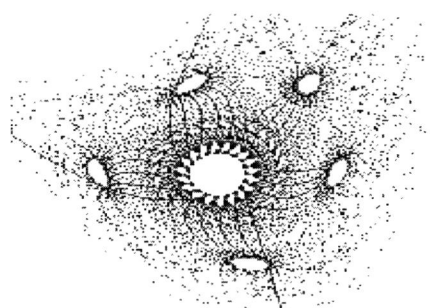

Figure D.6 A fractal by Henon's model.

List D.4
fractal_.m

```
%fractal_.m   Fractal image plot by Henon's model.
clf,clear, W=ones(201,201)*64; colormap(hot)
hold on
L=1;
for y=0.1:0.01:1
  L=L+10;
    for x=.1;0.01; 1.2 ;
```

---

[5]H. Lauwerier, *Fractals*, Princeton University Press, 1991.

```
        L=L+1; if L>64 L=1; end
      a=0.24; b=0.9708; alph=76.1135;
      for n=1:100
        xb=x;yb=y;
        x=a*xb-b*(yb-xb^2);
        y=b*xb + a*(yb-xb^2);
        if abs(x)>10 | abs(y)>10 break;end
        nx = fix((real(x)+1)* 100);
        ny = fix((real(y)+1)* 100);
        if nx<1 nx=1;end; if nx>200 nx = 200;end
        if ny<1 ny=1;end; if ny>200 ny=200; end
        W(nx,ny) = L;
      end
   end
end
image(W); axis([1,200,1,200]); axis('off'); hold off
```

Appendix E

GRAPHICAL USER INTERFACE

The readers of this book have probably used menu-driven software more than once. Almost all commercially developed programs are operated by menus. Microsoft Windows is an example. Macintosh programs are all menu-driven. MATLAB itself is menu-driven. Graphical user interface (abbreviated GUI) makes a program friendly. The objective of this appendix is to describe an easy introduction to graphical user interfaces that can be programmed with MATLAB.[1]

This appendix describes how to develop GUIs. Demonstration scripts in this appendix will not only help you understand the explanations, but could also be used as templates when readers develop their own GUI-based programs.

The GUI panel is developed in a figure window, and consists of the following components:

(a) User interface menu
(b) User interface control devices
(c) Axes to display plots or images

FLOW OF OPERATIONS WITH GUI

With a GUI, the flow of computing is controlled by the actions on the interface. While the flow of commands in a script is predetermined, the flow of operations with a GUI is undetermined. The commands to create a user interface is written in a script. Once the script is executed, however, the user

---

[1] *MATLAB: Building a Graphical User Interface* by MathWorks: www.mathworks.com, [2] Patrick Marchand, *Graphics and GUIs with MATLAB*, 2e, CRC Press, 1999.

interface remains on the screen even after execution of the script is completed. The user's interaction with the interface starts there and continues until the interface is closed.

Figure E.1 shows the basic concept of software operation with a GUI. When a selection is made on a menu, the program records the value of that selection and executes the commands prescribed in the call-back string. The user interface menu, pushbutton, popup menu, slider, and editable text are all devices to control software operations.

Upon completion of instructions in the call-back string, control is returned to the interface, so the next selection from the menu can be made. This cycle is repeated until the GUI is closed.

The call-back string consists of a single command or a sequence of MATLAB commands, or a function call. Using a function call is preferred, particularly when more than a few commands are necessary in the call-back string.

In order to understand how to write a GUI, the reader needs to understand only five commands: uimenu, uicontrol, get, set, and axes. Nonetheless, what makes these commands rather complicated is that there are so many different ways of using them. Writing all kinds of situations is im-

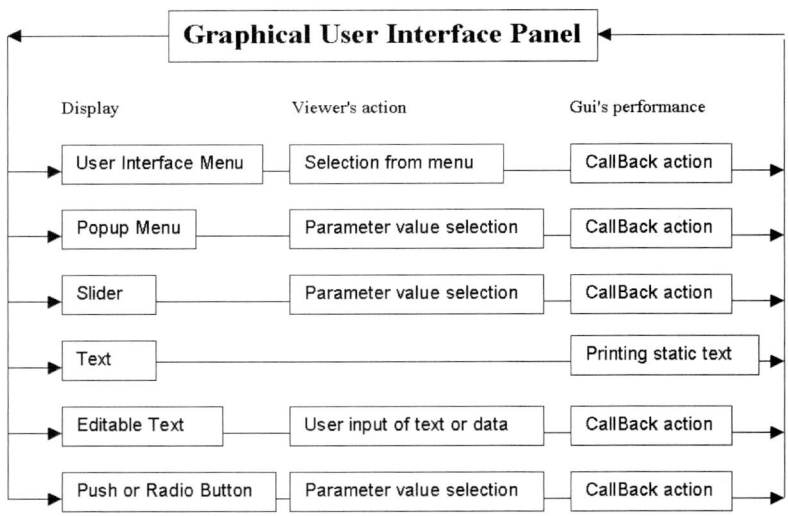

Figure E.1 Flow of operations with GUI.

possible, because it would take too much space and be very cumbersome to read. Therefore, this appendix tries to explain only the basic elements of GUI through examples. The reader should refer to *MATLAB: Building a Graphical User Interface* for more detailed information about the commands.

Here is one suggestion to make understanding GUI a bit easier. Run one or two sample GUI scripts in this appendix first. This is easy if the m-files for this book have been downloaded on your computer. Then try to understand the commands in the script. Trying to alter the scripts is an excellent method for fast learning. There are 18 demonstration programs in this appendix. To run a program in this appendix, type the name in the command window (assuming all the m-files in the diskette have been installed on your computer, or run the program directly from the diskette):

```
GuiDm_n
```
where n = 1, 2 .. 18.

USER INTERFACE MENU

The user interface menu is a menu or a group of menus in the top of a figure window. A menu rolls down when clicked by a mouse and shows a list of options. When a selection is made from the list, another level of menus may also roll down (if the menu is so designed).

A user interface menu is specified by `uimenu`. Its synopsis is as follows:

```
m1 = uimenu(gcf, ...
    'Label','label string 1',...
    'Position', [priority number (integer)],...
    'BackgroundColor',[r,g,b],...
    'CallBack','call-back string')
m2 = uimenu(gcf, ...
    'Label','label string 2',...
    'Position', [priority number (integer)],...
    'BackgroundColor',[r,g,b],...
    'CallBack','call-back string')
m3 = uimenu(gcf, ...
    'Label','label string 3',...
    'Position', [priority number (integer)],...
    'BackgroundColor',[r,g,b],...
    'CallBack','call-back string')
```

Here, three menus in one figure window are assumed. In the commands, m1, m2, ... are handles of the menus which often become necessary in `CallBack` as well as in other commands. The arguments after gcf are called *properties* of the menu and have the following meaning:

1. 'Label','label string' specifies the label of the menu that appears in the menu.

2. 'Position', k, determines the sequential position of the label in the menu, where k is an integer of the priority order.

3. 'BackgroundColor',[r,g,b] specifies the color of the menu background.

4. 'CallBack','call-back string' specifies the commands to be executed upon selection of the label.

In the foregoing synopsis, the lines of Position and BackgroundColor may be omitted if the default settings are acceptable. Furthermore, CallBack is not necessary if the menu is followed by a list of selections that opens when the menu is clicked.

Other properties may also be specified; however, the best way to learn such properties is to execute the get(handle) command after the uimenu command is executed, where handle must be similar to m1 or m2 in the earlier synopsis explanation. The get(handle) command returns the current properties of the menu, most of which are set by default, but can be changed in the arguments of the uimenu command statement.

The items for selections in the menu are also entered by uimenu. Considering the selection list for the first menu with handle m1, the synopsis involving three choices is as follows:

```
m1sA = uimenu(m1, ...
    'Label','Selection A',...
    'CallBack','call-back string')
m1sB = uimenu(m1, ...
    'Label','Selection B',...
    'CallBack','call-back string')
m1sC = uimenu(m1, ...
    'Label','Selection C',...
    'CallBack','call-back string')
```

All three selections belong to the first menu with handle m1. The properties Position and BackgroundColor are omitted, but can be included if desired.

Property CallBack here is important if the uicontrol is for the terminal level of the menu. The call-back string is a string that consists of a command, a set of commands, or a function call. All the computational jobs to be performed upon selection are specified in the string. The instruction(s) may range from a single command to multiple commands. For the simplicity of programming, however, it is desirable to write only a few commands, including one function call, in the call-back string. All details of the computations can be written in an m-file.[2]

A simple menu-driven program, GuiDm_1, plots $y = \sin(x)$ as illustrated in Figure E.2. The user can change the style of the curve, color, and line width[3] from the menu.

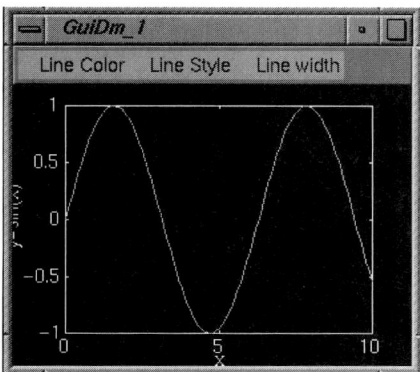

Figure E.2 User interface menu.

GuiDm_1.m

```
%GuiDm_1.m   Illustrates user interface menu.
close, clear
figure(1)
set(gcf,'Position',[100,300,300,220],...
    'NumberTitle','off',...
    'Name','GuiDm_1')
x=0:0.1:10;, y=sin(x);
p=plot(x,y);xlabel('x');ylabel('y=sin(x)');
stl = uimenu(gcf,...
      'Label','   Line Style',...
```

---

[2]The m-file can be a function m-file as well as a nonfunction m-file. In either case, `'call-back string'` is replaced by `'m-file name'`. The difference between using a function m-file and a nonfunction m-file is as follows. If a function m-file is used, the variables necessary in the function m-file must be given as arguments, because the variables in the calling m-file are not otherwise visible from the function m-file. On the other hand, if a nonfunction m-file is used, all the variables are visible from the called m-file. See more information on the m-file in Chapter 1, "MATLAB Primer."

[3]Line width did not change in the MATLAB version that the author used.

```
        'BackgroundColor',[0.8, 0.8, 0.8],...
        'Position',2);
clr = uimenu(gcf,...
        'Label',' Line Color',...
        'BackgroundColor',[0.8, 0.8, 0.8],...
        'Position',1);
lw = uimenu(gcf,...
        'Label',' Line width',...
        'BackgroundColor',[0.8, 0.8, 0.8],...
        'Position',3);
solid = uimenu(stl, ...
        'Label', 'Solid',...
        'CallBack','set(p,''LineStyle'','''-''')')
dotted = uimenu(stl, ...
        'Label', 'Dotted',...
        'CallBack','set(p,''LineStyle'','''':''')')
yellow = uimenu(clr,...
        'Label', 'Yellow',...
        'BackgroundColor',[0.9, 0.9, 0.1],...
        'CallBack','set(p,''Color'',''y'')')
green = uimenu(clr, ...
        'Label','Green',...
        'BackgroundColor',[0.1, 0.9, 0.1],...
        'CallBack','set(p,''Color'',''g'')')
red = uimenu(clr,...
        'Label', 'Red',...
        'BackgroundColor',[0.9, 0.1 , 0.1],...
        'CallBack','set(p,''Color'',''r'')')
solid = uimenu(lw, ...
        'Label', '0.5',...
        'CallBack','set(p,''LineWidth'',0.5)')
dotted = uimenu(lw, ...
        'Label', '1.0',...
        'CallBack','set(p,''LineWidth'',1.0)')
```

Notice that texts in the call-back strings must be enclosed with double quote signs.

Another example, GuiDm_2, plots one of the following functions at the user's choice from the menu:

1. $y = \sin(x)$

2. $y = \exp(-x)$

3. $y = \cos(x^2)$

4. $y = \exp(-x^2)$

Figure E.3 was plotted by GuiDm_2 (but the opened menu could not be shown).

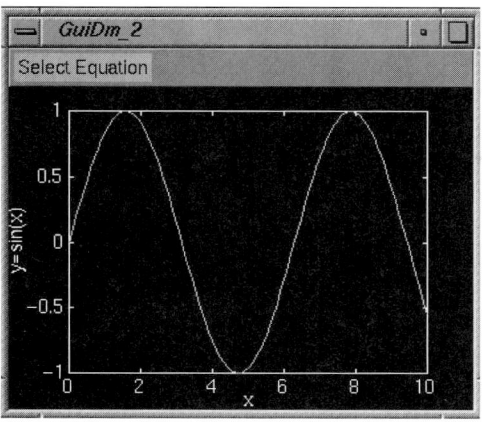

Figure E.3 Selection by menu.

GuiDm_2.m

```
%GuiDm_2  Demonstration of selecting equation form menu.
close, clear
fg=figure(1)
set(fg, 'Position',[150 150 350 250],...
    'NumberTitle','off',...
    'Name','GuiDm_2')
x=0:0.1:10;, y=sin(x);
p=plot(x,y);xlabel('x');ylabel('y=sin(x)');
stl = uimenu(gcf,...
     'Label','Select Equation',...
     'BackgroundColor',[0.8, 0.8, 0.8])
F1  = uimenu(stl, ...
     'Label', 'y=sin(x)',...
     'CallBack',...
  'plot(x,sin(x));xlabel(''x'');ylabel(''y=sin(x)'')')
F2  = uimenu(stl, ...
     'Label', 'y=exp(-x)',...
     'CallBack',...
  'plot(x,exp(-x));xlabel(''x'');ylabel(''y=exp(-x)'')')
F3  = uimenu(stl, ...
     'Label', 'y=cos(x^2)',...
     'CallBack',...
     [
      'plot(x,cos(x.^2));',...
      'xlabel(''x'');ylabel(''y=cos(x.^2)'')'...
     ])
F4  = uimenu(stl, ...
     'Label', 'y=exp(-x.^2)',...
```

```
              'CallBack',...
              [
               'plot(x,exp(-x.^2));',...
               'xlabel(''x'');ylabel(''y=exp(-x.^2)'')'...
              ])
```

The reader might combine the two foregoing scripts into one for exercise.

USER INTERFACE CONTROL

MATLAB user interface control is specified by the `uicontrol` command. The user interface control is similar to the user interface menu, but the former includes many styles. Its synopsis is

```
    k=uicontrol('Style','style spec',...
                'String','display string',...
                'Value', [value],...
                'BackgroundColor',[r,g,b],...
                'Max',[value],...
                'Min',[value],...
                'Position',[ left,bottom,width,height],
                'Callback','call-back string')
```

where 'style spec' is one of the following strings:

```
    popup
    push
    radio
    checkbox
    slider
    edit (editable text)
    text (static text)
    frame
```

Properties in `uicontrol` are similar to those in `uimenu`. The new properties that appear for the first time are:

1. 'Value',value: specifies default value of setting. For on/off switches, the value is 0 or 1. For a slider, it can be any value between the minimum and the maximum.

2. 'Min', value: sets the minimum value. Its meaning differs depending on the style.

3. 'Max',value: sets the maximum value. Its meaning differs depending on the style.

There are many more properties that can be written in the uicontrol commands just like the properties of uimenu, although in programming we desire to minimize the number of properties to make the script simple. To learn more about the additional properties, investigate using the get command.

In the following subsections, the styles will be explained in more detail.

Static Text

A static text can display some symbols, messages, or even numeric values in a GUI, and can be placed at a desired location. There is no call-back string with a static text. An example of a static text is shown here:

```
k1=uicontrol('Style','text',...
             'String','static text displayed',...
             'Position',[ 20, 50, 140, 30])
```

The contents of a displayed static text can be changed as needs occur. This is done by the set command. For example, execute the following command from the command window while the foregoing sample of uicontrol command is in effect:

```
set(k1,'String','A revised string is here now.')
```

To display numeric value(s) as a static text, write num2str(n), where n is a numeric value, in place of 'static text displayed' after 'String'. The output of GuiDm_3 is the top half of Figure E.4.

GuiDm_3.m

```
close; clf
h1=figure(1);
set(h1,'Position',[300,300,400,200],...
'NumberTitle','off',...
'Name','GuiDm_3  Numeric Value')
k1=uicontrol('Style','text',...
             'String',num2str(pi),...
             'Position',[ 20,50,140,30])
```

If multiple strings are to be displayed as a combined string, use brackets. For example, the second half of Figure E.4 is plotted by GuiDm_4.

GuiDm_4.m

```
% GuiDm_4  Combined strings in text.
close; clf
h1=figure(1);
set(h1,'Position',[300,300,400,100],...
```

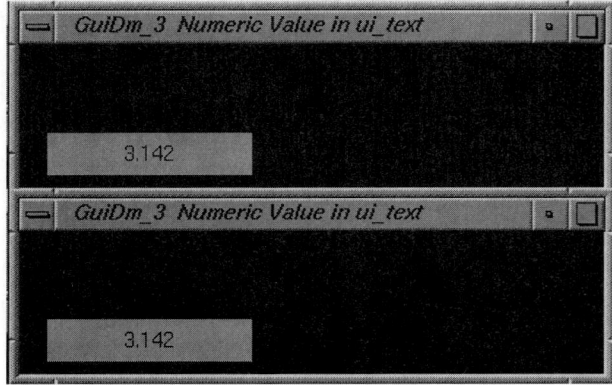

Figure E.4 Results of GuiDm-3.m and GuiDm-4.m.

```
        'NumberTitle','off',...
        'Name','GuiDm_4   Combined strings')
        k1=uicontrol('Style','text',...
                   'String',['pi=',num2str(3.14159)],...
                   'Position',[ 20,10,140,30])
```

Popup Menu

A popup menu is different from the user interface menu because the popup menu can be located anywhere in the figure window, while the user interface menu is located only at the top.

Suppose the popup menu is to offer a choice among A, B, C, and D. GuiDm_5.m illustrates how to write uicontrol for the popup menu. In order to run the script, a function task_1 is also necessary.

When GuiDm_5 is executed, a figure window will open with a small white label at the top left corner of the window (see Figure E.5). If the mouse is clicked while the pointer is within the white box, a menu will pop up in the middle of the figure window. Click A, B, C, or D, then a short message such as

        C is selected.

will be printed out on the command screen. For the simplicity of illustration, no other operation is performed, but task_1 can be much longer. Selections can be repeated until Close is selected in the menu.

GuiDm_5.m

```
%GuiDm_5 Demonstration of popup menu.
clf
h1=figure(1)
set(h1,'Position',[100,100,300,200],...
       'NumberTitle','off', ...
       'Name','GuiDm_5  Demo of Popup Menu')
k1=uicontrol('Style','Popup',...
             'String','A|B|C|D|Close',...
             'Value',  1,...
             'Position',[ 20,150,140,30], ...
             'Callback','task_1(h1,k1)')
```

task_1.m

```
%task_1.m
function task_1(h,k)
val = get(k,'Value');
    if val == 1, fprintf('A is selected\n')
elseif val == 2, fprintf('B is selected\n')
elseif val == 3, fprintf('C is selected\n')
elseif val == 4, fprintf('D is selected\n')
elseif val == 5, close(h)
end
```

Here, meanings of arguments for uicontrol in GuiDm_5.m are as follows:

1. 'Style', 'Popup': the style of user control is the popup menu.

2. 'String', 'A|B|C|D|Close': strings in the menu are A, B, C, D, and Close.

3. 'Value', 3: selects the third selection C as default.

4. 'Position', [20,150,140,30]: position of the menu is at (20, 150) in pixel units in the figure window, and the size of the menu is (140,30) in pixel units.

5. 'Callback', 'task_1(h1,k1)': when the popup menu is selected, command task_1 is executed, where task_1 is the function m-file.

Upon a selection on the popup menu (for example, we assume C is selected), function task_1 is entered and val is drawn. In the arguments of task_1, h and k are handles of the current figure and uicontrol, respectively. Command val=get(k,'Value') captures the value selected in the menu window, and val becomes 1 for A, 2 for B, etc. In this example, a message, 'C is selected', is printed out on the command window. If val=5, the figure window (of handle h) is closed and the GUI disappears. Otherwise, the program returns to the user interface, and the same procedure can be repeated.

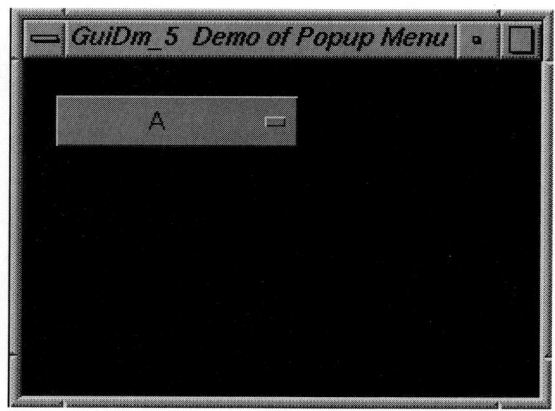

Figure E.5 Popup menu (1).

The figure window in the foregoing example (see Figure E.5) is awkward, however. Indeed, the size of the figure window is too large for just the menu, and more messages for users are desirable. In order to improve the figure window, we create GuiDm_6. The figure window size is reduced, while the background color is changed to green. The uicontrol with handle j is used to print out a message above the popup menu. Run GuiDm_6 to see the improvements (see Figure E.6).

GuiDm_6.m
```
% GuiDm_6 Shows improvements of GuiDm_5.
h1=figure(2)
set(h1,'Position',[30,50,280,100], ...
    'Color',[0,0.5, 0.5],'Name','GuiDm_6');
j=uicontrol('Position',[ 0,60,250,30], ...
    'String','Select from A, B, C, D or Close');
k=uicontrol('Style','Popup',...
        'String','A|B|C|D|Close',...
        'Position',[ 0,30,100,30], ...
        'Callback','task_1(h1,k)');
```

In the two foregoing examples, the call-back string is task_1; however, the contents of task_1 may be written directly in the call-back string. An example is

GuiDm_7.m
```
%GuiDm_7  Illustrates a long call-back string.
```

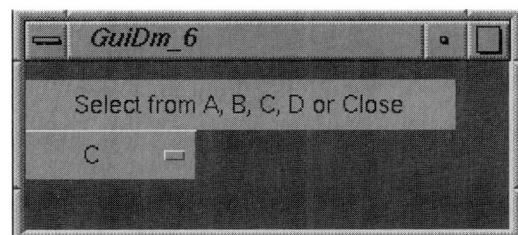

Figure E.6 Popup menu (2).

```
clf
h1=figure(2)
set(h1,'Position',[30,50,280,100], ...
    'Color',[0,0.5, 0.5],'Name','GuiDm_7',...
    'NumberTitle','off')
j=uicontrol('Position',[ 0,60,250,30], ...
    'Style','text',...
    'String','Select from A, B, C, D or Close')
k=uicontrol('Style','Popup',...
            'String','A|B|C|D|Close',...
            'Position',[ 0,30,100,30], ...
'Callback',...
[ ...
'val = get(k,''Value'');',...
'   if val == 1, fprintf(''A is selected\n''),',...
'elseif val == 2, fprintf(''B is selected\n''),',...
'elseif val == 3, fprintf(''C is selected\n''),',...
'elseif val == 4, fprintf(''D is selected\n''),',...
'elseif val == 5, close(h1),',...
'end' ...
])
```

Notice in the foregoing example, the call-back string is written in a row vectors of strings.

Push Button

GuiDm_8 illustrates the application of a push button; the result is shown in Figure E.7.

GuiDm_8.m
```
%GuiDm_8   Push Button
close;clf
h1=figure(1)
set(h1,'Position',[130,550,280,100], ...
    'Color',[0,0.5, 0.5],...
```

```
        'Name','GuiDm_8 Push Button',...
        'NumberTitle','off')
j=uicontrol('Position',[0,60,250,30], ...
        'Style','pushbutton',...
        'String','Push here to plot sin(x)' ,...
        'Callback',...
        [
         'h2=figure(2);x=0:0.1:10;plot(x,sin(x));,',...
         'xlabel(''x''),ylabel(''y''),'...
         'set(h2,''Position'',[130,310,280,200])'
        ])
```

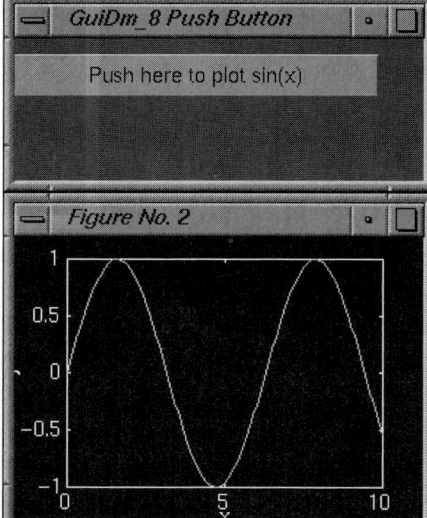

Figure E.7 Push button.

When executed, the window on the top side of Figure E.7 opens first. If the push button is then pushed, a new figure window (second window in Figure E.7) will open with a plot of $y = \sin(x)$. If you wish to quit the interface, type close in the command window.

Check Box

The check box is designed to provide on/off operations. The following script plots the sine function (see Figure E.8). Clicking on the bar located at the bottom of the figure toggles between the axis on condition and axis off conditions. The check mark in the box indicates that the position is on. The on/off positions are recorded in Value which can be found by get(handle, 'Value'). The commands axis on and axis off to toggle the axis are written in the call-back string.

GuiDm_9.m

```
%GuiDm_9   Check Box
close;clf
h1=figure(2)
set(h1,'Position',[130,450,300,200], ...
    'Color',[0,0.5, 0.5],'Name','GuiDm_9',...
    'NumberTitle','off')
hold on
x=0:0.1:10;plot(x,sin(x))
j=uicontrol('Position',[ 5,0,250,15], ...
    'Style','checkbox',...
        'Value',1,...
    'String','Push here to toggle axis' ,...
    'Callback',...
    [ ...
      'if get(j,''Value'')==0, axis off; ',...
      'elseif get(j,''Value'')==1, axis on, end' ...
    ])
```

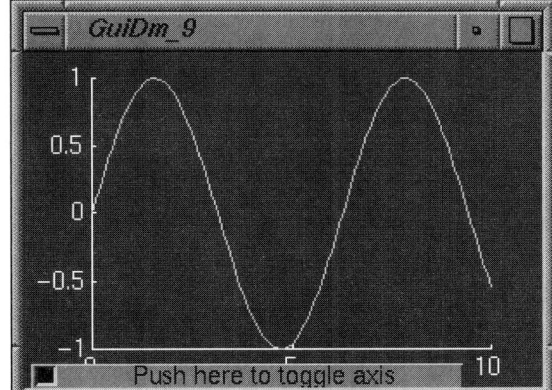

Figure E.8 Check box.

Radio Button

When only one radio button is used, there is no functional difference from a check box. On the other hand, radio buttons as a group are intended to be mutually exclusive (that is, if one button is on, all other buttons turn off), while check boxes are independent from each other. This exclusive feature of radio buttons can only be realized, however, by the user's own programming in the call-back strings (see *MATLAB: Building a Graphical User Interface*).

Slider

The slider is an analog device to change a parameter. The script of GuiDm_10 illustrates the application of sliders (see Figure E.9). The script demonstrates how an RGB color is affected by intensities of the three components, R, G, and B. The intensities are changed by sliders.

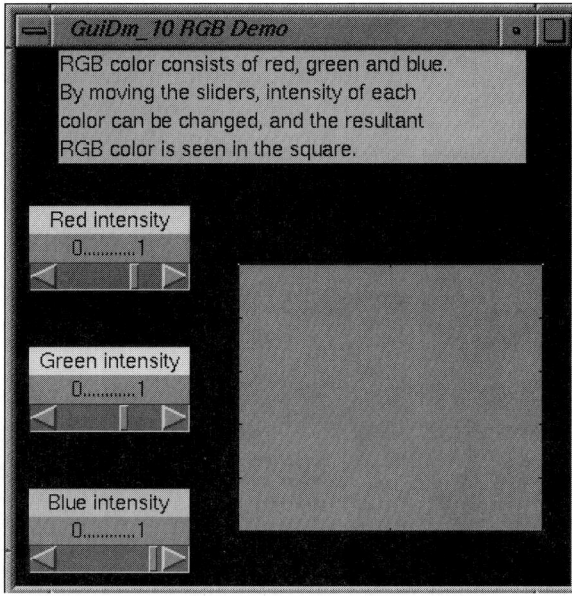

Figure E.9 Slider.

GuiDm_10.m
```
%GuiDm_10  RGB color demonstration
clf, clear
h6=figure(1);
clf
R=0;G=0.4,B=0;
set(h6,'Position',[60, 300,380,380],...
    'Name','GuiDm_10 RGB Demo',...
    'NumberTitle','off',...
    'Color',[ 0. 0.0 0.])
ah=axes( 'Position', [0.4 0.1, 0.55 0.50],...
    'Box', 'on', ...
    'Color',[R,G,B],...
    'XColor',[0,0,0],'YColor',[0,0,0])
%=============================
t1 = uicontrol(gcf,'Style','text', ...
    'String',...
        'RGB color consists of red, green and blue. ',...
    'HorizontalAlignment','Left',...
    'Position',[30,360,320,20],...
    'BackgroundColor',[0.8 0.8 0.8]);
t2 = uicontrol(gcf,'Style','text', ...
```

```
        'String',...
            'By moving the sliders, intensity of each ',...
        'HorizontalAlignment','Left',...
        'Position',[30,340,320,20],...
        'BackgroundColor',[0.8 0.8 0.8]);
t3 = uicontrol(gcf,'Style','text', ...
        'String',...
            'color can be changed, and the resultant  ',...
        'HorizontalAlignment','Left',...
        'Position',[30,320,320,20],...
        'BackgroundColor',[0.8 0.8 0.8]);
t4 = uicontrol(gcf,'Style','text', ...
        'String',...
            'RGB color is seen in the square.  ',...
        'HorizontalAlignment','Left',...
        'Position',[30,300,320,20],...
        'BackgroundColor',[0.8 0.8 0.8]);
%==============================Slider for Blue
b1 = uicontrol(gcf,'Style','text', ...
        'String','Blue intensity',...
        'Position',[10,50,110,20],...
        'BackgroundColor',[0.6,0.6,0.8]);
b2 = uicontrol(gcf,'Style','text',...
        'String','0............1',...
        'Position',[10,30,110,20]);
b3 = uicontrol(gcf,...
        'Style','slider',...
        'Min' ,0,'Max', 1, ...
        'Position',[10,10,110,20], ...
        'Value', B,...
        'CallBack', ...
        'B=get(b3,''Value'');set(ah,''Color'',[R,G,B])');
%==============================Slider for Green
g1 = uicontrol(gcf,'Style','text', ...
        'String','Green intensity',...
        'Position',[10,150,110,20],...
        'BackgroundColor',[0.6,0.8,0.6]);
g2 = uicontrol(gcf,'Style','text',...
        'String','0............1',...
        'Position',[10,130,110,20]);
g3 = uicontrol(gcf,...
        'Style','slider',...
        'Min' ,0,'Max', 1, ...
        'Position',[10,110,110,20], ...
        'Value', G,...
        'CallBack', ...
           'G=get(g3,''Value'');set(ah,''Color'',[R,G,B])');
```

```
%==============================Slider for Red
r1 = uicontrol(gcf,'Style','text', ...
   'String','Red intensity',...
   'Position',[10,250,110,20],...
   'BackgroundColor',[0.8,0.6,0.6]);
r2 = uicontrol(gcf,'Style','text',...
   'String','0............1',...
   'Position',[10,230,110,20]);
r3 = uicontrol(gcf,...
   'Style','slider',...
   'Min' ,0,'Max',1, ...
   'Position',[10,210,110,20], ...
   'Value', R,...
   'CallBack', ...
      'R=get(r3,''Value'');set(ah,''Color'',[R,G,B])');
```

Notice that slider values are captured using get with 'Value'.

Editable text

The editable text device allows the user to write a string input. Numeric values in vector or matrix form may be written as a string through the same device, which is converted to numeric values by the str2num command.

An example of uicontrol for editable text is:

```
ed1 = uicontrol(gcf, 'Style','edit', ...
      'Position', [10,260, 110,20],...
      'CallBack','inp_txt=get(ed1,''String'')')
```

The key words in the foregoing command are 'Style', 'edit', and get (handle,'String') which captures the text input. The following program (GuiDm_11) reads the user input of a matrix from the editable text (see Figure E.10), and computes eigenvalues of the matrix. The eigenvalues are printed on the command window.

GuiDm_11.m

```
% GuiDm_11  Editable Text
close,clf
```

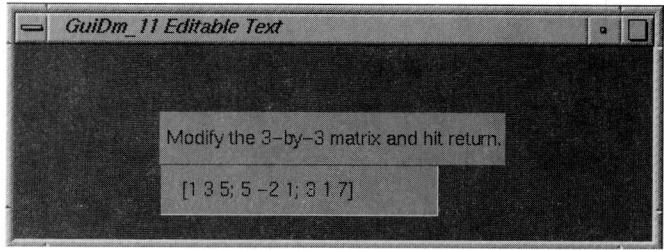

Figure E.10 Input of numbers through editable text.

```
h1=figure(2)
set(h1,'Position',[130,450,480,150], ...
    'Color',[0,0.5, 0.5],'Name','GuiDm_11 Editable Text')
ed0 = uicontrol(gcf, 'Style','text', ...
        'Position', [110,60, 260,40],...
        'String',...
        ' Modify the 3-by-3 matrix and hit return.')
ed2 = uicontrol(gcf, 'Style','edit', ...
        'Position', [110,20, 210,40],...
        'String','    [1 3 5; 5 -2 1; 3 1 7]',...
        'CallBack',['inp_txt=get(ed2,''String''),',...
        'eigenvalues=eig(str2num(inp_txt))'])
```

With the revised script, GuiDm_12, the eigenvalues are printed as static text within the GUI (see Figure E.11).

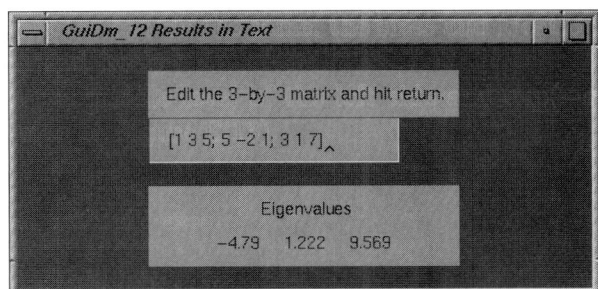

Figure E.11 Displaying results in static text.

GuiDm_12.m

```
% GuiDm_12    Results as static text
close,clf
h1=figure(2)
set(h1,'Position',[130,350,480,210], ...
    'Color',[0,0.5, 0.5],'Name','GuiDm_12 Results in Text',...
    'NumberTitle','off')
axis('off'); hold on
ed0 = uicontrol(gcf, 'Style','text', ...
        'Position', [110,150, 260,40],...
        'String',...
        ' Edit the 3-by-3 matrix and hit return.')
ed1 = uicontrol(gcf, 'Style','text', ...
        'Position', [110,50, 260,40],...
        'String',' Eigenvalues')
ed2 = uicontrol(gcf, 'Style','text', ...
        'Position', [110,20, 260,40],...
        'String',' ')
ed3 = uicontrol(gcf, 'Style','edit', ...
```

```
'Position', [110,110, 210,40],...
'String',' [1 3 5; 5 -2 1; 3 1 7]',...
'CallBack',...
['axis off; inp_txt=get(ed3,''String'');',...
'eigen=eig(str2num(inp_txt));',...
'ans=[num2str(eigen(1)),''      '',',...
'num2str(eigen(2)),''      '',',...
'num2str(eigen(3))];',...
'set(ed2,''String'',ans) '])
```

Frames

The `frame` style may be used to group devices such as radio buttons or check boxes.

MULTIPLE AXES

In developing a graphical user interface, it often becomes necessary to plot one or more graphs within the user interface. The `subplot` command may be used for this purpose, but the `axes` command is more flexible and allows versatile options for programmers.

The `axes` command opens an axis at a specified location within a figure window. Although multiple axes may be opened in a figure window by `axes`, we first consider only one axis. The following script plots a figure at the lower-left corner of the figure window, as shown in Figure E.12.

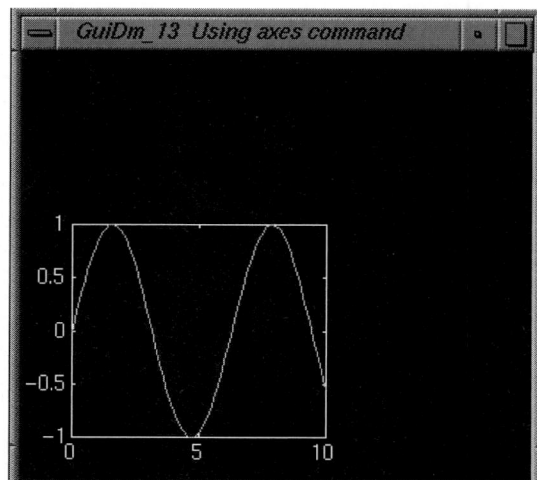

Figure E.12 Illustration of plot with `axes` (1).

GuiDm_13.m

```
% GuiDm_13: Illustrates axes command.
close,h1=figure(1),clf
set(h1,'Position',[300,300,350,300],...
       'NumberTitle','off',...
       'Name','GuiDm_13  Using axes command')
x=0:0.1:10;
axes('Position',[0.1, 0.1, 0.5, 0.5]);
plot(x,sin(x))
```

The location and size of the axis is specified by a vector following Position. The values in the vector have the same meaning as in uicontrol except the values are in the normalized scale (maximum is unity). The location and the size can be changed using different values in the position parameters.

The true power of the axes command is that it can open multiple axes at chosen locations. Although subplot can do the same, the sizes and locations of the subplots cannot be changed freely.

GuiDm_14 plots $\sin(x)$ in the middle level of the left side and $\exp(-x)$ at the right bottom (see left side of Figure E.13).

GuiDm_14.m

```
%GuiDm_14:  Illustrates multiple axes.
close,h1=figure(1),clf
set(h1,'Position',[300,300,350,350],...
       'NumberTitle','off',...
       'Name','GuiDm_14  Using multiple axes')
x=0:0.1:10;
```

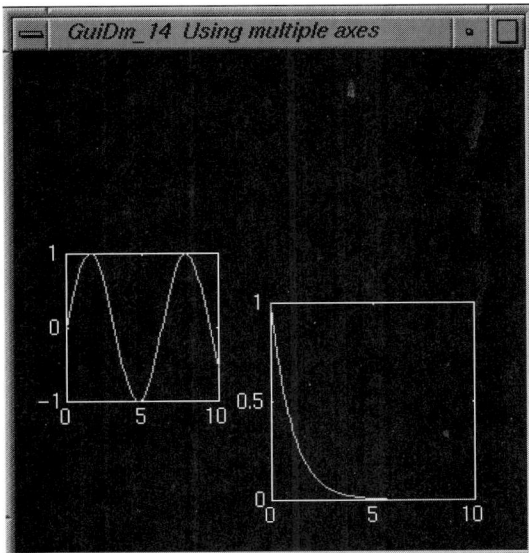

Figure E.13 Illustration of plot with axes (2).

```
axes('Position',[0.1, 0.3, 0.3, 0.3]);
plot(x,sin(x));
axes('Position',[0.55, 0.1, 0.4, 0.4]);
plot(x,exp(-x))
```

How can the first axis be reactivated as the current axis so that the graph may be revised by adding more curves or by erasing and redrawing? The answer is to use the `subplot` command to point to the desired axis. To do this, we have to use the handle assigned to each axis. Script GuiDm_15 plots two functions in each axis, as illustrated in Figure E.14.

GuiDm_15.m
```
% GuiDm_15  Using subplot with axes.
close,h1=figure(1),clf
set(h1,'Position',[300,300,350,350],...
       'NumberTitle','off',...
       'Name','GuiDm_15  Using subplot with axes')
x=0:0.1:10;
h1=axes('Position',[0.1, 0.3, 0.3, 0.3]);
plot(x,sin(x));
h2=axes('Position',[0.55, 0.1, 0.4, 0.4]);
plot(x,exp(-x))
%
subplot(h1)
hold on; plot(x,cos(x),':'); hold off
%
subplot(h2)
hold on; plot(x,sin(x.*x),':'); hold off
```

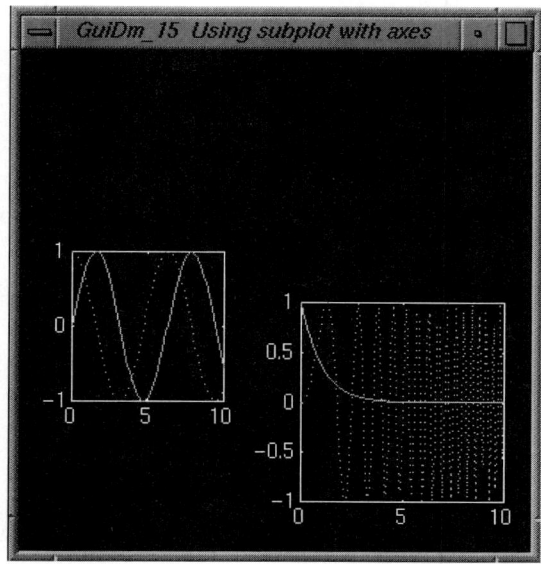

Figure E.14 Illustration of plot with `axes` (3).

APPLICATIONS

We illustrate three GUI applications that incorporate combinations of different devices.

Application E.1

Here, we develop script GuiDm_16 that displays a sphere (see Figure E.15) with choices for:

> Color map: hsv, flag, jet, and cool
> Type of display: mesh, surface, and surfl
> Shading: faceted, flat, and interp

GuiDm_16.m
```
%GuiDm_16   GUI to show 3D plots
clf, clear
h6=figure(1);
set(h6,'Position',[60, 300,380,380],...
       'Color',[ 0. 0.0 0.],...
       'NumberTitle','off',...
       'Name','GuiDm_16    3D plots')
[x,y,z]=sphere(10);
axes( 'Position', [0.4 0.2, 0.55 0.55],...
      'Box', 'on', 'Color','k')
surf(x,y,z,-z);
%==============================Slider control
```

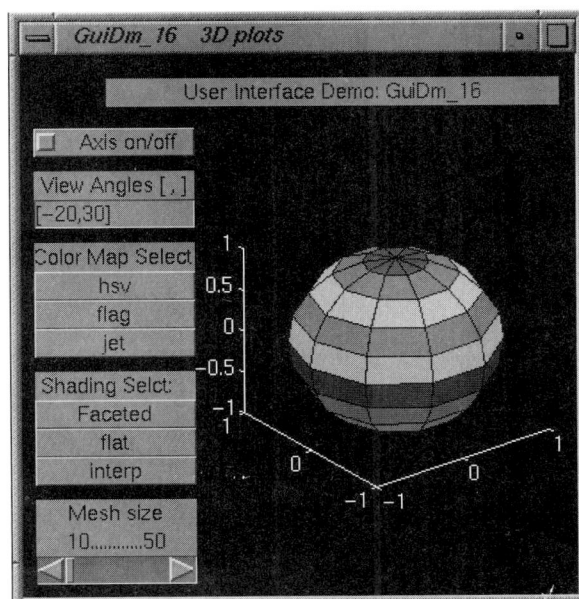

Figure E.15 A 3-D plot in a GUI.

```
txt_sl1 = uicontrol(gcf,...
        'Style','text', ...
        'String','Mesh size',...
        'Position',[10,50,110,20]);
txt_sl2 = uicontrol(gcf,...
        'Style','text',...
        'String','10............50',...
        'Position',[10,30,110,20]);
txt_sli = uicontrol(gcf,...
        'Style','slider',...
        'Min' ,10,'Max', 50, ...
        'Position',[10,10,110,20], ...
        'Value', -30,...
        'CallBack',...
  ['clear x y z; ',...
   ' [x,y,z]=sphere(ceil(get(txt_sli,''Value'')));',...
   ' surf(x,y,z,-z)'...
   ]);
%============================ Shading selection
push0=uicontrol(gcf, ...
        'Style','text',...
        'Position', [10,140, 110,20],...
        'String','Shading Select:   ',...
        'Value',0);
sym(1)=uicontrol(gcf,...
        'Style','push',...
        'Position', [10,80,110,20], ...
        'String','interp', ...
        'CallBack','shading interp ');
sym(2)=uicontrol(gcf, 'Style','push',...
        'Position', [10,100,110,20],...
        'String','flat',...
        'CallBack','shading flat ');
sym(3)=uicontrol(gcf, 'Style','push',...
        'Position', [10,120, 110,20], ...
        'String','Faceted',...
        'CallBack','shading faceted ');
%============================== Color Map Selection
push3=uicontrol(gcf, 'Style','push',...
        'Position', [10,170, 110,20], ...
        'String','jet',...
        'CallBack','colormap(jet)');
push2=uicontrol(gcf, 'Style','push',...
        'Position', [10,190, 110,20],...
        'String','flag',...
        'CallBack','colormap(flag)');
push1=uicontrol(gcf, 'Style','push',...
```

```
                'Position', [10,210, 110,20], ...
                'String','hsv',...
                'CallBack','colormap(hsv)');
push0=uicontrol(gcf, 'Style','text',...
                'Position', [10,230, 110,20], ...
                'String','Color Map Select:',...
                'CallBack','dummy=0');
%============================== View Angle Input
edtx0=uicontrol(gcf, 'Style','text',...
                'Position', [10,280, 110,20], ...
                'String', 'View Angles [ , ]');
edtx1=uicontrol(gcf, 'Style','edit', ...
                'Position', [10,260, 110,20],...
                'String','[-20,30]',...
                'CallBack',...
                ['v_ang=str2num(get(edtx1,''String''));',...
                 'view(v_ang) ']);
%============================== Axis on/off
ckbox=uicontrol(gcf, 'Style','checkbox',...
                'Position', [10,310, 110,20], ...
                'String','Axis on/off', ...
                'CallBack',...
                ['ckv= get(ckbox,''Value'');if ckv==1,',...
                 'axis on,elseif ckv==0, axis off, end ']);
%============================== Top title
title=uicontrol(gcf, 'Style','text',...
                'Position', [60,345, 310,20], 'String',...
                'User Interface Demo: GuiDm_16');
```

Application E.2

We revisit the electrical circuit of Example 10.16 and reorganize the script using GUI. The values of La, Lb, and Ra are determined by sliders, while Rb and C are selected from a popup menu. The circuit diagram and the ODE solutions are displayed in the GUI (see Figure E.16).

GuiDm_17.m

```
% GuiDm_17    Electric Circuit Analysis
clf, clear
h6=figure(1);
clf
R=0;G=0.4,B=0;
set(h6,'Position',[60, 300,680,380],...
    'Name','RGB_demo',...
    'NumberTitle','off',...
```

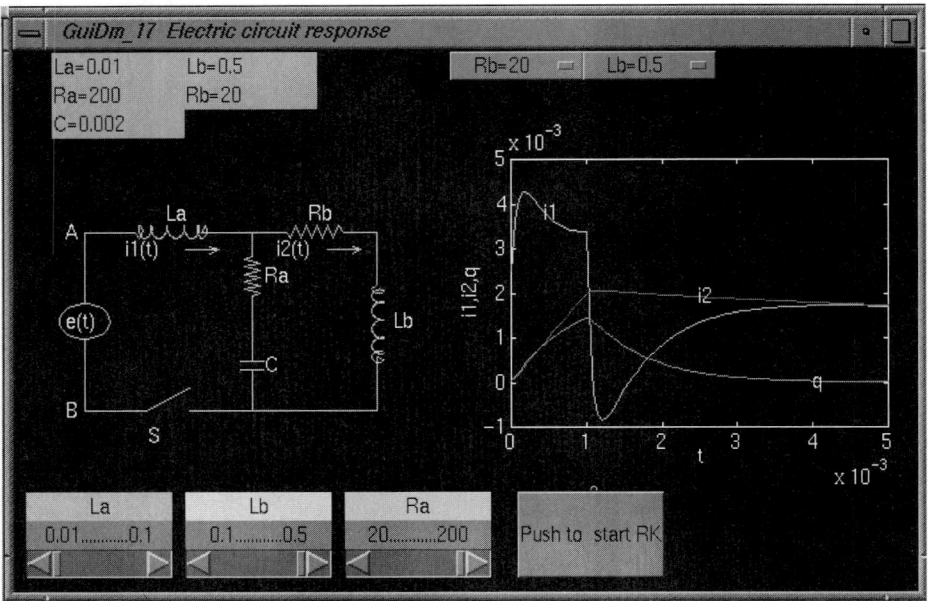

Figure E.16 GUI-guided circuit analysis.

```
            'Color',[ 0. 0.0 0.])
ah=axes( 'Position', [0.05 0.25, 0.4 0.50],...
   'Box', 'on', ...
   'Color',[R,G,B],...
   'XColor',[0,0,0],'YColor',[0,0,0])
ah2=axes( 'Position', [0.55 0.3, 0.42 0.50],...
   'Box', 'on', ...
   'Color',[R,G,B],...
   'XColor',[0,0,0],'YColor',[0,0,0])
subplot(ah); APE_circ  %calling APE_circ (diagram)
La=0.01; Lb=0.5;Ra=200;Rb=20;C=0.002;
subplot(ah2); APE_rk(La, Lb, Ra, Rb ,C);
                       %calling 2nd RK
%=============================
t1 = uicontrol(gcf,'Style','text', ...
   'String',...
      ['La=',num2str(La)],...
   'HorizontalAlignment','Left',...
   'Position',[30,360,100,20],...
   'BackgroundColor',[0.8 0.8 0.8]);
t1B= uicontrol(gcf,'Style','text', ...
   'String',...
```

```
            ['Lb=',num2str(Lb)],...
        'HorizontalAlignment','Left',...
        'Position',[130,360,100,20],...
        'BackgroundColor',[0.8 0.8 0.8]);
t2 = uicontrol(gcf,'Style','text', ...
        'String',...
            ['Ra=',num2str(Ra)],...
        'HorizontalAlignment','Left',...
        'Position',[30,340,100,20],...
        'BackgroundColor',[0.8 0.8 0.8]);
t2B = uicontrol(gcf,'Style','text', ...
        'String',...
            ['Rb=',num2str(Rb)],...
        'HorizontalAlignment','Left',...
        'Position',[130,340,100,20],...
        'BackgroundColor',[0.8 0.8 0.8]);

t3 = uicontrol(gcf,'Style','text', ...
        'String',...
            ['C=',num2str(C)],...
        'HorizontalAlignment','Left',...
        'Position',[30,320,100,20],...
        'BackgroundColor',[0.8 0.8 0.8]);
%==============================Slider control
b1 = uicontrol(gcf,'Style','text', ...
        'String','La',...
        'Position',[10,50,110,20],...
        'BackgroundColor',[0.8,0.8,1]);
b2 = uicontrol(gcf,'Style','text',...
        'String','0.01............0.1',...
        'Position',[10,30,110,20]);
b3 = uicontrol(gcf,...
        'Style','slider',...
        'Min' ,0.01,'Max', 0.1, ...
        'Position',[10,10,110,20], ...
        'Value', La,...
        'CallBack', ...
        ['cla;La=get(b3,''Value'');',...
         'set(t1,''String'',[''La='',num2str(La)]);',...
        ])
%=============================Slider for Green
g1 = uicontrol(gcf,'Style','text', ...
        'String','Lb',...
        'Position',[130,50,110,20],...
        'BackgroundColor',[0.8,1,0.8]);
g2 = uicontrol(gcf,'Style','text',...
        'String','0.1............0.5',...
```

```
            'Position',[130,30,110,20]);
    g3 = uicontrol(gcf,...
        'Style','slider',...
        'Min' ,0.1,'Max', 0.5, ...
        'Position',[130,10,110,20], ...
        'Value', Lb,...
        'CallBack', ...
        ['cla;Lb=get(g3,''Value'');',...
        'set(t1B,''String'',[''Lb='',num2str(Lb)]);',...
        ])
    %=============================Slider for RED
    r1 = uicontrol(gcf,'Style','text', ...
        'String','Ra',...
        'Position',[250,50,110,20],...
        'BackgroundColor',[1,0.8,0.8]);
    r2 = uicontrol(gcf,'Style','text',...
        'String','20............200',...
        'Position',[250,30,110,20]);
    r3 = uicontrol(gcf,...
        'Style','slider',...
        'Min' ,20,'Max',200, ...
        'Position',[250,10,110,20], ...
        'Value', Ra,...
        'CallBack', ...
        ['cla;Ra=get(r3,''Value'');',...
        'set(t2,''String'',[''Ra='',num2str(Ra)]);',...
        ])
    %=============================== Push button
    r1 = uicontrol(gcf,'Style','Push', ...
        'String','Push to  start RK',...
        'Position',[380,10,110,60],...
        'CallBack',...
        'disp([La,Lb,Ra,Rb,C]);APE_rk(La,Lb,Ra,Rb,C)');
```

APE_circ.m

```
% APE_circ.m    Draws an electric circuit diagram
cla
hold off
%axis('square')
axis([-0.3,4,-0.5,2.5]);
hold on
%battery_(0.1, 0.2, [0.0, 0], [0.0, 2]);
text(0-0.2 ,0, 'B')

text(0-0.2,2, 'A')
switch_(0.5, 1, [0,0], [2,0]);
capacitor_(0.1, 0.3, [2,0], [2,1])
```

```
resist_(6,0.5,   0.2, [2,1], [2,2]);
coil_(6,0.4, 0.07, [0,2],[2.,2]);
%coil_trad(4, 0.3, [0.8,2],[2.2,2]);
line_([2,0],[3.5,0])

resist_(6,0.5,   0.1, [2,2], [3.5,2]);
coil_(6,0.4, 0.07, [3.5,2],[3.5,0]);
text(2+0.19, 0.5,'C')
text(2+0.19, 1.5,'Ra')
text(0.8,-0.3,'S')
text(3.7,1,'Lb')
text(1., 2.2, 'La')
text(2.7, 2.2, 'Rb')
text(-0.2, 1.0,'e(t)')
text( 0.5,2.-0.2, 'i1(t)');
arrow_(0.4, [1.2, 2-0.2], [1.6, 2-0.2] )
text( 2.3,2.-0.2, 'i2(t)');
arrow_(0.4, [2.9, 2-0.2], [3.3, 2-0.2] )
axis('off')

line_([0,0], [0,0.8])
line_([0,1.2], [0,2])
ellip_( 0, 1, 0.3, 0.2)
```

Application E.3

Nozzles for gas flows are used in many aerodynamic devices; for example, jet engines, rockets, and wind tunnels. Here, we consider converging-diverging nozzles to produce a supersonic flow.

Students of fluid dynamics should know how to compute the Mach numbers in the nozzle using the isentropic air table and the normal shock table. The GuiDm_18 simulates the flow of air in a converging-diverging nozzle using GUI (see Figure E.17). (The list of GuiDm_18 is not printed here because it is lengthy, but it is available from the download site.) Although the nozzle configuration is hard-coded, it can be changed easily by modifying the m-file. The only user input is the back pressure of the nozzle, which is specified through an editable text window. As soon as the back pressure is typed in and the return key is hit, graphical results are displayed.

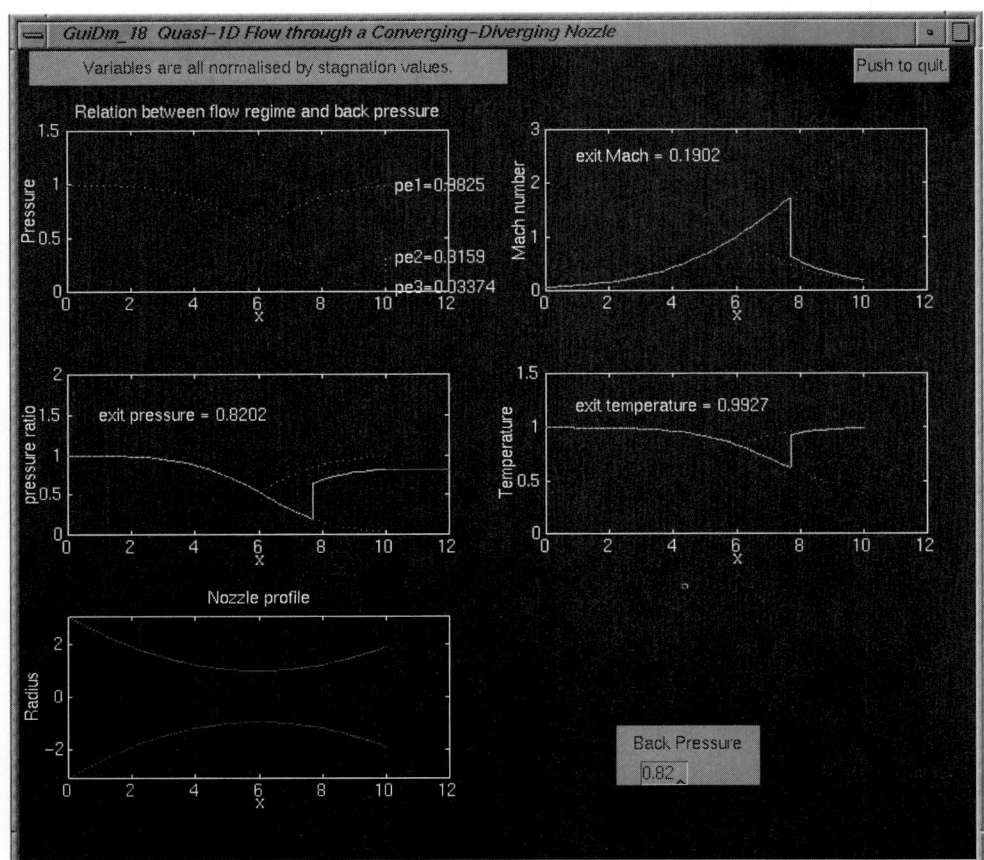

Figure E.17 GUI-guided analysis for nozzle aerodynamics.

Appendix F

ANSWER KEY

CHAPTER 1
(1.2)
  u=[y,x], v[x,y]
(1.3)
  [x;y]
(1.4)
  x=11:15
  z(k)=x.^2 + 2.3*x.^0.5
(1.5)
  x=[4 1 2]
  for n=1:length(x)
    z(n)=1/(1 + x(n)^2);
  end
  z
(1.6)
  a = [4 -1 2 -8 4 5 -3 -1 6 -7];
  for n=1:length(a)
    if a(n)<0, a(n)=a(n)*2;end
  end
  a
(1.7)
  a = [4 -1 2 -8 4 5 -3 -1 6 -7];
  b = [];
  for n=1:length(a)
    if a(n)<=0, b=[b,a(n)];end
  end
  b
(1.8)
  clear
  n=input('Type any odd number > 1: ')
  x(3:2:n)=2; x(2:2:n)=4;
  x(1)=1;x(n)=1;
  x
(1.9)
  clear
  n=input('Type any number for n: ')
  k=3*n+1;
  x(2:3:k)=3; x(3:3:k)=3;
  x(4:3:k-3)=2;
  x(1)=1; x(k)=1;
  x
(1.10)
  a = [4 -1 2 -8 4 5 -3 -1 6 -7];
  s=0;
  for n=1:length(a);
    if a(n)>0, s=s+a(n); end
  end
  s
  %s=21
(1.11)
  n=input('How may printers? ');
  s=0;
  for k=1:n
    if k==1, s=150;end
    if k==2, s=s+120;end
    if k>=3, s=s+110;end
  end
  s
(1.12)
  n=input('How many printers? ');
  s=0;
  for k=1:n
    if k==1, s=150;end
    if k==2, s=s+120;end
    if k>=3, s=s+110;end
    fprintf ...
      ('Number of printers %2.0f', k)
    fprintf ...
      (': Total price=$%3.0f\n', s)
  end
(1.13)
  n=input('How many cartridges? ');
  s=0;
  for k=1:n

```
        if mod(k,3)==1, s=s+50;end
        if mod(k,3)==2, s=s+35;end
    fprintf(' %2.0f cartridges',k)
    fprintf(': Total price=$%3.0f\n',s)
end
```
(1.14)
```
x=[7 1 2 4 8 5];
L=length(x);
for k=1:L
    c=0;
    for n=1:L-1
        if x(n)>x(n+1),
            temp=x(n); x(n)=x(n+1);
            x(n+1)=temp;
            c=c+1;
        end
    end
    if c==0 break, end
end
x
```
(1.15)
```
[1 2 5;3 1 2;4 1 3]
```
(1.16)
```
sum: 8 4 10
max: 4 2 5
min: 1 1 2
```
(1.17)
```
m=input('Type an integer: ')
p=0;
for n=2:m-1
    if mod(m,n)==0, p=1;break; end
end
if p==0, fprintf ...
    ('%3.0f is prime no.\n',m)
else fprintf ...
    ('%3.0f is not prime no.\n',m)
end
```
(1.18)
```
n=1:99;
for k=1:99
    if isprime(k)==1, n(k)=0;end
end
total=sum(n)
% The total is 3890
```
(1.19)
(a)
```
s=0;
for n=1:10; s=s+n/(n+1);end; s
```
(b)
```
n=1:10; sum(n./(n+1))
%x=7.9801
```
(1.20)
```
m=[1 2 5;3 1 2;4 1 3];
[ni,nj]=size(m);
for i=1:ni
    for j=1:nj
        if m(i,j)==1, m(i,j)=-1; end
    end
end
m
```
(1.21)
```
v='glacier';
L=length(v);
for m=1:L
    if v(m)=='i',
        fprintf('address = %1.0f\n', m)
    end
end
```
(1.22)
```
m=rand(4,4)
for i=1:4
    for j=1:4
        if m(i,j)<0.5,
            fprintf ...
            ('i=%1.0f, j=%1.0f\n', i,j);
        end
    end
end
```
(1.23)
```
function y = fun_es(x)
y = 0.5*exp(x./3) - x.^2.*sin(x);
```
(1.24)
```
function y = fun_lg(x)
y = sin(x).*log(1+x)-x.^2;
```
(1.25)
```
function x = quad_rt(a,b,c)
alen=length(a);
blen=length(b);
clen=length(c);
if (alen ~= blen | ...
    blen ~= clen | ...
    clen ~= alen)
fprintf ...
    ('Lengths of a,b,c inconsistent')
```

```
        return
    end
    x1 = -b/2./a;
    x2 = (-sqrt(b.^2-4*a.*c))/2./a;
    x=[x1+x2; x1-x2]
(1.26)
    function y = fun_ch(x)
    fprintf...
      ('Which  function to use?\n\n');
    fprintf(' fun_es\n  fun_lg\n');
    choice = ...
     input('Enter function name):',',','s');
     choice
    if (choice == 'fun_es'),
      y =fun_es(x);
    end
    if (choice == 'fun_lg'),
      y = fun_lg(x);
    end
    if (choice ~= 'fun_es' | ...
       choice ~= 'fun_lg')
       fprint('Invalid input. Stopped.\n');
    end
(1.27)
    x = 1:5
    y = [-1:-1:-5]'
    xsav=x, ysav=y'
    save f_asc xsav ysav -ascii
    clear
    load f_asc
    xloa = f_asc(1,:)
    yloa = f_asc(2,:)'
(1.28)
    A = [1 2 3 4 5 6 7 8 9 0];
    len = length(A);
    fprintf('Vector A is\n');
    fprintf('[ ');
    for i=1:len
       if (i < len)
          fprintf('%d,  ',A(i));
       else
          fprintf('%d ]\n',A(i));
       end
    end
    fprintf('Print completed.\n');
(1.29)
    dice_option = ...
```

```
     input('Enter 0 or 1:');
    if (dice_option == 1)
      fprintf ...
     ('Random no. (1 ~ 6): %f\n'...
        ,5*rand+1);
    elseif (dice_option == 0)
      break;
    end
(1.30)
    function f = fun_xa(x,n)
    f = 1;fac = 1;
    for i=1:n
      fac = fac*i;
      f = f + x^i/(fac);
    end
(1.31)
    function f = fun_xb(x,n)
    f = 0;
    for i=1:n
      f = f + (-1)^(i+1)*x^i/i;
    end

CHAPTER 2
(2.5)
  clear,close all
  delta=0.005
  x1a=0:0.01:pi-delta;
  x1b=pi+delta:0.01:3*pi-delta;
  x1c=3*pi+delta:0.01:4*pi;
  y1a=sin(x1a)./(1+cos(x1a));
  y1b=sin(x1b)./(1+cos(x1b));
  y1c=sin(x1c)./(1+cos(x1c));
  figure, plot(x1a,y1a), hold on
  plot(x1b,y1b),plot(x1c,y1c)
  axis([0 max(x1c) -10 10])
  title('(1)    y=sin(x)/(1+cos(x))')
  xlabel('x'); ylabel('y')
  plot([pi,pi],[-100,100],'k-.')
  plot([3*pi,3*pi],[-100,100],'k-.')
  plot([0, 20], [0,0],'k')
  hold off
  %
  x2=0:0.01:4;y2=1./(1+(x2-2).^2);
  figure, plot(x2,y2)
  title('(2)    y=1/(1+(x-2)^2)')
  xlabel('x'); ylabel('y')
```

```
%
x3=0:0.01:10;
y3=exp(-x3).*x3.^2;
figure, plot(x3,y3)
title('(3)  y=exp(-x)*x^2')
xlabel('x'); ylabel('y')
```
(2.6)
```
clg,clear;  x1=0; x2=pi/2-0.0001
dx=(x2-x1)/50; x=x1:dx:x2;
y=tan(x); plot(x,y); hold on
x1=pi/2+0.0001;
x2 = 3*pi/2-0.0001;
dx=(x2-x1)/50; x=x1:dx:x2;
y=tan(x); plot(x,y)
x1=3*pi/2+0.0001;
x2 = 5*pi/2-0.0001;
dx=(x2-x1)/50; x=x1:dx:x2;
y=tan(x); plot(x,y)
x1=5*pi/2+0.0001;
x2 = 10;
dx=(x2-x1)/50; x=x1:dx:x2;
y=tan(x); plot(x,y)
axis([0 10 -10 10]);
title('y=tan(x)');
xlabel('x'); ylabel('y')
```
(2.7)
```
close all,clear,hold off
x=0:0.05:6;a=3;b=1;
y=(x-1).*(x-2).*(x-4).*(x-5) ...
   /(a-1)./(a-2)./(a-4)./(a-5);
z=(x-2).*(x-3).*(x-4).*(x-5) ...
   /(b-2)./(b-3)./(b-4)./(b-5);
plot(x,y,x,z)
title('Problem 2.3');
xlabel('x'); ylabel('y')
axis([0 6 -20 20])
```
(2.10)
```
close all, clear
x=-1:0.01:1;
n=0;
figure(1)
for m=1:8
  n=n+1;
  if m==5, n=1; figure(2),end
  subplot(2,2,n)
  y=cos(m*acos(x));
  plot(x,y)
  title(['m=',int2str(m)])
  text(1.1,-1.2,'x')
  ylabel('y')
end
fprintf ...
  ('Move Fig 2 to see Fig 1.\n')
fprintf('Hit RETURN to end.\n')
pause
close all
```
(2.11)
```
clear, close all
x1=0.001:0.01:pi/2-0.001;
x1d=pi/2+ ...
    0.001:0.01:3*pi/2-0.001;
x1e=3*pi/2+0.001:0.01:5;
x2=0.0001:0.01:0.99;
x3=0.00001:0.01:2;
y1=tan(x1)./x1.^(0.3);
y2=exp(x2)./sqrt(1-x2.^2);
y3=x3.^(-x3);
figure(1); plot(x1,y1)
hold on
y1d=tan(x1d)./x1d.^(0.3);
plot(x1d,y1d)
y1e=tan(x1e)./x1e.^(0.3);
plot(x1e,y1e)
hold off
axis([0 5 -10 10])
title('(1) y=tan(x)/x^(0.3)')
xlabel('x'); ylabel('y')
figure(2), plot(x2,y2)
title('(2) y=exp(x)/sqrt(1-x^2)')
xlabel('x'); ylabel('y')
figure(3), plot(x3,y3)
title('(3) y=x^(-x)')
xlabel('x')
ylabel('y'); ylabel('y')
fprintf ...
  ('Move top fig to see another.\n')
fprintf('Hit RETURN to end.\n')
pause
close all
```
(2.12)
```
close all, clear
t=0:0.01:4*pi;
x=sin(-t)+t; y=1-cos(-t);
plot(x,y)
```

```
        title('Problem 2.6')
        xlabel('x'); ylabel('y')
(2.13)
        clear,close all
        a=[0 1 100]; b=[1 1 0];
        x=-3:0.01:3;
        y1=a(1)*x+b(1);
            z1=x+i*y1; w1=1./z1;
        y2=a(2)*x+b(2);
            z2=x+i*y2; w2=1./z2;
        y3=a(3)*x+b(3);
            z3=x+i*y3; w3=1./z3;
        plot(real(w1),imag(w1), '-')
        k=length(w1);
        text(real(w1(k))+0.05, ...
                imag(w1(k)),'1')
        hold on
        plot(real(w2),imag(w2),'--')
        k=length(w2);
        text(real(w2(k))+0.05, ...
                imag(w2(k)),'2')
        plot(real(w3),imag(w3),'-.')
        k=length(w3);
        text(real(w3(k))+0.05, ...
                imag(w3(k))+0.5,'3')
        hold off
        axis([-1.5 1.5 -1.5 1.5]), ...
                    axis('square')
        title('Problem 2.7')
(2.14)
        clear, close all
        [x,y]=meshgrid(-3:.2:3,-3:.2:3);
        z=0.2*cos(x)+y.*exp(-x.^2-y.^2);
        mesh(x,y,z)
    % Note the axes are different
    % if mesh(z) is used
        title('Problem 2.14')
(2.15)
        clear, close all
        [x,y]=meshgrid ...
           (0:.05:0.8,-0.35:.01:0.05);
        f=y.^2 + x.*exp(y) - tanh(x);
        cs=contour(x,y,f, [0,0]);
        title('Problem 2.15')
(2.16)
(2.17)
(2.18)
        clear, close all
        [x,y]=meshgrid ...
                (0:.2:5,0:.2:5);
        f = x.^2 - 8*x + y.^2 ...
            - 6*y -0.1*x.*y + 50;
        c = 0*x + 0*y + 23.7;
        meshc(x,y,f)
        % view(-90,0)
        % Remove the comment sign, then
        % you'll see the min. more clearly!
        text(2, 5, 50, 'min. cost ~23.8')
        text(2, 5, 45, 'x= ~4.5')
        text(2, 5, 40, 'y= ~3.2')
        xlabel('X'),ylabel('Y'),
        zlabel('f')
        view([30,30]);
        title('Problem 2.18')
(2.19)
        clear, close all
        [x,y]=meshgrid(0:.2:5,0:.2:5);
        f = x.^2 - 8*x + y.^2 ...
            - 6*y -0.1*x.*y + 50;
        fmin=min(min(f))+0.001;
        fmax=max(max(f))-0.001;
        df = (fmax-fmin)/10;
        level=fmin:df:fmax;
        c=contour(x,y,f, level);
        clabel(c)
        % view(-90,0)
        % Remove the comment sign, to
        % see the min. more clearly!
        hold on
        %mesh(x,y,c,8)
        hold off
        %text(2, 5, 50, ...
        %'min. cost ~23.8')
        %text(2, 5, 45, 'x= ~4.5')
        %text(2, 5, 40, 'y= ~3.2')
        xlabel('X'),ylabel('Y'),
        zlabel('f')
        % view([30,30])
        title('Problem 2.19')
(2.20)
        See or run h_faces.m in the
        Numerical Analysis and Graphic
        Visualization
        Toolbox.
```

(2.21)
(2.22) Left as a project.
(2.23) Left as a project.
(2.24) Left as a project.
(2.25) Left as a project.

CHAPTER 3
(3.1)
C =
5   3   5
3   3   5
3   1   4
D =
-3   1   1
-3 -1   3
3   -1   0
E =
10   8   10
3   6   9
12   5   10
(3.2)
B'A' =
10   3   12
8   6   5
10   9   10
(AB)' =
10   3   12
8   6   5
10   9   10
(3.3)
E =
16
9
11
(3.4)
D =
3   5   3   2
0   2   4   3
5   1   7   3
E =
-1 -1   3   0
0   0   4   1
1   -1 -3   3
F =
13   9   10
9   8   9

21   8   10
G =
10   9   20   12
6   8   19   10
6   1   8   8
3   7   13   5
H =
37
27
9
22
(3.5)
E =
14   6   15
-3   5   3
4   7   20
(3.6)
X1 =
1
3
2
X2 =
0.3625
0.2122
0.0911
(3.8)
a =
1 0 0   0.2500   2.0000   0.2500
0 1 0 -0.3125 -3.2500   1.6875
0 0 1   1.0625 -0.7500   0.0625
Therefore, the 3 sets of solutions are:
ans =
0.2500
-0.3125
1.0625
ans =
2.0000
-3.2500
-0.7500
ans =
0.2500
1.6875
0.0625
(3.9)
A =
7   1

```
            4       5
  The inverse of A is:
  ans =
    0.1613   -0.0323
   -0.1290    0.2258

  A*inv(A)=
    1.0000        0
    0        1.0000
  inv(A)*A=
    1.0000        0
    0        1.0000
(3.10)
  Inverse of A:
    1.0000  -1.0000        0        0
   -1.0000   2.0000  -1.0000        0
   -0.0000  -1.0000   2.0000  -1.0000
         0        0  -1.0000   2.0000

  Inverse of B:
   -0.0400    0.0400    0.1200
    0.5600   -1.5600    0.3200
   -0.2400    1.2400   -0.2800
(3.11)
  Inverse of M:
    0.5000   -0.5000    0.5000
   -0.5000    1.5000   -1.5000
    0.5000   -1.5000    2.5000
(3.12)
  The inverse of M is:
    0.9344   -0.5574    0.1475
    0.2295   -0.0492   -0.0164
   -0.1475    0.2459    0.0820
(3.13)
 (a)
  A =
     2   -1    0
    -1    2   -1
     0   -1    2
  l =
    1.0000        0        0
   -0.5000   1.0000        0
    0       -0.6667   1.0000
  u =
    2.0000  -1.0000        0
        0    1.5000  -1.0000
        0         0   1.3333
```

```
  ans =
     2   -1    0
    -1    2   -1
     0   -1    2
 (b)
  B =
     2   -1    0
    -3    4   -1
     0   -1    2
  l =
    1.0000        0        0
   -0.6667   1.0000        0
        0   -0.6000   1.0000
  u =
   -3.0000    4.0000   -1.0000
        0    1.6667   -0.6667
        0         0    1.6000
  ans =
     2   -1    0
    -3    4   -1
     0   -1    2
(3.14)
  x =
    2.5000
    4.0000
    3.5000
  x =
   -2
    2.3333
   10.333
(3.15)
  det(A) = -10
  det(B) = 7
  det(C) = 51
  det(D) = -199
(3.16)
  det(L)=(8)(8.75)(2.2)(4.9052)
  det(U)=1
  det(A)=det(l)det(u)=740
(3.17)
  (b)(c)(d) All fail.
(3.18)
  det(A) = 1/(det(B)det(C)det(D))
         = -4.9603e-04
(3.19)
  det(A)  = -2016
  det(A')= -2016
```

(3.20)
  hilb(5)
  (a) 1, 1
  (b) 1, 1
  hilb(12):
  (a) 0.9496, 1.1469
  (b) 226.29, 51.3998
(3.23)
  (b) poly([2 4 6; 1 -1 5; 2 0 1])
  ans=1.0000 -2.0000 -17.0000 -46.0000

CHAPTER 4
(4.1)
  ((((x-3)x+2)x+1)x+2),
  (((((3*x+0)*x+2)*x+1)*x+0)*x+7)
(4.2)
  First equation:
  Define roots of the polynomial as:
  r1 = 1.8463 + 0.8105i
  r2 = 1.8463 - 0.8105i
  r3 = -0.3463 + 0.6099i
  r4 = -0.3463 - 0.6099i
  Then, y=(x-r1)(x-r2)(x-r3)(x-r4)
  Second equation:
  Define:
  r1 = -1.1254
  r2 = -0.2821 + 1.2085i
  r3 = -0.2821 - 1.2085i
  r4 = 0.8448 + 0.7954i
  r5 = 0.8448 - 0.7954i
  Then,
  y=3(x-r1)(x-r2)(x-r3)(x-r4)(x-r5)
(4.3)
  Answer for the first equation:
  (a)
  Coefficients of the power series:
  5* poly([3 4 -1 -3])
  ans = 5*[1   -3   -13   27   36]
  (b)
  x=[3 4 -1 -3 0];
  y=[0 0 0 0 5*(-3)*(-4)*(3)];
  polyfit(x,y,4)
  ans =
      5   -15   -65   135   180
(4.4)
  (a) Coefficients of the power series:

c =
  -0.0523 -0.0472 -0.4129 0.9179
  (b) Clustered form:
  y(x) = -0.0523(((x + c2/c1)x + ...
                     c3/c1)x + c4/c1)
  where
    c2/c1 =0.9031,
    c3/c1=7.9005,
    c4/c1=-17.5619
  (c) Factorized form:
  y = -0.0523(x-r1)(x-r2)(x-r3)
  where
    r1 = -1.2102 + 3.1794i
    r2 = -1.2102 - 3.1794i
    r3 =   1.5174
(4.5)
  x= [1 2.5 4 5 6.1 7.2 10]
  y =[0 0   0 1 0   0   0]
  c=polyfit(x,y,6)
  ans =
      -0.0083 0.2545 -3.0427 17.8558 ...
  -53.2742 74.5124 -36.2975
(4.6)
  b=(5-1)*(5-2.5)*(5-4)*(5-6.1) ...
      (5-7.2)(5-10);
  poly([1, 2.5, 4, 6.1,7.2, 10])/b
  ans =
      -0.0083 0.2545 -3.0427 17.8558 ...
  -53.2742 74.5124 -36.2975
(4.7)
  c=polyfit([0, -2, 1, 2], ...
              [1, 0, 0, 0],3)
  ans = 0.2500 -0.2500 -1.0000 1.0000
(4.8)
  (a) c=-0.5000   1.0000
  (b) c= 0.6667 -3.0000   3.3333
  (c) c= 0.2500 -1.0000 -0.7500   2.5000
(4.9)
  (a) c= 1.5000   2.5000
  (b) c= 0.6250 -0.2500 -1.0000
  (c) c= 0.0000   0.5000   1.5000   0.0000
(4.10)
  clear, clf, dx=pi/4/50;
  x=0:dx:pi/4;
  y1=x/(pi/4)*sin(pi/4);
  plot(x,sin(x)-y1)
  max(sin(x)-y1)

ans = 0.0298
(4.11)
```
clear
dx=pi/4/50;   x=0:dx:pi/4;
e = abs(-0.5*x.*(x-pi/4)*(-0.3827));
plot(x,e), max(e)
ans = 0.0295
```
(4.12)
(a)
c = -0.1256 -0.3770 0.9130
(b)
f = 0.6416
(4.13)
c =
-0.0523 -0.0472 -0.4129 0.9179
(4.14)

f(x)	x
0.4137	0.9867
0.7233	0.4359
0.8501	0.1569

(4.15)
c =
 0.0840 -0.4100 0.4040 1.2100
f(1.75)=1.1116, f'(1.75)=-0.2592
(4.17) See (4.15) for f and f'.
(4.21)
(b)
y =
+(-1.3333x^3 + 6.0000x^2
    - 8.6667x + 4.0000)*y1
+(4.0000x^3 + -16.0000x^2
    +19.0000x - 6.0000)*y2
+(-4.0000x^3 + 14.0000x^2
    -14.0000x + 4.0000)*y3
+(1.3333x^3 + -4.0000x^2
    + 3.6667x - 1.0000)*y4

CHAPTER 5
(5.1)
(a)
Extended Trapezonidal Rule
for integrating f(x) = tan(x)

n	I
2	0.35901
4	0.34976
6	0.34800
8	0.34737

(b)
Extended Trapezonidal Rule
for integrating f(x) = exp(x)

n	I
2	1.75393
4	1.72722
6	1.72226
8	1.72052

(c)
Extended Trapezonidal Rule
for integrating f(x) = 1/(2+x)

n	I
2	0.40833
4	0.40619
6	0.40579
8	0.40565

(5.2)
Extended Trapezonidal Rule
for integrating f(x) = sin(x)

n	I	Error
2	0.94806	0.05194
4	0.98712	0.01288
8	0.99679	0.00321
25	0.99967	0.00033
100	0.99998	0.00002

(5.3)
Time needed to drain the water is 30.0hr.
(5.4)
  1.6231 1.9192 1.9997
(5.5) 0.3881 with 20 intervals
      0.3927 (exact)
(5.6)
I_romberg =   2.0265
(5.7)
  h = 0.25   0.5
  I = 0.6811125   0.676975
  I_romberg = 0.682492
(5.8)
```
clear
v1 =polyfit([-1,0,1], ...
            [1,0,0],2);
```

```
V1=poly_itg(v1);
   w1= polyval(V1,1) ...
       - polyval(V1,-1);
v2 =polyfit([-1,0,1], ...
            [0,1,0],2);
V2=poly_itg(v2);
w2=polyval(V2,1) - ...
       polyval(V2,-1);
v3 =polyfit([-1,0,1], ...
            [0,0,1],2);
V3=poly_itg(v3);
w3=polyval(V3,1) - ...
       polyval(V3,-1);
ans:
   w1 = 0.33333333333333
   w2 = 1.33333333333333
   w3 = 0.33333333333333
```

(5.11)
(a)
```
clear
for L=[2,4,8,16,32]
i=0:L; h=pi/L; x=0+ i*h;
f=1./(2+cos(x));
w(1:L:L+1)=1; w(2:2:L)=4;
w(3:2:L-1)=2;
I_a=(1/3)*h*sum(f.*w);
disp([L,I_a])
end
#intvl   I
    2    1.74532925199433
    4    1.80766243956556
    8    1.81376723628645
   16    1.81379936338045
   32    1.81379936423422
```
(b)
```
    2    0.61431587942640
    4    0.61428180399030
    8    0.61427949131182
   16    0.61427934338188
   32    0.61427933408061
```
(c)
```
    2    1.09083078249646
    4    1.11008073748169
    8    1.11072017850517
   16    1.11072073453917
   32    1.11072073453959
```

(5.12)
(a) n=2,   I=2.1376
    n=32, I=2.0973
(b) n=2,   I=1.2761
    n=32, I=1.2912
(c) n=2,   I=8.5770
    n=32, I=8.5527

(5.13)
56.52 m

(5.14)
291.6 m (Exact 291.86)

(5.16)
n=2: 18.805
n=4: 21.526
n=6: 21.540

(5.19)
```
h=0.1;
x=-10:h:10;
f=exp(-x.^2)./(1+x.^2);
h*sum(f)
h=0.1:  ans=1.34329342164674
  0.01:     1.34329342164674
  0.001:    1.34329342164672
```

(5.20)
a: 1.8138
b: 0.6143
c: 2.0973
d: -0.2400
e: 0.2329

(5.21) (a) 0.9063, (b) 3.1044

(5.22)
Applying the extended trapezoidal rule of 2 intervals for the integral on the x coordinate, the double integral can be written as
I = (0.5/2)[G(1)+2G(1.5)+G(2)]   (a)
where G(1) is the integral of sin(1+y) in the y-direction from y=0 to y=1. Each G can be calculated by the extended trapezoidal rule as
G(1) = (0.5/2)[sin(1+0)+sin(1+0.5)
              +sin(1+1)]=0.94644
G(1.5)=0.85364
G(2)=0.56184
So, (a) becomes
I = 0.80139 with trazepoidal

```
clear
x=1;
g1=0.5/2* ...
  (sin(x+0)+2*sin(x+0.5)+sin(x+1));
x=1.5;
g15=0.5/2* ...
  (sin(x+0)+2*sin(x+0.5)+sin(x+1));
x=2;
g2=0.5/2* ...
  (sin(x+0)+2*sin(x+0.5)+sin(x+1));
I=0.5/2*(g1+2*g15+g2)
```
(5.23)
```
Using the extended Simpson 1/3 rule,
I=(0.25/3)[G(0)+4G(0.5)+G(1)]
 =(0.25/3)[0+4(0.4309)+1.2188]
 =0.4904
%
clear
x=0;g0=0;
x=0.5;
g05=x/2/3* ...
  (sqrt(x+0)+4*sqrt(x+x/2)+sqrt(x+x));
x=1;
g1=x/2/3* ...
  (sqrt(x+0)+4*sqrt(x+x/2)+sqrt(x+x));
I=0.5/3*(g0+4*g05+g1)
```
(5.24)

2x2	2.6666
4x4	2.9760
8x8	3.0835
16x16	3.1211
32x32	3.1343
64x64	3.1390

(5.26)
I=0.36686
(5.27)
Using the extended Simpson's rule of 2 intervals,
I=(0.5/3)[1.9682+4(1.8154)+1.5784]
 =1.8014

CHAPTER 6
(6.1)
$y'(0) = 66.31$
$y''(0) = -263.86$
$y'''(0) = 576.11$
$y''''(0) = -891.18$
$y'''''(0) = 807.81$
$y'(0.5) = -10.06$
$y''(0.5) = 70.37$
$y'''(0.5) = 231.49$
$y''''(0.5) = -487.28$
$y'''''(0.5) = 807.81$

(6.2)
$y'(0) = 6.293e+003$
$y''(0) = -1.508e+006$
$y'''(0) = 2.485e+008$
$y''''(0) = -2.500e+010$

(6.3)

h	(a)	(b)	(c)
0.1	0.04293	-0.04113	0.900e-3
0.05	0.02125	-0.02080	0.225e-3
0.01	0.00421	-0.00419	0.900e-5
0.005	0.00210	-0.00210	0.225e-5
0.001	0.00042	-0.00042	0.900e-7

(6.4)
(a)

h	forward	backward	central
0.1	0.0119	-0.0132	-0.0006
0.05	0.0061	-0.0064	-0.0002
0.025	0.0031	-0.0032	-0.00004

(b)

h	forward	backward	central
0.1	0.0125	-0.0125	-0.0006
0.05	0.0063	-0.0063	-0.0002
0.025	0.0031	-0.0031	-0.00004

(6.5)
On the z coordinate, the coefficient of f_{-2} is a quadratic polynomial fitted to
  z=[-2 -1 0], g=[1 0 0]
that can be determined by the polyfit command. Similarly, the coefficient of f_{-1} is the quadratic polynomial fitted to
  z=[-2 -1 0], g=[0 1 0]. The coefficient of f_0 is also a quadratic polynomifal fitted to
  z=[-2 -1 0], g=[0 0 1].
The coeffcents in the polynomial form can be differentiated by the polyder command, and then evaluated for z=0 by the polyval

command. Script is:
```
c=polyfit([-2 -1 0],[1 0 0],2)
d=polyder(c); polyval(d,0); %0.5
c=polyfit([-2 -1 0],[0 1 0],2)
d=polyder(c); polyval(d,0); %-2.0
c=polyfit([-2 -1 0],[0 0 10],2)
d=polyder(c); polyval(d,0); %1.5
```
The final result is

Point	Coefficient
-2h	0.5/h
-1h	-2/h
0h	1.5/h

(6.8)

h	(a)	(b)
0.1000	0.0010	0.0015
0.0500	0.0003	0.0003
0.0250	0.0001	0.0001

(6.9)

h	(a)	(b)
0.1000	-0.0016	-0.0020
0.0500	-0.0004	-0.0005
0.0250	-0.0001	-0.0001

(6.10)
Script
```
x=[-2 -1 0 1 2];
c(5,:)=polyfit(x,[1 0 0 0 0],4);
c(4,:)=polyfit(x,[0 1 0 0 0],4);
c(3,:)=polyfit(x,[0 0 1 0 0],4);
c(2,:)=polyfit(x,[0 0 0 1 0],4);
c(1,:)=polyfit(x,[0 0 0 0 1],4);
c(:,2)*3*2
```
Ans:

term	coefficent
f(2h):	0.5000/h^3
f(h):	-1.0000/h^3
f(0):	0.0000/h^3
f(-h):	1.0000/h^3
f(-2h):	-0.5000/h^3

(6.12)
  (a) 0.5hf", hf"
  (b) alpha=2

(6.13) alpha=4/3

(6.16)

term	coefficient
f(-0.1)	-4/0.6
f(0)	3/0.6
f(0.2)	1/0.6

Error term
    (-1/3)(0.01) f'''

(6.17)
Error term
    (1/2)h^2f'''

(6.19)
(a) poly_drv([0, 0.001], ...
               [0, 0.4171],0)
    du/dy(0) =
    417.1 /s (approximately)
    shear stress =
      (0.001)(417.1) = 0.4171 N/m^2

(b)
```
c=polyfit([0, 0.001, 0.003],
          [0, 0.4171, 0.9080],2)
polyder(c)
```
or alternatively
poly_drv([0, 0.001, 0.003], ...
          [0, 0.4171, 0.9080],0)
474.3
du/dy(0) = 474.3 /s
         (approximately)
shear stress =
    (0.001)(474.3) = 0.4743 N/m^2

(6.20)
(a) (-0.2412*3+4*0.4767-0.7002)/(2*0.5)
    = 0.4830, or equivalently
    c=polyfit([0 0.5 1],...
    [0.2412, 0.4767, 0.7002],2)
    polyder(c)
    or alternatively
    poly_drv([0 0.5 1],...
      [0.2412, 0.4767, 0.7002],0)
    Ans=0.483

(b) (0.4547-2* 0.7002+ 0.9653)/0.5^2
    = 0.0784, or alternatively
    poly_drv([0.5 1 1.5], ...
      [0.4547, 0.7002, 0.9653],1)
    Ans=0.0784

(c) (-3*(-3*0.0775 +4* 0.1573 -0.2412)
    +4*(-3*0.1528+4*0.3104 -0.4767)-
    (-3*0.2235 +4* 0.4547 - 0.7002))
    /(2*0.5)/(2*0.5)
    = 0.3114

CHAPTER 7
(7.1) (a) 0.6772, 0.19068
 (b) 0, 0.7469
(7.2)
 (a) 4.428, 7.706
 (b) 0.5419
 (c) 0.8527
 (d) 0.3786
(7.3) Find the solution of
 $f(x)=\tan(x)-3.5=0$
 $x=1.2925$
(7.5) (a) 0.3, (b) 0.03389, 0.7652
(7.7) 0.2155, ideal gas: 0.2553
(7.8)
 (a) 0.6772, 1.9068
 (b) 0, 0.7469
 (c) -0.3714, 0.6053, 4.7079
 (d) 0.4534
 (e) 2
(7.9) (a) 0.5885, 3.0964
 (c) Graphic analysis, and very small h.
(7.10) 1.6581, 1.7362, 3.4829, 4.0287
(7.11) 2.3470, 5.4978, 8.6394
(7.12) $x=0.2967$
(7.13) $x=0.4717$
(7.16) (1) $f=0.05411$, (2) $f=0.01967$

CHAPTER 8
(8.1)
 $g(x)=1.9x+0.22$
(8.2)
 $g(x)=-10.012x+11.026$
(8.3)
 $g(x)=1.2070\exp(-0.4914x)$
(8.5)
 $g(x)=-0.2488x^2+2.632x-0.0333$
(8.6)
 $g(x)=-0.0027764x^3-0.002238x^2 + 2.576x - 0.01667$
(8.8)
 $g(x) = 240.2x + 0.1019$
 $g(x) = -13982.1x^2 + 352.06x - 0.0099565$
 $g(x) = -1019702x^3 - 1745.6x^2 + 316.98x - 0.00016729$
(8.9)
 $g(x) = 41.559x^3 - 101.60x^2 + 60.074x - 0.11771$
(8.10)
 $g(x) = -1.8576 + 3.8143x + 3.2418\sin(pi*x) + 1.0941\sin(2*pi*x)$

CHAPTER 9
(9.2)
Consider the x data and y data points as functions of equispaced s points:

s:1 2 3 4 5 6 7 8 9 10 11
x:0 1 2 3 3.5 3.7 3.5 3 2 1 0

s:1 2 3 4 5 6 7 8 9 10 11
y:0 1 1.5 1.5 1 0 -1 -1.5 -1.5 -1 0

We fit spline functions to each set with cyclic boundary conditions. Since spacing of s is unity, all h values in Eq.(9.1.14) are unity. So the coefficient matrix becomes

```
4 1                   1
1 4 1
  1 4 1
    1 4 1
      1 4 1
        1 4 1
          1 4 1
            1 4 1
              1 4 1
1               1 4
```

The right side becomes
6(x(10)-2x(1)+x(2))
6(x(1)-2x(2)+x(3))
6(x(2)-2x(3)+x(4))
6(x(3)-2x(4)+x(5))
6(x(4)-2x(5)+x(6))
6(x(5)-2x(6)+x(7))
6(x(6)-2x(7)+x(8))
6(x(7)-2x(8)+x(9))
6(x(8)-2x(9)+x(10))
6(x(9)-2x(10)+x(11))
6(x(10)-2x(11)+x(2))

The solution determines
dx^2/ds^2 for each point.
The matrix for y is the same.
The right side term is the
same as for x except x is
replaced by y.
%=================================
```
clear, close
s=[1 2 3 4 5   6   7   8 9 10 11];
x=[0 1 2 3 3.5 3.7 3.5 3 2 1  0];
s=[1 2 3   4   5 6 7 ...
              8   9   10 11 ];
y=[0 1 1.5 1.5 1 0 -1 ...
             -1.5 -1.5 -1  0];
for i=1:11
   A(i,i)=4;
   if i>1, A(i,i-1)=1;
       xm=x(i-1);ym=y(i-1);
   else A(1,10)=1;
       xm=x(10);ym=y(10);
   end

   if i<11, A(i,i+1)=1;
       xp=x(i+1);yp=y(i+1);
   else   A(i,2)=1;
       xp=x(2);; yp=y(2);
   end
    dx(i) =6*(xm-2*x(i)+xp);
    dy(i) =6*(ym-2*y(i)+yp);
end
xdd=A\dx';
ydd=A\dy';
x(12)=x(1);
xdd(12)=xdd(1);
y(12)=y(1);
ydd(12)=ydd(1);
for i=1:11
ax(i)=x(i);
bx(i)=(x(i+1)-x(i)) ...
      - (xdd(i+1)+2*xdd(i))/6;
cx(i)=xdd(i)/2;
dx(i)=(xdd(i+1)-xdd(i))/6;
ay(i)=y(i);
by(i)=(y(i+1)-y(i)) ...
      - (ydd(i+1)+2*ydd(i))/6;
cy(i)=ydd(i)/2;
dy(i)=(ydd(i+1)-ydd(i))/6;
end
[s',bx',cx',dx']
sr=0:0.1:10;
for k=1:length(sr)
    n=floor(sr(k))+1;
    h=sr(k)-floor(sr(k));
    xr(k)=ax(n)+bx(n)*h ...
         +cx(n)*h^2+dx(n)*h^3;
    yr(k)=ay(n)+by(n)*h ...
         +cy(n)*h^2+dy(n)*h^3;
end
plot(xr,yr)
hold on
plot(x,y,'*')
```

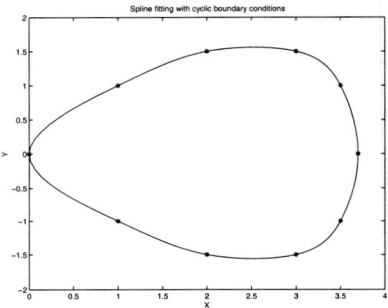

Figure F.1 b-spline.

(9.3)

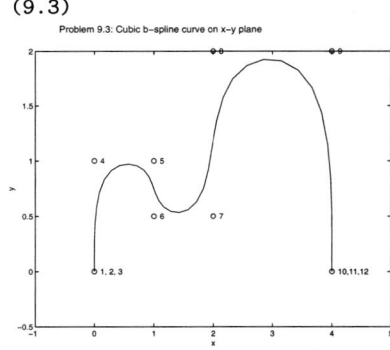

Figure F.2 b-spline.

(9.4)
```
a+c=0
a*exp(b) +c=2
```

```
    a*exp(5b)+c=4
    Solve
    f(b)=2exp(b)- exp(5b)-1=0
    by Newton iteration.
    b=-0.6563, a=-4.1563, c=4.1563
```

CHAPTER 10

(10.1)
With h=0.01:

Case	1	2	3
t	y	y	y

---

t	y	y	y
0	1.0000	1.0000	0.5000
1	1.3361	0.2073	0.4440
2	0.7765	0.06894	1.7903
3	0.4038	2.4885E-2	4.9169
4	0.2706	9.1376E-3	9.9632
5	0.2092	3.3607E-3	16.980

Case	4	5
t	y	y

---

t	y	y
0	1.0000	1.0000
1	0.4982	0.6109
2	0.3321	0.7439
3	0.2491	0.5006
4	0.1993	-0.2666
5	0.1661	-2.2338

(10.2)

---

t	y	z

---

t	y	z
0	1.0	0
1	0.9625	-0.1519
2	0.7726	-0.3000

(10.3)
With h=0.01:

Case	1	2	3	4
t	y	y	y	y

---

t	y	y	y	y
0	1.0	0.0000	1.0000	1.0000
1	-0.9514	0.8489	0.8797	1.0612
2	0.8102	0.9191	0.5383	1.3609
3	-0.5902	0.1359	0.3042	1.8860
4	0.3128	-0.7689	0.1760	2.5510
5	-0.0050	-0.9586	0.1032	3.2889

(10.4)
Solution for t=1 is obtained by
```
h=0.1;  y=[1,0]';
a=[ 4/h+3/2,  -7/2;  -2/2, 7/h+8/2];
b=[ 4/h+-3/2,   7/2;   2/2, 7/h+-8/2];
s=[0,0]';
for n=1:10
  y=a\((b*y)+s)
end; y
```

With h=0.1

t	y	z
0	1	0
0.5000	0.7277	0.0912
1.0000	0.5804	0.1213
1.5000	0.4901	0.1260
2.0000	0.4269	0.1205
2.5000	0.3780	0.1115
3.0000	0.3373	0.1016
3.5000	0.3022	0.0920
4.0000	0.2713	0.0830
4.5000	0.2437	0.0747
5.0000	0.2191	0.0672

(10.5) The velocity of water, v, is related
to the water level, y, by v^2=2gy, or
v=sqrt(2gy). Radius of tank is r=0.25y.
The mass balance equation is
   pi*r^2dy=-pi(0.02)^2vdt, or with
r=0.25y and v=sqrt(19.6y),
   0.25^2y^2dy = -sqrt(19.6y)0.02^2dt
or dy/dt=-0.0283340sqrt(y)/y^2
The tank becomes empty at
approximately 2.51s.

(10.6)

---

x	y (F. Euler)	y (Analytical)
1.0000	0.0434	0.0432
2.0000	0.0491	0.0491

3.0000	0.0499	0.0499
4.0000	0.0500	0.0500
5.0000	0.0500	0.0500

(10.7)
The computed results during the first 1 s are shown in the following table:

Time(sec)	y	y'
0.0	0.1	0.0
0.1000	0.0904	-0.1898
0.2000	0.0634	-0.3434
0.3000	0.0241	-0.4310
0.4000	-0.0200	-0.4356
0.5000	-0.0602	-0.3561
0.6000	-0.0890	-0.2077
0.7000	-0.1006	-0.0190
0.8000	-0.0928	0.1738
0.9000	-0.0671	0.3334
1.0000	-0.0284	0.4290

(10.8)
The computed results for the first 1 s are shown in the following table:

Time(sec)	y	y'
0.0	0.1	0.0
0.1000	0.0907	-0.1825
0.2000	0.0653	-0.3175
0.3000	0.0296	-0.3834
0.4000	-0.0088	-0.3732
0.5000	-0.0428	-0.2945
0.6000	-0.0662	-0.1671
0.7000	-0.0756	-0.0183
0.8000	-0.0703	0.1228
0.9000	-0.0523	0.2305
1.0000	-0.0260	0.2873

(10.9)

Time(hr)	N(iodine)
0.0000	1.0000E+05
0.5	0.9491E+05
1.0	0.9008E+05

(10.10)
The computed results are shown in the following table:

Time(hr)	N(iodine)	N(xenon)
0	1.0000E+05	0
5	5.9333E+04	3.3339E+04
10	3.5204E+04	4.2660E+04
15	2.0888E+04	4.1012E+04
20	1.2393E+04	3.5108E+04
25	7.3533E+03	2.8225E+04
30	4.3629E+03	2.1821E+04
35	2.5886E+03	1.6430E+04
40	1.5359E+03	1.2138E+04
45	9.1131E+02	8.8418E+03
50	5.4071E+02	6.3716E+03

(10.11) With h=0.5,
t=0.5 y=0.5833
t=1   y=0.3538

(10.12)
n=1: $y(1) = y\_1 = 0.9$
n=2: $y(2) = y\_2 = 1.6153$

(10.14)
$y(0.5) = y\_1 = 0.4375$
$z(0.5) = z\_1 = 0.7422$
$y(1) = y\_2 = 0.7468$,
$z(1) = z\_2 = 0.4869$

(10.15)
The computed results are

x	y	v=y'	w=y''
0	1	0	0
0.2	1	-0.02	-0.2
0.4	0.992	-0.08	-0.3996
0.6	0.968	-0.17976	-0.5964
0.8	0.920128	-0.31840	-0.7864
1.0	0.84072	-0.49408	-0.9641

(10.16)
(a) The concentration becomes 1/10 at approximately t=57min.

(b) The peak occurs approximately at t = 12min.

t(min)	y1	y2
0	10	0
2	9.231366	1.648955
4	8.521812	2.745326
6	7.866797	3.441559
8	7.262129	3.849981
10	6.703938	4.053222
12	6.18865	4.111933
14	5.71297	4.070513
16	5.273852	3.961353
18	4.868486	3.807974
20	4.494278	3.627362
22	4.148833	3.431688
24	3.82994	3.229584
26	3.535558	3.027089
28	3.263803	2.828346
30	3.012936	2.636116
32	2.781351	2.452163
34	2.567567	2.277528
36	2.370215	2.11274
38	2.188033	1.957966
40	2.019853	1.813121
42	1.8646	1.67795
44	1.721281	1.552086
46	1.588977	1.435094
48	1.466843	1.326499
50	1.354097	1.225808
52	1.250016	1.13253
54	1.153936	1.046178
56	1.065241	.9662828
58	.9833625	.8923951
60	.907778	.8240876

(10.17)
y(1) = 0.3307

(10.18)

t	h=0.5	h=1
0	0	0
1	0.32233	0.32388
2	-0.59577	-0.59636

(10.19)
The result of the second-order Runge-Kutta scheme is 393.07 m, while the third-order Runge-Kutta scheme gives 392.57 m.

(10.20)
(a) he local error of the second-order Runge-Kutta scheme is proportional to h3 so we can write the error for one step with a step size h as
$E(h) = Ah^3$
Therefore, considering the solutions for y(0.2) with h=0.1 and h=0.2, we can write
$y(0.2; h=0.1) + 2A(0.1)^3$
$= y(0.2; h=0.2) + A(0.2)^3$
Introducing the computed solution of the table to the foregoing equation yields
0.894672+0.002A
=0.8947514+0.008A
or after rewriting,
- 0.000079 = 0.006A
or
A = -0.000079/0.006
= -0.079/6= -0.01316
Therefore, an estimate for the error of y(0.2; h=0.1) is
$2A(0.1)^3 = 2(-0.013)(0.001)$
= -0.000026
(b) An estimate for the exact value is 0.8946720 - 0.000026 = 0.894646
(c) Because $E(h) = Ah^3$, set
$0.00001 = |-0.01316|h^3$
The solution is
$h = (0.00001/0.01316)^{(1/3)}$
= 0.091
which is slightly less than h=0.1.

(10.21)
With h=0.2, and h=0.1, the second-order Runge-Kutta scheme gives, respectively
h=0.2: y(0.2) = 2.4374
h=0.1: y(0.2) = 2.4832

(10.23)
(a) The second-order Runge-Kutta

scheme for one step is
$y_{n+1} = y_n(1 + ah + 0.5(ah)^2)$
(b) If a = -0.01 for example, the domain of instability is h>200.

(10.25)
T = 392.9 K at t = 10 min.

Chapter 11

(11.5)

i	T C
1	96.26
2	92.90
5	84.92
8	80.13
10	78.89

(11.11)

i	T
1	901.8
2	459.2
3	346.8
4	277.2
5	222.6

(11.12)

x	T K
0	773
0.01	662.1
0.02	579.2
0.03	516.7
0.04	469.5
0.05	434.0
0.06	407.8
0.07	389.1
0.08	376.5
0.09	369.3
0.10	366.9

(11.14)

i	phi
1	1.1845
2	2.2764
3	3.2672
4	4.1488
5	4.9131
6	5.5524
7	6.0596
8	6.4283
9	6.6531
10	6.7292

SUBJECT INDEX

A
airfoil, 448
    NACA0012, 305
Alchemy, image, 457
Arithmetic operators, 7
array
    arithmetic operators, 20
    multiplication, 52
    variable, 18
arrow, 66, 67
axes, 486
    property, 68
axis, 55
    -square, 55, 86

B
backward
    difference, 253
    Euler method, 361
bilinear interpolation, 192
bisection method, 283
Blasius equation, 432
boundary
    conditions, 415
    layer, 433
    -value problem, 351, 414
break, 15
bullet, 291
b-spline, 324, 331

C
Cartesian grid, 75
Cauchy integral, 268
caxis, 84, 440
central difference, 253
characteristic polynomial, 151

Chebyshev
    points, 183
    polynomials, 108
clabel, 71
clear
    command window, clc, 10
    variables, 10
clf, 55
clock, 5
close, 56
clustered form, 12, 161
Colebrook correlation, 308
color
    axis, 84, 440
    map, 84, 439, 489
    mesh and surf, 84
    plotting, 77
complex
    roots, 162
    variables, 8
condition number, 132
continuation mark, 8
contour, 70, 298
    curvilinear grid, 75
    triangular grid, 73
    with mesh plot, 80
    with surface plot, 80
conv, 166
converging-diverging nozzle, 495
cubic
    root, 287
    spline, 168
curvilinear grid, 75, 82
cyclic boundary condition, 328
cylindrical coordinate, 427

c-spline, 324

D
date, 5
deconv, 166
degrees, 1
demo, 6
derivative, 250
diagonal matrix, 128
diary, 6
difference approximation, 252
differentiation, 250
    of polynomial, 165
    of Lagrange interpolation, 181
diffuse, 82
diffusion, 464
disp, 18
division, polynomial, 166
double
    integration, 231
    precision, 140

E
eigenvalue, 152, 485
eps, 9
equal, not equal, 11
error
    bisection method, 283
    interpolation, 166, 168, 177
    Runge-Kutta, 395
    Euler method, 358
escape, 6
Euler method, 355
exponent operator, 7
e-format, 17

F
figure, 54
filename, 4
    of movie, 455
finite difference, 285
flopsn, 9
format
    long, 9
    short, 9
formatted output, 17
forward difference, 253
forward Euler method, 355

forward Euler method, 369
fourth-order Runge-Kutta, 385, 396
fprintf, 17
furfl, 82
furnace, 289
f-format, 17

G
Gauss
    elimination, 135
    Gauss-Jordan elimination, 141
    Gauss-Legendre quadrature, 240
getenv, 6
getframe, 453
GIF, movie, 455
Gifanime, 455
ginput, 92
global error, 362
greater than, less than, 11
Greek symbols, 63
grid on, off, 56

H
happy face, 85
harmonic oscillation, 154
heat transfer, 374
Henon model, 465
Hermite interpolation, 188
higher-order ODE, 367
Hilbert matrix, 118
hold on, off, 59, 85
hsv, 77
hue saturation value, 77

I
identity matrix, 112, 117
if/end, 11
ill-conditioned, 1, 130, 317
Image Alchemy, 455, 457
image format, 457
implicit function, plotting, 55, 71
inf, 9
initial value problem, 351
instability, 358
integration
    Lagrange interpolation, 181
    polynomial, 165
    two-dimensional, 231

interpolation
    bilinear, 193
    Chebyshev points for, 183
    cubic, 168
    Hermite, 188
    Legendre points for, 187
    linear, 166
    transfinite, 195
interp1, 328
inverse matrix, 118
inversion of matrix, 141
irreducible matrix, 149
iterative solution, 149

J
Jacobi iterative method, 149
Jacobian, 298
jet, 439
JPEG, 67, 455

L
label, contour, 71
Lagrange interpolation, 170, 174, 254, 330
    integration of, 181
    differentiation of, 181
    double, 194
least square, 309
legend, 60, 66
Legendre
    points, 187
    polynomial, 219
length, 13
light, surface plot, 82
line
    color, 53
    type, 53
linear
    algebra, 110
    combination, 319
    interpolation, 166
linewidth, 51
Lobatto points, 186
local error, 362
log, 1, 57
loops, 12
lower-triangular matrix, 129
LView Pro, 455

M
mark, 52
matlabpath, 4
matrix
    inverse, 119
    inversion, 142
    irreducible, 150
mesh, 69
meshc, 80
meshgrid, 69
method of lines, 402
modified Euler method, 358
movie, 453
moviein, 453

N
NACA0012 airfoil, 305, 448
NaN, 9
nargin, 9
nargout, 9
natural convection, 374
natural frequency, 281
Newton iteration, 285, 294, 342, 430
Newton-Cotes formula, 215
new-line operator, 17
nonlinear curve fitting, 314
nonlinear ODE, 429
nonuniform grid, 424
null matrix, 112
number-to-string, 61
num2str, 61

O
ordinary differential equation, 351
osculating polynomial, 187
overdetermined equation, 121, 127, 312

P
paper position, 64
path, 5
permutation matrix, 113, 128, 147
pi, π, 7
pivoting, 137
pivoting, 141
plot
    surface, 76
    3d, 64
polar, 56

poly, 163
polyder, 165, 182
polyfit, 164, 312
polynomial, 316
    Chebyshev, 183
    osculating, 188
    Legendre, 219
polyval, 164
popup menu, 476, 477, 486
position, 477
PostScript, 67
power function, 314
product, polynomial, 166
property
    figure, 64
    editor, 66
push button, 479

Q
quit, 3
quiver, 72

R
radio button, 481
rand, 118
random matrix, 118
residual, 127, 128, 310, 316
rgbplot, 439
Romberg integration, 211, 398
roots, 162
    of polynomial, 152
rotation, 88, 444
Runge-Kutta, 371
    fourth-order, 385, 396

S
secant method, 290
second-order ODE, 363
semicolon, 7
semilog, 57
shading, 85
shape function, 174
shooting method, 399
Simpson
    1/3 rule, 210, 383
    3/8 rule, 385
simultaneous equations, 291
single precision, 140

singular matrix, 119, 126
singularity, 282, 287
skydiver, 353
slider, 482
soap bubble, 86
SOR, 149
spaghetti rule, 128
specular, 82
spherical coordinate, 427
spline, b-, c-, 324
square matrix, 112
stretching function, 343
string, 18
string variable, 17, 23
subplot, 63
subscript, 63
successive substitution, 279, 291, 359, 430
superscript, 63
surface, 76
    plot, 82
surfnorm, 82

T
Taylor
    expansion, 257, 285
    polynomial, 270
text, 63, 66
third-order Runge-Kutta, 383
time interval, 395
title, 60
tolerance, 283
tranlation, 443
transfinite interpolation, 195
translation, 88
transpose, 117
    operator, 19
    matrix, 112, 311
trapezoidal rule, 205, 222, 372
triangular grid, 73
tridiagonal equation, 419, 422
trigonometric, 1
two-dimensional plot, 68

U
uicontrol, 474, 475, 478
uimenu, 474
UL decomposition, 145
underdetermined equation, 121, 127

upper-triangular matrix, 129

V
van der Waals equation, 305
vector, plot, 72
velocity vector, 72
version, 4
vi editor, 6
view, 78
Vinokur, 343
viewer's eye position, 78

W
while/end, 12
working directory, 2

X
xlabel, 60

Y
ylabel, 60

Z
zeros, 279
zoom, 56

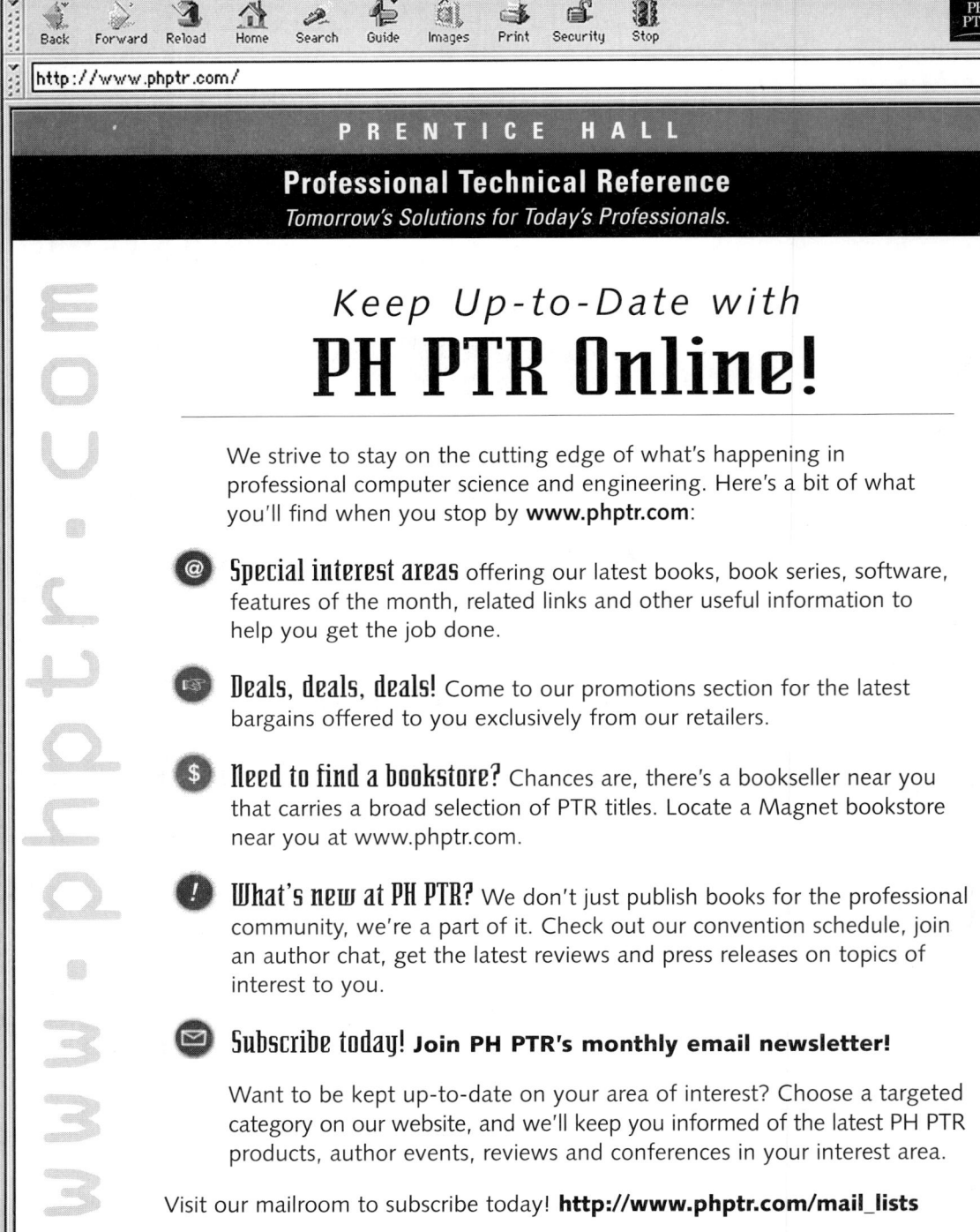